Engraved by J. C. Buttre

Geo M. Troup

THE LIFE

OF

GEORGE M. TROUP.

BY

EDWARD J. HARDEN.

SAVANNAH:

E. J. PURSE, No. 6 WHITAKER STREET.

MDCCCLIX.

TO

THOMAS M. FORMAN, Esq.,

AND

Dr. D. H. B. TROUP,

This Work

IS RESPECTFULLY DEDICATED.

PREFACE.

THE biography of GEORGE M. TROUP is submitted to the public, in the hope that it will be useful, and that its defects will be indulgently considered. Undertaken at the request of friends, whose opinions are worthy of regard, the work has grown to proportions not at first foreseen; and much of the labor has arisen from the difficulty of deciding what portions of a mass of materials, could, with least injury, be omitted. Taking into view the length of time Governor TROUP was before the public, and the important measures in which he acted, this difficulty is easily seen.

Little merit is claimed for the work, beyond the labor of a compilation. Governor TROUP is generally permitted to speak for himself: few speak so well; none more truthfully. It is possible, undue prominence has been given to some portions of his history; but it is hoped no important part of his public life has been omitted. His private correspondence must have been extensive; and, without doubt, much of it has been irrecoverably lost. Some of his letters, written in the privacy of friendship, are, for the first time, published; and they contribute no little to the interest of his biography. This interest would have been increased by the publication of other private letters—especially those relating to agriculture, in which their author felt deep concern; but this was forbidden by the prescribed limits of this volume.

To preserve connection in the history, and present its facts in their order, documents have been interwoven in the body of the work; and they constitute its principal value. With a view to bring the volume into suitable compass, and a desire not to give matters merely political too great preference, some of the documents have been put in an Appendix in small type.

It is scarcely necessary to state that the book has been printed wholly in Savannah; or to express the hope that it will be found as free from typographical errors as books usually are. Even in printed copies of the same document, disagreements have been found; thus adding greatly to the labor of determining the true reading. An abbreviated designation has been used to distinguish original notes.

The fac-simile of Governor TROUP'S signature, which accompanies the engraved likeness, is taken from a letter written in 1811. Some years later, and down to the period of his death, he usually, if not uniformly, employed only the initial letters of his given name.

To the many friends who have generously aided in the work, this occasion is taken to return sincere thanks; but these are especially due to Major W. J. McINTOSH, Hon. JOHN C. NICOLL, I. K. TEFFT, Esq., Dr. W. C. DANIELL, J. HAMILTON COUPER, Esq., Col. JAMES HUNTER, G. B. CUMMING, Esq., THOMAS M. FORMAN, Esq., Hon. JOSEPH HENRY LUMPKIN, Governor BROWN, R. B. HILTON, Esq., IVERSON L. HARRIS, Esq., Dr. JOHN G. SLAPPEY, STEPHEN F. MILLER, W. S. DANIELL and JOHN S. BRYAN, Esquires. The work itself will show a part of the indebtedness to Major McINTOSH, Dr. DANIELL, Mr. COUPER and Judge LUMPKIN; Dr. DANIELL having (besides other favors,) furnished about a hundred letters to himself from Governor TROUP, extending from 1825 to 1856; some of which will be found in succeeding pages. The earlier letters from Governor TROUP; were furnished by Mr. TEFFT, whose assistance has been otherwise invaluable, and from whom, as well as Judge NICOLL, important information has been derived. To Mr. HILTON, acknowledgments are due, for full files of the Georgia Journal from 1823 to 1827; to Gen. G. P. HARRISON and HENRY WILLIAMS, Esq., for valuable documents; to J. R. SNEED, Esq., for access to the files of the Savannah Republican; and to THE GEORGIA HISTORICAL SOCIETY, for the free use of its library and papers.

Savannah, 21st October, 1859.

NOTE.—The intelligent reader will not fail to correct small typographical errors. On page 190, fourth line from the bottom, for "after," read "during"; and on page 299, ninth line from the top, for "yourself," read "yourselves."

TABLE OF CONTENTS.

LIFE OF GEORGE M. TROUP.

CHAPTER I.

Birth, Parentage, Education, and First Appearance in Public Life.

By the Charter of the Province, the boundaries of Georgia included all that territory "which lies from the most northern part of a stream, or river there, commonly called the Savannah, all along the seacoast to the southward, to the southern stream of a certain other great water or river, called the Alatamaha, and westwardly from the heads of the said rivers respectively, in direct lines to the South seas; and all that share, circuit and precinct of land, within the said boundaries, with the islands on the sea, lying opposite to the eastern coast of the said lands, within twenty leagues of the same, which are not inhabited already, or settled by any authority derived from the Crown of Great Britain," &c.

By a royal proclamation, dated the seventh day of October, 1763, "all the lands lying between the rivers Alatamaha and St. Mary's," were added to the province of Georgia.

It is hardly necessary to remark that the term "South seas" * conveyed no definite idea of the western boundary of the province, or that the claim under that description never extended, practically, to the west of the Mississippi river. Accordingly, we find that, by the fourth article of the Treaty between the United States and Spain, dated the 27th October, 1795, "it is likewise agreed that the western boundary of the United States which separates them from the Spanish colony of Louisiana, is in the middle of the

* The Pacific Ocean was originally called the South Sea.—Ed.

channel or bed of the river Mississippi, from the northern boundary of the said States to the completion of the thirty-first degree of latitude north of the equator." And by the Constitution of the State of Georgia, adopted the 30th day of May, 1798, the boundaries of the State were set out as follows: "that is to say, the limits, boundaries, jurisdiction and authority, of the State of Georgia, do and did, and of right ought to extend from the sea, or the mouth of the river Savannah, along the northern branch or stream thereof, to the fork or confluence of the rivers now called Tugalo and Keowee, and from thence along the most northern branch or stream of the said river Tugalo, till it intersects the northern boundary line of South Carolina, if the said branch or stream of Tugalo extends so far north, reserving all the islands in the said rivers Savannah and Tugalo to Georgia; but if the head-spring or source of any branch or stream of the said river Tugalo does not extend to the northern boundary line of South Carolina, then a west line to the Mississippi to be drawn from the head-spring or source of the said branch or stream of Tugalo river, which extends to the highest northern latitude; thence down the middle of the said river Mississippi until it shall intersect the northernmost part of the thirty-first degree of north latitude; south by a line drawn due east from the termination of the line last mentioned, in the latitude of thirty-one degrees north of the equator, to the middle of the river Apalachicola or Chattahoochee; thence along the middle thereof to its junction with Flint river, thence straight to the head of St. Mary's river, and thence along the middle of St. Mary's river to the Atlantic ocean; and from thence to the mouth or inlet of Savannah river, the place of beginning; including and comprehending all the lands and waters within the said limits, boundaries and jurisdictional rights; and also all the islands within twenty leagues of the seacoast."

At the time of Gov. Troup's birth, 8th September, 1780, all the country west of the present western boundary of Georgia (except a small portion of West Florida,) and within the limits aforesaid, were within the acknowledged limits of that State. It was within the bounds of the present State of Alabama, then a part of the territory of Georgia, that he was born.

The following letter to Col. Pickett, the historiographer of Alabama, will show this fact and the precise spot of his nativity more clearly. The statement of Col. Pickett having been questioned, he wrote to Gov. Troup on the subject, and received the following reply:

VALDOSTA, November 5th, 1852.

Col. A. J. Pickett,

Dear Sir: I have uniformly said to those who have appealed to me for facts connected with the history of persons and things in past time, and particularly such as relate to myself and family, that I have not a scrap of paper in the form of a record, memorial or authentic manuscript, that has been preserved for the purpose, or, indeed, any whatever, to my knowledge, spared by time, or by those yet more active destroyers, rats and mice. I must except the Bible, treasured by every family, and thus saved from the wasting influences of both. I have one of these, an old Oxford edition of 1772, in which is found recorded, in the hand-writing (the most beautiful and legible I ever saw,) of my father, the birth-place of six of his children. I copied this, word for word, into a new family Bible, and now have both before me. The following is a literal extract from the former, and all that appears in my father's hand-writing.

"John McIntosh Troup, born the 3d of December, 1778, at Mobile in West Florida.

"George Michael Troup, born at McIntosh's Bluff, on the river Tombigby, 8th of September, 1780.

"David Troup, born at London, 8th November, 1781.

"Roderick William Troup, born at Charleston, South Carolina, on Friday the 28th of February, 1783, at half-past three o'clock in the morning.

"Robert Lachlan Troup, born at Savannah, the —— day of December, 1784.

"John James McGillivray Troup, born at Savannah, the 31st of August, 1786."

You would not receive an historical fact better authenticated. It was the possession of this Bible which emboldened me to send you anything for your history, touching the life of myself and family. Its chronology and register of places rendered it invaluable. It seems that mother or father, or both, were in Mobile in 1778; at McIntosh's Bluff, on the Tombigby, in 1780; at London in 1781; at Charleston in the early part of 1783; at Savannah in 1784, and in Savannah still in 1786; and, finally, that having removed from Savannah, he was (although not in his hand-writing, but in the hand-writing of his chief clerk, an enlightened and educated man,) in 1778 in McIntosh county, (old Georgia, if you please,) at his residence called Belleville, where he lived, died, and was buried.

Thus you have, upon what I consider unquestionable evidence, the fact of my birth-place, to which I never ascribed any importance, and in which I could not imagine that any, out of our family, would feel the least interest. I never, for any moment of my life, doubted that I was born on the Tombigby. I was as much a native of Georgia as if born on the southern bank of the Savannah river, where Oglethorpe built his town, whether in possession and under the jurisdiction of Spaniards, Englishmen or Americans. The English occupation was short-lived, and acquired by force. Our constitutional and chartered rights were undoubted, and were never to be surrendered without our consent. The civilians may differ, but, if driven to the wall, I would be a Georgian or Alabamian by the law of *Postliminium.* You will see that what the registry of the family Bible exhibits, I implicitly adopt. What I had presumed to submit to you from the store-house of my frail memory, I deemed unreliable, and already I think that errors may be detected in that part which relates to the connection and alliances between the different branches of the McIntoshes—a part which could only have been learned from my family and their friends, and in my earlier life.

Major William McIntosh, of Savannah, son of Col. John, and brother of the late Colonel who fell so gallantly under the walls of Mexico, can, better than anybody else, make the correction, and, if they interest you at all, you can use them as you please. There have been other mistakes besides the birth-place, and more amusing. Some of my kind friends, to assure themselves of my personal identity, have set me down in print and in writing with a middle name which I do not answer to, and McIntosh has been preferred to Michael, on account, I presume, of my mother's name and genealogy, and my known connection with that family.

But certainly I have written enough on this subject, writing from a sick bed, and snatching intervals of pain. First, your urgent request; second, the claims of truth, even in little things; and third, the gratification of gratifying the rational and harmless curiosity of esteemed friends, will be my apology, which will, I think, have been anticipated before you come to it. Yet I cannot close it without saying that my friend, Col. J. W. Jackson, had written a memoir, published in White's Statistics of Georgia, in which he not only eschews the mistake, but gives the true place and time as if from the original. No man is more sensitive to every omission or departure from truth, and it would have pained him to have committed the most innocent error. This work, entirely of his own observation and research, according to the best lights extant, (I could afford him nothing,) was the offspring of an affluence of friendship, was penned with a sedulous regard to matter of fact, and lofty disdain of everything that would savor of flattery or embellishment. Whilst he has most happily succeeded in the first, he may not, with all his care, have been so entirely successful in the last; but, as far as it goes, and as far as it purposed, it is a true history, and greatly better than any I could have written myself, and has saved me a vast deal of trouble.

Very truly and respectfully, your friend,

G. M. Troup.

P. S. It surprised me exceedingly, that you should have found among the old white Indian traders, any memorial or tradition of our family, although we had an uncle who was one of them—an uncle on our mother's side, and named McIntosh—a very respectable man, I believe, for I never saw him but once, when a very small boy, he came from the Nation on a visit to my mother. He must have been the son of Capt. John, of McIntosh Bluff. It is yet more remarkable they should have corroborated our Bible, as they assuredly did, when they said I was taken from the Tombigby when I was two or three years old. A few years after, I was a child at school with Miss Stuart at Savannah.

G. M. T.

The reader having been thus introduced to Major W. J. McIntosh, of Savannah, we prefer to continue this narrative in his own words, reduced to writing at the request of the author, and bearing date

SAVANNAH, 1st February, 1858.

Dear Sir: In compliance with your request respecting my recollections of the early life of the late Gov. Troup, of Georgia, I will reply briefly and as accurately as I can in connection with his family, but must go back prior to the first settlement of Georgia by its founder, General Oglethorpe, to trace his descent, especially on his mother's side, whose family was a branch of the McIntoshes of Borlam, Inverness, Scotland; and I feel myself also called on by Gov. Troup, in a letter to Col. A. J. Pickett, the historian of Alabama, to state the connection of the two families. And this induces me, necessarily, to introduce the name of McIntosh so prominently, in speaking of this truly great and good man.

Of his father's descent or history I know but little; though, when a young boy, I was often in his house, a playmate of his sons, at his residence called Belleville, a beautiful site on Sapelo river in the county of McIntosh—which name it still bears, but long since passed from the proprietorship of his family. The axe, neglect, and the ravages of time have left it but a faint picture of what it was when forest-clad, and under the improving hand of Mr. Troup. Here he became a planter, here he died, and here his remains were interred. He bore the reputation of a well-bred and honorable gentleman, born and educated in England; and at one period of his life was extensively and successfully engaged in commerce, but was never for any length of time confined to one locality. He married Catharine, the daughter of Captain John McIntosh, and we find from an old, well-preserved Bible—the family record—that although Mr. Troup had six sons, no two were born in the same place, except the two youngest. * * * *

These sons are all deceased. The Governor, who survived his brothers, was called George McIntosh Troup, from his known connection with the family, instead of George Michael, his real middle name. His eldest brother it was who bore the name of McIntosh after his grandfather. The initial of their middle names being the same, the unimportant mistake was easily made, but was never adopted or sanctioned by the Governor himself.

Mr. Troup, the father, married, as before stated, Catharine, the daughter of Captain John McIntosh, brother of the eccentric Captain Roderick McIntosh, of the British army, commonly called Rory, with whom the late Mr. John Couper, of St. Simon's Island, a distinguished and intelligent planter, was well acquainted during the Revolutionary war, and of whom he gives some amusing anecdotes in White's Historical Collections. Mrs. Troup's father and his eccentric brother were relations of John More McIntosh, the progenitor of the name in Georgia, and who served under General Oglethorpe, as commander of the Highlanders, in their battles with the troops of Spain in Georgia and in Florida. Many of this clan suffered severely in the Rebellion of 1715 and in that of '45, in consequence of their adhesion to the interest of the Stuarts, and taking up arms in their cause under the Earl of Mar against the Hanoverian succession to the crown of England; not because those

Highlanders believed in the "Divine right" of their kings, but the right to war against the usurpation of a throne, the rightful heir to which they believed to be a descendant of the House of Stuart.

Captain John McIntosh had also a son, William, brother of Mrs. Troup, and who was a captain in the British army, and also an agent of that government, under Col. Stuart, to the Muscogee or Creek nation of Indians during the Revolutionary war, and who was the father of the Indian Chief, Gen. William McIntosh, the friend of civilization among his own people, and the friend of Georgia, and who won for himself a Brigadier's commission from the United States, by bravely fighting against and subduing the hostile Indian tribes in Georgia, in Alabama and in Florida, under Gen. Jackson. This warrior-chief had a brother named after his grand-uncle, the eccentric Captain Rory, and who, it has been said, was in council what his brother was in the field. These men were the first (Indian) cousins of Gov. Troup, and it was remarked of their father, the Governor's uncle, that he was a "brave and generous man, and was qualified, physically and morally, to have figured in the most desperate strife." This gentleman, after the Revolutionary war, married a sister of the late Gen. John McIntosh, of the Revolution, which drew closer the connecting tie of the two families.

The father* of Gov. Troup, though often removing from place to place, was a lover of books, and had secured a well selected little library for his residence at Belleville, where his son George received the rudiments of his early education, under the guidance of a private tutor and the eye of his father; and in this library, where he had free access, he acquired the taste for reading, and that delight in books, not usual with boys of his age. His hours of relaxation from study were spent with his horse, his dogs and his gun, in the use of which he was indulged by his father, his oldest

* It seems that this gentleman was at one time engaged in mercantile business at Charleston, S. C., and Sunbury, Ga., with Col. John Baker, of Liberty county, who died in the year 1792.—ED.

brother having died early, and the others being too young to participate fully in their enjoyment. He was afterwards sent to school in Savannah, and, at a proper age, to Erasmus Hall, an academy then of great repute in Flatbush, on Long Island, New York, where many youths of the South were educated; at the head of which was Doctor Peter Wilson, an elderly and religious Scotch gentleman of great learning, afterwards of Columbia College in the city of New York.

The Doctor was a stern, unbending Republican, much respected by the students; and many of them here doubtless took their bias, and imbibed their predilections in favor of the cause he was known to espouse; and during the contest for the Presidency, between Mr. Adams and Mr. Jefferson, and when the excitement was high and boisterous in Flatbush, amongst the village politicians, there were frequent gatherings to discuss the claims of the candidates. When these were seen, and young Troup could by any means be present, there he would be, amongst the old men, ready to engage in argument, and could scarcely be restrained by older heads and less excited friends, from mingling in the crowd and taking part in the discussion, unmindful or regardless of the danger to which his youth and fiery zeal in favor of Mr. Jefferson, would expose him. I was at Flatbush with him, and frequently witnessed the great concern he manifested for the success of the Republican candidate.

He was of a slender frame, fair complexion, good figure, and rather handsome; of a feeling heart, and susceptible of the kindest emotions. He was studious, and of a warm temperament, polite and friendly to his fellow-students, but never seemed to have formed any close, boyish or bosom friendships, so common among youths of his age; inclined to taciturnity and reflection, though not backward in the enjoyment of the manlier sports of the time. He was exceedingly tenacious of his honor; and any reflection calculated to impair it, would be instantly met by a pungent reproof, in a seemingly quiet way, yet sufficiently significant of his determination, if the insult were not retracted, to proceed to extreme measures; and his decision of character was so well known, that he never had the trouble of doing more. I never knew him to be concerned in any senseless, wicked or mischievous act, that would reflect discredit on his name, or involve him in unpleasant scrapes, which were common enough then and there; and when he thought himself sufficiently advanced in his studies for college, he left Erasmus Hall, for Princeton, with an unsullied reputation. It was supposed, by his associates, that he would not look higher, on entering college, than the Sophomore class; but they were soon surprised, on learning, that, without difficulty, he became a member of the Junior class; and in due time he graduated with distinction.

He returned to Georgia, and commenced the study of law in Mr. Noel's office in Savannah; and, whilst so engaged, he wrote many political essays, over the signature of Z, much admired as coming from so young a man. About this time, he was appointed, by his friend and patron, Gen. James Jackson, then Governor of Georgia, and the scourge of evil-doers, his Aid, with the title of Colonel, then considered more honorable than now, from the indiscriminate manner in which the title is conferred.

* * * * * * * * * * *

Emerging from his minority, in 1801, he was elected to the Legislature, where he at once occupied a high position. In 1804, he removed to Bryan county, having previously married Miss McCormick; and, as soon as constitutionally eligible, was elected to Congress, of which he was a member until 1815, when he retired to private life. His support was given to the administrations of Mr. Jefferson and Mr. Madison; and he possessed the entire confidence of both these eminently great men, and was chairman of the committee on Military Affairs during the war—a position arduous and of great responsibility.

In the year 1809,* having been a widower for some

* The exact date of Col. Troup's second marriage was the 8th of November, 1809. The fact was thus announced in the Savannah Republican, of 25th November, 1809:

years, and without children, he married Miss Carter, a lady of Virginia, by whom he had six children, three of whom, two daughters and a son, arrived at maturity. The eldest daughter married Thomas Bryan, Esq.; by which union there were born to Gov. Troup several grand-children.

I find that I have already gone beyond the limit of your request, to wit, my recollection of Gov. Troup's early life, the characteristics of his boyhood, &c., &c. I trust an exact and impartial history of his public life, services and character, may soon be accessible to all.

Truly, your friend and obedient servant,

W. J. McIntosh.

The precise year of Gov. Troup's graduation at Princeton, was 1797, one year after that of his cotemporary, Judge Berrien, and two before that of Mr. Forsyth. On his return to Georgia, he entered the law office of the Hon. John Y. Noel, at Savannah. On the 29th day of May, 1800, he was admitted, before the Superior Court of Chatham county, the Hon. Thomas P. Carnes presiding, to plead and practice, as an attorney, solicitor and proctor, in the several courts of law and equity in the State, on the certificate of Thomas Gibbons, Charles Harris and William B. Bulloch, Esquires, stating, that, "after due examination, we conceive him fully entitled to admission, and recommend him accordingly." It does not appear that he ever practiced law to any extent. Even had his taste lain in that direction, his early connection with political and public life would have interfered with the duties and calls of a profession, requiring, for its active pursuit, all the zeal and energy of early manhood and mature life. In 1800, he declined an election to the Legislature, (at the call of the Republican

---

"Alexandria, Nov. 11.

"Married, on the 8th instant, by the Rev. Mr. Gibson, George M. Troup, Esq., member of the House of Representatives from Georgia, to the amiable and accomplished Miss Ann Carter, daughter of the late George Carter, Esq."

Besides Florida, (the wife of Thomas M. Forman, Esq.,) who died several years before her father, Col. Troup left, by this marriage, two other children—Oralie, who is yet living, and George M., who died within two years after the decease of his father. Mrs. Troup died in May, 1828, many years before the Governor.—Ed.

party of Chatham county,) on account of his minority. In 1801, he consented to serve, and was elected a Representative; and he was re-elected to the same post, in 1802, and again in 1803. The General Assembly then sat at Louisville; and there, on the 30th of October, 1803, he was married to Miss Ann St. Clare McCormick, eldest daughter of Dr. James McCormick, then late of that place. In 1804, he removed to the county of Bryan, and settled at a place, near Hardwicke, now known as Troup's Old Field. At this place, he had the misfortune to lose his wife, on 30th September, 1804, less than a year after his marriage.* The exact length of his residence in Bryan county is not known; but the county records show, that, in the year 1805, he was placed, by the Inferior Court, on the list of those owning slaves liable to do road duty, and that he was also put on the grand jury list; though the minutes of the Court do not show that he was drawn, or that he ever served, as a juror. It was probably because of his domestic loss, that he returned to Savannah, where he seems to have been residing at his election to Congress in 1806.

We may close this portion of the narrative, by remarking, that if, as a boy, his manner was reserved and unobtrusive, so, when he came to act a part in the drama of life, he seems to have been unconscious of possessing those qualities which endeared him to his fellow-citizens, and which were fitting him to pass, with honor, through scenes as trying as they were checkered.

From Pickett's History of Alabama, (vol. 2, beginning

* The circumstances connected with the death of this lady, possess a melancholy interest, and may not be out of place here. Colonel Troup had prepared himself for a life of conjugal happiness, and had fitted up his house with the luxuries as well as the comforts of life. Mrs. Troup having been taken suddenly ill, a physician was sought in vain. As the only resort, a neighbor, who had considerable experience in blood-letting, was sent for, as the symptoms seemed to warrant the belief that bleeding would relieve the patient. On his arrival, the neighbor proceeded to bind up the arm, and was about to apply the lancet, when, in his anxiety, Col. Troup asked: "W——s, do you think you can bleed her?" The reply was, "No!" The arm was immediately unbound, and the patient died. It seems that the question of the anxious husband conveyed to the mind of the proposed operator, a doubt whether the operation would be successfully performed; and, to use the language of the latter, so "unmanned" him as to destroy his confidence in his own skill. In relating these facts to the writer, nearly fifty years after their occurrence, the gentleman, to whom reference is made, did not seem to entertain any doubt that venesection would have relieved the patient.—ED.

at page 198,) published in 1851, we make the following extract:

"At the close of our last chapter, it was stated that the first American Court held in Alabama, was at McIntosh Bluff, which is situated upon the western bank of the Tombigby, between its confluence with the Alabama and the town of St. Stephen's. Connected with this Bluff, there is, to us, a pleasing historical reminiscence. Alabama has the honor of being the birth-place of George M. Troup, late Governor of Georgia, and who is one of the most vigorous and expressive political and epistolary writers of the age. His grandfather, Captain John McIntosh, the chief of the McIntosh clan, was long attached to the army of West Florida; and his valuable services were rewarded, by the King of England, with the grant of McIntosh Bluff, and extensive tracts of land upon the Mississippi. He had a son, who was also a British officer, and a daughter, a native of Georgia. The latter, while on a visit to England, married an officer of the royal army, named Troup. She sailed from England to Mobile, and, arriving at the latter place, entered a barge, and went up the Tombigby river to the residence of her father, at McIntosh Bluff, where, in the wilds of Alabama, Governor Troup was born, in September, 1780."

An article has recently appeared in a Georgia newspaper, from which the following is extracted:

"A paper was published in Louisville, Jefferson county, prior to 1800, by Ambrose Day. It was called the Louisville *Gazette & Republican Trumpet*, and George M. Troup, at that time a lawyer in Savannah, contributed to its editorial columns, although not generally known as the editor."

Having no reason to question the correctness of the above, in other respects, it is yet certain that Colonel Troup was not admitted to the Bar until 1800.

CHAPTER II.

Early Career as a Public Man.

THERE is every reason to believe that the subject of this memoir would have become eminent in the higher branches of the legal profession, had he devoted his manhood to the study and practice of law. Such was the opinion of his legal preceptor, a gentleman of distinction and of great acquirements in the science, and who was well qualified to form a proper judgment of the mental capacity of his student. The rigid course of preparation then necessary to bring a young man forward as a candidate for professional honors and emolument, favored the development of those qualities which are necessary to the successful practice of a science, in which, although many accumulate property, comparatively few acquire a solid or lasting reputation. The progress of this history will tend only to strengthen the opinion thus formed of Gov. Troup's talents, at a time when the future statesman contemplated probably little more than the strifes of the forum, and the promotion which, especially in a free Government, attends the career of the diligent and well-trained lawyer. His retirement from the bar, at an early period after his admission, was owing, perhaps, as much to want of taste for forensic display, as to the times when he graduated as a lawyer, and which were calculated to draw into the service of the State young men of talents and patriotism. His habits were always retiring; yet, the probability is, that, in weighing the chances of usefulness to the public, he settled down into a conviction that he could be more serviceable in political life; the more especially, as it was one from which, without injury to private interests, he could at any moment retire—as he always did—whenever no public emergency seemed to render his services necessary. That he deferred much to the judgment of his friends, in the estimate which he put upon his services, is true; and one of the beauties of his life seems to have been, that his patriotism was tempered by a modesty, which, whilst it was ready to yield to the suggestions of friendship, was still not of a kind to betray him into a want of proper confidence in himself when the occasion demanded a surrender of his time and talents to the public good. But, whether from taste or otherwise, it is certain he did not practice long enough to acquire reputation as a lawyer; and there is reason to doubt if he practiced at all. It is not improbable that he appeared as an advocate, on the criminal side of the court; but the records of the court, where he was admitted, do not show that he brought any suits there.

The year 1800 is memorable for the overthrow of the Federal party under John Adams, and the election of Thomas Jefferson. This was the first trial of strength between the two parties which openly succeeded the retirement of Washington from the Presidency; and the principles of which turned upon the different modes of construing the Federal Constitution. Those who favored a strong government, voted for Mr. Adams; the friends of a strict construction and of the rights of the States, voted for and elected Mr. Jefferson. We have seen that young Troup was a Republican at the school on Long Island. On his return to Georgia, he lost none of his zeal for the same cause. It was upon the principles of that party he planted himself, as soon as he could form a judgment for himself; and surely he never afterwards gave occasion to friend or foe to taunt him with abandonment of principle. His enemies being judges, he never advocated the principles of consolidation; and, in the judgment of his friends, if he erred at all, it was on the side of the rights of the co-equal and sovereign States of the Union.

But, independently of her federal relations, Georgia was in a peculiar and an interesting condition at home. Only a few years had elapsed since the honor of the State was tarnished by one of the most stupendous frauds recorded in history. This is known as the YAZOO fraud, a full narrative of which belongs rather to the documentary history of Georgia, than to a biography. We have seen that the western boundary of Georgia extended to the Mississippi River, and embraced the larger portion of the present States of Alabama and Mississippi. A small river, in the last mentioned State, gave the name to a transaction which brought deserved infamy upon its authors. The fraud has been thus briefly described: "Several projects for the sale of large tracts of country within the limits of Georgia, were, at different periods, presented to the Legislature. However contrary to good policy, they were listened to. But it is probable the majority of that body never had sagacity enough to foresee the rapidity with which population and wealth would increase, giving in their progress an immense value to what was then a wilderness. Be that as it may, however, we find them, in 1789, [Watkins' Digest, p. 387,] entering into a contract with these companies for the sale of fifteen or twenty millions of acres of land, including a vast tract bordering on the Mississippi River. But a dispute arose about the payment of the purchase money; and the condition upon which the grants were to issue, was not complied with. During the session of 1794–'5, the General Assembly passed an act conveying to four associations, called the Georgia, the Georgia Mississippi, the Upper Mississippi, and Tennessee Companies, about 35,000,000 of acres of land, lying between the rivers Mississippi, Tennessee, Coosa, Alabama and Mobile. The bill was warmly contested in both houses, and had also to encounter opposition from the Governor. It ultimately passed, however, by a majority of ten in the House of Representatives, and two in the Senate. The sale of so large a territory was received by the people with an almost unanimous burst of indignation, for it was soon known that nearly all the members who voted for the law, had been either directly or indirectly corrupted by the purchasers."*

The succeeding Legislature passed an Act, reciting,

* The consideration for this sale was five hundred thousand dollars. For the Act itself, see Watkins' Digest, pp. 557 to 566.—ED.

amongst other things, "Whereas the last Legislature of this State, not confining itself to the powers with which that body was constitutionally invested, did usurp a power to pass an act, on the seventh day of January, one thousand seven hundred and ninety-five, entitled 'An act supplementary to an act for appropriating a part of the unlocated territory of this State, for the payment of the late State troops and for other purposes therein mentioned, declaring the right of this State to the unappropriated territory thereof, and for other purposes;' by which an enormous tract of unascertained millions of acres of the vacant territory of this State, was attempted to be disposed of to a few individuals in fee simple, and the same is not only unfounded as being without express constitutional authority, but is repugnant to that authority as well as to the principles and form of government the good citizens of this State have chosen for their rule, which is democratical, or a government founded on equality of rights; and which is totally opposed to all proprietary grants or monopolies in favor of a few, which tend to build up that destructive aristocracy in the new, which is tumbling in the old, world; and which, if permitted, must end in the annihilation of democracy and equal rights, those rights and principles of government which our virtuous forefathers fought for and established with their blood"; and the Act proceeded to declare "the said usurped act" to be "null and void," and to annul all grants thereunder, and further, "that within three days after the passage of this act, the different branches of the Legislature shall assemble together, at which meeting the officers shall attend with the several records, documents and deeds in the Secretary's, Surveyor-General's and other public offices, and which records and documents shall then and there be expunged from the face and indexes of the books of record of the State, and the enrolled law or usurped act shall then be publicly burnt, in order that no trace of so unconstitutional, vile and fraudulent a transaction, other than the infamy attached to it by this law, shall remain in the public offices thereof," &c., &c.

Foremost and most effective in his opposition to this "usurped act," was Gen. James Jackson. Being then a Senator in Congress, he resigned his place, came home, was elected to the Legislature, and aided in passing the annulling law. The following account of the burning deserves a place here:

"Having determined that the act was 'usurped,' it was considered rightful that the records and documents pertaining to the sale should forthwith be destroyed. No monument of its wickedness should remain in the public offices, to give flattering assurance to the speculator that his corrupt machinations might *yet* be gratified. It was necessary to show to the universe, by decided conduct, that Georgia loathed the corruption, loathed the speculators, loathed the evidences of fraud, and would never abandon her ground! By order of the two Houses, a fire was kindled in the great square in front of the State House. Thousands of happy and elated citizens, who proudly conceived that their wrongs were redressed, had repaired to the spot, to witness the most remarkable spectacle ever presented within our limits. They were convened from every part of the State; and had, from the commencement of the session, remained at Louisville, intensely surveying the proceedings of each successive day. A circle was formed by the members, around the fire, the Governor and the high officers of the Departments being present. John Milton, the Secretary of State, and the Committee of Three who reported the mode of destroying the testimonies of our debasement, Mr. Sims, Mr. Few and Gen. Jackson, produced from the archives the enrolled bill and usurped Act. These were delivered to the President of the Senate, for examination. By him they were passed to the Speaker of the House, who handed them, after inspection, to the Clerk. He read aloud their titles, and gave them to the Messenger, who, committing them to the flames, cried out with loud and decisive voice,

'*God save the State, and long preserve her Rights, and may every attempt to injure them perish as these wicked and corrupt Acts now do!*' " *

* Savannah Republican, and Georgia Journal, for 1825.—ED.

Whilst these things were passing in Georgia, young Troup was quietly pursuing his college studies at Princeton. But he was not an inattentive observer of the political events in his State. His subsequent course in the Legislature showed that he was an enemy to the enemies of Georgia, and that the Yazoo fraud touched no chord of sympathy in his bosom. The imperfect history of the times does not enable us to state, with certainty, more than that, as a member of the Legislature in 1801, 1802 and 1803, he fulfilled the just expectations of his friends, giving his support to such measures as were calculated to advance the interests of the State, and maintaining those republican principles on which rests the liberty of the country. He was soon to be transferred to a wider if not a more useful field of labor, where we shall find him, as ever, the enemy of fraud* and the champion of liberty, justice and equality.

In 1806, Joseph Bryan, one of the Representatives from Georgia, having resigned his seat in Congress, Col. Troup consented to become a candidate for the vacant office, which the Governor had ordered to be filled by an election to take place on the first day of September. The following neat and just tribute was published, editorially, in a Savannah paper of that date:

[From "The Southern Patriot," September 1st, 1806.]

This day an election takes place for a member to represent this State in the Congress of the United States, for the residue of Mr. Bryan's term. Col. G. M. Troup is among the candidates, a gentleman whose republicanism, integrity and talents entitle him to claim a very distinguished place in the affections of the people of this county, as well as of his fellow-citizens at large. He has frequently represented the people of this county in the General Assembly of this State, and in that capacity has discharged his duty not only to the perfect approbation of his constituents, but in a manner highly honorable to his own firmness, consistency and

* A succeeding chapter is devoted to Col. Troup's course in Congress on the Yazoo fraud, and his speeches on that subject.—ED.

patriotism. It is expected that his old friends will not be backward or lukewarm at this important occasion, but that they will come forward with their usual alacrity and zeal. Col. Troup has never in a single instance deviated from the persuasion of a democratic republican; but if personal and political honesty, combined with the warmest and most enthusiastic attachment to the government and constitution of his country, are qualifications which *all virtuous men* wish to see concentrated in the character of a representative of the people, then this gentleman is entitled to the *respect* even of that class of his fellow-citizens between whom and himself there may be some shades of difference in political opinion.

The election resulted in the choice of Dr. Dennis Smelt; but, at the general election held just five weeks after, 6th October, 1806, Col. Troup was elected, with Dennis Smelt, William W. Bibb and Howell Cobb, a Representative for the full term to commence on the 4th of March, 1807; and he took his seat in the House of Representatives at Washington, on the 26th day of October, 1807.

The rapidity with which he had acquired the public confidence and risen to stations of honor and responsibility, whilst it did not inflate his pride, seems not to have excited the apprehension of his friends. If there were no other evidence of his integrity and talents, this sudden promotion to important stations, as soon as he was constitutionally eligible to them, would afford strong presumption that he possessed both qualifications; but the proof will be furnished when we come to consider his acts. It is believed that he never solicited an appointment of any kind; and this is known to be true of him in mature life. This was in the earlier if not the better days of the republic. How far such conduct may commend itself to the politicians of the present day, the future historian of the country must determine.

In 1824,* he said: "Our political morality will never be pure as long as offices are sought with the avidity and

* See his annual message, as Governor, for 1824.—ED.

importunity which now distinguish the canvass for them in all the States with the exception of New England. Whenever it is believed by the people that those who seek office with most eagerness, are frequently the most unworthy, the evil will have found its remedy. Merit is always conspicuous enough, and our people will be sufficiently enlightened to discover and appreciate it. The nomination, therefore, as well as the election of the candidate, ought to belong to them. The American historian will blush to record the scenes in which, within the passing year, candidates for the first dignity have not disdained to be actors. A practice, ripened into custom among a whole people, though proved to be a bad one, is not easily changed or discontinued. It is known that this must be the work of time, and of the intelligence and virtue of the people themselves. Whilst I am disposed to respect as I ought, long established habits and opinions, I would reproach myself were I to withhold a single sentiment, the expression of which it was believed the interest or honor of the country required."

At a subsequent period—one important in the history of Georgia—and when there was danger of conflict between Federal and State authority, he used this remarkable language, in a message to the Legislature, in reference to himself: "If it be possible, which I do not permit myself to believe, that a certain person filling a certain station, stands in the way of the peace and harmony which ought ever to subsist between this and the general government, and on this account valuable interests are endangered, that person will retire instantly, and with much more pleasure than he ever occupied that station."

Knowing the sincerity of Gov. Troup's heart, and the frankness of his character, the reader may well believe he spoke truly of himself, when, in his inaugural address of 1825, he said, "possessing no very great confidence in my own qualifications for the public service, I have not habitually or pertinaciously sought the public favor."

CHAPTER III.

State of the Country.—Mr. Troup in Congress.—His Course There.

THE year 1807 was an eventful one in the history of the United States. The two great belligerents of Europe, England and France, were contending for supremacy, and what the latter had gained on land, she had some time before lost on the ocean. England was the acknowledged mistress of the seas. For years previously, the neutral commerce of the United States had suffered by the desolating wars of Europe, to which we were no party. A detail of the consequences of this state of things, belongs rather to a general history of the country, but they will be noticed sufficiently, in the progress of this work, to give a general idea of the irritating causes which finally led to the war of 1812. It was in vain that the United States insisted upon their rights, as a neutral power, to carry on trade with either belligerent, or with any other European nation—contraband of war only excepted. Negotiation had failed, and was likely still to prove fruitless. As a last resort, Mr. Jefferson, in 1807, recommended an embargo. This was resisted by nearly the whole power of the Federal party, whilst the Republicans as generally supported it. In his message to Congress, of 18th December, the President said: "The communications now made, showing the great and increasing dangers with which our vessels, our seamen and merchandise are threatened on the high seas and elsewhere, from the belligerent powers of Europe, and it being of great importance to keep in safety these essential resources, I deem it my duty to recommend the subject to Congress, who will doubtless perceive all the advantages which may be expected from an inhibition of the departure of our vessels from the ports of the United States. Their wisdom will also see the necessity of making every preparation for whatever events may grow out of the present crisis."

A bill was accordingly introduced, the same day, to lay "an embargo on all ships and vessels in the ports and harbors of the United States;" and after a debate of four days, and sundry amendments, was passed in the House by a vote of eighty-two to forty-four—Col. Troup voting in the affirmative. It passed the Senate, the same day, with the amendments, and was immediately approved by the President. It provided, amongst other things, that "an embargo be, and is hereby laid on all ships and vessels in the ports and places within the limits or jurisdiction of the United States, cleared or not cleared, bound to any foreign port or place; and that no clearance be furnished to any ship or vessel bound to such foreign port or place, except vessels under the immediate direction of the President of the United States; and that the President be authorized to give such instructions to the officers of the revenue, and of the navy and revenue cutters of the United States, as shall appear best adapted for carrying the same into full effect: *Provided*, that nothing herein contained shall be construed to prevent the departure of any foreign ship or vessel, either in ballast or with the goods, wares and merchandise on board of such foreign ship or vessel, when notified of this act." The second section enacted, "that during the continuance of this act, no registered or sea-letter vessel, having on board goods, wares and merchandise, shall be allowed to depart from one port of the United States to any other within the same, unless the master, owner, consignee or factor of such vessel shall first give bond, with one or more sureties, to the collector of the district from which she is bound to depart, in a sum of double the value of the vessel and cargo, that the said goods, wares or merchandise shall be relanded in some port of the United States, dangers of the seas excepted, which bond, and also a certificate from the collector where the same may be relanded, shall by the collector respectively be transmitted to the Secretary of the Treasury. All armed vessels possessing public commissions from any foreign power, are not to be considered as liable to the embargo laid by this act."

This was the beginning of a system of commercial restrictions, intended, not so much as measures of retaliation, as an inducement to the two great belligerent powers of Europe to respect the rights of a neutral pursuing her lawful commerce without interference in the quarrels of the world, with which the United States were then at peace. The blow was virtually aimed at England, which the Federal party were supposed to favor; whilst they, in turn, accused the Republicans of too great partiality for France. That some measure of this sort was necessary, the judgment of the country has since proved; but it revived, at the time, all the bitterness of party spirit which had seemed to become dormant, to a great extent, on the re-election of Mr. Jefferson in 1804.

But another, and, for the time, a more serious occasion for alarm, grew out of the pretended right of Great Britain to search American vessels for British subjects. This doctrine of impressment was one to which the United States could never give their sanction. If a neutral flag could not protect neutral property, it was yet in the power of Congress, by a system of embargo, or non-intercourse, to make it the interest of the British people to respect the rights of neutrals; but the doctrine of impressment struck at the right of the government to protect itself from the violation of a fundamental principle of our national policy —the right of every citizen or subject to throw off his allegiance—in opposition to the English theory—*once a subject, always a subject.* But even if this theory were right, its application must be attended with difficulty. Who is to judge whether a man be a British-born subject or a native citizen of the United States? That the question under consideration led practically to gross oppression in many instances, was true. But injury to the rights of individuals was not the only consequence of the attempt to enforce this doctrine of impressment. It gave occasion for an act of atrocity on the part of Great Britain, equaled only by the acts of vandalism committed subsequently by her soldiery at the capture of Washington City. We refer to the affair of the Chesapeake. This occurred on the 22d of June. On the 30th of July, the President, by proclamation, required Congress to assemble on the 26th day of October, assigning as the reason that "great and weighty matters claiming the consideration of the Congress of the United States, form an extraordinary occasion for convening them." Congress convened accordingly. The Representatives from Georgia, as before stated, were William W. Bibb, Howell Cobb, Dennis Smelt and George M. Troup. In his opening message, the President said: "Circumstances, fellow-citizens, which seriously threatened the peace of our country, have made it a duty to convene you at an earlier period than usual. The love of peace, so much cherished in the bosoms of our citizens, which has so long guided the proceedings of the public councils, and induced forbearance under so many wrongs, may not insure our continuance in the quiet pursuits of industry. The many injuries and depredations committed on our commerce and navigation upon the high seas, for many years past; the successive innovations on those principles of public law which have been established by the reason and usage of nations as the rule of their intercourse, and the umpire and security of their rights and peace, and all the circumstances which induced the extraordinary mission to London, are already known to you. The instructions given to our ministers were framed in the sincerest spirit of amity and moderation. They accordingly proceeded, in conformity therewith, to propose arrangements which might embrace and settle all the points in difference between us, which might bring us to a mutual understanding on our neutral and national rights, and provide for a commercial intercourse on conditions of some equality. After long and fruitless endeavors to effect the purposes of the mission, and to obtain arrangements within the limits of their instructions, they concluded to sign such as could be obtained, and to send them for

4

consideration, candidly declaring to the other negotiators, at the same time, that they were acting against their instructions, and that their government therefore could not be pledged for ratification. Some of the articles proposed might have been admitted on a principle of compromise, but others were too highly disadvantageous, and no sufficient provision was made against the principal sources of the irritations and collisions which were constantly endangering the peace of the two nations. The question, therefore, whether a treaty should be accepted in that form, could have admitted of but one decision, even had no declarations of the other party impaired our confidence in it. Still anxious not to close the door against friendly adjustment, new modifications were framed, and further concessions authorized than could before have been supposed necessary; and our ministers were instructed to resume their negotiations on these grounds. On this new reference to amicable adjustment we were reposing in confidence, when, on the 22d day of June last, by a formal order from the British Admiral, the frigate Chesapeake, leaving her port for distant service, was attacked by one of those vessels which had been lying in our harbors under the indulgence of hospitality, was disabled from proceeding, had several of her crew killed, and four taken away. On this outrage no commentaries are necessary. Its character has been pronounced by the indignant voice of our citizens, with an emphasis and unanimity never exceeded."

The war spirit had been fairly aroused; and although no solemn declaration of war or other open acts of hostility were made for about five years afterwards, yet it was evident that war was inevitable, except by the sacrifice of the national honor, or by the retreat of England from her extravagant pretensions. War did follow, and the spirit which animated it was never allayed until that war was terminated in "*a blaze of glory at New Orleans!*"

We have seen that the embargo received the support of Col. Troup. On the 20th February, 1808, a bill supplementary to the embargo law being before the House, he observed that he had always thought the measure of the embargo was the best for our situation that could be devised, and had no doubt that if the measure had been followed up by a pertinent system of defence, it would have produced an honorable peace even by this time. For the same reason he wished the embargo to be rendered effectual.

Nor were the people of Georgia unmindful of the condition of affairs which were transpiring, or of the measures that it would be proper to adopt in case hostilities should become inevitable. On the 20th of December, 1808, the Governor approved an address to the President, which had been unanimously agreed to, and in which it was declared: "The Legislature of the State of Georgia, the immediate organ of the public will, think proper, at this all-important period of time, to address you. It is sensible, sir, that while the great powers of Europe are involved in a contest almost unexampled in magnitude, consequences and duration, that the people of these shores, though happily situated at a distance from the scene of carnage, yet being largely engaged in the pursuit of commerce, must from necessity suffer great privations from the want of a vent for the produce of a country fertile, extensive, and inhabited almost exclusively by agriculturists. But, sir, the citizens of this State, strong in their independence, and proud of their government, feel happy that a measure has been adopted which they conceive to be at once pacific and manly. They will never wish to see the lives and property of their brethren exposed to the insult or rapacity of a foreign power. And should this measure fail to produce the desired effect immediately, they will cheerfully submit to its continuance; *if, on the other hand, our present embarrassments should eventuate in a war, they will, in proportion to their number and resources, give zealous aid to the government of their choice*, confident that from the judicious management of the public funds, and the easy pressure of taxation hitherto, a conflict could be maintained to every advantage which pecuniary means would bring in support of a people patriotic and brave."

To understand the peculiar difficulties which embarrassed the United States in their relations to the European world, and which crippled their commerce, and finally led to the war of 1812, and to explain what follows in reference to those difficulties, it is proper to subjoin the following condensed statement of the policy and conduct of England and France, then the leading powers and the principal belligerents of Europe. The statement is believed to be correct in its main features:

"The battle of Trafalgar annihilated the united fleets of France and Spain; and all the principal ports of the French empire, with a long extent of seacoast, were held in rigorous blockade by the British squadrons. To retaliate on the British, the Emperor Napoleon devised a new plan of attack, which he called the *Continental System.* The object of this scheme was to cut off all intercourse between the continent of Europe and Great Britain, and thus weaken England by destroying this portion of her commerce. On the 21st of November, 1806, Napoleon, having defeated the Prussians, and entered Berlin, the capital of that kingdom, issued from the royal palace of that city his celebrated *Berlin Decree* *: by which he declared the British isles in a state of blockade, and, consequently, that every American or other neutral vessel going to, or coming from, these isles, was subject to capture. The same decree provided that all merchandise belonging to England, or coming from its manufactories, or colonies, although belonging to neutrals, should be lawful prize *on land.* This provision was carried into effect. General Armstrong, American minister at Paris, regarded the Berlin decree, at first, as inapplicable to American commerce, on account of the treaty then existing between the United States and France, but in October, 1807, in answer to his inquiry as to the effect of the decree, the French minister of foreign relations informed him of his mistake. The condemnation of American vessels commenced in November following. The British government, in retaliation of Napoleon's Berlin decree, issued

* Dated, "In our Imperial Camp, Berlin, Nov. 26, 1806."—ED.

their famous *Orders in Council*, dated November 11, 1807. By these orders, all direct trade from America to any part of Europe at war with Great Britain, or which excluded the British flag, was totally prohibited. Goods, however, were allowed to be landed in England, and, after paying duties, might be re-exported to Europe. On the 17th of December succeeding, the orders in council were followed by the *Milan Decree* of Napoleon, which declared that every vessel that should submit to be searched by a British man-of-war, or which should touch at a British port, or should pay any impost whatever to the British government, should be *denationalized*, and subject to seizure and condemnation. These edicts of the two belligerent powers were, of course, destructive to the principal part of the foreign commerce of the United States. American vessels trading directly with French ports, were liable to capture by British cruisers; and if they touched at a British port, they were confiscated on arriving in France. The British orders in council operated with the most severity on American commerce, as through their powerful navy the English possessed the means of enforcing them."

The session of 1807–8 closed on 25th April, 1808.

Early in the session of 1808–9, a resolution was offered, in the U. S. House of Representatives, to the effect that the act of the previous session, laying an embargo, and the supplementary acts, "ought to be immediately repealed." On the question whether the House would agree to consider the resolution, there were but nine votes in the negative—amongst them was that of George M. Troup. In explaining his vote, he said he felt himself bound at all times to treat with the greatest delicacy all motions and propositions of an ordinary nature. But there were times in which his feelings compelled him to depart from the ordinary rule. This was one. He had voted against the consideration of the resolution because he would reject, with that dignity which it deserved, an abstract proposition at this time to remove the embargo; and because he thought a prompt rejection would mark to the foreign world the temper of the country. He suggested, since it was to be discussed, that the discussion should be postponed a while, until time was given to digest the voluminous mass of documents laid before them. For in these documents were contained the best arguments in favor of the embargo.

Soon after this, the House Committee on Foreign Relations, having made a report, submitted a series of resolutions, one of which was as follows: "*Resolved*, That the United States cannot, without a sacrifice of their rights, honor and independence, submit to the late edicts of Great Britain and France."

The House being in committee of the whole,

Mr. Troup said he was extremely happy to agree in one thing with the gentleman who had just sat down, (Mr. Randolph) that the Southern had not suffered less by the operation of the embargo than the Eastern States; but when, in differing from the gentleman from Massachusetts, (Mr. Quincy,) on a point of still greater importance, he was also compelled to differ from the honorable gentleman from Virginia, he did so with the deepest regret. It has been said by the gentleman from Massachusetts, observed Mr. T., that for the last eleven months the country has suffered by this system of embargo the extreme of disgrace and humiliation, and the gentleman from Virginia has called it a measure of degrading submission. Sir, it is not a measure of submission; it is a measure of resistance, and of the most formidable resistance. Whatever may have been the object of the Executive in recommending the embargo, it has ever been supported by us as a measure of coercion—as a measure of justifiable retaliation. I contend that it is not submission. Acquiescence in the orders and decrees—submission to seizure and condemnation—would be submission to all intents and purposes; but that measure which keeps at home the ships and property which our enemies seek to capture on the high seas, is not submission, but resistance; and the gentleman from Massachusetts will find it so to his sorrow. Commerce, sir, is the life-blood of England; it is the foundation of her wealth, her prosperity and her maritime grandeur. But the gentleman says we have retired from the highway of nations, and left our great rival free to navigate it. True, we have retired from the ocean; we have left our rival free to navigate but very little more than between port and port of her own dominions. We have given the finishing stroke to her exclusion from the commerce of the civilized world; she has not one tittle of it left, other than what you yourselves would have if your embargo were raised to-morrow; and your committee have told you what that is—a scanty, contemptible commerce of seven millions of dollars. England lost one hundred millions when France shut the continent against her; she lost fifty millions by the occlusion of your own ports; and nothing of trade is left her but that she may drive with the native powers of Asia and Africa; with Sweden, and, precariously, with Spain, Portugal, and their possessions. No more, then, of raising the embargo to carry on commerce, when, without a sacrifice of independence—without a dishonorable submission to the Orders in Council—we cannot carry on more than seven millions of commerce. I know it is said that the people of the Southern States are the enemies of foreign trade—that their spirit and their interests are anti-commercial. Sir, in this sentiment, which is of itself without foundation—nay, without even the shadow of foundation—is to be sought that jealousy which has given rise to so many evils, and from which such serious evils are yet to be apprehended; but, sir, it is a mean, pitiful, contemptible jealousy. The Southern States are not the enemies of commerce. Indeed, how can it be said of a people who raise seventy millions of pounds of cotton, and for which they have not a home market for ten millions, that they are the enemies of commerce! No, sir; they have, from the beginning of your government to the present day, sacrificed as much to the prosperity of commerce as any people of the Union. They have been at all times as ready to go to war for commerce—on the attack on the Chesapeake they were even more forward to go to war for the honor and dignity of the flag than the people of the Eastern States.

A little more than was said by my friend from Virginia, as to the comparative operation of the embargo on the Eastern and Southern States. Compare the operation of this measure by the proper test—the only true and correct one—the depreciation of the respective staples of those two sections of the Union. Let the gentleman from Massachusetts state to the House what has been the depreciation of his beef, pork, fish, cheese, butter, onions, potatoes, and cabbages, and I will tell him what has been the depreciation of our great staples, cotton and rice. The ordinary market price of cotton is between eighteen and twenty-two cents; the embargo price is from ten to twelve. The ordinary price of rice is from five to six dollars; the embargo price is from two to three. Our people are, besides, in proportion to their number, more in debt than the people of the Eastern States.

But the gentleman from Massachusetts warns us against a perseverance in the system of embargo. A perseverance, according to the gentleman, is to be followed by open hostility to the laws. Sir, I dread no such hostility. We have no reason to dread it. It is altogether impossible that men who are actuated by the basest of human passions can make a serious movement in a revolution. No, sir; I insist upon it, that we have no cause to fear the anti-embargo men of Massachusetts. One brave, independent, generous yeoman of Massachusetts, would drive half a dozen such fellows into the ocean. But, the truth is, the gentleman seems to have wholly mistaken the condition of his countrymen. He told us that he had suffered everything but famine; that the distress and ruin were co-extensive with the country. They could not or would not suffer longer. Yet, sir, the gentleman was not well seated, before his colleague (Mr. Bacon) rose, and with equal claim to veracity, and the same opportunity of forming a correct opinion, told you that his honorable colleague had given a very high coloring to the picture; that the distresses of the people were by no means as great as they were described; and that if they were less prosperous and flourishing than before the embargo, they were far—very far—from the state of misery which his colleague had represented.

Sir, many of these observations have been made with extreme reluctance; they have been extorted under circumstances which must give pain to every American, but which cannot fail to kindle in him the liveliest indignation. No man can read without horror and disgust, in the papers of the day, the most treasonable and flagitious libel that ever disgraced our country—the anonymous publication circulated in Newburyport.

Sir, it is remarkable that we have been so gradually familiarized with British outrages, and have at length become so completely reconciled to the most extravagant excesses of them, that what two years ago you would have been willing to go to war for, would now be considered a matter of too trifling importance to merit your attention, much less your resentment. Two years ago you were willing to go to war to limit the right of search; you would have gone to war to prohibit the practice of impressment; you would have gone to war to overturn the lawless system of blockade; you would have gone to war for the colonial trade; for the attack on the Chesapeake; two years ago you would have gone to war for the Orders in Council; and now that all these outrages, and more than these, have accumulated on your head, until you are bowed down to the earth, you are content to beg a little commerce of England! You tell England, if she will be pleased to grant you a little trade, you will open your ports to her, and shut them against France! This last, this humiliating overture, she rejects with indignation. You have no choice left, as your committee has reported, but between war and embargo. We cannot go to war with one, without going to war with the other; because, the wrongs done by one are not less than the wrongs done by the other—unless, indeed you consider the shedding of innocent blood the greatest of all possible wrongs.

I know this measure of embargo has been condemned, loudly condemned ; but only by men who propose to re-seat themselves in power by an appeal to the feelings and interests of the community. In one part of the country this appeal has been made with effect. The avaricious have been corrupted, the ignorant have been duped. In all countries there are the avaricious and the ignorant ; and the passion of the one and the credulity of the other have been wielded with success by the anti-embargo men. Sir, the people have been led to believe that a great commerce could be carried on under the orders and decrees, when in fact no commerce could be carried on without compromitting the honor of the nation. They have been led to believe that a commerce could be carried on without hazarding the peace of the country, when in fact no commerce could be carried on without involving the country in war ; and whilst the great object of the government was to protect commerce, the embargo was said to aim a deadly blow at commerce. It is by such misrepresentations that the noisy enemies of the embargo out of doors have been deluded and corrupted. And are these the people to whom we are called on to turn a respectful and deferential ear? —the merest Shylocks—men who cry out, away with your honor, your independence, your neutrality—they are all stuff—give us gold!—British merchants, British agents, and malcontent Americans—the depraved of the cities, and the ignorant of the country—men who are ready to sacrifice the honor and independence of the nation for a little trade in codfish and potash! If we are thus degenerate—if we are thus fallen in thirty short years, it is high time to abandon your republican system of government. Sir, will posterity believe that this very people, who thirty years ago magnanimously offered up their lives and fortunes for the acquisition of independence, are now prepared to sacrifice that very independence to their avarice! Will posterity believe that this same people, in one short year, forgot the affair of the Chesapeake? That they were ready to shake hands with the murderers and robbers of their countrymen? I will not, for myself, assent to such a base barter of honor for gold. No, sir! If it has come to this—if we cannot for a year or two years endure the privations incident to a measure of embargo, if we cannot exist without the luxuries of life, notwithstanding the most imperious calls of honor and of duty, we are unworthy the blessings we enjoy—we have lost our virtue, and are ripe for the dynasty of the Bonapartes, or any other dynasty; and whether you are conquered by France into miserable servitude to-morrow, or corrupted to sell your country to England, is not worth a reflection. This accursed avarice will ruin you.

Sir, it is not to such a people as those—and I trust in God a majority of the people of New England are very different—that I would appeal to test the correctness of the measure of embargo. Were I disposed to test its correctness by its popularity, I would appeal to the people of Virginia, too honorable to be corrupted, too enlightened to be duped. I would ask them what they thought of the embargo, and they would answer with an almost unanimous voice—they would go further—they would be ready to support it with their lives and fortunes.

You have done everything for commerce—you have negotiated for commerce—you have jeoparded the peace of the country for commerce—you have passed an embargo to protect commerce—and commerce is the first to abandon you. God forbid that I should speak thus of the whole mercantile community. I have seen too many instances on this floor of noble and magnanimous sacrifice of private interest to the public weal; they are not the Smiths, or the Grays, or the Crowninshields of whom I speak.

If the embargo were raised to-morrow, none would trade but men of desperate character and bankrupt fortune—the real *bona fide* American merchant would not venture a ship at sea; and where would they trade? Why, to be sure, they might drive a trade in beef and pork and flour to the

West Indies, and some of our cotton and rice and tobacco would find their way to England, if the French privateers did not catch them; but the market would soon be overrun —it would be no better than the home market; and where would you trade to besides? If you are determined to pay the ninepence per pound tribute, for permission to re-export your cotton to the continent, the French decrees would take it; and, if they did not, the price of the article would be so enhanced by the tribute, that the market of the continent would be lost to you.

Permission to arm is tantamount to a declaration of war, and the people of this country want peace, as long as they can preserve it with honor. And do you think, sir, we are ready to plunge headlong into a ruinous war, naked and unarmed, to gratify a few bankrupt commercial speculators? It is easy to declare war; it is more difficult, under present circumstances, to maintain peace, and it is most difficult of all to wage a successful war. Sir, beware! It is the object of the gentleman from Massachusetts and his friends, to lead you, step by step, into a war, and if he can, into an unpopular war, which the moment you cease to conduct with effect, you are ruined, and he and his friends are exalted. To such an event, deplorable as it would be, I could be reconciled if I believed the gentleman and his friends would govern in the true spirit of the constitution; but liberty has been hunted down in the Old World—there is scarce a remnant of it left, save in America—here it is sustained by the ruling party; and, sir, the moment this party ceases to rule, Republicanism is gone, and with it the hopes of all good men forever. On this account I deprecate such an event.

It would appear to me from the tenor of the gentleman's remarks, (Mr. Quincy,) that he wants war with France and alliance with England. If this be the fact, the gentleman is not consistent. If he is really as much afraid of the gigantic power of France as he affects to be, (and I must confess, for my part, I am very much afraid of it,) assuredly it is not policy to provoke France—it is our policy to keep out of the way of both monsters as long as we can, and to husband our resources. And what would avail an alliance with England? You could only furnish men to be slaughtered on the continent. I can tell the gentleman from Massachusetts in what he would much better exemplify both his patriotism and consistency—in union, in uniting to call into activity the resources of the nation for its defence—in organizing and arming and disciplining; and, what is not less desirable, in adopting a system of finance, which would not fail you in any exigency; in short, in pursuing the course in which you are, which the soundest policy points to as the safest and the best, the course of impartial neutrality, if, indeed, neutrality has anything to do with it.

As to the embargo, so much has been said, both in and out of doors, in its justification, that I will forbear to touch it. It is only necessary to observe that it has been supported, and will be continued, as a measure of security and of just retaliation. As a measure of security, it keeps the property at home, which, but for it, would have enriched your enemies; as a measure of retaliation, it would have had its effect, but for the anti-embargo men of Massachusetts. If the gentleman will co-operate to make it efficient, he will soon find the great mercantile politicians of England, from Anderson down to McCall Bedford, have not been mistaken in the belief that this country can vitally affect the colonial and manufacturing interests of that, by an embargo system.

As to a declaration of war against France and Great Britain, and the policy of making it immediately, no local considerations should be permitted to enter into our view of it; but this much is to be said, that the Southern people are much more interested in raising the embargo than going to war; by the first, they would find a vent for a small proportion of their staples; by the latter, they could get nothing but taxes and fighting. The anti-embargo men of Massachusetts would not make more by the first than ourselves, and by the last they would make nothing more than their privateers would make for them; but the great object is to postpone the evil.

One word, before I sit down, as to what fell from the gentleman from New York. He proposes to repeal the embargo in relation to Spain and Portugal. Sir, is the political condition of those States characterized by a permanency and stability which would warrant commercial connection with them? Trade with the Junta of Seville—a mere political ephemeron—a being of a day! Sir, I wish the Spanish patriots success, with all my heart, but success is impossible. Ten thousand to one, that whilst I am speaking, this same Junta of Seville is imploring clemency at the footstool of the great usurper. Indeed, sir, if we are bound to consider this people of any definite description, we are to consider them rather as French subjects than Spanish patriots, for the only official paper in relation to them is the instrument of abdication and renunciation by which this unhappy people have been transferred over, like a flock of sheep, to the Emperor Napoleon, and by the very men for whose rights of empire they are said to be contending.

The question was taken, the next day, on the resolution under consideration, and it was passed without a division; but it is evident that the debate did not turn upon the resolution simply, and that the vote determined nothing in regard to the relative strength of the two parties—one, the Republican, ready to support the administration in all just measures to vindicate the honor of the country; the other, the Federal, bound by no sympathy for the party in power, or its leader, Mr. Jefferson, and ready at any moment to seize a favorable opportunity for bringing the administration and its friends into odium with the people.

The following letter, never before published, from Col. Troup to Charles Harris, Esq., will show the views of the former on our foreign relations, even before the meeting of Congress in 1807:

WASHINGTON, 14th Oct., 1807.

Dear Harris: This morning I paid a visit to the President. As we were alone, he was communicative. The substance of what passed, so far as I am at liberty, I give you.

Nothing decisive of the question of peace or war can transpire previously to the return of the Revenge. She is not expected short of a month, as even her arrival in England is not known to the government. England flatters our ministers, and they speak of her favorable disposition. She disavows absolutely any authority to Berkeley, and talks of atonement. But, my friend, the chances of war, notwithstanding, are beyond all comparison greater than those of peace. Our Spanish negotiation, which, during the absence of the Emperor, was suspended, is actively renewed, and before the end of the session the government has reason to look to a satisfactory issue. Heretofore, Spain has made no advances. I may conjecture that Bonaparte will speak for us in an audible and imperative tone.*

I give you nothing, perhaps, that you have not anticipated; but as it is stated on authority, it will afford you more solid foundation for your political lucubrations. This horrid scrawl is intended for Charlton, the Bullochs and Morel, as well as yourself, when you get together over some brandy and water. Have been sick, and can't write you all.

Your friend sincerely,

Geo. M. Troup.

* The President has nothing to do with this last sentence —remember!

To Gen. D. B. Mitchell, he wrote during the session, on the same subject, as follows:

WASHINGTON, 18th Feb'ry, 1808.

Dear Sir: * * * *

The House is this morning occupied in providing for the raising of several regiments (9) on a war establishment.

Mr. Rose's negotiation, it is understood, is brought to a close, at least for the present, and the Congress will in future be engaged as if war is inevitable. We have a French decree declaring England blockaded by sea and land. Whether it be genuine or forged is not certain.

Very respectfully, dear sir, your friend,

Geo. M. Troup.

WASHINGTON, 28th March, 1808.

Dear Sir: Your favor, of the 13th inst., came to hand last night. The tenor of the King's speech, which reached us at the moment of the rupture of Rose's negotiation, gave rise to but one opinion among the friends of our country—that war was inevitable. The only question seemed to be how we should wage it. I make no doubt in such event the defensive mode would be adopted in the first instance—prohibiting intercourse, preparing ourselves for attack, and organizing a force for the reduction of the British Provinces on the first offensive act of the enemy.

Three days since, dispatches were received from Mr. Pinkney, stating that the ministry had lowered their tone; and indeed, my friend, I sincerely believe if we have courage and perseverance, the bully will retreat from his high ground and give us by honorable treaty what the law of nations has decreed. And yet should such concessions settle us down in a permanent peace with that country, it is very questionable whether France would not take umbrage. The conduct of the Emperor of late is calculated at least to put us on our guard. *It is known* he is spoiled by fortune, that he is overbearing, and perhaps that he aims at universal empire. Be it so or otherwise, it becomes this government to act as an independent nation, uncontrolled by anything but a sense of justice and moderation. Could you see the whole ground, you would think the crisis as difficult as that of '77. Indeed, to think so you will require little more than the documents the publication of which is permitted.

The fate of the Bill authorizing a sale of arms to the State, is at least doubtful, and it is to be feared that if passed it will be under such modification as to render it of little importance to Georgia. (We may get 5,000 stand.) We were obliged in the House to go upon the beggarly system, which I did not like, and which of course gave a fine field to the Yazoo men and the rest. The Army bill is passed to its third reading. Congress has been occupied a week in reading the documents accompanying the President's communication. We may adjourn in three weeks.

Your friend, respectfully, GEO. M. TROUP.

Gen. D. B. Mitchell, Savannah.

The Army bill, to which reference is above made, being under consideration, 4th April, 1808,

Mr. Troup said, that after the very eloquent and patriotic speech of his friend from Virginia, (Mr. Randolph,) he felt it doubly incumbent on him to justify the vote he should give, by a few observations. I really cannot, said he, for my part, perceive, with the gentleman from Virginia, that a bright prospect of peace has suddenly opened upon this country. My views of things at this moment are very different; it really seems to me that the clouds are gathering about us darker and thicker every day. It must be, from the nature of things, extremely difficult to determine whether we shall have peace or war, because that event, I trust, depends on powers not to be controlled by us. But, however difficult it be to determine it, what security have we that we shall not be attacked? Are we certain that an act of hostility against this country will ever be preceded by a solemn and formal declaration of war? No, sir, all experience is against it. The Spanish frigates were attacked, and there was no declaration of war—nay, they were attacked in the midst of negotiation for peace, or rather in the midst of friendly negotiation; Copenhagen was attacked and in flames, and there was no declaration of war.* Recollect, when your measure of embargo begins to press hard upon the British colonies; when from that

* The reader will understand these references to be to the capture of Spanish Treasure Ships by the British, in 1804, and the bombardment and burning of Copenhagen, by the same power, in 1807.—ED.

salutary measure the colonies are reduced to the last extreme of wretchedness and want, the tigress will attack you for food for her young; it is not unlikely that she may steal upon you in the dead of night, and treat you as at Paoli. And pray, sir, what security have you against that Power which a gentleman from South Carolina (Mr. D. R. Williams,) so appropriately called the tiger? What security have you against France? Do you expect to sleep in profound tranquillity because Britain interposes between you and France her thousand ships? It would be idle and irrational to expect it. You had an instance, the other day, of the Rochefort squadron making its way in the face of the whole British navy, and, it is said, with five thousand troops on board, who might, for aught you could have done, be drawn up on your frontier.

But what is to be done in the present crisis of affairs? Is the nation to remain undefended merely because gentlemen entertain prejudices against a particular species of defence? On what physical force will you rely for defence? You can only choose between the militia and a standing army; and when, the other day, it was proposed, by an honorable gentleman from Virginia, to class and re-organize the militia, you refused to do so. And it is well known that the present defective system of militia, in our quarter of the country at least, is good for nothing. No man has more confidence in the militia than myself; I consider them the great and cheap defence of the nation; but you must class, arm and equip them, and, when they are so armed, classed and equipped, purge this country of that refuse of humanity, a British faction and a French faction —if, indeed, there be any such—and your militia will defend you against the world.

The jealousy of standing armies is characteristic of our people; it results essentially from their habits and political institutions; but this jealousy existing only in times of peace, is, in a season of public danger, always succeeded by that policy which reposes the safety of the nation in discipline, in habits of obedience, and in concert of operation. No man ever complained of a standing army when his country was invaded. No man complained of a standing army during the Revolution, though many complained, and causelessly complained, of the militia. The truth is, that the evil of standing armies is always effectually guarded when the regular force bears a very small proportion to the armed militia. By adopting such policy, by so proportioning your regular force to your militia, you will have nothing to do but to command it to lay down its arms, and it is done.

Circumstances render it necessary, at this moment, to create a war establishment, not so much for the purpose of defence against invasion, an event, perhaps, not so seriously to be apprehended, as was well observed by my friend from Virginia, but to preserve peace by preparing for war. It is at this time, and under such circumstances as the present, the maxim applies, to preserve peace or avert war, you must prepare for war.

As to confidence in men, under whom the force is to be wielded, and of which so much has been said, I will only observe, that I either have very great confidence or no confidence at all, and a sufficiency of it, on the present occasion, to believe that it will be neither misdirected nor abused; and I repose this confidence the more readily, as I am aware the army will be disbanded with the same facility it has been created, when the occasion for it ceases.

Although somewhat out of its chronological order, we have here inserted this speech entire, as it exhibits the foresight of its author, and is a just compliment to his sagacity and his patriotism. Three days afterwards, the bill passed the House by a large majority; and, having passed the Senate with the House amendments, was signed by the President on 12th April, 1808.

On the 9th of January, 1809, the Senate amendments to the bill from the House for employing an additional number of seamen and marines, being before the House,

Mr. Troup said he rose but for the purpose of stating facts which struck him as being applicable to the subject before the House. He referred chiefly to an extract of a letter written to himself, and published in the paper of to-day. [Mr. T. then read the extract which appeared in the National Intelligencer on the 9th instant.] In addition to these facts,* letters had been received, in the course of this morning, containing further particulars, which he begged leave to state to the House. After the officer (commander of a British armed vessel,) had been forced on board his vessel, and while lying in our waters and within our jurisdiction, he had fired several shots at pilot-boats passing and repassing, had been very abusive, and threatened the town with what he called vengeance; and, in addition to these facts, letters had reached Savannah from Liverpool, giving satisfactory information that vessels of fifteen or twenty guns had been fitted out for the purpose of forcing a cotton trade with South Carolina and Georgia. This information, Mr. T. said, came from unquestionable authority. And it was because he was unwilling that the people of this country should longer submit to the abuse of British naval officers; because he was unwilling that they should be exposed to the insolence of every British commissioned puppy who chose to insult us; because he was unwilling that armed vessels should force a cotton trade, when every man knew that nine-tenths of the people of Georgia would treat as traitors the violators of the embargo; it was for this reason that he was disposed to vote for the amendments from the Senate. The great objection which had been taken to them was the expense which they would produce. Economy, Mr. T. said, was a good thing in time of peace; but if this contracted spirit of economy predominated in our war councils, if we were forced into a war, so help him God, he would rather at once tamely submit our honor and

* The affair of the British war brig Sandwich is here referred to. Having anchored off Tybee, two of her officers came up to Savannah, and were immediately ordered off, because of the violation of the proclamation of the President, interdicting our harbors and waters to all British armed vessels. The vessel reluctantly put to sea; but, before doing so. fired several shots at a pilot-boat in the harbor, and committed other outrages.—ED.

independence than maintain them in this economical way. If we went to war, we ought not to adopt little measures for the purpose of executing them with little means; neither should we refuse to adopt great measures because they could not be executed but with great means. It was very true that, in war as well as in peace, calculation to a certain extent was necessary; but, if they once resolved on an object, it must be executed at whatever expense. He was no advocate for standing armies or navies, generally speaking; but, in discharging his duties here, he must be governed by the circumstances of every case which presented itself for his decision, and then ask himself, Is it wise, politic and prudent to do this or omit that? He said he would never go back to yesterday to discover what he had then said or done, in order to ascertain what he should now do or say. Political conduct must depend on circumstances. What was right yesterday might be wrong today. Nay, what was right at the moment he rose to address the House, might, ere this, be palpably wrong. Conduct depended on events, which depended on the folly or caprice of men; and, as they changed, events would change. It might have been a good doctrine long ago that this country ought to have a navy competent to cope with a detachment of the British navy; it might have been good doctrine then, but was shocking doctrine now.

At that time England had to contend with the navies of Russia, Denmark, France, Holland, Spain, &c. Now, England was sole mistress of the ocean. To fight her, ship to ship and man to man, (and it was impossible that gentlemen could think of fighting her otherwise, if they fought her at all,) we must build up a huge navy at an immense expense. We must determine to become less agricultural and more commercial; to incur a debt of five hundred or a thousand millions of dollars, and all the loans and taxes attendant on such a system, and all the corruption attendant on them. He should as soon think of embarking an hundred thousand men for the purpose of attacking France at her threshold, as of building so many ships to oppose the British navy. It was out of the question; no rational man could think of it. But that was not now the question. It was, whether we would call into actual service the little navy we possessed. It was not even a question whether we would have a navy at all or not. If that were the question, he would not hesitate to say that even our present political condition required a navy to a certain extent, to protect our commerce against the Barbary Powers in peace, and in time of war for convoys to our merchantmen. He only meant a few fast-sailing frigates, such a navy as we have at present, for the purpose of harassing the commerce of our enemies also. He therefore thought our present naval force ought to be put in service. As far as the appropriation ($400,000,) would go, it would be employed; but if Congress should hereafter see cause to countermand or delay the preparation, they would have it in their power to do so by refusing a further appropriation.

In perfect consonance with the foregoing, were his views in regard to the Gunboat system, which had been recommended by President Jefferson. The same subject being before the House, on 11th January, 1809,

Mr. Troup said he regretted exceedingly that he was under the necessity of again troubling the House, but he felt himself bound, in some measure, to state more particularly his reasons for voting for the bill, and to reply to some cogent objections made from a quarter of the House which he much respected. He stated anew the reasons which he had given why the United States should have a small naval force. He thought it indispensable at this time to man and equip our little navy, not for the one or the other general reason in its favor which he before stated, but to protect from violence and insult the territory of the United States; that territory which gentlemen in this House were so fond of calling the territory of the good old United States—he meant the marine league from the shore —as sacred and inviolable as any spot of earth within our limits. It was for the purpose of protecting this part of our territory, for removing those cruisers which are competent to blockade the mouths of our rivers, that he wished this navy to be equipped. Gentlemen said the gunboats were competent to the protection of our harbors. Mr. T. acknowledged it; he said he did believe that the invention of man never devised a more competent system than gunboats, co-operating with fortifications, for the protection of our ports and harbors, but they were calculated to act only on shoals and in smooth waters.* They were not fit for any other species of service; they could not stand the winds and the waves, the billows and the tempests. And notwithstanding our ports and harbors might well be defended by these gunboats, they were not competent to the purpose for which these frigates were to be manned, to prevent blockades of our own waters. [The rest of this speech is omitted for want of room.]

We cannot better conclude this chapter than by referring, briefly, to the position which Col. Troup occupied as a public man, even before he took his seat in the House of Representatives, on 26th October, 1807. Twelve days before, as has been seen by his letter to Mr. Harris, he is found in close, if not familiar, conversation with the President, Mr. Jefferson, on the subject of our foreign relations —then the absorbing question of the day. He had then just completed his twenty-seventh year, had not entered upon his Congressional duties, and it was no small compliment to have received, in advance, the confidence of so sagacious a statesman as the then chief magistrate of the Union.

The second session of the tenth Congress terminated, and the Congress itself expired, on 3d March, 1809.

The next chapter will be devoted to Col. Troup's opposition to the schemes of the Yazoo speculators.

---

* For the reasons which urged Mr. Jefferson to recommend this species of defence, see his special message of February 10th, 1807. Although much ridiculed by his opponents, at the time, experience has proved its efficiency, both in this country and Europe, as a means of defence.—ED.

CHAPTER IV.

Yazoo Fraud.—Claims growing out of it, before Congress.—Course and Speeches of Col. Troup thereon.

IT is necessary to go back somewhat, in the order of time, to consider the course of events flowing from an infamous fraud upon the people of Georgia, a brief statement of which we have already given. It is pleasant to reflect that although the escutcheon of the State was for a while tarnished by the bribery and corruption which attempted the alienation of an immense territory, for a consideration almost nominal, yet the people, rising in their strength, and with an honest indignation, rescued the character of the State from the disgrace which cupidity and corrupt speculation had essayed. Whilst the honest man would desire to turn his face from the subject, with loathing, still it is one so interwoven with the history of the country, and especially of the State of Georgia; that no historian can altogether pass it over, and no biographer of George M. Troup ought to do it. In his detestation of the fraud, he stood second to none; in effort and service against it, no man did more than he, unless we except General James Jackson. Like the record of the transaction which was burned with "fire from heaven," * it could be wished that the history of it had perished from the mind of man; but, like all monuments of human folly and human crime, it stands alike the memorial of wickedness and the beacon of warning against avarice.

About the time of the passage of the corrupt Act, the speculators engaged in the fraud deposited in the treasury the sum of five hundred thousand dollars, being the amount

* Until recently, the writer never heard a doubt expressed, that, on the occasion of the destruction of the record of the Yazoo Act, fire was kindled by a burning glass. All tradition confirms this idea; and whilst it may be true that the ordinary means of applying fire were used, on that occasion; yet there seems to be no reason to doubt that, during the solemnities of the occasion, and as expressive of public detestation of the Yazoo fraud, the sun-glass was also used.—ED.

of money consideration for which the grants were to issue. By a statement made to the Legislature, in 1813, by Gov. Mitchell, it appears that "the Yazoo Deposit was originated by five hundred thousand dollars and paid into our treasury by certain companies of men, in consideration of grants which they received from the State for a large tract of our western territory, since ceded by Georgia to the United States. This transaction took place in the winter of 1794. At the following session of the Legislature, in the winter of 1795, the grants issued to those companies were declared null and void, and provision was made for the repayment of the money to all those who should call at the treasury and produce sufficient evidence of the amount paid by them. Under these laws, many persons, as well original grantees as those called sub-shareholders, claimed and received from our treasury three hundred and ten thousand six hundred and ninety-five dollars, 13 10-12 cents, part of the original five hundred thousand, leaving a balance of one hundred and eighty-four thousand seven hundred and sixteen dollars, forty-seven and a half cents, which is the amount now in our treasury, subject to some deduction for guard expenses, &c."

In 1798 Georgia adopted a new constitution, by the twenty-third section of the first article of which the boundaries of the State were declared and defined as stated in the beginning of this work; and the said section proceeded to say:

"And this convention doth further declare and assert that all the territory without the present temporary line and within the limits aforesaid, is now of right the property of the free citizens of this State, and held by them in sovereignty, inalienable but by their consent. *Provided nevertheless*, that nothing herein contained shall be construed so as to prevent a sale to, or contract with, the United States, by the Legislature of this State, of and for all or any part of the western territory of this State, lying westward of the river Chattahoochee, on such terms as may be beneficial to both parties; and may procure an extension of settlement, and an extinguishment of Indian claims, in and to the vacant territory of this State, to the east and north of the said river Chattahoochee, to which territory such power of contract or sale, by the Legislature, shall not extend: *And provided also*, the Legislature may give its consent to the establishment of one or more governments westward thereof; but monopolies of land by individuals being contrary to the spirit of our free government, no sale of territory of this State, or any part thereof, shall take place to individuals, or private companies, unless a county or counties shall have been first laid off, including such territory, and the Indian rights shall have been extinguished thereto."

The twenty-fourth section of the same article declared:

"The foregoing section of this article having declared the common rights of the free citizens of this State in and to all the territory without the present temporary boundary line, and within the limits of this State, thereby defined, by which the contemplated purchases of certain companies of a considerable portion thereof are become constitutionally void, and justice and good faith require that the State should not detain a consideration for a contract which has failed; the Legislature at their next session shall make provision, by law, for returning to any person or persons who has or have *bona fide* deposited moneys for such purchases in the treasury of this State: *Provided*, that the same shall not have been drawn therefrom in terms of the act passed the thirteenth of February, one thousand seven hundred and ninety-six, commonly called the rescinding act, or the appropriation laws of the years one thousand seven hundred and ninety-six, and one thousand seven hundred and ninety-seven; nor shall the moneys, paid for such purchases, ever be deemed a part of the funds of this State, or be liable to appropriations as such; but until such moneys be drawn from the treasury, they shall be considered altogether at the risk of the persons who have deposited the same," &c., &c.

It was evident, then, that the Yazoo speculators were cut off from all hope of profit from any act of the government of Georgia; but, to put the matter beyond all dispute, the Legislature of 1798–9 not only passed an act to carry into effect the said twenty-fourth section of the third article of the constitution, for refunding the deposits in the treasury, but, on the 16th day of June, 1802, an act was passed, "to ratify and confirm certain articles of agreement and cession entered into on the 24th day of April, 1802, between the commissioners of the State of Georgia on the one part, and the commissioners of the United States on the other part," by which the State of Georgia ceded to the United States all her territory not included in the present limits of the State, but including the fraudulent grants to the Yazoo companies, and to which act of cession we shall have occasion more particularly to refer when we come to speak of the Creek difficulties. The consideration money to be paid for this cession, was one million two hundred and fifty thousand dollars; besides which, it was stipulated in the second condition of said articles of cession, "that all persons who, on the 22d day of October, 1795, were actual settlers within the territory thus ceded, shall be confirmed in all the grants legally and fully executed prior to that day, by the former British government of West Florida, or by the government of Spain, and in the claims which may be derived from any actual survey or settlement made under the act of the State of Georgia, entitled 'An act for laying out a district of land situate on the river Mississippi, and within the bounds of this State, into a county to be called Bourbon,' passed the 7th day of February, 1785;" and in the third condition it was further provided, "that the United States, for the period and until the end of one year after the assent of Georgia to the boundary established by this agreement, shall have been declared, may, in such manner as not to interfere with the above mentioned payment to the State of Georgia, nor with the grants herein before recognized, dispose of or appropriate a portion of the said lands not exceeding five millions of acres, or the proceeds of the said five millions of acres, or any part thereof, for the purpose of satisfying, quieting or compensating for any claims other than those herein before recognized, which may be made to the said lands or to any part thereof. It being fully understood that if an act of Congress making such disposition or appropriation, shall not be passed into a law within the above mentioned period of one year, the United States shall not be at liberty thereafter to cede any part of the said lands, on account of claims which may be laid to the same, other than those recognized by the preceding condition, nor to compensate for the same; and in case of any such cession or compensation, the present cession of Georgia to the right of the soil thus ceded or compensated for, shall be considered as null and void, and the lands thus ceded or compensated for, shall revert to the State of Georgia."

We have deemed it proper to premise so much, in order that the course of Col. Troup in the U. S. House of Representatives, in regard to the Yazoo speculation, might be better understood. But it is necessary to make a further explanation. Some of the speculators, or their assignees, having, after said act of cession, carried the matter before Congress, the Legislature, on the 23d day of November, 1807, passed the following preamble and resolutions:

"Whereas, in the year seventeen hundred and ninety-five, as will be recollected with emotions of indignation by every virtuous citizen of this State, a combination of influential and moneyed men, succeeded, by *bribery* and *corruption*, in obtaining the passage of an act, conveying the right of this State in a well known portion of the western country, called YAZOO, to several companies of purchasers; and whereas the succeeding Legislature, duly convinced of the flagitious agency which had procured the act aforesaid, virtuously determined, by a rescinding law, to prohibit all contracts, conveyances and grants originating in that fraud, from being carried into effect, it solemnly becomes this Legislature to support and preserve consistent the reputation of this State, by denying the statement of a band of speculators, combined from New Hampshire to the Mississippi, to embezzle the funds, either of this State or the United States, and to riot on the profits of an extensive tract of country, in alleging, *falsely*, that the State of Georgia contemplated in the articles of cession to the United States of her western territory, in eighteen hundred and two, *any compromise of the Yazoo claims in any way whatever.* And inasmuch as it is important to the decision of Congress on this subject, and greatly so to the dignity and justice of the State of Georgia, that the truth as it is in this matter should be fully and unequivocally defined; it is therefore unanimously

Resolved, *by the Senate and House of Representatives of*

the State of Georgia, in General Assembly met, That they have viewed and still view with abhorrence, the attempt made by a set of unprincipled men, commonly known by the appellation of Yazoo men, to corrupt a majority of the Legislature of this State in the year 1795; which attempt was rendered abortive by the virtue of the succeeding Legislature.

Resolved, That it never was the intention of the Legislature of this State, when they ratified certain articles of agreement and cession entered into by commissioners appointed by the State of Georgia and the United States, to evince any desire to compromise claims that originated in fraud, and which were rendered invalid by State sovereignty.

Resolved, That the thanks of the Senate and House of Representatives of the State of Georgia be given to John Randolph, member of Congress from the State of Virginia, and the late majority of the ninth Congress, for their virtuous and manly opposition to a compromise, which would in their opinion equally compromit the dignity of the government of the United States, and the sovereignty of this State.

Resolved, That the Governor be requested to transmit copies of the foregoing resolutions to Mr. Randolph, to the Secretary of State, the Secretary of the Treasury, and the Attorney General of the United States."

The claimants having therefore no hope of assistance from the State, applied to the federal government for relief. It is not necessary to trace in detail the rise or history of these applications to Congress. It will appear in the course of this history that the claims were pressed with pertinacity, and resisted with energy at every step. The commissioners of the United States, who had negotiated with the authorities of Georgia for the cession of the western territory, had, in their report to Congress as early as February, 1803, recommended an adjustment of the claims, and stated that "various equitable considerations, which may be urged in favor of most of the present claimants, render it expedient to enter into a compromise on reasonable terms." But they were doomed to encounter violent opposition, and in opposing these claims no one was more honest or zealous than the subject of this biography.

The Legislature of Georgia having publicly thanked the eccentric John Randolph for his "virtuous and manly opposition to a compromise," it will not be considered irrelevant if we give here some extracts from one of his speeches, especially as they serve to throw light upon what follows.

On the 29th March, 1806, the subject came before the House, on a message from the Senate, stating that they had passed a bill to carry into effect the provisions of the eighth section of the "Act* regulating the grants of land, and providing for the disposal of the lands of the United States south of the State of Tennessee." A motion was immediately made by Mr. Nelson, of Maryland, that the bill be rejected. Mr. Goldsborough, another member from Maryland, having made a fruitless motion to postpone, and having then requested to be excused from voting, Mr. Randolph said:

I hope the bill will be rejected. I have a very great respect for a full and fair discussion of every question brought before this assembly. But this is the third, and I do not know that I should be wrong in saying it is the fourth, session since this business has been pending before Congress. I believe that the report of the commissioners has been printed twice, if not three times, for the information of members. This bill, we are told, has been lying twenty days on our tables. But, had it come before the House but twenty minutes ago, when we advert to the history of the business, I am willing and anxious to give it a positive and prompt rejection. My memory is unfortunately bad. I do not, therefore, recollect when this subject, so well denominated the Yazoo subject, was first brought into this House. I know, however, it was several sessions ago, and I recollect that it was attended with some peculiar circumstances. I recollect that, important as the subject was, the discussion was smothered at the outset; and when I take into consideration that suppression of the discussion, with other facts in my own knowledge, there is the strongest *prima facie* evidence that it was designedly smothered.† But it may be said that the suppression of that discussion ought to render it more proper to discuss the bill before you.

* For this Act, see U. S. Statutes at large, vol. 2, pp. 229 to 235.—ED.

† In justice to the Reporter, it ought to be stated that he explained fully the reason why the debate was unavoidably omitted from the House proceedings.—ED.

On the contrary, the act of suppression, three or four years ago, drew the attention of the public to the subject, and caused the report of the commissioners to be republished, I believe, in every newspaper in America.

Now, what will be the consequence of this business, after having received the attention of one branch of the Legislature, and after having been slurred over by the other? I believe it would require no prophet to pronounce on the event. I have heard of a certain machine, which always gains and never loses—a machine which plain wagoners call a shuffling stick. Every step it gets up hill is sure, although the horse be restive, or the wagon be loaded too heavily, or the driver be incapable—still it cannot go back again.

I am for the rejection of the bill for another reason. This bill may be called the Omega, the last letter of the political alphabet; but, with me, it is the Alpha; it is the head of the divisions among the republican party; it is the secret and covert cause of the whole. This is the subject which has been shoved off from day to day, merely that we might get something from the other House, where its friends were more numerous. Yes, a union has been formed between Cape Ann and Marblehead, and the Rio del Norte, a union of the East with the West, which makes gentlemen more touchy and jealous of one acre of this territory than of all the real land of the United States. This has been seen, and the nation is sold. I say, *quoad hos* or *illos*, the nation is sold. We have heard of this thing two years ago, and it has come to pass. No prophets so true as those who have the means to bring things to pass. The Man of the Mountain is the truest prophet that ever lived. He had only to prophesy, to insure the perdition of any man.

What is the bill on which this House is called to act or not to act? If the gentleman will but use half the intelligence he manifests on other occasions, instead of asking to be excused from giving a vote, he will vote for an instantaneous rejection of this bill. The facts are simply these: That in 1794 and 1795, a project was set on foot to debauch and corrupt the Legislature of Georgia, and to obtain for the projectors a tract of country more extensive than any State in this Union, and more fertile than most of them; that this project succeeded; that the Legislature of Georgia was bribed; that for a mess of pottage, to be eaten by themselves, they transferred the birth-right of their countrymen. These facts are in proof to the House; and, instead of a postponement, gentlemen who want information have only to call for the reading of the records on your table. The sum stipulated to be paid for the country in question, embracing at the least forty millions of acres, was $500,000. This law excited, as it ought to have excited, in the people of Georgia, one general sentiment of indignation. But the corruption had pervaded and flooded and overflowed every* department of the government. Grants were made out, and the grantees held the parchments in their hands. The people of Georgia resolved to resort to first principles. It will be recollected that the corrupt law was passed in 1795. In the subsequent spring, the grand juries of the several counties made a unanimous protest against its passage; the succeeding Legislature repealed it, burnt the parchment, and exposed its authors. And what are we now about to do? Will we, after following an illustrious patriot† to his grave, sully the fairest page in his history by giving a sanction to this measure? The people will say you are mere mummers, actors that put on false garments for a particular occasion, and the moment after return to your original insignificance. The law was burnt—it was expunged from the records of the State, and the rescinding act incorporated in a subsequent constitution made by the people. But the grantees under the first act—under the corrupt act—had their post-horses and runners ready, who flew to the East and the West, the North and the South, and made sale of their grants. To whom did they sell? To persons apprised of the original invalidity of the act. But if they did not, does that change the question? Who are the Legislature of Georgia? The delegates of the people of Georgia. Who were the sovereigns of the several States before the Revolution? The representatives of the Crown. I will ask you, then, if one of these men had proceeded to give away the country, whether the Court of King's Bench would not have set aside the grant? They would. Subsequently to this, the United States received from the State of Georgia a grant of the country in question, and of other country not in question. In receiving this grant, they acknowledged the validity of the rescinding act of Georgia. The United

* In White's Statistics of Georgia, page 50, it is said, "no corruption was imputed to the Governor (Mathews). It is just to his memory—that of a soldier who had won a thousand laurels in the war of independence—to affirm that weakness of judgment, not corruption of heart, guided the pen which sanctioned the detested statute." There is a tradition, that his Secretary, to prevent the passage of the law, dipped the Governor's pen in oil; and that, after repeated trials, finding the pen would not write, the Governor seized another pen and signed the bill.—ED.

† Gen. James Jackson, a Senator from Georgia, who died in Washington City, on the 19th of March, 1806.—ED.

States, when they received the grant, were apprised of the preceding transfers, and the acceptance of the country from Georgia is unequivocal evidence of their opinion that the original act of 1795 was null and void. But in a country so extensive as this, in which some settlements had been previously made under British, Spanish, and other grants, from the State of Georgia, than those of 1795, it will be readily believed there were many antagonizing claims for lands. When, therefore, the United States received the country from Georgia, they entered into a compact with Georgia, or obtained permission from her, to give land not exceeding five millions, to satisfy claims not provided for in the original contract with her. Now the bill before you proposes to give this land as far as it goes, and to pledge the faith of the United States to that particular class of claimants whose pretensions arise under the act of 1795. These claims under the act of 1795, are the last class of claims under the State of Georgia, which, in my opinion, the United States are bound to satisfy. There is another description of claims, called the claims of 1789. And I am very glad the claims of 1789 are not included in this bill, because the joint interest of the two classes might possibly have an effect that in this House a single class would not. Well, Congress took the grant of the country in question from Georgia. They bound themselves to extinguish the Indian title to lands within the existing State of Georgia; to Georgia they stipulated to pay a certain sum of money, and they reserved the right of appropriating a quantity of lands not exceeding five millions of acres to satisfy claims not specially recognized in the contract with Georgia. The question now is, as I take it, whether these five millions shall go to satisfy the claims under the act of 1795. But if it should be the sense of the House that the bill includes those likewise of 1789, it will not alter, in my opinion, the question.

But I may be asked by men who profess not to be informed on this subject, what is this act of 1789, and who are the claimants under it, and how can there be interfering claims for the same land? The case is simply this: In 1789 two companies were formed, under the names of the South Carolina and the Virginia Yazoo Companies, who contracted for a great, and the greater part of the country afterwards purchased by the claimants under the act of 1795. But Georgia alleges that they did not comply with their contract, and that it was therefore set aside, and the same lands subsequently sold under the act of 1795. Be it remembered that the purchasers under the act of 1795 were men of understanding, of intelligence, of intrigue; designing men; speculators; not bullies, but swindlers; men not to be imposed on, but with their eyes open. They bought with a full knowledge of the equitable claims of 1789. When I say this, I do not mean to advocate the claims of 1789. When put to the test, one description of claims will be found as invalid as the other. But to whom did the grantees under the act of 1795, sell? After the presentments of the grand juries—after it had rung throughout the continent—that the whole was an imposition of corruption and fraud, and after there was every reason to believe they were acquainted with all the circumstances, deeds were given, one of which bears contemporaneous date with the rescinding act of Georgia. After this, what did they do? They went back to Georgia; there the money they had paid was still lying in the treasury of Georgia, with which Georgia said she would have nothing to do; after having sold the lands for which they had paid this half million, they drew this very money from the treasury of Georgia. Is this the say-so of an individual? The act appears in the report of your commissioners, composed of the Secretary of State, the Secretary of the Treasury, and the late Attorney General, in a report now on your table, and which has been twice published under the authority of this House. * * *

The bill was rejected, the same day, by a vote of sixty-two to fifty-four. Mr. Randolph then "moved that the House adjourn. He said that a few days ago the House had adjourned on account of the death of General Jackson. He hoped they would now adjourn on account of his resurrection. For he had told him, that if he could give a death-blow to the Yazoo business, he should die in peace. Adjourned, yeas fifty-eight."

This occurred before the entrance of Colonel Troup into Congress. During the session of 1807–8, the same subject came before the House, on a memorial signed by the Governor of Massachusetts by order and at the unanimous request of the Legislature of that State, "praying the attention of the National Government to the claim and rights of sundry citizens of the said State of Massachusetts in and to certain lands purchased under grants of the State of Georgia," &c. Mr. Bibb, of Georgia, immediately moved the rejection of the memorial. In seconding the motion, Col. Troup made a short speech, in which, amongst other things, he said:

The memorial, on a subject on which the House had before decided, and that on the most mature deliberation, was treating the House with disrespect; it was an attempt (it could be considered in no other light) to tease the House; to torture it into a compliance with the prayer of the petition. The House was to be provoked into a surrender of important rights to get rid of the memorialists. They were bound to listen to a memorial couched in decent, proper and respectful terms, but not to the language of insult—and this was an insult upon this body, calling upon it to sanction corruption so vile and infamous. With this impression he should second the motion of his colleague.

During the same debate, Col. Troup said:

He was extremely sorry that on this subject he should trouble the House—he felt at this time particularly disqualified. Was this business never to be finally disposed of? Did the claimants calculate their chances of success on the confidence, or rather on the audacity, with which they urged their claims? Was the justice of their claims to be estimated by the indefatigable assiduity with which they renewed their pretensions? and pretensions, too, which were audacious, unfounded and insolent—originating in fraud and corruption—embellished with murder, perjury, and every species of enormity! He trusted there was virtue sufficient in this Assembly to treat the claimants with contempt. He flattered himself that the Legislature would not degrade itself by a compromise with speculation and corruption; he presumed the Capitol was not the place where speculators were to seek indemnity. If it were, they had better appropriate five or six millions of acres to these injured persons—to these miscalculators of profit and loss, or rather to these men ruined by the unsuccessful exercise of the arts of bribery and corruption. What did the memorialists demand? That this House should indemnify them for losses sustained by the act of Georgia. Would they do it on the broad principle of relieving all speculators in distress, or from the cession to the United States, by the State of Georgia, of the land in question? On the last principle, they would not presume to attempt it; for they knew that they had not the power. On this account, he wished the memorial to be rejected. He was as much disposed as any gentleman on the floor to treat the State of Massachusetts with respect, as an integral part of the Union; but, he would ask, what right had the State of Massachusetts to interfere with an individual claim? None.

The subject again came before the House, on the 12th of February, 1808, on the memorial of Joseph (afterwards Judge) Story, as the agent of the New England Mississippi Company, praying that he might "be admitted to a hearing at the bar of the House of Representatives in behalf of said company, to state their rights and explain their claims," and a resolution offered to hear said agent. The mover of the resolution (Mr. Bacon, of Massachusetts,) said, "this was not a question which required any abstruse reasoning or deep research for facts. He had taken this resolution from a precedent, which he found recorded, of a similar indulgence granted to the South Carolina Company, who were heard at the bar of the House in support of their claim, by Mr. Moultrie, their agent, in a nearly similar case."

Mr. Troup hoped the resolution would not be adopted. The precedent adduced was not in point; that was in the case of an application to be heard on the subject of the old Virginia and South Carolina claims. It will be recollected by the House that the case adduced in precedent was an old, a dormant claim, which had slept long, and the principles of which were almost forgotten by members of the House, and, when application was made for hearing, they determined to hear all that could be said, that they might act understandingly on the subject. They did hear, and were satisfied; from that time to this the House had had no further trouble with it. The claims of these persons, however, have been turned over from session to session, canvassed over and over again; and the House are as well conversant with the merits of the claim as with its advocates. I do not know whether it is customary to admit within its bar the advocates of claims. For my part, I do not know, if such persons were admitted within the bar, that I would keep my seat and listen. It is impossible that this House could be so lost to a sense of its own dignity as to enter into a controversy on its own floor with speculators or their agents. In discussion of this subject among ourselves, our utmost coolness and care will be required to keep us in temper with each other; and the admission of a stranger within this bar, for the purpose of irritating, and, perhaps, insulting us—and I beg gentlemen to recollect that the theme is extremely delicate—will not increase the calmness which ought to be observed. What is the object of the present motion? Is it proposed, by admitting a practicing attorney on this floor, to enlighten us on a subject of which we are profoundly ignorant? No; with the principle of this claim we are all acquainted. Its object is to give some strength to a claim which has not the smallest foundation in justice, and they know it. They have no more claim on the United States than on you or me. Why, then, do they call upon us? Because the United States has an overflowing treasury. If I had it, they would make the same claim upon me. They are the cormorants which perch upon the treasuries of all nations; and as long as you have gold and silver, and manifest a disposition to give, they will stick to you. I thought, for my part, that one discussion would have sufficed for them; on the presentation of the original memorial, you listened to it, and submitted it to a Committee of the whole House. I was anxious that all discussion on this subject should have been waived: it might have been, and I had hoped it would. I myself would have submitted my individual feelings to the harmony of the nation, and am sorry that I am now compelled to speak.

On the same day, Col. Troup delivered another animated speech on the same subject. The question was taken on the resolution, and it was rejected by yeas twenty-eight to nays seventy-six.

In order to present here a general view of the further progress of this subject, it is necessary to go forward somewhat out of the chronological order of this biography. It is chiefly for the part which Col. Troup took, in opposition to these claims, that we have introduced the subject at all.

On the 17th December, 1810, he offered the following resolution in the House:

Resolved, That the Secretary of the Treasury be directed to lay before this House any information he may have touching any settlement, contrary to law, on the public lands in the Mississippi Territory; by whom, at what periods and extent, and what measures had been taken to remove such intruders on the public lands.

In explaining the resolution, he said his object was to obtain information as to certain lands in the Mississippi Territory; the title to which the United States had, on the one hand, declared to be vested in them, and the Supreme Court, on the other hand, had declared not to be in the United States, but in those persons claiming under the Yazoo speculation. This decision must either be acquiesced in or resisted by the United States. If acquiesced in, it must be in one of two ways. The United States must either permit the Supreme Court to execute its judgment in the ordinary course, or must permit quiet possession to be taken by the claimants. Whether they acquiesce in one way or the other, two distinct great rights were affected: first, the great interest of the whole people of the United States, claiming equal and common proprietorship of the soil; and, second, the great interest of the people of Georgia, to whom the United States had agreed to pay $1,250,000, out of the proceeds of the sales of these lands. If the decision of the Supreme Court of the United States was acquiesced in, the State of Georgia would be thus defrauded both of her land and money. But if the government of the United States would not submit to this decision, but resist it to the last extremity, what course could be taken but to employ the whole military force of the United States to eject all persons not claiming under the authority of the United States? If that description of persons claiming the territory, in whose behalf a decision was lately made, taking forcible possession, should obtain such a footing as to be able to oppose to the authority of the United States a considerable force, there would perhaps be no alternative but for the United States to remove them by an exertion of its military power, or tamely to acquiesce in the lawless aggression. It was from these considerations that he was desirous to have information on the subject of the late settlements there.

The resolution was adopted. The decision of the Supreme Court, to which reference was above made, is that in the case of Fletcher *v.* Peck, 6 Cranch's Rep., 87 to 148, at February term, 1810; a case originating in the U. S. Circuit Court for the District of Massachusetts, and which was brought to try the title to 15,000 acres of land situate on the Mississippi and Tombigby rivers, under and by virtue of sundry mesne conveyances founded on a grant from the State of Georgia under the act of 7th January, 1795. Those who are curious in such matters are referred to the decision itself for information on all the points adjudicated by the Court; but the following extracts we believe sufficient to show the general grounds on which the judgment in that case was rendered:

This (say the Court) is not a bill brought by the State of Georgia to annul the contract; nor does it appear to the court, by this count, that the State of Georgia is dissatisfied with the sale that has been made. The case, as made out in the pleadings, is simply this. One individual, who holds lands in the State of Georgia under a deed covenanting that the title of Georgia was in the grantor, brings an action of covenant upon this deed, and assigns, as a breach, that some of the members of the Legislature were induced to vote in favor of the law which constituted the contract, by being promised an interest in it, and that therefore the act is a mere nullity. This solemn question cannot be brought thus collaterally and incidentally before the court. It would be indecent, in the extreme, upon a private contract between two individuals, to enter into an inquiry respecting the corruption of the sovereign power of a State. If the title be plainly deduced from a legislative act, which the Legislature might constitutionally pass, if the act be clothed with all the requisite forms of a law, a court, sitting as a court of law, cannot sustain a suit brought by one individual against another, founded on the allegation that the act is a nullity in consequence of the impure motives which influenced certain members of the Legislature which passed the law. * * If a suit be brought to set aside a conveyance obtained by fraud, and the fraud be clearly proved, the conveyance will be set aside, as between the parties; but the rights of third persons, who are purchasers without notice for a valuable consideration, cannot be disregarded. Titles which, according to every legal test, are perfect, are acquired with that confidence which is inspired by the opinion that the purchaser is safe. If there be any concealed defect, arising from the conduct of those who had held the property long before he acquired it, of which he had no notice, that concealed defect cannot be set up against him. He has paid his money for a title good at law, he is innocent, whatever may be the guilt of others; and equity will not subject him to the penalties attached to that guilt. All titles would be insecure, and the intercourse between man and man would be very seriously obstructed, if this principle be overturned.

It is not proposed to combat the rulings of the court as the case actually stood before it upon the pleadings. The points decided by the Court, in the above extracts, appear to be these: First, Georgia not being a complaining party, the question could not be collaterally and incidentally decided. Secondly, For aught that appeared, the act was constitutionally passed. Thirdly, There was nothing on the face of the pleadings to show that the defendant was not a purchaser in good faith for a valuable consideration. The case was one of inference and presumption from the pleadings. How these inferences were met by the opponents of the act, amongst whom Col. Troup was one of the ablest, will now appear.

On the 19th of January, 1813, a bill passed the United States Senate, to carry into effect the report of James Madison, Secretary of State, Albert Gallatin, Secretary of the Treasury, and Levi Lincoln, Attorney General of the United States, Commissioners, &c., in the year 1803, recommending an equitable compromise with the Yazoo claimants. It passed a third reading in the Senate, against the votes of William H. Crawford and Charles Tait, Senators from Georgia. On the 20th of January, the bill was read a first time in the House, and on a motion to read it the second time and commit it, Col. Troup, having asked if a motion to reject the bill would not supersede a motion to commit, and being answered in the affirmative, said:

It is on no ordinary occasion, sir, I would permit myself to move the rejection of a bill on the first reading, coming from another branch of the Legislature, but the measure growing out of an hideous corruption, I owe it to you to move, because I think you owe it to your own dignity to reject the bill, not upon any dubious evidence of the fraud and corruption of the Georgia Legislature, but upon evidence satisfactory to you and to all mankind, spread upon your own records by commissioners of your own appointment, and which the clerk can be called on to read. The nature, the extent, the detail of corruption by which the Legislature of Georgia were induced to sell the public property, are there portrayed by your own commissioners. It is stated that more than two-thirds of the Legislature were bribed and corrupted, were interested in and parties to the purchase. They show you that A received 112,000 acres of land for his vote; that B received 75,000 acres for his vote; that C received 56,000 acres for his vote, and that none received less than 56,000 acres. It is upon this record evidence, then, that I move you to reject the bill. You rejected the bill from the Senate, on the first reading, for the suspension of the *habeas corpus* act. Why? Because the bill contained a principle violative of civil liberty. I move you to reject this bill! Why? Because it contains a principle destructive of republican government. The purity and incorruptibility of the representative character is the basis of our republican institutions—if there be one principle of our government more fundamental than another, it is that no benefit or profit or advantage shall result either immediately or remotely to any human being from the corruption of the representatives of the people. The bill proposes to give five millions of dollars to those claiming under the corrupters of representatives of the people. The corrupters only gave five hundred thousand dollars—the United States only gave twelve hundred and fifty thousand dollars to Georgia for her territory. The bill proposes to give five millions of dollars to the claimants—five millions of dollars to extinguish their claim. You are required to reward the claimants who bought of those who corrupted the Legislature of Georgia. We say, no! Let ruin overtake the corrupters of the representatives of the people and all claiming under them. The corrupters have made their fortunes, now you are called upon to make the fortunes of the claimants; this is to be precedent, this is to be example.

The claimants have hitherto urged their claim with indefatigable perseverance, they have teased and wearied you; you have constantly repelled them; they have seen their discomfiture in the justness and simplicity of your reasoning. You say to them, in substance, the Yazoo act having been fraudulently and corruptly obtained, was null and void, *ab initio*. All contracts founded in fraud are void. It could pass no right; if it could pass no right to the original purchasers, it is impossible that the original purchasers could pass any right to the claimants; and if no right passed to the claimants, it is impossible they can have a claim or shadow of claim against you. They constantly found themselves foiled by this honesty and simplicity of reasoning. Seeing you firm and inflexible, they turned about and addressed themselves to the Judiciary. They found in the law-books of England a maxim which suited them; two of the speculators combined and made up a fictitious case, a feigned issue for the decision of the Supreme Court.* They presented precisely those points for the decision of the court which they wished the court to decide; and the court did actually decide them as the speculators themselves would have decided them if they had been in the place of the Supreme Court. The first point was, whether the Legislature of Georgia had the *power* to sell the territory? Yes, said the Judges, they had. Second, whether by the Yazoo act an estate did vest in the original grantees? Yes, said the Judges, it did. Third, whether it was competent to any subsequent Legislature to set aside the act on the ground of fraud and corruption? No, said the Judges, it was not; an estate did vest in the grantees by the Yazoo act, which could not be divested by the act of any subsequent Legislature. No matter, say the Judges, what the nature or extent of the corruption, be it ever so wicked, be it ever so nefarious, it could not be set aside. The speculators had hunted up a maxim of the common law or equity courts of England, and the Judges wielded it for their benefit and to the ruin of the country—the maxim that third purchasers without notice shall not be affected by the fraud of the original parties. Thus, sir,

---

* In delivering his separate opinion in the case of Fletcher v. Peck, Mr. Justice Johnson said: "I have been very unwilling to proceed to the decision of this cause at all. It appears to me to bear strong evidence, upon the face of it, of being a mere feigned case. It is our duty to decide on the rights, but not on the speculations of parties. My confidence, however, in the respectable gentlemen who have been engaged for the parties, has induced me to abandon my scruples, in the belief that they would never consent to impose a mere feigned case upon this Court."—ED.

by a maxim of English law, are the rights and liberties of the people of this country to be corruptly bartered by their representatives. It is this decision of the Judges which has been made the basis of the bill on your table—a decision shocking to every free government, sapping the foundation of all your constitutions, and annihilating at a breath the best hope of man. Yes, sir, it is proclaimed by the Judges, and is now to be sanctioned by the Legislature, that the representatives of the people may corruptly betray the people, may corruptly barter their rights and those of their posterity, and the people are wholly without any kind of remedy whatsoever. It is this monstrous and abhorrent doctrine which must startle every man in the nation, that you ought promptly to discountenance and condemn. It is this doctrine, the basis and essential principle of the bill, that we call upon you to reject. Suppose, sir, the Legislature of Georgia, instead of selling the public territory, had corruptly sold the good people of Georgia and all their posterity into slavery, the consequences would have been the same, the judges would have decreed that an estate did vest in the original grantee, notwithstanding the corruption, which could not be divested by any subsequent Legislature. But, sir, let me state to you a case, exposing at once the flagrant enormity of the principle: it is a case as perfectly parallel as the human mind can conceive. Suppose, sir, that the twelfth Congress should corruptly sell the good people of the United States to England, and England should instantly sell to France—France would come upon the thirteenth Congress and demand possession; the virtuous thirteenth Congress would say, No! we will not give you possession; the twelfth Congress was bribed and corrupted to sell the good people of the United States; fraud vitiates every grant, and therefore you can have no right to demand possession. Ah! but, says France, I am an innocent purchaser, I purchased without knowledge of the fraud; and it is a maxim of the common law of England that third purchasers are not to be affected by the fraud of the original parties. Thus, sir, according to the Judges, would the good people of the United States be sold like a flock of sheep by the corruption of their representatives, leaving them, the people, without any kind of remedy whatsoever.

If, Mr. Speaker, the arch fiend had, in the bitterness of his hatred to mankind, resolved the destruction of republican government on earth, he would have issued a decree like that of the judges; he would have said, in the spirit and language of this bill, let the claimants under the corrupters of the representatives of the people be rewarded. In a nation of enlightened men, whose governments have their origin in and exist only by the will of the people, that will is contemned and held for nothing. Why, it may be asked, do the judges who passed this decision live and live unpunished? The answer is found in the mildness and moderation of our government. I thank God it is so. If, under a despotism, the *throne* of the monarch had been thus assailed, the judges would have perished. Here the foundations of the Republic are shaken, and the judges sleep in tranquillity at home. Take my word for it, Mr. Speaker—I beseech you to remember what I say—no party in this country, however deeply seated in power, can long survive the adoption of this measure. I remember a gentleman, once a member of this House; he had his seat on the opposite side of it; he was a man of the most vigorous intellect I ever knew; he had deeply studied human nature; to be sure his conduct was not always regulated by his knowledge of it; he was often imprudent and not unfrequently extravagant. Whenever this question was turned up, however, he used to address his political friends, "Gentlemen, I beseech you to withhold your countenance from this measure. It is founded in corruption, the people know it; they are not yet ripe for the supply of men who will support such measures. If you want to mount into power, if you wish to conciliate the affection of this people, you must assume a virtue if you have it not."

Mr. Troup said he wished it understood that in moving the rejection of the bill, it was not his design to enter at all into the merits of the Yazoo claim. The few observations he had submitted, were directed to the principle contained in the bill. If, however, the House should in its discretion determine to sustain that principle, and to enter into the merits of the question at large, he should, notwithstanding it had been so often discussed and was so well understood by every man in the nation, have no objection to meet it. He would then undertake to show to the House, 1st, That the Legislature of Georgia had no constitutional power to sell the public domain. 2d, That if it had, it could not sell fraudulently and corruptly. 3d, That these claimants had notice of the fraud, and, having notice, are, according to the maxim of the judges themselves, without claim or shadow of claim.

The bill was not rejected, but was referred to the Committee on Public Lands, which afterwards made a report recommending a modification of the terms of the bill, and proposing amendments accordingly. On the 8th of March, 1814, the Senate bill again coming up before the House, Col. Troup said:

He rose with great reluctance to move to reject the bill. There were only two considerations which could induce him to depart from the respect due to another branch of the Legislature; either that a measure emanating from it was unconstitutional or corrupt. It was because this measure had its origin in corruption he moved to reject the bill. When I say, sir, that this measure has its origin in corruption, I do not mean to be understood as charging corruption on the Senate—all I mean to be understood as saying, is, that this measure flows from corruption, as a stream flows from its source; it flows from the corrupt act of the Legislature of Georgia of 1795. The bill proposes to give five millions of dollars to the Yazoo claimants. The Yazoo Legislature sold for five hundred thousand dollars—Georgia sold to the United States for one million two hundred and fifty thousand dollars only, and you now propose to give five millions to the claimants to compromise their claim. How will we be able to account for this? How will posterity be able to account for it? Posterity will say that these claimants, like the gods of Milton, carried the mountains in their hands, and wielding the fifty millions of acres under the decision of the Supreme Court, have carried everything before them.

You know the history of this transaction, sir. On the 7th of January, 1795, the Legislature of Georgia sold to certain individuals, called the original grantees, fifty millions of acres of land for five hundred thousand dollars. Every member who voted for the law, except one, whose name does not appear, was bribed and corrupted, that is to say, was interested in, and the party to the purchase. On the 13th of February, 1796, the subsequent Legislature declared the corrupt act null and void; ordered the record to be burnt, and authorized the grantees to withdraw the purchase money. The convention of the whole people soon after confirmed the rescinding act. On the same day, that is to say, on the 13th of February, 1796, the Yazoo claimants purchased from the original grantees. The claimants say that they are innocent purchasers, without notice of the corruption—that an estate vested notwithstanding the corruption, and that they have a good title against you. It may be well to observe here that the claimants have constantly shifted their ground. At first they insisted that the Yazoo act of 1795 was a fair and honest act of legislation. As soon, however, as the report of your Commissioners, which exhibited the fraud in its nakedness, drove them from this ground, they insisted on the innocency of their purchase. Driven from this ground, they throw themselves on your mercy. Do not believe, sir, that the corruption in which this transaction was engendered, was a corruption of any ordinary character; it was a corruption without example in history; may it never find a parallel! Not merely were the corrupted corrupted by the corrupters—the corrupters cheated the corrupted—the corrupters cheated one another, and the corrupters, as they say, cheated these claimants. The members of the Legislature were bribed with land and money; in some instances the member gave his vote, and the corrupter withheld the bribe; the member went home—he had lost his character—he had lost his bribe, and he died broken-hearted in the bosom of his family. When the rescinding Legislature, in a spirit of liberality which became them, decreed that the original grantees might withdraw the purchase money, on producing certain evidence of their having made the deposite—such a scene of fraud, iniquity and depravity was exhibited, that the Governor, familiar as he had been with such scenes but a short time before, blushed and shut the doors of the treasury against them. Men concerned in this transaction, but who had not deposited one dollar, by perjury, forgery, or some other crime, drew thousands from the treasury; those of the speculators who had actually paid the money, were then defrauded by their brethren. On the other hand, some of the original grantees allege that they were cheated by these claimants—that the claimants gave them paper for their land, which paper turned out good for nothing. Thus, sir, you see this Yazoo transaction is a circle of fraud. It no doubt had a beginning, but it is certainly without end, unless you consummate it by this measure.

As good fortune will have it, Mr. Speaker, this is one of the plainest cases that can be presented to the understanding. The claimants either have a claim, or they have not. If they have a claim, you may compromise a claim; if they have no claim, you cannot compromise no claim. If they have a claim, it is a claim to fifty millions of acres of land, and you ought to give it to them, and say no more about it. Could you entertain a thought for one moment to avail yourself of your power to do wrong and injustice to these impotent individuals? Surely no man will have the hardihood to say that the magnitude of the claim ought to weigh one tittle in the scale of justice. The claimants either have a title to fifty millions of acres, or they have not a title to a square foot. How do they derive the title? From the original grantees. How do the original grantees derive title? From the Yazoo Legislature of '95. Their title, therefore, must depend on the validity or invalidity of the Yazoo act of the Legislature of Georgia—it can depend on nothing else. If the Yazoo act was a good and valid act, an estate vested in the original grantees; the grantees passed the estate to these claimants, and the claimants have a good title against you. If the Yazoo act was a null and void act, no estate vested in the original grantees; if no estate vested in the original grantees, they could pass none to these claimants, and if no estate passed to these claimants, on what pretense can they set up the title against you? Are the Congress of the United States prepared to say that the Yazoo act, notwithstanding the corruption of the representatives of the people, was a good and valid act? That it divested the public property out of the people and vested it in the grantees? Are the Congress of the United States prepared to say, that the representatives of a free and virtuous people may fraudulently and corruptly betray that people, and barter their rights, and that the people are without remedy? That an estate did vest by the Yazoo act, which could not be divested by any subsequent act! Sir, it is impossible. This doctrine is too monstrous to be entertained by a moral people, who love liberty—it strikes at all virtue, at all morality—it overturns Republican governments. You can not, you dare not, sanctify this doctrine. If you dare, one of two things must happen; the people are ready to approve it, or they are not—if they are, they have lost their virtue, and we must seek shelter under despotism; if they are not, you will go out and other men will come in. Not the gentlemen on the other side of the House—they never can come in—men will come in who will discountenance corruption, cherish virtue, and preserve the principles of the government pure and uncorrupted. I address myself to the Republican party: let them remember how they came into power. The Federalists had been charged with monarchical attachments; with cherishing corrupt principles of government. The people believed it. They said the government was not safe in such hands—they turned them out. You succeeded.

The people said to you—take this sacred trust, do your duty faithfully; preserve the principles of this happy government pure and uncorrupted, and be ready to hand it over to your successors whenever you shall be required, more pure and uncorrupted than when you received it. Will you do so when you have decreed that the representatives of the people may corruptly divest the estate of the people, and that they are without remedy? Yet, sir, this you must do the moment you decide to compromise this claim. But you have no reason, no motive, no apology, for thus deciding. I will take away from every unprejudiced man in the country every pretext, every apology for compromising this claim. I insist that the Yazoo Legislature had no constitutional power to sell the land.

1st. I contend that the Legislature had no constitutional power to sell.

2nd. That if they had constitutional power to sell, they could not sell fraudulently and corruptly.

3rd. That if, notwithstanding the fraud and corruption, an estate did vest in the original grantees, according to the decision of the Supreme Court, these claimants having notice of the fraud, are parties to it, and without title in law or equity.

There is no power given in the Constitution of Georgia, and without an express grant of power the Legislature cannot possess it. This is the doctrine distinctly, clearly, and unanimously maintained by the writers on public law. The reasons on which it is founded are as distinctly given. The people are seized, collectively and individually, of the public territory—it cannot be taken from them without their consent—it cannot be taken from them without their express consent—consent shall not be implied. 1st, because the power to sell the public domain is not a power incidental or necessary to the power of legislation. 2ndly, because it is too important a power to be derived by implication or construction. Not only is this the universal doctrine of the publicists, of Grotius, Puffendorf, Vattel, Burlamaqui, and others, but it is the doctrine to which all our political institutions have conformed. In the constitution of the United States, as well as the constitutions of the States, you see the doctrine clearly recognized. In the constitution of the United States it is said, "Congress shall have power to dispose of, and make all needful rules and regulations concerning the public property." Why was this power expressly granted? Because the Convention knew that if not expressly granted it could not be derived by implication or construction. So, in the State constitutions, the doctrine is recognized: "the power to dispose of the public domain being in the people, cannot be taken from them without their consent." I know it may be said that there is a difference between the United States and State constitutions, in the character of their powers—that in the United States constitution all powers not delegated are reserved—that in the State constitutions all powers are delegated but those which are reserved. This is true, but by all powers is meant only all ordinary powers, all powers that are essential and necessary or incidental to the general power of legislation; extraordinary powers, powers not essential to the general power of legislation, are, even in the States, retained by the people, and cannot be divested out of them without their express consent. This power to dispose of the public domain is an extraordinary power; for, say the publicists, one and all, this power is so essentially in the people, that even under the violent governments of Europe, the despot has no power to dispose of the public domain without the express consent of the people. I know, too, it will be said that the State Legislatures have in some instances disposed of the public property without an express grant of power to warrant it. I answer that in every such instance the Legislature was guilty of usurpation, and the people not bound—that if the people pleased to yield a tacit acquiescence, well and good—they did so because their attention had not been called to the usurpation by a flagrant and palpable corruption—but will you believe that if in any such instance the usurpation had been coupled with a notorious corruption of their representatives, they would not have resisted—that they would not have risen in mass, as did the people of Georgia, to put down the corruption and the corrupted? A people who would not, must have lost their virtue and been ready for a tyrant. I say, therefore, the Yazoo Legislature of Georgia had no power to sell the public property.

But if the Legislature had constitutional power to sell, it could not sell fraudulently and corruptly. Do you ask proof of this?—fraud and corruption vitiate every act, render it null and void *ab initio;* no contract, no obligation, can grow out of it. The powers granted by the people to their Legislatures, are granted in confidence that they will be fairly and honestly exercised. What would you think of the declaration of a constitution, "the powers herein granted shall be honestly exercised"? Would you not consider such a declaration ridiculous, and ridiculous because superfluous? Is not the implication as strong as any expression could be, that every fraudulent act of legislation is merely void? Suppose it were written in any constitution, "the Legislature shall have no power fraudulently and corruptly to betray the people," would you not, too, consider this ridiculous, and ridiculous because superfluous? Suppose it were written in any constitution, "the Legislature shall have power fraudulently and corruptly to sell the public property," would not such a grant of power be merely void, though proceeding from the highest human authority, the people themselves? And why void? Because repugnant to the laws of God and nature. Nay, sir, I go further; I say the great God of Heaven himself could confer no such power—if the great God of Heaven were to decree, "the Legislature shall have power fraudulently and corruptly to sell the public property," the decree would be merely void, because inconsistent with His holy attributes. And yet, sir, the Senate require of us to do that which the God of Heaven himself cannot do—legalize fraud and corruption—they require us to declare that, notwithstanding the fraud and corruption of the Georgia Legislature, an estate did vest in the original grantees, which it was competent to the grantees to transfer to the claimants; that the claimants have a title against you, and that to relinquish that title we must give them five millions of dollars. This is making war upon the people with a vengeance. To talk of the rights of the people after this, is insult and mockery. But why is it that the corrupt act of the Representative is not binding on the people? For this plain reason, the corruption of the Representative must precede the corrupt act; the moment he has betrayed his constituents, all ties and connection between them are dissolved, and he is no more capable of binding them than the merest stranger. Any other doctrine makes Republican government a farce—makes morality and religion idle sound. If corruption can divest the estate of the people, it can do any other act—it can legalize murder, robbery, treason—it can give universal license to crime. I say, therefore, that if the Legislature of Georgia had constitutional power to sell, it could not sell fraudulently and corruptly. The Yazoo act was merely void, and the rescinding act which declared it so, was only form; the people were in possession, continued in possession, and were not divested by it.

3rdly. If, notwithstanding the fraud and corruption, an

estate did vest in the grantees, yet, the claimants having notice of the fraud, are, according to the decision of the Supreme Court itself, guilty purchasers, without claim or shadow of claim. I say, sir, the claimants had notice. Let it be remembered, Mr. Speaker, that our government differs from all other governments in this singular but valuable characteristic—it is limited by written constitutions. In other countries it is said the acts or the grants of the government speak for themselves—nothing shall be admitted to contradict them. Not so in our country; every act or grant of the government must be consistent with the written constitution. Every man is presumed to carry the constitution in his head or in his pocket, that he may at all times be ready to compare the acts of government with the constitution. If the claimants had done this, if they had compared the Yazoo act with the constitution of Georgia, they would have found no power in the constitution authorizing the Legislature to sell, and this circumstance alone would have put them upon their guard—at least, this would have been the effect on all rational and prudent men.

But there was cause of suspicion on the very face of the act itself. The Legislature sold fifty millions of acres of as fine a country as any on the globe, for five hundred thousand dollars. Would not prudent men, looking at this single fact, have inquired how comes this? Would not prudent men, about to embark in a speculation so enormous, have thought it worth their while to send an agent from Boston to Georgia, to scrutinize and investigate the merits of this transaction? But, sir, these are circumstances to excite suspicion only. The people of Georgia themselves gave to the claimants the most prompt, direct and unexceptionable notice. Remember that more than a year elapsed between the passage of the Yazoo act and the purchase by the claimants. The events which followed the passage of the Yazoo act portended a revolution in Georgia, as terrible and as bloody as the revolution of Paris or of La Vendee. If the claimants had lived in the farther India, if they had lived in the islands of the Pacific Ocean, they would have received notice long before they purchased. Scarce had the Yazoo act passed the Legislature, when the whole country was in a ferment. The great body of the people, who, unlike their Representatives, remained uncorrupted and faithful to themselves, were everywhere in motion to counteract the projects of the traitors. Their grand juries and committees everywhere denounced the act a usurpation, called upon the country to assert its rights, and to put down the corruption and the corrupted. General Jackson—sir, I cannot think of Gen. Jackson without speaking of him as a man of rare patriotism and integrity—a man who, if he had lived in the days of Rome's greatness, or, rather, of Rome's virtue, would have had his bust in the Capitol—I speak of him thus, because his memory is intimately connected with this transaction; he was the only man I ever did know who was at all times ready to lay down his life, to sacrifice his wife and children and his fortune, to his country. General Jackson was at that time a Senator in Congress at Philadelphia; he was called by the people of Georgia, publicly called, from his seat in Congress to aid in rescinding the usurped act—he obeyed. The address of the people and his answer were published in all of the newspapers of the day. A man by the name of Thomas, one of the corrupted Senators, was murdered in his own house, that he, together with his testimony, (for he bore witness to the corruption and threatened to confess,) might be consigned to oblivion. By some it was said the speculators had murdered him, by others that his indignant constituents had done the deed. The truth is that the greatest efforts were necessary to restrain the people from acts of violence. Now, sir, all these things were done, not in secret to deceive the innocent purchasers of New England; they were done publicly and in the face of day; they were published in all the newspapers of the time, from Boston to Savannah; and yet these things were to the innocent purchasers of New England as if they had never been. Yes, sir, if you believe the claimants, they were as ignorant of them as the people of Crim Tartary. They tell you they never read newspapers. The mail running weekly between Boston and Savannah—the coasting trade open—and yet the claimants are innocent purchasers; for one whole year they heard not a word of what was passing in Georgia. If the mails had been stopped, if the coasting trade had been interrupted, if all communication had been cut off, this plea of ignorance might have been set up. In the then state of intercourse of the civilized world, if the claimants had lived in Batavia, they would have had notice long before they purchased.

But there is other evidence of notice still more conclusive. On the 17th of February, 1795, that is to say six weeks after the passage of the Yazoo act, General Washington sent to Congress a public message to the following effect:

"I have received copies of two Acts of the Legislature 'of Georgia, one passed on the 28th of December, the other 'on the 7th January last, for appropriating and selling the 'Indian lands within the territorial limits claimed by that 'State. These copies, though not officially certified, have 'been transmitted to me in such a manner as to leave no room 'to doubt their authenticity. These Acts embrace an object 'of such magnitude, and in their consequences may so 'deeply affect the peace and welfare of the United States, 'that I have thought it necessary now to lay them before 'Congress."

Here then was notice to all the world, notice at least that something was wrong. General Washington, from the elevation of his high office, standing as it were on the top of Mount Sinai, with an angel voice, reaching the extremities of the earth, proclaimed, beware! A more distinct, audible, universal notice could not have been given to all mankind. The claimants heeded no more the warning of General Washington than they did the barking of a foist. Congress referred the message to a committee. The committee reported a resolution and bill authorizing the Executive to extinguish the title of Georgia to the country in question. With the Yazoo act before them, the committee did not deign to speak of the sale to the claimants, but, treating the Yazoo act as null and void, proceeded to treat with Georgia for the extinguishment of her title. The claimants say they never heard of the proclamation of General Washington. They never read newspapers.

But this is not all. The claimants stand convicted under their own hands and seals; they are guilty purchasers on the face of their own title deed. Not only did their title deed not contain a general warranty in their favor, it contained an express stipulation that in no event would they, the claimants, go back upon the grantees from whom they purchased, for even the consideration money, on account of any defect in their title. Under their own hands and seals did the claimants covenant and agree that the grantees of whom they bought should not be liable to refund the purchase money, if their title turned out to be defective. Sir, this is a fact so extraordinary and incredible, that if it were not recorded on the title deed itself, I would hesitate to declare it. It is without example in transactions between man and man. Do you not see, but for this, the claimants would have resorted to the original grantees for their purchase money, with interest and damages; that is to say, they would have resorted to the same remedy as all other men do under like circumstances in every country; they would have recovered their purchase money paid for a consideration which had failed, for a title which had proved defective, with interest and damages—they would, in fact, have had all the remedy to which innocent purchasers, without notice, are entitled by the laws of any country? But they precluded themselves by their own act and deed; and, because they have done so, are we bound to indemnify them? They have as much right to apply for indemnity to the Emperor of China. But there is another fact: the rescinding Legislature met in the beginning of January, '96—the claimants purchased on the 13th of February, '96—on the opening of the Legislature, the preparatory motion was made to rescind the usurped act; the claimants, therefore, had six weeks to inform themselves of what was doing and what was about to be done in the Georgia Legislature, before they purchased. But there is another fact, which ought to be conclusive on this point—a gentleman from Massachusetts, many years a member of this House, resident in the neighborhood of Boston, uniformly declared they had notice; that gentleman, respectable for his good sense and integrity, intimately acquainted with the parties, constantly passing in and from Boston, perfectly familiar with the circumstances of the purchase, constantly affirmed that he was himself knowing to the corruption of the Georgia Legislature at the date of the purchase, and that the claimants were as knowing to it as himself. Here, then, is the testimony of a disinterested man. You oppose to it the declarations of the interested claimants. The truth is, the claimants had knowledge of the fraud. Like other speculators, they bought to sell again; all they wanted was the wax and the parchment. They cared not a straw for anything else, for fraud and corruption, or defect of title; if it answered the purpose of the grantees, it would answer the purpose of the claimants; the claimants took the title deed for better, for worse, and if they had not known that Congress might be teased and worried out of anything, they never would have had the effrontery to set up a claim against you.

But, it is said the commissioners reported in favor of a compromise. What does this amount to? No more than a report of a committee of the House, which you respect only as its merits entitle it to respect. The commissioners investigated the claims; laid before you in all its nakedness the fraud and corruption, from beginning to end, and came to the conclusion which no man of common sense could avoid, that the claimants had no title whatsoever. Here, sir, the commissioners ought to have stopped; but, strange to say, they suggested to Congress the expediency of a compromise. What! you ask, is it possible that such men as Mr. Madison, Mr. Gallatin and Mr. Lincoln, should have followed up such a conclusion by such a suggestion? No title, and yet recommend the compromise of a title! Never were two propositions more inconsistent. You will say there must have been some reason for this. I will tell you the reason: it was the same reason that operated on the 10th Congress to surrender the embargo—the clamor of a formidable party. The commissioners were surrounded by a host of claimants, as we are now; they found them a troublesome set, growing every day stronger and stronger. They yielded—they said, though they have no title, yet you had better give them money and send them about their business. This is all that can be said now.

But, it has been alleged that the United States have engaged to compromise. Not so. The United States are as free to compromise, or not to compromise, as if nothing had been said or done on the subject. It is said that the United States are bound to compromise, because five millions were set apart by the articles of agreement and cession, for the indemnification of these and other claims. True! But on condition only, that Congress should, upon an investigation of the claims, believe that in right and justice they ought to be compensated. The history of this part of the business is simply this: When the commissioners of the United States and of Georgia were negotiating the terms of purchase of the Mississippi Territory, the claimants got about them and harrassed them with incessant importunity. The commissioners of the United States said to the commissioners on the part of Georgia, You see how we are embarrassed by these claimants; will it not be better to quiet them, by making a reservation in their favor? Never! indignantly answered the Georgia commissioners; we will never consent to compromise the infamous corruption. But, said the commissioners of the United States, will you not agree to make a conditional reservation, leaving it to the United States to make them compensation, or not, upon an investigation of the merits of their claim? To this the commissioners of Georgia could have no objection; it was a matter for the United States. They did object, however, to give any pledge whatsoever to compromise the claim. Nay, more; they insisted that if Congress did not within a year set apart the five millions of acres, it should never be in the power of Congress to compensate them at all, under any circumstances. The commissioners on the part of Georgia said to the commissioners of the United States: If the United States choose, at any time, to compromise this corruption, we cannot help it; but we will never give our sanction or countenance to it, because we believe the claim unfounded in right, justice or morality; if you, upon investigation, think otherwise, here are the five millions of acres set apart, out of which you may compensate; if you can, even *in foro conscientiæ*, consent to compromise this corruption, be the shame and scandal of it upon you. The United States did, accordingly, within one year set apart the five millions of acres to compensate this and other claims, but upon the same conditions and in the same words as the articles of agreement and cession; that is to say, upon condition that the United States, upon an investigation of the merits of the claims, should determine they were founded in right and justice. The question is now, as it has always been, are the claims founded in right and justice?

But to remove every impression that the United States are pledged in the remotest degree, I refer you to Mr. Gallatin himself, and to the report of a committee of the House, at the last session. Mr. Gallatin, in his letter addressed to Mr. Dana, the chairman of the Yazoo Committee, dated 9th January, 1805, says, (speaking of the object of the reservation of the five millions,) "to leave it in their 'power to compromise with that description of claimants, 'by allowing so much of the surplus of five millions of 'acres as they might think proper, without, at the same 'time, pledging Government to enter into a compromise, 'if, upon a full view of all the circumstances of the case, a 'different course was thought more eligible." Thus you see, according to Mr. Gallatin, the United States are at perfect liberty to compromise, or not, at their discretion, as if no articles of agreement and cession had ever been entered into; as if no law had ever been passed setting apart the five millions of acres. Your committee appointed on this subject at the last session of the last Congress, say the same thing. Their language is, "Congress is not bound 'to compromise, if, upon an investigation of the merits of 'the claims, they shall be found unsupported by right and 'justice." The assertion, therefore, that the Government is pledged, is a mere pretext, as is every other reason assigned for the compromise.

But it is contended that the Supreme Court have decided

in favor of the claimants and against the United States; that it is better to give up a part than to lose the whole. Sir, there is no danger of our losing the whole or a part, if we will do our duty to ourselves and to the country. The Supreme Court cannot decide the rights of the United States in a case to which the United States not only were not a party, but to which they cannot, by any constitutional possibility, be a party without their consent. The case of Fletcher and Peck was a decision of a feigned issue, made up between two speculators, to decide certain points, in the decision of which they were interested. Will any man, in his senses, say that the right of the United States to the public property could be affected by such decision? This doctrine is almost as shocking as the other doctrine set up in support of the compromise—the representatives of the people may betray the people, and the people are without remedy. I trust, sir, that neither the one nor the other will be countenanced by you; but that you will, without hesitation, reject the bill. Whenever it is conceded that it is competent to the Supreme Court, in a case between A and B, to take from the United States fifty millions of acres of land, it will be time for the Government to make a voluntary surrender of the public property to whosoever will have it. The public property would be nothing but an expense, an incumbrance, which it would be profitable to shake off with as little delay as possible. No, sir; the Government is the guardian, the trustee, of the public property. Like all governments, they must of necessity determine their own rights of property; and if they remain faithful to those rights, all the decisions of all the judicial tribunals under Heaven cannot deprive you of a square acre of the public land. But, sir, I am tired and disgusted with this subject. I hope the bill will be rejected.

The bill was not rejected. It had previously passed the Senate, by a vote of twenty-four to eight—the two Senators from Georgia, Messrs. Bibb and Tait, having voted against it—and on the 26th March, 1814, after several slight amendments, it passed the House, by a vote of eighty-four to seventy-six—the Representatives from Georgia, Messrs. William Barnett, Alfred Cuthbert, John Forsyth, Bolling Hall, Thomas Telfair and George M. Troup, voting against it. The act was approved by the President on the 31st of the same month.

11

These votes show the unanimity of the people of Georgia against a compromise of these claims. They, as well as their Representatives, believed that the honor of the country required that the claims should not be acknowledged or compromised. The case was a novel one; but it is believed that if ever a great public exigency demanded a refusal of any sort of claims, or pretended claims, this was it. The evidence contained in the previous portion of this chapter, appears conclusive on this point. Nevertheless, in addition to the report of the United States Commissioners, Messrs. Madison, Gallatin and Lincoln, stating their belief "that the interest of the United States, the tranquillity of those who may hereafter inhabit the (Mississippi) Territory, and various equitable considerations which may be urged in favor of the present claimants, render it expedient to enter into a compromise on reasonable terms"; two several committees of the House had reported to the same effect, from the last of which (15th March, 1814,) we make the following extract:

The committee have had the subject of the said (Senate) bill under their consideration, and are of opinion that it is expedient for the government of the United States to enter into a compromise with the persons claiming lands in the Mississippi Territory, under and by virtue of the act of the Legislature of Georgia, of the 7th January, 1795. *The reasons for this opinion do not rest on the strict legality of the title of these claimants to the lands in question*—though the committee cannot forbear remarking that that title appears to have all the sanction which can be derived from a solemn decision of the highest judicial tribunal known to our laws—they are grounded on considerations connected with the permanent interests of the United States, as they relate to the Mississippi Territory; with the quiet and speedy settlement of that Territory; with the more easy extinguishment of the Indian title to the lands contained in it; with the security against all future Indian wars in that quarter, which the settlement of the Territory must afford; with the extensive navigation connecting parts of the Western States with the Ocean, which must be opened when the population of the Territory shall be adequate to such an object, and with the strength and safety which such a population must confer on the Louisiana portion. It may, in addition, be remarked that there are equitable considerations connected with the present claims, which, in the opinion of the committee, strongly recommend them to the favor of Congress. Although the original act of the State of Georgia might have been procured by fraudulent and corrupt means, it satisfactorily appears to the committee, as far as their inquiries have been extended, that the present claimants, or those under whom they hold, were bona fide purchasers of the immediate grantees of Georgia, without notice of any fraud or corruption in the original grant.

The part of the above extract which we have italicized, shows that the adjustment was recommended more on the idea of a *compromise*, than on any view of the strict rights of the claimants. It was, perhaps, well for the peace of the country that the controversy had been transferred from Georgia to Washington City, and that the United States, in a moment of generosity, could not, and pretended not to, exhibit that generosity at the expense of Georgia more than of any other of the States. A people that had destroyed the record evidence of their betrayal, would hardly have made provision for claimants, the *bona fides* of whose titles was, at least, questionable, and the assertion of which title caused patriotic Georgians to recoil with horror at the name of a transaction which threatened to undermine representative government. Georgia had not been heard before any judicial tribunal; she could never have been made a party there without a sacrifice of her dignity; but there was no time when she could not, with safety to her honor, trust her cause in the hands of her faithful Representatives, foremost among whom was George M. Troup.

The bill,* as it finally passed, provided for settling the claims, under the provisions and restrictions therein mentioned, in the following proportions:

* The reader is referred, for further information on the subject of this bill and the acts amendatory thereof, to the United States Statutes at Large, Vol. 3, pp. 116, 117, 118, 119, 120, 192, 193, 235, 236, 294, 295.—ED.

To the persons claiming in the name or under the Upper Mississippi Company, - -	$ 350,000
Tennessee Company, - - - -	600,000
Georgia Mississippi Company, - -	1,550,000
Georgia Company, - - - -	2,250,000
Citizens' Rights, - - - -	250,000
Making an aggregate of - - -	$5,000,000

CHAPTER V.

Re-Election to Congress.—State of our Foreign Relations.—Preparations for War.—Colonel Troup's Course.—Bank of the United States, &c.

IN October, 1808, Colonel Troup was re-elected to Congress, and on the 22d day of May, 1809, took his seat in the House of Representatives as a member of the eleventh Congress. His colleagues, as in the previous Congress, were William W. Bibb, Dennis Smelt and Howell Cobb.

Mr. Madison had been inaugurated President of the United States. In his opening message at the special session then begun, the President said: "On this first occasion of meeting you, it affords me much satisfaction to be able to communicate the commencement of a favorable change in our foreign relations, the critical state of which induced a session of Congress at this early period."

On the first of March, 1809, the retiring President, Mr. Jefferson, had approved an Act "to interdict the commercial intercourse between the United States and Great Britain and France, and their dependencies, and for other purposes," by which commerce with those nations was closed, and the entrance of the harbors and waters of the United States interdicted to all public vessels belonging to those nations, or private vessels sailing under the flag of either, except vessels forced in by distress or charged with dispatches from the government to which they belonged, &c.; but with authority to the President, "in case either France or Great Britain shall so revoke or modify her edicts as that they shall cease to violate the neutral commerce of the United States, to declare the same by proclamation; after which, the trade of the United States, suspended by this act, and by the act laying an embargo on all ships and vessels in the ports and harbors of the United States, and the several acts supplementary thereto, may be renewed with the nation so doing"; and, by the last section of which, it was provided that said non-intercourse act should continue in force until the end of the then next session of Congress, when the embargo acts were, by the same section, to expire.

The message continued to say: "In consequence of the provisions of the act interdicting commercial intercourse with Great Britain and France, our ministers at London and Paris were without delay instructed to let it be understood by the French and British governments, that the authority vested in the executive to renew commercial intercourse with their respective nations, would be exercised in the case specified by that act. Soon after these instructions were dispatched, it was found that the British government, anticipating, from early proceedings of Congress at the last session, the state of our laws, which has had the effect of placing the two belligerent powers on a footing of equal restrictions, and relying on the conciliatory disposition of the United States, had transmitted to their legation here, provisional instructions, not only to offer satisfaction for the attack on the frigate Chesapeake, and to make known the determination of his Britannic majesty to send an envoy extraordinary with powers to conclude a treaty on all the points between the two countries, but, moreover, to signify his willingness, in the mean time, to withdraw his orders in council, in the persuasion that the intercourse with Great Britain would be renewed on the part of the United States. These steps of the British government led to the correspondence and the proclamation now laid before you, by virtue of which the commerce between the two countries will be renewed after the 10th day of June next."

The sequel shows that these anticipations were not to be realized.

During this session, Colonel Troup, although not a frequent, was an occasional, speaker; but there is nothing in the reports of his speeches which makes it important to transcribe what he said.

[1809.] On the second day of the session he was placed upon the committee on Elections; and, on the 26th May, upon the committee on Foreign Relations. Congress adjourned on the 28th day of June, the most important act of the session being "An Act to amend and continue in force certain parts of the Act, entitled 'An Act to interdict the commercial intercourse between the United States and Great Britain and France, and their dependencies, and for other purposes';" of which it is only necessary to say that it modified the non-intercourse act of 1st March, in conformity with what seemed to be a returning sense of justice on the part of Great Britain, and with what was hoped from that country and France in regard to their previous policy towards the United States.

The act was approved by the President on 28th June. On the passage of the act, Colonel Troup was not present, and therefore gave no vote.

[1809.] Congress assembled again on 27th November.

Colonel Troup was re-appointed on the committee on Elections, and was also placed upon the committee on Post Offices and Post Roads.

On the 29th of November, the President sent in his annual message to the two Houses, from which the following extracts are made, showing the change which had come over the aspect of our foreign relations:

"At the period of our last meeting, I had the satisfaction of communicating an adjustment with one of the principal belligerent nations, highly important in itself, and still more so as presaging a more extended accommodation. It is with deep concern I am now to inform you that the favorable prospect has been overclouded by a refusal of the British Government to abide by the act of its Minister Plenipotentiary, and by its ensuing policy towards the United States, as seen through the communications of the Minister sent to replace him. Whatever pleas may be urged for a disavowal of engagements formed by diplomatic functionaries in cases where by the terms of the engagements a mutual ratification is reserved, or where notice at the time may have been given of a departure from instructions, or in extraordinary cases essentially violating the principles of equity, a disavowal could not have been apprehended in a case where no such notice or violation existed, where no such ratification was reserved, and more especially where, as is now in proof, an engagement, to be executed without any such ratification, was contemplated by the instructions given, and where it had, with good faith, been carried into immediate execution on the part of the United States. These considerations not having restrained the British government from disavowing the engagement by virtue of which its orders in council were to be revoked, and the event authorizing the renewal of commercial intercourse having thus not taken place, it necessarily became a question of equal urgency and importance, whether the act prohibiting that intercourse was not to be considered as remaining in legal force. This question being, after due deliberation, determined in the affirmative, a proclamation to that effect was issued. It could not but happen, however, that a return to this state of things, from that which had followed an execution of the arrangement by the United States, would involve difficulties. With a view to diminish these as much as possible, the instructions from the Secretary of the Treasury, now laid before you, were transmitted to the collectors of the several ports. If, in permitting British vessels to depart without giving bonds not to proceed to their own ports, it should appear that the tenor of legal authority has not been strictly pursued, it is to be ascribed to the anxious desire which was felt that no individuals should be injured by so unforeseen an occurrence; and I rely on the regard of Congress for the equitable interests of our own citizens, to adopt whatever further provisions may be found requisite for a general remission of penalties involuntarily incurred. The recall of the disavowed minister* having been followed by the appointment of a successor†, hopes were indulged that the new mission would contribute to alleviate the disappointment which had been produced, and to remove the causes which had so long embarrassed the good understanding of the two nations. It could not be doubted that it would at least be charged with conciliatory explanations of the steps which had been taken, and with proposals to be substituted for the rejected arrangement. Reasonable and universal as this expectation was, it also has not been fulfilled. From the first official disclosures of the new minister, it was found that he had received no authority to enter into explanations relative to either branch of the arrangement disavowed, nor any authority to substitute proposals as to that branch which concerned the British orders in council; and, finally, that his proposals with respect to the other branch, the attack on the frigate

* Mr. Erskine.—ED.

† Mr. Jackson.—ED.

Chesapeake, were founded on a presumption repeatedly declared to be inadmissible by the United States, that the first step towards adjustment was due from them; the proposals at the same time omitting even a reference to the officer * answerable for the murderous aggression, and asserting a claim not less contrary to the British laws and British practice, than to the principles and obligations of the United States. The correspondence between the department of State and this minister, will show how essentially the features presented in its commencement have been varied in its progress. It will show also, that, forgetting the respect due to all governments, he did not refrain from imputations on this, which required that no further communications should be received from him. The necessity of this step will be made known to his Britannic majesty through the minister plenipotentiary of the United States at London. And it would indicate a want of the confidence due to a government which so well understands and exacts what becomes foreign ministers near it, not to infer that the misconduct of its own representative will be viewed in the same light in which it has been regarded here. The British government will learn, at the same time, that a ready attention will be given to communications through any channel which may be substituted. It will be happy if the change in this respect should be accompanied by a favorable revision of the unfriendly policy which has been so long pursued towards the United States."

We have thus made copious extracts from the message, in order to show generally the true state of the relations between the two countries. To go into details would require an examination into the diplomatic history of the times, and the foreign policy of the government. Enough has been said to shed light on the subjects of a national character in the discussion of which Colonel Troup took part, and on which we shall soon permit him to speak for himself. We have seen that as early as October, 1807, he believed *the chances of war, beyond all comparison, greater than those of peace.* But things had now reached a point where even the cautious policy of Mr. Madison failed to avert the inevitable consequence of British denial of "*free*

* Admiral Berkeley.—ED.

trade and sailors' rights." Preparation—actual preparation—for war, was now necessary, and for this the Republican party set about in earnest.

Early in the session,

Mr. Troup begged leave to submit to the consideration of the House, several resolutions, which had for their object the vindication of the commercial rights of the United States, against the belligerent nations of Europe. He submitted them at this time, with less reluctance, because the introduction of them was in no wise inconsistent with the most friendly negotiations which might be pending with foreign governments. It is high time, said Mr. T., in my opinion, that these commercial rights were either vindicated or abandoned. The remnant of commerce which the joint operation of the belligerent decrees has left to us, is scarcely worth carrying on. To designate what this little is, would be no difficult matter, but it would be superfluous; every one that hears me understands it.

But, it would be well to inquire on what principle the belligerents pretend to justify these commercial restrictions? The avowed principle is retaliation, but is it the true principle? Unquestionably not. And why? Because it is equally asserted by both belligerents. Both cannot be retaliators; one must be the aggressor, the other the retaliator. If this principle, then, be equally urged by both, who is to judge between them? If the alleged principle of retaliation be not the true one, what is? As respects France, the true principle of her decrees is to be sought in the policy of embarrassing England by excluding from the continent British merchandise; and as to Great Britain, the principle of her Orders in Council may be found in the consideration of her interest and her power. She avowedly contends that it is her interest to engross the commerce of the world; that she has the power to engross it, and, therefore, she will engross it.

But, what are the principles more specifically asserted by Great Britain? First, the right of blockade by proclamation; second, the right to turn your vessels into her ports to pay duty and take out a license. This right of blockading by proclamation is not a right growing out of a state of war; it is no belligerent right; it is a pretension, as applicable to a state of peace as to a state of war, and if we submit to it in a state of war, we must submit to it in a state of peace. The only principle of blockade which we recognize, is that which gives to belligerents a right to turn from ports so closely invested as to make the entry of them dangerous; and, after due warning, vessels bound to them. But the right asserted by Great Britain to blockade by a piece of parchment or paper, issued from her council chamber, a port or ports, a kingdom or kingdoms, a continent or continents, is a right no more relative to a state of war than to a state of peace; and, if we submit to the pretension in a state of war, we must equally submit to it in a state of peace. It is founded on the most arbitrary tyranny, it goes to the annihilation of your commerce. As to the other right, of forcing our vessels into her ports, to pay duty and take out license, this is equally applicable to a state of peace as to a state of war. We acknowledge the right of Great Britain, or any other nation, to shut her ports against us, provided there be no treaty stipulation to the contrary. But the right of Great Britain or of France to shut the ports of any other nation against us, is a right no more appertaining to a belligerent than to a neutral. If we submit to it in war, we must equally submit in peace; and this right, like the other, is founded in the most arbitrary tyranny. What right has Britain to tyrannize on the ocean, and prescribe limits to our trade? She will not permit to us a trade which she cannot herself enjoy. She prohibits to us a trade which our government permits, because it is her interest to monopolize it. It is equally our interest to monopolize, and, therefore, if you please, sir, we will prohibit the trade which her government permits, and which it is our interest to monopolize.

If Great Britain can rightly prohibit our trade, because it is her interest to prohibit it, have we not the right to prohibit her trade for the same reason? If she, with right and justice, can stop and seize and confiscate our vessels because they attempt a trade which she forbids, and only because she forbids it, cannot our government do the same in relation to her trade? If she can turn our vessels into her ports to pay duty and take out license, what prohibits us from doing the same as to her vessels? England is a nation, so are we. England is independent, so are we. What prohibits us from doing to England what England does to us? Unquestionably nothing. To say that we have no right to do to England what England does to us, is to acknowledge our inferiority; it is to acknowledge that she may demand without hesitation, and that we are under obligation to submit without hesitation.

I am aware that it may be objected to the resolutions that the adoption of them would lead to hostility; but the same objection is equally applicable to any resolution which would go to the vindication of our commercial rights. They ought not to lead to hostility; they are merely retaliatory. They follow the spirit of the British Orders in Council and French Decrees, and therefore cannot be complained of by either power. There is a great and profitable commerce, and rapidly increasing, passing not indeed before our doors, but near enough to make the capture of vessels engaged in it convenient to us, which the resolutions have chiefly in view. I allude to the Brazil and Spanish Main trade.

Is it not matter of surprise, that a commerce so profitable, so extensive, and so convenient, should have been permitted to a Government which permits no commerce to us but what her convenience and her interest suggest? Is it not strange that we should have suffered that Government to participate in a commerce which both our interest and our convenience stimulate us to engross? But, above all, is it not inexplicable that we should passively have suffered the monopoly of it by her, when we ourselves were willing and able to engross it? The House will perceive, on the face of the resolutions, that, as they regard France, they are not equivalent to a war measure—neither by a war measure, nor by that which I have the honor to submit, can we come in contact with France; she has no commerce on the ocean. In relation to England, it is short, infinitely short of war; because by war her continental colonies would fall; her West India Islands would be distressed, and our privateers would cut up her commerce; but the resolutions propose merely to retort the evils of her own injustice, to do to her what, and no more than what, she has done to us. Reserving, for another occasion, any further remarks, I beg leave to read the resolutions to the House.

Mr. T. then read the following resolutions:

Resolved, That it is expedient to authorize the President, by law, to instruct the commanders of the armed vessels of the United States to stop and bring into the ports of the same, all ships or vessels, with their cargoes, the property of the subjects of the King of Great Britain and of the Emperor of France, bound to ports other than those within the dominions or colonies of either.

Resolved, That it is expedient further to authorize by law the detention of all ships or vessels, with their cargoes, the property of the subjects of the King of Great Britain, until the duties to be regulated and ascertained by law shall be first levied and collected upon the goods and merchandise whereof the said ships or vessels shall be laden, and until the said ships or vessels shall have received due license to depart.

Resolved, That it is expedient further to authorize by law the detention of all ships or vessels, with their cargoes, the property of the subjects of the Emperor of France, brought within the ports of the United States, there to abide the final decision or order of Government in relation to the same.

Resolved, That an ad valorem duty of ——— be levied and collected on all the goods, wares or merchandise, of British product or manufacture.

Resolved, That it is expedient further to authorize the President, on payment of the duties authorized to be levied and collected on the goods laden on board vessels the property of the subjects of the King of Great Britain, forthwith to grant a license to such vessels to depart and to proceed to the port of original destination, without further hinderance or molestation.

The House having agreed to consider these resolutions,

On motion of Mr. Troup, they were ordered to lie on the table, as he stated, to give every member the same time to consider them as he had himself taken.

It does not appear that the mover of these resolutions ever afterwards called them up. The country was not prepared for them. And yet, on a survey of the then existing state of things, it is difficult to perceive why the measures indicated by them would not have been the best for the country. On principle, they would have given as good pretext for a declaration of war by France, as by England, against the United States. In our defensive mode of conducting the war which did ensue, the former power could, without a navy, have inflicted but little injury on us, and there seems to have been no reason why we should not have been as well prepared for war with Great Britain in 1809 as in 1812. We had submitted to insult after insult, from that power; our foreign commerce was almost annihilated by her; and what little remained became well-nigh unavailable, because of the retaliatory measures to which our own government felt compelled to resort, whilst it was hesitating between an open declaration of war and a system of commercial restrictions; or, rather, whilst, by a resort to the latter, it was weakening its own resources and creating discontents at home by measures more injurious to our own people than detrimental to our enemies. Indeed, one serious ground of objection to the war, when at last it was declared, was that it came too late to avenge the wrongs of the country, and at a time when a large portion of the people indulged still the vain hope that negotiation would do for us what we had not as yet tried by open hostilities.

First and last, Colonel Troup was the open advocate of his country's rights; and although he foresaw the impolicy or futility of mere commercial restrictions so long adhered to, yet, when the conflict came, it found him the same undaunted supporter of a vigorous war, that he had been of a line of policy that would have hastened the crisis or have altogether averted it. His speeches and votes show that whilst he often differed from his political friends, in matters of detail, he never deserted the Administration of his choice, which was honestly endeavoring to promote the best good of the country. On 17th February, 1809, he had "condemned the proposed non-intercourse system as submission, without even money in return for it," and on the 27th of the same month he voted against the bill. His opinion was, as we have seen, that, short of more decided measures, the embargo, properly enforced, and followed up by a pertinent system of defence, was "the best for our situation which could have been devised."

Having already referred to the general provisions of the non-intercourse act of 1st March, 1809, (which was amended and, as to certain parts of it, continued in force "until the end of the [then] next session of Congress," by the act of June 28, 1809,) we cannot do better than make the following extracts from a letter of Col. Troup to Gov. Mitchell, dated

WASHINGTON, March 17, 1810.

My Dear Sir: I offer you my sincere congratulation on your elevation to the chief magistracy, but especially on the prospect which is every day opening before you of uniting more various and stronger interests in your support than several of your immediate predecessors. The people of Georgia, if I understand them rightly, will only require the firmness and moderation and dignity with which you set out, to yield that support as liberally and as heartily as ever they accorded it to our old and excellent friend Jackson. * * * The Southern States require all the qualities which command respect, to oppose a successful resistance to the Eastern and mercantile interests in Congress. The rights of the former are every day shamefully sacrificed to the undue weight of the latter. By superior intelligence, by cunning, by stratagem, individuals are detached from the Southern and Western interests, and made to unite in measures which have for their object the prosperity merely of New England navigation and fisheries. The rest call in vain for union and concert in behalf of the interests of Southern agriculture. The Yankees, with these stragglers, carry the day, and laugh in their sleeves at the zeal with which Georgia and South Carolina support all the measures of the general government. It is thus we have been saddled so long with non-intercourse, and it is thus that non-intercourse is proposed to be followed by another frivolous system of commercial restriction. I have long witnessed these projects with indignation, and seeing that in all of them nothing was consulted but the local interests of the day, I too have looked to local interests. It is therefore that I have been for war or free commerce. The non-intercourse co-operates with the Orders of Council, 1st, to carry on a round-about trade with Great Britain in her own vessels; 2dly, to prohibit all trade with France or Holland or Italy. The effect on us is to give to the British the monopoly of our cotton at eleven cents, and a monopoly of the supply of broadcloths at fourteen dollars the yard. Whilst the Yankees can freight their vessels to smuggle British property into the continent, they care not two straws about the rest. The wheat-grower and the tobacco-planter have been doing well under the non-intercourse, and they too are content. This is the cause of our stupid perseverance in non-intercourse. Now it will be repealed, or suffered to expire on the close of the session. The Senate and House are at variance on Mr. Macon's Bill. In the conference, the managers of the Senate propose to incorporate the convoy principle; the managers on our part dissent, but the report has not been acted on by either. The result is problematical. As we hourly expect to hear from our ministers at Paris and London, there is no desire to hurry the Bill—perhaps it is well. * * * *

With best wishes for you and yours, I am, my dear sir,

Respectfully, your friend,

GEO. M. TROUP.

The bill, to which reference is made in this letter, had been reported by Mr. Macon, from the committee on Foreign Relations, as early as December 19th. The following was the substance of it:

[1809.] The first section prohibited all public vessels of Great Britain or France from entering the harbors of the United States, subject to certain exceptions. The second section prescribed the punishment for violation of that provision. The third section prohibited all vessels sailing under the flag of Great Britain or France, or owned in whole or in part by any citizen of either, from entering the harbors of the United States. The fourth section prohibited the importation into the United States of goods from Great Britain or Ireland, and France, and their colonies, or of goods from any foreign port, the growth, product or manufacture of Great Britain or France, unless in vessels owned wholly by citizens of the United States. The above provisions to take immediate effect. The fifth section prohibited, after the 15th of April, the importation of goods from Great Britain and France, and their colonies, unless imported directly therefrom. The next three sections affixed penalties for infraction of these provisions. The ninth section authorized the President, in case either Great Britain or France so revoked or modified her edicts as to cease to violate the neutral commerce of the United States, to declare the same by proclamation; after which, the prohibitions of the bill, on the commerce of the nation so doing, should cease. The next section repealed the act of 28th June, 1809, to amend and continue in force certain parts of the non-intercourse act of 1st March, 1809. The last section limited the operation of the act to the end of the then next session of Congress.

In consequence of disagreement between the two Houses, the bill was finally lost. After sundry amendments, it had passed the House—all the Representatives from Georgia voting for it, except Colonel Troup. In the debate on the disagreement of the two Houses,

Mr. Troup remarked that gentlemen, in speaking of the bill as it went from this House, seemed to have forgotten the contents of that bill. It was spoken of as a bill full of resistance. If any such principle was contained in the bill, he had no recollection of it. If he recollected right, the part struck out proposed a direct commerce to the ports of the belligerents in our own vessels. Was this the principle of resistance? He had thought that, last winter, non-intercourse was resistance. But it seemed that what was resistance then was submission now. If the Senate was disposed to resist in reality with cannon and ball, and therefore would not take the milk-and-water resistance of this bill, he did not feel disposed to blame them.

[1810.] On the question of insisting on the disagreement to the amendments of the Senate, Colonel Troup again voted in the negative—the rest of the Georgia delegation voting in the affirmative. The following speech, delivered on the 27th of March, will explain the reasons for his votes, and throw light on the subject under consideration. The question recurring on adhering to the disagreement to the Senate's amendments,

Mr. Troup said, if it was the object of gentlemen to get rid of all commercial restrictions, they could only do so by concurring with the Senate. If they adhered, their object would indeed be defeated. The non-intercourse would be saddled on the country so long as the law continued in operation. Look at the sections of the bill as it went from this House, said Mr. T. It is true that one of these sections repeals the non-intercourse, but it is also true that another section substitutes a measure, which, if retaliated, must revive the non-intercourse in fact. Not only are these provisions inconsistent, but another section of the bill recognizes that inconsistency, and provides a remedy, by authorizing the President to execute the law within four leagues of the coast, by employing the public armed vessels of the United States to detect smugglers. Now, I say, sir, that the amendment of the Senate, which goes to the destruction of these sections, has for its object the destruction of the non-intercourse law. Sir, no man can contemplate the non-intercourse law in a light more serious as an evil to the people of this country, than myself. There never was a measure adopted more deleterious in its operation on the morals and interests of the people. The single effect of it has been to depreciate the staple commodity of the country at the rate of one hundred per cent., and exalt the British manufactures in the same ratio; to make cotton sell at eleven cents a pound, and to make the growers of it pay fourteen dollars a yard for broadcloth. Look at the practical operation of it. A cargo of cotton from a southern port is landed at Amelia Island.* If British goods are there, ready for exchange, they are taken in exchange for the cotton, and smuggled into the country. If there be no goods there, they bring back no return, except the freight for the short navigation to Amelia Island. The cargo is landed, a duty of eight per cent. paid on it, besides commissions, &c., and a duty of eight or ten per cent. more on re-exportation, and what freight the British ship-holders choose to demand. This is not only the effect of the non-intercourse. It must be the effect of every system of commercial restriction short of the measure of embargo; because all the penalties and sanctions which you can possibly devise for carrying that system into operation, must operate on a class without the reach of those penalties; people who are without your jurisdiction; people, too, who tell you, in the plainest language, they have no country, that they are governed by no sentiment of honor or principle of patriotism, that commercial gain is the sole object of their consideration, and that every other object will be sacrificed to it. Does not every day's experience apprise you that this is the truth? Look at the common practice and habits of those called ship-owners. Are they not every day lending their vessels to the British merchants for the purpose of violating the continental policy, to the French, the Dutch or any other merchants, for the purpose of violating the British Orders in Council, or to British and French merchants, for violating the laws of their own country? And is it possible, sir, that you expect to execute, with any degree of success, a system which is to operate on the belligerents, when the penalties for a violation of the system are to operate on this class? It is impossible; such a system must be futile and inefficient. Because, then, I am disposed to get rid of the non-intercourse and

* Then a dependency of Spain.—ED.

every sort of commercial restriction, considering it injurious only to ourselves, can it be said that I am disposed to submit to the orders and decrees of the belligerents? No, sir; those gentlemen have surrendered the rights and interests of the country, who did originally submit to an abandonment of the embargo. It is true now, and it was true then, that there was nothing between you and the British Orders in Council, but either embargo or war.* You repealed the embargo, and refused to go to war, and now, as then, there is no remedy short of war or embargo. Propose what other remedy you please, and it is only calculated to excite ridicule abroad. If you propose to convoy—what! it is asked, will you convoy a trade to every quarter of the globe with six, eight, or ten frigates? If you propose to arm the merchantmen—what! it is asked, will you arm your merchantmen against the British navy? If we are to have neither embargo nor war, I, for one, am willing to get rid of the non-intercourse, and not substitute anything for it. To obtain this object, there is no mode left but to concur with the Senate in their amendments, and strike out those clauses which can have no other effect than to perpetuate the system of non-intercourse.

In all this, Colonel Troup was consistent. We have seen that he opposed and voted against the repeal of the embargo. That he differed from a majority of both Houses and the President, is no evidence that he was wrong. In his conduct on this, as on all other subjects, we have the highest evidence of an independent and self-relying spirit. Beyond its principles, party had no trammels for him. In the House, Dr. Bibb voted with Col. Troup, Dr. Smelt voted the other way—Mr. Cobb was absent. In the Senate, Gov. Milledge voted for the bill, and Mr. Crawford against it.

During the session of 1809–'10, the question of the recharter of the Bank of the United States came before Congress. In the first section of the bill, there was a provision that the President and Directors should "pay into the Treasury of the United States one million two hundred and fifty thousand dollars, *as the price and equivalent for the renewal and continuance of their charter as aforesaid.*" On this subject,

* Did not subsequent events fully justify this prediction?—ED.

[1810.] Mr. Troup said gentlemen might pass the bill, but for the Constitutional question. If they did pass it, he hoped they would not permit themselves to become the retailing hucksters of the community for the sake of bank charters. In the name of common honesty, said he, I beseech you, what power have you to sell a charter? There is power in the Constitution to sell the public property; but there is certainly no power to sell privileges of any kind. I therefore move you to strike out the bribe, the douceur, the bonus, as gentlemen call it, of $1,250,000.

On the same day, (April 21,) he spoke as follows:

Mr. Troup said he forbore at present going into the question of constitutionality. He had no idea that he could, with any efficiency whatever, stand up on this floor, with such a weapon as an argument, to contend with a moneyed institution of ten millions. If I am not disposed to go into the general question of constitutionality, said he, I am as certainly indisposed to derive this power from the power to pass all laws necessary and proper. I am the more reluctant to do so, because it is a dangerous power, and ought not to be derived by implication. I say that the power is dangerous, for if it be conceded that the Congress of the United States have a right to erect a moneyed institution with a capital of ten or twenty millions, it is competent to erect one with a capital of one hundred milions. It may be competent, therefore, to the United States to raise a corporation more powerful than itself—a moneyed institution which may absorb all the powers of the State. And this principle as a precedent will be more dangerous in this case, because the temptation is so much greater in proportion to the amount of capital. I do contend that if the Constitution did intend to grant the power of chartering moneyed institutions, it did not intend to grant it for the purposes of speculation, and of speculation merely. Sell privileges! Sell, for $1,250,000, the exclusive privilege of taking usurious interest on money! I thought, sir, that the power of selling privileges and indulgences was exclusively the right and power of the Pope. I ask gentlemen on what authority they act? On none of morality, certainly—but on what authority? On that of the corrupt government of England. Servile imitators of England, we must have a national bank! And why not an East India Company? We could sell a charter, tomorrow, for millions. We could sell chartered privileges for almost as much as we should choose to ask. If we become the retailers of privileges, we shall go on to sell them till we overdo the business; and when this great national source of revenue, after becoming our chief and only resource, had failed, to what resources for revenue should we be driven? Is it not a very rational inference, that it will be to the sale of all privileges we can derive from the Constitution a power to dispose of? If, sir, on any occasion you would set up, in the market, privileges for sale to the highest bidder, even do so with respect to privileges of every description. You would no more hesitate to set up, for sale, privileges of nobility than this privilege—but (I thank God!) the Constitution has prohibited you. But for that, we would sell them now as we do bank privileges; we should go on to make it our chief resource, till, by the cheapness of the title, we should destroy the value of the trade. If we can draw money into the Treasury, by bargain and sale of privileges, let it be understood that we shall continue to foster it as our chief national resource. Having done with internal and direct taxes of all descriptions, because we consider them oppressive, this sale of privileges will be made the chief national resource.

I will add but one thing. The moment you accept this $1,250,000, you are bribed in the same manner as the British Parliament have suffered themselves to be corrupted. Like them, we not only shamefully partake of the crime, but on our statute book acknowledge the fact.

In continuation of the debate, the same day, and in reply to Mr. Key, of Maryland,

Mr. Troup observed that the gentleman had said that the power to incorporate a bank was derived from the power to lay and collect revenue; and that the power ought to be exercised, because banks give a facility to the collection of the revenue. If the power be exercised, it must be necessary and proper. If it be necessary to the collection of the revenue, the revenue cannot be collected without it. The gentleman from Maryland might say a bank institution was useful. He might say it would give facility to the collection of the revenue; but facility and necessity are wholly different, and the Constitution says that a power, to be incidental, must be necessary and proper. If facility be a ground of action, we are greatly wide of the true policy. We ought to adopt that measure which shall give the greatest facility. The ingenious gentleman himself could sit down and in fifteen minutes devise half a dozen modes which would give infinitely more facility than a bank to the collection of the revenue. He might farm out the revenue; establish farming districts; put a farmer-general at the head of them, with a corps of Janizaries. The Secretary of the Treasury would have nothing to do but draw on him for a sum of money, and require it or his head. This, sir, is a plan which would give the greatest possible facility. You could command money of the farmer-general, or you could require his head. Himself and his Janizaries could always send the money; or, if he did not, the people and the Janizaries could send his head.

Such is a synopsis of the argument against a Bank of the United States. Col. Troup was always opposed to the measure. It was enough for him to know that the question of Constitutional power was a doubtful one. His argument always was, in reference to a doubtful power, *forbear to exercise it*, BECAUSE *it is doubtful*. Let those who pretend to believe that his doctrines, in their practical enforcement, lead to anarchy, remember that whilst he honestly believed the tendency of our federative system was towards consolidation, he steadily maintained, practically and in theory, that the proper and only way to keep up the Constitutional equipoise, was in adhering strictly to the letter of the compact, without encroachment by the States or usurpation by the Federal Government. If he ever maintained any other doctrine, the fact is unknown to those who most closely watched his political career, and have since most honestly studied his recorded opinions. Such a system of government is that which the framers of the Constitution intended; and he is the enemy of that instrument who would degrade the States to a blind and passive submission to any encroachment upon their rights which a corrupt or interested majority in Congress should choose to enact.

Yielding to the pressure of the times, many honest men of the Republican party were led to support a National Bank—amongst others, the late President, Mr. Madison; but Col. Troup was not in Congress when the act of incorporation was passed in April, 1816; and his last recorded vote on that subject, in the House,* was on the 17th day of February, 1815, when he voted, with the majority, to postpone indefinitely a bill to incorporate a Bank of the United States.

[1810.] The second session of the Eleventh Congress closed on the 1st day of May.

At the third session, which began on 3d December, Col. Troup was re-appointed on the committee on Elections, and was also placed on the standing committee on the Post Office and Post Roads.

The President's Message showed that no improvement had occurred in the aspect of our relations with Great Britain and France.

The most important act of the session was one entitled "An Act supplementary to the Act, entitled 'An Act concerning the commercial intercourse between the United States and Great Britain and France, and their dependencies, and for other purposes,'" the second section of which was as follows:

"That, in case Great Britain shall so revoke or modify her edicts, as that they shall cease to violate the neutral commerce of the United States, the President shall declare the fact by proclamation; and such proclamation shall be admitted as evidence, and no other evidence shall be admitted of such revocation or modification in any suit or prosecution which may be instituted under the fourth section of the act to which this act is a supplement. And the restrictions imposed, or which may be imposed, by virtue of the said act, shall, from the date of such proclamation, cease and be discontinued."

[1811.] For this bill Col. Troup voted. He took, however, little part in debate. The most important subject on which he spoke was the motion made on 21st January, to postpone indefinitely the consideration of the bill for re-chartering the Bank of the United States.

* On the 11th day of June, 1832, Gov. Troup voted in the Senate against the re-charter of the United States Bank; but the bill, having passed both Houses, was vetoed by President Jackson, on the 10th of July; and, on the 13th of the same month, the question coming up whether the bill should become a law, notwithstanding the President's objection, it was decided in the negative—Gov. Troup voting to sustain the President.—ED.

Mr. Troup conceived the motion now made to be perfectly proper. He felt, however, under no obligation to accommodate the bank. The act granting an act of incorporation was entirely a voluntary act, and the duration of it limited in the act itself to a term of twenty years. If the bank had acted the part of an ordinary or discreet merchant, it would have taken care, before the expiration of its charter, to have wound up its business and be prepared to meet the event; because the Legislature was not bound to renew it, not having, either by the original charter, or by any subsequent act, given any pledge that it would do so. The bank not having received any pledge of renewal, ought to have been prepared for its dissolution. If the institution had done what it ought to have done, the Government, so far as it is concerned, would have prepared itself against the event, as he was told it was now about to do, by substituting arrangements with the State banks for arrangements with the Bank of the United States or its branches. Mr. T. could therefore see no difficulty in assenting to this proposition, whether as respected the Government or as respected the individuals concerned in the Bank.

On the 24th of January, the question was decided in the affirmative—yeas sixty-five, nays sixty-four—Col. Troup voting with the majority.

The third and last session of the Eleventh Congress terminated 3d March, 1811.

CHAPTER VI.

Col. Troup's Re-Election to Congress in 1810.—State of the Country. Declaration of War.—Course in Congress.

IN October, 1810, the people of Georgia elected, as their Representatives in the Federal Legislature, William W. Bibb, Howell Cobb,* Bolling Hall and George M. Troup. Col. Troup was at this time residing in Montgomery County.

The first session of the Twelfth Congress began on the fourth day of November, 1811, pursuant to proclamation of the President; and on that day the above named Representatives from Georgia took their seats in the House. The aspect of our foreign relations had not improved. In his opening Message, (Nov. 5,) the President said:

"In calling you together sooner than a separation from your homes would otherwise have been required, I yielded to considerations drawn from the posture of our foreign affairs; and in fixing the present for the time of your meeting, regard was had to the probability of further developments of the policy of the belligerent powers towards this country, which might the more unite the national councils in the measures to be pursued. At the close of the last session of Congress, it was hoped that the successive confirmations of the extinction of the French decrees, so far as they violated our neutral commerce, would have induced the government of Great Britain to repeal its orders in council, and thereby authorize a removal of the existing obstructions to her commerce with the United States. Instead of this reasonable step toward satisfaction and friendship between the two nations, the orders were, at a moment when least to have been expected, put into more rigorous execution; and it was communicated through the British envoy just arrived, that while the revocation of the edicts of France, as officially made known to the British government, was denied to have taken place, it was an

* On 27th November, 1812, William Barnett took his seat in the House of Representatives, as a member of the Twelfth Congress, in place of Howell Cobb, resigned.—ED.

indispensable condition of the repeal of the British orders that commerce should be restored to a footing that would admit the productions and manufactures of Great Britain, when owned by neutrals, into markets shut against them by her enemy ; the United States being given to understand that, in the mean time, a continuance of their non-importation act would lead to measures of retaliation."

After further enumeration, the message proceeded:

"I must now add, that the period is arrived which claims from the legislative guardians of the national rights, a system of more ample provisions for maintaining them. Notwithstanding the scrupulous justice, the protracted moderation, and the multiplied efforts on the part of the United States, to substitute, for the accumulating dangers to the peace of the two countries, all the mutual advantages of re-established friendship and confidence, we have seen that the British cabinet perseveres not only in withholding a remedy for other wrongs, so long and so loudly calling for it, but, in the execution, brought home to the threshold of our territory, of measures which, under existing circumstances, have the character as well as the effect of war on our lawful commerce. With this evidence of hostile inflexibility in trampling on rights which no independent nation can relinquish, Congress will feel the duty of putting the United States into an armor and an attitude demanded by the crisis, and corresponding with the national spirit and expectations."

The Message then recommended, more in detail, such measures of preparation as the exigency of the times seemed to demand.

Thus we see that the anticipations of Colonel Troup, in regard to the futility of the non-intercourse measures, either in securing our rights or preventing a war, were about to be realized. But preparation for war required the raising of means to carry on the war; and this, except by the temporary expedient of a loan, could be done only by taxation.

In answer to a letter of inquiry from the House committee of Ways and Means, the Secretary of the Treasury, Mr. Gallatin, submitted on 10th January, 1812, an estimate of the amount, and the mode of raising a revenue, sufficient for the wants of the country.

And here it is proper to introduce a letter from Colonel Troup to Governor Mitchell, altogether characteristic of the writer, and which shows his position and views in reference to the then state of public affairs:

WASHINGTON, 12th February, 1812.

Dear Sir:—I had the pleasure to receive your favor yesterday. Your sentiments on our national affairs are always welcome. They are particularly so at this time. The public mind had proceeded, with slow step, from doubt to resolution; and when, at last, it settled in conviction, it was not to be supposed that anything short of the attainment of its object would have satisfied it. This may be true yet; but it does not seem as palpably true now as a few weeks ago. To say that the retrograde step is commenced, or will be commenced, would be saying too much; but that the war mercury has sunk a little, nobody here can doubt. The letter of the Secretary of the Treasury has done this.

What—you will ask—men ready to go to war who are not ready to vote taxes? Yes; the very name is more terrible than 50,000 British bayonets. But not so much the taxes: there is the excise, and the stamp, and the salt duty. We can get along without them; loans are better; Treasury notes are better than loans, &c., &c. Can a system grow out of this discordance?

There are only two alternatives: the expenses being already authorized by law,* we must repeal the law or raise the money. To repeal the laws, will be to abandon, in the most deliberate manner, the contest; and money to a limited amount only can be raised by loans. A majority, therefore, will be found at last to unite in a system of taxation, direct and indirect. The subjects of the former will be, probably, spirits, carriages, refined sugars, licenses to retailers, stamps on *Bank paper.*

Is it surprising, then, that in the midst of this perplexity we should require your countenance and encouragement? For myself, I denounce all further temporizing or indecision; and, our Foreign relations continuing the same, nothing but a declaration of war or an open abandonment of the contest will satisfy me. Nothing short of this can satisfy the just expectations of the Southern people, who have been bearing the brunt of the restrictive system from the beginning.

* Referring to "An Act to raise an additional Military force," approved 11th January, 1812, and "An Act authorizing the President of the United States to accept and organize certain Volunteer and Military corps."—ED.

We have much to hope from the diplomatic skill of Mr. Barlow: but should he fail in relieving our cotton from the prohibitory duty, there will be little scruple among Southern men in "recurring to measures not *literally* warranted by the *bargain*."

The Officers of the 25,000 have been apportioned among the respective States, and to our share has fallen the appointment of one Lieutenant-Colonel, one Major, seven Captains, and a proportionate number of subalterns. The first has been given to General Jack, the second to Mossman Houstoun.

Some doubts are entertained of the practicability of raising men on enlistment for five years. This may give rise to a bill for raising a certain number on short enlistment.

On the subject of the ensuing Congressional election: my interest, you know, imperiously demands my attention at home. If we have war, it will be a duty to continue; if we have not, I will eagerly seize the opportunity to retire. In any event, I do not wish to occasion the least embarrassment or trouble to our friends.

With best wishes for you and yours,

I am, dear Governor, very sincerely,

GEO. M. TROUP.

On the 29th November, 1811, the committee on Foreign Relations made a report to the House, in which they briefly but forcibly reviewed the causes and state of our differences with Great Britain, and which they concluded by recommending,

"1st. That the Military Establishment, as authorized by the existing laws, ought to be immediately completed by filling up the ranks, and prolonging the enlistment of the troops; and that, to encourage enlistment, a bounty in lands ought to be given in addition to the pay and bounty now allowed by law.

"2d. That an additional force of ten thousand regular troops ought to be immediately raised to serve for three years; and that a bounty in land ought to be given to encourage enlistments.

"3d. That it is expedient to authorize the President, under proper regulations, to accept the service of any number of volunteers, not exceeding fifty thousand; to be organized, trained, and held in readiness to act on such service as the exigencies of the Government may require.

"4th. That the President be authorized to order out, from time to time, detachments of the militia, as in his opinion the public service may require.

"5th. That all the vessels not now in service, belonging to the Navy, and worthy of repair, be immediately fitted up and put in commission.

"6th. That it is expedient to permit our merchant vessels, owned exclusively by resident citizens, and commanded and navigated solely by citizens, to arm, under proper regulations, to be prescribed by law, in self-defence, against all unlawful proceedings towards them on the high seas."

The report led to an animated debate, (December 12th,) during which, the question being on agreeing to the second resolution,

Mr. Troup rose to make an effort to put an end to the debate; a debate in which the great mass of the House were enlisted on one side, against the solitary gentleman from Virginia (Mr. Randolph) on the other. I trust, sir, the period has arrived when the House will feel itself bound, by the imperious calls of the country, to act, and to act promptly. I am ready to go heart and hand with the advocates of the resolution; all I ask is, that they will lead with prudence and discretion; deliberate when deliberation is useful, act when action is necessary. But, if the spirit of debate, as in former times, has seized upon us; if idle verbiage and empty vociferation are to take the place of manly and energetic conduct, I enter, at this early stage of the proceeding, my solemn protest. I cannot, I will not, share the responsibility of this ruinous course. Indeed, sir, so conscious do I feel of the evil—nay, of the danger to the country, from the course which has been adopted, I shall be constrained to call for the previous question, unless my friends shall interpose the more pleasant corrective, their own good sense, to stop it. I know, sir, they have been impelled by the most honorable sentiments, the most generous passions, patriotism, honor, zeal for their country, rage against her oppressors. They are good reasoners, they are eloquent—but of what avail is argument, of what avail is eloquence, to convince, to persuade, whom? Ourselves, the people? Sir, if the people are to be reasoned into a war now, it is too soon, much too soon, to begin it. If their Representatives here are to be led to it by the flowers of rhetoric, it is too soon, much too soon, to begin it.

When the honorable Chairman of the Committee of Foreign Relations (Mr. Porter,) reported the resolutions, I had hoped he would have made a motion to go into conclave, or, if that had not been deemed advisable, that at least the resolutions, when taken up with open doors, would have been treated as a system of defensive measures called for by the exigency of the times, and affording no just ground of complaint to any Power which might please to consider itself the object of them. Such a course would have been not less consistent with the report of the committee itself, than with the letter and spirit of the President's Message. The President himself would have been fortified by it. When the British Minister called, as he undoubtedly will, upon the President, to demand the causes of these warlike preparations, he might have been answered: Sir, they are no other than what they purport on the face of them to be, a system of defence on the part of the American Government, called for by the state of the world; or, if he pleased, he might have said, called for by the attitude which his Britannic Majesty had assumed, the propriety of which no nation had a right to question. But, instead of this, what had been done? Why, at the very outset, we have been told the measures were intended as measures of offensive hostility; that the army was to be raised to attack Canada; nothing short of it; all the advocates of the resolution declared it. Now, sir, could a more public or formal declaration of war have been made? Contrary to the practice of all nations, we declare first and make preparation afterward. More magnanimous than wise, we tell the enemy when we will strike, where we will strike, and how we will strike! Do we mean a mere bravado? Impossible. No man who knows the advocates of the resolutions would suspect it; but we hope the enemy will recede; he may; but if he should not, let gentlemen look to the consequences; let them look well to the character of that enemy: is he feeble, spiritless, destitute of resources, without courage, without honor? No, sir; with two hundred and fifty thousand regulars and all the munitions of war in store, his fleets and transports manned, equipped and provisioned; their sails bent to every wind, they ask but one hundred and twenty days to reinforce Quebec, to fortify Montreal, to gain the passes into Canada, to march the supernumeraries to Boston. Here we sit in idle debate. Sir, I do contend, most seriously, that ten thousand regulars can march to Boston in defiance of the militia of Massachusetts, well armed and organized as I know them to be. Now, sir, suppose this should happen, and more wonderful things have happened, what will be said? What will my friend from Virginia say to the first victims of the war? Why, he will say, "This is no war of mine; I exerted all my strength to turn these people from their mad and desperate career!" The gentleman from Virginia exonerates himself from all responsibility by the very act of opposition; but, what can be said of us, the advocates of the resolution, to whom all responsibility attaches? That "we had not finished our war speeches!"—that "we could not begin to raise men until we had finished them!" Sir, believe me, the people of this country want no such speeches; they will go for war, because they believe war is necessary to the preservation of their honor and substantial interest; they want men and arms to defend them—not words. If gentlemen persevere in the debate, I will call the previous question. The safety of the state, after what has been said and done, demand it, and all considerations must yield to that.

The resolutions were all afterwards carried, (the first having been previously adopted,) and a bill or bills ordered to be brought in, pursuant to the sixth resolution. On the 2d of January, 1812, a bill from the Senate, "to raise an additional military force," being before the House, and an amendment having been offered,

Mr. Troup observed that, if it were found, some time hence, that 25,000 men were unnecessary, Congress could at once say that only a certain part should be raised. It had, in his opinion, been correctly said that if we do not want 25,000 men, we do not want one man. Can the gentleman from Pennsylvania (Mr. Smilie, the mover of the amendment,) doubt that 5,000 men will be wanted for the defence of New Orleans? And is it not stated by the Secretary of War, that 12,000 men will be wanted for the fortifications on our seaboard, exclusive of the aid to be derived from the militia, which takes 17,000 out of the 25,000 men? And is there a man, who has a knowledge of military affairs, who would be willing to sit down before the Gibraltar of America, Quebec, with less than 20,000 men? In his mind, however, the capture of Halifax would be more important than Quebec, as from thence may be expected the chief attacks upon our commerce; but Halifax could not be taken until Quebec was first secured. He could see no reason for adopting the amendment.

On the 9th of the same month, a question being before the House on receding from some amendments (in regard to appointment of officers,) to which the Senate would not agree,

Mr. Troup was in favor of receding, because, in doing so, he believed the raising of the troops would be expedited; for, if two hundred officers could raise ten thousand men in a given time, four hundred officers could raise twenty thousand in the same time. He could not help replying to a remark of the gentleman from Pennsylvania, (Mr. Smilie) that gentlemen were all for economy. Mr. T. was not for a war of economy, but a war of vigor. All wars are necessarily expensive. The more feeble and protracted they are, the greater will be the expense; and the expense is less, in proportion, as they are short and vigorous. If we are not to have an energetic war, let us have no war. He believed the resources of the country are adequate to any war. Compare the situation of the country with what it was in 1775. Our population now consists of seven millions of active, enterprising individuals, carrying on a commerce second only to one nation in the world; then, our population was only three millions, with a feeble colonial commerce, and the people miserably poor in everything but a spirit of liberty. What did they do? If gentlemen will recur to the Journals of that day, they will discover that, when Congress had a formidable army ready to march, they had not a dollar of revenue, and the people were too indigent to raise money. Congress had to issue bills of credit to the amount of two millions of dollars. If it be thought we cannot raise the necessary supplies, we had better do at once, what, perhaps, we shall find it necessary to do, if we refuse to recede from these amendments—*submit*.

[1812.] The bill to authorize the President to accept and organize certain volunteer corps, being before the House on the 11th of January, a question arose as to the power of the President to employ this force out of the limits of the United States. Col. Troup spoke as follows:

Mr. Troup said, it was evidently an object with the Convention who formed the Constitution, to repress, as much as possible, in the new government, the power of making conquests. History had informed them that conquests had always been injurious to every country which had engaged in making them; they, therefore, by their provisions, endeavored to repress this spirit. They say, in so many words, "If you will indulge in this spirit of conquest, which has been the bane of every nation which has indulged in it, you shall carry it on by an army, and an army only." And why? Because an army could only be raised by putting the country to great expense, and this was the limitation which the Convention thought proper to put to the spirit of conquest. A large army, maintained for this purpose, would be viewed with jealousy by the people of the United States; and of this the members of the Convention were well aware. There was, on the face of the Constitution, Mr. T. said, an obvious distinction made between the Army and the militia. Power is given to Congress to raise armies. For what purposes? For all military purposes. Congress shall have power to call out the militia. For what purposes? To suppress insurrections, execute the laws, and repel invasions. If it had been the design of the Convention to have given Congress the same power over the militia as over the Army, would they not have said so in express terms? But there was another good reason for withholding this power from Congress. The States relied upon the militia for their protection against any attempt at usurpation by the General Government. If gentlemen will turn to one of the amendments of the Constitution, they will find it declared, "that a well regulated militia is necessary to the security of a free State."

But there is another wide distinction between the Army and militia, from the different characters of the persons who compose the two bodies. What are the militia? They are yeomanry; citizens of the country, called from their homes and their families, in cases of emergency, for the defence of their country. Would it be reasonable to vest the power in Congress to carry these men from their homes and their families, for foreign invasion or foreign conquest? It could not have been the intention of the Convention that these men might be shipped off against Jamaica or Vera Cruz—for if, by any construction of the Constitution, the militia can be sent one foot beyond the limits of the United States, they might be sent to Chili or Paraguay.

If, then, the militia cannot be sent out of the country, and these volunteers are militia, neither can they be so disposed of. But are they militia? He did not know how they could be distinguished from them. They now form a part of the militia, under the officers of the respective States, and they are so to remain. They are, therefore, volunteer militia, and nothing else.

But gentlemen say, these volunteers can be marched out of the country by their own consent. Will consent make any difference? Will it make an act of government constitutional, which, without it, would be unconstitutional? The government of the United States and these volunteers are not the only parties concerned. The people of the United States were the makers of the Constitution, and not these individuals and the General Government; and the respective States cannot surrender their militia, which they have a right to hold for their own security.

But the gentleman from the State of Maryland, (Mr. Wright,) says, that the militia may be called out by the General Government to execute the laws; that the President may be authorized to take possession of Canada by law, and that the militia may be called upon to execute this law. This, he considered as an unfounded construction of the Constitutional provision. It was surely never meant that the militia should be called upon to execute the laws without the Union, but within it. The law alluded to by the gentleman would be a declaration of war, and not a law of the Union, for the execution of which the President has power given to him to call out the militia.

If the militia can be called out to repel invasion, they can be called out to the seaboard or garrisons, for the purpose of repelling invasion, whenever well-founded apprehensions are entertained of such an event; and if they go beyond the territory, it would be no less an act of repelling invasion than was the first onset.

If, said Mr. T., these volunteers are to be organized as regular troops, not for five years, like the other regulars, but for one year, then whatever men enter the service of the country, will go into this corps; and the army provided by law to be raised, would not be enlisted.

Mr. T. was willing to authorize the President to accept of the service of fifty thousand volunteers for the defence of the country, under the bill as it now stands, which would leave the government at liberty to send the regular troops abroad, if they found it necessary to do so.

Imperfectly reported as these speeches probably were, they serve to show the consistency, foresight and patriotism of their author. From the first, he had looked to the contingency of war as not only probable, but highly so; he had been opposed to a temporizing policy; he had denounced the non-intercourse system as futile, and calculated to bring the country into contempt with her enemies; and now that war was inevitable, he was in favor of an immediate preparation for and vigorous prosecution of it. When the shock came, and the roar of the battle drowned the clamor of foes and hushed the feeble voices of the timid advocates of the nation's honor, his voice and his example served, in the din of the conflict, to give confidence to the brave, and to animate the drooping courage of his countrymen.

[1812.] In addition to other speeches which he made during this session, Col. Troup spoke at length, on 30th April, in favor of a bill to appoint Assistant Secretaries of War. In concluding his speech, he said: "no man in the country is equal to one half the duties which devolve on the present Secretary." The bill passed the House, but was afterwards indefinitely postponed in the Senate.

President Madison sent in to Congress, his "War Message," on the 1st day of June. After reciting the wrongs under which the United States had suffered, the message proceeded: "Whether the United States shall continue passive under these progressive usurpations and these accumulating wrongs, or, opposing force to force in defence of their national rights, shall commit a just cause into the hands of the Almighty disposer of events, avoiding all connections which might entangle it in the contests or views of other powers, and preserving a constant readiness to concur in an honorable re-establishment of peace and friendship, is a solemn question which the Constitution wisely confides to the legislative department of the Government," &c., &c.

On the 4th day of June, the House, by a vote of 79 to 49, passed a bill declaring war between Great Britain and the United States. It passed the Senate, with amendments, on the 17th; the amendments were concurred in by the House on the 18th, and on the same day the bill became a law by the signature of the President to it.

On the 6th of July, the first session of the Twelfth Congress terminated by the adjournment of both Houses.

We here present to the reader a letter written by Col. Troup to Gov. Mitchell, dated

WASHINGTON, 6th Sept., 1812.

Dear Sir: I arrived here yesterday. The President is on a visit of a week to his country seat.

Col. Monroe, with whom I conversed, yesterday, on our Georgia affairs, assures me you shall be supported. The negotiation for Florida, at which I hinted when I saw you, is not relinquished, and hope is still indulged from it. Take no notice of the order of the Secretary to Col. Smith. Though acknowledged to be irregular, Col. Monroe insists it was inadvertent.*

Mathews and——————————have not yet arrived.

Hull, with a superior force well armed and provisioned, surrendered in a most dastardly manner, at a time when he had the power to make himself master of Upper Canada. He might have taken Malden at any day between his departure from and return to Detroit. The British would have surrendered after a show of resistance. Harrison and Winchester will speedily recover the lost ground.

With high consideration and sincere friendship,

G. M. TROUP.

His Excellency Gov. Mitchell,
Milledgeville, Georgia.

[1812.] The second session of the Twelfth Congress began on the 20th day of November. On the 6th of that month, Col. Troup was appointed second on the House

*This portion of the above letter refers, probably, to the part which Gov. Mitchell took, at the instance of the President of the United States, in an effort to procure from the authorities of East Florida—then in a state of supposed revolution, growing out of the "patriot" difficulties—the annexation of that province to the United States. Gov. Mathews, who was first appointed for that purpose, had been superseded, on the ground of an alleged excess of the powers confided to him, and Gov. Mitchell was put in his place, and at once proceeded to St. Mary's for the purpose of negotiation. In his message of 1812, Gov. Mitchell said: "On my arrival at that place, I found the progress of the revolution stopped before St. Augustine, the patriots being unable alone to attack that formidable post, and the American troops not permitted to act on the offensive. In a short time I sent to Augustine, in compliance with the instructions I had received, and a correspondence between the person then acting as governor, and myself, commenced, which, however, soon terminated, in consequence of the Span-

committee to which so much of the President's message as related to the militia, volunteers and the Army of the United States, &c., was referred.

On the 19th, Mr. Williams, of South Carolina, chairman of the committee, reported "a bill concerning the pay of the non-commissioned officers, musicians, privates and others of the Army of the United States, and for other purposes." The third section of the bill was as follows: "That, during the said war, every person above the age of eighteen years, who shall be enlisted by an officer, shall be held in the Army of the United States during the period of such enlistment; anything in any act to the contrary notwithstanding." On the 20th, the House being in committee of the whole, a motion was made to strike out the third section—the principal grounds of objection to it being that the enlistment of minors tended to violate the public morals—that it interfered with public economy—and violated the spirit of the Constitution. In reply to these arguments,

Mr. Troup said, the objections to this provision were lame in their nature; he only wished they were half as sound as they were novel. It was the result of the experience of men older than themselves in military concerns, that this very description of population, between eighteen and twenty-one, constituted the strength and vigor of every war. What was the fact as respected France? So just was this principle in the contemplation of France, that her whole army is made up of these young men; and yet an attempt is made to deter us from using them, by a flimsy pretext, that to employ them would be violating the obligations of a contract and the principles of morality. If our feelings and sympathies be suffered to influence us in favor of the individual who voluntarily enlists, the reasons are much stronger in favor of discharging one half of those already in your ranks, than the description just spoken of.

iard preferring the application of force to remove the American troops, which he actually tried on the 16th May, to the more tedious operation of having it done by negotiation in a peaceful manner. The experiment, however, did not succeed, and the troops kept their ground."

Col. Smith was the commander of the American forces, and these forces were not withdrawn for some time after. It would appear, from Col. Troup's letter, that Gov. Mathews was alive at its date, although it is stated in Gov. Gilmer's work, "Georgians," that he died at Augusta, March, 1812, "whilst on his way to Washington city to *thrash* the President.—ED.

There is scarcely any man over the age of twenty-one years, between whom and other individuals there is not some strong obligatory moral tie, which we ought not to sever if we could conveniently avoid it. Look at the case of a husband deserting his wife and children, or of a man, above twenty-one, deserting his aged parent, dependent on him for subsistence. Are not these cases equally strong? The doctrine of the gentleman, whether on the score of morality or expediency, will apply to cases above as well as below the age of twenty-one. As respects the young men of our country, there is no fact better established than that, at the age of eighteen, they are, as respects physical power, as well qualified for the fatigues of the camp, as in other countries at twenty-one. Their services are more valuable than those of any other class, and he was not willing to dispense with them when we had the greatest occasion for them.

On the 21st, he spoke as follows:

Mr. TROUP.—If a stranger in the gallery had listened to the member from Massachusetts, (Mr. Quincy,) he would have supposed that the provision of the bill against which the gentleman's anathemas were most vehemently leveled, authorized the recruiting sergeant to enter the house of the citizen, drag from it the young man, and transport him, loaded with chains, (as is said to be the practice of one nation of Europe,) to the armies. Who would have supposed that the provision merely authorized the recruiting sergeant to accept the voluntary service of the young man, between eighteen and twenty-one? The service due to the country, prior in point of time, paramount in obligation, must yield, says the gentleman, to the service due to the master, the parent, ro the guardian. If, sir, in the days of Rome's greatness, if in the proud days of Grecian glory, the man could have been found base and hardy enough to withhold the young men from the public service, to turn them from the path of honor, or to restrain them from the field of fame, he would have been hurled from the Tarpeian Rock or consigned to the Cave of Trophonius. The young man is preferred here, not because he is preferred in France, but because his physical constitution and his moral temperament peculiarly qualify him for the arduous duties of the field and camp; bodily vigor and activity, ardor, enterprise, impetuosity; without family, and therefore without the cares which family involve: No wife, no helpless children. Without care, but for his country; without fear, but for her dishonor; he is most eminently qualified for the duties of the camp and the field; all experience has proved it.

But the gentleman is not content with opposing himself to the patriotism of the young men; he is not less opposed to the increase of pay. Mr. T. thought, from the conduct of the House the other day, that the provision had been universally approved. He was the more surprised at the opposition of the gentleman, because it was this provision of the bill which meant to eradicate that vice and immorality of the Army, which the gentleman affected so much to deplore. The increase of pay had two objects, the filling the ranks, and the general respectability of the Army. The recruiting service had suddenly stopped; it stopped only because all the men which were to be had for sixteen dollars bounty, and five dollars and one hundred and sixty acres of land, were already picked up; to get more, nothing could be done but to increase the pay; the quantum of increase was the only question. The difficulty of enlisting men was not peculiar to us; it was felt by every nation. Military wages bore no equitable proportion to the ordinary wages of the country. In the stronger and more despotic governments of Europe, force was resorted to; in the more mild and moderate, stratagem and fraud and trick. Who had not heard of the tricks of recruiting sergeants? Under our own government, enlistments, to be lawful, must be fair and free and voluntary; hence, the only remedy left us was increase of pay. But the filling of the ranks was by no means the most important object. The increase of the general respectability of the Army was of infinitely more importance. The regular service had been brought into universal disrepute in the country. The cause is obvious; it was the five dollars per month, and nothing else. There was nothing ignominious or disgraceful in the nature of the employment; on the contrary, it is honorable, it inspires honorable sentiments. Ask the farmer why he does not encourage his son to enlist in the service of his country? He answers at once, that he can make ten dollars a month on the farm; that if he has honesty and industry, anybody will hire him for ten dollars. Can there be any doubt that, by increasing the pay, you will increase the numbers of the Army? Not only so; in the exact proportion as you increase the pay, will you increase the respectability. It is self-evident. Suppose, instead of sixty dollars, or ninety dollars a year, you would agree to give them five thousand dollars, there is no doubt your ranks would soon be filled.

You would have the silk-stocking gentry, (I do not know that the Army would be much better for that,) you would chance to have a few members of Congress, perhaps a Secretary of State, perhaps an ex-President; you would at least enlist honesty and industry. I say, sir, the increase of the respectability of the Army at this moment is of infinite importance. With every disposition to rely on the militia for defence and offence, we are not permitted to do so; the militia are withheld by some of the States. The gentleman and his friends have withheld the militia of Massachusetts; he would now withhold the regulars. Give character and respectability to the Army, and when, in a spirit of jealousy or disaffection, or treason, the militia should be withheld, you are still independent; you are still a government for all the objects of government. If Massachusetts and Connecticut—but I forbear.

On the 30th of December, the House being in committee of the whole on the bill to raise an additional military force, and a proposition being made to postpone the further consideration of it,

Mr. Troup said, he would have no objection to grant the postponement asked by the gentlemen, (Messrs. Gold and Quincy,) if their object was consistent with that of the committee. The object of the committee was to combine a union of council and energy of action in favor of the war. The next campaign must be opened with vigor, and prosecuted to success. With this view, the committee had presented a system; gentlemen might, if they pleased, call it a system of the Executive. They submitted it to the House, not as the very best which it was possible for human ability to devise, but the best which, under all circumstances, they were able to present: they asked gentlemen on the opposite side, to take it, not word for word, as it was submitted, but to take it for as much as it was worth; to amend it if defective; to substitute one in lieu of it if radically wrong. Their argument would be listened to with pleasure—their amendment or substitute respectfully considered. But the motion to postpone was inadmissible, because the motive was incorrect; procrastination in the present state of the country was death. Gentlemen would neither amend the system with a view to make it better, nor would they substitute one in lieu of it. They were opposed to the war; they disavowed any responsibility for its origin, progress or consequences—it was a war of wickedness against innocence. Gentlemen had expressly said so; they would not give you a dollar or a man to carry it on. Yet are we asked to postpone the bill—to hear the argument—to risk the loss of another campaign. If there be anything which can endanger the system, it is delay. A week or a day is of great importance. It is a Parliamentary rule, that he who is radically opposed to a bill shall not amend it. It is a good rule that he who is opposed to the war shall not plan the campaign. A gentleman on the other side of the House, (Mr. Potter,) had said, in a spirit of frankness and candor which did him honor, that, having opposed the war, he was opposed to the ways and means of conducting it, and therefore to any object of expenditure connected with it—to a navy, an army and everything else. He was happy to find, however, that there were some gentlemen on the same side of the House who would not act with him; who would not sacrifice the country to the passions of party. Mr. T. only asked that the majority, to whom the responsibility attached, should be permitted to proceed in furnishing the Executive with the means of conducting the war.

But the most considerable, and perhaps the ablest speech which Col. Troup delivered during and in defence of the war, was on the 6th of January, 1813, pending the discussion of the bill just noticed, to raise an additional military force of 20,000 men for one year.

He spoke as follows:

Mr. Troup said, that observations had fallen from certain gentlemen, which merited reply and deserved correction. The two gentlemen who had just sat down, (Messrs. Grundy and Archer,) had noticed some of those observations in a handsome manner, and had given the appropriate answer. There yet remained some points which it would be proper to notice; it was the comparative decorum with which they were made that entitled them to respect. The gentleman from Connecticut, (Mr. Pitkin,) had declared that this government had insisted in past time, and did still continue to insist, that the American flag should cover all descriptions of persons sailing under it, and that this perseverance in an erroneous principle had been the cause of the war, and of all the calamities the nation had suffered. Mr. T. said, he was the more surprised to hear a round, unqualified declaration of this kind from the gentleman, because he had given repeated proofs to the House of the attention which he bestowed on the public documents, and the assiduity with which he had studied them; there were two of them, especially, which the gentleman must have read, and, reading, could not fail to have remembered; one of no very remote date, the other very recent, and very interesting; it would be doing injustice to the gentleman to believe they were not strongly imprinted on his memory, yet did both those documents more plainly and directly contradict the allegation of the gentleman. Long before the period, however, to which I refer, Mr. King, our Minister at London, had written to the Secretary of State, "that, on this subject, (viz., impressment,) we had again and again offered to concur in a convention, which we thought practicable to be formed, and which would settle these questions in a manner that would be safe for England and satisfactory to us." (Letter 15th March, 1799.) The first document after this is a letter of instruction from the Secretary of State to Mr. Monroe, Minister at the Court of St. James, dated May 29th, 1807, soon after the failure of the treaty concluded by himself and Mr. Pinkney, and is to the following purport:

"It is agreed that after the term of——————months, computed from the exchange of ratifications, and during a war in which either of the contracting parties may be engaged, neither of them will permit any seaman, not being its own citizen or subject, and being a citizen or subject of the other party, who shall not have been for two years at least, prior to that date, constantly and voluntarily in the service or within the jurisdiction of the parties respectively, to enter or be employed on board any of its vessels navigating the high seas; and proper regulations, enforced by adequate penalties, shall be mutually established for distinguishing the seamen of the parties, respectively, and for giving full effect to this stipulation."

Here, then, is documentary evidence that, so far back as the year 1807, the American government had tendered to the British cabinet a proposition, the effect of which was to exempt from the protection of the American flag, or, what is the same thing, to exclude from the American service, every description of persons, saving American native-born and naturalized citizens. Does the gentleman insist that the naturalized citizen should not be protected? If he does not, will he authorize the British to search and impress, though the American government should prohibit, by all the penalties of law, foreigners of any description from entering into the service of her merchant vessels? Does he mean that we shall be exposed to the vexatious practice of search and impressment, notwithstanding the government shall do everything in its power to prevent British subjects from entering into its service? But, Mr. Speaker, if the proposition of Mr. Monroe did not go far enough for the gentleman, the proposition of Mr. Russell unquestionably did. Here it is:

"I finally offered, in order to answer at once all the observations and inquiries of Lord Castlereagh, that the proposed understanding should be expressed in the most general terms; that the laws to take effect on the discontinuance of the practice of impressment, should prohibit the employment of the native subjects or citizens of the one State, excepting such only as had already been naturalized, on board the private or public ships of the other; thus removing any objection that might have been raised with regard to the future effect of naturalization, or the formal renunciation of any pretended right."

The effect of this proposition of Mr. Russell, sir, is not only the exclusion of British subjects from American employ, but the exclusion of British subjects who may in future be naturalized in the United States. Hence, our flag would have covered none but native Americans, and such British subjects as had been before naturalized. Having employed the power of the country; having resorted to all the pains and penalties which the law can provide to prohibit this description of persons from serving on board American vessels; will the gentleman, notwithstanding, insist that British commanders shall enter our vessels to make search for seamen? If, notwithstanding the prohibition, it were permited to British officers to make search for seamen, the prohibition had better not be made; the practice might as well go on in all the latitude of tyranny and oppression which has distinguished it.

The gentleman from North Carolina (Mr. Pearson) has been pleased, in the course of his observations on this subject, to offer to the House a project for a peace. He would have the Legislature to pass laws prohibiting the employ of British seamen in our service, leaving the President to make a tender of those laws, through fit and proper characters, to the British government, as the basis of an adjustment. The gentleman is to accomplish two objects by his project—a union of parties, and a peace with the enemy; both objects, sir, are not less interesting to me than to the gentleman; but, I very much doubt, Mr. Speaker, whether either of them be attainable. The gentleman not only requires a specific form to be given to the proposition itself, but it is an essential condition on which he is to enter into the union, that the proposition be tendered to the British government by such characters as he will approve; by men, as he says, without office and without expectation of office. Now, sir, although it may not be very difficult to find men who do not hold office, it would seem to me to be extremely difficult, if not impossible, to find men without expectation of office; and yet the gentleman would be under no obligation to unite with us, unless his project were tendered to the British government by such men. Mr. Pinkney had passed for a Federalist, both in this country and England; he had tendered a very important proposition to the British government; but, as the gentlemen on the other side had always doubted the sincerity of the government in making that overture, it is to be presumed that whatever confidence they might have had in Mr. Pinkney as a politician, they had ceased to respect him as a fit person to make propositions to the British government. Sir, I fear it is as difficult to unite parties as to conciliate the British government. Both the gentlemen from Connecticut and North Carolina have mistaken the character of that government; she is not to be conciliated. If they sincerely want peace, they must employ the resources and energies of the country to coerce it. This is susceptible of proof; repeated overtures have been made in the most amicable spirit, and have been uniformly rejected, and under circumstances which left no doubt of the lurking hostility which dictated the rejection.

The proposition of Mr. Monroe, of 1807, had failed; the proposition of Mr. Pinkney, of 1810 and 1811, had failed; the recent proposition of Mr. Russell had failed. Of the first, I have already spoken. Give me leave to say something of the second. The failure of the second proposition, viz.: to continue the non-intercourse against France, repealing it as to England, provided England would rescind her Orders in Council, is one of the most extraordinary and unaccountable occurrences in political history. Be it remembered, sir, that this proposition was substantially a proposition to go to war on the side of England against France, provided England would rescind her orders—France continuing her decrees. I say this was the proposition, substantially, because this was the inevitable effect of it, to place the United States in the same relation to England as they are now placed in relation to France—not with a view, Mr. Speaker, to an alliance with either; far from it; but to the ultimate vindication of their own just rights against the aggressions of either of them—warring for themselves, and for themselves making peace. But, most strange to say, Mr. Speaker, this voluntary tender of our friendship was disdainfully rejected; at a period, too, when England, pressed by a formidable war, was standing as it were on her last legs—all Europe united against her—and when, according to her own declaration, her very existence was at stake; when, too, the single condition of this friendly proposition was, that England should recall a measure, which, but a short time after, she was forced to abandon to the clamors and distresses of her own people. No, said England, we want not your friendship; it is of no value to us; you have not courage and fortitude to defend, manfully, your own just rights, and how can I expect that you will render important service to me? It is altogether impossible, sir, to account for the conduct of England, without supposing her to have entertained such sentiments. And will the gentleman from North Carolina flatter himself with the belief, that, after the failure of such a proposition, England is to be conciliated by his project—a project substantially the same as that of Mr. Monroe, of 1807, and identically the proposition of Mr. Russell in 1812? But the gentleman derives hope from the ground on which Mr. Russell's proposal was rejected. Mr. Russell, says the gentleman, was not regularly commissioned, nor was he formally instructed to make the proposition in the latitude in which he tendered it. But, sir, was not the letter of the Secretary of State a sufficient commission for him? And, suppose Mr. Russell, consulting the spirit rather than the letter of his instructions, had given to the proposition a somewhat more liberal character, it was not on this ground the proposition was rejected; it was rejected, as Lord Castlereagh expressly said, because England would never consent to entertain any proposal which went to abridge her right of impressment; that any arrangement for the limitation of this right was impracticable, and had always been so; that it was true, on this subject, their *friends in Congress*—meaning the *Federalists*—had believed in the practicability of an arrangement, but they were mistaken; Mr. King was as far from accomplishing it as Mr. Monroe: that, in fact, it was in vain to negotiate about it; popular feeling would not permit them to make any concession upon the subject. This is the language of Lord Castlereagh. But suppose it had not been: If the British cabinet were sincerely disposed to listen to the proposal, they would have said so, notwithstanding any objection which could have been taken to the authority or power of Mr. Russell. Lord Castlereagh would have said, for instance, that the proposition was a fair one; that, if offered by an agent with full powers, it would be entertained; if inconvenient to make it the basis of negotiation at London, it might be made the basis of negotiation at Washington. But this, sir, never entered into the head of Lord Castlereagh. The answer to Mr. Russell was, that the thing was wholly impracticable, and had always been so. But, the gentleman desires us to repeat the same proposition, that we may receive the same answer.

I trust, sir, by this time, I have been able to satisfy the gentleman that England is not to be conciliated. Will the gentleman and his friends unite with me in a project of coercion—a project in which I have no less confidence than the gentleman from North Carolina in his own? Yes, sir, so much confidence that I would almost be tempted to make a bargain with the gentleman to take any of their projects, however fanciful, if, within a reasonable time, the enemy did not yield to united councils and an active war. My project is, *embargo*—an immediate, entire and rigidly executed embargo, embracing as well the coasting as foreign trade, and, if you please, sir, a provision by law for naturalizing British seamen, voluntarily entering into the service of the United States, *during the war*—the converse of the proposition of the gentleman. An embargo may be resorted to at this moment with comparatively little sacrifice; the foreign trade is inconsiderable, the coasting trade is almost entirely interrupted. The effect of an embargo would be;

1. To keep our own commerce safe at home, leaving the commerce of the enemy exposed to the assaults of our privateers and public vessels;

2. To distress the enemy at home, in his colonies, and on the Peninsula;

3. To give ten-fold vigor to the war, by making a diversion of men and of capital in favor of our privateers, and of men in favor of our public vessels;

4. To facilitate the reduction of Canada, by creating partial scarcity, at least—perhaps absolute distress.

Now is the moment, Mr. Speaker, for this embargo. The British papers announce that the price of bread has risen on the heel of the harvest, though the harvest has been described as abundant. The proclamations of the Prince Regent prohibit the conversion of grain into starch, and the use of grain in the breweries. Can we have stronger evidence of apprehended scarcity? Sir, of the force and effect with which this measure may be wielded against the enemy, we do not want more decisive proof than that which the enemy himself has furnished—proof which is a source of triumph and exultation to every American. Two facts were unfolded. First, by the examination before the British House of Commons, it had been shown that, if the British people were not at all times and under all circumstances absolutely dependent on us for a market for their manufactures, they were at this time and in the present state of the world absolutely dependent; second, that if not always, and in every state of things, absolutely dependent on us for supplies of provisions, they were in the present state of Europe absolutely dependent. I beseech the gentlemen, therefore, to take the embargo as a sure measure of attaining what they profess so much to desire—peace. But, sir, the other measure which I tender to the gentlemen, though not so powerful and efficient against the enemy, is not less interesting: the protection of seamen of every description, during the war, who shall be found fighting under the American flag—to naturalize the seaman voluntarily enlisting on board the armed vessels of the United States, and, having naturalized, to protect him with the power of the country. Whatever, Mr. Speaker, have been our misfortunes or reverses on the land, we may enjoy the consolation that the gallantry and skill of our seamen will make the war, if not a short, yet certainly an honorable, one for the country; the war was undertaken chiefly for them; they will be chiefly instrumental in waging it, and I have no doubt they will make it a glorious one for themselves and for all of us; but they ought to be protected. Whatever be the description or character of the seaman fighting under the American flag, that seaman ought to be protected. Not a hair of his head should be touched by the enemy with impunity. In considering, Mr. Speaker, the right, propriety and justice, of adopting this regulation, we are naturally led to advert to the British doctrine and practice on this subject; and here I beg leave to remark that it is scarcely possible for the imagination to conceive anything more inconsistent and contradictory than the British doctrine and practice. She sets up a principle of public law—be it arbitrary or be it sound, no matter—she requires the observance of it from all other nations as a settled principle of public law. So long as it suits her to respect, she respects it; whenever it suits her to violate, she violates it; her principle is, that allegiance is natural, perpetual and inalienable; that it is born with the subject, and descends with him into the grave; that once a British subject, always a British subject. She enforces this doctrine when she impresses from American vessels naturalized citizens; she enforces it when she threatens with death, as the Prince Regent has recently done in his proclamation, the British seaman of any description who may be found fighting under the American flag. She violates the doctrine, she tramples it under foot, when she declares, by statute, that the American seaman entering voluntarily into her service, and continuing two years, is *ipso facto* naturalized. She violates the doctrine, she tramples it under foot, when she declares, by statute, that the American seaman contracting marriage with a British subject, is *ipso facto* naturalized. Thus, while in practice she contemns her own doctrine, she holds out every lure and temptation to the American seaman to desert the service of his country. It is not of much importance to us, Mr. Speaker, what doctrine the British government may set up; all we ask is, that, whatever the doctrine be, she will herself respect it. While her Government is in the habitual practice of naturalizing American seamen, she insists that our Government shall not naturalize her subjects. Assuredly, Mr. Speaker, it cannot be unlawful for us to do in relation to her what she does in relation to us. If she violates the public law in relation to us, that very public law authorizes us to violate it in relation to her. This is the law of retaliation. If she can naturalize our seamen serving two years on board her vessels, or contracting marriage with her subjects, we may naturalize her seamen entering voluntarily into our service; the period of two years, prescribed by the British statutes, makes no difference; it affects not the principle; it is entirely arbitrary; she might as well have prescribed two months, or two days, or two hours.

You will observe, Mr. Speaker, that the British Government, in executing this regulation, has no regard to the character of the American seaman. It is unimportant to her whether the seaman be a deserter or not from the American service; it is immaterial whether he deserted before or after the war. Indeed, no questions are asked; it is sufficient for the purpose that he is an American citizen, willing to enter into her service, contracting marriage with a British subject, or serving two years on board her public ships. We demand nothing but reciprocity; there is no justice or equity where there is no reciprocity; and between nations there must be reciprocity, because there is perfect equality. Hence, Mr. Speaker, the justice, the lawfulness, the propriety of the regulation which I propose to you. Let us for a moment consider its expediency. Engaged in a war with a formidable Power, we find ourselves in one important respect occupying a vantage ground. Shall we avail ourselves of it to the injury of the enemy, or shall we voluntarily abandon it? The advantage results from the nature of things. The temptation to British seamen to enter the American service is stronger than the temptation to American seamen to enter the British service; and the fact is that more British seamen enter the American service than American seamen the British service. Shall we, I repeat, avail ourselves of this advantage during the war or not? Not, Mr. Speaker, that we want her seamen; not that they are essentially useful, much less necessary to our service; but that, by taking them from the enemy, we wound, and wound her where she is most vulnerable; the loss to her is much more important than the gain to us. She sets the example, too; and when we offer, as a condition of peace, to prevent her seamen from entering into our service, we are instructed by her conduct that she chooses rather to enforce her practice of impressment, by arms, than to rely on any pledge which we can give for the exclusion of her seamen from our employ.

I entreat gentlemen, therefore, to take my project of coercion instead of their project of propitiation. I have endeavored to show that the enemy is not to be conciliated;

First, Because the conciliatory overture of 1807, substantially the same with the proposition of the gentleman from North Carolina, was rejected;

Second, Because the overture of Mr. Russell, of 1812, identically the proposition of the gentleman, was rejected;

And, third, above all, that the overture repeatedly pressed by Mr. Pinkney, in 1810 and 1811, the inevitable effect of which would have been to throw us into the war on the side of England against France, was rejected.

Sir, it will be asked, with wonder and astonishment, how an overture of this character, so favorable to the obvious policy and interest of England, could have been thrown back upon us with disdain; incredible as the fact is, it is true. The cause, I repeat it, is only to be sought in the ineffable contempt in which she has held us; looking at our party divisions, and calculating on the weakness and fluctuation of our councils, she indulges a confident belief that the fatal and vibratory policy which yielded the old embargo to the clamors of a petty faction, would forever distinguish our cause. Yes, sir, it is to the forced repeal of the old embargo that we must look for the causes of our protracted quarrel with England. We had given no incontestable evidence before of the influence of faction upon our councils; from that moment, however, she ceased to respect us; from that moment, she never dreamed that it was possible for us to go to war. When the war came, she let go the Orders in Council, to be sure, but she still continued to believe, and yet continues to believe, that the same spirit of faction, which forced the repeal of the old embargo, would drive you out of the war. She has been looking with hope and with confidence to the issue of the late elections. Now that she is disappointed in the result, there is no saying what she will do. Our safest and wisest course is, however, to combine the resources of the country to give force and vigor to the war.

The objections to this bill, sir, are so various and contradictory, that one is at a loss in what manner to consider them. By some, it is said the force is too great; by others, it is too small; by some, the term of enlistment is too short; by others, the innocent Canadians are to be overrun with it directly; and others, again, are opposed to it, because standing armies are dangerous to republics, and because they confer great patronage and power.

We are embarked in the war; a military force is necessary to carry it on: it must be one of two descriptions—*militia* or *regulars*. When we ask gentlemen for the militia, they say no!—the militia belong to the States; they are constitutionally under the control of the State authorities for local defence; you shall not have them. Well, sir, in this, for the present, we have seemed to acquiesce; but, gentlemen, if you will not give us the militia, pray give us a regular force. No, say gentlemen, regular armies are dangerous to Republics; they confer too much patronage. Well, if you will neither give us regulars nor militia, what will you do? And here, sir, at last we have extorted *their system*. Will you believe it, sir?—it is to repeal the declaration of war, lay down our arms, and throw ourselves upon the generosity of the enemy—he is a noble and generous foe, and will grant you reasonable terms. Thus, sir, are we to be bound hand and foot, with our locks shorn, and delivered over to the Philistines. We answer: this, gentlemen, may be a very good system for you, but it is a very bad one for us; if you will be united against us, we will endeavor to be united for the country against you; and when we negotiate, to negotiate with arms in our hands.

Sir, there is one argument which, on this subject, I think, merits attention. As the power of declaring war is lodged with the Legislature, so the power of conducting it is vested in the Executive. He is, constitutionally, the sole conductor of war; he has the planning of the campaign, the adaptation of force, and the uncontrolled direction of it in the field. The object of the war is a speedy and honorable peace, and it is his duty so to direct the national force, that the object be attained in the best manner, and with the least possible delay. He is responsible to you, therefore, for the wise and judicious application of the force; he is responsible to you by election, and by impeachment. Is not this *responsibility* of some value to you? Does it not become you to maintain and cherish it? You can only cherish it by granting, and granting liberally, the supplies asked for. If you withhold the supplies, you destroy the responsibility, you assume it to yourselves. If you grant the supplies with a niggardly or parsimonious hand, you impair the responsibility, you diminish it essentially. Liberal supplies of men and money are necessary to success; your armies and navies must be well found, or they are inefficient. How comes it the Emperor of France marched fifteen hundred miles from home, and vanquished forty millions of people, before we reduced a petty province of the enemy, with a population of only three hundred thousand, and lying at our very door? Military skill out of the question—it is because of his ample command of men and money. How is it that England makes such vast efforts on the Peninsula? It is because the Parliament never hesitates to grant the supplies, and to grant them liberally. But the term of enlistment is too short; so it is, if we want this force for the general purposes of the war; for the general purposes of the war, five years' men are infinitely better; but we do not want more five years' men than are already provided for by law. The Executive asked this force, in addition, as a peculiar force, and for a temporary occasion; they say, everything considered, it is best adapted to their object. Will we believe them? Will we give them what they ask? Or, will we give them what they do not ask?

Mr. T. concluded his speech, by adverting to the alleged misfortunes of the war, and attributing much of the delay of operations on land to the unwarrantable efforts of party, in introducing insubordination and disaffection in the Eastern States, &c.

[1813.] The bill passed the House on the 14th of January, under the title of "An act in addition to the act, entitled 'An act to raise an additional military force, and for other purposes,'" was slightly amended in the Senate, and was finally approved by the President on the 29th of the same month.

The second and last session of the Twelfth Congress terminated on 3d March, 1813.

CHAPTER VII.

Col. Troup's Re-Election to Congress.—Sessions of Thirteenth Congress.—Progress and close of the War.—Conscription.—Retirement of Col. Troup from the House of Representatives, &c.

ON the 24th day of May, 1813, the first session of the Thirteenth Congress began. Mr. Madison had been inaugurated, for the second time, as President, on the 4th of March preceding. The Representatives from Georgia, elected on the first Monday of October, 1812, were William Barnett, William W. Bibb, John Forsyth, Bolling Hall, Thomas Telfair and GEORGE M. TROUP.

On the 26th of May, Col. Troup was appointed Chairman of the Committee on Military Affairs, and in this position he continued during the war. A better selection could not have been made. It is admitted that he possessed military talents of a high order. His advocacy of the war was based upon principle, and he was for pressing it with vigor. In afterwards reviewing his political life, "he was better satisfied with his speeches and efforts in Congress, in bringing on the last war with Great Britain, after her dastardly and disgraceful attack upon the Chesapeake, than any other portion of his past political life."* He possessed all the talent, foresight and firmness necessary for the post; and when we consider the distinguished ability on the Republican side of the House at that time, his appointment may be considered anything else than an empty compliment.

It is not consistent with the plan of this work to go into a detail of the events of the war. Up to this period, the land forces had met with some reverses and some successes, and our gallant little navy had already given earnest, in a

* See letter of Hon. Joseph H. Lumpkin, in a subsequent chapter.—ED.

few brilliant victories, of a future career of renown as remarkable as it was unexpected.

This session of Congress was adjourned on the second day of August. Several important acts were passed for the defence of the country, the prosecution of the war, raising taxes, &c.

[1813.] On the 14th of June, Col. Troup, from the Military Committee, introduced a bill to provide for the widows and orphans of militia slain, and for militia disabled in the service of the United States; and, on the 22d, he introduced a bill to continue in force, for a limited time, certain acts authorizing corps of rangers for the protection of the frontiers, &c.; and, on the 23d, a bill supplementary to the act in addition to the act to raise an additional military force; also one in relation to the regulation of the ordnance; and, on the 30th, a bill making further appropriation for fortifying the ports and harbors of the United States. But it would be useless to go into a consideration of the various measures proposed by him, from the appropriate committee, during the session. The reports of proceedings do not show that he took much part in debate. Indeed, this seems to have been a working and not a debating session. Such was the progress made in business, that, on the 16th of July, in secret session of the House, Col. Troup, from the committee on Military Affairs, made the following report:

The committee on Military Affairs, to whom was referred a resolution of yesterday, having relation to the present movements of the enemy, report:

That they have examined into the state of preparation, naval and military, made to receive the enemy, and are satisfied that the preparation is, in every respect, adequate to the emergency, and that no measures are necessary, on the part of the House, to make it more complete.

[1813.] On the 6th of December, Congress re-assembled. The President congratulated that body on the success of our arms—the splendid victory of Perry on Lake Erie, of Gen. Harrison at the battle of the Thames, &c., &c. No man felt more keenly than Colonel Troup the reverses which our land and naval forces sometimes experienced, and no one rejoiced more heartily at the successes which crowned the efforts of the Administration and its friends to wage an unequal war against a haughty foreign foe, and insidious enemies at home. Late in the previous session, Mr. Bradley, of Vermont, had offered a resolution of inquiry "into the causes which led to the multiplied failures of the arms of the United States on our Western and North-western frontier," &c. The resolution had been laid on the table, and a resolution to print it negatived.

At the present session, a resolution, of the same import, but calling on the President for information, not improper to be communicated, was offered by the same member. In voting against the resolution,

Mr. Troup said, that if an inquiry of this sort was expedient at all, the shape of the proposition was perhaps as little exceptionable as could have been given to it. But a military inquiry, under any circumstances, was a matter of so much delicacy that it ought to be well weighed and entered into with much caution and circumspection. This arose from the nature of such inquiries. Secrecy was the soul of military operations. Their details ought to be known to those concerned only; for, if imparted to others, perchance they might find their way to the enemy. It was very well known that military investigations frequently took place in the British House of Commons; but the invariable object of them was to turn out the Ministry. Such an inquiry, however common, rarely was instituted even there; and, whenever successfully urged, it had invariably been when the object of an expedition or campaign had been abandoned. Mr. T. said he should have liked to have heard from the mover of the resolution something like argument; that much more of advantage would result from the adoption, than of evil that might ensue from it. Suppose any possible result of the inquiry—suppose, for instance, that by the communication, in answer to this resolution, it should be shown that General Wilkinson had been prevented by bad weather from commencing his operations in due season; that, when he reached St. Regis, General Wilkinson, without forming a junction with Gen. Hampton, had proceeded on Montreal; or that, even having formed such a junction, it would have been unmilitary for him to proceed onwards; suppose it should turn out that there had been the best military conduct possible on the part of all our Generals; or, that the object of the campaign failed to be accomplished in consequence of the misconduct of either of them, or was the result of cowardice or treason; suppose any result, probable or improbable, and where is the constitutional remedy? How would the gentleman lay his hand on the delinquent? An investigation, it appeared to him, could not properly be made by a tribunal which had not the power to apply the remedy. The investigation, as well as the remedy, rightly belonged to another department of the government. Martial law was the only proper corrective to be applied to misconduct of military men. Not, Mr. T. said, that he was opposed to every species of military inquiry. Far from it. There were certain species of inquiry which it might be perfectly proper to institute. For the purpose of new-modeling an army, abolishing certain descriptions of force or grades of office, such inquiries might be necessary. But, said he, for the purpose of reaching any particular military commander, who is supposed to have forfeited the confidence of the people, the remedy is not yours; it belongs to the Executive. Not having the remedy in our hands, the inquiry cannot be productive of any advantage to the public concerns. But with respect to some evils which may result, Mr. T. said he would add a few words. What description of evidence would be necessary to the intelligent prosecution of such an inquiry? Nothing short, certainly, of the plan of the campaign, the correspondence with the Generals, and the correspondence of the Generals with each other, &c. Mr. T. dwelt on the evils which would result from exposing to the enemy a plan of the campaign, &c. Unfortunate as the termination of this campaign might have been, it would become more so by exposing to the enemy the official details of its plans and progress. Wherever we had experienced, during the war, anything of disaster or defeat, it was attributable to our ignorance of the force of the enemy. It was therefore obviously important to us to follow the example of the enemy in this respect, and keep him as much as possible in ignorance of our military operations. He may occasionally derive information from a traitor or deserter; but information so acquired bore no comparison to the injury which would result from affording the enemy official information on these matters; and such official information, he presumed, would alone satisfy the object of the gentleman's motion. He hoped therefore it would not pass.

The resolution was passed by a large majority, but against the vote of Col. Troup and the two next to him on the Military Committee.

[1814.] On the 7th of January, Mr. Grosvenor, of New York, offered the following Resolution:

"That the committee on Military Affairs be instructed to inquire into the acts, rules and regulations, by which furloughs and leave of absence from the Armies of the United States are obtained by officers thereof, and whether the said acts, rules and regulations ought to be revised, altered and amended; and that they have leave to report by bill or otherwise."

Mr. Troup objected to this motion, as traveling out of the province of the Legislature into that of the Executive. To Congress was granted the power of raising armies and granting supplies for them; but to the Executive were confided the exclusive control and direction of the armies when raised. To enable him properly to execute this duty, the President had been vested with the most arbitrary powers—the power of dismissing without assigning a cause, and, jointly with the military courts, of cashiering, and inflicting on officers other punishments, even unto death. The power, then, of controlling military movements, said Mr. T., is not with us, but with the Executive. He may dismiss any officer of the Army, and even the Secretary of War, for misconduct; and the power of control, possessed by this House, is the power of impeaching the President, if he fail in the performance of his duty. True it was, the enemy had, on a recent occasion, suprised us, found us slumbering in our beds in a thoughtless manner—but it was not for him to say where the blame lay of that occurrence. In relation to the officers now absent from the Army, he could only say that he had heard—and he had heard because, in his capacity of Chairman of the Military Committee, it had become his duty to inquire into the matter—that when the Army lately went into cantonments, there were found to be a considerable number of supernumerary officers attached to it. An order had been issued by the commanding General to consolidate the troops into full and complete regiments, and allot to each of the regiments so formed its proper complement of officers. That order being properly executed, the supernumerary officers were thrown out of employ—and orders were given to them to repair to the different recruiting stations, where unquestionably they would be occupied more beneficially to the service than in any other way. This was the fact in relation to the absence of the officers generally who were not in the Army. It struck him, Mr. Troup said, that there was something objectionable in the object of the resolution. It proposed to make the manner of granting furloughs a matter of legislative provision, when in fact it was a thing which could not properly be legislated upon, depending so entirely, as it did, on circumstances and on the state of the Army. If Congress were to make a law that no furlough should be granted, there was not an honorable man in the country who would accept a military office. This being his view of the subject, he hoped the resolution would not pass.

In rejoining to the member from New York,

Mr. Troup deprecated the disposition which appeared to prevail in that House to interfere in the management of the Army. If the members of this House undertook to make themselves judges of the manner in which the war ought to be conducted, there would be about as many opinions as there were members in the House; and at last, after all their opinions, the war must be conducted by the Executive, in such manner as he might deem most consistent with the public interest. The gentleman last up had fairly avowed his ignorance of existing regulations on the subject. Mr. T. rose to inform the gentleman and the House of their nature; by whom it would be agreed they were as comprehensive as anything could be. Mr. T. read the following article from the regulations issued from the War Office:

"No furloughs shall be given during a campaign; nor any, but by the General commanding the district or army, and for the cause of disability, which disability shall be certified by regimental or hospital surgeon.

"Furloughs shall, besides expressing the term of time granted to absentees, express also an order to join the regiment, post or garrison, to which they may belong.

"No order shall be given to officers seeking a furlough for their own convenience, which shall have the effect of entitling them to an allowance for transportation of baggage."

This provision, Mr. T. said, was as imperative as it could be, and had all the force of law. There was, therefore, obviously, no amendment necessary to the existing provisions. In inquiring into the non-execution of this provision, if such was the object, the House assumed a duty not belonging to it, and must go upon the principle that it had a right to punish officers for misconduct; otherwise, it was not within its province to inquire into their conduct in this respect.

The resolution was laid on the table.

These speeches are given, not merely on account of their intrinsic excellence, but to show the zeal and activity of Col. Troup in that particular branch of the public service which had been so largely entrusted to his vigilance, and to show, also, his familiarity with the duties and details of his responsible post.

Besides many plans and propositions which he presented to the House, for carrying on the war, he spoke, during the session, on various subjects—most of them connected with the absorbing topic of the war. But we do not deem it necessary to refer particularly to them. This session closed on the 18th of April, 1814.*

Congress was again convened, by the President, on the 19th of September, of the same year, by proclamation dated the 8th of August. Before the meeting of Congress, however, to wit, on the 23d of August, the British had taken possession of the city of Washington, burned the Capitol and other public buildings, and committed other acts of outrage unknown to civilized warfare.

In his message to Congress, the President thus alluded to these outrages:

"In the events of the present campaign, the enemy, with all his augumented means and wanton use of them, has little ground for exultation, unless he can feel it in the success of his recent enterprises against this metropolis and the neighboring town of Alexandria, from both of which his retreats were as precipitate as his attempts were bold and fortunate. In his other incursions on our Atlantic frontier, his progress, often checked and chastised by the martial

*During this session, a new embargo act was passed, entitled "An Act laying an embargo on all ships and vessels in the ports and harbors of the United States," and was approved by the President on the 17th day of December, 1813. It was of short duration, however, having been repealed on the 14th day of April, 1814, by the decisive vote, in the House, of one hundred and fifteen to thirty-seven. On the question of repeal, the Georgia delegation stood: YEAS—Messrs. Alfred Cuthbert, Forsyth and Telfair; NAYS—Messrs. Barnett, Hall and TROUP.

Dr. Bibb had been elected, on 6th November, 1813, to the Senate, in place of Hon. William H. Crawford, resigned; and Mr. Cuthbert took his seat in the House, on 7th February, 1814, in place of Dr. Bibb.—ED.

spirit of the neighboring citizens, has had more effect in distressing individuals, and in dishonoring his arms, than in promoting any object of legitimate warfare. And, in the two instances mentioned, however deeply to be regretted on our part, he will find in his transient success, which interrupted for a moment only the ordinary public business at the seat of government, no compensation for the loss of character with the world, by his violations of private property, and by his destruction of public edifices, protected, as monuments of the arts, by the laws of civilized warfare."

Although not strictly pertinent to a biographical work, we cannot here omit the insertion of one of the many incidents of brutal outrage, which so excited the American people at the time, and the recollection of which at this day causes the patriotic heart to rejoice that the time has passed, when England, with all her boasted strength, can further outrage the feelings of a generous but then comparatively impotent foe. Although anonymous, the article appears to be truthful, and has been recently republished, substantially, in one or more of the newspapers of this country. It is as follows:

To the Editors of the National Intelligencer:

Among the deeds of vandalism committed during the late invasion of the city, by the enemy, I know of none more base and wanton than the mutilation of the monument at the Navy yard. This elegant monument of the liberality and gallantry of our naval heroes, has been shamefully defaced by the hand of some barbarian. On the base, the Genius of America is represented by a female figure pointing to an inscription and raising a view of the battle before Tripoli, instructing her children who are standing beside her. The pointing finger and thumb have been cut off. History, a female figure, who is represented as recording the event, has been robbed of her pen—and the figure of Fame, who is represented as descending in a cloud covering the deeds of her sons with the palm and crown of glory, has been robbed of the palm at the expense of the hand that held it. From every inquiry it is possible to make, there is no reason to doubt that it was the deliberate act of some of the British officers, as several of them were seen to be on the base of the monument, by the neighbors around the yard.

The deed itself appears to have some allusion to the time when it was perpetrated; but poor indeed must have been the inspiration of the poet, not to have foreseen, in the victories of McDonough, Warrington and Blakeley, how soon History might resume her employment, and Fame cover our heroes with, I trust, an imperishable palm of victory.

AN OBSERVER.

Colonel Troup was at the seat of the national government when the capital was taken. As chairman of the Military committee of the House, he probably deemed it his duty to be there. His proud spirit was fired with indignation at these atrocities. We have it from good authority,* that, amongst the few persons in Washington at the time, who did not forget their propriety in the general panic which pervaded all classes, were JAMES MONROE, then Secretary of State, and GEORGE M. TROUP.

In consequence of the destruction of the Capitol, Congress convened in a public building of the city which had been used for the Post and other public offices.

On the 26th of September, a resolution was offered, "That a committee be appointed to inquire into the expediency of removing the Seat of Government, during the present session of Congress, to a place of greater security, and less inconvenience, than this city, with leave to report by bill or otherwise." On this resolution, five of the members from Georgia, to wit, Messrs. Cuthbert, Forsyth, Hall, Telfair and TROUP, voted in the negative.

During this session, Col. Monroe (who had succeeded John Armstrong as Secretary of War,) addressed the following communication to the Military Committee of the House:

DEPARTMENT OF WAR, October 17, 1814.

Sir: The great importance of the subject, and the other duties of the Department, which could not fail to be very sensibly felt, at so interesting a period, by a person who had

* Gen. Thomas S. Jesup, of the U. S. Army, who stated the circumstance to two gentlemen of Savannah, in 1854.—ED.

just taken charge of it, are my apology for not answering your letter of the 24th of September, at an earlier day, on the defects of the present Military Establishment.

Due consideration has been bestowed on the subject-matter of that letter, and I have now the honor to submit to the Committee the following report:

1. That the present Military Establishment, amounting to sixty-two thousand four hundred and forty-eight men, be preserved and made complete, and that the most efficient means authorized by the constitution, and consistent with the general rights of our fellow-citizens, be adopted, to fill the ranks, and with the least possible delay.

2. That a permanent force, consisting of at least forty thousand men, in addition to the present Military Establishment, be raised for the defence of our cities and frontiers, under an engagement by the Executive with such corps that it shall be employed in that service within certain specified limits, and that a proportional augmentation of general officers of each grade, and other staff, be provided for.

3. That the corps of engineers be enlarged.

4. That the ordnance department be amended.

Respecting the enlargement of the corps of engineers, I shall submit hereafter a more detailed communication.

For the proposed amendment of the ordnance department, I submit a report from the senior officer of that department in this city, which is approved.

I shall be ready and happy to communicate such further remarks and details on these subjects as the Committee may desire, and shall request permission to suggest hereafter the result of further attention to, and reflection on, our Military Establishment generally, should anything occur which may be deemed worthy its attention.

I have the honor to be, &c.,

JAMES MONROE.

Hon. G. M. Troup,
Chairman Military Committee.

This letter was accompanied by "Explanatory Observations," which, after other remarks on the occasion, the nature and the exigencies of the war, spoke as follows:

"It follows, from this view of the subject, that it will be necessary to bring into the field, next campaign, not less than one hundred thousand regular troops. Such a force, aided, in extraordinary circumstances, by volunteers and militia, will place us above all inquietude as to the final result of this contest. It will fix on a solid and imperishable foundation, our union and independence, on which the liberties and happiness of our fellow-citizens so essentially depend. It will secure to the United States an early and advantageous peace. It will arrest, in the further prosecution of the war, the desolation of our cities and our coast, by enabling us to retort on the enemy those calamitiesw hich our citizens have been already doomed to suffer; a resort which self-defence alone, and a sacred regard for the rights and honor of the nation, could induce the United States to adopt."

Four plans were then submitted, with a view to carry out a system of national defence; and, on the 27th of October, Col. Troup, from the committee on Military Affairs, reported a bill making further provision for filling the ranks of the regular Army, by classifying the free male population of the United States. The bill proposed, generally, to provide for the division of the whole free male population of the United States, by the assessors, into classes of twenty-five men each; each class to be compelled, under a penalty of——hundred dollars, to furnish, within——days after such classification, an able-bodied recruit, for the service of the United States, &c., &c.

It is hardly necessary to state that this whole system of raising men by draft, instead of recruiting, (which had very much failed in consequence of domestic opposition, especially in New England, to the war,) was denounced by the Federalists as a CONSCRIPTION; or that the occurrence of peace, soon afterwards, rendered the further consideration of the drafting system unnecessary—a system which seems to have met the approbation of General Washington,* in 1790, and which the great military powers of Europe have practically, although not always humanely, enforced, as necessary to successful military operations.

It is only fair to let Col. Troup speak for himself on this and other plans, then before Congress, for the conduct of

*For a full consideration of these plans, the reader is referred to the Annals of Congress, 1814—'15, vol. 3, pp. 482 to 491—Niles' Weekly Register, vol. 7, pp. 294 to 301—Encyclopedia Americana, Article CONSCRIPTION.—ED.

the war. On the same day that he reported the bill for classifying the militia, (27th October,) he also reported a bill "to authorize the President of the United States to accept the services of volunteers who may associate and organize themselves, and offer their services to the government of the United States;" also a bill "to provide for the further defence of the frontiers of the United States, by authorizing the President to augment the present Military Establishment."

On the 2d of December, the House being in committee of the whole on these several bills, as well as two bills from the Senate on that subject, the Senate bill authorizing the President to call into service 80,430 militia, to serve two years, for the defence of the frontiers, being in order,

Mr. Troup said, that the bill before them being a bill from the Senate, which had not been referred to the Military Committee, but which had been taken up on the motion of the gentleman from South Carolina, (Mr. Calhoun,) the Military Committee, as such, were strangers to its provisions. It was not to be expected, therefore, that he could give to the House an exposition of its principles and details. The gentleman from South Carolina was, no doubt, prepared to do so. For himself, Mr. T. said, he was opposed to the measure of the Senate, and would therefore move to strike out the first section of the bill; it would try the principle. The measure of the Senate, he humbly conceived, was inadequate to the object. It proposed to give you a militia force, when you wanted not a militia but a regular force. He respectfully suggested to the House, in considering this subject, the propriety of endeavoring, in the first place, to establish the principle on which they would rest their military measures for the further prosecution of the war; whether it were the principle of classification and draught, or classification and penalty; whether the principle proposed by the Senate, or any other principle, they could not, he humbly conceived, arrive at any conclusion satisfactory to the House, or useful and honorable to the country, without adopting this mode of proceeding. Having established the principle, the Committee of the Whole, or a select committee, might consider the details.

Mr. T. said, he very well knew that mankind were governed by their hopes and fears; more by their hopes than their fears; and he was not insensible of the effect which the dispatches received yesterday from our Ministers at Ghent might have on the measures under consideration. He should be very sorry if the effect would be to induce the Legislature to discontinue or relax the preparations necessary for a vigorous prosecution of the war. If such should be the effect, the enemy might have good reason to exult in the success of a diplomatic trick played off at Ghent, which, lulling us into a false security, would enable him to strike us at the opening of the next campaign, unarmed and unprepared. If he should be able to do so, he would begin to consider himself a match for the Yankees in cunning, and we would repent when it was too late. Mr. T. said he did not mean to say we would not have peace—politics were too uncertain to justify such a declaration—we may have peace in a few weeks. He only meant to say, that calculations founded on events which may happen at Ghent or at Vienna, and which would induce the Legislature to relax in the necessary preparations for the next campaign, ought not to be indulged; measures ought to be taken, not on a supposition of speedy peace, but of protracted war. If peace happened, the preparation for war would do no harm. If peace did not happen, the want of preparation would do much harm; it might lose the next campaign, and losing the next campaign might lose the objects of the war. I only suggest, therefore, sir, that it is wise and prudent to act as if the negotiations at Ghent would certainly fail. In submitting, sir, to the committee, the few observations with which I intend to trouble them on this motion, I will endeavor to satisfy them that the measure proposed by the Senate ought not to be taken, because it places our reliance for a successful prosecution of the war on irregular militia; whereas, our reliance ought to be placed on disciplined troops, and that some other measure, therefore, ought to be resorted to—some measure calculated to fill the regular ranks and augment the regular establishment.

In making provision for the further prosecution of the war, there would be but one object common to all—to bring the war to a speedy and honorable termination by all the means in the power of the Legislature. At least, it would be an object common to every genuine American, because every American had an interest in it. The war was a war for the country, and the result of it, whatever it might be, whether glorious or inglorious, would determine the character of the country and government. If glorious, every American, without distinction of party, would participate in that glory; if inglorious, every American, without distinction of party, would participate in the infamy of it. He knew very well that certain gentlemen had said the war was a party war, a war for the administration—but gentlemen would find, ere long, their mistake. They would find that Europe, the civilized world, who will alone be competent to pass judgment upon this subject, will not stop to inquire by what party in America this war was declared—by what party it was prosecuted—by what party brought to its termination. No, sir, they will look to the result, and to the result only, and as that result is glorious or inglorious for the country, so will they determine the character of this country and government. Every American, therefore, is interested to bring the war to an honorable termination by all the means in his power. But how is this to be done? I answer, in the spirit and language of perfect simplicity, by endeavoring to create a motive in the enemy to discontinue the contest. But how is this to be effected? I answer, in the same spirit and language, by endeavoring to wound him where he is vulnerable. The enemy is vulnerable in two points; in his commerce on the ocean—in his territorial possessions neighboring to us. If, by any possibility, (which I do not admit,) he should succeed so effectually to blockade our ports and harbors as to shut up completely our public and private armed vessels, he will cease to be vulnerable in his commerce; he will remain vulnerable in his territorial possessions only. There, sir, I would carry the war without hesitation; there I would endeavor to create a motive in him to discontinue the contest. In proportion as he values his territory, in the same proportion will he make sacrifices to preserve it; as you endanger the existence of his territory, in the same degree will be his motive to discontinue the war to preserve it. That he sets a high value on his territories you have the strongest evidence. He has already made great exertions to preserve them; he has been able to preserve them only because you have not made great efforts to conquer them. You never will conquer them by taking the measure of the Senate. Will any man believe we can induce the enemy to discontinue the war, by manning the lines of our frontiers—standing on the defensive—receiving and repelling his blows as well as we can? No, sir, so far from inducing the enemy to abandon the contest, this mode of prosecuting the war would only increase his motive to continue it, whilst the motive on our part to discontinue it would be daily and hourly increasing. A dishonorable peace would terminate the contest—the surrender of our independence would terminate it—nothing else could. I would, therefore, carry the war into the enemy's country, and with a force enabling you to wound him there. But the military force of the enemy has been greatly augmented. It is unnecessary to speak of the events by which this augmentation has been brought about—it is sufficient that we know and feel it. Ordinary prudence requires that your own military force be augmented; not merely in the same proportion—in a much greater proportion. In a much greater proportion, because, all other things being equal, he has one decided advantage over you—an advantage which we can neither destroy nor remove—I mean the command of the ocean, by which he compels you to stand upon the defensive on a line of frontier of 2000 miles, and to defend that line with 100,000 men against 10,000 afloat. He comes, no man can tell when, no man can tell where; and, to be prepared at all, he compels you to be prepared at all points. I say, therefore, your augmentation ought to be in much greater proportion than his augmentation. But what description of our military force will you augment? Sir, if, after what has happened, I could for a moment believe there could be any doubt or hesitation upon this point, I would consider everything as lost; then, indeed, would there be an end of hope and of confidence—then, indeed, would there be nothing before us but gloom and despondency, and the horror of despair. But you will not doubt—you will place your reliance on a disciplined regular force; upon a regular disciplined force alone can you rely for success. It matters not whether you determine to conduct the war offensively or defensively: if you determine to prosecute it offensively, you ought to rely mainly on a regular force—because, to be successful, you must meet and beat in the open field the regular veteran troops of Europe. Not one step can you advance in the conquest of Canada, until you are prepared to do this. This can only be done by regular disciplined troops. If you determine to prosecute the war defensively, you ought to rely mainly on regular troops; for you must expect to meet and to repel regular disciplined troops–and this can be done most effectually with regular disciplined troops. It will be done, not only more effectually, but more economically; not only more economically, but more conveniently for the country. It will save the militia of the country, and in saving the militia it will save the active industry of the country—it will save, of course, the product of that industry; the product of that industry is national wealth—it will save the national wealth.

But not only do these considerations urge you, in my humble opinion, to resort to all the means within your power to fill the ranks and augment the regular establishment; other considerations call upon you to make the army as respectable in number as it is already in character—considerations growing out of that character. An army little better than two years old, collected hastily from the plough, the loom and the workshops—without discipline, without even the rudiments of the military science—the officer to be instructed, that he might be qualified to instruct the soldier—this army has performed deeds of heroism and of gallant daring that would have done honor to the best days of Greece and Rome, that will adorn the page of your own history. It is true that this army has not from the beginning every where triumphed; it is true, it has not from the beginning carried everything before it; it had not strength, it had not numbers. But this much may be said of it, and with truth, that, from the beginning to this moment, it has in no one instance dishonored the standard which it bore; unless, indeed, a solitary instance may be appealed to as an exception—an instance as yet of doubtful and undecided character. More recently, its triumphs have been more brilliant; in open field, man to man, it has vanquished the conquerors of the conquerors of Europe. Who can hesitate, therefore, (the war continuing,) to make this army as respectable in number as it is already in character, to enable it to continue these triumphs? The bill from the Senate, instead of proposing this, proposes to authorize the President to call upon the States for eighty thousand raw militia; and this is to be our reliance for the successful prosecution of the war. Take my word for it, sir, that if you do rely upon it, (the military power of the enemy continuing undivided,) defeat, disaster and disgrace must follow. As an auxiliary or secondary force, the militia may be relied on; as principal, in a contest with regular troops, never. But the state of the army: upon this part of the subject, sir, I will say nothing, because I can say nothing that you are not already in possession of. You have authorized a force of sixty odd thousand men; you have raised thirty odd thousand; you have a deficiency of twenty odd thousand to supply; these thirty odd thousand men, already raised, are distributed over a line of four thousand miles of frontier; is it any wonder, then, Mr. Speaker, that Canada has not been conquered? No, sir, the wonder is not that Canada has not been conquered: the wonder is that this little army has been able to keep its ground; the enemy has been stronger in regular troops at all points from the beginning, and the very annunciation of this fact is enough to cover our little army with glory. You have a deficiency of twenty odd thousand to supply; how will you supply it? Assuredly the bill from the Senate will not supply it; will the mode heretofore resorted to, supply it? Will the recruiting system supply it? No, sir; the recruiting system has failed; I mean it has failed to fill your ranks. What are the facts upon this subject? They are, that two millions of dollars have been applied, since January last, and thirteen thousand men have been enlisted; this, it may be said, is doing very well. So it is; but what is the general result? The general result is, that our army is very little stronger now than it was this time last year; and in testing the operation of the system, it is to the general result we must look. At the rate of thirteen thousand men per annum, it would take five years to raise the authorized force; the recruiting system therefore has failed, it has failed to fill our ranks. I do not mean to say, sir, that the recruiting system, with the present high bounty and encouragement, would not eventually fill our ranks; I am not disposed to say that it would not (provided the power of the enemy had continued broken and divided by the troubles of the continent,) have answered our purpose; but I do say, that under existing circumstances and for our present purpose, the recruiting system ought not to be relied on; it cannot be relied on to fill our ranks by the opening of the next campaign, and to risk the loss of the next campaign is to risk the loss of everything. But is there no mode to which you can resort for filling the ranks, but voluntary enlistment? I would be extremely sorry if we could not. I have always thought this Government, when administered in the true spirit of the Constitution, the strongest government in the world, even for the purposes of war; but if the doctrine set up of late be true, this is the weakest and most contemptible government on earth; it is neither fit for war nor peace; it has failed of all the ends for which governments are established. It cannot be true that this Government, charged with the general defence, authorized to declare war and to raise armies, can have but one mode of raising armies, whilst every other government that has ever existed has had an absolute power over the population of the country for this purpose, and has actually exercised it. But this question is not properly before the House, and I will not go into an argument to show that you can, like other governments, resort to other modes of raising armies than that of voluntary enlistment; that you can resort to classification and draft, to classification and penalty, or any other mode which a sound discretion may in a particular state of the country dictate and justify. All I intend to say at present is, that you have an absolute power over the population of this country for this purpose, and that in the present state of the country it is wiser to resort to classification and draft, than to resort to the bill from the Senate; the one will give the men certainly and expeditiously, the other will not. But, sir, compare the measure of the Senate with the measures proposed by your own committee, and which are before you. The measure of the Senate proposes to authorize the President to call out eighty thousand militia for two years, and this is called a remedy for the evil of State. Now, sir, the evil of State, as I understand it, is not the want of a militia force, but the want of a regular force. The evil of which the country complains, of which the Government complains, of which the militia themselves complain most grievously, is the number of militia in service; the incessant harassment, vexation and oppression of the militia, and the extraordinary and burdensome expense of that particular service. As a remedy for this grievance, the Senate propose to detach eighty thousand militia. The President has at command, and has always had at command, a million of militia; and in this extraordinary crisis of our affairs, when pressed by a formidable enemy, and surrounded with difficulties, the remedy proposed by the Senate is eighty thousand militia, which, it must be admitted on all hands can be no better, for at least the next campaign, than raw militia called out in the ordinary way. But the bill proposes to furnish regular troops. How? By holding up *in terrorem* a militia classification and draft; exempting every three classes which shall furnish two regular soldiers, from the liability to furnish three militia men. Do the friends of this measure believe —will they with any degree of confidence assert, that it will have the effect, even partially, to fill the ranks? I think not. And suppose it should fail to furnish regular soldiers, what will be our condition in the months of July and August next? Much worse, sir, than our condition in the months of July and August last. The war continuing, the power of the enemy unbroken, our condition will be desperate. The regular force every day falling off, (for be it remembered these eighty thousand militia will be withdrawn from the operations of the recruiting service,) we shall have to oppose to the enemy a remnant of regular troops, and these eighty thousand raw militia—and who will answer for the consequences?' In the months of August and September last, we had in the field the regular army and upwards of one hundred thousand militia, and we nowhere found ourselves too strong. It is true, the Senate propose to improve the recruiting system—an improvement which two years ago this House proposed to the Senate, but which the Senate then thought proper to reject. I mean the enlistment of young men between the ages of eighteen and twenty-one. But if these eighty thousand militia for two years should happen to be, as they are likely to be, that very description of population upon which this system would otherwise operate, what hope can be entertained that the recruiting system, even with its improvements, will be as productive the next year as the last?

I humbly conceive, Mr. Speaker, that the measure of the Senate, proceeding from the best intentions, will fail in the accomplishment of our object. I conceive, with much deference to the House, that the measures reported by their own committee are much to be preferred. They propose—first, to augment the regular establishment to one hundred thousand men; second, to authorize the President to accept, under liberal encouragements, the service of volunteer corps; third, to authorize the President to receive into the service of the United States, State troops, which may be made to serve in lieu of the militia of such States. The principle of the system is, to substitute, as far as we are able, a regular force for a militia force, as more efficient, more economical, and, for the militia themselves, more convenient—and one hundred thousand regulars would take the place of two hundred thousand militia—two hundred thousand militia would cost as much as three hundred thousand regulars. If we can command an hundred thousand regular troops, it may, notwithstanding, be necessary, on particular emergencies, to resort to the militia. To enable the government still further to spare the militia, volunteers are authorized. They also will be more efficient than ordinary militia. It is impossible to say to what extent these corps will offer themselves—to whatever extent the government is enabled to avail itself of their services, to the same extent will the militia be saved. If government should derive no aid from this source, it has another resource in State troops. They also will take the place of the militia. The militia will still continue the bulwark of the country. Whenever the existence of the country shall be endangered, it is the militia that must save it. The system proposes to relieve them from the constant harassment of which they complain, and justly complain. To raise the regular troops, you have the alternative, proposed by the Secretary of war, or the committee. The plan of the Secretary of War, is the only effectual one. If we have energy and spirit to take it, it will fill our ranks and augment our regular establishment, certainly and expeditiously. The people will justify the measure, because they will feel that it is necessary to the maintenance of the honor, the character and independence of the country. The plan of the committee, though less efficient, is, in my humble opinion, better than that of the Senate. Where it fails to give you men it will give you money. It will be certain to give some men and some money. I hope the House will agree to strike out the section.

After a long debate upon the Senate bill above referred to, it passed the House on the 14th of December, with sundry amendments; but it was, on the 28th of the same month, postponed in the Senate, in consequence of its disagreement to the amendments, until the second Monday of March, when the session would have ended, and it would be otherwise unnecessary to consider the question. During the discussion, the system of conscription, as it was called, was attacked and defended with great warmth and signal ability; but, happily for the country, the time was approaching when neither enlistment nor drafting would be longer wanted. On the consideration of the bill for "making further provision for filling the ranks of the Army of the United States," a Federal member from Massachusetts, Mr. Cyrus King, exclaimed, "*James Madison, President of the United States, is the father of this system of conscription for America, as his unfortunate friend Bonaparte was of that of France;*" but Mr. C. J. Ingersoll, of Pennsylvania, afterwards, referring to an act of Parliament for recruiting the regular army, enacted in 1756, and to another act passed in 1757, said, "*thus, sir, it appears that*

Lord Chatham planned and Wolfe executed a precedent for Bonaparte's conscriptive system."

The following letter from Colonel Troup to Gen. D. B. Mitchell, deserves insertion here:

WASHINGTON, Dec. 18th, 1814.

Dear Sir: I have received your favor of the 28th ult. I will cheerfully embrace the first opportunity that presents itself, to recommend young Foster for a commission.

Congress, as you perceive, make little progress. The Taxes and Bank will be the prominent measures of the session. It is not reduced to certainty that the latter will pass, though I think it probable. We must rely on voluntary enlistment to fill our ranks, Congress not having firmness to resort to any other more effectual measure. Another dispatch vessel is looked for daily. What will be the accounts from Ghent, you can as well conjecture as myself, having all the information we have here. It would be unreasonable to say we cannot possibly have peace.

Yours, very respectfully and sincerely,

G. M. TROUP.

Having deemed it an act of justice to Gov. Troup to refer thus at length to his connection with the much abused and misrepresented subject of conscription, it is also due to him that the further history of the system before Congress be here also inserted.

[1815.] On the fifteenth of February, the Committee of the Whole House, to which the bill reported by him for classifying the Militia had been referred, were discharged from its further consideration, and the bill was indefinitely postponed.

On the 6th of the same month, the same subject, in somewhat different form, had been brought before the House, on the following resolutions submitted by Mr. Rich, of Vermont:

Resolved, That the committee on Military Affairs be instructed to inquire into the expediency of providing, by law, for arranging the citizens subject to the direct tax, into classes, in such manner that each shall, as far as may be practicable, consist of persons residing contiguous to each other, and from which together —— hundred dollars shall be due; and of permitting each class to furnish one man for the regular Army, within a given number of days, in lieu of said tax.

Resolved, That the said committee be instructed to inquire into the expediency of augmenting the direct tax for the present year, so as that it may be sufficient to procure —— thousand men at —— hundred dollars each.

The resolutions were denounced, amongst other reasons assigned, because of their alleged tendency to obstruct the recruiting service; and the plan proposed was denominated a "wild project."

The House having agreed to consider the resolutions,

Mr. Troup (the chairman of the Military Committee,) said that, being a member of the committee to whom it was proposed to refer this subject, it did not become him to express any decided opinion on it. All he hoped was, that the House would not instruct the committee on this head, unless determined to perfect the proposition into the shape of a law; inasmuch as the committee, in its ministerial capacity, had already cognizance over this subject, and could report on it without instruction, if deemed by them expedient. With respect to the military subjects of the present session, the House could not fail to recollect that the report of the Secretary of War had stated what force we had, and what addition to it was desirable for the further defence of the country. It had been proposed to Congress to augment the regular force to one hundred thousand men, for which purpose it was proposed to resort to the most energetic means. It was necessary for the committee of this House, said Mr. T., to endeavor to ascertain the opinion of both branches of the Legislature as to the different modes of raising men. We did so; and found that no efficacious measure, calculated certainly and promptly to fill the regular army, could be effectually resorted to. Measures were matured and proposed by the committee, but were not pressed on the House from the solemn conviction that there was no disposition in the Legislature to act finally on the subject. This being ascertained, other measures were adopted to improve the recruiting service, to authorize the acceptance into the service of volunteers and State troops in the nature of regulars. If the whole number authorized of the two latter could be commanded, together with the sixty thousand regulars, (supposing the ranks to be filled,) it would give an effective force of one hundred and forty thousand men, and might be reasonably expected to produce one hundred thousand; as great a number, perhaps, as, under present circumstances, the finances of the country would bear. Even at this late day of the session, however, Mr. T. said, he was willing to resort to the only certain and effectual mode of augmenting the regular army to a hundred thousand men, to the support of which the finances of the country might, before the adjournment, be made adequate. He hoped, at least, the House would so decide on this question, as to make the vote on it decisive of their real views in regard to it.

The resolutions were, finally, referred to a committee of the whole House; but the foregoing speech of Col. Troup gives the best and the true reasons why they were never afterwards called up or acted on.

On the same day that he reported the bill for classifying the militia, (27th October,) he had also, as we have seen, reported a bill "to authorize the President of the United States to accept the services of volunteers who may associate and organize themselves, and offer their services to the Government of the United States"; also a bill "to provide for the further defence of the frontiers of the United States, by authorizing the President to augment the present Military Establishment." The former of these two was, after amendment, passed into a law on the 27th of January afterwards; and, at a prior day of the session, an act was passed making further provision for filling the ranks of the Army of the United States. These were, it would seem, the "other measures" to which reference is made in the foregoing speech, and which rendered useless any effort to raise troops by drafting or conscription. Let those who might be disposed to censure the Secretary of War and the Chairman of the Military Committee for proposing this plan for conducting the war, remember the actual condition of the country at the time, the difficulties attending the recruiting service, and the levy of troops in any other way; and that the judgment of eminent military men has been in favor of this method as the proper one for raising the most effective military force.

[1815.] On the 8th of January the battle of New Orleans was fought and won. Resolutions of thanks and congratulations were introduced in both Houses—in the Senate by Mr. Giles, and in the House by Col. Troup. A treaty of peace had been signed at Ghent, on the 24th of December, but the news of it did not reach this country until the 11th of February. On the 20th of that month, the President laid before Congress copies of the treaty, the ratifications of which had been duly exchanged.

On the 16th of February, the resolutions from the Senate expressive of the thanks of Congress to Gen. Jackson and the troops under his command, being amended and coming up before the House on the question of ordering them to a third reading,

Mr. Troup, of Georgia, said that he congratulated the House on the return of peace; if the peace be honorable, he might be permitted to congratulate the House on the glorious termination of the war. He might be permitted to congratulate them on the glorious termination of the most glorious war ever waged by any people. To the glory of it General Jackson and his gallant army have contributed not a little. I cannot, sir, perhaps language cannot, do justice to the merits of General Jackson and the troops under his command, or to the sensibility of the House. I will therefore forbear to trouble the House with the usual prefatory remarks; it is a fit subject for the genius of Homer. But there was a spectacle connected with this subject upon which the human mind would delight to dwell—upon which the human mind could not fail to dwell with peculiar pride and exultation. It was the yeomen of the country marching to the defence of the city of Orleans, leaving their wives and children and firesides, at a moment's warning; on the one side, committing themselves to the bosom of the mother of rivers; on the other, taking the route of the trackless and savage wilderness for hundreds of miles; meeting at the place of rendezvous—seeking, attacking and beating the enemy in a pitched battle—repulsing three desperate assaults with great loss to him—killing, wounding and capturing more than four thousand of his force—and finally compelling him to fly, precipitately, the country he had boldly invaded: the farmers of the country triumphantly victorious over the conquerors of the conquerors of Europe. "I came, I saw, I conquered," says the American husbandman, fresh from his plough. "The proud veteran who triumphed in Spain, and carried terror into the warlike population of France, was humbled beneath the power of my arm. The God of Battles and of Righteousness took part with the defenders of their country, and the foe was scattered before us as chaff before the wind." It is, indeed, a fit subject for the genius of Homer, of Ossian or Milton.

We should be pleased to give this speech entire; but it is unnecessary. The war was closed; and to Col. Troup the country was much indebted for wise and calm counsels devised in the committee-room, and for many stirring appeals on the floor of the House—all calculated to bring to a happy issue a contest in which his intellect and his heart were united in vindicating the honor of his land. He had not been a candidate at the election in 1814, and, as the thirteenth Congress was about to expire, he was on the eve of retirement to private life, entitled to and fully enjoying the confidence and respect of his countrymen. Before retiring, however, he felt that he had a duty to perform to the brave army whose operations he had so essentially aided. He, accordingly, on the 22d of February, reported, from the Military Committee, a bill fixing the Military Peace Establishment of the United States. The bill provided that the Military Peace Establishment should consist of such proportions of artillery, infantry and riflemen, not exceeding in the whole ten thousand men, as the President should think proper; the corps of engineers to be retained; the general officers to consist of two Major Generals and four Brigadier Generals; the President to cause selections to be made of officers from the existing force, and to cause the supernumerary officers to be discharged as soon as circumstances should permit; three months pay to be given to each officer, &c., so honorably discharged, and, in addition, to each officer and private a donation of land, &c., &c.

The bill seems to have passed the House substantially as it was reported, and afterwards passed the Senate, with amendments, the principal of which was that striking out donations of land to disbanded officers and soldiers. On the question that the House recede from their disagreement to this amendment, Col. Troup voted in the negative. The motion, however, prevailed, and the Act was approved by the President on the third of March.

When the bill was before the House, Col. Troup made a long and able speech in its support, which deserves to be recorded here, but which is reluctantly omitted because of the space already devoted to military subjects.

The House adjourned, *sine die*, on the third of March, 1815, and Colonel Troup, having thus finished forever his connection with that branch of Congress, retired to his plantation in Laurens County.

CHAPTER VIII.

Col. Troup's Election to the United States Senate.—His Course in that Body.—Resignation.—Election as Governor of Georgia, &c.—Internal Improvement.—Land Lottery.

THE retirement from public life which Colonel Troup had proposed to himself, was to be of no long duration. The Legislature of Georgia assembled in November, 1816; and one of the duties devolving on them was the election of a Senator in the Congress of the United States, for the term which was to begin on the 4th of March, 1817.

We have already seen that Dr. William W. Bibb had been elected to fill the residue of Hon. Wm. H. Crawford's* term, made vacant by the appointment of the latter as Minister to France. Colonel Troup having been urged to become a candidate for the full term, he wrote, as follows, to his friend Governor Mitchell:

LAURENS, Oct'r 30th, 1816.

Dear Sir: Having lately suffered a severe cut on the second finger of my right hand, which is not yet healed, I hold the pen with great difficulty in answering your friendly letter of the 19th instant.

To the solicitations of my friends, heretofore, I have uniformly opposed the resolution, together with the motives, with which I retired from Congress. They have ceased to operate with their original force, but I cannot disguise that it is with great reluctance I have answered to their more recent requests on the subject of the approaching election for the Senate, that "they might command my services." My name will by no means be used for any office, unless it should seem to be the general wish.

If the state of my hand permit, I will have the pleasure to see your Excellency in the course of the ensuing week.

* On the resignation of Mr. Crawford, William Bellinger Bulloch, of Savannah, was appointed in his place, on the 8th of April, 1813, by the Executive of Georgia, and took his seat in the Senate on 24th May, and continued there until the adjournment of Congress on the 2d of August. Dr. Bibb was elected, in November following, Mr. Bulloch being no candidate.—ED.

In the mean time, I remain, my dear sir, most respectfully and sincerely, Your friend and servant,

G. M. TROUP.

His Excellency, Gov. Mitchell,
Milledgeville.

On the 8th of November, 1816, the election came on, and resulted in the choice of Col. Troup over Dr. Bibb. The latter immediately resigned his seat for the unexpired term, and Col. Troup was, on the 12th November, elected in his place. It is said that Dr. Bibb had made himself unpopular by voting for the "compensation law;" in other words, for a bill which, amongst other things, provided for payment "to each Senator, member of the House of Representatives, other than the Speaker, and delegate, the sum of fifteen hundred dollars," annually, in lieu of the usual *per diem* pay. There is no doubt that the people of the country were very much excited at the passage of this law; and yet, as it would seem, for very little cause. The act was passed in March, 1816, and was soon after made the subject of presentment by grand juries in different parts of the State.

The following sketch from Gov. Gilmer's work, entitled "Georgians," pages 108 and 109, is deemed appropriate here:

Dr. Bibb was a member of the Georgia Legislature at a very early age for entrance into public life. William H. Crawford and John Forsyth had, perhaps, more of the confidence of the authorities of the State than Dr. Bibb. George M. Troup alone rivaled him in the love of the people. He was elected a member of the House of Representatives in 1806, and, some years after, Senator in Congress. He was a very influential member during the restrictive commercial policy of Mr. Jefferson's administration, and afterwards one of Mr. Madison's most confidential advisers. The passage of the compensation law excited the indignation of the people to such fury, that all the members of Congress from Georgia, except one, were turned out of office, though the measure was not voted for by some of them; because, as the people said, they talked at all times, upon every subject, but objected not a word against getting increased pay per day. Mr. Madison soothed Dr. Bibb's mortification for this withdrawal of their confidence by his constituents, by appointing him Governor of Alabama Territory. He accepted the appointment, and removed to Huntsville. Two years after, the people of Alabama organized a State Government. Dr. Bibb was their first Governor. During the summer of 1820, whilst riding rapidly to escape from a shower of rain, his horse stumbled, and injured him so that he died.

On his way to Washington, Col. Troup came to Savannah, where, after some necessary preparation, he embarked by *sailing vessel* bound for the Chesapeake. He arrived at Washington on the 11th of December, and on the next day took his seat in the Senate, when, also, the credentials of his election for six years from the 4th of March, were read and filed. On the 13th, he was placed on the Finance, and also the Military, Committee. During this session, he submitted a resolution, which was adopted, instructing the committee on Claims to inquire into the expediency of authorizing the payment to Georgia, of certain claims, for the services of militia called out under the authority of the United States, during the years 1792 and 1793, for the defence of said State against Indian invasion. An act was also passed for the payment of a sum of money to the State of Georgia, under the articles of agreement and cession between the United States and Georgia; also an act authorizing the Secretary of the Treasury to pay to the State of Georgia fifteen per centum upon the quota of direct tax, for the year 1816, assumed and paid by Georgia. He voted for a repeal of the compensation law; and, at every stage, against a bill "to set apart and pledge, as a permanent fund for internal improvements, the bonus of the National Bank, and the United States' share of its dividends." After sundry amendments, the bill passed both Houses,* but was arrested by the President's veto, because of the "in-

* On the passage of this bill in the Senate, Judge Tait, the other Senator from Georgia, voted for it; on its passage in the House, every member from Georgia voted for it, except Hon. Alfred Cuthbert, who was absent.—ED.

superable difficulty" felt by that officer "in reconciling the bill with the Constitution of the United States."

Congress adjourned on the 3d of March, 1817, and the Executive session of the Senate terminated on the 6th of the same month.

[1817.] The first session of the Fifteenth Congress began on the first day of December. Col. Troup took his seat on the 10th. He was appointed to a place on the Committee on Foreign Relations, and was made Chairman of the Military Committee of the Senate.

On 31st December, the following resolution was submitted by Mr. Burrill, of Rhode Island:

Resolved, That the committee to whom was referred the petition of the committee of the yearly meeting of the Society of Friends, at Baltimore, be instructed to inquire into the expediency of so amending the laws of the United States, on the subject of the African slave trade, as more effectually to prevent said trade from being carried on by citizens of the United States, under foreign flags, and also into the expediency of the United States taking measures, in concert with other nations, for the entire abolition of said trade.

[1818.] The resolution coming up for consideration, on the 2d of January, and having been read,

Mr. Troup rose to object to the last clause of the resolution, which contemplated a concert with foreign nations. He thought this a most extraordinary proposition, and asserted that, according to his apprehension, no measure could be adopted more replete with danger to the welfare, to the very existence of this country, than a formal coalition, for any purposes, with any foreign nation whatever. It was a policy, a resort to which ought always to be resisted, and he hoped would be resisted, with a firmness not to be overcome. The object of the first part of the proposition, for making our laws against the slave trade more perfect and more effectual, Mr. T. approved, and was willing to co-operate in it. He was ready to go as far as any one, in enforcing, within our own jurisdiction, the abolition of the African slave trade. Within our land line, or water line, even on the high seas, he was willing to enforce our own laws on the subject; but to direct the President to enter into any compact or concert for this object with any foreign nation or individuals, was a step he would never consent to. He could not separate from foreign alliances the idea of foreign politics and foreign wars; and the proposed measure he should view as the commencement of a system of foreign connections, tending to foreign alliance, to which Mr. T. expressed great repugnance. Unless, therefore, the propositions embraced by the resolution were separated, he should be obliged to vote against it.

Mr. Burrill having spoken on the subject,

Mr. Troup replied, that the proposed concert for abolishing a particular traffic on the high seas, pre-supposed resistance, and resistance was to be repressed by the united means of the nations entering into the compact. This, certainly, Mr. Troup said, was one step towards, and might be the prelude to, alliances with foreign powers. Besides, he said, this was not one of those traffics proscribed by the law of nations, though prohibited by our statutes; and he doubted the expediency of such a combination to put down a trade which was thus permitted. If motives of humanity are urged in favor of this measure, let us, said Mr. T., begin at the fountain head. If the policy of this country is to be changed; if the well-remembered parting advice of a wise and good man is to be departed from, and we are to commence a system of "entangling alliances," let us look for some objects worthy of the change; let us aim at the abolition of impressment, and free our seamen from that odious tyranny; or, let us enter into the cause of South American emancipation; let us not enter, for the first time, upon a system so fraught with danger, without some such great justifiable motive; without the certainty of accomplishing some object of an importance corresponding with the sacrifice we are to make.

Mr. Burrill having read the tenth article of the Treaty of Ghent, to show that the proposition was not a novelty, and that the United States were specifically pledged to Great Britain to use "their best endeavors" to abolish the trade,

Mr. Troup replied that, in the very provision referred to, the Executive had cautiously and pointedly abstained from compromitting the country to any connection for this object —the article of the treaty stipulating simply that each party would, with good faith, carry into effect its own statutes on the subject of this trade. The article, in short, engaged the parties to do that which, Mr. T. said, would have been done by the United States without any such stipulation.

The same subject coming up again on the 12th January,

Mr. Troup said he had no intention, when he objected the other day to a part of the resolution, to involve the Senate in a debate upon it; and he very plainly perceived that, at this stage of it, it would be considered premature to discuss at large the merits of the question. But he would submit to the Senate if it were competent to them, in union with the President, to pledge the arms and resources of the country, in a concert with foreign Powers, for any object whatsoever. He denied that it could be done in the spirit of the Constitution. It would be a pledge of that which we had not. The arms and resources of the country were confided elsewhere; they were deposited, not with the two, but the three, branches of the Legislature; and, in fact, were not even to be found there. The people were essentially the depositary of them, and their Representatives the organ. Yet it was proposed to pledge, by an act of the Executive power only, the arms and resources of a nation, in concert with foreign Powers, for the abolition of the slave trade. Gentlemen seemed to entertain very different significations of the term concert; for his part, Mr. T. said, he knew of but one signification, which, in its application to the present subject, could legitimately attach to it; a signification sustained equally by the law of nations, the law of diplomacy, as far as he knew such a law, and the universally received acceptation of the term—concert with foreign nations. Sir, what is it but a term for common councils and common efforts? The gentlemen propose to themselves a great object—no less than the universal abolition of the slave trade; other nations, they acknowledge, hold out against them. Will they be content, then, with a concert of common councils? Assuredly they will not. Between nations, common councils mean nothing, unless sustained by common efforts; and common efforts between nations mean nothing less than war, if war be necessary for the object. War must be necessary, so long as other nations assert the right and hold to the practice of the slave trade. It is true that you may begin with negotiation, but it is certain that, if negotiation fail, you must resort to war. What would avail a treaty stipulation which would pledge the United States to exert, in concert with Great Britain, their advice and persuasion to induce Spain and Portugal to abolish the slave trade? Spain and Portugal would care nothing about your advice and persuasion, especially when you told them that you intended nothing more. Rhetoric and eloquence are not the instruments of nations for the execution of grand projects. He was well persuaded that the gentleman from Rhode Island meant to deal in something more substantial; idle and insignificant verbiage could not suit his purpose; for, if it did, he already found it in a treaty. This word concert, therefore, Mr. President, means something—it means connection, combination, alliance, for a given object; it means entangling alliance. You are admonished against entangling alliances; for what reason? Because our Government is of its own kind, insulated, the only Republic in the world, between which and other governments there is no common principle, no common feeling, no common sympathy; they may combine for their own interests; they may enter into concert for your destruction; they will not be so ready to combine with you either to promote your interests, or interests common to you and them. You propose a concert with crowned heads! They never concert with themselves, but broils, and quarrels, and wars follow in the train. History is full of them; and, if entangling connections, sir, between monarchs, who wield the sword and the purse, who make peace and war at their will, be fruitful of these mischiefs, what may we not expect when you enter the lists without the means of doing what you engage to do? Gentlemen will say this mode of reasoning is entitled to little weight; it is speculative—admit it; the argument of experience is alone admissible, and the argument of experience is decisive. The only instance which I recollect, sir, of a concert between this country and any foreign Power, is that of the French Treaties of 1778. It was a concert, and it turned out a most entangling one. It was a concert, too, for an object near and dear to the American heart; a concert for liberty and independence. A more important object can never present itself. In the one treaty, we stipulated the guaranty of the French American possessions; in the other, we stipulated that France (being in a state of belligerency with any other Power,) might use our ports freely with her ships of war and prizes. Now, sir, I pray you, how did we fulfil our stipulations? We did not fulfil them at all. We got out of the difficulty, I will not say dishonorably, but as well as we could. I believe, sir, the men who presided over our councils, at the time of which I speak, were honorable men, and were willing to do whatever they could to carry into effect, in good faith, what they engaged to do; but, sir, they could not; they wanted the sword and the purse, and the Constitution had intrusted them to others; they were intrusted to the people. I sincerely believe, sir, that France saw the embarrassing dilemma, and took pity upon us. She saw we could not execute the guaranty without going into the war, and she forbore to press it. But, in consequence of her thus forbearing, she thought she might the more rightfully demand the rigid execution of the other article. We had stipulated to allow French ships of war and prizes to go and come freely, and to remain at pleasure; it was a stipulation partial in effect. France being at war with England, it admitted to France what it refused to England. It was inconsistent, too, with the spirit of President Washington's proclamation of neutrality. France, having abandoned her claim for the fulfillment of the guaranty, thought she was entitled to a favorable construction of the article relating to ships of war and prizes. She demanded the right of arming, and fitting, and commissioning in our ports. We resisted, and eventually we found ourselves in a war with France. This, sir, is the only instance of a concert between this country and a foreign Power which I recollect; such has been the result of it, and such will ever be the result. It is unavoidable from the nature of our political institutions. We enter into embarrassing stipulations; we are called upon to execute them; we call uponthe people to draw the sword and advance the purse; they answer us, No! we have nothing to do with your treaties of concert or your guaranties; if you are unwise enough to enter into them, you may get out of them as well as you can; you shall not do so at our expense, or with our aid and assistance. And so, sir, they will answer always. They will go to war for rights which belong to them; for their honor, their independence; for interests entirely their own; they will not for rights and interests which are extraneous, and in which they feel no concern. This was the lesson taught by the people to the men who directed our councils on the occasion to which I referred; an awful warning never to put to hazard the peace of this country by connections with foreign Powers for any objects whatsoever, much less for objects foreign to our interests and our feelings. The treaties adverted to were negotiated under the former government. It is believed that nothing similar has occurred under the present. Mr. T. said he would no longer tire the patience of the Senate with such desultory remarks: but he could not forbear the expression of his surprise that the proposition of the gentleman should be urged with so much zeal and earnestness, when it was well known to the Senate and the world, that from the origin of the present Government, almost up to the present moment, American citizens, the flesh and blood of the land, had been seized by the Algerines, handcuffed and chained, incarcerated and enslaved, four thousand miles from their homes and the bosoms of their families, and no instance is recorded of a proposition having been submitted to the Senate to advise the President to enter into concert with foreign nations for the abolition of Algerine slavery.

The course and speeches of Colonel Troup, on this subject, evince the soundness of his judgment, and his political forecast. His warnings and predictions have been justified and fulfilled by events occurring at the present day. It is only during the last year, 1858, that Great Britain, on pretence of a right to visit American vessels for the purpose of capturing slavers, under the "concert" treaty between the two governments for suppressing the African slave trade, carried this assumed right so far as to endanger the peace of the two countries, and was at last compelled to acknowledge the justice of our complaints against the insolent exercise of a pretended right which the United States never admitted, and which our ancient enemy has been at length compelled to abandon.

This session of Congress closed on the 20th of April. It is unnecessary to dwell upon the proceedings, or to specify the measures of the session in which Col. Troup took part. He had left his home reluctantly; private and domestic considerations required his presence there; and, bidding farewell once more to public pursuits, he resigned his place in the Senate, and retired to his home in Laurens.

At the time of which we write, there was, politically speaking, but one party in Georgia. As the best evidence of the fact, the Legislature of 1816, which elected Colonel Troup to the Senate, not many days afterwards elected Gen. John McIntosh, Charles Harris, H. Mitchell, Jared Irwin, John Rutherford, Gen. David Meriwether, John Clark and David Adams, Electors of President and Vice

President; and who, though belonging to different local parties in Georgia, were known to be favorable to the election of Mr. Monroe and D. D. Tompkins to the two highest offices in the gift of the people. Mr. Crawford was the acknowledged leader of one local party, and Gen. John Clark of the other. They were personal enemies, and, in one sense, political rivals. The towering intellect and high position of Mr. Crawford, put him, in some respects, far above the men of his day in Georgia, and her people looked forward to the time as not far distant, when, besides the lofty positions already occupied by him, the highest honor of the republic would almost certainly be conferred on him. In biding his time as the looked-for successor of Mr. Monroe, his prospects became blasted by sudden and severe disease, which, in the judgment of many of his friends and warmest admirers, unfitted him for the first place in the gift of his countrymen. For several years he had been unconnected with active participation in the local politics of Georgia. Soon after his return from France, he was appointed Secretary of the Treasury, and was in the discharge of the duties of that office at the period to which we refer. Nevertheless, his name and his character were potent in Georgia. As a general thing, his friends were the friends of Col. Troup; and it was the wish of these friends, and of Mr. Crawford also, that Col. Troup should become a candidate for the Gubernatorial Chair of Georgia.

The time for which Gov. Rabun had been elected, expired in November, 1819. That gentleman had died in October, just previously to the meeting of the General Assembly which was to elect a Governor. Gen. Clark and Col. Troup were the opposing candidates—the latter "induced by urgent application of his friends to consent to become a candidate." It does not become us to speak of the comparative merits of the two men. The bitterness of the times has passed away, and it is the duty of all, but especially the impartial historian, to tread lightly over the ashes of the dead. Born in Revolutionary times, and trained, under the eye of his patriotic father, to the use of arms in defence of his country, Gen. Clark had done service to the State. Inferior to Col. Troup, in education, though equally brave, he had the same good fortune to enlist troops of ardent and devoted friends.

The election resulted in the choice of Gen. Clark, by a majority of thirteen votes. The probability is, that this result was, for private reasons, gratifying to the defeated candidate, although mortifying to his friends. The main reason which induced his retirement from the Senate—domestic affliction in the loss of his wife's health—still operated with full force to check political aspiration, if he had any. His consenting to serve, if elected, showed a disposition to yield rather to the advice and solicitations of friends, than to obey his own inclinations.

The same result occurred in 1821. Gov. Clark was re-elected by a majority of *two* votes—Clark 74, Troup 72. The late Hon. Joseph W. Jackson, than whom none better understood or appreciated the character of his friend, and who was a member of the House at the time, thus wrote:

"The writer of this memoir well remembers the intense excitement that preceded this election, and the course of Col. Troup at Milledgeville. His supporters urged him to visit the members, and to canvass for their votes. He refused, alleging, truly, that *a candidate for the Executive chair should not debase that high office by seeking to influence the Legislative votes. He had refused, through life, to electioneer, and he was too old to do it now.*"* In looking back at these reverses, the intelligent reader cannot fail to perceive that, as events afterwards proved, the time had not come when Col. Troup's talents and firmness were absolutely needed at the helm of state. There was then no imminent peril, no impending crisis, which required them.

The following letter to Gen. D. B. Mitchell, will show that Col. Troup was not inattentive to the interests of Agriculture:

* White's Statistics of Georgia, page 553.—ED.

LAURENS, Decr. 12, 1822.

Dear Sir:—The enclosed letter for General McIntosh,* is without the proper direction, because I do not know either the place of his common residence, or the means by which it may be most expeditiously conveyed to him. I take the liberty to trouble you with it, that it may reach him certainly and without delay.

The object of it is to procure horses for the plough—Indian Tackies, young and sufficiently strong—say 10 or 12 of them. I presuppose they may be bought low; and that, being much in the habits of trade, he can furnish them as cheap as any body. Be so good as to charge yourself with the receipt of his answer, and forward it to me.

Pray, what is the state of the atmosphere at Milledgeville, or have you been much there ?

Your friend and serv't,

G. M. TROUP.

[1823.] The gubernatorial contest was renewed in 1823; but Gov. Clark was no longer in the field. The rival candidates were George M. Troup and Hon. Matthew Talbot—the latter a friend and supporter of Gov. Clark. The election took place on Thursday, the 6th day of November, in the Representative Hall, by joint ballot of the two Houses. The result was as follows:

For George M. Troup, - - - - - -	85
" Matthew Talbot, - - - - - -	81
Majority for Col. Troup, - - - - - -	4

The inauguration of the new Governor took place, with the usual solemnities, on the 7th, when he delivered the following admirable

INAUGURAL ADDRESS:

FELLOW CITIZENS:—I come to the administration of your affairs with unfeigned diffidence of my own ability to manage them to your advantage. The indulgence which you have shown me, on every past occasion, is my inducement to undertake it, and my incentive to persevere. At every

* The Indian Chief, Gen. William McIntosh, already noticed, and who figures in a succeeding portion of this history.—ED.

step of my progress, there will be errors to extenuate—weaknesses to overlook. Nevertheless, I come into office free and unfettered, without passions to gratify or pledges to redeem; and what is deemed to be right, under the Constitution and the laws, will be done.

I have nothing to promise but good intention—save only, that I will endeavor that the laws be executed, the public functionaries, so far as depends on me, held to a strict accountability, and the State, according to its means, defended against its enemies.

The season of peace, gentlemen, in which we find ourselves, is the season for the cultivation of the arts of peace; and what is wanting in the works of Providence, designed for the purposes of man, 'tis for the industry of man to improve; and to improve what God has bountifully given, is gratitude to God. In the measures, therefore, which you may deem proper, to extend or facilitate the great work of internal improvement, you may, at all times, rely on my hearty and zealous co-operation. With regard to the other measures, embracing the leading interests of our country, that *in them* we will move in harmony and in concert, I have the best assurance in the patriotism and intelligence with which I am surrounded.

Fellow-citizens—let us cease our strifes—let our divisions be at an end. The march of science is so steady—the progress of illumination so irresistible in this great and growing country, that the generation to come may look back upon our foibles with pity and compassion. Let us discard our selfishness, therefore, and let our motto be—GOD AND OUR COUNTRY.

The following message of the Governor to the Legislature, is so characteristic of his honesty and his aversion to political intrigue, that we insert it for the benefit of the reader. The caucus referred to was one for the nomination of persons to be voted for as President and Vice President of the United States. The rest is explained by the message.

EXECUTIVE DEPARTMENT, GEORGIA,
Milledgeville, 16*th Dec.*, 1823.

Having been made the instrument of conveying to you the accompanying document transmitted to me by Gov. Carroll, of Tennessee, at the request of the Legislature of that State, I would cheerfully have submitted it to you without comment; but, as forbearance in this respect might be construed into approval on my part of any thing contained in it, I do not hesitate to lay before you the crude suggestions to which it has given rise, trusting that they will be regarded with all the indulgence to which good intention may entitle them.

This paper purports to be a formal act of the Legislature of Tennessee, and its object the denunciation of what it pleases to call a Caucus, which may possibly be held at the city of Washington, by members of Congress, for certain purposes. What precise and definite meaning the Legislature of Tennessee designed to attach to the word Caucus, I cannot conceive. It is not an English word. It is not to be found in our dictionary, and, being an uncouth word and of harsh sound, I hope never will. It is not to be found in either the Constitution or laws of Tennessee, and being a mere abstract conception, cannot become a subject of legislation at all.

The paper evidently refers to a contemplated meeting of members of Congress, to influence a decision on a certain question. Can any act of the Legislature of Tennessee affect the persons of members of Congress, or others at the city of Washington? There it has no more jurisdiction than it has beyond the sea. Members of Congress, like all other officers of government, stand in two relations to society; the one public, the other private. They forfeit nothing of their rights as individuals, by assuming public duties, and the most arbitrary despotism could not prevent their assembly for purposes not expressly inhibited by the laws. Such an assembly for convivial or social purposes, might intermingle with its amusements the gravest discussions, and, among these, the very question the discussion of which by that assembly the Legislature of Tennessee so ardently denounces. It would give to itself a name other than that of Caucus, and then the vain, unprofitable resolution of the Legislature of Tennessee would not have even a shadow on which to fix itself.

It is thus that Legislatures, on the eve of great elections, stepping aside from their legitimate province, enter the field of contention, inflame the angry passions, making the contention more fierce and the tumult more boisterous; and it is thus, that instead of seeing a great and wise people moving with calmness and deliberation to the election of their first magistrate, the political arena presents a scene, where, as in the turbulent days of Rome, the bitterest feelings of human nature are in conflict; which, from idle agitations grow into tempest, and, when they do no worse, make us discontented with ourselves and bring representative government into disrepute everywhere.

G. M. TROUP.

The direct reference made by the Governor, in his inaugural, to the question of Internal Improvement, the importance of the subject, and a disposition not to break the connection in the narrative of political matters in subsequent chapters, induce us to give here a brief but connected view of that subject, and the important part which Governor Troup acted on it.

The position of Georgia, in regard to the trade of the West and the commerce of the Ocean, had called the attention of her people and her politicians to the subject of internal communication long before any regular system was devised. To go no further back, the Legislature of 1820 passed joint resolutions looking to the gradual but certain introduction of such a plan ; and, on the 22d December, of that year, Gov. Clark approved an act for the appointment of "a fit and competent person for topographical and civil engineer of the State of Georgia," at a salary of three thousand dollars, and providing that "the duties of the said topographical and civil engineer shall consist in surveying the navigable rivers and waters of this State; in exploring the obstructions of the same; reporting the best plans for removing them; suggesting the practicability and utility of internal improvement; in directing and superintending the application of such appropriations as the Legislature may make from time to time for the purpose of internal improvement; in rendering an annual report to the General Assembly of his official transactions, and of the transactions of his department; and in such other duties as are usually imposed upon such officers, and as may be imposed on him, from time to time, by law."

In his annual message of 1823, Governor Clark said:

"I am constrained to inform you that I have not, during my administration, been able to select a suitable character, who would accept the appointment of civil and topographical engineer. There have been, notwithstanding, several applications made for the appointment of gentlemen of respectable character and standing, but not of experienced knowledge, which I deem an indispensable requisite in the person on whom it is conferred. I am still of the opinion which I had the honor of suggesting to the last Legislature, that it would be advisable to unite with the State of North Carolina in procuring the services of Mr. Fulton.*"

In his annual message of 1824, Governor Troup said:

The period has arrived when Georgia can no longer postpone the great work of internal improvement. If considerations of the highest order could not prevail, State pride would be a motive sufficiently strong to determine her. Some of her sisters are already far in advance of her. Almost all of them have, to a greater or less extent, embarked in it. She sees the most enterprising and persevering among them already deriving advantages from it, which place them in the first rank of opulence and power. A State, therefore, like Georgia, blessed by Providence with the means of reaching the highest commercial prosperity, by a road plain, direct and practicable, will no longer linger in the rear. She will begin, and, with a little patience and perseverance, instead of decaying cities and a vacillating trade, and, what is most humiliating, that trade seeking an emporium elsewhere than within her own limits, she will witness the proud and animating spectacle of maritime towns restored and flourishing, new ones rising up—her trade steady and increasing—her lands augmented in value and improved in cultivation—the face of the country beautified and adorned; and she may witness what was once deemed impossible to human efforts, the Western waters mingling with her own, and the trade of Missouri and Mississippi floated through her own territory to her own seaports, and all this within the compass of her own resources, provided the ordinary economy, prudence and foresight be employed to husband, cherish and improve them. The first and most important step will be to command an engineer of science and practical skill, and measures have been taken to procure the services of such an one. As it is indispensable that he rank among the highest of his profession, it follows that his compensation should be fixed at such a rate as other States have assigned to the like order of talents and qualification. I am persuaded you will not hesitate to do this. The Legislature of Georgia is too enlightened to undervalue the services of

* Hamilton Fulton; afterwards appointed Chief Civil Engineer by Governor Troup.—ED.

mind; and, looking to her true interest in this particular, she will find the best economy in the highest compensation. The critical accuracy necessary in every stage of the proceeding, the minuteness of observation, the correctness of calculation, and the application of the mathematical science to the whole, require the first order of cultivated mind, and under the direction of such a mind there is moral certainty that mistakes or errors of a fatal character will not occur. In avoiding these you save an expenditure, in comparison with which the salary of a lifetime would be as nothing. The laborious topographical explorations and surveys which must precede the plans and estimates for the execution of the great works, will also require time; for they are these which will determine what ought first to be undertaken—what most beneficial—what most practicable—what least expensive.

In his message at the extra session in May, 1825, the Governor again referred to the subject; but as this portion of the message is intimately connected with the Indian controversy, and the whole of it may be found in a subsequent chapter, we forbear extracts here.

At the regular session of 1825, he spoke thus, in his annual message:

A resolution of the Legislature, instructing the Governor to authorize the survey of the intermediate country, with the view of connecting by a canal or road, or both, the waters of the Gulf and Atlantic—a work of not less importance to the Union than the connection of the two seas by the Isthmus of Panama, and of most easy execution, has not been carried into effect. The opinion of the Executive on this subject has been made known to the Legislature. The authorities of Georgia cannot pass beyond their own limits into the territory of any other State, or of the United States, for any such objects, without committing trespass, and it is not understood that the most practicable line of communication between the two waters would fall wholly within the jurisdiction of Georgia. In truth, this is most appropriately a work for the United States, without any constitutional hinderance or impediment; a short cut through her own soil would accomplish it, and the whole Union would immediately partake the benefits. The attention of the President had been invited to this subject before, and whilst he acknowledged the great importance of the work, it is not known that any measures have been taken in relation to it. His attention was called, at the same time, to the practicability of uniting the eastern and western waters, by a canal turning the base of the Apalachian mountains at their southern extremity; an operation of more obvious utility, because of less doubtful practicability, than the contemplated one for connecting the Chesapeake and Ohio. A promise was given that this also should receive early consideration, but nothing more has been heard of it. Without bringing into question here the power of the General Government to make canals at pleasure within the jurisdiction of the States, it would, perhaps, be more advisable for the State governments to depend for internal improvements on their own powers and resources; and I am happy to inform you that the State of Tennessee, having a common interest with ourselves, has given unequivocal indications of her willingness to co-operate with us in this undertaking. We have continued assurances that a civil engineer of competent qualifications may soon be commanded for the service of the State. To give you an outline of the views of the Executive on the general subject, I have caused the instructions, which, in the absence of the Legislature, would have been given him, to be laid before you. And here permit me to suggest the policy of applying a portion of the fund set apart for internal improvement, to the construction of roads which shall so traverse the country as to make the communication between the different counties and the commercial towns, more safe, easy and expeditious. Considering climate and localities, it may be deemed expedient to invest the capital in a description of labor, which, under proper direction, would not only be efficient for the accomplishment of the work, but could be ultimately made to return to the treasury a large proportion of the amount invested.

From the "instructions" we make the following extracts, which are deemed appropriate here:

The first movement will be the exploration of the country, with a view to make yourself master of its topography; and, as our large rivers have their rise in the north-western extremity of the State, there I would first invite your attention, that you may discover the facilities and difficulties offered by the ground—the water which may be commanded for all purposes, and the points at which the rivers may be most usefully connected by a grand transverse canal. To ascertain these with precision, surveys are to be made, levels to be taken, and estimates formed; and these, with the utmost diligence, will require time. This first movement will have steadily in view an eventual communication between our own waters and those of Tennessee or Alabama, and the connection of both by a grand canal with the Atlantic, from which, as a great artery, the lateral ones will proceed, connecting the various sections and interests of the country, so that it may be said by each and by all that none have been neglected, and that nature and art had combined effectually to make of a great community one family, between the most distant members of which the intercourse would be safe and easy always. The Alabama and Chattahoochee, which empty into the Gulf of Mexico—the Tennessee, which disembogues into the Ohio, and the Savannah and Alatamaha, which discharge into the Atlantic, all take their rise at the foot of the Apalachian mountains, and may almost be said to have a common source. How far the union of these may be practicable—at what points it would be most feasible, and at what labor and expense it may be accomplished, are objects not now claiming your attention for any other purpose than, by a bird's-eye view of the country, to ascertain what may be done at a future day, either by the General Government, or by the States more immediately interested in opening the communication, and at what points either the Savannah or our extreme western waters may first receive either the water of the Tennessee or Alabama. So far from details being required in relation to these, general conclusions and conjectural estimates, formed from your observation of the country, will be considered satisfactory.

On the 20th December, 1824, a joint resolution had been approved, authorizing and requesting the Governor "to engage the services of a competent civil and topographical engineer, on such terms as may be deemed advantageous, and that he cause the said engineer, with the necessary aid, to make such surveys, estimates and reports as may be practicable, in pursuance of the laws of this State, in order that the same may be laid before the Legislature with a view to the commencement of a system of internal improvement, and that the sum of ten thousand dollars be appropriated to carry this resolution into effect." The appropriation was accordingly made during the same session.

On the 21st of December, 1825, an act was passed, "to create a Board of Public Works, and to provide for the commencement of a system of Internal Improvement." It provided for the election, by joint ballot of both houses, at that session, and annually thereafter, of seven persons, who, together with the Governor for the time being, should constitute "The Board of Public Works of the State of Georgia," one Commissioner to be chosen from each Congressional District, the Governor to be *ex-officio* President of the Board, which was to be a body corporate, &c.; and it was declared that "the Board shall, as soon as may be, cause the necessary surveys, estimates and reports to be made and presented to the Legislature, with reference to the opening, improvement and construction of roads, bridges, navigable waters and canals in this State," &c., &c. Fifty thousand dollars were appropriated to the purposes of the act. Under this act, the following persons were elected Commissioners: John Elliott, for the first, John Schley, for the second, John G. Pitman, for the third, Wilson Lumpkin, for the fourth, Joel Crawford, for the fifth, Elijah H. Burritt, for the sixth, and James Hamilton Couper, for the seventh, Congressional District.

It is evident, from what has been said, that a great system of canalling was in the contemplation both of the Governor and the Legislature. Rail Roads were then hardly thought of in this country, or in any part of the world. The success of the New York and Erie Canal had prepared the minds even of the Southern people for most extravagant expectations from that branch of internal improvement. The result is too well known to be here particularly mentioned. But no less praise is due to those patriotic men who devised the first grand scheme of internal communication, under the administration and the auspices of Governor Troup.

Pursuant to a call of the Governor, the first meeting of the Board took place at Milledgeville, on the 20th of March, 1826. It was addressed by the Governor, its *ex-officio* President, in a speech which we would gladly transcribe, if we had room for it. The following extract will be read with interest:

"Fortunately, a happy concurrence of opinions between the Legislative and Executive branches of the government, has relieved us, for the present, from the embarrassment of rival claims and conflicting interests. Expanded views have been preferred to a narrow and contracted policy, and we commence our labors untrammeled by local projects or undigested details. The outlines are marked, and the sub-divisions are to be sketched and filled up by degrees. Our resources are not to be exhausted by idle or vain experiments, or dissipated by the heedless policy of attempting everything and perfecting nothing. We are to proceed cautiously, that we may proceed safely, giving our undivided means and labor to a single work of approved utility, until it is done and well done. The Eastern and Western waters are to be united, and to the accomplishment of this every minor interest is made subservient. The large rivers are to be connected with each other and with the sea, by a grand transverse canal, as nearly central as practicable, from which the lateral ones are to flow, as the legislative authority shall from time to time decree. Railways and roads are subjects of your jurisdiction, and within the scope of your powers either to construct or to improve them—and, for these, funds are at your disposal—corporate powers given to you—and the geometric skill and engineering science of the country placed within your reach. Your first measures will be chiefly preparatory—to appoint the artists necessary to carry your orders into effect—to cause to be made topographical examinations and surveys of the country least explored—to direct the routes to be traced—the levels to be taken, and the estimates of expense, whether the communications be opened by roads or by canals, and to calculate the relative advantages in different positions of roads, canals or railways, will be among the first of them; and to these objects, as limited by law, your measures will be confined for the present year."

The Governor informed the Board of his intention to appoint Hamilton Fulton principal Engineer; and, after the adoption of necessary resolutions, appointment of committees and the transaction of other business, the Board adjourned to the fourth Monday in October. During the recess of the Board, William Terrell, of Sparta, and Alexander Telfair, of Savannah, were appointed in the room of Joel Crawford and John Elliott, respectively, who had resigned.

[1826.] The Board met, pursuant to adjournment, at Milledgeville, on the 23d of October, and, after a session of twelve days, adjourned, having first adopted an able report to the Legislature, drawn by Mr. Couper, accompanied by the report of the Chief Engineer. Our regret at not being able to give the proceedings of the Board entire, is much diminished by having it in our power to furnish the following condensed statement of its operations and the results, furnished the writer by Mr. Couper, in a letter dated St. Simon's Island, August 14, 1858:

"By the Act of the Legislature of 1825, establishing the Board of Public Works, Gov. Troup became, ex-officio, its President; and he presided at most, if not all, of its meetings. He took an active and leading part in all of the proceedings, and the influence of his opinions was felt in the most important decisions of the Board. Upon the most vital question which arose,—and that which has shaped the course of the public improvements of Georgia, the co-operation of Gov. Troup decided the action of the Board, and subsequently that of the State. To illustrate this, I must go into some detail, and incur your suspicion of my egotism. I refer, however, to the printed proceedings of the Board, for the principal facts in support of my assertions.

"By the Act of the Legislature establishing the Board of Public Works, an extensive system of *Canals* was contemplated, extending, in the one direction, from the Tennessee river to the Atlantic, and, in the other, from the Flint to the Savannah river; and the first duty enjoined on the Board was to make the requisite surveys for both. At the first session of the Board, two corps of Engineers were organized to make the surveys; and they were employed, during the summer of 1826, on them. At the next session, in the autumn, reports were made by the Engineers to the Board, and it then devolved on the latter to present their report to the Legislature. At this stage, I presented my views to the Board, in opposition to the system of canals, and in support of the substitution of rail roads in their place.

"A recent visit to England had demonstrated to my own mind, that, except for heavy transportation, rail roads were destined to supersede canals; and I was most anxious that the State should not involve herself in a work of very great expense and of very doubtful advantage. The subject being new, I found myself, at first, in a minority; but, being ably supported by the concurrent opinion of the Chief Engineer, Mr. Fulton, and ultimately receiving the support of Gov. Troup, I was authorized by the Board, in the Report which I made to the Legislature, as Chairman of the committee, to recommend the abandonment, for the present, of the system of canals, and a trial, on a limited scale, of rail roads as a substitute.

"The quarrel among the Engineers, and the enlistment of the two dominant parties in it, occasioned the dissolution of the Board, and the abandonment of the system of Internal Improvement. This was fortunate, as the public mind was not then prepared for rail roads, and a perseverance in the construction of the grand system of canals would have cost the State from $10,000,000 to $15,000,000.

"After a very earnest conversation with Gov. Troup, he at last said to me: 'Well, Mr. Couper, I will go with you in favor of rail roads; but what power do you contemplate?' My reply was, 'locomotives, of course.' 'Good God,' said he, 'I cannot stand that; I will go to the extent of horse-power.' This was in 1826, when there were only 22 miles of rail road in the whole world. What a contrast a *third* of a century has produced!"

It should be mentioned that three days after the passing of the act creating the Board of Public Works, to wit, on the 24th December, 1825, the General Assembly passed an act "to lay out a central Canal or Railway through this State," the main purpose being stated in the act to be "the ultimate object of joining the waters of the Tennessee or Mississippi rivers"; with canals to unite with the Central Canal, &c., and with liberty to the Board of Public Works to take into consideration the comparative advantage of railways over canals, &c., &c. Still, as has already been said, railroads were hardly in the contemplation of the authorities of Georgia at that time, as a part of the permanent internal improvement of the State. The gradual substitution of this system for canals, the awakening of public attention to its superiority, and the extension and perfection of that system, are subjects of curious consideration. That Governor Troup was one of the first to be convinced of this superiority, is shown by the letter of Mr. Couper. To these two gentlemen, perhaps, more than to any others of their compeers, belongs the credit of having saved the State from the ruinously expensive system of canalling, worthless anywhere in comparison with railroads, and especially in a southern country.

In his annual message of 1826, Governor Troup said:

"After a tedious correspondence with several of the most distinguished of the Engineers of the United States, from which no satisfactory result could be promised, Hamilton Fulton, Esq., a gentleman of known integrity of character, and recommended by the most eminent of the Engineers of England, was appointed to the office of Chief Civil Engineer. It is hoped that Mr. Fulton will not disappoint the just expectations of the public. The proceedings of the Board of Public Works, after their first organization, are submitted to you. A plan* of Internal Improvement having been digested and prescribed by the Legislature, nothing remained for them but to adopt the most prompt and appropriate measures to carry it into effect. The report of the Board and of the Chief Engineer will disclose the first practical operations under them, and will enable you to decide upon the merits of the past, and what for the future, in furtherance of the plan, the public interest shall require. To open new sources of commerce, and give facilities to those already open, are the great objects of the system. If, by a communication between the waters of Tennessee and those of Georgia, the trade of the Mississippi and Ohio can be diverted to our Atlantic ports, the freight and commissions would more than suffice to replace, with the ordinary interest, the capital which might be employed in effecting that communication; and, if this were true at the beginning, the progressively increasing commerce which an almost unbounded region, with rapidly augmenting population, would supply, might convert a

* The act of 24th December, 1825, already cited, contained this provision: "That the Board of Public Works shall not enter on any further plan or scheme for internal improvement, till the duties imposed by this act are fulfilled, unless they are so directed by the Legislature of this State."—ED.

channel of intercourse into a permanent source of revenue to the State. Whatever can be realized in this respect, will depend on the facilities given by the projected canal across the Peninsula of Florida, which, forming a line of steamboat communication between the Western waters and our Atlantic ports, cheap, continuous and comparatively safe, may have advantages over the short and more direct route, not open to this valuable instrument of conveyance. As connected with such an undertaking, the States of Alabama and Tennessee have been consulted, and their views in relation to it, so far as communicated, are submitted. With respect to that part of public improvement designed to facilitate the intercourses of trade within our own limits, the obvious rule will be to adapt our measures not only to the actual state of the trade and commerce of the country, but to the means which we can command to give efficacy and success to them; and whether canals, or rail roads, or turnpikes shall, in different situations, be considered as best adapted to this end, to limit both capital and labor to a single object at a time, until that object is accomplished." Then follow these remarkable words: "*It need not excite surprise, if, before a long time, with the exception of the level alluvial country, the* RAIL *will universally supersede the* CANAL, *having the advantage of cheapness, expedition, healthfulness, safety and certainty.*"

On the 26th of December, 1826, the act creating the Board of Public Works, and that to lay out a Central Canal or Railway, were *repealed.*

The following extracts from Governor Troup's message of 1827, contain his last official views and his parting advice on the subject of Internal Improvement:

I invite your attention again to the subject of Internal Improvement, and to the dangers inseparable from a longer postponement of a judicious system adapted to the wants and resources of the State. It is mortifying to our pride, and it will prove ruinous to our interest, that every State in the Union and every State in Europe, advancing in the course of improvement, opening communications between the most distant parts of its territory, cheapening its transportation, augmenting its trade and commerce, and cementing the union of its people, give signs of increasing illumination, whilst Georgia, with some claims to intelligence and public spirit, has not yet executed a solitary work or raised a single monument in illustration of her devotion to the agricultural and commercial prosperity of her people. We must soon withdraw from the rivalry of trade, or share it on the most unequal terms. No fertility of soil, no geniality of climate, can compensate to Georgia a difference of freight of five to one against her, in a competition with her neighbor States. Her industry will be paralyzed, and her capital exhausted. Already, the wheat-grower of the western parts of New York, from which formerly a bushel of wheat was not exported, supplants the wheat-grower of Georgia in his own market; and, ere long, the cotton market reduced to the lowest price at which the article can be raised, Georgia, with such fearful odds against her, will be forced to abandon the cultivation. In this, as in all the articles of a bulky or weighty carriage, the cotton States will undersell her in the same proportion which their facilities of transportation bear to her difficulties; and, when reduced to the ultimate point of stagnation and depression, she may awake from her repose with regrets and lamentations, but without the means or the resources to remedy the evil. You are not invited to premature or unprofitable efforts. You are asked to keep pace with your sisters in the improvements which correspond to the actual state of the trade, wealth and population of the country; and, if nothing more, at least to make the high roads the avenues of a cheap and expeditious transportation at all times, and the navigable streams likewise in the degree and to the extent of which they are susceptible. The Report of the Chief Engineer, who has continued in the public service at my particular request, will show what, with very limited means, has been done or attempted, during the past season, and what it may be useful or profitable to do hereafter. It is not to be expected that this or any other competent officer will devote himself to the service of the State, for a compensation scarcely sufficient for the maintenance of his family, when the same qualifications in other States find a double or triple allowance. It would be wiser to abolish the office.*

It is unnecessary to pursue this subject further. Enough has been said to exhibit the views of Governor Troup on this subject; and although subsequent events showed, and the sentiment of the country is now in favor of, the propriety of entrusting works of internal improvement to private enterprise, yet, in looking back to the history of

* The office was afterwards abolished, under a joint resolution passed in 1828.—ED.

such works, whether public or private, it must be admitted that the course of Governor Troup on the subject had no little influence, at the time, in rousing public attention to the great system of works which have conduced to place Georgia amongst the foremost States of the Union, and that the influence of his example has been felt for good to the present time.

In addition to what has been said on the subject of internal improvement, it is proper to present to the reader the following letter from Gov. Troup to a committee of gentlemen at St. Mary's:

EXECUTIVE DEPARTMENT, GEO.,
Milledgeville, 26*th July*, 1824.

Gentlemen:—I have received your resolutions and memorial. On the subject of Internal Improvement they speak my own sentiments.

Every argument will be urged upon the Legislature, and of course will not be urged in vain, to do its duty in this respect. Until they decide, your wishes can in no respect be gratified. No power is reposed here to gratify them.

You ask the appointment, *pro tempore*, of a special Engineer to make the surveys and estimates of the works which will be necessary to accomplish the connection between the waters of the St. Mary's and Suwanee—no such power is lodged with the Executive. It is due to your very respectful and respectable memorial, to make known to you what the Executive has deemed it his duty to do in this respect.

The resolution of the Legislature which authorized the Governor to appoint an Engineer, has been unavailing for that purpose, as might have been easily foreseen. A salary which it authorized, of $3,000, could not be supposed to command adequate qualifications, when such qualifications were compensated by other States at the rate of from 5 to 10,000. All the efforts, therefore, made in past time by my predecessor, failed of effect. They have not been renewed by me, on the same ground, because on the same ground they would have been equally unavailing. But, trusting and believing that the Legislature would, upon their first meeting, place this business on the only basis upon which it should rest, I have been unremittingly engaged in employing all the means left me to procure a competent Civil Engineer for the great objects of Internal Improvement in the State of Georgia. No man is worth employing who is not, scientifically and practically, an Engineer of the first order. No mistakes or errors must be committed in the outset, as, in the state of public opinion, they would have the effect of devolving on posterity what it is both our interest and our duty to undertake ourselves.

A Civil Engineer of these qualifications is in a fair way of being engaged conditionally, but conditionally only. If the Legislature should adopt my recommendations, he will be employed, and under the most favorable auspices for the permanent benefit and advantage of the State.

With respect to the subject to which you have more especially invited my attention, I have only to say, that on the very first opening which presented itself of executing the resolution by means which did not depend upon ourselves, I availed myself of it by addressing a letter to the President himself, requesting that, under the late act of Congress, competent Civil Engineers should be dispatched to Georgia to attend to her interests under that act, and more particularly invited his attention to the survey, plans, estimates, &c., of the grounds and works for connecting the St. Mary's with the Suwanee. To this communication, though made many weeks ago, no answer has been received.* When received, whatever may be the purport, it will be made known to you through the public prints.

Very respectfully, gentlemen,

Your ob't serv't,

G. M. TROUP.

Messrs. Belton A. Copp and
Bachlott, Committee, St. Mary's.

* Just received and will be published in the next papers. —G. M. T.

The correspondence with the President, to which reference is above made, is here inserted in full. It will be found referred to in the Governor's annual message of 1824; and it will be seen that the Governor's application did not at all commit him to an admission of the power of Congress to legislate in cases not falling within the letter of the Constitution.

EXECUTIVE DEPARTMENT, GEO.,
Milledgeville, 29*th June*, 1824.

Sir:—The Congress having thought proper to pass the act of the 30th April, which authorizes the President to procure the necessary surveys, plans and estimates for roads and canals, and feeling it to be my duty to ask for Georgia a proportionate share of the benefits or advantages which may result to the Union from such a measure, I beg leave to call your attention to the importance of connecting the waters of the Savannah with those of the Tennessee river—the waters of the St. Mary's with those of the Suwanee in East Florida, and of directing to be made any other surveys, plans and estimates in which Georgia may take an interest, and which the President may think proper to order under the act of Congress.

With great consideration and respect,

G. M. TROUP.

The President of the United States,
Washington City.

DEPARTMENT OF WAR, July 15th, 1824.

SIR:—The President of the United States has transmitted your letter, of the 29th ult., to this department, with instructions to inform you that in carrying into effect the act of Congress, of the 30th April last, directing surveys to be made for the purpose of constructing roads and canals, the interest of all the great sections of the country will be duly attended to, comprehending those of the Southern States, and, in connection with their interests, as well as that of the nation, he has determined at an early period to direct a survey for a national road from the seat of government to New Orleans.

In relation to the objects to which you call his attention, as being particularly connected with the interest of the State of Georgia, he deems them to be important and worthy of the attention of the nation; but it will be impossible, under the general arrangements which have been made to carry into effect the act above referred to, to bestow immediate attention on them.

I have the honor to be, sir, with great respect,
Your obedient servant,

J. C. CALHOUN.

His Excellency G. M. Troup, Governor of the
State of Georgia, Milledgeville.

The reader will find the Act of Congress, to which reference is made in the preceding correspondence, in the U. S. Statutes at large, vol. 4, pages 22 and 23, entitled "An Act to procure the necessary surveys, plans and estimates upon the subject of roads and canals"; and, on pages 139 and 140, of the same volume, another act, entitled "An Act for the survey of a route for a canal between the Atlantic and the Gulf of Mexico." It needs scarcely be added that nothing practical ever resulted from these acts, at least so far as concerned the development of the resources of Georgia.

Having thus referred to Governor Troup's connection with Internal Improvement, it is proper here to notice another subject which has always divided the public mind of Georgia as to its advantages and evils—we mean the Land Lottery system—one to which Governor Troup publicly and officially gave the sanction of his name in 1825. For his views thus announced, we must refer the reader to his message at the extra session of the Legislature in that year. The first act passed by the General Assembly for disposing of the public lands, was approved by Governor Milledge on the 11th day of May, 1803, and was entitled "*An Act to make distribution of the late cession of Lands, obtained from the Creek Nation by the United States Commissioners, in a Treaty entered into at or near Fort Wilkinson, on the sixteenth day of June, eighteen hundred and two.*" Gov. Troup was then a member of the Legislature; but whether he voted, or how he voted, we have now no means of knowing. That he was opposed to a distribution of the public lands without important reservations for the great interests of public education, internal improvement, &c., may be seen by the message to which reference has just been made. The whole subject was one of delicacy; and whilst the opponents of the system were neither few nor wanting in intelligence, yet they were most decidedly a minority of the people. Governor Troup's approval of the Lottery act of 1825, is no evidence, however, that the details of the bill were in consonance with his own opinions. The probability is he would have made larger reservations for public purposes. Still, he deferred, on this as on other occasions, to the will of the people as expressed through their representatives. "The lands," said he, "belong to them in joint and several property, and none but themselves or their immediate representatives can rightfully dispose of them."

But, independently of other considerations, there were grave political reasons why Georgia should come into full possession of the territory acquired from the Creeks in 1825. These reasons will appear in the sequel; and it may suffice here to say that the time seemed fully to have come when all hope of remaining longer within the constitutional boundaries of the State, against the spirit of the articles of cession of 1802, should be taken from savages, whose residence in Georgia was not only of no benefit to either the white man or the red, but was actually detrimental to the true interests of the former. A survey, and early settlement of the lands by lottery, seemed to give better promise of this result than any other mode; and, right or wrong, that system has been heartily approved by a large majority of the people of Georgia.*

As the biographer of Governor Troup, the writer confesses to a suspension, if not an entire change, of opinion, on the subject, since he undertook this work; and he feels that he cannot do a better service to the public than by giving the following views of the origin, policy and propriety of the land lottery system, from the pen of a gentleman † whose opportunities have been ample, and who seems to have given to the subject the most careful consideration:

"The peace of 1783 found a population of some 35,000 or 40,000 thinly spread over about one-third of our State as

---

* Such was the popularity of the Lottery system, that, out of fifty-three who voted in the Senate, at the extra session of 1825, only three voted against the bill; and, in the House, only ten out of ninety. The Senators were James Bozeman, of Baldwin, John J. Maxwell, of Bryan, and John Whitehead, of Burke. The Representatives were William Law, Mordecai Myers and Robert W. Pooler, of Chatham, Joseph Quarterman and George W. Walthour, of Liberty, Belton A. Copp, of Camden, S. M. Ingersoll, of Bibb, Simeon Oliver, of Elbert, I. H. Saffold, of Washington, and James Rembert, of Wilkes.—ED.

† Dr. W. C. Daniell—in a letter to the editor, dated 7th May, 1859. It is due to this gentleman to state, that, whilst he admits a change of opinion in regard to the Land Lottery, he speaks, in his note to the editor, of the foregoing contribution "as the best and only *amende* which I can now make to a profoundly wise policy, which I prejudged because I did not comprehend it in its full bearings."—ED.

now defined, with a western frontier running from the St. Mary's river to the Currahee mountain, some four hundred miles, and that frontier rendered insecure by the presence of tribes of Indians, who could not be trusted as friends nor subdued as enemies. The Federal Government was unable to supply the protection claimed, and Georgia was left to her own inadequate resources. Indian incursions were not infrequent. A law of the State, still on our statute books, requires that every man capable of bearing arms shall take them with him, with a specified amount of ammunition, when he shall attend public worship. Cannon were stationed at intervals, on a line parallel to the Oconee river, and near it, to give the alarm upon the appearance of the Indians in the settlements, so that families near these stations should seek refuge in the block-houses built for that purpose chiefly by individual enterprise. The farms were cultivated in succession, by their owners in a body, with their arms stacked at a convenient distance for alarms to be given by their vigilant and faithful dogs. Occasional forays were made by the Indians, to kill, scalp, burn and carry away. Then the men in the neighborhood would assemble, usually at a block-house as a central point—appoint their officers and dash off in hot pursuit. Sometimes they would overtake the retreating marauders—at times encumbered with prisoners and spoils—attack and usually disperse them, with more or less of mutual loss; at other times, they would follow the trail to the Indian village, attack it, disperse the inhabitants, burn their wigwams, destroy the standing crops, and carry off recovered prisoners and stock.

"About 1837, in returning from a visit to the bereaved family of my deceased brother, who had died in the Petit Gulf Hills, Mississippi, I stopped to dinner at the house of a Mrs. Collins, in Emanuel or Bulloch county, who had been scalped in one of these Indian forays late in the last century. She was a tall, stately woman, upwards of eighty years old, and wore a handkerchief on her head to conceal the loss which she had sustained from the scalping-knife of an Indian warrior.

"There was no established peace between the frontier Georgians and Creek Indians, from the Revolutionary war until after the close of the war of 1812–'15 between the United States and Great Britain, after which they were well whipped and virtually destroyed or dispersed by the Hero of New Orleans. During the colonial government in Georgia, as in other British American provinces, the great demand was for occupants for the boundless domain of forest land, and the latter was freely distributed to all who would occupy but a small portion of the large grants freely supplied to settlers at nominal prices. This policy necessarily scattered the population thinly over the territory. Here, this condition was rendered still worse by the sale, at nominal prices, of a body of land acquired by the Crown, early in the Revolution, from the Indians, and now embraced in the counties of Washington, Hancock, Taliaferro, Greene, Oglethorpe, Clark and Jackson, east of the Oconee and Apalachee rivers, and to which we are indebted for the introduction of a word into our expansive language. It was sold in large bodies, at nominal prices, soon after Peace, chiefly to wealthy emigrants from, and to land speculators in, Virginia and North Carolina; and, held by such men and in such bodies, how could it be rendered a barrier to the powerful and hostile tribes of Indians who fished and hunted on the western banks of these streams? Fauche's troop of one hundred mounted men, raised to guard the four hundred miles of frontier, even with all his energy and tact, and all their industry and endurance, could supply but a very inadequate protection. The Federal Government was in its swaddling clothes, and did little or nothing in reply to appeals for protection against the Indians, which went up to distress and harass the great and good Washington almost daily from the frontier settlements extending from Florida to Canada.

"Georgia, the youngest of the thirteen colonies recently admitted to their Independence, possessed of a large territory occupied by a small and sparse population by no means homogeneous, was left to her own resources to provide that protection to herself which the Federal Government was unable to furnish. How was that necessity to be supplied? Near twenty weary years of occasional conflicts and continual insecurity had failed to build up a barrier population on the boundary rivers, when the settlement of the Yazoo controversy by the treaty of 1802, which divested Georgia of the territory now composing the States of Alabama and Mississippi, supplied the means of acquiring the Indian land west of the Oconee and east of the Ocmulgee rivers; and the distribution of that land in small parcels or tracts, by Lottery, was determined on as the best mode of establishing a barrier population against the aggressive Indians.

"It has never been denied that the purpose sought in the Lottery was fully and promptly accomplished; but it has been contended that the land should have been sold, and the money received applied to Education, Internal Improvements, &c., &c. It has long been affirmed, and is, I believe, almost annually repeated, that the Land system of the United States does not pay. With us, even after the gift of the land in lots, the sale of the fractions, (the small portions cut off in the surveys by straight lines,) yielded a fund which has been in part wasted in various schemes of opening rivers, &c., and in part applied to the uses of the University, county academies and poor schools; with how much success, I leave to those to say who have administered these bounties or partaken of the benefits of the provision. One thing is certain: small as was the proportion of the land sold, to the whole, the purchasers of the fractions were enabled to obtain of the Legislature indulgences on their notes given in payment, from time to time, until this action became annual and chronic; and the applications ceased because the debtors were deceased and their estates distributed, or had been hurried Westward by the spirit of enterprise so characteristic of us. In 1833, I saw amongst the assets of the Central Bank—then virtually the State Treasury—notes of various denominations, dated in the early days of this century, and held as part of the proceeds of the fractional sales—where, doubtless, your eminent Collector of Autographs could add even to his collection. If we admit that all the money applied to the improvement of our rivers, has been as successful as wise men anticipated, and that devoted to Education has accomplished all that the ambitious promised and the good expected, we must still believe that if all the land had been sold, it would have yielded less money than the sales of the fractions have brought into the Treasury, and that here, at least, part has been greater than the whole. If the purchasers of one or five per cent. of the land, controlled the Legislature to the extent of a virtual remission of ten or fifty per cent. of the purchase money, how much would the State have received, had she sold all the land? And then she would not have established on the east bank of the Ocmulgee that barrier of stout hearts and strong arms—the necessity of that day in Georgia. That was no Whitefield enterprise to build an Orphan House before the children were begotten or their parents had mated, but a self-reared protection to a recent and sparse population—to save feeble woman and helpless infancy from the scalping-knife and the firebrand of a border savage enemy. That was achieved; and how can we measure that by money, or weigh the lives of the previous generation from whose loins we have sprung, in the balance with any measures involving merely ameliorations of our condition, whether real or imaginary?

"May we not indeed say that our Land system has been wiser than that of the United States, which, thus far at least, has been a tax upon the Treasury, whilst ours has paid something above and beyond the protection which it gave to our frontier?

"You will see that I have spoken of our Land Lottery policy as a system originating, as I think, in a clear and wise view of our condition, when it was introduced. Of the abuses to which it is said to have given rise, I need not speak. They affect not the principle. How often is it that what was at first a pure and simple good, becomes the nucleus around which errors and abuses gather—parasites that exhaust the vitality of the tree—vermin that devour the life-blood of the animal!"

CHAPTER IX.

Beginning of Indian Difficulties.—Cherokee Controversy.—Federal Relations.—Slavery Agitation by Ohio Legislature.—Gov. Troup's first Annual Message.—Election of Governor given to the People.—Commissioners appointed to treat with the Creeks.—Governor requested to receive La Fayette, &c., &c.

IN this and succeeding chapters, we are to consider that portion of the life of Gov. Troup which is admitted to have been the most interesting in his history, not only because of the conspicuous part which he acted in the important events of that time, but because of the events themselves; and however some may affect to sneer at what they pretend to consider a small matter—one which, as is further pretended, might have been consummated under the direction of some other and less sagacious and determined statesman—yet, it will be found, on investigating the origin and results of the Indian, and especially the Creek, controversy, that great moral and political truths underlay the whole, and that the development and practical application of them were owing more to Gov. Troup than to any other man of his day. No history of this period could be complete without the most frequent reference to him; and his biography for that period is a history of Georgia for the same time. Fortunately, this history is enveloped in no doubt; the evidence speaks for itself; and, like all history depending upon documentary evidence for its elucidation, the chronicler is relieved from vague and empty speculation; and, instead of mere surmising, he has only to quote the well authenticated records of the day as the best vindication of the truth of his story.

Reference has already been made to the cession by Georgia, in 1802, to the United States, of all that portion of her western territory lying west of her present western boundary, and east of the Mississippi river—an immense tract of valuable land, embracing almost the entire extent of the present States of Alabama and Mississippi. The land, thus ceded, amounted to about fifty millions of acres, and the consideration to be paid to Georgia was the sum of one million two hundred and fifty thousand dollars. The fourth article of the act of "agreement and cession" was in the following words:

"That the United States shall, at their own expense, extinguish, for the use of Georgia, *as early as the same can be peaceably obtained on reasonable terms*, the Indian title to the county of Tallassee, to the lands left out by the line drawn by the Creeks in the year one thousand seven hundred and ninety-eight, which had been previously granted by the State of Georgia; both which tracts had formerly been yielded by the Indians; and to the lands within the forks of the Oconee and Ocmulgee rivers; for which several objects the President of the United States has directed that a treaty shall be immediately held with the Creeks, *and that the United States shall, in the same manner, extinguish the Indian title to all the other lands within the State of Georgia.*"

It would be going beyond the design of this work, and lead to undue prolixity, to give a history of the measures by which Georgia, at various times between the act of cession and the beginning of Gov. Troup's administration, came into possession of lands in the occupancy of the Indians at the time the cession was made, to wit, 24th April, 1802;* or to enumerate the various excuses made for the delays in extinguishing the Indian title to *all* the lands within the boundaries of the State as laid down in the articles of cession and defined in the constitution of Georgia; or to specify the various appeals which, in the mean time, were made, to induce the General Government to do an act not only of simple justice but of plighted faith. We cannot, however, omit a special reference to "the memorial, remonstrance and protest" of the Legislature, to the Presi-

*The cession was ratified by the Legislature of Georgia on the 16th of June, 1802.—ED.

dent of the United States, approved by the Governor, Gen. Clark, on the 22d December, 1819, from which we make the following extract:

"Your memorialists are impelled, by a sense of duty which they owe themselves and the people of Georgia, again to call the attention of your excellency to a subject in which they consider their best and most permanent interests involved. It has been the unfortunate lot of our State to be embroiled in the question of 'territorial right,' almost from the commencement of her existence. The feelings excited by such warmth and succession of contest, have been heightened and aggravated by inconveniences and exposures incident to our frontier situation. To alleviate this condition, to circumscribe our extent of settlement and become more defensible; and finally, to settle the questions of *territory*, limits and boundaries, were the prevailing inducements to the vast relinquishment made by Georgia to the United States, in the articles of agreement and cession of 1802. Abstractedly from these inducements, it will not be contended that other considerations could have produced the effect. The period has now arrived, when, in the opinion of your memorialists, the subject is no longer to be regulated by the rules of policy and convenience, but has assumed the more definite and substantial shape of positive right. It has long been the desire of Georgia, that her settlements should be extended to her ultimate limits; that the soil within her boundaries should be subjected to her control, and that her police, organization and government should be fixed and permanent. For the fulfilment of these desires, we have waited the tide of events, and observed the march of time for seventeen years. Within this period, we have witnessed with much gratification the spread of the Union, and the accession of States and Territories greater in extent than the original confederation. Two of the members of this vast family are the descendants of Georgia; yet, Georgia loses her strength and influence as a member of the Republic, retarded, as she is, in her growth and population, and denied the fostering aid of her common parent."

After eloquently narrating some of Georgia's grievances in the premises, the remonstrance added:

"Your memorialists respectfully solicit, that Commissioners acting under the authority of the United States, may treat with the Creek and Cherokee nations of Indians, for further cessions of territory for the use of Georgia."

On the 8th of January, 1821, a treaty* was concluded at Indian Spring, with the Creek Indians, by which a considerable cession of land was made to Georgia, and of which land the (original) counties of Dooly, Houstoun, Monroe, Fayette and Henry were laid off by act of the Legislature passed 15th May, 1821. The Creeks and Cherokees, however, still remained in possession of a large portion of the best territory of Georgia.

In this posture Governor Troup found affairs when he assumed the duties of the executive government in 1823. In December, of that year, he sent the following message to the Legislature:

EXECUTIVE DEPARTMENT, GEORGIA,
Milledgeville, 15*th Dec.*, 1823.

The repeated remonstrances to the general government, urging the extinguishment of Indian claims to lands within our territorial limits, have only resulted in partial concessions of territory. Notwithstanding the pledged faith of the general government in the articles of agreement and cession, frequent occasions have been omitted to fulfil her obligations to Georgia. It is mortifying enough to advert to the single one of 1814,† when, disregarding positive

---

* For this treaty, see U. S. Statutes at Large, vol. 7, pages 215, 216.—ED.

† The occasion to which reference is here made, is evidently the treaty at Fort Jackson, dated 9th August, 1814, by which not only was a large cession of land, now lying within the State of Alabama, made to the United States, as "an equivalent for all expenses incurred in prosecuting" a war against the Creeks, whilst what was then considered a comparatively worthless portion was acquired for Georgia, but in the second article of which the United States agreed to "guarantee to the Creek nation, the integrity of all their territory eastwardly and northwardly of" a certain line. It was in reference to this treaty, that Mr. Bevan, in his report to the Governor, in 1825, said: "*it is well known*, THAT at Fort Jackson presented to the General Government a favorable opportunity for a full compliance with all the stipulations of its agreement with Georgia; but the United States (although bound to us,) owed money to others, which consideration, blending itself with other views of *policy* or *expediency*, (synonymous terms,) induced them to extinguish the Indian title to a very great quantity of rich land in Alabama, while Georgia was told that she must be content with a portion of pine-barren territory," &c., &c.

For the Resolution, Memorial and Remonstrance of the Legislature of Georgia, against this treaty, in 1816, the reader is referred to Lamar's Digest, pp. 1168, 1169, 1170 and 1171. In the memorial and remonstrance, the Legislature said: "No crisis ever presented such prospects of an advantageous extinguishment of Indian title, as the period of the treaty referred to. A severe chastisement had been inflicted on the Creeks; their power was broken—their arrogance subdued; and it only became necessary, under these circumstances, to have demanded and obtained an accession to such terms as the United States, looking to their compact with Georgia, might have thought proper to have dictated."—ED.

obligations to Georgia, as stipulated by compact, the United States suffered a large extent of Indian country to pass into the hands of others to whom she was not bound by engagements of any kind. The same treaty ought to have extinguished for Georgia the Indian claims to all the lands within her limits—she was not noticed in it. In every subsequent negotiation with the Indians, it would have been as easy to have acquired the whole, as part of the territory. The failure is to be sought in the parsimonious appropriations of money on the part of the United States, and the consequent limited instructions to her agents. A wise economy would have dictated the application of abundant means under favorable auspices, to do at once what she knew sooner or later she would be obliged to do. From the moment the general government entertained a belief that Georgia would be satisfied with small appropriations of money for the acquisition of small portions of lands, things have been growing worse and worse. The general government itself is daily multiplying obstacles (innocently, to be sure,) to the further acquisition, and its practice is so far variant from its theory, which teaches that a concentration of the tribes is one of the most effectual modes of advancing their civilization. Georgia has given to the United States 50,000,000 of acres for 1,250,000 dollars. The United States have gratuitously given to the Yazoo claimants between four and five millions dollars besides; and when you have added to this the paltry sums she has paid in extinguishment of Indian title within our limits, you will find a net balance in her favor to the amount of twenty millions of dollars at least. The words, "as soon as may be," in the articles of agreement and cession, will no longer avail the United States any thing; the operation of these has been long since estopped by time. It was never in contemplation of either of the parties to that agreement, that twenty years should elapse, and that Georgia should find herself in possession of only one half of her reserved territory. Indeed, further procrastination, as inconsistent as it is with justice to Georgia, can subserve no useful purposes to the United States, or to the Indians themselves. The latter have discernment enough to perceive that, soon, very soon, Georgia must have what is her own. The United States recognize in practice, and in theory, the allodiality to be in Georgia, the temporary usufruct only in the Indians. Of what value is this right of use within our limits, in the present exhausted state of the game? If the passion of the hunter is to be gratified, send him across the

Mississippi; if the mind is to be improved into civilization, limit him to the pursuits of agriculture. Blending justice with authority, the United States have but to command, and the claims of Georgia will be satisfied. The treaty lately held with the Seminoles is in illustration. The United States had little else to do than to prescribe the limits within which those tribes were to retire.

I recommend to you, therefore, to address yourselves, once more, and for the last time, to the justice of the United States, in language firm but respectful; to demand and insist on, 1st, A liberal appropriation of money to extinguish the Indian claims to all the lands within our territorial limits—2dly, Commanding instructions to her agents, whoever they may be, that what of right ought to be done, shall be done.

G. M. TROUP.

The message having been referred, in the Senate, to the joint committee on the State of the Republic, they made a report,* on the 18th December, which finally passed both Houses, and was approved by the Governor on the 20th. From the report we make the following extracts:

The Committee on the State of the Republic, to whom was referred the communication of his Excellency the Governor, on the subject of the extinguishment of Indian claims to the lands within the territorial limits of Georgia, beg leave to report:

That they have derived much gratification from the perusal of this interesting document. It presents to them an unequivocal manifestation of the disposition of the Executive to sustain the just rights of the State on the important subject of the extension of jurisdictional limits, with a firmness which is tempered by discretion, and a zeal which is guided by intelligence—a disposition, to which, in the unanimous opinion of this committee, every suggestion of duty, and every feeling of honorable pride, on the part of this Legislature, will be accordant and responsive. The committee do not deem it necessary, in this report, to enter into a minute examination of the luminous exposition of the rights of this State, which is contained in the communication of his Excellency the Governor. Adopting it as unanimously as they do, and in its whole extent, they believe

* This report, although not presented by Judge Berrien, who was second on the committee, yet bears unmistakable marks of his pen. It deserves to be inserted at length; but want of space forbids.—ED.

they will best perform the duty which is assigned to them, by recommending that an address be presented to the President of the United States, based on the principles and fortified by the arguments of this communication.

Then follows an eloquent address to the President, the conclusion of which is as follows:

These memorialists have seen with what facility, the United States, "blending justice with authority," have been enabled to prescribe to the native tribes inhabiting the contiguous Territory of Florida, the limits of their range, and they do not doubt that a similar exercise of a legitimate authority, equally tempered by justice, will suffice to obtain for Georgia all which she desires. They ask, therefore, from the government of the Union, certainly with the respect which they have always felt, and which they have omitted no proper occasion to manifest, to the government of their choice and of their confidence, but at the same time with the earnestness which is authorized by the justice of their claim, and demanded by the necessities of their constituents, that a liberal appropriation may be made for the extinguishment of the Indian title to all the remaining lands within the limits of Georgia, and that commissioners may be appointed, with instructions in every event to effect this indispensable object, by a proper representation to the Indian tribes of the just claims of Georgia—of the solemn obligation of the United States—and of the improvement in their own condition, which will result from their acquiescence.

The report was agreed to, *unanimously*, in the Senate, and probably in the House also, although the journal of the latter body simply shows that it was passed without division.

During the same session, the Governor approved joint resolutions embodying a memorial and remonstrance of the Legislature to the President of the United States, "relative to the claims of the citizens of Georgia, under the treaty made at the Indian Springs on the eighth of January, eighteen hundred and twenty-one," drawn by Judge Berrien, and to which reference is made in the Governor's annual message of 1824.

Appended to the report already noticed as having been

approved by the Governor on 20th December, was a resolution, "that a copy of the foregoing memorial and remonstrance be forwarded to the Senators and Representatives of the State of Georgia in the Congress of the United States, and that they be requested to use their exertions for the attainment of its object." The Governor accordingly communicated the proceedings of the Legislature to the Georgia delegation in Congress, and the same were immediately thereafter made known to the government at Washington. On the 17th of February, 1824, the Secretary of War addressed the following note to Gov. Troup:

DEPARTMENT OF WAR, 17th February, 1824.

Sir:—I am directed by the President of the United States to enclose for your information, copies of a communication from the Cherokee delegation, now at this place, the answer of this department to their communication, and the reply, by which you will perceive that the nation is very adverse to making any additional cessions of land to the United States. I avail myself of the opportunity, to assure you that it will afford the President much pleasure to adopt any measure, in his power, which may tend to the fulfilment of the convention with the State of Georgia, with the least possible delay. With this view, he would be gratified to receive the aid of your opinion on a subject so interesting to the State over which you preside.

I have the honor to be
Your most obedient servant,
J. C. CALHOUN.

Accompanying this letter was one to the President, dated January 19th, 1824, signed by John Ross, Geo. Lowrey, Major Ridge and Elijah Hicks, calling themselves "the delegation of the Cherokee nation," and in which, amongst other things, they say, "the Cherokee nation have now come to a decisive and unalterable conclusion not to cede away any more lands." In his answer to them, the Secretary, after stating, "you must be sensible that it will be impossible for you to remain, for any length of time, in your present situation, as a distinct society, or nation, within the limits of Georgia, or of any other State," &c., &c., added, "it remains for the Cherokee nation to decide for itself, whether it will contribute most to their own welfare and happiness for them to retain their present title to their lands, and remain where they are, exposed to the discontent of Georgia and the pressure of her citizens, or to cede it to the United States for Georgia, at a fair price to be paid, either in other lands beyond the Mississippi, or in money to be vested in lands to be purchased for them, as individuals, within that or any other State. Should the nation decide to relinquish its present title, and to adopt either of the alternatives suggested, this government is disposed to act generously with them," &c., &c. In their reply, "the delegation of the Cherokee nation," amongst other things, said, "we beg leave to say to the President, through you, the Cherokee nation are sensible that the United States are bound, by its compact with Georgia, to extinguish, for the use of that State, the Indian title to lands within the limits claimed by the State, as soon as it can be done *peaceably* and on *reasonable* conditions; and are also sensible that this compact is no more than a conditional one, and, without the free and voluntary consent of the Cherokee nation, can never be complied with on the part of the United States; and having been duly authorized to make known to the government of the United States the true sentiments and disposition of the nation on this subject, the President has been informed that 'the Cherokees have come to a *decisive* and *unalterable* conclusion *never* to *cede away* any more lands. And as the extinguishment of Cherokee title to lands can never be obtained on conditions which will accord with the import of the compact between the United States and Georgia, it is desirable that the government should adopt some other means to satisfy Georgia, than to remain any longer under anticipation of being enabled to accomplish the object of purchasing the Cherokee title." The reply further suggested that the limits of Georgia, if too small, might be increased by an *addition from the Floridas*, and that the Cherokee nation might one day "enter into a treaty with the United States, for admission as citizens under the form of a Territorial or State government!"—although they admitted that "the situation of the nation is not sufficiently improved in the arts of civilized life to warrant any change at present."*

The Senators from Georgia, at that time, were John Elliott and Nicholas Ware; the Representatives were Joel Abbott, George Cary, Thomas W. Cobb, Alfred Cuthbert, John Forsyth, Edward F. Tattnall and Wiley Thompson; Col. Tattnall was sick and absent. In their letter to the Governor, after referring to an interview which two of their number had had with the President, and to the "correspondence which had been held between the Secretary of War and certain Cherokee Chiefs," they added, "we shall not attempt to describe our surprise at the *novel* character of this correspondence." In conclusion, they said, "should the President address a message to Congress on the subject, our course will be a plain one. If he should not, it does not appear to us proper to do more than we have done, as a correspondence has been opened between your Excellency and the Secretary of War, at the request of that officer, no doubt acting under the direction of the President."

The *aid of Gov. Troup's opinion* having been invoked by the letter of the Secretary of War, he promptly addressed to that officer the following communication:

EXECUTIVE DEPARTMENT, GEO.,
Milledgeville, 28th February, 1824.

SIR:—I have received this day your letter of the 17th instant. Be pleased to present to the President my acknowledgments for the attention which he has given to the requisition of Georgia, and especially for the manifestation of his sincere desire to adopt any measure in his power which may tend to the fulfilment of the convention with the State of Georgia, with the least possible delay.

In compliance with his wishes, I hasten to lay before him my views and expectations, as connected with this fulfilment. In your effort to open a negotiation with the Cherokee delegation, for extinguishment of claims, you are met by a flat negative to two fair and liberal propositions:

* It was strongly suspected, at the time, that the Indians were influenced to this course of conduct by designing white men. The history of their race shows conclusively that they cannot endure too close proximity with a superior race. Gov. Troup lived to witness the peaceable removal of the "Cherokee nation" beyond the Mississippi.—ED.

the first, to purchase for valuable consideration in money; the second, to accommodate them with equivalent territory in a favorable situation beyond the Mississippi. Unreasonable as the answer has been, my mind was fully prepared for such an one. It had been made known to me, some time before, that a council had been formed in the nation, for the special purpose of coming to the resolution that the State of Georgia should never acquire, for any consideration, another acre of Cherokee land, either through the agency of the United States or otherwise; and, in conformity with this resolution, all the measures were preconcerted to enable the Chiefs to present themselves before the President, with a boldness bordering on effrontery, and to receive his first advance to negotiation with the emphatic no! a word easily pronounced, but in this instance most unadvisedly: not the spontaneous offspring of Indian feeling and sentiment, but a word put into his mouth by white men, who are nourished and protected by the power of the United States; who have no common interest or sympathies with those whom they instigate to use it; and who, fixed upon the soil almost without mete or bounds, regard it as a goodly heritage for their descendants, which no power can limit or take away.

From the day of the signature of the articles of agreement and cession, this word ceased to be available to the Indians, for any permanent interest of their own. From that day, the power of protestation which they have so recently interposed, departed from them, and could never be used but for a little delay, or for a better bargain. On that day the fee simple passed from the rightful proprietors to Georgia, and Georgia, after a lapse of twenty years, demands nothing of the competent authority but the amotion of the tenants in possession. The answer is not only no! but never. And is this a fit and proper one to be given to the demand of the people of Georgia, who have endured so long and so patiently? who have parted with an empire for a song? who have waited to see the United States reimbursed all their expenses, and a net revenue flowing into their coffers from the land which was their birthright? a people who, having made a little reservation for themselves by compact, are now told, in answer to their just and reasonable demand, that this compact is only conditional, depending for its fulfilment on the will and pleasure of the Indians? that the primitive aboriginal rights are such now as they were before the discovery of the country, and that, if Georgia wants land, the United States have enough in

Florida or elsewhere to give her? How is this insult and mockery to be repelled, proceeding as it does from the polluted lips of outcasts and vagabonds, who make the Chiefs the instruments of reiterating it at Washington? No, sir; this trick of vulgar cunning is only to be met by the firmness and dignity which become the United States government, which it has never failed to manifest on every occasion calling for it, and which he, who is the special depositary of all these sacred qualities, has always displayed to so much advantage to his high office and to the country. The Indians must be made to understand that no talks will be listened to but such as proceed from councils strictly Indian in character and composition; that the compact with Georgia is a very different instrument from that which has been represented to them; that by it the word of the United States is passed, and that nothing can redeem it but the cession of all their lands within her limits; that the time has come when to postpone this redemption would be essentially a breach of faith, of which the United States will never permit herself to be suspected; that, consulting the comfort and happiness of the Indians alone, the United States have omitted to press this measure upon them until the very last hour; that the United States have made sacrifices for Indian interest, and will expect some small ones from the Indians in return; that, if they desire civilization, nothing is more consistent with it than concentration; and that, without regard to the acquisitions of territory, the United States have acted upon this principle from the beginning, as a fundamental one in their system of improvement; that beyond the limits of Georgia, and within the territory proper of the United States, there are lands enough for the Cherokees and all their generations to come, of which the United States possess the full and absolute dominion, where they may sit down in quiet and peaceful enjoyment, and where none can come to make them afraid; that, on the other hand, if tired of the arts of civilization, they will betake themselves to their old pursuits, you have made a fair and liberal offer of wilderness enough, abounding in game, where the white man will not speedily come to trespass or to annoy; that, in presenting these honorable overtures, you are actuated by a sincere regard to Indian interest; that, in the rejection of both, you can perceive nothing but an unfriendly spirit; and that, finally, if they persevere in this rejection, the consequences are inevitable: 1st, that you must assist the Georgians in occupying the country which is their own, and which is unjustly withheld from them;

or, 2ndly, in resisting the occupation, to make war upon and shed the blood of your brothers and friends.

Having said so much, it remains only to advert to the other topics contained in your letter to the Indian delegation, and for these a word will suffice :

1st. The reservation of part of our territory for the settlement of the Indians ;

2nd. Their incorporation into and amalgamation with our society.

As to the first, the answer is, the articles of agreement having made no provision for such reservation, none can be made without the consent of Georgia, and that Georgia will never give her assent to any without an equivalent, (if she would, with one,) is absolutely certain. With regard to the second proposition, the answer is, that if such a scheme were practicable at all, the utmost of the rights and privileges which public opinion would concede to Indians, would fix them in a middle station between the negro and the white man, and that as long as they survived this degradation without the possibility of attaining the elevation of the latter, they would gradually sink to the condition of the former; a point of degeneracy below which they could not fall. It is likely that before they reached this, their wretchedness would find relief in broken hearts. Most assuredly, nothing will contribute so essentially to that scanty share of human happiness which is left them, as their concentration and insulation, where, having enough for the wants of agriculture, they will, in their seclusion, afford no pretexts for the intrusions or annoyances of the white man.

Thus frankly, in compliance with the request of the President, I submit to him my general views on this interesting subject. Thus frankly I will deem it my duty to submit them to the Legislature of the State. They are such, no doubt, as have already suggested themselves. They seem to me the only ones which the attitude assumed by the Indians will suffer us to entertain. I am sorry I cannot support them by matter-of-fact information of official character. To me this is impossible. I can only say, generally, that among men best informed on Cherokee affairs, the minds of a majority of the nation are well prepared to receive your proposition for removal.

In conclusion, I must state not only my hope, but my conviction, that the President will perceive, in every movement on our part in relation to this business, a sincere desire to harmonize with the Union; to maintain peace and tranquillity with the Indians, until longer forbearance will cease to be a virtue; in fact, to lend ourselves, as we have always done, heart and hand, to the support of every wise and virtuous administration of the General Government. But the President will, at the same time, consider that Georgia has a deep stake in the prompt decision of the present question. Of all the old States, Georgia is the only one whose political organization is incomplete; her civil polity is deranged; her military force cannot be reduced to systematic order and subordination; the extent of her actual resources cannot be counted; the great work of internal improvement is suspended, and all because Georgia is not in the possession of her vacant territory; a territory waste and profitless to the Indians; profitless to the United States; but, in the possession of the rightful owner, a source of strength, of revenue, and of union.

Whilst you present to the President my respects, be pleased to accept for yourself the offer of my high consideration for the part you have taken in this transaction.

G. M. TROUP.

Hon. John C. Calhoun,
Secretary of War,
Washington City.

[1824.] On the 30th of March, the President sent a message to Congress, transmitting "certain papers enumerated in a report from the Secretary of War, relating to the compact between the United States and the State of Georgia, entered into in 1802, whereby the latter ceded to the former a portion of the territory then within its limits, on the conditions therein specified." Giving a synopsis of the fourth article of the compact, the message stated that the papers would show the measures adopted by the Executive of the United States in fulfilment of its conditions, from its date, and particularly the negotiations and treaties with the Indian tribes for extinguishing their title, and the sums paid for the lands acquired; also the posture of affairs with the Cherokees, "and the inability of the Executive to make any further movement with this tribe, without the special sanction of Congress." The President further stated his full conviction that the best efforts of his predecessors had been exerted "to execute this compact in all its parts, of which, indeed," said he, "the sums paid and the lands acquired during their respective terms, in fulfilment of its several stipulations, are a full proof." He further stated that he had been animated by the same zeal since he came into office, enumerated some of the means that had been lately used to induce the Cherokees to remove beyond the Mississippi, their refusal to cede any more land, &c. Whilst his impression was strong "that it would promote essentially the security and happiness of the tribes within our limits, if they could be prevailed on to retire west and north of our States and Territories, on lands to be procured for them by the United States," he said, "I have no hesitation, however, to declare it as my opinion that the Indian title was not affected in the slightest circumstance by the compact with Georgia, and that there is no obligation on the United States to remove the Indians by force. The express stipulation of the compact, that their title should be extinguished at the expense of the United States, when it may be done *peaceably* and on *reasonable* conditions, is a full proof that it was the clear and distinct understanding of both parties to it, that the Indians had a right to the territory, in the disposal of which they were to be regarded as free agents. An attempt to remove them by force, would, in my opinion, be unjust. In the future measures to be adopted in regard to the Indians within our limits, and, in consequence, within the limits of any State, the United States have duties to perform and a character to sustain, to which they ought not to be indifferent. At an early period, their improvement in the arts of civilized life was made an object with the Government, and that has since been persevered in. This policy was dictated by motives of humanity to the aborigines of the country, and under a firm conviction that the right to adopt and pursue it was equally applicable to all the tribes within our limits." He submitted the matter to Congress, to "decide whether any measure on the part of Congress is called for at the present time, and what such measure shall be, if any is deemed expedient."

The report of the Secretary of War reviewed the state

of affairs with the Creeks and Cherokees at the date of the convention with Georgia, in 1802, and the subsequent measures taken to obtain cessions of land, and the supposed grounds of failure in many instances. The following statistical extracts will be interesting:

"At the date of the convention, the Indians owned, within the limits of Georgia, 25,980,000 acres, of which 19,578,-890 acres belonged to the Creeks, and 7,152,110 acres to the Cherokees, which tribes owned, besides, a considerable extent of country in the States of Alabama, Tennessee and North Carolina. Between both of those tribes and the United States there were subsisting treaties, at the time of the date of the convention, which, among other things, fixed the limits of their respective territories, and guarantied to them the lands within those limits. [See 1st vol. U. S. Laws—Treaty with the Creek Indians, p. 361, art. 5. Treaty with the Creeks, ratified 7th August, 1790. Same, page 327, Treaty of Holston, 1791, art. 7. Same, page 332, Treaty of 1798, near Tellico, articles 1 and 2.] In fulfilment of the stipulation of the 4th article with Georgia, there have been held seven treaties with the Creeks and Cherokees; of which five were with the former; two of which were previous to the late war with Great Britain, in 1812, and three since. By the two preceding the declaration of war, there were ceded to Georgia 2,713,890 acres, and, by the three latter, 12,034,-800 acres, making together 14,748,690 acres. With the Cherokees there have been held two treaties, both since the late war, by which Georgia has acquired 995,310 acres, which, added to that acquired by treaties with the Creek nation, make 15,744,000 acres that have been ceded to Georgia since the date of the convention, in fulfilment of its stipulations. In acquiring these cessions for the State of Georgia, the United States have expended $958,954.90; to which should be added the value of 995,310 acres, which were given in exchange with the Cherokees, on the Arkansas river, for a similar quantity ceded by the Cherokees to Georgia, by the treaties of 1817 and 1819, which lands, estimated at the minimum price of the public lands, would make $1,244,137.50. If to these we add the sum of $1,250,-000 paid to Georgia under the convention, and $4,282,151,-12 1-2 paid to the Yazoo claimants, it will be found that the United States have already paid, under the convention, $7,735,243,52 1-2, which does not include any portion of the expense of the Creek war, by which upwards of seven millions of acres were acquired to the State of Georgia."

The following is the conclusion of the report:

"In performing the high duties of humanity to the wretched aborigines of our country, it has never been conceived that the stipulation of the convention with Georgia, to extinguish the Indian title within her limits, was contravened. The government has been actuated solely by a desire to perform the obligation which considerations of humanity imposed on us, in relation to these unfortunate people. Their situation, at best, is wretched, and can only be rendered tolerable by the perpetual exercise of that humanity, kindness and justice which has ever characterized the acts of the government towards them."

The foregoing extracts and synopsis may suffice to explain some portions of the previous letter of Gov. Troup to the Secretary of War, and as an introduction to that which follows:

EXECUTIVE DEPARTMENT, Ga.,
Milledgeville, 24*th April*, 1824.

Sir:—I cannot refrain from the expression of my surprise at the late communication which the President has thought proper to make to Congress, on the subject of the claims of Georgia against the United States, under the articles of agreement and cession of the year 1802.

Assuming, as it does, principles which I controvert; asserting facts which I cannot permit myself to admit, it becomes my duty in the recess of the Legislature of Georgia, to enter my protest in behalf of the people of this State against them, in the same manner as I believe they would themselves do, if they had an opportunity of speaking by their immediate Representatives. The avowal of these principles, the assertion of these facts, involves the destruction of the compact between Georgia and the United States, makes it null and void, and leaves no alternative to Georgia but acquiescence or resistance.

If nullified by the act of one party, the other party is absolved, and both are free to declare the resumption of their original rights. Will this cancelment make for Georgia or the United States? Give us back our lands; we give you back your money; and, without making war upon the States of Alabama and Mississippi, we will run the risk of concluding with them the best bargain we can. It would be a better bargain for Georgia, than that the execution of which we urge upon the General Government. But, before this, we will have to ask a little money of you.

Refund to Georgia the five millions which you gratuitously presented to certain persons, the price of the pacification of New England, and which you paid from the proceeds of our lands. And is it come to this? Is it discovered at last that Georgia has no claims either upon the United States, or upon the Indians, under the compact of 1802? That it is all a dream, a vision, a phantasma, with which the deluded people of Georgia have been plaguing themselves for twenty years! And I pray you of what other construction is the Message to Congress susceptible? Are not the Indians there treated as allodial proprietors? As an independent people, having *plenum et absolutum dominium*, and seized *per my et per tout;* and that therefore Georgia can take nothing but at their will and pleasure?

The United States have promised, in the compact, to extinguish for Georgia the Indian claims to the lands reserved, as soon as it could be done peaceably and on reasonable terms. The President, in his message, construes this into a stipulation, to do in this respect whatever it might please the Indians at any time to do. Of what value was such a stipulation to Georgia? She could take nothing by it which she had not without it. Georgia might, according to the President, entreat the United States to ask the favor of the Indians, to sell peaceably and on reasonable terms, and if the Indians pleased to answer No! Never! the just claims of Georgia were satisfied now and forever. Was ever such a stipulation heard of before, either in compact between government and government, or in contract between man and man? Georgia has not required the United States to invade Indian rights, to satisfy her claims. She has only asked of the United States to do for her what she has done for herself; acquire Indian lands whensoever and wheresoever she wanted them; employ the same means for us in the fulfilment of Treaty obligation, which you habitually employ for yourselves without any such obligation. In short, do as you did in the case of the Florida Treaty and others. When the President says he and his predecessors have invariably done so, may he not have forgotten the Treaty of 1814, when a commanding word to General Jackson would have procured for us the Creek lands within our limits, on at least as good terms as it did procure other lands for the United States beyond them? I appeal to the records of your office, sir, as the voucher of the fact, that when that treaty was negotiated, the obligations of the United States were no more remembered than if the compact of 1802 had never existed. Make an estimate from the same records of what you, since 1802, have acquired for yourselves, and compare it with what, under the pledges of the agreement, you have acquired for Georgia. The difference will be about as one hundred to an unit. And yet it is asserted that the United States have sought every opportunity to fulfil the stipulations of the compact. And may I ask the favor of you, sir, to put your finger on that particular part of them, where it is shown that a proposition to extinguish claims in your behalf, has been answered by the potent monosyllable No! and that you have been content? The history of the Plymouth Colony and of William Penn might have been illustrated by the patience with which such an answer had been borne. The United States have never pretended, until now, that it would be borne at all. Now we turn over a new leaf—the principle of the old treaty of Philadelphia, the *quid pro quo* principle, must govern all treaties and satisfy all consciences. Would it had been so from the beginning. I confess to you, sir, I do not like this kind of half honesty. If the principle of Penn's Treaty was right, that of every other which followed, was wrong, and he who has done wrong is in point of conscience bound to get back to right. To undo promptly and directly what you have unrighteously done, is a dictate, I think, of the Platonic and Socratic school; undoubtedly that of a much higher, the Christian.

Begin, therefore, with Georgia, if you please, to unsettle all that has been settled; but let not Georgia be the first and the last. Say, in a spirit of repentance, that what we have taken unlawfully we will restore; that the edict of Pope Alexander, of pious memory, shall pass for nothing; the proclamations and charters of divers Kings of England for nothing; priority of occupation, priority of civilization, priority of Christianity, all nothing; Spanish precedent, which, by the law of force, took everything and gave in return stripes and blows, of course for nothing; and, beseeching the forgiveness of sins, return to the principles and practices of William Penn.

But then is not atonement still due to the Aboriginal? How (if you take the rule of the message for your guide,) can you repair the wrongs of all kinds done him since the landing on the rock of Plymouth? Your whole substance would not compensate them by one half. But, sir, not even the Puritans and the Quakers will consent to give up now, and, if things are to remain as we find them, why is Georgia to be selected as a propitiary offering? It is a fact unquestionable, that for fifteen or twenty years past, well knowing your obligations to Georgia under the compact, you have encouraged the Cherokees to make progress in all the arts of civilized life of first necessity and comfort, within the acknowledged limits of Georgia. They have been rearing flocks and herds, constructing comfortable buildings, making agricultural improvements of various kinds, organizing a government adapted to the grade of civilization they had reached, with schools and religious establishments appurtenant, &c., &c. And you encouraged the beginning and progress of these things, with certain foreknowledge they could by no possibility endure. They have been taught by the United States to value them as they ought; if they had not been taught altogether at our expense, and without our consent, we would have had no objection. But this has been the sole cause of the unwillingness of any part of the Cherokees to move. The United States, therefore, create the cause—the Cherokees avail themselves of it, to turn their backs upon your propositions for negotiation, and you have no means of escaping the difficulty, but by asserting for the Cherokees rights which they have not, and denying rights to Georgia which you ought to know she has.

I do most earnestly wish, sir, that this subject could be disposed of forever. It never recurs but the heart sickens at the recollection of the crimes connected with it. And are the wrongs of Georgia never to have an end? When the proclamation of '64* gave to Georgia the country between the Atlantic and the Mississippi, it was thought we took something by it. It was not believed it gave us what we and all mankind had before, the right to ask the Indians to sell lands in fair market. We not only thought differently, but acted differently. We knew that the whole country was ours in virtue of the very best kind of title then recognized by civilized Europe, and, paying proper respect to the occupation of Indians, we exercised all the rights of sovereigns and masters, until Mr. Adams conceived a notion that part of the country belonged to him. So he said to us: That part which you occupy you may keep—the rest I will take to myself. Accordingly he sat down with his army on the banks of the Mississippi, and erected a Territorial Government; Georgia was in no condition to resist. She began therefore to supplicate; from supplication she passed, by an effort of great courage, to

* The royal commission to Gov. Wright, in 1764, is probably here meant, and not the proclamation of 1763.—ED.

remonstrance, and thence suddenly into the articles of agreement and cession, where we still find her. But, in the mean time, what had happened? I blush to think of it. The evils of that sore and nameless iniquity are felt at this hour in all the ramifications of society. The instigators and plotters of it you paid handsomely. How, I will not say; the secret is yet to be revealed. The purity of the President has no doubt kept him a stranger to it, to this moment. But, after all, having proceeded in a course of piece-meal execution of the Articles for twenty years, why do you stop short, and say to us—all this has been gratuitous; we owed you nothing, and we have paid you a great deal; your restlessness and inquietude and importunities; our harassments and perplexities and expenses, have all been the results of false conceits and hallucinations, and they must have an end. Accordingly, it is recommended to end them, by proposing a removal of the Indians, with their consent; not because the United States are bound by the compact to take this, or any other measure, to place Georgia at once in possession of her territory; but because of considerations confined exclusively to the welfare and prosperity of the Indians. I am, notwithstanding, gratified that the President and myself, differing unfortunately on other points, should concur in this as a measure indispensable to the improvement of the condition of the Indians, and necessary to secure their permanent peace and happiness. But why this could not have been accomplished without the intervention of Congress, I cannot easily conceive. A treaty for the *exchange* of lands would seem to me to be as obviously within the compass of Executive powers, as a treaty for the *purchase* of lands, or any other object. If the instrument of persuasion is the only admissible one for the attainment of the end, I do not know how Congress can, by any act of theirs, make that which is already in the hands of the President, more efficient for your own purposes. Delay is certain to follow, and, anxious as we are to know our fate, it is delay we deprecate.

The first detachment from the body of the Cherokees, moved across the Mississippi, on the naked promise or suggestion of Mr. Jefferson; a majority of the Cherokees would do so now.

One more instance, if you please, of the unkind and unfriendly treatment recently received at the hands of the United States. The President, in the course of the present session, has considered it his duty to recommend to Congress to make provision for the claims of the Massachusetts militia; claims which Congress had hitherto refused to recognize, because, with very few exceptions, that militia, (in the late war with England, *flagrante bello*,) were arrayed against the constituted authorities of the Federal Government.

Georgia, too, has militia claims against the Federal Government, of some 20 or 30 years standing, which have been constantly urged upon the justice of Congress. I remember to have introduced them before the Senate, and, so unexceptionable were they deemed by that enlightened body, their validity was sanctioned without a dissenting voice. They would have passed the House of Representatives, also; but, on their way, they fell into bad company; they fell in with the Massachusetts claims, then most obnoxious, and shared their fate. They were claims for services faithfully and patriotically rendered in defence of our frontier against the Indians. They amount to $120,000, at least. When we press the United States for payment, the answer is: These claims, and all other claims of Georgia, were merged in the articles of agreement and cession; and, when we go to look for the article in which this supposed mersion is to be found, we will as readily find it in that very important one which gives to us the right to ask the lands of the Indians, and to the Indians the corresponding right to answer no! as in any other.

I will trouble you no further on this unpleasant subject. The causes which lead me to the expositions and references contained in this paper, are not of my seeking. I would willingly have avoided them. The absolute denial of our rights, as we understand, and have long understood them, at the moment when we believed they would have been most respected, is a subject of mortification and regret. So far as I participate these feelings with my countrymen, I assure you, sir, they are not the offspring of this day or this hour. Smarting under a sense of our wrongs, within the first hour I set my foot on the floor of the Senate Chamber, I had occasion to expose the wrongs of Georgia, and to apprise the Senators that I would never vote for an Indian treaty, until the claims of Georgia were satisfied. My convictions and my feelings remain the same to this day. Nevertheless, my sentiments towards the President are unchanged. Who can be exempt from error, amidst the cares and troubles of such an office? What heart so callous as not to pardon injuries inflicted by it? We forgive, but our rights are still our rights. At what time and in what manner they will be asserted, must depend upon the representatives of the people.

Respectfully, G. M. TROUP.

The Hon. J. C. Calhoun,
Secretary of War, Washington.

The Georgia delegation* in Congress were not inattentive to passing events. On the 10th of March, they addressed a letter to the President, from which we extract the following:

To the President of the United States:

The Secretary of War has addressed to the gentlemen composing the Georgia delegation to Congress, copies of the extraordinary documents furnished by persons who are called the *Cherokee delegation.* As this is believed to be the first instance in which a diplomatic correspondence has been held with *Indian Chiefs*, and in which they have been addressed by the Department of War, in the same terms with those used to the *representation of a State*, it becomes a subject of inquiry in what light the Cherokees are at present viewed by the government of the United States. If, as an independent nation, to be treated with all the forms of diplomatic respect, the negotiation with them should be transferred to the Department of State, and will, no doubt, be preceded by a proper examination into their authority to speak for the Cherokee tribe, on matters affecting its prosperity and existence. If to be viewed as *other Indians;* as persons suffered to reside within the territorial limits of the United States, and subject to every restraint which the policy and power of the general government require to be imposed on them, for the interest of the Union, the interest of a particular State, and their own preservation, it is necessary that these misguided men should be taught by the General Government that there is no alternative between their removal beyond the limits of the State of Georgia and their extinction. The government of the United States will deceive them grossly, if they are led to believe that, at this day, *their* consent is necessary to the fulfilment of *its* obligations to the State of Georgia. Their will must yield to the paramount duties of the general government to itself and to each member of the confederacy. The Cherokees allege, (if, indeed, the representation is made with their authority,) that they are resolved neither to leave nor sell

* Col. Tattnall was absent from indisposition.—ED.

the lands on which they reside—lands which belong to the State of Georgia; over which Georgia did claim sovereignty until the adoption of the federal Constitution, and over which she will exercise her powers whenever any administration of the general government resolves to fix permanently upon them any persons who are *not*, and whom she will never suffer to *become* her citizens. The doctrines of the general government, sanctioned by the highest tribunals, vindicate the claim of Georgia to the ownership of the soil. The Indians are simply *occupants*—tenants at will—incapable of transferring even their naked possession, except through the instrumentality of the United States, to the State of Georgia. Aware of the tenure by which their temporary possession is held, their head men have sought, in many instances, to secure from the United States a title to the soil itself. Stipulations have been entered into by the general government, equally contradictory to the rights of Georgia and the obligations of the United States; stipulations, however, which show that the general government have the acknowledged right to transfer the possession of the Cherokee lands to the State of Georgia. The power which takes from the Cherokee *tribe* a portion of soil to confer it on a Cherokee *chief*, under a different tenure, can rightfully take from the Cherokee nation for the benefit of a State.

It is with deep concern that the necessity is felt, of pressing upon the general government the considerations that are due to its character for good faith in its contracts with a member of the Union. Since the year 1802, implicit reliance has been placed in the general government; and the just expectation has been indulged, that, in the execution of its high duties, the executive administration would carefully and steadily pursue the object for which the faith of the Union was pledged—the *peaceable extinguishment*, on *reasonable terms*, of the *Indian title* to all the lands within the territorial limits of Georgia. In 1817, the public declaration of the President to Congress, that an arrangement had been made, by which, in exchange for lands beyond the Mississippi, a great part, if not the whole, of the lands possessed by the Cherokee tribe eastward of that river, in the States of North Carolina, Tennessee and Georgia, and in the Territory of Alabama, would be soon acquired, gave a just expectation that the national pledge given to Georgia would be redeemed. In the eight years which have succeeded, these anticipations of the President have been realized everywhere but in Georgia. The successive purchases made, since that period, have crowded the Cherokees out of Tennessee, North Carolina and Alabama, almost altogether into Georgia; and the terms upon which they have been made, have created all the difficulties now encountered in the *peaceful acquisition*, on *reasonable terms*, of the land upon which the Cherokees are now permitted to remain; difficulties which are every hour increasing, from the policy pursued by the general government. * * *

If the Cherokees are unwilling to remove, the *causes* of that unwillingness are to be traced to the United States. If a peaceable purchase cannot be made in the ordinary mode, nothing remains to be done but to order their removal to a designated territory beyond the limits of Georgia, and give an ample equivalent for the territory left by them, and an ample support to the territory granted to them. An order of this kind will not be disregarded by the Cherokee tribe, whose interest will be essentially promoted by a compliance with it, (whatever may be the effect of it upon a few *chief men*, who seem to consider *their own interest* as separate and distinct from that of their brethren,) as it must be obvious that a tranquil and undisturbed possession of a permanent property can alone enable them to acquire the arts of civilized life, and to secure to them its benefits.

Our duty is performed by *remonstrating* against the policy heretofore pursued, by which the interests of Georgia have been disregarded, to the accomplishment of other objects of general interest; and a compliance with a solemn promise postponed, for the acquisition of territory for the general government; and by *insisting*, as we do most *earnestly*, upon an immediate fulfilment of the obligations of the articles of cession, concluded in 1802, as the only means by which justice can be done to the State we represent, and the character of the general government be vindicated.

J. ELLIOTT,
N. WARE, } Senators.

JOEL ABBOTT,
GEO. CARY,
TH. W. COBB,
A. CUTHBERT,
JOHN FORSYTH,
WILEY THOMPSON, } Representatives.

Washington, 10*th March*, 1824.

Nothing special seems to have been done in regard to this matter, during the then session of Congress, except to refer it in the House to a select committee, of which Mr. Forsyth was chairman.* On the 14th of April he made a long report, which, on his motion, was referred to a Committee of the Whole on the state of the Union. In regard to the right of Georgia to sovereignty and soil, the report said:

"The State of Georgia claimed, on the establishment of the Independence of the United States, all the lands now forming the States of Georgia, Alabama and Mississippi, with the exceptions of those portions of the two last States which formed a part of Florida and Louisiana. This claim was founded upon the charter of incorporation of the proprietary government; on the royal commissions issued to the Governors of the State, after the proprietors had surrendered their charter to the Crown. The claim was disputed by South Carolina, and by the United States. The conflicting claims of South Carolina and Georgia were adjusted by a convention between them, in 1787. The United States recognized, by the treaty with Spain of the year 1795, the claim of Georgia, [Journals of old Congress, vol. 13, pp. 49, 50,] having refused, in 1788, a cession from the State, on account of the remoteness of the lands, and of the terms proposed by Georgia. In April, 1798, Congress passed a law [Laws of United States, vol. 3, p. 39,] in relation to the western part of the territory of Georgia, with a reservation of the rights of Georgia to the jurisdiction and soil. In May, 1800, another act [Laws of United States, vol. 3, p. 380,] was passed, containing a similar reservation. In December, 1800, Georgia remonstrated against these acts, as a violation of her right of sovereignty and soil. [Reports of Con.: 2d sess., 6th Cong., p. 87.] The compact of 1802 put an end to the disputes which were likely to arise out of this collision between the General and State governments. By this compact, the United States obtained a surrender of the right of Georgia to the sovereignty and soil of two States, containing, by estimate, eighty-six millions of acres of land, for the paltry consideration of the payment of $1,250,000, *out of the proceeds of that land*, and of a promise to extinguish the Indian title to the land within the territorial limits not ceded to the United States, as soon as it could be done *peaceably and on reasonable*

* The committee consisted of Messrs. John Forsyth, Alfred Cuthbert and Thomas W. Cobb, of Georgia, George McDuffie, of South Carolina, and John Long, of North Carolina.—ED.

terms. The execution of this compact produced no change in the right of Georgia to the sovereignty and soil of the land within her newly defined boundaries. Its only effect was to throw upon the United States the expense which might attend the extinguishment of the Indian title, an expense which, but for this compact, must have been borne by the State. Nor did this compact, in the slightest circumstance, add to the title of the Indians; it recognized the claim only they, as Indians, were allowed to have, according to the usages of the States, and the liberal policy adopted towards them by the general government."

After an able review of the whole subject, the report said:

"The committee do not, however, believe that any serious difficulty now exists to the peaceable extinguishment of the Indian title, on reasonable terms. An order from the general government, for their removal, would be cheerfully acquiesced in, if accompanied by the necessary preparation for the prosperity of the tribe, and a just equivalent for the temporary inconveniences they might suffer."

The report concluded with recommending the following resolutions:

"*Resolved*, That the United States are bound, by their obligations to Georgia, to take, immediately, the necessary measures for the removal of the Cherokee Indians beyond the limits of that State.

"*Resolved*, That such an arrangement with the State of Georgia should be made, as may lead to the final adjustment of the claims of that State, under the compact of 1802, with the least possible inconvenience to the Cherokee and Creek Indians within the boundary of the State.

"*Resolved*, That the sum of   dollars should be appropriated for the purposes expressed in the above resolutions."

[1824.] In the U. S. Senate, on the 16th of April, a communication was received, in the form of a memorial, from John Ross, George Lowrey, Major Ridge and Elijah Hicks, "delegates from the Cherokee nation of Indians," animadverting on the letter of Governor Troup to the Secretary of War, of 28th February, and the letter of the Georgia delegation to the President, and in which, speaking of the emigration of the Cherokees, they said, "*such an event will never take place.*"

The memorial having been read,

Mr. Elliott, of Georgia, said he objected to a contest of this character, in this place, with the *Cherokee delegation*. He knew them only as other Indians, and to be treated with as such. If they claim to represent an independent nation, why do they address this body directly, and not through the Department of State? But, if they seek to be heard in their real character, they should present their claims to our consideration through the War Department. The course now attempted is novel and inadmissible, and he hoped the communication would lie on the table. It was then ordered to lie on the table.

As no treaty was made with the Cherokees during the administration of Governor Troup, and their removal to the West belongs to that part of the history of Georgia subsequent to his retirement from the public councils, we must here dismiss this subject, recurring to it only so far as it becomes connected with his messages to the Legislature or his official correspondence. In his first annual message, the subject is presented prominently, and the views therein expressed have, in principle, relation as well to the Creek as the Cherokee Indians.

The running and marking the dividing line between Georgia and Alabama having been brought to the notice of the Legislature, a resolution was adopted, at the session of 1823, for continuing the exertions which had already been commenced for that purpose; and early in the year 1824 Governor Troup opened a correspondence with the Governor of Alabama and the President of the United States, on this subject, the result of which will be found in his annual message.

The General Assembly met on the 1st of November; on the second, the Governor sent in his first annual message, as follows:

EXECUTIVE DEPARTMENT, GEORGIA,
Milledgeville, 2d Nov., 1824.

Fellow-Citizens of the Senate
and House of Representatives:

It is a matter of gratulation, that since the last assembly

of the Legislature, the United States have continued in a state of peace with all nations, courting amicable relations with all by a just and impartial system, and exhibiting at the same time the armor necessary to command respect to our rights everywhere. Connected with such happy auspices, the present year has been made memorable by the landing of General, late* Marquis, La Fayette, on the soil where the first years of his distinguished life were devoted, by purse and sword, to defend all that we held sacred of political and civil rights. It was due to him to be invited by the chief magistrate, in the name of the people of the State, to our bosoms, and it was accordingly done.

When it is said the United States have so far caused their rights to be respected by all nations, it is by no means to be understood that such a state of things can be lasting. The wisest policy—the most pacific dispositions, will not assure us against a change. At this moment, an organized confederacy of despots in Europe, more formidable than ever known before, shake their bloody sceptre at all nations who contend for freedom and the rights of man. The United States and Great Britain present the only barrier to the destruction of liberty, else the spirit which animates the Greek, in his glorious struggle with the Turk, would have been extinguished, South America subdued, and our firesides assailed. So long as the United States and England are leagued against them, these enemies of the human race dare not commit themselves to the seas. Meanwhile, the progress of mind, always seeking liberal principles, will make the cause of right and justice stronger every day, until this array of tyrants shall be broken and scattered, and liberation from thraldom be complete and universal.

The strongest operative principle of the American institutions in diffusing blessings of all kinds among savage and civilized men, is the principle of universal toleration, religious and political. This principle, having its foundation in the American constitutions of government, is dispensing its beneficent influences everywhere, to the uttermost ends of the earth; and, in perfect accord and harmony with the precepts of the gospel, it will make that gospel more and more active in the reclamation of human nature in regions

* This is consistent with the usual accuracy of Gov. Troup. It may not be generally remembered, that when, at the period of her Revolution, France attempted Republican government, La Fayette, in 1790, took the oath of fidelity to the constitution, having, some months before he took the oath, renounced his hereditary title, which he never afterwards resumed.—ED.

where the rose never blossomed, and where the savage continues to hunt his fellow-man as the beast of the forest. In fact, for the spreading of the benign doctrines of Christianity among the idolater and heathen, there is reason to believe that an All-foreseeing Providence has made this great, and, I hope, unambitious nation, its chief instrument. If the millennium is to come, American institutions, under the same direction, will bring it to pass. Then, for the first time, comes the epoch of universal peace. Before that, it is our business and our duty to be prepared for war. No sovereign State, whatever be its relation to others, should suffer itself to be wronged or insulted. The weaker, the more strenuously it should insist on its rights, the more vigorously defend them. The Romans never counted the number of their enemies, and it is better that all perish than that one tittle of honor be surrendered. Maintaining, however, with reason, justice and firmness, those rights which belong to us, we ought to make it our care scrupulously to respect the rights of others.

I call your attention, therefore, to the state of our Militia—under a good system, a bulwark—under a bad one, a rope of sand. It is recommended to you, most earnestly, to revise your system. Pains have been taken to give it all the efficacy of which it was susceptible. Wanting an energetic principle to enforce itself, it would not have been made available for even a temporary organization, but for the virtue and patriotism of our citizens. These virtues, in some degree, supplied the defects of the law, and will enable me to make a tolerably satisfactory estimate of the military power of the State. I cannot, in a message like this, enter into detail; but you have accompanying documents which will suffice to show partially the defects and the remedies. But suffer me to entreat, that in this revision you look to a military system purely abstracted from, and having no connection with, the civil polity. The citizen is a different being from the soldier. Carry the civil law into the camp, the latter becomes a fungus upon the State. Instead of perfect subordination and discipline, which regard his own preservation and the safety of the country, he looks constantly to his civil privileges—makes the law for his own government, and decides when he shall look the enemy in the face—when betake himself to flight. In no country can such a military system be maintained as a reliance for defence. Even under the laws of the United States, when the militia take the field, they are subjected to martial law. It is the novelty of this restraint which in war gives rise to so many difficulties, and causes so many embarrassments before the militia are qualified for active service; and how easy for the citizen to learn that, consulting his own safety and the safety of the State, the moment he takes his position in the ranks, his first duty and his first virtue is obedience, and how habitually easy in war will be the practice thus acquired in time of peace. It will be vain to attempt to discipline the militia in times of peace, unless the strictest subordination and obedience can be commanded among all ranks, from the general to the private. The basis of any good system is organization. Without permanent organization, it need not be attempted to uniform, equip, arm or discipline. The organization of the company is the basis of the whole, and it is ascertained by sufficient experience that it is extremely difficult to maintain a complete organization of companies under the present system. The supineness and indifference of the people who elect the company officers in a period of peace, their carelessness in attending elections at all, and consequently the very improper selections which are frequently made, have had a tendency to impair the value of the commission, which ought always to be held honorable. The uncertainty of preferment, too, which ought to be the sure reward of merit, deters young men of good character from seeking commissions of the lower grade. In fine, the numerous resignations constantly occurring, and the disinclination frequently manifested for this service, show the defect to be radical, and to require an effectual remedy. A uniform prescribed for the militia, cheap and equally useful in the ordinary occupations of life, would have a tendency to diffuse more generally that military pride so essential to the character of the soldier. The time, it is hoped, will arrive, when, under the wise provisions of the act of Congress for this purpose, the whole body of the militia of the United States will be supplied with arms and equipments. In this event, it will be desirable to establish in each county a central depot of arms, to be used on field days, and as the public service may require.

As one of the prominent evils of the existing system is the habitual non-execution of the sanctions and penalties prescribed by the laws, you will find it indispensable, as well for the enforcement of these, as for the uniform and regular execution of their general provisions, to provide for the appointment of an Adjutant-General, with adequate rank and emoluments, having his office at the seat of government; and, if it be thought proper to establish drill schools for the officers in central points of divisions or brigades, their general superintendence and direction should be confided to him under the orders of the Commander-in-Chief. The reports of Major-General Newnan and Brigadier-General Harden, merit your attention.

Intimately connected with the defence, is the public education of the country. Every citizen to be qualified efficiently to defend his rights and those of his country, should possess intelligence enough clearly to understand them; and this, in the complex relations of our political system, is at once the more necessary and the more difficult. The rich and the poor now unite in the acknowledgment of the advantages accruing from an enlarged system of education, which will qualify them equally for all the occupations, civil and military, to which the State may call them. In the front of the higher academic institutions already organized, you will take pleasure to recognize Franklin College, an ornament, and, under proper endowment, an institution of first utility to Georgia. Next, the academies of counties, only requiring a fostering hand to cause them to flourish and produce fruits worthy of the fathers who laid the foundations. I recommend to you to give to these institutions liberally and unsparingly, according to their wants. But, above all, I recommend that to the poor of our fellow-citizens you extend a bountiful hand. A poor and honest man is the noblest work of God. How much more worthy your care the children, who, under your protecting auspices, might be the best of men, under your neglect, the worst. Nothing is more easy than to comprehend all under the expanded wings spread over these institutions by the Constitution and the laws, which limit your discretion in nothing but the duty always imposed upon you to take care that, of public moneys appropriated to any object, a strict accountability be exacted. The rule of apportioning, annually, a specific sum among the different counties, in proportion to representation, as adopted by an act of the last Legislature, is not only a fair one but of easy execution.

[This paragraph of the message relates to Internal Improvement, and has already been copied into the preceding chapter.]

In calling your attention to the Judiciary, I am only directing it to objects with which it has been familiar. To bring justice as near as possible to the home of every citizen, at the least possible expense, and with the greatest possible expedition, are maxims of the common law, sound and salutary. The best maxims upon paper are of but little value, unless carried into practical effect. In England, where they have been long disregarded, but whence we derive our models, they have, at this moment, the worst system* of practical municipal jurisprudence of any country on earth, and this, chiefly, from the neglect of those very maxims. The delays and expenses of justice are ruinous ; so much so, that the very best part of their system, the High Court of Chancery, has become a nuisance to the country. Of what avail are the best principles of juridical science to any people, if in practice they are constantly abused ? In our system there is quite enough of delay and expense, and these may be diminished by discarding some silly maxims of the common law. But again, it is to be considered that justice should not only be rendered cheaply, expeditiously and conveniently, it should be rendered also with uniformity —that is, in all like cases, there should be like decisions. In the practice under our system, it is impossible to assure this desirable result, from two causes: 1st. From a number of Judges acting separately and apart; 2nd. From a want of time to mature their decisions in the most important cases. It has, no doubt, fallen within the observation of all of you, that frequently the most difficult and complex questions arise before our judges, and they have no more time for the investigation of them than for the decision of the most plain and simple ones. I advise you, therefore, if, for the sake of uniformity, always so desirable in the administration of justice, you deem it expedient to organize a Court of Errors—that you so organize it as not to enhance the expense to suitors. It is before such courts, as commonly organized, that this evil is so sorely felt by the citizen. The expense is increased. An argument is admitted: and this is the source of the expense. The argument is good for nothing. The parties before the

* In vol. 17, p. 91, of Georgia Reports, published in 1856, Hon. Joseph Henry Lumpkin says: "this complaint is well brought under Jones' Forms. And so far from construing the Act strictly, it should be liberally interpreted, intended as it was to facilitate the recovery provided by law for the redress of wrongs. And it is a feather in the cap of its author, that the Commissioners sent to this country from England, to look into the mysteries of American Law Reform, have transmitted a copy of this Act home, and it now stands upon the Statute Book of the British Parliament as a law of the Realm." The Act referred to is that of 1847, "to simplify and curtail pleadings at law," of which Hon. John A. Jones is the author.—ED.

court want not the argument—they want the decision. They will be quite content with the argument of the judges; and if the judges, selected for their legal wisdom specifically to decide questions of law submitted by the records of the courts below, cannot decide correctly without a labored re-discussion of such questions, not by themselves, but by others who ought not to be their superiors; such a court will only be an evil, by the amount of the unnecessary expense thus incurred.* Otherwise, much of good might result from it; more especially, if it be made the duty of the court to pass finally upon all questions at the first term.

The compilation and digest of the Statute Law of England in force in this country, has been confided, according to your direction, to William Schley, Esq. And Charles Harris, Thomas U. P. Charlton and William Davies, Esqrs., gentlemen of distinguished eminence at the bar, have been appointed with supervisory powers to advise, from time to time, alterations or amendments as the work progressed; so that, whilst by this concert and co-operation it will be rendered more perfect and complete, its final adoption as part of the code of this State will also be rendered more certain. In connection with this important subject, may I be permitted to suggest a like revision and digest of its companion, the common law?—or, returning to the dark ages what belongs to them, would it not be worthy of the generation in which we live, if Georgia, by embodying the best parts of the common and statutory law of England, the Roman civil law, and the Napoleon code, (the last by far the best system extant,) were to supply for herself a code of Jurisprudential Ethics, which, having their foundations in reason, justice and common sense, would be alike applicable to all times and all circumstances, and, relieving Georgia from a dependence on foreign legislation, relieve her from reflections humiliating to her pride and mortifying to her self-love?

The mollified penal code of Georgia had two humane objects in view—1st, To spare the life of the criminal

* In these last views of Gov. Troup we cannot concur. The saving of expense to the suitor is very desirable; but that suitor is yet to be found, who would be willing to submit his case, involving doubtful facts or intricate questions of law, without the aid of argument from his counsel. Besides, competent Judges would not undertake such a task. They want the light of every good argument that can be adduced, even "by others who ought not to be their superiors." It is a blot on our present system, that even a synopsis of the arguments of counsel is excluded from our Reports. If this were the place to suggest law reforms, we might attempt the showing of another way to save expense to suitors.—ED.

whenever it could be done with safety to society; 2d, To reform him by confinement and hard labor—a system which is constantly exhibited in contrast to the bloody one of England, and which, from its congeniality with the American character and feeling, it would be desirable to perpetuate. Our code, however, is, in its theoretical detail, defective, and I have no doubt that our Judges, who are most familiar with its virtues and its faults, will pronounce it so. Its mode of execution is at least equally so. The remedy of both is within your power, and, to apply it, it is only necessary to understand clearly what the defects are. It will be seen, on the most superficial survey, that we passed at once from the extreme of severity to the extreme of lenity. It was never believed that, under any tolerable system of criminal jurisprudence, punishment could be dispensed with, and yet the object of reform accomplished. This, however, is our system in practice. There is not even the appearance of punishment connected with our Penitentiary establishment, unless the restraint upon the liberty of roaming at large for the commission of crime, be considered so. The far greater proportion of the convicts at all times are better fed, clothed and lodged, than they have been accustomed to be; and, whilst they perform the work necessary to keep the body in a healthful state, they enjoy not merely the benefits of society, but exactly that description of it, which, in or out of the establishment, they would seek and court. The punishment, in ordinary cases, should be hard labor and solitary confinement—hard labor by day and solitary confinement by night. The practice of crowding four or six convicts in the same dormitory, is replete with evils which inevitably and directly defeat the very end of the institution. Not only is vice rendered more vicious by it, but the hope of reformation is forever cut off from those who, not hardened in iniquity, are willing to contemplate, in darkness and solitude, their first offences against the law, and the gloomy consequences which never fail to follow them. Every species of association or intercourse between the convicts ought to be suppressed, unless it be that kind of it which is indispensably necessary to the performance of the work in which they are engaged. Some lessons have been taught by the experience of the oldest institutions in the United States, which ought not to be lost to us in looking to the improvement of our own. The oldest and most obdurate offenders acknowledge that continued solitary confinement is the severest, the most irksome and most tedious of all the punishments they have suffered; nevertheless, they continue obdurate and unreclaimed. This fact, whilst it affords additional proof of the policy which would prevent association or intercourse between older and younger offenders, and between these and strangers of every description, may show also the expediency of dispensing with continued solitary confinement in most of the aggravated cases, and, in place of it, prolonging the time for which they are committed. The report of the Principal Keeper of the Penitentiary will disclose some judicious observations relative to the present state of the police, discipline and financial economy of the institution, and certain suggestions for reform and improvement in each.

With unfeigned regret I feel myself constrained to expose the state of the controversy in which Georgia has been reluctantly involved with the United States. That every disposition existed originally on the part of this government to pursue our claims against the general government with moderation and good temper, is manifest from the proceedings themselves. The Executive branch of it unequivocally disclaims to have been prompted on his part by any other than the most friendly feelings towards the constituted authorities of the United States; and he fondly trusts that whatever of irritation has been engendered, or unkind sentiments expressed, the cause is to be sought exclusively in the deep conviction felt by the government of Georgia, that Georgia was about to suffer flagrant wrong and injustice by the course of policy adopted by the United States in their intercourse with the Indians. Nor were any complaints elicited of this, other than such as were made in the most decorous and respectful terms, before the delegation of Georgia found themselves in an attitude of humiliation at Washington, by the comparison, forced upon them, between their own relation and that of a certain other delegation,* to the Executive government of the United States, in their intercourse with it. Nor was any measure resorted to here, of an uncourteous character, until the President of the United States, in a message to Congress, had so treated the claims of Georgia and the rights of the Indians, as to foreclose the former forever from making any further claim or demand upon the latter, provided there should be a recognition by Congress or by Georgia of the doctrine asserted by that message. The Governor would

* The reference here is to *the Cherokee delegation*, mentioned in a preceding part of this chapter, and composed of Ross, Lowrey, Ridge and Hicks.—ED.

have been wanting in duty to the people, whom on that occasion he represented, if he had not seized the first moment to protest, in the strongest language, against such doctrines; and whatever may have been offensive in the manner of the protest which he interposed, he insists that, in regard to the matter, truth was in every part of it maintained with the most scrupulous fidelity. The principle asserted by the message was, essentially, that the Cherokees were now the fee simple proprietors of the soil they occupy, and of consequence that no right of territory could lawfully pass from them without their voluntary and express consent —a principle so strange and novel, asserted for the first time in the history of the government, connected as it was with the declaration just previously obtained from the same Indians, that they never would consent to part with another foot of territory, amounted to an absolute denial of our rights and the destruction of our claims either upon the United States or upon the Indians now and forever. It was in contestation of this novel and strange principle, the Governor of Georgia found it to be his duty to address himself to the Executive government of the United States, in very plain language. The United States government seemed not to have understood our motto or our emblem, or, understanding, to have disrespected them. All our obligations, therefore, to the United States and to ourselves, our love of peace, of harmony and of union, prompted to this as the only means of warning the United States government, in due time, that they were precipitating themselves upon a crisis, the least deplorable of the results of which would be the entire ruin and destruction of the weaker party—results which could not be sought by the United States, and which we, on our part, had the strongest motives to avoid. There is yet time to avert them, and it is confidently believed they will be averted. It is impossible for the United States, upon a deliberate re-examination of the subject, ever to persuade themselves that it would be possible for the State of Georgia, or any other State possessing even limited sovereignty, to make a tame abandonment and surrender of indisputable and sacred territorial rights, to such pretensions as the United States government have thought proper to urge in behalf of the Cherokees. The documents having relation to this unpleasant subject, accompany this message, and I will add little else to the matter of them, save a single fact, to show how much the United States government have deceived themselves by asserting the principle just adverted to. In the year 1785, the United States concluded a treaty at Hopewell, with the Cherokees, in the first article of which it is declared, "that the United States give peace to them and receive them into the favor and protection of the United States," and, in the fourth article of which it is further declared, that "the boundary allotted to the Cherokees for their hunting grounds, shall be" so and so, comprehending these very lands which we now demand of the United States. And this concession of even a usufructuary interest is made on certain conditions stipulated in the treaty, and which, of course, if violated on the part of the Cherokees, would cause a forfeiture of even this right of hunting. The treaties of Galphinton and Shoulderbone, between Georgia and the Creeks, held in the years '85 and '86, contain similar stipulations, recognizing the right of soil, sovereignty and jurisdiction to be in Georgia and the United States, and the right of hunting only in the Indians, and within such limits as Georgia and the United States have designated. You will perceive, therefore, that whatever might have been the kind of tenure by which lands were acknowledged to be holden by the Indians before the treaty of Hopewell, after that treaty, so far as respects the Cherokee title to their lands, the tenure was definitively settled. If the fee simple had been with them before, from that moment it departed from them, and vested in Georgia. It could vest nowhere else, because the United States at that time recognized the paramount claim of Georgia. Now, it would behoove the United States to show how Georgia was divested of this title. She could not be divested but in virtue of her own express consent, and then it behooves the United States to show the treaty, grant or concession, in which such consent was given. So far from the United States being able to do this, we produce the articles of agreement and cession, to show a confirmation to us of this same territory thus acquired by the treaty of Hopewell. Suffer me to add that the United States have, in theory and practice, uniformly acted upon the principle of the treaty of Hopewell with regard to all other Indians; that is to say, conceding the right of use to the Indians, they have reserved to themselves the allodial title, with which are essentially connected jurisdiction and sovereignty; and that, for some reasons or other altogether unexplained, the case of Georgia has been made an exception, both in theory and practice.

The Commissioners of the United States, in their negotiations at Ghent, asserted the rights of the sovereignty and soil of all the Indian country within their boundaries, to be in the United States, and, consequently, that the Indians were mere tenants at will. They asserted, moreover, what is undoubtedly true, that the system adopted by the United States towards the aborigines, is more liberal and humane than that practiced by any other nation before them. The treaty of Hopewell is the basis of all other treaties with the Cherokees. Its provisions are confirmed expressly by the subsequent ones of Philadelphia, in '94, Tellico, in '98, and Tellico in 1805. Disregarding the stipulations of these treaties, the United States acknowledge the fee-simple to be in the Indians. The Indians, therefore, may rightfully cede certain portions of territory, in fee-simple, to private citizens of Georgia. Georgia, in the last resort, is forced to draw the sword against her own flesh and blood. The United States will then be the primary agent in fomenting civil war between the citizens of Georgia; and, what will be more unnatural—the citizens of Georgia resident in the Cherokee country, will appeal to the government of the United States to vindicate their supposed rights, against the assaults of their own brothers. Thus, the United States, by their new doctrine, overthrow the entire system of polity before established in their intercourse with the Indians, and will, if they persevere, reduce Georgia to the necessity of resorting for redress to measures depending on herself alone.

As to the guaranties contained in these treaties, they are guaranties to the Indians of the right of hunting on the grounds allotted them as securities against the trespasses of the whites, who might interfere with that use, and not guaranties of fee-simple title. How could the treaties expressly take from the Indians the fee-simple in one article and guaranty it to them in another? If the United States have encouraged the Cherokees to make expensive improvements on the lands of Georgia, and such improvements are assigned as the reason for not making the relinquishment, the United States are bound in honor and justice to pay the full value of them, and to give to the Cherokees territory of their own elsewhere, corresponding in extent and fertility with that which they abandon. The government of Georgia solemnly disavows any intention to do the least injustice to the Cherokees. On the contrary, it would respect their rights as it would those of any other people, and will contribute its full quota at all times, as it has done in past times, to civilize, improve and perpetuate a race of men of great nobleness of spirit, and with whom she has generally lived on terms of peace and friendship; but it can scarcely be expected by the Cherokees themselves, that obvious and indisputable rights of citizens of Georgia should be yielded to any interest of theirs, whether real or imaginary.

The government of the United States have thought proper to state an account current* with the State of Georgia. In this account, Georgia is charged with an aggregate of $7,735,243, made up of the following items, viz: $1,250,000, under the articles of agreement and cession—$958,954 paid in extinguishment of Indian claims—$1,244,137, for 995,310 acres of Arkansas land at the minimum price of $1,25—and $4,282,151 paid to the Yazoo claimants. It is perfectly fair and quite consistent with usage, that Georgia, on her part, should state an account also; and, taking the rule adopted by the United States, viz: the present minimum price of the public lands, the account would stand thus:—80,000,000 acres ceded to the United States, at $1,25 per acre, $100,000,000—from which deducting the above amount, charged to Georgia by the United States, there will be left a net balance of $92,264,757, gratuitously presented by Georgia to the United States. It will be recollected, however, that from the date of the contract with Georgia, in 1802, until the 24th day of April, 1820, the minimum price of public lands had been fixed at $2 per acre, and when it is considered that between the two periods no lands were sold for less, and large quantities were sold for more, the account can thus be stated:—80,000,000, at $2 per acre, $160,000,000; making the same allowance for Arkansas lands exchanged with the Cherokees, and giving credit to the United States for $1,990,620, instead of $1,244,137, the balance due to Georgia would be $151,518,274. The whole revenue of the United States would not pay it in seven years; to pay it in one year would involve the mass of the population of the United States in infinite distress. The interest would have enabled Georgia to dispense with taxes—to educate all her citizens at the public expense—to have armed and equipped her militia—to have made a garden of the face of the country, intersected everywhere by turnpikes and canals, and studded with the monuments of art. Foregoing these advantages for the benefit of the United States, Georgia would have been the last to remind the United States that sacrifices had been

* Referring to the report of the Secretary of War, of 29th March, 1824, from which we have already extracted, and the account annexed thereto.—ED.

made on their account, if the Federal government, postponing the rights and interests of Georgia to the imaginary rights of the Indians, had not forced upon her a comparison of what she is, with what she might have been.

But it cannot even be conjectured upon what grounds Georgia has been charged with the amount paid to the Yazoo claimants. Georgia was not consulted in the compromise with those claimants. She never, therefore, gave her assent to the compromise. On the contrary, so far as she could, she did by her delegation in Congress resist it.— Georgia, so long as she remained a moral agent, could never assent. The act was, in effect and substance, a formal decree of the highest authorities known to the constitution of the United States, in perpetual testimony of the reward which awaits those who shall in future time successfully bribe and corrupt the representatives of the people to sell their country; and, as in this case it was the Legislature of Georgia which had been so bribed and corrupted, it could not be expected by the United States that her assent ever would be given. It would have been equally reasonable, if the United States had surrendered the whole country to the claimants, and charged Georgia with the value of it.

No time was lost in transmitting to the President the memorial of the last Legislature on the subject of citizens' claims against the Creek Indians, which had been provided for by the treaty concluded at the Indian Springs.* The answer of the President, communicated through the Secretary of War, is submitted. You will see that the decision of which we complained, is considered final, and that no revisal of it need be expected. The provision of the treaty was undoubtedly designed to cover the whole amount of claims of every description and of every date, up to the year 1802, the justness and fairness of which could be substantiated by sufficient evidence. Nevertheless, the President has thought proper to reject claims for property taken and destroyed, only because it happened to be destroyed, although the broad and comprehensive words of the treaty are "property taken or destroyed"; and he has moreover resorted to the rules of interpretation prescribed by the law of nations, to expound treaties concluded with savages, by which a farther considerable amount is deducted from the claims of Georgia, pre-existing treaties not having, according to those rules, specifically provided for them. This con-

* The reader will not confound this treaty, made in 1821, with the subsequent treaty of 1825.—ED.

struction is the more unreasonable, as those treaties were concluded, not by Georgia, but by the United States, who ought not now to cause the citizens of Georgia to suffer by their own neglect or omission. Georgia, however, having improvidently assented to refer those claims to the arbitrament of the President alone, without appeal, whatever reason she may have to complain of the injustice of the decision, she is precluded from resorting to any measures of her own for redress. The Indians well understanding that the aggregate of the claims amounted to more than $250,-000, intended that the entire sum should be applied to the satisfaction of them. According to the rules adopted by the President, claims to the amount of $100,000 only, have been admitted. Whether the balance, viz: $150,000, will be credited to the Indians or will pass into the treasury of the United States, is not known to me.

I announce to you, with pleasure, that in compliance with the request contained in the memorial of the last session, and in fulfilment of the stipulations of the articles of agreement and cession, a treaty is about to be holden with the Creeks for the extinguishment of their claims to all the lands within our limits. May we not flatter ourselves that this friendly measure is the precursor of the final adjustment of all differences between the general government and the State of Georgia; and that, in a like treaty with the Cherokees, we may see all difficulties removed—the relations of the two governments restored to what they ought to be, and an old contract which has contributed so much to disturb them, carried into complete and final execution?

It gives me great pleasure, also, to be able to inform you, on the authority of our agent, that the claims for militia services, which have been earnestly and repeatedly pressed upon the Federal Government for some 20 or 30 years past, and which have so far remained unsatisfied, will be likely to find a gracious reception at the ensuing session of Congress. To promote this desirable result, I recommend to you to continue the services of Col. Hunter on the part of the State. The justice of these claims is so undoubted, that, to be universally acknowledged, they need only be understood.

As soon as it was ascertained that Congress had passed an act authorizing the President to procure the necessary surveys, plans and estimates for roads and canals, &c., I addressed a letter to the President, requesting that Georgia should be admitted to a participation of any benefits or advantages which might result to the Union from that act, and called his attention particularly to the importance of connecting the waters of the Savannah with those of the Tennessee, and the waters of the St. Mary's with those of the Suwanee. His answer, given through the Secretary of War, is transmitted herewith. It was presumed that the Congress had derived its power to pass the act, from the provisions of the Constitution which authorize it to regulate commerce between the different States, and which confide to it the defence of the country; and that no operations would be attempted under it which would be confined exclusively to the limits and jurisdiction of any particular State.* Taking this for granted, so far from opposing obstacles to its execution, I thought it my duty to interpose our claim for that proportion of any good resulting from it, which might rightfully belong to Georgia. And here permit me, as connected with this subject, to ask your attention to a resolution of the last Legislature, which authorizes the Governor to direct a survey to be made between the navigable waters of the St. Mary's and Suwanee rivers, for the purpose of connecting them by a canal—a measure of great interest to Georgia, and unquestionably of first importance to the United States—but certainly one which can be carried into execution by the United States alone. The territory through which the canal must pass, is the property of the United States, within their exclusive jurisdiction, and any survey attempted there, under the orders of the Governor of Georgia, would be considered a trespass and perhaps resented accordingly, Whilst, therefore, I feel the utmost solicitude that this work should be undertaken promptly, and believe, too, that the United States cannot engage in one which will contribute so importantly to the interests and safety of the whole Union, I humbly submit to you the reconsideration of the measure referred to, that, if you concur in opinion with me, the resolution may be rescinded. Georgia will not voluntarily place herself in the wrong with the United States, whilst points in controversy of a delicate nature remain unadjusted between them.

In executing the resolution of the Legislature, relative to the running of the line between this State and the State of Alabama, it was discovered from the correspondence

* In the language of President Monroe, in his veto message of 4th May, 1822, "of general, not local, national, not State benefit." See also President Jackson's Maysville road veto message, of 27th May, 1830.—ED.

between the two governments, that the Executive of the United States had never been informed of the desire of the State of Alabama to have the line run. And, for this reason alone, did the United States object to take any agency in the work. It is true they assigned the additional one of the United States being under no obligation to do so by the articles of agreement and cession, as the Legislatures of Georgia and Alabama had believed. Those Legislatures were mistaken; but the United States were, nevertheless, bound by considerations of interest to see that the line, when run, was truly run and marked. The country coterminous with that of Georgia, belongs, as yet, to the United States, and not to Alabama; and, when looking to the ultimate interests of Alabama, we invited her, in the spirit of sisterly affection, to unite and co-operate with us, it was not expected that the principal obstacle to the execution of the work would be found in the denial by the government of the United States that Alabama wished it, especially when it was known here, that, so long ago as January, 1823, the Legislature of Alabama had come to resolutions expressive of their utmost solicitude that the line should be speedily run, and that copies of the same should be transmitted by the Governor, without delay, to the President of the United States and to the Governor of Georgia. A copy having been received in due time at this department, it was presumed that one had also been received by the Executive of the United States. It was not for the Governor of Georgia to inquire whether, in conformity with the requisitions of the resolutions, a copy had been forwarded to the President of the United States, or whether, if forwarded, it had been received. It is sufficient that the United States government may now know that the assent of Alabama to the running of the line is not wanting; and it only remains for me to assure the Legislature, that, whenever it becomes necessary to the interest of the State to cause the line to be run, such measures as they think proper to adopt, will be carried into execution effectually and without delay. The State of Alabama will, of course, be invited to concur, and both will consider it due to the United States to give them timely notice. The correspondence on this subject with the government of the United States and that of Alabama, is submitted.

It is with great reluctance I feel myself constrained to call your attention to the general relations between the Federal and State governments. These relations, instead of being fixed and permanent as the Constitution itself, are changing every day, although the instrument which defines them does not change. There is in all political bodies, however organized, an instinctive passion for the accumulation of power. Those of the United States have not been backward in exhibiting this trait, and, as this, like most other strong passions, acquires strength by indulgence, it is not a subject of wonder that at this day it should be displayed with a force and effect calculated to awaken the most fearful apprehensions. Under its impulses, if not restrained, the States will be ultimately stripped of the powers once considered essential to their sovereignty, and be doomed to move in the humble and subordinate spheres of corporations merely municipal. Without referring to the series of measures which (derived by latitude of construction,) have had a tendency to weaken the powers of the States, and to strengthen those of the general government, it will be sufficient to advert to those of more recent occurrence, because of more alarming character. They are the attempted restrictions upon the State of Missouri as conditions of her admission into the Union—the repeated and partially successful assertion of absolute and uncontrollable power over Internal Improvement,—and, lastly, but least to be expected, the bold assumption of the power to regulate, at pleasure, by duties, restraints and prohibitions, the entire industry of the country, and eventually, of course, to prescribe the direction which the labor of every man shall take, whatever be his own natural inclination or propensity. It was confidently believed, before, that if there was any one political feeling cherished by the people of the United States more universally than another, it was that the freedom of industry, that is to say, the right of every man to betake himself to any honest employment whatever, as best suited his inclinations or interest, was absolutely secured against the possibility of encroachment from any quarter. The confiding American people no more thought of guarding this right of freedom of industry against the invasion of their representatives, than of prohibiting them from contaminating the purity of the atmosphere they breathed, or poisoning the fountains of water from which they drank. Nevertheless, this sacred right, derived immediately from Deity, and which no human institutions could take away, did not present even an impediment to the giant strides of the Federal Government. In thus defying nature and transcending the limits of the Constitution, what apology could be found for poor, frail, misguided man, but the one which the advocates of this system have sought for themselves—a refuge in the exploded doctrines of the sixteenth century—a refuge, indeed, because covered with a veil of thick darkness? But, to our shame be it written, the descendants of the very people of Europe who were enchained for ages by this system, rise up in our day, with uplifted hands and voices against it. It is this, say they, which confined our fathers to their work-shops—which cut off all intercourse between man and man, by which intellect could be improved—which made the son to tread in the footsteps of the father—and which left him no ideas, no sentiments, no feelings, but what belonged to his family and to his trade. The American Congress, who ought to be in the van of everything liberal in politics, in commerce and in the arts, go back to this era to seek lessons of instruction for their constituents. As Providence will have it, these constituents are three hundred years in advance of them; and, unless they give lessons to their representatives in turn, they will find the general government very soon employed in making roads and digging canals within their own exclusive limits and jurisdiction—levying taxes on one portion of the community for the single purpose of giving encouragement to the industry of another portion of the same community, and finally passing an act of universal emancipation, which would undoubtedly be the last. If the Legislature of a State should resolve to resist such assumed powers, the United States government would be reduced to the unpleasant alternative, either of enforcing them because they were clear, manifest and explicit ones, or of revoking them, as of equivocal and doubtful character, and not justifying a recourse to civil war to maintain them. And it would seem that this single consideration would be sufficient to deter any wise and prudent administration of government, under our constitution, from acting upon such constructive powers at all.

I recommend to you to avoid the unnecessary multiplication of laws, as well as their frequent alteration and amendment. In framing such as are necessary, too much caution cannot be observed. Discourage divorces,* seldom creditable either to those who ask, or to those who grant them, and always indicating a depraved state of society. Give the more important elections to the people, and confide to others the less. Duties ought never to be required of them,

---

* When will this stain upon the Statute-Book of Georgia—granting divorces for causes not warranted by the law of God, or agreeable to any enlightened system of morals—be wiped out once and forever?—ED.

which they are unable or unwilling to perform. If the people desire to retain the inferior and less important elections, undoubtedly their wishes ought to be consulted. It is believed they do not. Of this, however, you are the best judges. The election by the people should be real, not nominal. They should have motives sufficiently propulsive to turn out in their strength, whenever the laws require it. It is believed that the civil and military elections which devolve upon the people, would, if they were compelled to attend them, stop the plough one-fourth part of the year, bring great distress on families of the poorer class, and subtract in the same proportion from the product of the national industry. Our political morality will never be pure as long as offices are sought with the avidity and importunity which now distinguish the canvass for them in all the States with the exception of New England. Whenever it is believed by the people, that those who seek office with the most eagerness are frequently the most unworthy, the evil will have found its remedy. Merit is always conspicuous enough, and our people will be sufficiently enlightened to discover and appreciate it. The nomination, therefore, as well as the election of the candidate, ought to belong to them. The American historian will blush to record the scenes in which, within the passing year, candidates for the first dignity * have not disdained to be actors. A practice, ripened into custom among a whole people, though proved to be a bad one, is not easily changed or discontinued. It is known that this must be the work of time, and of the intelligence and virtue of the people themselves. Whilst I am disposed to respect, as I ought, long established habits and opinions, I would reproach myself were I to withhold a single sentiment, the expression of which it was believed the interest or honor of the country required.

It will be your duty, under the constitution and laws, to proceed at an early day to the election of nine Electors of President and Vice President; and, during the session, to the election of a Senator † of the United States to succeed the Hon. John Elliott, whose term of service expires on the

* The reference is to the Presidential election of that year,—Mr. Adams, Mr. Clay, Mr. Crawford and Gen. Jackson having been the candidates; the result of which was the election, in February, 1825, of Mr. Adams, by the House of Representatives, although he had not received a plurality of votes in the Electoral Colleges. Few, if any, ever supposed he was the choice of the people.—ED.

† Hon. John M. Berrien was elected, without opposition, to succeed Mr. Elliott, and Hon. Thomas W. Cobb in place of Mr. Ware. Mr. Cobb having resigned his seat in the U. S. House of Representatives, Hon. R. H. Wilde was elected in his place, on 13th December, 1824.—ED.

third of March next—also a Senator to fill the vacancy occasioned by the death of the Hon. Nicholas Ware, and three Brigadier Generals, viz: for the first brigade of the second division, vice Thomas Glascock, resigned—for the second brigade of the second division, vice John Irwin, deceased—and for the second brigade of the third division, vice Elias Beall, removed.

The clauses in the public acts, which authorize free persons of color to be sold into slavery,* ought to be expunged from them, as repugnant to the constitution and the laws of God.

The report of the Treasurer will exhibit the state of our finances. The aggregate of sales of the last fractions amounted to $262,325,25. The commissioners who superintended them, deserve well for the assiduity, fidelity and integrity with which they discharged the laborious duties.

A statement of the votes taken at the late general election, in conformity with a resolution of the Legislature, with a view of ascertaining the popular will in relation to the mode of choosing Electors of President and Vice President, is submitted; from which it appears that a preference has been given to that by popular election, and by a large majority.†

[These three paragraphs of the message, being of local or temporary interest, are omitted.]

A resolution of the Legislature of Ohio, is submitted, recommending the abolition of slavery. Whilst it affords evidence that our sister has not interests of her own to occupy her, and that she manifests very tender concern for ours, we cannot forbear saying that our property will be safe in our own keeping for the present. It is mortifying that our rights of private property should, in violation of every sentiment of delicacy and propriety, be canvassed and passed upon by strangers of every description, and in every possible form of combination and conspiracy. We must arrest this nuisance, or throw it back upon the aggressors. That self-created societies, prompted by false conceits of philanthropy and benevolence, should officially intermeddle in a matter which it is impossible for them to comprehend because of the dense atmosphere of prejudice which surrounds them, would be unpardonable,

* A repeal took place, accordingly, on 20th December.—ED.

† An act was passed on 18th December, giving this election to the people; and this mode of choosing the Electors of President and Vice President has been ever since continued.—ED.

31

if it were not known that, upon certain subjects and in the most enlightened communities, there are to be found the greatest enthusiasts and fanatics. But that the enlightened State of Ohio should assume the prerogative of dictating to Georgia what disposition she shall make of her own domestic property, is passing strange. Georgia has never attempted to interfere, directly or indirectly, with the internal polity, local institutions, or rights of property of any of the States, and it was hoped that the same delicacy and forbearance would have distinguished the conduct of other States in relation to herself. The respectable State of Ohio ought to remember that there may be some things, connected with her own institutions and manners, not very agreeable to the people of Georgia, and that the work of retaliation is always an easy one. She must learn, too, that the question which she has taken the liberty to present to the Legislature of Georgia, is one which Georgia will never permit herself to receive at the hands of strangers —that she will make it for herself whenever it may be proper to make it at all, and exactly at the time and after the manner she shall deem best; and, repulsing all foreign interference as obtrusive, will take to herself exclusively the good and the merit, as she will certainly be obliged to take the evil, which may come of it. Our sister of Ohio will understand, for the future, that this is a subject *sui generis*, which only ourselves can comprehend; that the efforts of others to better the condition of the negro have invariably made it worse, and that the negro has never yet found a sincere friend but his master.

I lay before the Legislature, at the same time, sundry other resolutions of the States of Ohio, Massachusetts, Maine, New York and Mississippi.

The returns of the different Banks in which the State has an interest, are submitted. Two of them have not been made in conformity with the terms of the resolution of the last session, and have been so notified. All of them should resume specie payments without delay. Whatever may be the state of debit and credit in the course of trade between this and other States, producing an unfavorable rate of exchange, that exchange will always be augmented in proportion to the real or supposed depreciation of our paper. And if there exists no cause for the real, the Bank should furnish no pretence for a constructive, depreciation—a consequence inevitable from a failure to pay in specie, and which will be a clear subtraction from the wealth of Georgia, to the amount of that depreciation.

Finally, I recommend to you to bring to the consideration of the subjects submitted, calmness of temper, and more especially a kindly feeling and forbearance towards each other; so that, from the measures which follow, we may be able to render an account of our stewardship, creditable, if not to our understandings, at least to our hearts. Unless I deceive myself, you may safely count on similar feelings predominating here; and if, from this concert and concurrence, benefits do not ensue, it will be more our misfortune than our fault. Whatever of error or omission may result, good intention and the love of country will atone for. You will see, indeed, indications of unpleasant feelings, the offspring of our controversy with the United States. Entertaining, we are bound in honesty to express, them. The highest considerations and the warmest sympathies attract us to the great centre of our social system. That centre, however, must revolve on its axis in the place assigned to it. The primary and secondary bodies must move, each in its own orbit. It is our duty, in keeping the even tenor of ours, to contribute to the order and harmony of the whole, and this duty we will endeavor to fulfil. That no baleful comet may, in its irregular course, strike one of them from its place, and, deranging the system, bring all back to chaos and confusion, is the fervent prayer of your fellow-citizen,

G. M. TROUP.

The Representatives from Georgia, elected to Congress, this year, were John Forsyth, Edward F. Tattnall, George Cary, Wiley Thompson, Alfred Cuthbert, James Meriwether,* Charles E. Haynes—the two last in place of Mr. Cobb and Mr. Abbott, who declined being candidates for re-election.

A committee of the Senate, to whom had been referred so much of the Governor's Message as related to the Ohio resolution on the subject of slavery, made a report, which passed both houses, and was approved by the Governor on the 7th December. In their report, the committee, amongst other things, said:

"While your committee contemplate, with no ordinary emotions, the ameliorated condition of the slave in the

* Appointed 16th July, 1824, with Duncan G. Campbell, to treat with the Creeks.—ED.

Southern country, they view with regret this unnecessary interference on the part of a sister State, so well calculated to excite the anticipations and hopes of the slave, and impel him to those acts, which, instead of bettering his condition, must augment his misfortunes. Your committee, therefore, consider the resolution as violative of the true dictates of humanity; and this idea is supported by a contrast of the slave population of the South, with the wretched and miserable condition of the free people of color who crowd the houses of punishment and correction in some of our sister States. If, in the South, they do not revel in liberty, they are at least supplied with the necessary wants of life."

A resolution, appended to the report, disapproved the Ohio resolution, and requested the Governor to transmit a copy of the Georgia resolution to the Governor of each of the States.

Resolutions were passed, at the same session, authorizing and requesting the Governor to receive General La Fayette, "in such manner as, in his judgment, may evince the gratitude of the people of this State for his distinguished services," and authorizing the Governor to draw on the contingent fund for such sums of money as might be necessary to carry into effect the resolution for reception.

During the session of 1823, a bill was passed to alter and amend the second section of the second article of the Constitution of the State, so as to make the Governor elective by the people. In 1824, it was again passed by a constitutional majority, in both Houses, and was approved by the Governor. In the Senate, there were only *nine* votes against it—in the House, *ten*.

[1824.] In his annual message of 7th December, the President announced to Congress that Commissioners had been appointed, and negotiations for a treaty with the Creek Indians were then pending. The Commissioners appointed on the part of the United States, were Duncan G. Campbell and James Meriwether, of Georgia.

The Governor sent in the following message to the Legislature:

EXECUTIVE DEPARTMENT, GEORGIA,
Milledgeville, 17*th Dec.*, 1824.

As a reasonable expectation ought to be indulged that the treaty now holding with the Creeks, after the negotiation has been thus far protracted, will terminate in a further acquisition of territory, I recommend to you, before your adjournment to pass a provisional resolution, requiring the Governor, in such event, to convene the Legislature, and at such season as may best comport with your convenience.

G. M. TROUP.

Each House, therefore, passed a resolution for the calling of an extra session in May following.

The preliminaries, for a treaty, to which the Governor referred, were then being carried on at a place called Thle-cath-ca, or Broken Arrow, on the Chattahoochee; but these negotiations, which were begun early in December, failed, as will be seen in the sequel. Pending the negotiation, Gov. Troup addressed to the Commissioners, the following letter:

EXECUTIVE DEPARTMENT, GEORGIA,
Milledgeville, 9*th Dec.*, 1824.

Gentlemen:—The Legislature will probably adjourn about the 18th instant; and, as much anxiety is manifested to know whether you have any prospects of concluding a treaty, I have sent an express, that this letter may be safely delivered into your own hands. If there are no prospects of bringing your mission to a favorable termination, be so good as to apprise me of the obstacles you have had to encounter. If you found yourselves anticipated and forestalled by the Indian Council held in the Spring, of which we received the first notice, recently, through an Alabama print, inform me, if you please, by what authority that council was held? —whether with the knowledge, countenance or encouragement of the Agent?* Was the Agent present at that council, and what part did he take? Who drew up their state paper? Were the proceedings of that council made known by the Agent to his government, without delay, and was it with a knowledge of these proceedings that you were appointed? Were any allusions made to them in your instructions? You will pardon the trouble I give you. There

* John Crowell, appointed Agent to the Creek Indians early in 1821, in place of Gen. D. B. Mitchell.—ED.

is no absolute right, on my part, to propound these questions; no obligation on yours to answer them. Nevertheless, you are citizens of Georgia, and, if your negotiations fail, you will see how necessary for me to receive true and correct answers to these questions, from such authority as will enable me to use them in vindication of our rights, to the best advantage. You will not infer, from any of them, that hasty inferences have been indulged to the prejudice of the government of the United States. Hope is still entertained that all will be right; and in no event will anything be sought to inculpate the government of the United States, but strict matter of fact.

With great consideration and respect,

G. M. TROUP.

The Commissioners, in their reply of the 14th December, said: "We are not without our difficulties in determining what shall be our answer to the several inquiries which you have propounded. These do not arise, however, from any reluctance to make to you a full disclosure of our proceedings, and the obstacles which we have had to encounter, but from an apprehension that, by such communication, we might, *for the present*, weaken the means of which we hope successfully to avail ourselves." And again: "The proceedings which you have seen published, as occurring at Tuckabatchee and Pole Cat Springs, were evidently intended to forestall us. They have, in a great measure, had the effect, by spreading alarm throughout the nation, by the miserable farrago of threats which they contain. For some time past, the Cherokees have exerted a steady and officious interference in the affairs of this tribe. That this has derived additional impulse, and that we are now encountering a daily interference, most active and insidious, we have no doubt."

Anticipating our narrative a little, it may be proper here to state that on the 11th January, 1825, after the failure at Broken Arrow, Col. Campbell, one of the commissioners, submitted to the Secretary of War the following proposition: "The facts, heretofore disclosed, show a willingness, on the part of the Indians within the Georgia limits, to cede their territory, and to emigrate; but insurmountable obstacles present themselves to the acceptance of a treaty thus concluded. It is now proposed to re-assemble the Chiefs of the whole Nation; to renew the offers already made; to obtain the entire Creek country, if practicable; but, if this cannot be effected, then to accept a treaty signed by the Chiefs within the limits of Georgia, provided such treaty be accompanied by the assent of the other Chiefs, that the land to be abandoned by the emigrating party shall be immediately subject to the disposition of the Government." In his reply, of 18th January, the Secretary of War, after stating that the President had "deliberately considered" a former "proposition submitted by the commissioners to treat with the Creeks, of holding a separate treaty with Gen. McIntosh," &c., &c., and that the President's opinion was "that he cannot, with propriety, authorize the treating with Gen. McIntosh alone, as proposed by the Commissioners," &c., &c., yet added: "the President can see no objection to a renewal of the negotiation, as proposed in your letter of 11th instant, in order to obtain an arrangement with Gen. McIntosh, with the consent of the nation, for the cession of the country in question; and you are, accordingly, in conjunction with Major Meriwether, as commissioners, authorized to renew the negotiation. You will, however, distinctly perceive, in the remarks which have been made, that, whatever arrangement may be made with Gen. McIntosh, for a cession of territory, must be made by the Creek nation, in the usual form, and upon the ordinary principles with which treaties are held with the Indian tribes."

The Legislature of 1823 having appointed the late Hon. William Schley * "to compile and digest the statute laws of England" then "of force in the State of Georgia," and having authorized the Governor to have the same "exam-

* This gentleman is well and honorably remembered as having been afterwards Judge of the Superior Courts of the Middle Circuit, a Representative in Congress, and Governor of Georgia from 1835 to 1837. He died at Augusta, on 20th November, 1858, much esteemed by all who knew him.—ED.

ined by a committee of three learned in the law," after which he was to "approve or disapprove of the same," Governor Troup appointed, as that committee, Messrs. Charles Harris, William Davies and Thomas U. P. Charlton. In 1826, the work was approved by the Governor, and it has since been known to the legal profession and the public as "Schley's Digest." The following is his letter to Judge Charlton on the subject. It will be seen that he indulges in some pleasantry in regard to the compensation which he was authorized to make to the committee for their services.

VALDOSTA, Laurens, 12th April, 1824.

Sir: I received your letter, yesterday, on the subject of a Compilation and Digest of the Statute Law of England in force in this State, and concur entirely in the views you have taken of it.

I can easily conceive that the work may be either worthless or highly valuable. The competency of the hands to which its execution has been confided, is ample security that the latter result will be attained. There can be no doubt of the extent of your powers over it—to approve or disapprove are terms equally applicable to every part as to the whole; and, as the greater power is always construed to include the lesser, you are, of course, invested with that of revision and correction; and this is in perfect consonance with what I understand to be Mr. Schley's own views of your several duties under the resolution; so that you cannot fail to move harmoniously in the execution of the work, and make it in the end what you desire it should be.

As to the compensation for your services, all I can say at present, is, that I will endeavor to be as liberal as possible; but, if in attempting what I wish in this respect, my courage should fail me, I would turn you over to the Legislature, backed by as strong a recommendation as any Governor, elected by the Legislature, dare.

This letter is intended as well for Messrs. Harris and Davies as for yourself.

Respectfully yours, G. M. TROUP.

Thomas U. P. Charlton, Esq.,
Savannah.

Before proceeding, as we shall in the next and succeeding chapters, to give a somewhat detailed account of the

Creek controversy, it is proper to make reference to the relations subsisting between the Executive of Georgia and Col. Crowell, whose appointment as Indian Agent has been already noticed; and, the more especially, as the inquiries in Gov. Troup's letter of 9th December, 1824, to the U. S. Commissioners, implied doubt of the Agent's fidelity to the interests of Georgia; and the following extracts of a letter from the Governor to the President—containing serious charges against the Agent—will be found so frequently referred to hereafter, as to make it almost necessary that portions of it be inserted here.

On the 3d of March, 1817, the eastern part of the Mississippi Territory was, by act of Congress, made a separate Territory, called Alabama; and on the 16th day of November, 1818, Col. John Crowell took his seat in the House of Representatives, at Washington, as its Delegate. On the 14th December, 1819, Alabama was admitted into the Union; and, as already seen, Col. Crowell was, early in 1821, appointed Agent to the Creek Indians.

On the 8th of January, 1824, Rev. William Capers, as Superintendent of the Creek Indian Mission, and Chairman of the Missionary Committee of the South Carolina Conference, addressed a long letter (verified by affidavit) to the Secretary of War, complaining of the Agent, charging that he could not do justice where religion was concerned; that he was believed to be an enemy to the Gospel, abusing his authority and his influence to oppugn it, &c. This letter was handed to Governor Troup, for transmission to Washington; and, in forwarding it to the Secretary of War, the Governor wrote as follows:

MILLEDGEVILLE, 16th January, 1824.

Sir: In submitting to you a complaint against an officer under your authority, it will not be understood that I am actuated by any other motive than the desire of making you intimately acquainted with a man who would seem so far to be an utter stranger to you. You will see, in the sequel, dark and mysterious things unveiled, and upon such high authority that no man dare to shut his eyes against them. The naked statement which I make, will pass for nothing

—it is so intended—but the sacred and solemn appeal which I know has preceded it, will make an instantaneous and lasting impression. It comes from a sacred source, where piety and devotion unite with patriotism to bring culprits of every kind to justice.

You are no stranger to the virtues of Mr. Capers, who, blending the finest talents and accomplishments with no ordinary eloquence, stands first among Christian ministers in this Southern country. I have said to him, that his oath, which he has tendered in support of his memorial, is no better than his word, and that you will so consider it; so of the rest—he is the voucher for them all, and a better you cannot have. * * *

Mr. Crowell, the Agent, not being an inhabitant of the State of Georgia, but an officer of the United States, abandoning his station, did, for political purposes, repair to the seat of government of Georgia, with the sole view and intent to use his influence in behalf of one of the candidates at the late election for Governor, and did so use it in the most open, public, and grossly indelicate manner; thus intermeddling in the political affairs of a State to which he ought to have been, as he was, in fact, a stranger and an alien; and thus compromitting the Government, whose agent he was, in a matter in which the highest interests of the States were involved; no less interests than the freedom and independence of the elective franchise.

Very respectfully, &c., &c.,

G. M. TROUP.

The Hon. J. C. Calhoun,
Secretary of War.

To these things, Col. Crowell replied, on 18th March, denying what he called "the unfounded and frivolous charges" of Mr. Capers, and retorting upon the Governor with considerable acrimony. In noticing the charge of interfering with the political affairs of Georgia, he said:

"That I am no inhabitant of Georgia, is not correct; the seat of my agency being within the chartered limits of that State. That I am an officer of the United States, is true; but that I, in a 'grossly indelicate manner,' opposed his election, I deny. That I *openly* and *boldly* did so, I admit. In doing this, I may have acted imprudently, by provoking his resentment; but how my doing this could compromit the Government, whose agent I am, in relation to the free and independent exercise of the elective franchise, in Georgia, I confess I have yet to learn. * * There is, certainly, then, no express or implied incompatibility between the office of Indian Agent and that of opposer to Governor Troup, in his canvass for public suffrage."

In answer to the letter of Mr. Capers, the Secretary of War, under date of 30th March, said:

"The President regrets that there should be any misunderstanding between yourself, and the society of which you are a member, and the Agent. But, after a careful examination of the charges, and the reply, he is of opinion that there is no foundation on which to take any measure against him, particularly, as his general conduct, in the discharge of his official duties, has been marked by promptitude and accuracy, as far as they have come within the knowledge of the Department," &c.

And, in writing to the Agent, on the same day, the Secretary of War said: "You will give a decided countenance and support to the Methodist Mission, as well as to any other society that may choose to direct its efforts to improve the condition of the Creek Indians," &c., &c.

As introductory to what follows in succeeding chapters, it is proper to present a concise view of the relations existing between the Creek nation of Indians and the United States, for some time before and at the conclusion of the treaty of the Indian Springs, in February, 1825.

On the 30th of August, 1813, occurred the terrible massacre at Fort Mims on the Alabama river. The attacking party was led by the celebrated Weatherford, instigated by British agents. Even before this time, the Creeks were divided into two parties—the peace party, or Friendly Indians, supported by McIntosh and his friends—and the war party, or *Red Sticks*, so called from the painted color of their war clubs. The former—sometimes called Lower Creeks—resided almost wholly in Georgia; the latter—or Upper Creeks—lived almost, if not altogether, in Alabama. The war which ensued between the Red Sticks and the United States, and the victories gained by Gen. Floyd, of Georgia, Gen. Andrew Jackson and others, over these hostile Indians, find their appropriate place in the general history of the country. Vanquished in battle, and broken in spirit, the hostile Creeks yielded in 1814, and the treaty of Fort Jackson, already noticed, was the result. The war party were a conquered people; and yet they were afterwards the almost unyielding enemies of the Georgians and Alabamians.

The brave McIntosh was ever the friend of Georgia and the Union. In the subsequent war with the Seminoles of Florida, who were aided and encouraged by some of the Red Sticks, McIntosh commanded a brigade of Friendly Creeks, and did effective service against the Seminoles and their allies.

From a report made by Joseph V. Bevan, Esq., in October, 1825, to Governor Troup, by appointment of the Legislature, we make the following extract. Referring to a difficulty between the Indian Agent and McIntosh, in 1824, Mr. Bevan said:

Somewhat before this period, McIntosh proposed, in a Council of the Cherokees, that they, the Creeks, the Chickasaws and Choctaws, should emigrate westward of the Mississippi; and there that these four nations of Southern Indians should form one consolidated government. It is needless to say that these propositions were rejected—this was not all: McIntosh, (who had been constituted a Cherokee Chief, in consequence of intermarriage with one of their women,) was degraded, and denounced to his own countrymen as an enemy to the Red People. These sentiments were speedily adopted by the Big Warrior,* who assembled a few of the Upper Creek Chiefs at the Pole Cat Springs, where, with the assistance of his son-in-law, (who was also sub-agent under Col. Crowell,) those celebrated resolutions were passed, which are now held to justify the murder of all those who signed the treaty. It was then that parties began really to be distinguished; the Upper Creeks or *Alabama Indians* inclining to the Cherokee talks; the Lower Creeks, or Georgia Indians, to those of McIntosh: and it was in this state of things, that McIntosh came to the determination that he would conclude

* This Chief, although not one of the Red Sticks, belonged to the Upper Towns. He died at Washington city on the 8th of March, 1825.—ED.

the treaty, (as he and the Little Prince * had done but four years before,) without waiting for the consent of those Towns situated on the waters of the Coosa and Tallapoosa. To this measure, it appears that he was strongly influenced by three considerations:

1. That the Cowetuh Towns, being the oldest in the nation, were at one time sole owners of the country, and, as such, by the custom of the nation, have absolute authority with regard to the disposition of land.

2. At all events, that each town, retaining its original rights with regard to territory, inviolate, and having never surrendered them, (such as they were,) to the National Council, had full authority to dispose of its own domain.

3. That the Upper Towns had forfeited their rights, if they ever had any, by their treason during the war; which had caused the cession or surrender of all the lands mentioned in the treaty at Fort Jackson.

There are also three important facts belonging to the history of this transaction, which it would be as well to take along with you:

1. That the few friendly Indians among the Upper Creeks, during the late war, were either in the power or possession of the hostiles, until relieved by McIntosh and his Cowetas.

2. That neither the Big Warrior, the celebrated *Hopoithle Yoholo*, nor any other Chief of the Upper Creek Nation, signed the treaty of 1821—a treaty whose validity has never been questioned.

3. That at the treaty held by Messrs. Campbell and Meriwether, the *Cussetuhs* had already *taken the talk* of the Commissioners, before their departure over night, which, being the Indian mode of accepting a proposition, was held by McIntosh as sufficient to justify its formal conclusion according to the mode of the white people, without obliging all his heathens to affix the signature of the cross.

* Another celebrated Chief of the Upper Towns, and who was after, if not before, the death of Big Warrior, their head Chief, and who figures largely in subsequent transactions. His Indian name was Tustennuck Opoyow, or Tustunnuggee Hopoie. He was, by some, regarded as "Head Chief of the Nation."—ED.

CHAPTER X.

Treaty concluded with the Creek Indians.—Disturbances growing out of it.—Murder of McIntosh.—Governor's Reception of La Fayette.—Extra Session of the Legislature.—Governor's Message.—His Recommendations.—Views on Slavery Question.—Proceedings of the Legislature.—Governor's Correspondence with the President, Gen. Gaines and others, begun, &c., &c.

The causes of the failure of negotiations at Broken Arrow, will appear by reference to the documents published in this chapter. Negotiations were then transferred to the Indian Springs, after the following notification had been given to the Agent of Indian Affairs.

WASHINGTON CITY, January 12, 1825.

Sir:—The Commissioners on the part of the United States have come to the conclusion of assembling the Chiefs of the Creek nation, for the purpose of submitting to them matters of importance to themselves and the Government. The day of convention will be the 7th of February next, Monday, at the Indian Springs. We are desirous that all the Chiefs of the nation should attend, who are in the habit of transacting public business, and of signing treaties. You will cause the enclosed invitation to be circulated, forthwith, among the chiefs, and broken days issued accordingly. On my return to Georgia, which will be in a few days, I shall probably have occasion to address you further upon the subject of the negotiation.

I am, sir, your obedient servant,

DUNCAN G. CAMPBELL.

Col. John Crowell,
Agent Indian Affairs.

The "invitation" or circular, dated the same day, and signed by Col. Campbell, in behalf of himself and the other Commissioner, addressed "to the Chiefs of the Creek Nation," was in the following words:

"By the authority of the President of the United States, you are requested to convene at the Indian Springs, on

Monday, the 7th day of February next. Matters of great consequence to the Nation and the United States, will be laid before you. We shall expect all to be present, on the day appointed, who are in the habit of transacting the business of the Nation, and of signing treaties."

On the 7th of February, the Commissioners met at the place appointed, but, as few of the Chiefs had arrived, no business was then done. The Agent was present, and on the same day addressed a note to the Commissioners, in which he said: "Having been informed by the War Department of the renewal of the negotiation with the Creek Indians, for a cession of land, and being instructed to obey your orders in relation to the negotiation, I now have the honor to inform you that I will, in compliance with my instructions, obey such instructions as I may receive from you in the fulfilment of your duties under the instructions of the War Department, and cheerfully co-operate with you in bringing to a successful termination the present negotiation."

On the 10th, the Commissioners finding that Chiefs and Head Men, to the number of nearly four hundred, had convened, a meeting was had, except with the Tuckabatchee Chiefs, who sent a message "that they were not ready, and were not disposed to meet in the room prepared for the council, but were disposed to hold meetings at their own camp." The Council, nevertheless, proceeded to business, and after "a long and friendly talk" by the Commissioners to the Chiefs, a treaty was concluded, and, after being discussed and explained, was signed, on the 12th, [Feb., 1825,] "by all the chiefs present, except the delegation from Tuckabatchee, and one chief from Talladega." In the mean time, however, a part of the Chiefs of two of the towns had left, mysteriously, and the only explanation of this movement, obtained at the time, was that the "order" for their departure was given by William Hambly, United States Interpreter, aided by the advice of Stedham, a Chief of one of the towns.

It is not important, here, to particularize the terms of the treaty, except to state that, for a consideration named, the Creeks ceded to the United States "all the lands lying within the boundaries of the State of Georgia as defined by the compact" of 1802 between the United States and Georgia, in exchange for lands of "the like quantity, acre for acre, westward of the Mississippi;" and that the period of their removal was not to "extend beyond the first day of September, in the year eighteen hundred and twenty-six." It is important to state that this treaty, signed by the United States Commissioners, by William McIntosh, "Head Chief of Cowetaus," and fifty-one other Chiefs, was "executed on the day as above written, *in presence of* JOHN CROWELL, *Agent for Indian Affairs.*"

Whatever may have been the truth of the charges brought against this Agent, or the extent of his connection with the subsequent troubles in the Creek country, there is no doubt that, after having been thus present at the council and the execution of the treaty, and having *signed his name as a witness to it*, he wrote, the very next day, a letter to the Secretary of War, of which the following is an extract:

"Yesterday a treaty was signed by McIntosh, and his adherents, alone. Being fully convinced that this treaty is in direct opposition to the letter and spirit of the instructions, which I have a copy of, I feel it to be my bounden duty, as the agent of the government, to apprise you of it, that you may adopt such measures as you may deem expedient, as to the ratification; for, if ratified, it may produce a horrid state of things among these unfortunate Indians. It is proper to remark that, with the exception of McIntosh, and perhaps two others, the signatures to this treaty are either chiefs of low grade, or not chiefs at all; which you can perceive, by comparing them to those to other treaties, and to the receipts for the annuity, and these signers are from eight towns only, when there are fifty-six in the nation."

Now, assuming all these things to be true, the question is, why did not the Agent decline any participation in the business?

Col. Campbell, one of the Commissioners, wrote thus, to the Secretary of War, on 16th February:

"On the 13th instant, we had the honor of enclosing to you, from the Indian Springs, the copy of a treaty which had been concluded, the day previously, with the Creek nation of Indians. On Monday morning, the 14th, a supplemental article was added, which has exclusive relation to two reservations claimed by the Indian chief, General McIntosh. I am gratified at the opportunity which I now make, of transmitting to the Department, by our Secretary, Major Hay, the original treaty and the Commissioners' Journal. On reference to this last document, you will discover under what circumstances the negotiation was renewed, and how it progressed and terminated. There is nothing of singular import in the whole proceeding, except the sudden and mysterious departure of the Cussetaus, at night, after solemn assent to a treaty. The explanation given to this movement, by the report of Col. Williamson,* at the conclusion of the Journal, I hope will be found satisfactory. The step was far from being voluntary. These chiefs, doubtless, were deluded by a wily and perfidious individual in the service of the government, as interpreter. His opposition to a treaty was notorious. His life and character have been too much diversified, and too strongly marked, to make him a fit officer of public trust. The attendance of the Chiefs was a full one; much more so than is usual when *Chiefs only* are invited. The opposition was feeble, and seems to have been dictated by the Big Warrior. The death† of this Chief, I conceive, puts the question at rest. That all opposition will now cease, and that the dissenting party will now treat and reunite themselves with the majority, I have no doubt. To meet this expected contingency, a portion of the appropriation has been reserved."

The foregoing extracts show the opinion of the Commissioners, or, at least, one of them, in regard to the fairness of the treaty; but events were in progress of maturity and development, for which neither they nor the public were then prepared.

Whatever may have been thought of the course of President Monroe with reference to the recent demonstration of

* This gentleman had been employed by the U. S. Commissioners to ascertain the reason of the departure of certain Chiefs from the treaty ground; and it was upon information given him, that Hambly and Stedham were implicated.—ED.

† It has been seen that he was not then dead. His Indian name was Tustunnuggee Thlucco.—ED.

the so called "Cherokee delegation," he soon after signalized the close of his administration, in regard to the Indians, and especially those resident in Georgia, by an admirable message which he communicated to Congress on the 27th of January, 1825. We make the following extracts:

"For the removal of the tribes within the limits of the State of Georgia, the motive has been peculiarly strong, arising from the compact with that State, whereby the United States are bound to extinguish the Indian title to the lands within it, whenever it may be done peaceably and on reasonable conditions. In the fulfilment of this compact, I have thought that the United States should act with a generous spirit, that they should omit nothing which should comport with a liberal construction of the instrument, and likewise be in accordance with the just rights of those tribes. From the view which I have taken of the subject, I am satisfied that, in the discharge of these important duties, in regard to both the parties alluded to, the United States will have to encounter no conflicting interests with either. On the contrary, that the removal of the tribes from the territory which they now inhabit, to that which was designated in the message at the commencement of the session, which would accomplish the object for Georgia, under a well-digested plan for their government and civilization, which should be agreeable to themselves, would not only shield them from impending ruin, but promote their welfare and happiness. * * A negotiation is now depending with the Creek nation, for the cession of lands held by it within the limits of Georgia, and with a reasonable prospect of success. * * To give effect to this negotiation, and to the negotiations which it is proposed to hold with all the other tribes within the limits of the several States and Territories, on the principles and for the purposes stated, it is recommended that an adequate appropriation be now made by Congress."

The following is the Governor's letter to the Commissioners, on the subject of the message:

EXECUTIVE DEPARTMENT, GEORGIA,
Milledgeville, 8th Feb., 1825.

Gentlemen: Within this hour, the mail has brought an important communication, made by the President to Congress, on the 27th ult., and connected with the objects of your commission. Fearing a copy may not have reached you, I hasten to forward, by express, a newspaper which contains it. He can be with you early to-morrow morning.

With consideration and respect,

G. M. TROUP.

D. G. Campbell, J. Meriwether, Esqrs.,
U. S. Commissioners for holding treaty with the Creeks,
Indian Springs.

The Commissioners replied, on the 9th, from Indian Springs:

It affords us much pleasure to acknowledge the receipt of yours of yesterday, enclosing a special message lately made by the President to the Senate of the United States. We were aware that such communication was intended to be made, and had arranged for its transmission to this place. It had not arrived, however, which makes the arrival of your express the more acceptable. The Chiefs of the nation are coming in, in considerable numbers. We discover distinctly the decided hostility of a large deputation from Tookaubatchee, but are of opinion that in council we have the ascendency in numbers and in grade. We cannot admit the possibility of defeat, yet such may be the result. Our expectations are founded upon facts which amount to strongest assurance of success, and we must indulge the gratification, that even "while Troup is Governor," * the policy and obligations of the United States will be effected, and the rights of Georgia obtained.

The Governor wrote again to the Commissioners:

EXECUTIVE DEPARTMENT, GEORGIA,
Milledgeville, 12*th Feb.*, 1825.

Gentlemen: Accept my thanks for your last letter by express. A dispatch from Mr. Forsyth has this moment reached me, and, believing it may be of service to you, I hasten, by another express, to place you in possession of it. Our delegation, as was expected, are resolved to do their duty; it is known to me you will do yours to all parties, and I will endeavor not to be wanting in mine. There can be no doubt of the correctness of the suggestion of Mr. Forsyth, that a treaty concluded with that portion of the tribe resident in Georgia, for the cession of all the lands within our limits, would be approved by Congress.

With great respect and consideration,

G. M. TROUP.

* Referring to a remark attributed to the Agent, that "Georgia should get no land from the Indians while Troup was Governor;" showing the suspicion of the Agent's hostility to the treaty even before it was signed.—ED.

To which the Commissioners replied:

INDIAN SPRINGS, Feb. 13th, 1825.

Sir: Your express has this moment reached us, and delivered your communication covering the proceedings of Congress upon the Indian question. We are happy to inform you that the "long agony is over," and that we concluded a treaty, yesterday, with what we consider the *Nation*, for nearly the whole country. We enclose you a copy, also dispatches for the Government. These last are addressed to your care, to secure their certain transmission by to-morrow's mail. The original Treaty will be conveyed by our Secretary, to Washington City, by the stage leaving Wilkes, on Thursday next. We are still in time for ratification by the present Senate, and beg to offer you our sincere gratulations upon the more than successful issue of a negotiation in which you have been an ardent co-worker.

With great consideration and respect,

DUNCAN G. CAMPBELL,
JAMES MERIWETHER.

His Excellency G. M. Troup.

Soon after the failure of negotiations at Broken Arrow, Gov. Troup had addressed a letter to the President, dated 23d December, 1824, complaining of the conduct of the Agent, and in which, speaking of that conduct, he said: "you had timely and sufficient warning, by a communication which I had occasion to make the Executive Government, some twelve months since, and which was answered by the confirmation of this same man in office."*

Having received information of the signing of the treaty, Gov. Troup addressed the following letters to the Georgia delegation in Congress:

EXECUTIVE DEPARTMENT, GEORGIA,
Milledgeville, 15*th Feb.*, 1825.

Gentlemen: From what I have learned, unofficially, of the late conduct of the Agent at the Indian Springs, his hostility to the interest of Georgia has suffered no abatement. I can by no means vouch for the accuracy of the reports connected with it. The Commissioners must know,

* The sub-Agent, Walker, was dismissed from his office, by the Secretary of War, in January, 1825, on the ground that, "so far from contributing to effect the object of the government, your influence has been used in defeating the successful termination of the treaty."—ED.

and, if founded in truth, you will be satisfied, that the Agent will leave no efforts unessayed to detain the Creeks in their own country, to the last hour limited by the treaty, if he be longer continued in office. McIntosh and all his people are willing to hurry away—the Agent can retard or detain them, by the multiplication of obstacles which will be insuperable to them. We are much concerned in their speedy removal.

With great consideration and respect,

G. M. TROUP.

EXECUTIVE DEPARTMENT, GEORGIA,
Milledgeville, 17*th Feb.*, 1825.

Gentlemen: What was stated in my letter of the 15th, in relation to the conduct of the Agent at the Indian Springs, as rumor, is confirmed as matter of fact. Professing good dispositions, and tendering hearty co-operation to the Commissioners, he was secretly engaged in undermining them. The Chiefs were all, the Tookaubatchees excepted, ready to sign the treaty, and whilst the Commissioners were occupied in the preparation of it, the Agent ordered a portion of them to depart by night. When the Commissioners, to their astonishment, discovered this secession, they dispatched Col. Williamson in pursuit, and to advise them to return; but their resolution was fixed, and, when it was asked why they had thus precipitately turned their backs upon the Commissioners, on the very eve of the signature, their answer was, one and all, "by order of the Agent." You see, therefore, that but for this perfidious interference, the treaty would have been concluded by the entire nation, and with an unanimity almost unexampled. This last act of the Agent proves that he is yet animated by the same inveterate hostility to the interests of Georgia, which signalized his conduct and defeated the treaty at Broken Arrow. It is the interest of Georgia, as I believe it is the wish of her people, that the territory be organized as speedily as possible, consistently with the treaty; and as, in expediting the removal of the Indians, much will depend on the facilities afforded by the Agent, it is presumable that he will not fail to take the necessary measures to detain them to the last hour limited by the treaty. I understand, further, that those of the tribe who refused their assent to the treaty, threaten injury to McIntosh and his Chiefs. Should the execution of these threats be attempted, (the treaty having been ratified,) I will feel it to be my duty to punish, in the most summary manner, and with the utmost severity, every such attempt, as an act of hostility committed within the actual territory and acknowledged jurisdiction of Georgia; and thus, whether the Agent of the United States may think proper to deport himself as a neutral or a partisan.

With great respect and consideration,

G. M. TROUP.

P. S. Dr. Meriwether, the Secretary to the Commissioners, I learn, proceeds to Washington with the treaty. He will, no doubt, be able to give you any information which you may require touching the proceedings at the Indian Springs.

G. M. TROUP.

The Hon. Senators and Representatives in
Congress, from Georgia,
Washington City.

The Secretary of the Commission was Major Hay, and not Dr. William Meriwether, who was present, however, and afterwards made an affidavit, from which the following is an extract:

"After the whole treaty had been gone through and explained, it was signed and sealed by the parties. There was no objection whatever made by Col. Crowell, or the Interpreter, when called upon to witness the treaty, nor did this deponent ever hear from Col. Crowell the slightest suggestion that the Chiefs present were not competent to make a treaty, nor does he believe that any such suggestion was made."

On the 28th of February, 1825, the President sent to the Senate, "a treaty lately concluded at the Indian Springs, by Commissioners of the United States, duly authorized, with the Chiefs of the Creek Nation, assembled in council, with the documents connected therewith."

So it appears that Col. Crowell's letter, of 13th February, complaining that the treaty was "in direct opposition to the letter and spirit of the instructions," had no effect upon the Executive Government at Washington. On the 3d of March, the Senate advised and consented to the treaty, and the same was duly ratified and confirmed by Mr. Adams, (who had succeeded Mr. Monroe, in the Presidency, on the fourth of March,) four days afterwards, that is, on the seventh day of the same month."*

On the 21st of March, the Governor issued his proclamation, which, after reciting the ratification of the treaty, &c., said:

"I have, therefore, thought proper to issue this, my proclamation, warning all persons, citizens of Georgia and others, against trespassing or intruding upon the lands occupied by the Indians, within the limits of this State, either for the purpose of settlement or otherwise; as every such act will be in direct violation of the provisions of the treaty aforesaid, and will expose the aggressors to the most certain and summary punishment by the authorities of the State and of the United States."

A proclamation was also issued by the Governor, on the 18th day of April, reciting the ratification of the treaty, the importance "that the territory aforesaid should be organized and settled with as little delay as may comport with the provisions of the treaty; and, to this end, the assent of the Indians having been obtained, to the running and survey of the country under the authority of the State"—he, therefore, by authority of the Legislative resolve, called an extra session of the General Assembly, to meet at Milledgeville on the 23d day of May.

Meanwhile, a storm was gathering, which was soon to burst on the head of McIntosh, and to produce scenes of disorder seldom witnessed amongst civilized or savage men. With the calmness and foresight for which he was so remarkable under the most adverse circumstances, Governor Troup had contemplated the prospect, and, with his usual energy, had determined to prevent the threatened outbreak,

* The vote, in the Senate, on advising and consenting to the treaty, was as follows: YEAS—Messrs. Barbour,† Bell, Benton, Bouligny, Brown, Clayton, COBB, Dickerson, Eaton, Edwards, ELLIOTT, Findlay, Gaillard, Hayne, Holmes, of Me., Holmes, of Mississippi, Johnson, Johnston, Kelly, King, of Ala., Lanman, Lloyd, of Md., Lloyd, of Mass., Lowrie, McIlvaine, McLean, Macon, Mills, Parrott, Ruggles, Seymour, Smith, Talbot, Tazewell, Thomas, Van Buren, Van Dyke, and Williams,—38. NAYS—Messrs. Barton, of Missouri, Branch, of North Carolina, Chandler, of Maine, and DeWolf, of Rhode Island—4.—ED.

†The same person who, afterwards, whilst Secretary of War, negotiated the second, or "new" Creek treaty—ED.

if possible. On the 17th February, certain Chiefs of the friendly Indians met the Governor in his office, and made an address to him, in which they said:

"We meet you to-day, in your office, to express our opinion as principal chiefs of Coweta; which expression we have considered best to give you in writing, that you may know when we act contrary to our talk. Eighteen hundred and thirteen was the beginning of the hostile party, and General McIntosh was the first red man who joined the United States, and spilt his blood in her defence; at that time we were warriors under General McIntosh, and fought for our country; and, after peace was made, we were appointed Chiefs by General McIntosh, not by Little Prince or the Big Warrior; therefore we love said McIntosh until death, and will hold fast to his talks, because we know he acts agreeable to our father's talks, and by him we gain our protection from our father the President. Looking back to 1813, we believe that but for the relations which McIntosh sustained to the United States, we should have lost our lands without getting a penny for them.

FATHER: At the late treaty of the Indian Springs, a good many hostiles, as usual, objected to it. If that party should attempt to breed a disturbance with the friendly Indians, we shall inform you for protection; and we hope you will protect us, in case the hostiles should intrude on us, as we look for protection from you, as we have been trying to gratify the wishes of our father, the President. We hope he loves us as his red children; and we hope you love us as friends of justice, as friends of good order and friends of harmony."

Three days after, they again addressed the Governor, and, amongst other things, said:

"OUR FATHER: At the treaty of Broken Arrow, the chiefs got jealous of McIntosh, and threatened to kill him; the charge against him was that he wanted to sell land to the commissioners of the United States. In 1824, a few chiefs met at a place called the Pole Cat Springs, and passed a law that if any person should sell or offer land for sale, guns and rope should be their end. This law was intended to prevent General McIntosh from selling land; but it was not agreeable to the laws of the nation. If it was intended to be the national law, it ought to have been read before the national chiefs, and let them determine it—not collect a few chiefs to make a law. Could an individual State pass a law to extend all over the United States, or one county make and enforce a law for the government of the whole State? The guns and rope are taken from the pattern of the Cherokees. Therefore we do not consider it a law of the nation to be enforced; it is merely law among themselves; but those who signed their names to the pattern of the Cherokees, determine to execute the law. This is the report from some of our friends. If they determine, we are ready to defend ourselves, and, with your assistance, they will find a great difference in numbers. Our characteristic disposition is to treat all mankind as friends, brothers and relations. We determine never to impose on any man, but treat all as friends."

It appears, by the Executive Journal of that date, that on the 19th of February, several of the Chiefs of the Creek nation, Gen. McIntosh among them, went to the Executive chamber to hold a "talk" with the Governor, the substance of which was that they had consented to give up their lands and move across the Mississippi—that they expected, before they left, to encounter difficulties and privations; notwithstanding which, they were willing to listen to the advice of their great father, and give up the lands; but, in doing this, offence had been given to some of their people; and, as there were bad white men among them, who were endeavoring to stir up their own people to do them harm; and, more especially, as the Agent was among their worst enemies, and they could expect no protection or support from him, they wanted to know whether they could be certain of protection from the government of the United States, and from that of Georgia, &c., &c.—that to this the Governor replied, stating the happiness he felt at their determination to remove, &c., &c.; that, with regard to protection against their own people who were hostile, or against the whites, he had no doubt the President would afford them all the protection their situation might require; that, as to the State of Georgia, they should, so far as depended on him, find protection at all times; and, so long as they conducted themselves well, the people of Georgia would be ready to support him in it, with all their hearts; for they had for a long time been the friends of Georgia in peace and war, and that they themselves had fought and bled for Georgia in the last war, and that the Georgians could not forget them, &c., &c. There was some further talk not important for insertion here—the foregoing being generally a substantial, and, for the most part, a literal, extract from the Journal referred to.

With commendable promptness, the Governor dispatched one of his Aids-de-camp, Col. Henry G. Lamar, to the Creek country, with the following message to the hostile Indians:

EXECUTIVE DEPARTMENT, GEORGIA,
Milledgeville, *26th Feb.*, 1825.

In consequence of the apprehensions expressed in a talk delivered by the friendly Chiefs of the Creek Nation, on the 19th instant, the written communication delivered at the same time, and another on the 21st, by Etome Tustenuggee, of the hostile intentions of the unfriendly party in said Nation, toward McIntosh and his friends, in consequence of the late treaty; and, in compliance with the promises given them, that every aid should be afforded them within the power of this government, it is thought proper to send a friendly talk to the Chiefs of Tookaubatchee and Kussetau, at the same time forewarning them of the danger to which they will expose themselves by any outrage committed on McIntosh, or any of the friendly Indians, in consequence of said treaty. Accordingly, Col. Henry G. Lamar is dispatched with a talk to said hostile Chiefs, in the following words, to wit:

To the Chiefs and Headmen of
Tookaubatchee and Kussetau:

I hear bad things of you. You threaten McIntosh and his people, because they listened to their father, the President, and ceded the lands to the Georgians. They acted like good and dutiful children. You opposed yourselves to the wishes of your great father, who was doing the best for the interest of his red people, and would not sign the treaty. But this you did, as I believe, under the influence of bad men, who pretended to be your friends, but who cared nothing about you. Now I tell you, take care and walk straight. McIntosh and his people are under my protection, as well as under the protection of the United States. If any harm is done by you, or any of your people, to McIntosh or his people, I will treat you in the same way as if you were to come into our white settlements and do the like. I will pursue you until I have full satisfaction. Do not let bad men persuade you that because you live in and near to Alabama, you will be safe. If you commit one act of hostility on this side the line, I will follow and punish you. But I hope there will be no occasion for this, and that you will take counsel of wise and good men, and so conduct yourselves for the future, as to receive the approbation and protection of your father, the President, and that I also may look upon you as friends and treat you accordingly. This message will be delivered to you by my Aid-de-camp, Col. Lamar.

G. M. TROUP,
Governor of Georgia.

In his instructions to Colonel Lamar, the Governor, amongst other things, said:

From the moment of the ratification, the territory will be considered as belonging to Georgia, in all respects, excepting merely the temporary occupancy of the Indians, and any act of disorder or violence committed there, will be treated as committed within the actual jurisdiction of the State, and, of course, the Indians committing it, pursued and punished wheresoever they may go.

You will meet them with friendly dispositions: say to them, in accordance with the spirit of the message which you carry, that it is the settled opinion of all the wise and good men of the United States, that the Indians, looking to nothing but their own interest, present and future, ought to move, without delay, beyond the Mississippi. They already know this to be the advice of their great father. They will soon know it to be the advice of his great council, the Congress. None but bad men, hostile to their true interests, will ever advise them to the contrary. You will take with you the published documents, showing the views of the President in relation to the conduct of both the Agent*

* In his report, of 8th January, to the War Department, written at Washington City, Col. Campbell, speaking of the failure of negotiations at Broken Arrow, attributed the failure to certain unfavorable influences which had been produced by (amongst others,) John Ross, a Cherokee Chief, and Walker, the sub-Agent of Indian Affairs These influences caused a meeting of a portion of the Creeks at Tookaubatchee, in May, and at Pole Cat Springs, in November, 1824. At the former, a resolution was passed to "follow the pattern of the Cherokees, and, on no account whatever, to consent to sell one foot of land, neither by exchange nor otherwise," and "this meeting was attended exclusively by Chiefs within the Alabama limits." Referring to the proceedings at these meetings, Col. Campbell said: "Of the existence of these proceedings, by which the question was prejudged, and the commission forestalled, we had no knowledge until we obtained it casually on our way to the treaty. Under these disadvantages the negotiation was commenced; and the journal of our proceedings, herewith furnished, will

and Cherokees at Broken Arrow, the indignation with which he viewed their conduct, and, of course, the indignation with which he will regard the conduct of the Indians hostile to the treaty, if they do not in future deport themselves as men deserving his love and friendship; and another paper, less authentic, but not altogether unofficial, taken from the National Journal, in which they will see that the Indians west of the Mississippi, without foreknowledge of the views or plans of the President, have adopted the same views, and are concerting the same measures for bringing all the Indians together on the west of the Mississippi; and that soon, very soon, they will all go; so that a red man will not be seen between the Mississippi and the lakes.

Pursuant to his instructions, Col. Lamar proceeded immediately to the Creek country. He visited the towns of Kussetau and Tookaubatchee, held a talk with the Indians, endeavored to compose the excited feelings of the discontented, &c., &c. On the 10th of March, he made a report to the Governor, but we can copy only the concluding part, as follows:

"My own opinion, which is partly conjectural, and in part formed from observation and conversations had with some of the Indians, is this—leave them to themselves—if they clearly understand what are the wishes of the President, they will conform to them. I speak of them collectively, as a people. They have no correct notions of our government and their relative connection with it. Their conclusion is, that the powers of the President are absolute, and that he has an unquestionable right to coerce obedience. But, independent of this notion of fear, the unlimited confidence reposed in the wisdom and virtue of the President,

serve to show, to some extent, the manner in which it was pursued. The Commissioners were dependent solely upon their own exertions. They derived no aid from the principal Agent, and encountered the perfidious opposition of his assistant." On the 13th January, Mr. Calhoun, the Secretary of War, writing to Col. Campbell, and referring to the conduct of the Agent, said: "It was not doubted by the Department but that he would zealously co-operate in effecting the object of the government in authorizing the treaty to be held. It appears, however, by the report, that the Agent neglected to inform you of the previous meetings and decision of the Creek Chiefs at Tookaubatchee and the Pole Cat Springs, which had so material a bearing on the negotiation; and that the Commissioners had to rely solely upon their own exertions, without aid from the Agent, who assumed a neutral position. It also appears, from the journal, that, in the opinion of the Commissioners, the Creek Indians have been misled by the Cherokees, and *others, whose duty it was to have instructed them better*. It is the desire of the President, before he makes any decision on the conduct of the Agent, to be put in full possession of all the facts and circumstances which may enable him to form a correct opinion as to his conduct and motives in withholding his co-operation," &c., &c.—ED.

is a sure guaranty of the successful accomplishment of his wishes. In order to destroy the effects of this influence, I discover that the belief has been imposed upon them, (at least to some extent,) that the Commissioners, being Georgians, were only subserving the interest and wishes of Georgia. There are a number of white men settled among them, who heretofore looked with pleasure on their prospects of enjoying the benefits of a permanent location, who have acquired their confidence by the connections they have formed, and I have no doubt that their influence is secretly exerted to excite discontent, and inculcate opinions adverse to the interest of Georgia and the policy of the General Government. There is another prevailing feeling among them. They indulge the belief, should they move beyond the Mississippi, that a perpetual warfare with the tribes inhabiting that country would be the inevitable consequence. You will discover in my talk to them, with the view to produce a complete reconciliation, I endeavored to refute that opinion. If the treaty is ratified, I have no doubt that all clamor will cease ; for, in proportion as they understand the wishes of the President, and the course of conduct our government adopts towards them, in the same degree will all other influence be diminished. Added to this, what has been done, was done, no doubt, with the view to prevent its ratification. The cause, therefore, which produced the excitement, will cease to exist after that desirable object is accomplished."

It is proper also to remark that Ho-poth-le-Yoholo and Little Prince, then the principal men of Tookaubatchee and Kussetau, both denied to Col. Lamar any hostility to M'Intosh and the other friendly Indians, for having signed the treaty.

But there were secret and malign influences at work, which it was not in the power of the Governor to counteract successfully. A week after penning his instructions to Col. Lamar, he received the following letter :

NEWNAN, 3d March, 1825.

Governor: I take the authority to inform you, since we left you we haven't got home in consequence of the hostiles. I met my friends at Flint River, Mr. Miller and A. Tustunnuggee, and they tell me that they run them off—threatened to kill them—cut their throats and set up their heads by the road for a show—they are determined to die on their own country, and they have appointed men to kill seven

Chiefs, Gen. McIntosh, myself, Joseph Marshall, Samuel Hawkins, James Island, Etome Tustunnuggee and Col. Miller. Since the treaty, the hostile party have been in council a second time at Broken Arrow, and are now at Tookaubatchee, holding a council—they have not broke up yet. We understand they have sent a memorial on to the President not to interfere with them or assist us—to let them settle it among themselves. No doubt they are determined to destroy us if they can. Myself and father parted at the Indian Springs, on our way home—since I heard the news, I have dispatched a runner to him, not to stay one moment at home, but to meet me at this place. Excuse my handwriting. This is not half I know, but the bearer of this is in a hurry.

I remain your son,

CHILLY MCINTOSH.

His Excellency G. M. Troup.

It will be remembered that the writer of the above, Chilly McIntosh, was the son of General William McIntosh, head Chief of the Cowetas, and that all the threatened Chiefs above named, belonged to the McIntosh or friendly party—several of them having signed the treaty. The Governor, in his reply, dated 5th March, said:

"Your letter of the 3d came safe to me this moment. I am sorry to hear that the hostiles continue to be such fools and madmen. They will soon be taught better. If they do not listen to my talks sent by Col. Lamar, I will send a military force to the line, to keep them in order and punish offenders. Col. Lamar left this for Kussetau and Tookaubatchee last Sunday, the 27th February. He must have arrived at the council before this. It is as I told you it would be; the hostiles have been set on by bad white men. I hope your father will keep out of their way until they are brought to their senses."

The following letter was written by Gen. McIntosh to the Governor:

CHATTAHOOCHEE, 29th March, 1825.

To His Excellency G. M. Troup:

Sir: I take the liberty of sending Samuel Hawkins to you, seeing in the newspapers your proclamation stating that the treaty was ratified by the President and Senate. We see in the papers, also, where Crowell had wrote to the

Department that Chiefs of the lowest grade had signed the treaty, and we see where he says there will be hostilities with us if the United States sign the treaty. We are not any ways in danger until he comes home and commences hostility, and urges it himself on us. If the treaty is ratified, if you can let Samuel Hawkins have two thousand dollars, or stand his security in the Bank to that amount, we will send men on now to look at the country to try to move away this fall; the money, if loaned to us, will be paid back as soon as the money comes on to pay the first payment of the treaty.

Any information that you can give him will be satisfactory to us.

Your dear friend, &c.,

WILLIAM MCINTOSH.

The same day, Governor Troup wrote to McIntosh, as follows:

EXECUTIVE DEPARTMENT,
Milledgeville, 29th March, 1825.

Dear General: You will have seen by my proclamation of the 21st inst., that I have resolved, in fulfilment of the stipulations of the treaty, to maintain inviolate all your rights reserved by it, so that you suffer no detriment or loss by the trespasses or intrusions of the whites as long as you continue to occupy the country.

It is important that the territory acquired by the late treaty should be organized as speedily as possible, consistently with the provisions of that instrument; and, not doubting that your assent will be given to the survey of it before your removal, I have dispatched a messenger to you, that your resolution may be communicated to me without delay. It is not presumed that the least inconvenience can result to you from this measure. Besides my own determination to cause the rights of the Indians to be respected in their persons and property at all times, there will be a future and ample security and protection in the selection of the officers who shall be charged with the duty of running the lines, who shall be responsible, not only that no depredations are committed by themselves, but that none shall be committed by others, without their giving prompt notice to the lawful authorities, so that the offenders may be brought to justice.

You will understand that there is no intention on my part to hurry your departure; the period of this will be left to your considerations of interest and convenience under the treaty; but as the survey is a work of time, this time can be saved to us; so that, having completed it, nothing will remain but to occupy and settle the country after you shall have left it. I wish you by all means to give me your final answer by this express, that I may know what measures it will become my duty to adopt.

Your friend,

Gen. William McIntosh, G. M. TROUP.
Creek Nation.

The following is the reply to McIntosh's letter:

EXECUTIVE DEPARTMENT,
Milledgeville, 4th April, 1825.

Dear General: I have received your letter of the 29th ult., by Col. Hawkins. There will be no danger of any hostility in consequence of the ratification of the treaty. You will find everything going on peaceably and quietly. If bad white men intermeddle to stir up strifes and excite bad passions among the Indians, I will have them punished. The President will do the same. My agent has reported that the Indians opposed to the treaty are quite friendly; that they think of no mischief; that they love you, and will do whatever their father, the President, advises. The Senate ratified the treaty, without any difficulty, although the Agent was opposed to it. I write, this morning, to the United States Commissioners, to furnish you with the necessary funds to enable your Commissioners to explore the country west of the Mississippi, so that you may make your arrangements to move during the next fall. As soon as I hear from them, you shall know it. I wish you to inform me, as early as possible, of your resolution about the running and survey of the country, as mentioned in my letter by express.

You will have seen, by my proclamation, that I have determined the Indians shall suffer no loss or injury from our white people, if I can help it. It is intended to guard them against those people whom they will themselves consider as trespassers and intruders; and not to prevent white people from going into the Nation, with honest intentions, to make purchase of stock or property of any kind which you can lawfully dispose of; all such persons will be suffered to pass and repass without molestation. We will endeavor, too, to appoint good and honest men for our Surveyors, so that they will do no harm themselves, and suffer none done to the Indians.

Your friend,

Gen. William McIntosh, G. M. TROUP.
Creek Nation.

McIntosh wrote again, on the 6th, as follows:

ACORN BLUFF, 6th April, 1825.

Governor Troup:

Dear Sir: I received your letter of the 29th March, by the hands of your messenger, which gave me pleasure to get. On the 10th of this month the Chiefs will be here, when I will lay your letter before them, after which I will inform you what we shall agree to without delay. When this meeting is held, if we agree to the running of the lands, it is my wish that the Surveyors should get their support from the red people.

I am, dear sir,
Yours with respect,
WILLIAM McINTOSH.

On the 9th, the Governor again wrote to McIntosh, sending an express, the next day, to learn the deliberations of the Council, and also to inform the General that the money asked as an advance for the exploration of the country west of the Mississippi, would be ready whenever sent for through an authorized agent, &c.

McIntosh replied, on the 12th of April, to the Governor's letters of 29th March and 4th April. After referring to the supposed friendly feelings of the Indians who opposed the treaty, and the danger to which the friendly party might be exposed, as well as the disposition of the Governor and the President to protect them, he said:

"I have been, however, at some loss in making up my mind, and must confess to you the embarrassment I have labored under. Ever since the President of the United States has had agents residing among us, we have universally considered it our duty to consult him on all important matters that relate to the General Government or the government of any particular State, considering him the legal and proper organ through whom all official correspondence should pass, in relation to our interests appertaining to the treaties made with our nation and the United States. Some differences existing between the present Agent of the

35

Creek nation and myself, and not having any confidence in his advice, I have determined to act according to the dictates of my best judgment, which results in the determination to agree to the request of your Excellency, in giving my consent, and, in behalf of the nation who signed the treaty, their consent that the land lately ceded to the United States, at the Indian Springs, may be run off and surveyed whenever you may, or the General Government, think proper to do so. If the general government of the United States have no objection, and the Agent of the Creek nation, with the party he influences, does not make any objection or opposition to running and surveying the land, myself and the Chiefs and Indians, who were in favor of the late treaty, do not object. We give our consent."

At the same time, McIntosh wrote to the Governor, sending a memorial of Chiefs to the Legislature, requesting that it be laid before the General Assembly, &c. It abounded in expressions of good will, and was called their "last and farewell address." Although too long for transcription, we cannot omit the following excerpts:

"The country which you now possess, and that which we now remain on, was by the Great Spirit originally given to his red children. Our brothers, the white men, visited us when we were like the trees of the forest. Our forefathers smoked the pipe of peace and friendship with the forefathers of the white man, and when the white man said, we wish to live with the red man and inhabit the same country, we received their presents, and said, welcome; we will give you land for yourselves and for your children. We took the white man by the hand, and held fast to it. We became neighbors, and the children of the white man grew up, and the children of the red man grew up in the same country, and we were brothers. The white men became numerous as the trees of the forest, and the red men became like the buffalo. *Friends and Brothers:* You are like the mighty storm; we are like the tender and bending tree; we must bow before you; you have torn us up by the roots, but still you are our brothers and friends. You have promised to replant us in a better soil, and to watch over us and nurse us. * * * The day is come when we surrender the country of our forefathers—land of our nativity; our homes, the places of our youthful diversions. We surrender it to our brothers and friends, and our hearts are glad that we are not forced to do so by our enemies. We go; our people will seek new lands; our hearts remain with you."

The memorial was signed by McIntosh and fifteen other Chiefs.

The Governor replied as follows:

EXECUTIVE DEPARTMENT,
Milledgeville, 16*th April*, 1825.

Dear General: Your two letters, of the 12th instant, have just been received, by which it is made known to me, that, in council, you have given your consent to the survey of the lands. Your memorial to the Legislature will be presented, according to your request, and the notice you wish published, in relation to purchases of property of any kind, improvements, &c., &c., will, in the same words as you have written, be printed in our next papers.

I hope that you will meet the Little Prince and council, in good friendship. I wish to see you all united in brotherly affection before you move, and am convinced the President desires the same.

Your friend, G. M. TROUP.
Gen. William McIntosh, Creek Nation.

In his letter of 12th April, from which we have already quoted, McIntosh had written to the Governor:

"I have this moment received notification from the Little Prince, inviting me and the chiefs in this quarter, to attend a meeting of the nation at Broken Arrow, on the 19th instant. My own health will not permit me, probably, to attend the meeting in person, but all of my Chiefs will go. I have determined, if my health permits, to accompany the delegation to the Western country, in our exploring tour, so soon as we receive the money which we desired you to obtain for us through the Commissioners."

The following correspondence explains itself:

MILLEDGEVILLE, 18th April, 1825.

Dear General: In one of your late letters, you say something about the consent of the United States, or if the agent and the hostiles do not make opposition. Pray, explain to me your meaning. We have nothing to do with the United States, or the agent, or the hostiles, in this matter; all we want is the consent of the friendly Indians who made the treaty. If we wanted the consent of the United States, we could ask it.

Your friend, G. M. TROUP.
Gen. William McIntosh, Creek Nation.

CREEK NATION, 25th April, 1825.

Dear Sir: I received your Excellency's request, yesterday, dated the 18th inst., and hereby state to you that my only meaning was not to act contrary to stipulations made between our nation and the United States government; and we do hereby, absolutely, freely and fully, give our consent to the State of Georgia, to have the boundary belonging to said State surveyed at any time the Legislature of Georgia may think proper, which was ceded at the late treaty of the Indian Springs.

Signed in behalf of the Nation, and by the consent of the Chiefs of the same.

I have the honor to be, sir, with great esteem,

Yours respectfully,

WILLIAM McINTOSH.

His Excellency Geo. M. Troup.

The writing of this letter was one of the last acts of McIntosh. On the night of the 29th or the morning of the 30th of April, he was cruelly murdered, at his own house on the Chattahoochee, by a band of the hostile Indians. Tome (or Etome) Tustunnuggee, an old chief of Coweta, shared the same fate; and Samuel Hawkins, son-in-law of McIntosh, perished some hours later. Chilly McIntosh escaped, by jumping through a window, and fled, with the news, to the Governor. Gen. Ware wrote, as follows, to Gov. Troup:

LINE CREEK, Fayette County, Ga.,
May 1st, 1825.

Gov. Troup: The information you have no doubt received by Chilly McIntosh and other Indians, will be confirmed by the following relation of the circumstances attending the horrid transaction on the Chattahoochee and Tallapoosa, in the Creek nation. On the morning of the 30th April, several neighbors of mine who lodged on the bank of the Chattahoochee, this side of McIntosh's, about day-break heard the war-whoop, and they suppose from two to four hundred guns were fired—the houses were on fire when they set off. An intelligent Indian, Col. Miller, who has fled to my house, together with about 150 others, states that he supposes there are upwards of 400 warriors of the hostile party embodied on the Chattahoochee, at McIntosh's, feasting on all the cattle they can find, hogs, &c.,

belonging to the friendly party—states, also, that they have taken McIntosh's negroes and all other property they can find—they, he states, intend marching toward the settlement of the whites in three days. In this I am a little incredulous; though, as far as the resources of our country will afford, I will be prepared. Major Finley Stewart is collecting some volunteers to go out and reconnoitre the country; he will set off as soon as practicable. He, Col. Miller, supposes, including numbers long cloaked under the garb of friendship, who, since the death of McIntosh, have joined the hostile party, that the hostile party in the nation largely exceeds 4000 warriors, and that the friendly party amounts now to only 500. They implore protection —they need it—they are constantly coming in—say the road is covered with others.

Yours respectfully, ALEXANDER WARE.

Some provision ought to be made to supply those refugees with food. A. W.

Governor Troup addressed the following letter to the President:

EXECUTIVE DEPARTMENT,
Milledgeville, *3d May*, 1825.

SIR: Yesterday, Chilly McIntosh, son of the General, and bearer of this, came with other Chiefs to announce the death of his father. On the night of the 29th ult., whilst reposing in his bed, the savages hostile to the treaty, in great numbers beset and fired his house, and this chieftain, whose virtues would have honored any country, perished by the flames or tomahawk. The old Chief of Coweta, who was pursued with the same vengeance,* and for the same objects, perished with him. The crime of McIntosh and Tustunnuggee is to be sought in the wise and magnanimous conduct which, at the Indian Springs, produced the treaty of the 12th of February, and which, in making a concession of their whole country, satisfied the just claims of Georgia, reconciled the State to the Federal Government, and made happy, at least in prospect, the condition of the Creeks. When, by the last of his generous actions, he had

* Those who desire to see a detailed statement of these murders, are referred to the letter of Col. A. J. Pickett, of Alabama, in White's Historical Collections, pp. 170, 171, 172, and 173. It seems that the body of McIntosh was not burned, but that his scalp, "which was suspended upon a pole in the public square of Ocfuskee, (a Creek Town on the Tallapoosa River,) was the spectacle of old and young, who danced around it, with shouts of joy"; and that Tustunnuggee and Hawkins were also scalped, and their scalps carried to the Tallapoosa.—ED.

given his consent, in union with his Council, to the survey and appropriation of the country, only to gratify the wishes of the Georgians, and was on the eve of departure to explore the new home, where the future fortunes of all were to abide, he met the stroke of the assassin, and the bravest of his race fell by the hands of the most treacherous and cowardly. The guilty authors of this massacre it will be for you to detect and punish. I have done my duty.

You will soon read, in my official correspondence with your government, the Indians and the Commissioners, the beginning, the progress, and the end of this frightful tragedy, in which the catastrophe was foreseen, of which, ever and anon, the government of the United States was distinctly forewarned, which by the breath of its nostrils might have been averted, but which was not averted. In despite of every thing attempted to the contrary, I had before succeeded in maintaining peace. Even now, at the very moment I write, a message, of which you have a copy, is dispatched to the surviving Chiefs to forbear hostility. I believe the advice will be taken as an order; but, it is my duty to inform you, that to keep this peace longer than I can hear from you, will be impossible to any efforts of yours or mine, unless the most ample satisfaction and atonement shall be made promptly for the death of McIntosh and his friend.* The Legislature will convene in a few days, and on this account I have deferred any measures, either of retaliation or protection,

With great respect and consideration,

G. M. TROUP.

The President of the United States,
Washington City.

The following is the "Message to the surviving Chiefs," referred to in the preceding letter:

EXECUTIVE DEPARTMENT,
Milledgeville, 3d *May*, 1825.

Friend: I heard with sorrow, yesterday, of the death of our common friend, McIntosh. All good hearts among the whites deplore it as much as you. Satisfaction will be demanded, and satisfaction shall be had—but we must not be hasty about it. We will be cool and deliberate in the

* It is apparent from this and other expressions in the letter, that the Governor had not then heard of the death of Hawkins—Chilly McIntosh having left before that took place, and even before the manner of McIntosh or Tustunnuggee's death was known, it being clear that neither of them died by "flames or tomahawk."—ED.

measures we take, and then we will be certain to be right. You be peaceable and quiet until you hear from me, in the same manner as if nothing had happened to McIntosh or Tustunnuggee; but depend on it, my revenge I will have —it will be such as we have reason to believe the Great Spirit would require—such as our Christ would not think too much, and yet so much that I trust all red and white men will be content with. Mind what I say to you until you hear from me.

G. M. TROUP.

Col. Joseph Marshall,
Creek Nation.

The following orders were promulged on the 5th:

HEAD QUARTERS, Milledgeville, 5th May, 1825.

ORDERS.

The Commander-in-Chief having received information of the existence among the Creeks of the most frightful anarchy and disorder, and of the recent massacre of General McIntosh and the old Chief of Coweta, within the actual limits of Georgia, has thought proper to adopt precautionary measures without delay, so that if the United States, bound, by the Constitution and the treaty, to repress and punish hostility among the Indians and maintain peace upon our borders, shall, by any means, fail in their duty in these respects, a competent force may be held in readiness to march at a moment's warning, either to repel invasion, suppress insurrection among the Indians within our own territory, or give protection to the friendly Creeks, and avenge the death of McIntosh, who, always a firm friend to Georgia, fell a sacrifice in her cause:

Ordered, That Major-General Wimberly, Major-General Shorter, and Major-General Miller, of the 5th, 6th and 7th Divisions, forthwith proceed to take the necessary measures to hold in readiness their respective Divisions, to march at a moment's warning, either by detachments or otherwise, as they may be commanded by authority of the Legislature, or of the Commander-in-Chief.

By the Commander-in-Chief:

SEABORN JONES,
Aid-de-Camp.

In his orders, of same date, to each of the above named Generals, he said:

In carrying into effect the enclosed General Orders, you

will keep a watchful eye to the frontier of our white settlements, so that you may be able, without communicating with me, to repress, on its first occurrence, any commotion which may happen there in consequence of the state of things prevailing in the nation. These infuriated and misguided people may have the temerity, before the General Government can interpose, to pursue the Indians within our organized limits. You will, therefore, in the spirit of these instructions, give your orders corresponding with them to your most confidential officers resident near the frontiers, who, on any sudden emergency of this character, may, without consulting you, proceed instantly to their execution. A copy of General Ware's letter, received after my general orders were issued, will assure you of the nature and extent of the danger to be apprehended, and of the promptitude with which they are to be carried into effect.

To Brigadier-General Ware he wrote, as follows, on the same day:

I have this moment received your letter, and at the very time when I had issued orders to Major-Generals Shorter and Wimberly, with corresponding instructions to meet the very exigencies which, from your information, you have reason to anticipate. They will have the contents of your letter communicated to them, that their orders may be dispatched with the least possible delay. I wish you to take measures, and the best you can, for the comfortable maintenance of our unhappy friends, whilst they seek refuge among us and are protected by our arms. Additional orders will be immediately given to Major-General Miller to hold his Division in readiness. The expense of supporting the Indians will be incurred by the State, in the first instance, and reimbursed to her from the first instalment payable to them by the United States. You will, therefore, hold me responsible for any contract you may make on this account, whilst, at the same time, I ask the favor of you to cause them to be made on the best possible terms.

I sincerely trust, if these infuriated monsters shall have the temerity to set foot within our settled limits, you may have the opportunity to give them the bayonet freely, the instrument which they most dread, and which is most appropriate to the occasion.

The same day he wrote to the War Department, as follows:

EXECUTIVE DEPARTMENT,
Milledgeville, 5th May, 1825.

Sir: I lose no time in communicating, for the information of the President, a copy of a letter received this morning from Brigadier General Ware, commanding the second brigade of the 5th division of the militia of this State, and to advise you that measures have been adopted for the adequate protection of the frontiers, and for the safety of the friendly Indians seeking refuge within our limits, until the authority of the United States can be effectually interposed for these purposes; and that, therefore, the expenses incurred in the mean time will be considered chargeable to the United States. In due time the measures referred to will be laid before you *in extenso*.

With great consideration and respect,

The Secretary of War. G. M. TROUP.

Col. Hawkins, the interpreter, and friend of McIntosh, has shared his fate.

Brigadier-General Charles J. McDonald having written the Governor a letter, dated 6th May, referring to the "disturbances among the Creek Indians," and especially the supposed danger to Col. Crowell, the Agent, from the alleged hostility to him of "those friendly and those hostile to the treaty," the Governor wrote him as follows, on 7th May:

"Your letter of the 6th instant, by express, is this moment received. I am happy to learn from him that he bore to you orders from Gen. Wimberly, in consequence of my general orders to him. You are, therefore, already on your guard, and you will not hesitate a moment to take the necessary measures, first to make safe the frontier, and then to give to the Agent any protection which, according to the evidence before you, his safety shall demand; and of which, from your proximate situation to him, you will be the exclusive judge. I hope that no harm has befallen him; and, if not, you may assure him that any force which may be necessary to reduce to order and obedience any militant tribes of the Creeks within our limits, shall be furnished promptly, under the command of a trusty officer, who will be charged with full power to act efficiently, under any exigencies that may arise.

I thank you for the promptitude with which you have communicated this new information—at the same time I indulge hope that the cause of alarm has been exaggerated. It is scarcely to be believed that the Agent, from whom nothing has been heard, well knowing the contentions which agitate the country, and the imminent perils which surround him, should not have dispatched runners to make known to this government, officially, and without delay, the circumstances which your letter discloses upon the authority of a respectable traveler. The express which brought it, carries the answer."

The Governor's surmises were right in regard to the "cause of alarm." He therefore, on the 10th of May wrote to Gen. McDonald, and, after referring to a letter from the third party, said:

"You will immediately, therefore, on the receipt hereof, arrest the progress of any measures you may have devised for the security of the Agent, and return to the position in which you found yourself before you received my last instructions. You will, however, under the general order, received through Major-General Wimberly, still continue to hold your brigade in readiness to march to any point of the frontier, at short notice, lest we may be deceived by appearances, and surprised."

In his letter of 9th May, to the Secretary of War, forwarding a copy of Gen. McDonald's letter and his reply, the Governor said:

"The friendly Indians continue to desert their homes, and seek protection within our limits. Our arms are open to receive them at all points, and the necessary measures taken for their maintenance; the expense of which will devolve on the United States, or the Indians; it is hoped, on the former."

In a postscript, he added: "Up to this time not a word has been received from the Agent."

We have been thus minute in details regarding the sudden emergency which arose, not only for the purpose of exhibiting the patriotic promptness of Gov. Troup on an occasion of great interest to the country, but also to explain the sequel of a controversy in which it is proper that the course of the Governor, especially towards the Indian Agent, may be fully borne out by the record. That unjust suspicions rested upon this Agent, in regard to some matters, may be conceded; but it is also believed that an impartial survey of the whole ground would lead to the irresistible conclusion that he was not the man for the station, and that, in compliance with the request of the Governor, his commission should have been revoked.

The murder of McIntosh and his friends, was made the subject of a special presentment by the Grand Jury of the U. S. Sixth Circuit Court at Milledgeville, May term, 1825; but we have not space for extracts from it.

It would be useless to attempt a notice of all the proceedings, official and unofficial, which grew out of the excitement in the Indian country. The messages of Gov. Troup and the official letters to and from him, on this subject, would fill a considerable volume; and it shall be our duty, in succeeding pages, to make such extracts from them as will illustrate his history in respect to this Indian controversy.

The following tribute to McIntosh and his friends, taken from an article (in White's Statistics of Georgia, pp. 555, 556,) from the pen of the late Hon. Joseph W. Jackson, deserves a place here:

"This brave warrior and the other treaty-making Indians had borne arms for the United States; those opposed to the treaty had been hostile in the war with Great Britain in 1812, '13, '14 and '15. So faithful had he been to us, that British blandishments had failed to affect his attachments; and, as a just reward for his fidelity and bravery, a brigadier-general's commission had, in that war, been sent to him from Washington. Again, in 1817 and 1818, he served under Gen. Andrew Jackson, against the Indians of Florida. The Indians friendly to the treaty were the same who had made previous cessions, against their power to make which no word had been uttered. They were the proprietors and occupants of the ceded lands, and in battle had conquered, in times past, the recusant Indians: those opposed were inhabitants of the interior country, altogether in Alabama, and little concerned with the question. But a few years before, General Jackson had treated the latter as a conquered people, and had prescribed to them their bounds."

On the 18th of May, a committee of the chiefs and headmen of the friendly Creeks addressed a communication to

Gov. Troup, enclosing an address, which they desired him to publish, the principal object of which seems to have been a denial of certain statements said to have been made by the Agent, in a letter published in a Macon paper, one of which was, "that the party of Indians friendly to Gen. McIntosh had threatened his life." The address further said: "We also see, in the same paper, information derived from the Agency, that the killing of McIntosh, Tome Tustunnuggee, and the two Hawkins, was not intended as hostilities against the whites; that it was only a fulfilment of their own laws, and a law which Gen. McIntosh himself had signed, and declared in the square at Broken Arrow, during the late treaty at that place. This law was, that if any Indian Chief should sign a treaty of any lands to the whites, that he should certainly suffer death. This statement is positively false; and it is only made use of as a pretext for the cruel murders which have been committed."

The Governor replied as follows:

EXECUTIVE DEPARTMENT,
Milledgeville, 21*st May*, 1825.

My Friends: I have this moment received your letter, with the paper which it enclosed, and will, as you request, cause them to be published in the next papers. I hope now that the worst is over. 'T is true that McIntosh and his friends, who have been so cruelly murdered, cannot be restored to life—but the Great Spirit, who is also good and merciful, will look down upon your sufferings with pity and compassion—he will wipe the tears from your eyes, and soften the hearts of even your enemies among the whites—so that, if your great father should turn his ear from your complaints, or shall fail to punish the white men, who in his name have disturbed your peace, and brought the heaviest afflictions upon you, he will have to answer for it, both to his white children and the Great Spirit. It cannot be doubted, therefore, that all will yet be right. In the mean time, continue to do as I have advised you, and until you hear from me. My officers everywhere are ordered to take care of you and make you comfortable. As soon as Chilly returns, you shall know it.

Your friend,
G. M. TROUP.

The Chiefs and Headmen of
the Friendly Creeks.

[1825.] Independently of their complicity with the hostile Creeks, the Cherokees were again disposed to give trouble on their own account. On 24th March, Mr. Forsyth wrote a letter to the Governor, enclosing the copy of the letter which the former had "written to the Secretary of War since the adjournment of Congress, on the subject of the execution of the recent treaty with the Creek Indians, and the formation of a treaty with the Cherokees," &c., with the Secretary's answer and several papers received with it. In his letter to the Secretary, dated 9th March, Mr. Forsyth urged the removal of the Creeks without unnecessary delay; and, in regard to the Agent, he said: "The conduct of the Creek Agent, who has spared no pains to prevent the formation and ratification of the treaty, justifies an apprehension that he will not fail to obstruct, as far as is in his power, the accomplishment of the wishes of the State. Under this conviction, a request that the conduct of the Agent may be watched, and that no confidence shall be reposed in him that can be consistently withheld, is dictated by the interests of Georgia, the wishes of the Creek tribe, and the honor of the General Government." Referring to the Cherokees, he said, after a brief but interesting examination of their relations to Georgia, "my own opinion is, that the President may, without injustice to the Indians, without violating either principle or usage, cause a purchase to be made of the Cherokees residing in Georgia, of the lands lying in Georgia;" and he concluded with expressing "the hope that a new effort with the Cherokees will have as fortunate a termination as the recent effort with the Creeks."

Mr. Barbour, the new Secretary of War, replied, on 23d March. He said, after acknowledging the receipt of Mr. Forsyth's letter, &c.:

"The treaty of the Indian Springs having been ratified, will be carried into effect; measures having been already taken in conformity to its provisions. Upon the second subject referred to in yours, I have the honor to state, in reply, that the President, as well from inclination as a sense of duty, is disposed to carry into effect the conditions of the compact of Georgia, whenever that can be done consistently with its provisions. In this spirit, and in conformity to your suggestion, a letter was addressed from the Department to the delegation of the Cherokees in this place, a copy of which, marked A, is herewith enclosed; also, a copy of their answer, marked B, to which is added a copy of a communication, marked C, addressed by the Cherokee chiefs to the President. You will readily perceive, from this correspondence, the determined opposition of the Cherokees at this time to the cession of their lands. I am directed by the President to state, that he entirely accords in the policy recommended by Mr. Monroe to Congress, at their last session, on the subject of the general removal of the Indians to the west of the Mississippi—a policy believed to be alike advantageous to the citizens of the United States, in their neighborhood, and the Indians themselves. This object, as far as it lies within the sphere of his power, will be promoted, and on every suitable occasion its beneficent effects will be particularly inculcated on the Cherokee nation."

It is not important to refer specially to the documents accompanying the letter. Ross, Lowrey and Hicks, "the delegation of the Cherokees," declared their sentiments in regard to a cesssion of lands to be the same as those formerly expressed to Mr. Calhoun, and that they were "unchangeable;" and, in an insolent letter to the President, hoped that measures might be "adopted by the United States and the State of Georgia, so as to close their compact without *teasing* the Cherokees any more for the lands."

The following is the Governor's reply, which, although addressed to Mr. Forsyth, was, as will be seen, intended for the Secretary of War:

EXECUTIVE DEPARTMENT, GEORGIA,
Milledgeville, 6th April, 1825.

Sir: Your letter, of the 24th ult., covering a correspondence between yourself and the Secretary of War, and other papers connected with the fulfilment of the stipulations of the Articles of Agreement and Cession, was received yesterday. Accept my thanks for your unremitted attention to the interest of the State. They are due, from the people, to you and the rest of the delegation, for your generous and patriotic devotion to their rights, and for the firmness and dignity with which, on every occasion, you have supported them. On the opening of a new administration of the General Government, soon after one important concession had been made to our just demands, it is scarcely necessary to inform you how eagerly I sought repose from the painful altercation which it had been my imperious duty to wage with the constituted authorities of the Union, and with how much of hope and anxiety I looked forward to the future, trusting that, in better and improved relations, we would find a kindly and conciliatory spirit succeeded to troubled feelings; the sense of wrong on either side consigned to forgetfulness; and the claims of Georgia recognized in all the extent which reason, justice and good faith would warrant. I trust that for these, more has not been asked—that less will not be received.

It cannot be dissembled, however, that in the answer given by the Secretary of War to your communication of the 9th ult., presupposing the best disposition to do right, a course of policy is indicated which must infallibly terminate in wrong. It is of kindred spirit with that, which, for a time, kept us in abeyance with the Creeks, and held the State suspended between the most fearful alternatives. On the 12th of March, the delegation of Cherokees at Washington, laid before the President their customary annual protest against a cession of lands on any terms, now or hereafter. On the same day, they are asked, by order of the Secretary of War, if they will sell lands; they answer, no, and this answer is echoed by the Secretary of War to you. I hope it is not considered, as it purports to be, *final*. Should the proposition be renewed, another and very different character must be given to it. The Cherokees must be told, in plain language, that the lands they occupy belong to Georgia; that sooner or later the Georgians must have them; that every day, nay, every hour, of postponement of the rights of Georgia, makes the more strongly for Georgia, and against both the United States and the Cherokees. Why conceal from this misguided race the destiny which is *fixed* and *unchangeable?* Why conceal from them the fact that every advance in the improvement of the country is to enure to the benefit of Georgia; that every fixture will pass with the soil into our hands, sooner or later, for which the United States must pay an equivalent or not, to the Indians, according to their discretion? The United States are bound, in justice to themselves, instantly to arrest the progress of improvement in the Cherokee country; it is the reason constantly assigned by the Cherokees for their refusal to abandon the country. The force of the argument, therefore, if good now, increases with the progress of improvement; the progress of improvement will be accelerated by the irresistible force of the argument. Thus, by a double ratio of geometrical progression, known only to the logicians of modern times, Georgia will find herself in a predicament, in which, whatever may have been the aggravation of her wrongs, she never before stood—disseized of both the argument and the lands. Why not, therefore, in common honesty and plain dealing, say to the Indians, remove now, or stay the hand of improvement forever; now we will give you the full value of improvement; hereafter we will give nothing, because we cannot afford to pay for improvements from which no benefit will result to us, which will belong to the Georgians, and which you were forewarned, in good time, not to make? Let them say, now is the appointed time; we offer you acre for acre, and we change your tenancy at will into a fee simple, which will descend to your posterity forever. If you accept, well and good; if you refuse, we are not bound to make you the same offer again. You were once without a country;* you sought refuge among the Creeks; they received you with open arms, and gave you the lands you now occupy; take care that you are not without a country again—you may find no more Creeks—no more lands.

Is it to be conceived that such an argument would be wasted on the Cherokees? What motive would be left them to continue in a state so precarious, when, every incentive to human industry being destroyed, the barn, the dwelling, the out-houses, the fencing, falling into decay and ruin, the wretched Indian scatters upon an impoverished and exhausted soil the seed from which it is even doubtful if he is permitted by the impatient white man to reap the scanty harvest?

Is it forbidden to speak the language of truth and frankness? It may be that all will avail nothing. If all should, it will be because the Cherokees distrust the sincerity of the United States. That they have reason for distrust, even

* Having doubts as to the reference in this part of Gov. Troup's letter, the Editor applied to Gov. Gilmer, who, in a note dated 27th Feb., 1859, says: "I suppose that the Cherokees had occupied, for an unknown time, the territory which they possessed in the upper parts of North Carolina, South Carolina and Georgia, when they became known to the Colonists," &c. And again: "Gov. Troup's expression, which you quote, refers, I suppose, to that part of the Cherokee territory which had, at one time, been occupied by the Creeks."—ED.

in the conduct of the United States towards themselves, is undoubted. When they were willing to cede lands, the United States would not take them. In the conduct of the United States towards the Creeks, they think they see abundant proof of the lukewarmness and indifference of the General Government in carrying into practical effect, so far as concerns Georgia, the plans which they devised for the removal of the Indians. It is of no consequence that the Indians are deceived by appearances—the appearances would deceive any body. They see the Agent for the Creeks, well knowing the officially expressed will of the Government, opposing himself to that will, holding councils of the Indians for the very purpose of anticipating and forestalling the Commissioners of the United States, by inconsiderate and violent resolves, the same as those of the Cherokees themselves. When the treaty is holden at Broken Arrow, the Cherokees are present, by their emissaries, under the eye of the Agent, busied to defeat, by the most wily machinations and contrivances, the objects of the treaty. They witness the failure of the treaty, and by these means. Is such a case explicable before the Indians? —the servant setting at naught the will of the master, and the master countenancing the servant in defying that will: the government itself, when asked for the resolution of these mysterious things, resolves them into a misconception of duty. On the renewal of the treaty at the Indian Springs, the like scenes are presented both to whites and Indians—the Agent professedly aiding the Commissioners, secretly undermining them, dismissing in the dead of night the Chiefs who had agreed to sign the treaty; protesting the treaty, after having affixed his own signature to it as a witness, on the ground that these very same Chiefs did not subscribe to it; announcing to his government that the treaty was in direct violation of its own instructions; insinuating very strongly that improper means had been adopted to procure it, and denouncing the hostility of the Indians in the event of its ratification.

The poor Cherokees knew, as well as the most enlightened member of the Cabinet, that if a foreign minister of the first grade had dared the one-half of this, he would have been dismissed with disgrace. Yet the Agent, opposing himself to his government, as it would seem, certainly opposing himself to the Commissioners appointed by that government, passing on to Washington for the avowed purpose of preventing the ratification of the treaty, meets a cordial greeting of his employers there, and when the President, discrediting every word of the Agent, had submitted the treaty to the Senate—when the Senate, in like manner, trusting nothing to the Agent, and reposing confidence in the declarations of the Commissioners, had ratified it, he is permitted to depart for his Agency, if not with new demonstrations of affection, without, so far as I know, the slightest reprehension or blame; and, what is worse than all, after having placed himself at the head of a party adverse to that which is now dominant, and which had recently ceded the country to us, he is appointed the guardian of the whole, to conduct to their new and distant home this hapless race; to command their destinies through untried and checkered scenes, and to make his distance from the controlling power an absolute security against all scrutiny and responsibility. The only apology attempted by the Agent for any allegation of misconduct or aberration from duty, in these respects, has been—'t was not I, 't was the sub-Agent—'t was not I, 't was the Interpreter. The United States might possibly be the voluntary dupe of such shallow pretences; certainly not the Cherokees or the Georgians. Ask the Commissioners, if, but for the interference of the Agent, there would have been serious difficulty at Broken Arrow. Ask them, if, at the Indian Springs, an almost unanimous concurrence of the Chiefs might not have been commanded, but for the counterplots and underworkings of the Agent. Ask any member of the cabinet, notwithstanding the farrago of resolves and protestations to the contrary, if he may not command a treaty, on a given day, upon just and reasonable terms, for a cession of all the lands claimed by the Cherokees.

Be pleased to present a copy of this note to the Secretary of War. Upon the general subject, everything has been heretofore said which it was proper or becoming to say; and I had resolved not to resume it, unless invited on the part of the Federal Government, or commanded by the Legislature of the State. The more recent events may not have been portrayed, before the present Cabinet, in the same light in which you and myself cannot fail to regard them. The gentlemen who have recently* come into it, I know person-

* The new members then recently appointed by Mr. Adams to places in his Cabinet, were Henry Clay, Secretary of State, Richard Rush, Secretary of the Treasury, and James Barbour, Secretary of War. Mr. Southard and Mr. Wirt, the other members of the Cabinet, had been appointed Secretary of the Navy and Attorney-General, respectively, by President Monroe, and were continued in office by President Adams. Hon. John McLean, also appointed under the previous administration, was continued as Post-Master-General; but that officer was not then one of the Cabinet.—ED.

ally, and will be very much deceived if they are not deserving our highest confidence, as intelligent, upright and patriotic men. If they understand this matter correctly, they will see that it is not a question about some five or six millions of acres of land; it is one of principle and of character, connected with the honor of the government, and therefore above all price.

The people of the United States, content with their political institutions, ask nothing of their rulers but purity in the administration of their affairs—disinterestedness, singleness of purpose, for the public weal, sincerity and plain dealing on the part of all the functionaries, from the highest to the lowest, fidelity to every trust, and strict accountability in the fulfilment of every duty, to the exclusion of selfishness, intrigues, tricks, and devices of low cunning, to gratify party passions and subserve sordid interests, hucksterings and barterings, and all the rest, which they will cheerfully leave to the mountebanks and jugglers to whom they appropriately belong.

With great consideration and respect,

G. M. TROUP.

The Hon. John Forsyth,
Washington City.

It is time, now, to turn from scenes of agitation and strife, to contemplate, for a moment, one of a different sort—a holiday scene—a pageant never to be forgotten in the history of Georgia or of the Union; we mean the visit and welcome of the great and good La Fayette to our shores. Returning, after a period of nearly half a century, to the country which he had largely contributed by his valor to rescue from the grasp of oppression, and to set up and establish as an independent nation, he was everywhere received with acclamations, amidst the booming of cannon and the most lively demonstrations of joy. Slowly pursuing his journey through the North, he turned his face toward the plains and cities of the South, and, on the 19th day of March, 1825, reached Savannah and stood upon the soil of Georgia. Pursuant to a joint resolution of the General Assembly, Governor Troup was there to welcome him as the guest of the State. As the General reached the top of the bluff at the eastern end of the city, he was welcomed by the Governor in the following eloquent strains:

Welcome, La Fayette!

General: 'T is little more than ninety years since the Founder of this State first set foot upon the bank on which you stand. Now, four hundred thousand people open their arms to receive you. Thanks to a kind Providence, it called you to the standard of Liberty in the helplessness of our early revolution—it has preserved you, that, in your latter days, the glory of a great empire might be reflected back upon you, amid the acclamations of millions.

The scenes which are to come, will be, for you, comparatively tranquil and placid—there will be no more of dungeons—no more of frowns of tyrants. Oh, sir, what a consolation for a man, who has passed through such seas of trouble, that the million of bayonets which guard the blessings we enjoy, stand between you and them!

But, enough—welcome, General! welcome—thrice welcome to the State of Georgia!

During his stay in Savannah, Governor Troup joined in the festivities of the occasion, and reviewed the squadron of cavalry.

He was also selected to deliver to the Colonel of the first Regiment, a stand of colors wrought for it by the lady of the Brigadier-General. The following was the address, delivered in presence of General La Fayette, the military, and a vast concourse of citizens:

Colonel: I present to you, by command of Mrs. Harden, a Standard of Colors for the first Regiment, worked by her own hands. It is a fine offering from the fair to the brave, in the presence of the veteran hero whom all hearts delight to honor. I am happy to be the instrument of unfurling them for the first time before the Regiment. They are consecrated by the fair donor and the presence of the Nation's guest. The hand which executed this beautiful work, has painted, in indelible colors, the emblems* which will guard them. Look on this picture, or on that—this repels dishonor, that animates to patriotism and to deeds of

* The principal emblems were, on one side, the arms of the State, the Constitutional arch being supported by three female figures representing "Wisdom, Justice and Moderation"; and, on the reverse, a bust of La Fayette, (in the old Continental uniform,) and which is being crowned with a laurel wreath by the American Eagle.—ED.

valor. They cannot be tarnished. Death before their inglorious surrender.*

[1825.] Pursuant to the Governor's proclamation, the General Assembly convened, in extra session, at Milledgeville, on Monday, the 23d day of May. There being a quorum of both Houses present, the Governor, on the same day, sent in the following message, which we cannot consent to abridge:

EXECUTIVE DEPARTMENT, Ga.,
Milledgeville, 23*d May*, 1825.

Fellow-Citizens of the Senate
and House of Representatives:

In calling you together, I have not been unmindful of the personal inconvenience and of the public expense which attend it. Consulting both, little will be submitted to your consideration disconnected with the main subject of your deliberation.

The recent acquisition of our vacant territory in the occupation of the Creeks, is that subject, and the survey and appropriation the objects, which will claim your attention. For the first, we are chiefly indebted to the Commissioners of the United States, Colonel Campbell and Major Meriwether. Too much praise cannot be given to these gentlemen, for the firmness and intrepidity with which they met the most formidable obstacles, and for the untiring zeal and patient labor, with which they conquered them. That of this praise there can be no waste or misapplication, you will read in the various documents and correspondence connected with it, and which are submitted. You will distinctly see that the principal difficulties which embarrassed them from beginning to end—which defeated the first treaty at Broken Arrow, and which were well nigh producing a rupture of the last, at the Indian Springs, proceeded from a quarter, the least of all to be expected—from officers in the pay and confidence of the Federal Government, who, instead of rendering to the Commissioners the most cordial co-operation, had organized an opposition, thereby exposing to suspicion their own Government, which, in justification of itself, was finally obliged

* Gov. Troup accompanied La Fayette to Augusta; and, at Milledgeville, entertained him, at the Executive Mansion, as the guest of the State. At the public dinner to La Fayette at the latter place, Gov. Troup gave the following toast: "A union of all hearts to honor the Nation's guest—a union of all heads for our country's good."—ED.

to avow that the perfidious plots and devices contrived by it, were unknown and unauthorized at Washington, at the same time the authors and contrivers were permitted to escape but with little observation, and certainly without merited punishment.

The Delegation in Congress, always faithful to their trust, have seconded, by active and incessant labor, the measures taken by this Government to support not only this important right, but all other rights and interests of the State; and, in the delicate and critical relations which these involved, have so deported themselves as to command the confidence of ourselves, and the respect of all who know them.

In disposing of the territory thus acquired, it is recommended to you to consult the will of your constituents, so far as that will can be distinctly ascertained. The lands belong to them in joint and several property, and none but themselves or their immediate representatives can rightfully dispose of them. Recognizing this as a fundamental principle, you have, in the exercise of a sound discretion, to look as well to ulterior and remote, as to immediate interests; interests which the people themselves cannot fail to appreciate and cherish, because they directly and equally concern each and every of them now, and their posterity hereafter. They are those of Public Education; of Internal Improvement; of relief from taxation, when taxation would be most required and most burthensome; the efficiency of a military system for defence, in providing arms and arsenals and all the materiel of war, for which no State ought to be dependent on another, and indeed every subject, which, in peace or war, can conduce to the safety or prosperity of the State, and requiring for its most useful and energetic application, the propulsive instrument, money. To dilate upon these topics, would be to consume your time uselessly. Your own wisdom will better supply the argument in support of each. Suffice it to say, that the accumulation of a fund for internal improvement on an extended scale, will, by its judicious application, so multiply your resources, and augment your income, as to enable you, eventually, to replace that fund; provide abundantly for all the wants of the State; dispense with taxation; and place you, in all these respects, on a footing with the most favored of your sister States, who, with less means, have accomplished more.

These are no idle speculations. The results are about to be realized in an illustrious instance, where a great member of the Confederacy has made herself greatest by perfecting what nature had roughly sketched, and thus fulfilling, by a no very complicated process, the highest duties to herself and to God. Our physical advantages are scarcely inferior; and, when it is believed to be quite practicable to divide with her the trade of the Western world, our temptations cannot be less. Pre-supposing, therefore, that the system hitherto adopted, for the settlement of our territory, will be pursued, I advise that the fee upon the grant be fixed at a rate which, whilst it makes the grant essentially a donation, and takes nothing from the pockets of the poorest of our citizens, but what will be paid without inconvenience or complaint, will, at the same time, bring something into the Treasury, in aid of the general fund appropriated to these objects. To this the proceeds of the fractions and of any reservations you may think proper to make, will importantly contribute.

Having advocated the present system from the beginning, there has been no reason to change any opinion formed of it. Men and the soil constitute the strength and wealth of nations: and the faster you plant the men, the sooner you can draw on both. No new country has been peopled faster than the territory acquired from time to time by Georgia; none more rapidly improved with the same established modes and customs of improvement. The speculations by which its principle has been vitiated, it is our bounden duty to discourage and repress; they defeat the very end of it, because, whilst you contemplate the advantage of the poor, the speculator preys upon the poor, and fattens on it.

Having foreseen that troubles might arise in the Indian country from the proceedings at Broken Arrow, and the Indian Springs, I sought an early opportunity, after the first indications of them, to dispatch my Aid-de-camp, Col. Lamar, into the nation, with a talk for that portion of the tribe which had menaced McIntosh and his friends with injury. This duty was performed entirely to my satisfaction, as you will perceive by the report of Col. Lamar. They professed the most friendly sentiments, both toward the whites and toward McIntosh, and gave assurances that they were meditating harm to neither. It is believed, from recent information, that they acted in perfect sincerity and good faith, and that the subsequent departure from it was the result of the active and malignant interference of white men. In my solicitude for the peace and happiness of this afflicted race, who were about to leave us to try new fortunes in a distant land, I issued the Proclamation of the

21st of March, which immediately followed the ratification of the treaty, and thus transcended the obligations enjoined by strict duty.

Having their own pledge that the peace should be kept among themselves, I wished to see no interruption of it by the Georgians; and, honorably for them, there has been none. I verily believe, that but for the insidious practices of evil-minded white men, the entire nation would have moved harmoniously across the Mississippi. The massacre of McIntosh and his friends is to be attributed to them alone. That chieftain, whose whole life had been devoted to Georgia as faithfully as to his own tribe, fell beneath the blows of the assassins, when reposing in the bosom of his family, upon the soil of Georgia; the soil which he had defended against a common enemy and against his own blood; which he had relinquished forever to our just demands; and which he had abandoned to our present use, only because we asked it. So foul a murder, perpetrated by a foreign force upon our territory, and within our jurisdiction, called aloud for vengeance. It was my settled purpose, having first consulted the Government at Washington, to have dealt out the full measure of that vengeance; so that honor, humanity, justice, being satisfied, whatever stain may have been left upon our soil, none should upon the page of our history.

But the Representatives of the people were about to assemble, who would bring with them feelings and sentiments corresponding to the occasion, tempered by a deliberate wisdom and a sound discretion; the task is cheerfully resigned to them, and whatever in the last resort they will—that will be done.

The consternation and alarm which immediately followed the death of McIntosh, rendered necessary measures of precaution, as well for the security of the frontier as for the protection of the friendly Indians, who, deserting their homes, fled, with their wives and children, before the hostile party, and presenting themselves destitute and defenceless at various points of the frontiers, asked bread of our humanity, and protection of our arms. The Quarter-Masters were directed to supply the one, and our Generals ordered to afford the other; and both at the expense of the United States, of which they had due notice. The orders and instructions to Major-Generals Wimberly, Miller and Shorter, with the correspondence, &c., are laid before you.

The United States Government has been again advised of the earnest desire of the Government of Georgia, that the line between this State and the State of Alabama should be run and marked. The United States answer to this last request, that it is a concern of the two States exclusively, in which the United States will not interfere. On the former occasion, as you will remember, the General Government declined a participation, and upon the allegation singly that the State of Alabama had not given her assent. The State of Alabama had, in fact, given her assent, and had sought, with much solicitude, the concurrence of Georgia. Very recently, her former resolutions upon this subject have been rescinded, and Georgia is left free to run the line with or without her co-operation, as she may deem best. The correspondence with the General Government, and the letter of the Governor of Alabama, are submitted.

Our claims to the lands occupied by the Cherokees within our limits, as well as those on account of Indian depredations, provided for by the first treaty at the Indian Springs, are adverted to only to inform you of the actual state of those interests, and for this purpose the various papers connected with them are laid before you.

Since you were last in session, much anxiety and concern have been manifested for all the interests connected with the Bank of Darien. The origin of the excitement, and consequent depreciation of the paper of that institution, may be considered fit subjects of investigation. The report of a committee appointed to examine the state of its affairs, having been reviewed and adopted by you, left at the close of the session the solvency of the Bank indisputable. When, on a subsequent occasion, it became necessary for the Executive to pass an order connected with this depreciation, and the administration of the finances, I did not hesitate so to act as to conform the order both to your expressed opinion and the practice of the Treasury. As no change had been made in the condition of the institution, I would suffer none to be made in the payments and receipts of its bills at the Treasury, until you should order otherwise; and, whilst I would not permit any measure to be taken which would be construed into depreciation at the Treasury, I would suffer none that would have the least effect to embarrass the operations of the other institutions; and this was the more proper, because the difficulties of the one institution might be ascribable, in some degree, to remissness or indiscretion in the management, for which it was certainly not entitled to favor, whilst the operation at the Treasury still continued favorable to it, inasmuch as, the receipts and payments being confined to Darien bills, and the receipts exceeding the payments, there would be a constant accumulation of such bills, and consequently a subtraction, to that amount, from the circulation of the country.

In every other State of the Union, where bank credit has been sustained, these institutions mutually aid and assist each other, and by harmonious co-operation maintain unimpaired the circulating medium of that State. Those of Georgia must profit of this wise example. Interest and credit are not to be found in rivalry and discord, and it is sincerely hoped and believed that, in this instance, conflicting opinions have been the result of misapprehension or mistake. The great institution of the United States keeps them all in check, and should, at the same time, keep them all in union.

The expenses incurred by the reception of General Lafayette, amount to $7,198 32, as you will see by the accounts and vouchers which are exhibited. The Executive had, in this instance, received an unlimited power over the public treasure, which ought never to be confided but upon very extraordinary occasions. It is due to the public, as well as to the officer charged with the disbursement, to institute a strict inquiry into the expenditure; thus exacting, as far as practicable after the expenditure, that accountability which, in ordinary cases, ought to be secured before. The orders given to my Aids-de-Camp, who were charged with their execution, enjoined on them the strictest economy: and, all circumstances considered, they have not disappointed my expectations.

Since your last meeting, our feelings have been again outraged by officious and impertinent intermeddlings with our domestic concerns. Besides the resolution presented for the consideration of the Senate, by Mr. King, of New York, it is understood that the Attorney-General of the United States, who may be presumed to represent his Government faithfully, and to speak as its mouth-piece, has recently maintained, before the Supreme Court, doctrines on this subject, which, if sanctioned by that tribunal, will make it quite easy for the Congress, by a short decree, to divest this entire interest, without cost to themselves of one dollar, or of one acre of public land. This is the uniform practice of the Government of the United States; if it wishes a principle established which it dare not establish for itself, a case is made before the Supreme Court, and, the principle once settled, the act of Congress follows of course. Soon, very soon, therefore, the United States

Government, discarding the mask, will openly lend itself to a combination of fanatics for the destruction of every thing valuable in the Southern country. One movement of the Congress unresisted by you, and all is lost. Temporize no longer—make known your resolution that this subject shall not be touched by them, but at their peril. But for its sacred guaranty by the Constitution, we never would have become parties to that instrument; at this moment you would not make yourself parties to any Constitution without it; of course, you will not be a party to it from the moment the General Government shall make that movement.

If this matter be an evil, it is our own—if it be a sin, we can implore the forgiveness of it—to remove it, we ask not either their sympathy or assistance: it may be our physical weakness—it is our moral strength. If, like the Greeks and Romans, the moment we cease to be masters, we are slaves—we thenceforth minister, like the modern Italians, to the luxury and pleasures of our masters—poets, painters, musicians and sculptors we may be—the moral qualities, however, which would make us fair partakers of the grandeur of a great empire, would be gone. We would stand stripped and desolate, under a fervid sun and upon a generous soil, a mockery to ourselves, and the very contrast of what, with a little firmness and foresight, we might have been. I entreat you, therefore, most earnestly, now that it is not too late, to step forth, and, having exhausted the argument, to stand by your arms.

Your fellow-citizen,

G. M. TROUP.

The reading of this document produced a profound sensation in both Houses; and the message became at once an important topic of comment in and out of the State. It was not to be expected that the political party opposed to the Governor would say much in its praise; whilst, with his friends, it served to increase, if possible, their admiration for the man and the magistrate. It was freely and unsparingly commented on by Northern journals, the conductors of some of which professed to regard its author as the *mad Governor of Georgia.*

The portion of the message which produced most excitement out of the State, was that which related to the question of slavery; and it is due to the Governor and the then Attorney-General of the United States, that some special reference be here made to it. On the 18th of February, 1825, Hon. Rufus King, of New York, laid on the table of the U. S. Senate, for "future consideration," the following resolution:

"*Resolved by the Senate of the United States of America*, That, as soon as the portion of the existing funded debt of the United States, for the payment of which the public land of the United States is pledged, shall have been paid off, then and thenceforth, the whole of the public land of the United States, with the net proceeds of all future sales thereof, shall constitute and form a fund, which is hereby appropriated, and the faith of the United States is pledged, that the said fund shall be inviolably applied to aid the emancipation of such slaves, within any of the United States, and to aid the removal of such slaves, and the removal of such free persons of color, in any of the said States, as, by the laws of the States, respectively, may be allowed to be emancipated, or removed to any territory or country without the limits of the United States of America."

This, although not the origin of the slavery agitation, was certainly a bold movement in support of the fanaticism which has ever since disturbed the peace and threatened the integrity of the Union; and fully justified the withering denunciation and haughty defiance of Governor Troup.

The House of Representatives having requested the Governor to lay before it "the evidence on which he founds his remarks, in his message relative to the interference of the United States government with our domestic affairs," he returned the following message:

EXECUTIVE DEPARTMENT,
Milledgeville, *7th June*, 1825.

I had hoped that in submitting to the Legislature the resolution of Mr. King, the abstract from the government paper, the several resolutions of the legislatures of certain States, and the reference to the doctrines maintained by the Attorney-General before the Supreme Court at Washington, in cases involving the question of slavery or no slavery, and had expressed my own opinions upon them, I had done enough. In cheerful compliance, however, with the expressed wishes of the House of Representatives, I make this further communication.

Even from the moment we became parties to the Union, notwithstanding the guaranties of this interest by the Constitution, efforts have been made to render unavailing those guaranties, to make inroads upon the subject of them, in various modes, sometimes by open assaults, sometimes by covert acts, equally injurious to the interests involved as disgraceful to the parties inflicting the injury. Throughout this period and to the present moment, we have defended ourselves by memorial, remonstrance, resolutions, supplications, &c. All reflecting men had foreseen that these might serve the purposes of the times, because, as God would have it, for those times the strength and courage were with us. Now, the times are changed. The strength has departed, and they would destroy the interest, that they might destroy the moral principle which sustains it. The spirit which animates these disturbers of our peace, is of no ordinary kind—it is the same as that which rallied under the banner of the cross, and propagated religion by the sword—it sticks at no measures, it weeps over no distress; but, believing all means justifiable and holy and consecrated, marches to its object without regard to age or sex, and wars even with the sleep of the cradle. This is the very spirit of fanaticism. But the other day, I sent you the resolution of the State of Delaware, formerly with us—now against us. Maryland, losing her interest, will soon follow her example. The resolution of Mr. King, preposterous as it is, is just as likely to succeed as any other silly thing.

Mr. King, certainly one of the most able men in council that his country has produced, proposes to buy out our interest with our own property. Mr. King, in token of the high value set upon this special service, is sent Ambassador to England, to refresh his memory there with the law in Somerset's case, * which is also a favorite one with our learned Attorney-General. The government paper at Washington, daring more than had ever been dared, announces that this

---

* Reported as Somerset vs. Stewart, in Lofft's Rep., 1. Chancellor Kent says of it: "In the case of Somerset, in 1772, who was a negro slave, carried by his master from America to England, and there confined, in order to be sent to the West Indies, he was discharged by the K. B., upon *habeas corpus,* after a very elaborate discussion, and upon the ground that slavery did not and could not exist in England, under the English law." 2 Kent's Com: 248. —ED.

is the appointed time.* The Attorney-General, representing the United States, says before the Supreme Court, in a ripe and splendid argument, that slavery, being inconsistent with the laws of God and nature, cannot exist. Do we want more, or shall we wait until, the principle being decided against us, the execution issues, and the entire property, put up at public auction, is bought in from the proceeds of our public lands? This is left to your decision. The United States can choose between our enmity and our love; and, when you offer them the choice, you perform the last and holiest of duties. They have adopted a conceit, and, if they love that more than they love us, they will cling to it and throw us off. But it will be written in your history, that you did not separate from the household without adopting the fraternal language—choose ye, this day, between our friendship and that worthless idol you have set up and worshipped.

G. M. TROUP.

Accompanying this message, was a correspondence between the Governor and Col. Seaborn Jones. In his letter to Col. Jones, dated 6th June, Gov. Troup said:

"Be pleased to state if you were not present at Washington, during the late session of the Supreme Court, and if, in a cause or causes depending therein, and involving the question of *slavery or no slavery*, you did not understand the Attorney-General to assume and maintain the general doctrine that slavery could not exist consistently with the laws of God and nature, &c."

In his reply, Col. Jones said:

"I have just received your note of to-day, inquiring for what I heard from the Attorney-General of the United States, on the subject of slavery. I regretted very much, at the time the argument was made by Mr. Wirt, in an African case, involving the question of slavery, that I did

* The *National Journal*, a paper then recently established, and understood to be the organ of Mr. Adams, had, a short time before, said: "The sovereignty of St. Domingo in the possession of the blacks, the freedom accorded to that description of persons in various parts of South America, the incipient measures adopted by the English Government for the liberty of the slaves in the British West India Islands, and the sympathy felt by all Christendom for the sufferings of that unfortunate race of beings, can only terminate in their liberation from bondage. Such an event, which will but remotely affect the pride, and not at all the safety, of the European nations, must necessarily have a powerful influence on the feelings and welfare of the United States. *It is time, therefore, to look seriously to this matter, and to come to some definite resolution as to the continuance or total abolition of slavery among us*," &c., &c.—ED.

not hear the whole of it. It was my good fortune only to hear a part of his argument, and I cannot say definitely and certainly that, in the part of the argument I heard, he did advance and maintain the position that slavery was contrary to the laws of God and nature. After his argument was over, I certainly heard, in general conversation, that he had assumed such a position; and, on the next day, when Mr. Ingersoll, of Philadelphia, argued the Portuguese claim for the claimants, he made his argument an answer to the one the Attorney-General had made in the Spanish claim, (on the part of the United States,) he distinctly stated that Mr. Wirt had laid down such a doctrine, and he proceeded to combat it. Whether Mr. Wirt did or did not do so, I am unable positively to state—but he was present when Mr. Ingersoll stated it, and did not object to the statement. I have the more distinct recollection on the subject, as I then thought that the Virginian and Pennsylvanian had changed sides."

Besides the foregoing, the Governor stated, substantially:

That a few days before the meeting of the Legislature, he conversed with the Hon. J. M. Berrien, Senator in the Congress of the United States, on the subject of our slave property, and the danger to which it was exposed by the repeated attacks of other States and of the United States: he said the crisis was an awful one, and that no time was to be lost in taking measures of defence; he had very recently the best opportunity to understand the views of the General Government in relation to it; that the doctrines delivered by the Attorney-General, before the Supreme Court, were extreme, and of the most alarming character—neither more nor less than that slavery could not exist, being contrary to the laws of God and nature, &c.; that he was engaged as counsel in one or more of the cases involving this doctrine, and that he regretted exceedingly that the reply had not been allowed him—he said the Legislature should take up the subject seriously; that he (the Governor,) answered that he was determined to present it in the strongest light, &c., &c.: that Judge Berrien adverted particularly to the great excitement against us, produced by these appeals both to the court and auditory.

Mr. Wirt having afterwards denied that he uttered the sentiments imputed to him, it is, perhaps, due to the memory of Judge Berrien and that of Gov. Troup, that the following correspondence should appear in the biography of the latter. It occurred before the publication of Mr. Wirt's denial, but was not made public until afterwards.

SAVANNAH, 28th June, 1825.

My Dear Sir: I have seen, in the Georgia Patriot of the 14th inst., an article, purporting to be a statement made by you to the Legislature, of a conversation between you and myself, which occurred during my last visit to Milledgeville, and cannot avoid expressing to you the surprise and regret it has excited. When I saw, in your first communication, the manner in which you had noticed the subject of the interference of other States in our domestic concerns, I was struck with the singularity of your having transferred (what I presumed you believed to be,) the substance of a private, unofficial conversation, to a public, official document, without consulting me to know whether your recollection of that conversation was accurate—whether I would consent to be brought before the Legislature in that manner —or, in fact, giving me the slightest intimation of your intention thus to present me to the public. When, subsequently, a call for information was made on me by the Chairman of a committee of the House of Representatives, I was forced to the conclusion that you had given my name to that committee; and, in my reply, written at the instant, after mentioning this impression, I proceeded to make a brief statement of what I had said. If that letter was shown to you, as, from reference to some circumstances, it seems may have been the fact, before your statement, of the 6th June, was made, I have then to complain that you should have persevered in that statement, after my explanation to Mr. Lumpkin; and with the disposition, in relation to me, which such a measure would manifest on your part, I should, of course, be relieved from the feeling towards you which now embarrasses me. I prefer to adopt the contrary conclusion. I am unwilling, perhaps unable, at the moment, to shake off the feelings springing from a friendship of more than twenty years; and I cannot forget that, under the operation of these, and from a belief that the public interest would be promoted by your success, I omitted no honorable exertion to aid your election to the office which you now fill. Under the combined influence of these considerations, I am extremely unwilling to do any thing of which your enemies might avail themselves to your injury. But the situation in which I am placed before the public, by your communication, and subsequent statement, is one in which I cannot consent to remain. I have made no such assertions as may be inferred from that statement. On the contrary, you have misunderstood both the tenor and object of my observations. The African case, in which I am of counsel with the State, having been the subject of conversation between us, I was naturally led to advert to the disposition to interfere with our domestic concerns of that sort, which I thought had been manifested during the last winter at Washington. I considered the resolution of Mr. King as strongly evincing such a disposition, and I thought that the sentiments which I heard expressed, and those which I understood were expressed in the case of the Ramirez,* and the conversations out of doors, to which the argument of that case gave rise, were calculated to excite a restlessness among our colored population, which might be productive of the most awful consequences. I, therefore, suggested to you, as I had done to others, my opinion that these consequences ought to be met, and would be most effectually averted, by concurrent resolutions of the Legislatures of the Southern States, declaring this subject to be exclusively within their own particular cognizance, and asking Congress to abstain from intermeddling with it. I spoke to you of the purport of the arguments of counsel, so far as I had heard them, and of those which had been ascribed to counsel whom I did not hear. I told you that I considered the doctrines advanced, as alarming, and that, with the feeling which, as a Southern man, they excited in me, I should have been glad of an opportunity of replying, which the order of the discussion did not allow to me; but I told you, also, that I was not present when the argument of the Attorney-General was delivered; that the Supreme Court did not sustain these doctrines; and I expressed to you no opinion that the government of the United States had any concern in urging this discussion. I could entertain no such opinion, as I had been informed that the Attorney-General had, at a previous term, given up the case on the part of the government, and that it was retained at the instance of a member of the Colonization Society. I had not the most distant conception that any observation of mine could have led you to think of intimating to the Legislature that an appeal to arms might become necessary. I

* Reported as the Antelope, in Wheaton's Reports of the decisions of the U. S. Supreme Court, vol. 10, beginning at page 66.—ED.

had in view, simply, a decisive, but temperate, expression by the Legislatures of the Southern States, of their feelings on this subject; and, so little did I anticipate such a course, that when you suggested the inquiry, whether you ought not to communicate the subject to the Legislature, at their extra session, I told you I thought it was unnecessary, as the regular session would occur before the meeting of Congress, and the Legislatures of other States would then be convened.

With this view of the conversation which I had with you, and without insisting, as I think I might do, that you should not have drawn me before the public, unless with my own consent, I now simply repeat that I cannot agree to stand before that public in the attitude in which I am placed. If you can suggest any mode which I can with propriety adopt, by which I can retire from it, without injury to you, I shall be gratified. Acquitting you, as I do, unhesitatingly, of any intention to misrepresent me, I regret very much that this misconception should have occurred at a moment when the circumstances may, by perversion, be used to your injury; but the views which you have received from this conversation, and have communicated to the Legislature, are so variant from those which I entertained, and which I have thought, and still think, best calculated to rally the Southern States around a cause which is common to them all, that I cannot consent to diminish the little prospect which I have of being in any degree useful in the National Councils, by being considered as having originated them.

Pray let me hear from you, soon, and believe me

Yours, truly,

JN: MACPHERSON BERRIEN.

Governor Troup.

MILLEDGEVILLE, 2d July, 1825.

My Dear Sir: I received your letter of the 28th ult., this morning, and am sorry that any misconception of the conversation in relation to the slave question, should have occurred or given you the least inquietude. The purport of the conversation on your part, was nothing, as I understood, but a recapitulation of circumstances which occurred at Washington, of public notoriety there, as they soon would be everywhere, and the impression which those circumstances made on your mind. I did not suppose you further acquainted with the views of the general government than those circumstances disclosed, or the opportunities which your presence there might afford you of acquiring them, much less with any definite or specific projects which that government might have in contemplation; and I distinctly remember you to have said that the decision of the Supreme Court had not sanctioned the doctrines of the Attorney-General, a fact very well understood when the message was penned. Indeed, in all these things you are at liberty to consult your own memory, as equally good with mine; but, suffer me to say, you have adopted a very erroneous conclusion in believing that an impression may have been designed to be made, that the particular part of the message to which you have referred, and which has given rise to so many and such liberal remarks, was the offspring of your suggestion, or in consequence of anything emanating from you. So far from it, the disclosures made by you in that conversation, formed but a small part of the matter upon which that part of the message was, after mature deliberation, framed. I assure you that I would not, on any account, that you should participate, in the least degree, the responsibility of the adoption and promulgation of that sentiment—nor shall any body else. I claim both the idea and the language embodied there, as my exclusive property; and, in the enjoyment of it, I do not see that there is much likelihood of my suffering interruption. Nevertheless, it is a sentiment approved by every re-consideration of it, and one which will be sedulously impressed upon my children.

That the resolution of Mr. King, and the sentiments you heard expressed, connected with it, and those which you understood were expressed in the case of the Ramirez, and the conversations out of doors, to which the argument of that case gave rise, were calculated to excite a restlessness among our colored population, which might be productive of the most awful consequences, and your considering the doctrines advanced by the Attorney-General and others, as you understood them, alarming, were all the facts of any importance, according to my estimate of them. It was well known that they were the views of the general government only, from which we had anything to fear; and whether you expressed any particular knowledge of these views, or not, we were at liberty to infer them from the facts disclosed. Neither in dictating that part of the message, therefore, nor in devising a remedy for the evil complained of, were you or any body consulted, or more than a due weight given to your disclosures.

Reference was unhesitatingly made to that conversation, because that you were a Senator of this State in the Congress of the United States, and it became your duty to make known to this government whatever transpired at Washington prejudicial to its interests. Having sought an early opportunity, informally to do so, I thought you entitled to credit; and, accordingly, at the call of the Legislature, submitted to it the paper to which you have alluded.

Cordially reciprocating the friendly sentiments you express,

I remain, very truly, yours,

G. M. TROUP.

The Hon. J. M. Berrien.

P. S. You are at liberty to use this letter as you please.

G. M. T.

On the 2d of July, 1825, Mr. Wirt addressed a letter to the Chief and Associate Justices of the Supreme Court, to the Reporter, and to Thomas Addis Emmet, Esq., as follows:

"In a late official communication by Gov. Troup to the Legislature of Georgia, I find myself charged with having maintained before the Supreme Court of the United States, at the last term, the proposition 'that slavery, being inconsistent with the laws of God and nature, cannot exist.' Will you do me the justice to say, in reply, whether, either your notes of argument, or your recollection, impute that proposition to me, or any sentiment or opinion that slavery, as it now exists in the several States, could or ought to be abolished, or be attempted to be abolished, or interfered with at all by the authority of the government of the United States."

We have not space for the full replies given to this inquiry. The following extracts may suffice. The Chief Justice said:

"I have no recollection of your having uttered, in any form, the sentiment imputed to you. The impression on my mind is, that you denounced the slave trade, not slavery; the practice of making freemen slaves, not that of holding in slavery those who were born slaves."

Judge Washington said:

"I feel no hesitation in answering, that no part of your

argument maintained any or either of these propositions directly, nor did the general scope of it warrant, in my opinion, the deduction of any such sentiment."

Judge Duvall said :

"I answer, without hesitation, that I have no recollection whatever that you maintained the proposition imputed to you by Governor Troup, in the argument of the cause before-mentioned, or in any other cause. * * * * * If you had made use of such an argument, it would not have escaped my notice. You contended that the slave trade is not countenanced by the law of nations; that, by the existing law of nations, it is unlawful; that these Africans were under the protection of the laws of the United States, and, *prima facie*, free by those laws, &c., &c."

Judge Thompson said:

"I have looked over my notes of your argument in the case referred to, and do not find that I have noted any such unqualified proposition being laid down by you. Nor have I the least recollection of your urging any such sentiment in the sense imputed to you. And I am persuaded it would have made a strong impression on my mind, if you had endeavored to establish the proposition that slavery did not, at this time, legally exist in our country, or that the courts of justice were not bound to recognize its existence, and to respect and enforce the laws in relation to it. And I think your argument could not, in justice, warrant a conclusion that you intended, in any manner whatever, to call in question the laws of the Southern States on the subject of slavery."

Mr. Emmet (who stated, also, that the "recollections" of Mr. D. B. Ogden agreed with his own,) said:

"So far as relates to what is there ('the official communication from Governor Troup,') imputed to you, I can confidently say that the statement is incorrect. * * * * You spoke of slavery in the United States, as an evil inflicted on the colonies by the mother country, and for which they ought to be pitied, and not blamed; and though I cannot cite your words, I collected, from what you said, that you regarded it as an evil which must be submitted to. I am confident you expressed no opinion *that slavery, as it now exists in the several States, can be or ought to be abolished, or attempted to be abolished, or* *interfered with at all, by the authority of the Government of the United States.*"

[The italics are Mr. Emmet's.]

Mr. Wheaton, the Reporter, said:

"I have great pleasure in being able to state, both from recollection and from my notes taken at the time, that neither of those propositions was maintained by you before the Court."

Now, assuming it to be true that the Attorney-General, in no part of his argument, "maintained (in the language of Judge Washington,) any or either of these propositions directly," and that the denial of Mr. Wirt, who was a Christian gentleman, is sufficient to show that he did not admit the right of the Federal Government to interfere with the institution of slavery in the States, yet it appears equally clear that, in the case actually before the Court, it was entirely unnecessary for him to speak of "*slavery in the United States as an evil inflicted on the colonies by the mother country, and for which they ought to be pitied.*" Was not this declaration calculated to "excite a restlessness" to which Judge Berrien referred? That Mr. Wirt, in the "ripe and splendid argument" which he delivered, used expressions which he ought ever to have regretted, and which he did regret, seems probable; that some of his remarks were injudicious, is proved by the letter of Mr. Emmet.

In the letter from which we have already quoted, Judge Marshall said: "You stated, in terms, that you had no authority to speak the sentiments of the Government; and that the arguments you should use were to be considered as entirely your own." And the *National Journal*, Mr. Adams' reputed organ, and the paper in which Mr. Wirt's defence appeared, referring to this declaration, stated: "This declaration, we are told, was elicited by a paragraph which appeared in one of the papers of this city, on the morning on which the Attorney-General was expected to speak, intimating that the public could now have an opportunity of hearing, through the Attorney-General, the sentiments of the Executive on the subject of the slave trade, and by a similar suggestion from one of the counsel opposed to him." Still, the inquiry remains: why, even in the face of these suggestions, this solemn disavowal of his "authority to speak the sentiments of the Government," if what he was about to say was only such as became a Southern man, and especially in a cause in which it appears the Government had no concern? If Governor Troup was wrong in saying, of the Attorney-General, that he was one "who may be supposed to represent his government faithfully and to speak as its mouth-piece," it does not thence follow that he erred in denouncing what he believed to have been dangerous doctrines publicly uttered by a man holding office under that government.

We have given to this subject more space, probably, than it deserves; and we dismiss it with the remark, that, whilst the occasion of the Governor's denunciation is regretted, that regret is diminished by the consideration that it afforded Governor Troup the opportunity of putting upon record, in an official form, the most eloquent of all his noble admonitions to the people of Georgia.

The main object of the assembling of the Legislature in extra session, having been the disposition of the lands lately acquired from the Creeks, a bill for that purpose passed both Houses, and was approved by the Governor on the 9th of June; for the details of which, reference must be m de to the Act itself. Criminal jurisdiction over the territory was attached to the counties of Dooly, Houstoun, Pike and Fayette.

The joint Committee on the state of the Republic, "to whom was referred the subject of the conduct of the Agent of Creek Indian affairs, in relation to the late treaty in that nation; and also in respect to the murder of General McIntosh and others of the Creek Chiefs," after hearing testimony, made a report, which was agreed to in the Senate, 31 to 18, and concurred in by the House, 64 to 28, and approved by the Governor on the 11th June. In the report, the Committee said they did "not see, in the evidence, sufficient proof to justify them in presuming that the Agent ordered, contrived, or instigated the murder of General McIntosh." It concluded with resolutions censuring the conduct of said Agent, in regard to the treaty, requesting his removal by the President; and, in order that "all due and proper proof of his delinquency" might be made, instructing the Governor to "appoint two or more fit and proper persons to collect evidence therein," &c., &c., and requesting the Governor to transmit to the President a copy of the report, &c., with the accompanying documents, or such parts thereof as were not then in his possession, &c., &c.

On the 7th of June, Col. Crowell published a card or address to the public, dated the 3d. Speaking of the Governor, he said: "And now at his instigation the Legislature have taken up the subject, and are, as I understand, examining witnesses against me, without apprising me of their design." After protesting against this course, and entreating a suspension of opinion, he added: "An Agent from the government of the United States is now here, commissioned with full powers to examine into all the circumstances connected with it, and report to his government."

During the same session, a resolution of thanks was passed to Messrs. Campbell and Meriwether, "for the firmness, perseverance, zeal and patriotism which they have displayed in procuring a cession of territory so favorable to the interest of Georgia." Of the Governor, the Legislature said: "*Our thanks are also tendered to his Excellency the Governor, for his active and patriotic efforts in expediting the settlement of said territory.*"

The Agent, to whom Col. Crowell referred in his card, as having been sent on to examine into affairs connected with the Indian Agency, was Major T. P. Andrews, who arrived at Milledgeville, in May, with dispatches to the Governor from the War Department. On the 31st May, he communicated his dispatches, and, in his letter of that date, said to the Governor:

"I presume you will be informed, by the dispatches now handed you, that I have been appointed by the President of the United States, to examine into certain implied charges against Col. Crowell, the Indian Agent, contained in your Excellency's letter to the President, of the——— inst., as well as others of a direct and specific character, made by Chilly McIntosh and other Chiefs of the Creek Nation, at Washington. To enable me to perform this delicate and responsible trust with effect, I have the honor to request that you will be pleased to furnish me with any charges and specifications which you may have to make against the officer referred to, accompanied by any evidence in your Excellency's possession, relating thereto, or references to the sources whence such evidence may be derived," &c., &c.

He also stated that he would exercise the discretionary power vested in him of discharging the Agent, should the charges, or information in possession of the Governor, demand it.

The Governor replied as follows:

EXECUTIVE DEPARTMENT,
Milledgeville, 31*st May*, 1825.

Sir: Immediately on the receipt of your communication of this date, I proceeded, in compliance with the wishes of the General Government, to charge the Agent superintending the affairs of the Creek Indians, with:

1st. Predetermined resolution to prevent the Indians, by all the means in his power, from making any cession of their lands in favor of the Georgians, and this from the most unworthy and most unjustifiable of all motives.

2dly. With advising and instigating, in chief, the death of McIntosh and his friends.

You are referred to the documents connected with my late message to the Legislature, and to the testimony disclosed and to be disclosed before the committee charged with the investigation of the subject to which they relate, and which are submitted to you.

Respectfully, your obedient servant,

G. M. TROUP.

To Major Andrews,
Special Agent of the U. S.,
Milledgeville.

The following is the dispatch of which Major Andrews was the bearer, announcing his own appointment as special agent to inquire into the charges against the Indian Agent, and the appointment of Gen. Gaines to inquire into, and check, if possible, the troubles in the Creek country:

DEPARTMENT OF WAR, May 18, 1825.

SIR: In answer to your several letters received at this Department on the 15th and 17th inst., I am instructed by the President to express his deep regret at the deaths of General McIntosh and the other Creek Chiefs, and the shocking circumstances with which they were attended. While your Excellency is understood to ascribe the cause of these events to the criminal conduct of the Agent, he, by dispatches received some few days past, states to this Department that your purpose of entering upon and surveying their territory, as made known by your proclamation, had produced in the Chiefs, who received it when assembled in general council, for the purpose of receiving their annuity, feelings of melancholy and great distress. Exceptions to your measures were then taken by them: they declared their assent had never been given, and that it had not been asked. Those exceptions were communicated by the Agent in the letter above referred to, together with the request of the Chiefs that the Government would interpose its authority, and put a stop to the contemplated survey.

Whatever cause may have produced the disturbances and bloodshed which followed so soon upon the breaking up of that Council, has now become a matter of very subordinate consideration, compared with the means necessary to be adopted to prevent their repetition. Remote from the theatre of action, with but little information, and that uncertain, (for we have not a word from the Agent,) as to the extent of the designs of the Indians, or the scale on which their operations will be conducted, the President has deemed it advisable, and has ordered accordingly, General Gaines, distinguished alike for his military skill and for his discretion, now in Georgia, to repair forthwith to Milledgeville, for the purpose of consulting with your Excellency, on the measures proper to be adopted in reference to the actual posture of affairs on his arrival. To him a discretion has been given, if in his judgment the occasion requires it, to call on you for such portion of the militia of Georgia, to be placed in the service of the United States, as he thinks necessary; to march, also, such portions of the regular force as may be convenient, to the scene of operations, and to take command of the whole. By his instructions, he will be ordered to repel any hostile. attempt that may be made by the Indians on the people of Georgia, and to chastise them by measures of retaliation for such attempt, till their sufferings and submission shall entitle them to clemency. If their violence has been limited to their own tribe, the course to be pursued is not without its embarrassments. The Government of the United States, since its establishment, has, in no case, it is confidently believed, forcibly interposed in the intestine feuds of the Indians. They have limited their interference to good offices and friendly advice. To depart from this policy, strengthened by time and the approbation of the American people, involves a high and delicate responsibility. On the other hand, to surrender the Indians, friendly to the views of the United States, to the unrestrained ferocity of the hostile party, is too shocking to humanity to permit. Amid these opposing difficulties, the General is instructed to enter the territory of the Creeks, and extend protection to the friendly party, but not commit hostilities on the Indians, unless provoked thereto by acts, on their part, which may justify such hostilities. A special messenger will be dispatched to Milledgeville, on Friday, at farthest, with General Gaines' instructions.

The President, not yet being informed of the measures adopted by your Excellency, cannot, at this time, take any step thereon. Your promised communication will relieve him from this difficulty, and immediately on its arrival will receive his prompt attention.

I am instructed to say to your Excellency, that the President expects, from what has passed, as well as from the now state of feeling among the Indians, that the project of surveying their territory will be abandoned by Georgia, till it can be done consistently with the provisions of the treaty.

From the charges made by your Excellency, and the Deputation here, against the Agent; Major Andrews, possessing, from his high character, the full confidence of the Executive, has been deputed to the Agency to inquire into these charges and to adopt the course, in reference to the Agent, which he may deem best calculated to promote the public service.

Major Andrews is the bearer of the dispatches to Gen. Gaines, and, as he will pass through Milledgeville, if you have any facts calculated to criminate the Agent, an opportunity will be furnished your Excellency to communicate them.

I have the honor to be your obedient servant,

His Excellency G. M. Troup, JAMES BARBOUR.
Governor of Georgia, Milledgeville.

The Governor replied, as follows:

EXECUTIVE DEPARTMENT.
Milledgeville, June 3d, 1825.

Sir: I have received, by Major Andrews, your letter of the 18th ultimo. The dispositions manifested by your Government to do right in all the matters connected with the subject of my late communication, are only in accordance with my just expectations. I am happy that, in the general, the measures deemed best appear to be appropriate and judicious. Pardon me for making an exception. In searching the archives of your office, you will find, at divers times, and on various occasions, representations, made on the conduct of the Agent, all or any of which should have disqualified him as a competent witness against the government of the State of Georgia. On the recent one of the ratification of the treaty of the Indian Springs, yourselves pronounced upon that incompetency in terms not to be mistaken. The Agent protested against the treaty; the President submitted it to the Senate, and the Senate ratified it in contempt of that protestation. If a single declaration of the Agent had been accredited, the President would not have submitted it, the Senate would not have ratified it. The last of your prominent acts, therefore, in relation to this individual places him in an attitude before yourselves, which should have decided you to listen with great caution and reserve to any suggestions of his, connected with any subject whatsoever. Whilst, on the one hand, he presents himself before you as an accuser of the chief of the government of Georgia, and the accusation is neither more nor less than that the measures taken on his part have been the only exciting causes to the mischiefs and crimes perpetrated in the nation; and you, on the other hand, so far sustained him in this position, as not only to receive it willingly, and to specify it distinctly, but to make it the basis of a most erroneous construction of the treaty; and in consequence of that construction, to address to me a most extraordinary request of the President, affecting important interests here, I must pray you to excuse me, when I say to you in answer, that I do not feel myself treated in a very kindly or very generous spirit, and that, if treated in the most kindly and most generous, such an expectation would be pronounced at once as unreasonable on your part, and certainly not to be fulfilled on ours. Is it possible that the President could have consulted the Indian treaty, and compared its provisions with those of the articles of agreement and cession, and, at the same time have indulged this expectation? Without troubling you with the argument, permit me to state the fact. By the treaty of the Indian Springs, the Indian claims are extinguished forever. The article is worded in the present tense.* On the instant of the ratification, the title and jurisdiction became absolute in Georgia, without any manner of exception or qualification, save the single one which, by the eighth article, gives to the United States the power to protect the Indians in their persons and effects, against assault upon either, by whites or Indians. For this purpose, your powers are quite ample; and, in proceeding to the survey of the country, you will only find aids and guaranties on the part of this government for the faithful execution of the article. Beyond this you cannot pass. Soil and jurisdiction go together, and if we have not the right of both at this moment, we can never have either by better title. If the absolute property and the absolute jurisdiction have not passed to us, when are they to come? Will you make a formal concession of the latter—when and how? If the jurisdiction be separated from the property, show the reservation which separates it—'t is impossible. You have the same remnant of it in this case, as you have by constitution and treaty in all similar cases, where, treaties having guarantied the rights and privileges of aliens, those rights and privileges find their protection under the supreme law of the United States, within the jurisdiction of the several States. If the President believes that we will postpone the survey of the country to gratify the Agent and the hostile Indians, he deceives himself. To these poor deluded men, who have been hostile in peace and hostile in war, and the opponents of the treaty, Georgia could make no appeal. From McIntosh and his friends, who made the treaty, we sought permission to make the survey, and obtained it. Scrupulously regardful of the stipulation of the treaty, we asked them, in substance, if the survey would, in any manner, interfere with their convenience or

* The first Article of the treaty begins, "The Creek nation *cede* to the United States all the lands," &c.—ED.

security, and they answered, no—a ready answer, because the survey would in fact contribute importantly to both.

The frequent recurrence to the conduct of the Agent, may induce a belief that the influencing motives here are impure or tainted with prejudice—it is not so. As an individual, no angry feelings have been indulged toward him, or any harm desired—as a public officer, the most indignant sentiments have been awakened from the beginning, because, as soon as I entered upon the duties of this office, it was known to me that he had come to the resolution to prevent the Indians from ceding any lands to Georgia, so long as I continued in it; a resolution so ungenerous and unworthy of any officer, in any station, that I determined to employ all honorable means to effect his removal as absolutely necessary to the prosperity of the State. You ought to have removed him long ago, and thus have spared us all the evils which have followed your omission.

Be pleased to present my respectful compliments to the President, and assure him of my good wishes and regards. The frankness with which it is my duty to communicate with him, can have no tendency to weaken them on my part, or to excite distrust of their sincerity on his. Even upon the subject* of intensest interest to us, upon which the opinions of the President are known, many allowances are made for the immeasurable distance which separates us. In treating it, I have used strong language, but he will not on this account believe that I make light of the Union. I would offer up my life, with pleasure, to sustain it for a single day. The fearful consequences, constantly in sight, keep us in a state of agitation and alarm. I strive to stave them off; and it is for this that language is employed, sickening to the heart and most offensive to a vast portion of the common family. Who can help it, when they see wise men engaged in a playfulness and pastime like this, indulging their whims and oddities and phantasies, and causing this Union to tremble upon a bauble?

With regard to the expenses attendant on our measures of defence, of which you are instructed to say nothing until those measures are submitted to you in detail, I have to congratulate you and myself that they will be so inconsiderable in amount as not to cause much trouble or anxiety to either of us. Whilst I took the precautionary measures to make safe the women and children upon the frontiers, I

* Gov. Troup refers here, of course, to the subject of slavery; and, in the next sentence, to the "stand by your arms" part of his then recent message.—ED.

remember very well that we had been pleading at your treasury, for thirty years, for similar expenses incurred in defending ourselves against the same Indians. I feel much more anxiety about the expenses which may be incurred by the friendly ones, who have sought refuge within our settlements, which they are quite willing to defray from their own scanty means, but which justice and humanity require you to defray for them.

With great consideration and regard,

G. M. TROUP.

The Hon. James Barbour,
Secretary of War,
Washington City.

Accompanying the Secretary's letter to the Governor, were the following documents: A letter from Chilly McIntosh to the Secretary, announcing the murder of General McIntosh and Tustunnuggee, and the destruction of his property, and asking protection for the friendly Indians, revenge for the murders, and indemnity for property destroyed, &c.: the answer of the Secretary, expressing sympathy, promising protection, and that the matter of remuneration would be recommended to the favorable consideration of Congress, &c.: two letters from Chilly McIntosh and three other chiefs of the friendly party, to the Secretary—one asking for revenge for the blood that had been spilt, an investigation into the Indian disputes, and protection for the friendly Indians—the second, complaining of the conduct of Col. Crowell, the Agent, stating that the Agent "is not trusted by us, and we do not feel safe in his hands." They said, further: "Col. Crowell has always been opposed to General McIntosh since 1823, when he tried to have him broke as a Chief of the Creek nation, and threatened to destroy his property. He was offended at Gen. McIntosh for refusing to give up a man named Stinson, without an order from the head Chiefs of the nation. Stinson was afterwards delivered into the Agent's custody, and tried for selling goods in the nation without a license, of which he was acquitted by the Federal Court, in Georgia," &c., &c. It further said: "Col. Crowell was opposed to the treaty at the Indian Springs, and tried to prevent the Creeks from selling their lands to the United States. He sent William Hambly, United States Interpreter, to the Council, to say that he wanted to see the Chiefs, but was jealous of the Commissioners. He told them that they should not give any long answer to the Commissioners, but only say 'they had no lands to sell.' That the Commissioners would threaten, but their threats would end in words, as soon as they heard from the government. Even after the treaty was freely agreed to, he did not cease his opposition. He sent a message by William Hambly, the Interpreter, to tell some of the Indians that they should go away across the line, that night, or they would be taken and shut up until they signed the treaty. This party went off in the night, as they were told. The next morning three men were sent after them to know why they had gone away; they told those men the message they had received from Col. Crowell, which was the reason of their going. One of these messengers, Ben Daulawza, is now in Washington." After other complaints, the letter ended: "Now, sir, we beg our father, the President, to send an Agent who will be a friend to all the nation equally; and one in whose hands we can feel safe to go west of the Mississippi. If Col. Crowell is continued Agent, we fear that the friends of Gen. McIntosh will be sacrificed:"—also a letter from the same chiefs, to the Secretary, inquiring if Col. Crowell had received the annuity money, for 1825, agreed to be paid by the treaty of 1821 at the Mineral Springs, and stating: "Col. Crowell, at Broken Arrow, informed the Council that he had made an arrangement with the government of the United States, that every individual of the nation should receive an equal share of the money which was to be paid under the late treaty. If he did make this arrangement, the party of us going to the western country, will not get enough to pay our expenses. If Col. Crowell did make this arrangement with you, not one would go to the western country; because they have no money to bear their expenses, and none to pay for their improvements. We beg also to know if the United States will not pay our expenses here, on the business which has brought us to Washington. It is business in which the United States are concerned equally with the Creek nation." They begged to be informed, that day, what would be done, as they were to leave Washington next day.

To this, the Secretary replied, the same day, expressing the President's regret at the rupture, and the death of McIntosh and others—that measures had been taken, which, it was hoped, would quiet disturbances and give security from future violence—that an examination would be had into the charges against the Agent, as well as the subject of the recent calamity, &c.—that such measures would be taken as should seem best calculated to reconcile the existing difficulties, to punish those who might appear to have promoted them, as might be in the province of the government to punish, &c.—that the expenses of their visit to Washington would be paid, on an approved estimate of them being presented, and that the request to have an Agent to accompany them in search of a country for their future residence, was granted.

This correspondence was all dated the 17th of May, 1825, and, with the Governor's correspondence with the Secretary of War and Major Andrews, the foregoing abstracts will serve to explain the following message of the Governor to the Legislature, dated 3d June, 1825.

The papers now communicated would have been laid before you as soon as received, but, the measures to be taken in carrying into effect the wishes of the President, depending on the arrival of Major-General Gaines, then daily expected, it was deemed best to withhold them until that arrival, when both the views of the General Government, and the measures consequent upon them could be fully disclosed. It being understood, however, that much public anxiety is manifested for their publication, they are transmitted to you. You will perceive by those views, that if the General Government, assuming the exclusive right to expound and carry into effect the treaty of the Indian Springs, shall persist in giving to it the construction which is to be found in the letter of the Secretary of War, and elsewhere, it would have been better for all parties that the treaty had never been concluded; for it is quite obvious to you, that, admitting the power and the construction, the execution of it may be indefinitely postponed at the will of the United States. According to that will, we are not to survey the country, because the hostile Indians who opposed the treaty have also opposed the survey; they continue to oppose both treaty and survey, and to conduct themselves in the most hostile and offensive manner. The hostile Indians would prohibit us from passing to and fro through the country, and the prohibition would be equally reasonable; the act of survey, so far as regards the security and peace of the Indians under the treaty, is as innocent as the act of passing to and fro. Whilst, therefore, by the treaty we have the absolute title to the soil, and the absolute jurisdiction, with the reservation merely of temporary occupation by the Indians, and of power in the United States to protect them in their persons and effects, the right of survey, even when the consent of those who ceded the country, is denied to us; and this denial founded on an assertion utterly destitute of truth, viz:—that the troubles in the nation have been caused by the act of this Government, which procured the consent of the Indians to survey the country. In the absence of all other testimony, to show that these troubles had their origin in other, and very different, causes, it is sufficient to inquire what assignable connection exists between the survey of the country and the hostility of the Indians? The survey could neither expedite nor retard the removal of the Indians; the Indians were not certain that even with their consent the survey would be attempted. Surely, therefore, if this had been the cause of excitement, the Indians would have waited the event. It is conceivable that the cession of the lands might have produced hostilities—but failing to do so, it is inconceivable how the consent to survey them, which had no relation to their eventual surrender and abandonment, could produce that effect. The object of the Government of Georgia, in procuring the consent, was not to settle the country one day sooner than the provisions of the treaty would authorize; but, in surveying the country, to save the time consumed in that operation, to extend its laws over it and to settle it immediately on the departure of the Indians—and this was of the more importance, because the Government was to expect in a short time the arrival of their Civil Engineer; and as that was to be the field of his first and most interesting operations, it was necessary to place him there under the guardianship and safety of our own laws. But so it happens, that this act of survey in which no body before ever saw harm or cause of offence, is suddenly magnified into an evil prolific of all other evils, and this merely because the Government of the United States is so informed by its Agent—that Agent who stands conspicuously charged as the prime mover and instigator of them all—who opposed the treaty from the beginning—protested against it to the last, foretold the mischiefs which were to come of it, and is yet the confidential, trusty and impartial witness upon whose dictum the United States Government accuses the Executive Government of Georgia. The Executive of Georgia will not retort the accusation—it will not say that the Government of the United States is responsible in the sight of Heaven and of the world, for the crimes (if any) committed by the Agent—because the Government of Georgia is not in the practice of thus treating the Government of the United States—but it must be permitted to say distinctly, that, upon the naked information and advice of the Agent, the Government of the United States has suffered itself so far to enter into the views, and to adopt the feelings, of the Agent, in relation to the late events connected with the treaty, as to have given, already, expositions to two of its important articles most palpably erroneous and unwarranted by the letter or spirit of either. The one is of that article which cedes absolutely the territory, and therefore, of course, cedes the jurisdiction—the other of that which stipulates the payment of the money to the Indians. Of the first, enough has been said for a message; of the second, it is sufficient to say that the United States Government has given such a construction to this article, that the hostile Indians, those which remain, as well as those which remove, will share equally with the friendly Indians, the money stipulated to be paid by it. The money is not given in consideration of the lands—the consideration of them is other lands, acre for acre in fee simple—the money is given expressly for improvements abandoned, losses suffered by removal, and to defray the expenses of removal. That portion of the tribe which will not remove, is to share it with that which does remove. This, to be sure, is no concern of ours—but you will see by the letter of Gen. Chilly McIntosh, that if this construction is persisted in, the consequences may be of the most deplorable character—a gross breach of treaty on the one side, a consequent refusal to comply on the other—

power enough on the one to enforce compliance—on the other, weakness, innocence, wretchedness and woes innumerable.

Permit me to add, that there is something strange and inexplicable in this conduct of the General Government to the Chief Magistrate of Georgia. On the 31st day of March last, my application to the Indians for permission to survey the country, and my intention, if that application succeeded, to convene the Legislature, were made known to the President. Although one communication at least was subsequently received from the War Department, not one word was said in objection to the survey. If any had been made, I would have discussed it calmly and temperately; and if, in the result, I had found myself in the wrong, it would have been a question whether, for other objects, an extra session should be called. Now that you are assembled, and in progress upon public affairs of deepest interest, it is attempted most unexpectedly to cross and embarrass you; but the Legislature is not to be frightened from its duty by an angry look. I invite you to proceed, therefore, in the course which you have taken, and, keeping strictly on the side of right, and within the pale of the Constitution and the laws, you will, under the most adverse circumstances, find the most cheering consolations. You cannot thus proceed without the countenance and support of your constituents, and I doubt not they will be readily yielded. If it be possible, which I do not permit myself to believe, that a certain person, filling a certain station, stands in the way of the peace and harmony which ought ever to subsist between this and the General Government, and on this account valuable interests are endangered, that person will retire instantly, and with much more pleasure than he ever occupied that station.

G. M. TROUP.

Before adjournment, the General Assembly adopted a report and resolution, to the effect that the running of the line between Georgia and Florida was not of sufficient importance to require legislative interference before the regular session; that, in regard to the boundary line between Georgia and Alabama, it was a subject of much greater importance, and required their immediate attention—that if an act * should be passed, as contemplated, for surveying and

* This Act was passed, and has been noticed.—ED.

disposing of the Creek country, it would become essentially necessary to have the line ascertained; and that, as it appeared from the documents, the government of the United States and Alabama had been consulted and declined any agency on the subject, they required the Governor, as soon as practicable, to procure the services of some competent person or persons to ascertain the boundary line between Georgia and Alabama, according to the compact of 1802, with the United States, notice being first given to the Governor of Alabama, that he might, if he should deem it necessary, appoint Commissioners to co-operate with those to be appointed by Georgia.

They passed, besides those already noticed and others not important for insertion, a resolution, authorizing and requesting the Governor "to take, forthwith, efficient measures to protect the Georgia frontier against the depredations or encroachments of the Creek Indians, by calling out a sufficient military force for that purpose, if found necessary."

This resolution was passed in consequence of a message from the Governor, dated 6th June, 1825, in which he said:

"I communicate, for the further information of the Legislature, two letters this moment received from our frontiers, which indicate the urgency of interposing a sufficient force for the protection of our inhabitants."

The letters conveyed information of hostile intentions which appeared to have been manifested by the Indians opposite the counties of Dooly and Early, creating alarm amongst the whites. The Governor promptly issued the necessary military orders for protecting the frontiers, and, on the 9th, sent in the following additional message to the Legislature:

Before your adjournment, it is due to you to place you in possession of all the information received at this department, and, so soon as received, of the actual state of things upon our frontiers, and from which, as by the information hitherto disclosed, the most unpleasant tidings may be daily expected. Without adverting to the causes or origin of them at all, I must say to you that it is my deliberate opinion that the United States government will be directly answerable to Georgia for every drop of blood shed upon this occasion; and I further say to you, what has been more than once said, that no State having pretensions to even limited sovereignty, ought to be dependent on another for the protection which is due from a government to its citizens, much less for that which, from the information communicated, seems to be urgently demanded for our frontier inhabitants. It is scarcely necessary to add that there are no measures which you may constitutionally authorize, which I will not execute with promptness and energy.

The Legislature adjourned on the 11th June, 1825.

General Gaines arrived at Milledgeville on Sunday, the 12th of June, and on the morning of the 13th had an interview with the Governor. On the same day he wrote to the Governor:

HEAD-QUARTERS, EASTERN DEPARTMENT,
Georgia, June 13th, 1825.

SIR: I have the honor to acknowledge the receipt of the correspondence referred to by your Excellency, in your verbal communication of this morning, representing the indications of hostility recently manifested by the Indians on the Western frontier of this State, numbered 1 to 4 inclusively; together with your instructions to Capt. Harrison, of the 10th of the present month. Of this paper, which I return herewith, I have to request the favor of a copy, with such information as that officer shall communicate, touching the execution of the important duty assigned to him.

With the greatest respect,
I have the honor to be
Your Excellency's ob't serv't,
EDMUND P. GAINES,
Maj-Gen. Com'g.

His Excellency Gov. Troup.

The Governor replied, the same day, enclosing a copy of his instructions, of 10th June, to Capt. James Harrison, commanding Twiggs County Cavalry, the substance of which was: that in carrying into effect the orders of Gen. Wimberly, he would be "careful to act strictly on the defensive, until circumstances shall arise to justify an opposite conduct;" that if he should, on arrival at the frontiers, find that the Indians had committed no outrages, &c., he would endeavor to pacify them, by assuring them that his presence there was not to make war upon them, but to "protect our people and others within our limits, in their persons and effects, against any assault or inroads upon either, and to chastise those who shall be mad enough to attempt them;" if, however, he should find they had committed hostile acts of unequivocal character, he should treat them as enemies, "pursuing them, if necessary, into the country occupied by them, and punishing them there," &c.—that if the Indians should merely have committed depredations on property, he should, whilst taking measures to recover the property, remember that the jurisdiction of the State had been established and its criminal laws extended over the country, so that the offenders could be seized and tried in the ordinary way; that the deluded Indians were objects rather of pity than resentment; and that, finding them in the wrong, the officer would endeavor to keep them so; that the officer should take the earliest occasion to inform himself correctly of the actual state of things, and that if it should appear expedient to do so, three companies or more of infantry or riflemen would be marched to his support; that the money advanced should be expended to the best advantage, proper vouchers taken so as to enable the State to charge the General Government with the amount, &c., &c.

The day after enclosing, to General Gaines, these instructions to Capt. Harrison, Gov. Troup wrote to the former, as follows:

It may be important to you to know, before you communicate with your Government and proceed to meet the Indians in convention, that the laws of Georgia are already extended over the ceded country, and of course that it is my bounden duty to execute them there. The statutory provision on this subject will be found in the papers of the morning, and in the act entitled "An Act to dispose of and distribute the lands lately acquired," &c.

The day previously, he had written to Gen. Gaines, and said:

In the course of the desultory and informal communication with you of to-day, my desire was intimated that the line between this State and Alabama should be run as early as possible, and I requested the favor of you to make known to your Government this desire, and without delay. A letter will be immediately dispatched to the Governor of Alabama, to apprise him of the resolution of the Government of Georgia to run that line, and to ask his concert and co-operation. If that concert and co-operation be refused, we will proceed to run the line without them, as we will also proceed in due time to make the survey of the lands within our limits, disregarding any obstacles which may be opposed from any quarter. You will see, therefore, how highly important it is that upon these points the two Governments should understand each other immediately.

In his letter to the Governor of Alabama, written 14th June, Gov. Troup said:

The enclosed resolution of the late Legislature will inform you that the Executive of Georgia is charged with the running of the line dividing this State and Alabama. As it is more than probable that I will take measures to carry their wishes into effect, very soon after the U. S. Government shall have had opportunity to quiet the disturbances which prevail in the Indian country; and as it is very desirable that the Government of Alabama shall harmoniously co-operate with that of Georgia in the execution of the work, I will thank you to inform me whether you feel yourself authorized to appoint Commissioners on your part to meet the Commissioners of Georgia, so that the operation may be a conjoint one, and satisfactory in its results to both parties.

To this letter, Governor Pickens, of Alabama, replied, on 3d of July, that he was "altogether unauthorized to appoint Commissioners or otherwise to co-operate in the desired work"—that the omission of the Legislature to act in the premises was not owing to any indifference to participating in the operation, or "indisposition to co-operate liberally and harmoniously in the execution of the work, whenever any practical benefit to either State might be promised." He further stated that until very recently the country on both sides the proposed line, was, for its whole extent, within the territory allotted to the Creeks and Cherokees, and for many months yet must continue in their occupancy, and that up to the period of the adjournment of the Legislature, no disposition for a cession of land had been evinced by either tribe; that, a treaty of cession having now been made, he felt assured the Legislature of Alabama would, at its next session in November, act with promptness in the premises, and presumed that action then would "be in very convenient season to meet the views of the Government of Georgia," &c., &c.

Governor Troup replied, on 10th August, and said:

"In compliance with the wishes expressed by your Excellency, I will cheerfully postpone the operation until November, confidently relying on the assurance that the Legislature of Alabama will, on its first meeting, take prompt measures to co-operate with Georgia in the execution of the work."

To the Governor's letter of the 13th June, Gen. Gaines replied, from his "Head Quarters" at Milledgeville, June 14th, 1825, and, amongst other things, said:

Your letter, which I shall without delay refer to the Department of War, announces your intention to cause the line to be run between this State and Alabama, and to survey the public land of the State within the late ceded territory. Upon the last mentioned subject, I am distinctly authorized to state to the Indians, that the President of the United States has suggested to Governor Troup the necessity of his abstaining from entering into and surveying the ceded land, until the time prescribed by the treaty for their removal.

There is, perhaps, no principle of national law better established, or more universally admitted, than that the contracting parties to a treaty possess the right, and, in a case like the one in question, the exclusive right of expounding and carrying into effect such treaty.

The decision of the President in this case must govern me in my intended conference with the Indians: and this conference must necessarily take place before the subject can be submitted to the President; nor is it probable that, if it were submitted, it would undergo any change.

I cannot, therefore, but express a confident hope that your Excellency may see the propriety of abstaining from the proposed survey, both of the boundary line and of the land within the late ceded territory, until the period arrives at which the removal of the Indians is required.

Immediately on receipt of this letter, Governor Troup addressed a communication to General Gaines, dated 15th June, in which he said:

I have this moment had the honor to receive your communication of the 14th inst., on the subject of the survey of the ceded country and the running of the dividing line between Alabama and Georgia, and in which you request that, in conformity with the expressed will of your government, both the survey and the running of the line may be forborne "until the period arrives at which the removal of the Indians is required."

It would give me great pleasure to be able to comply with any request made by yourself or your government. You would make none that did not, to your apprehensions, seem reasonable and proper. As, however, there exist two independent parties to the question, each is permitted to decide for itself, and, with all due deference to yours, I must be permitted to say, that my apprehension of the right and of the wrong leads me to the opposite conclusion—the conclusion to which the Legislature of Georgia, upon mature reflection, recently arrived by an almost unanimous voice, and which was made the foundation of my late communication to the Secretary of War, and my more recent one to you upon the same subject. I would deeply lament if any act proceeding from myself, should cause the least embarrassment to yourself or your government, especially considering the critical relations in which the United States stand to the Indians, and the great interest which the government of Georgia feels in their early and satisfactory adjustment; but it cannot be expected by your government, that important interests are to be surrendered, and rights deemed unquestionable, abandoned by Georgia, because of any embarrassment which may arise in the intercourse and negotiations between the United States and Indians. I set too just a value on your high character, to believe that you would willingly create them. I am equally persuaded that none will be suffered to exist which can with propriety be removed; and I know you will pardon me when I take the liberty of saying, that those to which you refer ought not to exist for a single moment. Upon every principle and practice of diplomacy, the particular instruction of your government, which has given rise to these embarrassments, ought at this moment to be taken and held as no instruction at all; for it is now known to you, that what purports to be an instruction, was given upon information which was believed to be true, but which has turned out to be false; and the presumption is irresistible, that, the state of things being changed, your government so far from desiring to press the execution, would gladly withdraw the instruction, and that, without any, the least responsibility, you are at perfect liberty to consider it withdrawn. It is not for me to instruct, but to derive instruction from you in everything connected with the military art; and you know as well as I, that no principle is better settled than the one which justifies disobedience to positive orders, under a change of circumstances. I say that the instruction had its origin singly in a falsehood imposed upon your government by its own Agent; and that, but for that falsehood, the instruction would not have been given. You have the proof in common sense, and in the documents and evidence connected with the late disturbances—if you want more proof, look into the gazettes of yesterday, where you find a Council of hostile Indians assembled by the Agent, proclaiming by acclamation his innocence of the death of McIntosh, because that death followed not from the survey but the law of the nation.

Your Government is informed by the Agent, that the hostile Indians are in array against us, because the Government of Georgia interfered to procure the consent to the survey. The same Indians testify to the falsehood of the declaration; and the dilemma is, that if the Agent is to be believed in the one case, the Indians cannot in the other. You see, therefore, Sir, plainly, the result—the Government of the United States, identifying itself in all things with the Agent, assumes for granted what is false; issues, in consequence thereof, a peremptory order to this Government to forbear an act which it feels it is its right and its duty and interest to perform. The falsity is made known to the officer instructed to carry that order into effect—the officer feels it to be his duty to proceed in the execution of the order, notwithstanding the change of circumstances which produced it. On the part of the Government of Georgia, the will of its highest constituted authority has been declared, upon the most solemn deliberation, that the line shall be run and the survey executed. It is for you, therefore, to bring it to the issue—it is for me only to repeat that, cost what it will, the line will be run and the survey effected. The Government of Georgia will not retire from the position it occupies, to gratify the Agent or the hostile Indians; nor will it do so, I trust, because it knows that, in consequence of disobedience to an unlawful mandate, it may very soon be recorded that "Georgia was."

Suffer me to say, also, that your Government has acted very precipitately and unadvisedly in this affair: after receiving notice of my intention to make the survey, it interposed no objection, though it had time to do so. A considerable interval elapsed, and it receives false information from the Agent, upon which it issues its peremptory order—soon after, it receives further false information from the same Agent, upon which it issues other orders confirmatory of the first, and which you seem to consider final.

But for my direct and active interference, hostilities would have immediately followed the death of McIntosh, and of a character so inveterate as to put at defiance any interference whatever, even on your part. Your powers, not your influence, might have been availing, to be sure, but your power was not here; and for preserving this peace you know what a respectful testimonial I have of the thanks of your Government, couched in the most delicate and complimentary terms.

The suggestion you make in derogation of our claim to participate in the construction or execution of the treaty, giving to that suggestion its utmost force, is merely that we are not nominally parties to the treaty—whilst the answer to it is, that we are party in interest deeper tenfold than they who appear upon the paper, and that the paper, in virtue of another paper to which we are parties, both nominally and in interest, passed a vested right of soil and of jurisdiction to Georgia, which none but the great Jehovah can divest.

You will be pleased to understand that there is no inclination here to urge hastily either the survey or the running of the line, so as to interfere in the least with the measures to be taken to pacify and tranquilize the Indians. On the contrary, all the facilities we can give for this object, will be readily afforded; but it is believed that in reasonable time this happy result can, with wise and prudent measures, of which your special Agent was advised yesterday, be easily accomplished; but never to be accomplished if the condition of that accomplishment be the abandonment of the survey and running of the line.

What, in our verbal conferences, had been promised, is now repeated, that the military requisitions which, in compliance with your instructions, you may think proper to make upon the Government of Georgia, will be promptly attended to, and the force placed under your command with the least possible delay. The implicit reliance in your high sentiments of honor, is my sufficient security that, that force, if it could, will in no event be employed against us.

On the 11th of June, the Governor had written to Messrs. Warren Jourdan, William W. Williamson, Seaborn Jones and William H. Torrance, informing them of their appointment, under authority of the resolution of the Legislature, to receive and take testimony in the case of the Agent for Indian affairs. He said: "as the party concerned disclaims the authority of the State to interfere, it is not to be presumed that application will be made to you for leave to cross-examine. Should, however, such application be made, you will not hesitate to grant it, giving timely notice of persons to be examined, and the time and place of such examination," &c., &c.

CHAPTER XI.

Canvass for Governor—Gov. Troup and Gen. Clark rival Candidates—Political excitement—Indian difficulties continued—Gen. Gaines and Major Andrews—Governor's correspondence with them and with the President, Secretary of War, &c.—Result of election for Governor—Governor's Inaugural, and Message to the Legislature—Action of the Legislature—New Counties laid out, &c., &c.

On the 5th day of April, 1825, the following announcement appeared in the Georgia Journal, a leading newspaper published at Milledgeville, and possessing the confidence of the Governor:

"☞ Gov. TROUP is a candidate for re-election to the office he now holds.

"☞ We are requested to state that Gen. CLARK is a candidate for the office of Governor."

The canvass had now opened, and the contest was to be the hottest ever witnessed in Georgia, and the excitement more intense than upon any other occasion of a civil nature, unless, perhaps, that which sprang up out of the Yazoo fraud. In consenting to an election by the Legislature, in 1823, Gov. Troup had so far put himself at the service of his friends, as to impose upon himself a sort of moral obligation to yield to their wishes in a canvass before the people. Besides, it was due to himself not to retire from a contest, the great interest and excitement of which had grown out of his own firm and manly administration of the affairs of the State. Whilst he had no particular ambition to gratify by a re-election to the office of Chief Magistrate, it was natural that he should desire to see his measures of government passed upon with approbation by the people whom he had so faithfully served; and he had too little fear of defeat, and too much confidence in his fellow-citizens, to decline a contest so much desired by his friends, and so proper under all the circumstances by which he was encompassed.

Nothing was more natural than that the opposition should bring out their well-tried and veteran leader. He had been Governor two consecutive terms; but what of that? There was no legal, no constitutional ineligibility. Gen. Clark had given his name to the party opposed to Mr. Crawford and his friends, long before Col. Troup had been named in connection with gubernatorial honors, or had evinced his remarkable talents for executive duties. "Troup and Clark" now rang through the State; and, whilst it was clear that the friends of the former had nothing to rely upon, in support of their chief, but his talents, virtues and great public services, it was certain that in the latter they had to encounter a foeman, who, to abilities of no ordinary sort, and long public services in the field and at the council-board, had the faculty of winning support where less sagacious politicians would have failed. Whatever faults Gen. Clark may have had—and who is free from them?—he was never charged with want of fidelity to his friends, or the lack of power to conciliate where success was possible by worthy means. Hence, he was beloved by his party, and was a dangerous competitor with any rival.

Before the close of the contest, Gov. Troup was running under and against a combination of circumstances that seemed little favorable to his re-election. Independently of the great popularity of his rival, he had to contend against the sympathies and probably the patronage of the Federal Executive; many weak-minded and timid persons thought his administration too bold; many honest men, whilst they could not, in calm moments, believe his motives to be impure, yet thought or feared he might precipitate a crisis, that would result in civil strife between the United States and Georgia. Besides having to encounter much of the hereditary hatred which the Clark party bore to Mr. Crawford and his friends, he had to stand the brunt of all the opposition which his controversy with General Gaines,

Major Andrews and Col. Crowell, had engendered. Add to all this, his contempt for those little arts and blandishments which politicians know so well how to use, and by which temporary success is often gained—and, to a casual observer, his chance might have seemed hopeless. But this was only the outside view. He had then had much experience in the public service, had never disappointed public expectation; and though it could not be said of him, as some one has remarked of Mr. Jefferson, *that he never made a speech, founded a sect, or fought a battle;* yet, like that great statesman, he had rarely misjudged men or measures, and could show a political record, as remarkable for its consistency, as it was untarnished by any, the slightest taint of dishonor. If ever a statesman, in our times, passed through a long public life, with clean hands and a good cnscience, that man was George M. Troup.

We proceed now to the course of the Governor in regard to the Agent of Indian affairs, and his correspondence with the special Agent on that subject. On the 8th of June, he wrote to Major Andrews to learn whether he had not, in a certain conversation, stated that the evidence submitted to him did not furnish even probable cause to suspect the Indian Agent as guilty under the charges exhibited against him in the Governor's letter of 31st May, &c.

In his reply, the same day, Major Andrews denied the justice of the inference deduced from that conversation, and stated his recollection of the result of that conversation to be, that, until he was furnished with the documents and evidence referred to in the Governor's letter of 31st May, he did not consider himself at liberty to form any opinion, even as to the propriety of suspending the Agent, &c.

He added:

I beg the attention of your Excellency to my letter, of the 31st May, by which you will perceive I expected to be able to furnish the Agent, in case his suspension was decided on, with a copy of the charges and specifications made against him, immediately on his being suspended, that "he might be able to defend himself before his government with as little delay as possible;" and that his suspension would also depend on the present state of excitement among the Indians. This course, your Excellency will do me the justice to believe, is in strict accordance with the instructions of my Government. I have delayed all proceedings, (even to a formal acknowledgment of the receipt of your letter of the 31st ultimo,) waiting to be furnished with the documents and evidence promised in it. So soon as I shall be honored by its receipt, (if General Gaines shall have arrived,) I will immediately proceed to execute the intentions of the President, as made known to your Excellency.

On the 13th of June, the Governor wrote a letter to Major Andrews, in which he said:

"In compliance with a resolution of the Legislature of the State of Georgia, I place you in possession of the report of a committee, the resolutions which follow, and the evidence which supports them, in the case of the Agent for Indian Affairs, whose conduct, in connection with the late disturbances in the Creek nation, has been recently a subject of investigation before that Legislature.

He wrote again, as follows, on the 14th:

In the conversations held with yourself and Gen. Gaines, in relation to the objects of your mission, you were pleased to express a desire to receive from myself any views or suggestions which might usefully contribute to the results which were most desirable. These, in passing, have been hitherto frankly given. As it is determined that one or both of you will proceed to attend the convention of the Indians about to be holden at Broken Arrow and the Indian Springs, it becomes my duty to disclose to you, in a special manner, the opinions entertained of this first and most important movement, so that, if miscarriage follow, the councils of Georgia will share in no degree the responsibility of that miscarriage. It is known to be one of your objects to elicit from the convention the truths connected with the late and present disorders in the nation—a development which the councils of Georgia cannot fail to regard with very deep concern. It has been more than once asked of you, therefore, if, preparatory to this movement, it did not seem to you as indispensable to suspend the Agent from his functions, under the authority vested in you by your Government. The answers given have been received with pain and regret, because they indicated an intention to forbear the exercise of the power, at least for the present, whilst it is plainly foreseen that the present is the only moment at which the exercise of it would be of any value to you, or to us, in the fulfilment of the objects of your mission, and for this very obvious reason: the Agent, in virtue of his official power, exercising a controlling influence over one portion of the nation, has already assembled that portion, and you see in the morning's paper by what a formidable and imposing array of Chiefs he stands exculpated and acquitted. Now, Sir, I appeal to your good sense to inform me of what avail will be the contemplated convocation and catechising of the Indians, the Agent holding to his commission and wielding his accustomed powers? Is it to be believed that, under like circumstances, they will reconsider their minutes and alter their verdict? Not so. In matters even of this kind, they have sagacity and shrewdness, and a decent regard for the opinions of the world. Not doubting that your object is the ascertainment of truth, it is hoped that you will suffer no obstacles to impede your course to it; the most formidable of all stands directly in your way. 'T is impossible that the faintest ray of light can reach you, when it is known that, in despite of all that has transpired of crimination, of investigation, of evidence, and of exposure, the Agent is present to the Indians in his robes of ermine, yet sustained by the Government of the United States, as if his purity were spotless and his name unsullied—the same in authority as he always has been—the same whom they behold in prospect to be their leader through new trials, their counselor in evil times, and the supreme director of their destinies in all times. Can it be presumed that, under such circumstances, the Indians will speak to you without restraint? The documents of incontestable authority prove to you that they will not. No, Sir; the way to the accomplishment of the ends of your mission, is open—suspend the Agent—make atonement to the friends of McIntosh for the blood shed by the guilty instruments of white men—restore the friendly chiefs to their political rank and power, and, my word for it, you will find truth, and enough of it, for any purpose—peace, reconciliation and union.

To this letter and that of the 13th, Major Andrews replied, from the Creek Agency, Flint River, on the 18th, stating that he had not received an official copy of the documents promised in the Governor's letter of 31st May —urging that they be furnished, and also that the Agent of the Government be furnished with any additional testimony which the Governor might wish to offer against the Indian Agent, &c., &c. He stated, further, that he entertained different opinions from those expressed in the Governor's last letter, and especially in regard to the suspension of the Agent—that, after a careful examination of the testimony taken by the committee (of the Legislature,) he did not think that the suspension was demanded on the ground contemplated in his letter of 31st May, and by the Government—that he did not think the presence of the Indian Agent at any place, or under any circumstances, would be prejudicial to truth—that he had hoped, as the Governor's message of 3d June implied doubt of the Agent's guilt, and he had been acquitted generally of one of the charges, by the report adopted by the Legislature, but still had the influence and power of the Executive and Legislature against him, and that, too, on *ex parte* testimony, that the Agent would not, on his trial, have to complain of any acts, on the part of another, that might appear to partake of oppression. Nevertheless, "in courtesy" to the Governor's fixed opinion, &c., he would suspend the Agent; but thought that public opinion should not be forestalled by the publication of *ex parte* testimony against the Agent, &c., &c.

Gov. Troup replied, on 20th June, and said :

I have, this moment, received your letter, of the 18th instant, dated at the Creek Agency. The printing of the documents and evidence having relation to the disorders in the nation, and to the charges exhibited by this Government, will be completed, it is understood, in the course of the day, so that a copy will be forwarded for your use, in the course of to-morrow. The commission authorized by the Legislature to take further testimony, will, for that purpose, proceed, forthwith, to the nation, and under orders to make all possible dispatch.

You have widely mistaken me, if you believe that any disposition exists here, to withhold from the Agent the most ample means of justifying himself to his Government; much less any desire for the performance of an act on your part that would savor of oppression: on the contrary, this Government desires that the fairest opportunity shall be afforded the accused, of profiting of every description of testimony which may be available for his complete vindication, free from any obstacles or embarrassments which it might have the power to interpose. It was in this spirit that my instructions to the Commissioners were drafted; and, although it was known that the Agent had disclaimed the authority of the Government of Georgia to interfere, and that, therefore, there was little probability of his seeking the benefit of a particular instruction; nevertheless, an instruction has been given, which will admit him, at his pleasure, to be present at the investigation on our part, and to exercise the right of cross-examination freely. Moreover, I can add, with great sincerity, that it will give me pleasure, at any time, to contribute aids and facilities to his defence; for, whatever I may believe of the guilt or innocence of the Agent, I trust that one and all of us, for the honor of our own human nature, would gladly see him vindicated and justified against such charges as have been preferred by this Government. Whilst, however, this assurance is given, it is nevertheless true that you have very much misconceived the sentence of my message, which, according to your construction of it, implies doubt of the guilt of the Agent—no such doubt exists. It was not said that the Agent had committed crimes, because it was not intended to say so; it was enough that the Agent had been charged with the commission of them; and, having exhibited the charges, I presume you would not have been insensible to the indelicacy of the accuser passing sentence upon the accused. But, whilst this was purposely avoided there, I can very freely make known to you here, that if, instead of passing upon the guilt or innocence of the accused, I had been stating my belief from the evidence even now disclosed, and *ex parte* as it may be, I would have said, without hesitation, that, with respect to the one charge, I believed him guilty of that beyond the possibility of refutation, and that with regard to the other, he was so far innocent only as he was not present at the time and place, inflicting the blows with his own hands. Taking very opposite views of the subject, you seem to have yielded a reluctant and ungracious assent to the suspension of the Agent, and indeed to indulge a little the language of complaint, lest injury might by possibility result from it to the accused.

Be persuaded, sir, that this act of suspension is in no respect personally gratifying to me; nor were feelings of any kind connected with my suggestion of the propriety of it, but those which yourself must have indulged for the successful fulfilment of the objects of your mission. I repeat what was before alledged in support of that suggestion, that it could not be conceived how it would be possible for you to make any, the least, advance to the attainment of truth, or to the pacification of the Indians, without it as a first and indispensable measure. The friendly Chiefs had already given your Government to understand that they would never consent to commit themselves again to the protection of the Agent; and you were almost present to witness that, by the power and influence of his office, the hostile Chiefs had been convoked, and a declaration of the innocence of the Agent either extorted or otherwise obtained; and this, too, just before the period had arrived at which General Gaines and yourself were to convene the same Indians, for the purpose of obtaining from them fairly and honestly the truth; a fact well known to the Agent, but which fact did not prevent him from thus forestalling and anticipating you.

When you permit yourself to say that the Agent "has not, so far as the investigation has been pursued by the authorities of Georgia, been informed of the nature and cause of the accusation," you will suffer me to answer, that this has been no omission of ours, but of yours. It was part of your duty to have notified the Agent, so soon as the charges were received, of the existence of those charges; and, with regard to specifications, I assure you that, unless for some very useful purpose to the interests of Georgia, I would not take the trouble to sit down to paper to make them. The Agent is charged with instigating the Indians to the commission of the crime of murder, and with predetermined resolution to prevent the Indians from making cession of the lands so long as a certain person was at the head of the Government of Georgia; and these, in all reason, are specifications enough. We are not exhibiting charges against the Agent as offending the martial law, to which a long detail of specifications, according to custom, must be subjoined. If your Government wants further specification, it must seek it elsewhere; and this, sir, is obviously the mistaken bias under which you and your Government labor. You are willing to resolve every thing into prejudice against the Agent, for his protection—whereas, it is notorious that the prejudice of your Government has been so far advantageous to him, that it is very difficult to subdue it by any kind of evidence. With respect to "the right of confrontation with the witnesses against him," there is abundant time for that, when, after finding a true bill, he shall be arraigned at the bar of justice—and, with regard to his "not having compulsory process for obtaining witnesses in his favor, as required by the sacred instrument which guards the rights of all," I pledge you my word of honor, that whenever I shall hear of such gross injustice being done him by any competent and authorized tribunal before which he may be cited, I will consider it as an injury done to myself; and, if done by a tribunal within our jurisdiction, and of course punishable for offences committed under our constitution and laws, so far as depends on me, the utmost efforts will be made to bring to punishment all or any public agents concerned in so offending.

The documents are in a course of publication, by order of the Legislature. Having been previously made public by that body itself, in the most formal manner, it is not seen that any further publication of them can operate injuriously to the Agent; for it would seem to be better, even on his own account, that after so much had been made known of their contents, all should be known, and that nothing should be left for inference or conjecture; especially, too, as the public, understanding the character of the evidence to be *ex parte*, will be able to estimate it at what it may be worth. It may be proper to add that, by a special and positive resolution, the Governor is directed to cause them to be distributed through all the counties, as soon as they are printed, and you are already informed that the printing will be complete in the course of to-day.

Major Andrews, replied, from the Creek Agency, on 23d June, disclaiming any intention to express a belief that the authorities of Georgia were disposed to withhold from the Agent the means of justifying himself; yet expressing his conviction that their course towards him must operate oppressively, &c. He then corrects an error into which the Governor had fallen; by showing that the convocation of the Chiefs by the Agent, and the procuring by him of documents from them, for his vindication, occurred "before it was possible for the Agent to know that Gen. Gaines or an

Agent of the government were ordered here." He insisted that specifications were necessary, as an act of justice, to a fair trial of the Agent, &c., and that before the *trial* of the Agent his punishment had been demanded—to wit, his dismissal, &c., &c., and that the publication against which suggestion was made, was the publication in the news papers and not in pamphlet. The writer concluded with a respectful protest against the imputation of prejudice to the General Government, &c.

The Governor replied as follows:

EXECUTIVE DEPARTMENT,
Milledgeville, 27*th June*, 1825.

SIR: I have this moment received your letter of the 23d inst. It gives me great pleasure to correct, without delay, an error into which I had fallen, and in consequence of not adverting particularly to the date of the certificate obtained from the Indians by the Agent, and published as part of his defence in one of the last papers. From a comparison of dates, it does appear that that certificate was obtained before the Agent knew that yourself and General Gaines would proceed to Broken Arrow to convene a Council or institute an inquiry. Whilst this correction, therefore, is most cheerfully made, you cannot but admit the utter immateriality of it to the Agent for any objects or interests of his; for the fact still turns out to be, that whilst the Agent, in procuring that certificate, did not intend to forestall, in particular, General Gaines and yourself, in making a certain examination, he did well know that it would forestall General Gaines or yourself or any others whom your Government might at any time depute to make an examination there; and this is the fact, and the only fact, of any consequence to the argument.

On the subject of specifications to which you have again called my attention, I have only to remark, that, if your Government pleases to forbear further inquiry or investigation into the conduct of the Agent, either because it derives no specifications from me, or because those specifications are not precisely such, in manner and form, as are agreeable to itself, it has the power to do so. But if your Government has not found matter enough for specifications, (if indeed they be at all important,) in the published accredited documents, or, finding it there in abundance, shall not choose to frame them for itself, I assure you, Sir,

I would not know where to proceed to look for it, even if I believed it (as I do not,) to be my duty to furnish those specifications. When time shall have disclosed that I was mistaken in attributing prejudice to your Government in behalf of its Agent, although that belief has not been assumed upon light ground, and is so far sustained by the occurrences of every day, I assure you, Sir, I shall proceed, without delay, to render to it the fullest measure of justice which injured honor could require from a deceived accuser.

Very respectfully,
Your obedient serv't,

T. P. Andrews, G. M. TROUP.
Special Agent.

Frequent reference having been made to the certificate of the Indians in behalf of Col. Crowell, it is proper to insert it here. The following is all that is necessary:

We, the undersigned, chiefs and head-men of the Creek Nation, do certify and declare that we determined, of our own free will and accord, to put to death the Chief McIntosh, and that neither the Agent, John Crowell, or any other white man, were the instigators or abettors—nor do we know or believe that he, the Agent, knew that we had any such design—nor did we communicate it to any but a few old and head-men. We determined to put him to death for a violation of a law first proposed by him and sanctioned by the Big Warrior and Little Prince—and then the different towns were called up, and the lawyers, who had been previously made by McIntosh, Big Warrior and Little Prince, were directed to put into execution this law, against any chief or other person who broke it, however great he might be, even Big Warrior, Little Prince or McIntosh.

To this were added the following statements in the form of question and answer: 1st. That the law "to take the life of a Chief of this Nation who should sell the lands of the Nation without the consent of the nation," was first made "on the west bank of the Oakmulgee, at the time the land belonged to them, the Indians." 2d. If the Agent had directed the killing of McIntosh, "we would not, (have done it) for he was not placed here for that purpose." No white person knew it, "but James

Hutton, who was born and raised in the Nation and considered as one of us, who we took as an interpreter." It was further stated that "the Chief who commanded the party that executed McIntosh, was asked if he told McIntosh's wife, or any person, that the Agent directed him to do so," replied, "No, and that he did not believe his men had done so, nor had he heard anything about it—and the Chief, after hearing what Chilly McIntosh had said, relative to their shooting at and pursuing him to the river, contradicted it, and said they neither shot at, nor pursued him, in short made no exertions to ketch (catch) him." The whole was signed by Little Prince and 36 others, and was dated the 14th May, 1825.

The following is inserted somewhat out of its chronological order, but in its appropriate place:

EXECUTIVE DEPARTMENT,
Milledgeville, 18*th June*, 1825.

SIR: From the course recently pursued by the Agent, in procuring from the Chiefs of the hostile Indians, under the influence of his office, and from the Missionaries, their attestation to his innocence, the Commissioners appointed under the authority of the Legislature, are directed to proceed to Broken Arrow, to participate in the councils to be holden there on the 25th inst. So far as they have for their objects the collection of facts and development of truths, as connected with the late disturbances in the Nation, and the charges exhibited by this Government against the Agent of the United States for Indian Affairs—they are instructed specially to avoid any interference, unless solicited, with the political arrangements or negotiations between the United States and the Indians, which appertain exclusively to the relations and interests subsisting between them, and to which the State of Georgia is no party. It is hoped and expected that this measure will meet your concurrence and approbation.

With great respect, &c.,

G. M. TROUP.

Maj. T. P. Andrews,
Special Agent.

On the morning of the 28th of June, the following letter

from Major Andrews to Col. Crowell, appeared in one of the public newspapers at Milledgeville :

CREEK AGENCY, Flint River,
June 21, 1825.

Sir : You have been advised of the measures heretofore taken by the President of the United States and the Secretary of War, in relation to the charges, specific and implied, made against you as Indian Agent. I have now to inform you, that a suspension from the exercise of your functions as Indian Agent, (until all the testimony to be collected in the Indian nation has been obtained and examined,) has been decided on. I herewith send you a copy of the evidence collected by a committee of the Georgia Legislature, and their report as adopted by the Legislature. Copies of other documents, promised me by the Governor of Georgia, shall be furnished you as soon as those documents are received. You will accordingly turn over the Agency to the sub-Agent, Captain Triplett.

In resorting to the discretionary power vested in me by the President, I feel it due to you to state frankly, that this determination does not proceed from any present impression unfavorable to your innocence. I am not at liberty, in my present peculiar situation, to form a settled opinion on the charges made against you, until all the evidence to be collected from every quarter has been received and carefully examined. But I feel it due to you to say, that so far as I am at liberty to take up a present impression, it is in favor of your integrity and honor. I feel it due to you to make this statement in consequence of the course (which must be considered an unjust one, if not oppressive,) pursued towards you by the authorities of Georgia—my impressions too being chiefly grounded on the *ex parte* testimony taken against you.

Your suspension is made from courtesy to the authorities of Georgia, who have repeatedly and urgently demanded it—on the ground that it would be impossible to elicit unbiased testimony in the Indian Nation, whilst you are in the exercise of your functions. It is done, too, from a desire to do away all pretexts which might otherwise hereafter be seized on to destroy confidence in the results of the examinations. The suspension will be withdrawn so soon as those examinations are concluded, should they result in establishing your innocence.

As the object of the General Government, in this examination, is the ascertainment of truth, it could not but give me pain, as its Agent, to find that in taking testimony against you, all the usual prerequisites were lost sight of by the authorities of Georgia. You were neither "*informed of the nature and cause of the accusations*," or *confronted with witnesses against you*, nor had you "*compulsory process for obtaining witnesses in your favor!*" The evidence on which the harshest opinions have been formed and expressed, was not only *ex parte*, but it has been spread before the public, in the newspapers, before you had been informed of its character or had an opportunity of making your defence; and public opinion thereby forestalled, before the General Government, under which you hold your appointment, has had an opportunity of examining the testimony of either party. The course which you have determined to pursue, as made known to me in the copy of your letter, of the 20th, to the Commissioners appointed by the Governor of Georgia to take further evidence against you—in inviting them to be present at the examination of your voluntary witnesses—is of an opposite character, and cannot fail to strengthen the belief of your conscious innocence.

It is scarcely necessary to add that in the exalted character of the President of the United States and the Secretary of War, you have the surest guaranty of a fair trial, and a just decision on it.

Very respectfully, sir,
Your most obedient servant,
T. P. ANDREWS,
Special Agent.

Col. John Crowell.

In giving this letter to the public, Col. Crowell, in his card, said, amongst other things: "Indeed, the untiring zeal manifested by Gov. Troup in the accomplishment of his purpose, has rarely been equalled and never surpassed—it stands without a parallel in the annals of persecution;" and he afterwards spoke of "the inquisitorial proceedings of the Governor and Legislature of Georgia."

On seeing Major Andrews' last letter, in print, the Governor immediately addressed the following note to Major Andrews:

EXECUTIVE DEPARTMENT,
Milledgeville, 28*th June*, 1825.

Sir: I call your attention to a letter purporting to be yours, and addressed to the Agent, in extenuation of your conduct for the act of suspension, and published in a paper here of this morning, called the Patriot. If this letter be authentic, you will consider all intercourse between yourself and this government suspended from the moment of the receipt of this.

G. M. TROUP.

T. P. Andrews,
Special Agent United States, Creek Agency.

And, on the same day, he wrote to the Secretary of War, enclosing, "for the information of the President," the paper containing Major Andrews' letter "in extenuation of his conduct in suspending" Col. Crowell "from his functions," under "instructions," and said:

"If, in writing such a letter, the Special Agent has so acted as to find himself within the letter or spirit of those instructions, it is obvious that the question which he was charged to investigate had been prejudged at Washington, before his departure from that city; and that, consequently, the Government of Georgia can no longer, consistently with its dignity, hold intercourse with that officer," &c., &c.

On the 4th of July, Major Andrews addressed a long letter to Gov. Troup, avowing the authorship of the letter to Col. Crowell, "with the exception of a few typographical errors," and sending the Governor a corrected copy. He said:

"It is such a letter as my sense of justice imperiously called on me to address him in performing a harsh act towards him—was approved of by my best judgment, such as it is—is approbated by a man,* who, for wisdom, stands inferior to few, and in honor to none; and such an one as, I confidently trust, will receive the approbation of my Government. It is such a letter as, from my letters of the 31st of May, 8th, 18th and 23d of June, to yourself, and our frequent verbal communications, as well as those verbal and written to your Aid-de-Camp and friend, Col. Lumpkin, you ought, in my opinion, to have anticipated; and such an one as I was convinced, "for the honor of human nature," (to use your own eloquent expression,) you expected."

He spoke, also, of the Agent's "inflexible integrity and firmness in stemming a torrent of corruption, disgraceful,

* Gen. Gaines, no doubt.—ED.

in my opinion, to the national character;" and this, after the examinations, "both numerous and important," had progressed.

Pending his correspondence with Major Andrews and Gen. Gaines, the Governor, on 18th June, addressed a letter to the Georgia Commissioners, Messrs. Jourdan, Jones, Torrance and Williamson, in which he said:

You are requested to proceed to the Indian Springs, to attend a Council of the friendly Indians to be holden there on the 20th inst. As it is presumed that every concert tendered on the part of this Government to assure a full development of the facts connected with the late disturbances in the Creek Nation, and also such as may more particularly affect the guilt or innocence of the Agent, under the charges exhibited against him by the Governor of this State, will be gratifying to Major-General Gaines, you are hereby authorized and empowered, under the authority vested in you by the Legislature, to employ all lawful means for the furthering of the objects aforesaid, avoiding at the same time any interference whatever with that Council in matters disconnected with the objects of your mission, and which appertain exclusively to interests and relations purely political subsisting between the General Government and Indians.

From the Indian Springs you will proceed to attend the other Council of Indians to be holden at Broken Arrow on the 25th inst. Your presence there will be of more importance, because more immediately connected with the investigation of the conduct of the Agent, as arraigned by the Governor, at the instance of the President of the United States, and by the Legislature of the State. You will no doubt be admitted to a free participation of that Council, and will be suffered to take with you, under sufficient safeguard, any of the friendly chiefs whose presence there you may consider necessary to the accomplishment of the objects which the United States and this Government have in view. There can be the less doubt of this, because, the charges having been already made both by the Executive and Legislative authority of Georgia against the Agent, and the Agent having so far thought proper to have recourse to the Missionaries and hostile Indians in the Nation, for his defence, and that defence being already before the public, at the instance of the Agent, in which it would seem that both being under the control and influence of his office, any direction most suitable to his views may be given to their opinions and feelings; it is only an exercise of strict right on the part of the Government of Georgia that it be heard before that Council, by its Commissioners, who are instructed to give and receive explanations for the purpose, in common with the Agents of the United States, of arriving at truth and doing justice to all parties. Should such participation be denied you, you will enter your formal protest against that denial, and proceed to avail yourselves, within the jurisdiction of Georgia, of all the testimony you can obtain.

In reply to the Governor's letter of 15th June, (copied in the preceding chapter,) Gen. Gaines wrote, the next day, stating that he had not permitted himself to be "influenced by any statements from Col. Crowell, although not prepared to condemn that officer without a hearing," &c. —that his impressions led him "to the conclusion that the proposed surveys, with the consequent influx of white men, strangers to the Indians, during the existence of feuds amongst them, would not fail to fan the flame of discord," &c,; expressed the hope that the Governor would soon hear, fully and satisfactorily, from the proper department; thanked him for the promptitude with which he had furnished him with information in regard to the late disturbances on the frontier, and stated his readiness to co-operate with him in the discharge of his duties; expressed the hope that the spirit of hostility might soon be restrained amongst the contending parties of the Indians; but, as a precautionary measure, desired the Governor to furnish, from the militia or volunteers, one regiment of cavalry, and one of infantry, to be held in readiness, &c., &c.

On the same day, he said he would take an early occasion to advise the Governor "of the result of the intended conferences with the Indians," &c.

On the 16th of June, the Governor wrote to Gen. Gaines that he had issued orders for the required military force &c.; and, on the 18th, he wrote him that the Georgia Commissioners would acquaint the General with the Governor's instructions to them; and expressed the hope that, "by concert and co-operation, such aids and facilities" might "be afforded as would be desirable" to Gen. Gaines, &c. The letter concluded:

From what has occurred, it is highly important that this Government should be represented at the Council to be held at Broken Arrow on the 25th. The many inconsistencies in the conduct of the Indians to be explained and reconciled, and their recent convocation by the Agent for the purpose of repelling charges made against him by the Governor of this State, at the instance of the Government of the United States, make it indispensable for the attainment of truth and justice, that the Commissioners should be present there. If, for this purpose, it should be thought advisable to take with them some of the friendly Chiefs, who are deeply interested in vindicating their characters against reiterated attacks upon them by the hostile party, it is hoped that this, likewise, will meet your concurrence, and that they will be placed under your safeguard and protection.

In reply, Gen. Gaines wrote from Indian Springs, on 22d June, and said: "I have to observe that, however much I might be aided by the experience, talents and integrity and honor of the Commissioners referred to on the part of the State of Georgia, I do not feel myself authorized, without new instructions from the Department of War, to comply with the demand contained in their letter of yesterday's date, 'to be admitted to a full and free participation of the Council of Indians,'" &c., &c.—that the Indians were "still laboring under some delusion and excitement," which "would be increased rather than diminished by adding to the number of individuals by whom they are to be addressed, or by any addition or multiplication of the matters of controversy to which their attention may be called"—that he was "fully authorized and instructed by the government of the United States, to protect the friendly Indians, to mitigate their calamitous condition; and, in the event of hostilities having ceased on the part of the opposite party, to restore harmony between them," &c., &c., &c.—that his sense of the responsibility of the high trust reposed in him, suggested clearly the propriety of his "having the entire control of every individual white man allowed to address the Council," and that he "should, moreover, have the control of every expression uttered to the Council by any citizen or officer of the United States" —that, without such control, confusion might ensue and the benevolent objects of the government be defeated; and added: "To avert an evil so pregnant with mischievous consequences to the Creek Nation, to the peace and honor of my country, and to my own reputation, I must decline the demand of the Georgia Commissioners;" but that, if "instructed by the proper authority to recognize the proposed co-operation of the Georgia Commissioners," he would "take great pleasure in serving with them;" and that his whole duty as a public officer was comprised in one single word, which suggested the propriety of the course pursued by him on that occasion—"and that word is *obedience*—obedience to the laws and the orders of the authorities placed over me." In the same letter, he stated that hostilities had ceased, and that he had received "satisfactory assurance of an earnest desire on the part of the Chiefs of both parties to remain at peace with each other," and that it therefore became his duty "to make peace upon just principles, and consequently to avoid an Indian War."

It is not important to notice, particularly, the action of the Georgia Commissioners, as that will appear substantially in the letters, &c., of Gov. Troup, which follow; and, however desirable it might be, we have no room for their correspondence with Gen. Gaines, Major Andrews and Col. Crowell. On the 28th of June, the Governor notified the Commissioners that "the dignity of Georgia requires that it no longer continue to recognize him (Major Andrews,) in his official character of Special Agent."

Three of the Commissioners, on the 20th June, addressed a note, at the Indian Springs, to Gen. Gaines, in which they said: "It is important to the Commissioners that your answer to the application of his Excellency the Governor to admit the Commissioners to a full and free participation of the Council of the Indians, should be received as early as practicable." The next day, Gen. Gaines replied, declining the application, his reasons for which will appear in his letter, of 22d June, to the Governor. This called forth a second letter from the Commissioners to Gen. Gaines, in which, after stating the object and importance of their mission, and especially in reference to the investigation of the conduct of the Indian Agent, they said:

"To arrive at the certainty of all these facts, in the most imposing and official manner, it was considered by our Government necessary to constitute the present mission. It was further determined, by the same Government, to be of the first consequence that the members of that mission should present themselves, clothed in their official character, in the Council of the Indians to be convened by you; believing that in those Councils information might be elicited material to the points in issue between the State of Georgia and the Agent for Indian affairs. For this purpose and no other, we have been directed by our Government to repair to this place, and to inform you of the same, and to respectfully ask your permission for admittance therein. We have done so by request only; we have not demanded it: that permission has been denied us. We therefore, in pursuance of our instructions, as also a proper sense of duty towards our Government, do hereby enter our formal protest against such denial, believing that, in consequence of being debarred the participation in those Councils, the State of Georgia will unquestionably be deprived of that which is to her of vital interest and great magnitude."

On the 20th of June, Col. Crowell addressed a note to the Commissioners, offering them permission to cross-examine his witnesses. He added:

"In giving you this invitation, I wish you distinctly to understand that it is not given under the impression that it is your right—since I have not been confronted with the witnesses against me. But it is given under a full conviction of being able fully to establish my innocence, by witnesses who shrink not from the ordeal of cross-examination, and to show you that my defence rests not, like the accusations against me, upon the flimsy foundation of garbled evidence, arbitrarily taken and improperly reported."

45

In accepting the invitation, by letter of 25th June, the Commissioners said:

"We shall be happy on our part to cross-examine any witnesses you may deem necessary. On our part, we would observe, that the Government of Georgia feels no disposition to deprive you of any and every means of justifying yourself. We have no doubt that you would have been permitted to be present and cross-examine the witnesses before the committee of the Legislature, had a request been made by you, and we have been particularly instructed by his Excellencythe Governor to afford you that privilege."

On the 25th of June, the Commissioners again called the attention of Gen. Gaines to that part of the Governor's instructions requesting that they be allowed a free participation of the Council of the Indians to be convened at Broken Arrow, and that then lately held at Indian Springs, and repeated the request to be admitted to the Council at the former place. To this Gen. Gaines replied, in a long letter of 26th June, declining the request. In his letter he said: "It affords me pleasure to profit by the *suggestions* of my fellow-citizens; but those *suggestions*, to be acceptable to me, must be free of anything like official power or control."

We copy the following letter from the Commissioners to the Governor, dated Fort Mitchell, 28th June, 1825.

By the return of your express, we advised you of our movements up to that date. Finding ourselves completely forestalled in every operation here, by the directions of Gen. Gaines and the Agent, we determined in Council that a part of the mission should proceed forthwith to Alabama,* believing the testimony to be obtained in that quarter more important than any we could collect here. In furtherance of these views, Cols. Jones and Torrance left here, yesterday evening, and will return with all possible dispatch to join us. The other two members of the mission continue to occupy their situation. The Indians will probably go into Council to-morrow. As yet we know nothing of the import of their deliberations, and as yet we can say nothing favorable of the object of our mission.

* Fort Mitchell was then supposed to be in Georgia; but the subsequent running of the line between the two States, showed it to be in Alabama.—ED.

Meanwhile, the Governor kept up a regular communication with the Commissioners. The following is one of his letters to them:

EXECUTIVE DEPARTMENT,
Milledgeville, 28th June, 1825.

Gentlemen: It would be desirable, if you have an opportunity to do so, to impress upon the Indians the innocence of the intention as well as the innocence of the act of survey, on our part, as their rights or interests of any kind can in no manner be affected by it. The measures of the United States will undoubtedly have a tendency to excite them against us; and if the United States should not take part with them in resisting the survey, humanity would dictate the propriety of forewarning them of the consequences, after placing them in possession of the facts and principles which govern our conduct.

Very respectfully,
G. M. TROUP.

The Georgia Commissioners,
at Broken Arrow.

Again, on the 1st of July, he wrote them:

"Perceiving by your peculiar situation in the Nation, that more of efficiency and dispatch may be given to your proceedings, by enabling you to detach members of your Board whenever it shall be deemed necessary, you are hereby further instructed to make such detachment at discretion—provided that not less than two shall be competent to proceed to business at any particular place, whose report shall in all cases be made to the Board for its adoption or rejection, and that no such proceeding shall be considered final and conclusive until it has received the sanction and approbation of the Board."

The following letters from two of the Commissioners, deserve a place here. The first gives, perhaps, the earliest official information which the Governor received of an expectation or attempt to *abrogate the treaty*.

CRABTREE'S, CREEK NATION,
June 30th, 1825.

His Ex. Geo. M. Troup:

Sir: Difficulties and obstructions having been thrown in the way of the early fulfilment of the objects which called us to this place, we have to request of you to detain any witness or witnesses who may attend at Milledgeville, for examination, until our arrival. The hostile part of the Nation have, for some time past, been deluded with the expectation, nay, almost certainty, of the abrogation of the treaty. We have great pleasure of informing your Excellency, that General Gaines took occasion, yesterday, while in council, to state distinctly such a hope was illusive—that such an occurrence was unknown in the history of diplomacy, and earnestly urged them to become reconciled to the treaty, and the policy of the General Government. We take occasion to assure your Excellency of our high consideration and respect.

WARREN JOURDAN,
WM. W. WILLIAMSON,
Commissioners.

CRABTREE'S, CREEK NATION,
July 2d, 1825.

His Ex. Geo. M. Troup:

Sir: We have the honor to acknowledge the receipt of your several enclosures by express.

In conformity with your wishes, a talk was immediately drafted, expressive of your views in relation to the survey of the country forthwith, accruing to Georgia by the late treaty concluded at the Indian Springs. As Gen. Gaines had, from the beginning to the end, disclaimed the authority of Georgia to an interference with the "delicate and important trust confided to him," we deemed it respectful to submit it to his examination and decision before we proposed it to the Council. We had the mortification to receive, in this as well as in every other application which was calculated to facilitate the objects of our mission and to elicit truth, the continued and reiterated declaration, "it will conflict with our instructions, it is therefore inadmissible." We have accomplished but little; our way has been obstructed and hedged in on all sides. We have been engaged indefatigably to promote the well-being of the State we have the honor to represent on this occasion. Our labors have been unsuccessful and mortifying to an extent unknown in the history of diplomacy. You shall hear from us in detail at a proper time.

Your Excellency's most obliged and humble servants,

WARREN JOURDAN,
W. W. WILLIAMSON,
Commissioners.

It is now time to return to Gen. Gaines. On the 1st of July, he wrote to the Governor:

I had promised myself the pleasure of sending you a detailed account of my conference with the Indian Council at this place, by this day's mail; but the mail is on the point of closing, and my account is not ready. I have, therefore, only to say that the Council here promise to be peaceable, and to settle their differences with the friends and followers of General McIntosh upon just principles.

They protest against the treaty.

They refuse to receive any part of the consideration money, or to give any other evidence of their acquiescence in the treaty. But they have, in the strongest terms, deliberately declared that they will not raise an arm against the United States, even should an army come to take from them the whole of their country; that they will make no sort of resistance; but will sit down quietly and be put to death where the bones of their ancestors are deposited; that the world shall know that the Muscogee nation so loved their country that they were willing to die in it, rather than sell it or leave it. This was their mode of expression, as interpreted in presence of Ben Hawkins, and several other interpreters, who were instructed to state whether or not the public interpreter did his duty.

The Council, fully attended, has thus appealed to our magnanimity; an appeal which never can be unavailing when addressed to citizens of the United States.

The Governor replied, as follows:

EXECUTIVE DEPARTMENT,
Milledgeville, 4th July, 1825.

Sir: I had the honor to receive your letter, of the first instant, this morning, for which be pleased to accept my thanks.

How does the obstinate refusal to remove consist with the universal consent given at one time to the treaty at the Indian Springs, with the exception of the Tookaubatchees, or with the report made by Hambly to Col. Williamson, that he had the yea or nay in the matter, and by the authority of these same people, or the placid content and good feeling for McIntosh, manifested in their talk to Col. Lamar? &c., &c. I much fear this ardent love of country is of recent origin; we can scarcely believe that the *amor patriæ* is all upon the one side, and that side the hostile one. Will you not be able to discover, in the course of your investigation, that everything had been said and done by white men to prejudice them against their new home? It is, indeed, a pity that these unfortunate men should be the dupes of the most depraved of our own color, and so far the dupes as to be made to act in direct repugnance to their own best interests; it is more to be lamented that the impostors and knaves cannot be dragged from their hiding places and punished. Presupposing these unhappy people to continue blind and obdurate, the utmost which your government can do, in the spirit of magnanimity and forbearance, will be to relinquish the benefit which would result to it from the execution of the treaty, and guaranty to them, for their permanent home, the lands west of the Georgia line. If the Cherokees continue to conduct themselves in like temper, the like provision may be made for them. But how will this accord with the recent policy adopted by the United States, or with the substantial and lasting interests of the Indians? In every estimate of humanity, it would be better that this deceitful charm, by which they are bound, should be broken and dispelled; that, after adjustment and reconciliation of differences, the entire body should move without sorrow to the country alloted to them. I am persuaded that no efforts of yours will be unessayed to accomplish this most desirable and holy end; holy, I say, because it is the only one which can consist with their peace, safety and happiness. Pardon me for throwing out these hasty and desultory reflections; they have no doubt already presented themselves to your own mind.

Presuming that the followers of McIntosh, who almost exclusively occupy the Georgia lands, will remove; and that, in their present unsettled condition, it would be very desirable to them to do so, whilst it would save the United States the expense of their maintenance and support here, I would feel myself obliged, if, consistently with your duty, you would give every encouragement to such dispositions.

With great consideration and respect,

G. M. TROUP.

Edmund P. Gaines,
Major-General Com'g,
Fort Mitchell.

On the 10th of July, Gen. Gaines wrote to the Governor, apologizing for not having written as often or as fully as he had been desirous of doing, in consequence of "the excessive heat of the weather," and "many inconveniences and interruptions," &c. He then proceeded to communicate the result of his conferences with the Creeks—that he had met the Chiefs of the McIntosh party, heard their respective statements, with the evidence for and against each party, and urged an adjustment of differences, to which they had mutually assented; that the McIntosh party demanded retaliation for their fallen Chiefs, and the immediate restoration of their property taken or destroyed, &c., &c. He added: "The reputed hostile party consists of all the principal Chiefs, and of nearly *forty-nine fiftieths* of the whole of the Chiefs, Head-men and Warriors of the Nation: among whom I recognize many who were in our service during the late war, and who, to my certain knowledge, have been for twenty years past, (and I think they have been at all times,) friendly to the United States as any of our Indian neighbors could have been known to be. I met them at Broken Arrow, the usual place of holding the great Council of the Nation: I could not, therefore, but view the supposed hostile party as in fact and in truth the *Creek Nation*, and altogether free of the spirit of hostility ascribed to them"—that he had "received from them, in Council assembled, the most deliberate assurance of their determination to be peaceable and friendly towards their absent people, as well as towards the United States. They regretted the necessity which, they contend, existed for the strong measures they adopted against Gen. McIntosh, and others, who, they affirm, forfeited and lost their lives by having violated a well known law of the Nation;" that they had "engaged to restore all property taken, and to pay for all that has been destroyed contrary to law," &c.—that "the Council strongly and unanimously objected to the late treaty, as the offspring of fraud, entered into contrary to the known law and determined will of the nation, and by persons not authorized to treat;" that they refused "to receive any part of the consideration money due under the treaty, or to give any other evidence of their acquiescence in it"—that they had "expressed the hope that their white friends would pity their deplorable condition, and would do them the justice to reconsider and 'undo that which has been wrongfully done'"—that he had endeavored, without success, to convince them "of the fallacy of their objections to the treaty, and to dissipate their delusive hopes that it can ever be annulled," &c., &c. The letter stated that there would be no occasion for the militia or volunteers of the State, and concluded thus:

"The certificate, of which I enclose herewith a copy, marked A, added to the declarations of the Chiefs in Council, of whom Joseph Marshall was principal and Interpreter, proves that your Excellency has been greatly deceived in supposing that the McIntosh party ever consented to the survey of the ceded territory being commenced before the time set forth in the treaty for their removal. This fact, giving altogether a new aspect to the subject of the proposed survey of the land, added to a strong conviction on my mind that the attempt to make the survey would be a positive violation of the treaty, and will, under existing causes of excitement, be certain to produce acts of violence upon the persons or property of unoffending Indians whom we are bound to protect, it becomes my duty to remonstrate against the surveys being commenced until the Indians shall have removed, agreeably to the treaty. I cannot doubt that the facts disclosed by the accompanying certificate, with the concurrent testimony of the Chiefs in Council, to which I have adverted, will induce your Excellency, without hesitation, to abandon the project of surveying the land before the month of September, 1826. This would be particularly gratifying to me, as it would relieve me of the painful duty of acting, not in concert with the venerated authorities of an enlightened and patriotic member of the United States, to whom I stand pledged, by every principle of honor, under the solemnity of an oath, to serve them honestly and faithfully."

The following is the certificate referred to by Gen. Gaines:

We certify that we accompanied the express from Governor Troup to Gen. McIntosh, conveying the request that he would allow the survey of the land acquired by the treaty at the Indian Springs, to be immediately commenced.

Gen. McIntosh replied that he could not grant the request, but would call the Chiefs together, and lay it before them —which was never done.

WM. EDWARDS.
JOSEPH MARSHALL.

At Portess, Upson Co., July 9, 1825.

I certify that this is a correct copy of the original certificate signed in my presence.

E. G. W. BUTLER,
Aid-de-Camp.

The following is Governor Troup's reply:

EXECUTIVE DEPARTMENT,
Milledgeville, July 16th, 1825.

Sir: I have only a moment left to say one word in answer to that part of your letter I had the honor to receive yesterday, which relates to the assent given by McIntosh to the survey of the country. The certificate of Marshall, no matter how procured, is one of the most daring efforts that ever was attempted by malignant villainy to palm a falsehood upon credulity. Now, Sir, that you may be at once undeceived with regard to this trick, which has been played off by somebody, I have to assure you that, independently of the assent three times given by McIntosh, under his own hand, which I have in my possession, this same man, Marshall, has repeatedly declared to me, that there was not a dissentient voice from the survey, among the friendly chiefs. All the chiefs I have seen, have uniformly declared the same; and so they have declared to others, both in and out of council; and for this you have my word of honor, and may have my oath. I very well know, from the late events which have transpired under the eyes of the Commissioners, that the oath even of a Governor of Georgia may be permitted to pass for nothing, and that any vagabond of the Indian country may be put in requisition to discredit him. But I assure you, Sir, if that oath should not weigh one feather with your Government, it will weigh with the people of this State, who, so far as I have a knowledge of their history, have never refused credence to the word of their Chief Magistrate, and I believe will not to the present one, unworthy as he may be. Permit me to say, in frankness, that I do not like the complexion of things, at all, as disclosed by the Commissioners on the part of the State, and sincerely hope that you may never have cause to regret the part you have taken in them. Every prepossession here was in your favor, and it would have given me great pleasure to cherish it in behalf of an officer who had rendered signal service to his country through many a perilous and trying scene.

Very respectfully,
Your obed't serv't,

G. M. TROUP.

Edmund P. Gaines,
Major-Gen. Commanding, Indian Springs.

To this letter, Gen. Gaines wrote the following as a reply; but which he caused to be published in a Milledgeville paper, instead of sending it by mail, or private hand, to the Governor. It is published here, in full, not as a specimen of eloquent composition or of polite diplomatic style, but that the reader may form a tolerable judgment of the propriety of the Governor's suspending, as he had done in the case of Major Andrews, all further official intercourse with the "Major-General, Commanding."

HEAD-QUARTERS, Eastern Department,
Indian Springs, *28th July*, 1825.

Sir: I have to acknowledge the honor of your Excellency's letter of the 17th of this month, by which it appears that you had "only a moment to say one word," in answer to mine of the 10th. Your one word, comprehending, however, two pretty closely written pages, coming as it does from the Chief Magistrate of an enlightened and patriotic member of the United States, demands my attention.

Not being disposed, however, to follow your example as to *time*, I have permitted your letter to lie on my table for a week past, in the expectation that a little reflection would suggest to you the propriety of correcting some expressions apparently hasty, and calculated to call forth an answer partaking of the climate and heated atmosphere in which I find myself: against which it has been my constant purpose to guard; but your letter having made its appearance in a newspaper just now handed to me by a friend, I can no longer see the propriety of withholding a reply. You say, "the certificate of Marshall, no matter how procured, is one of the most daring efforts that ever was attempted by malignant villainy to palm a falsehood on ignorant credulity."—"*No matter how procured!*"

I will first state to you the manner in which that frightful certificate was "procured," and then proceed to show that its "daring" character consists in its *truth*, and its direct tendency to expose in part the "*malignant villainy*" which has been extensively practiced on the credulity of many of the good citizens of Georgia, and other States, in reference to the Indians and the treaty. The facts contained in the certificate in question, were voluntarily, and, to me, unexpectedly communicated by Mr. William Edwards and Joseph Marshall, whose signatures it bears.

Of the character of William Edwards, who is a citizen of this State, I have had no means of knowing much personally. He has been represented to me by Col. Brodnax, of Pike, and by Col. Phillips, of this county, as a man of *truth*—poor, but honest and upright; a description of character applicable to a large class of the inhabitants of this and other parts of our western border, in whom I have usually found as much devotion to truth, as in any other class of American citizens.

Joseph Marshall is personally better known to me. He is a Creek half-breed, and is deemed to be a good interpreter; and however deficient, as I know he is, in education, and refined moral sentiments such as have obtained the sanction of civilized society, I have no doubt that he is one of the most upright Chiefs that ever belonged to the *little treaty-making party*. Neither of these men, Edwards or Marshall, appeared to me at all qualified for what you denounce their certificate to be, "the most daring effort that ever was attempted by malignant villainy."

Their statements were simple and apparently unprejudiced and unimpassioned; they were made after the principal business of the council had been brought to a close, and in the presence of many of the respectable citizens of Pike county.

Convinced of the propriety of all my duties with the Indians being performed in *open day*, and in the presence of as many as would attend, of all states and all colors, I took care that the certificate should be taken and explained in presence of the council, and of all others who had seen fit to attend.

I had no secret project to promote, nor any "*secret griefs*" to remedy, or secret hopes to gratify; and consequently had no occasion for separating the Chiefs, or for secret examination. The certificate was written as it was dictated, as I believe word for word, by my Aid-de-Camp, Lieut. E. George Washington Butler, a young officer of accomplished military education and talents—with unbending integrity and spotless honor; and who is as incapable of giving countenance to a *trick* or *misrepresentation*, as was the beloved Father of his country, with whose name he is honored, and whose patriotism and virtue he constantly scrupulously imitates. Having thus explained to you the means employed to obtain the certificate in question, for which I hold myself responsible, I have now to remark that, although I have never entertained a doubt that you were deceived into a belief that Gen. McIntosh had consulted the few Chiefs of his party, and had obtained their assent in Council to the immediate survey of the ceded land; yet I have found no satisfactory evidence of such Council, consisting of the Chiefs of the ceded territory, having ever acted at all upon the subject. And it is apparent from McIntosh's letters, "*no matter how procured*," (I will offer no apology for making use of your Excellency's pregnant phrase,) or by whom written, that he himself considered the permission to survey as merely conditional. But I contend that neither General McIntosh nor his *vassal Chiefs* had any right to give such permission: for the treaty, "no matter how procured," had become a *law of the land*: its provisions could not therefore be changed or rendered inoperative by any correspondence, or any subsequent agreement between your Excellency and any part or the whole of the individuals of one of the contracting parties, without the consent of the other.

The treaty makes it our duty to protect the Indians against the whites and all others; to protect them from the whites, it is necessary and proper that we should maintain the usual line of demarkation between them and the whites.

I am charged with their protection.

To accomplish this important duty, my first object has been to take effectual measures to prevent all intercourse between them and the whites, excepting only such as is sanctioned by the laws of the United States.

You say, "I very well know that from the late events which have transpired under the eyes of the Commissioners of Georgia, that the oath of a Governor of Georgia may be permitted to pass for nothing, and that any vagabond of the Indian country may be put in requisition to discredit him; but I assure you, sir, if that oath should not weigh a single feather with your government, it will weigh with the people of this State, who, so far as I have a knowledge of their history, have never yet refused credence to the word of their Chief Magistrate." To this apparently very serious, but certainly very vague, charge, I cannot undertake to reply, until you do me the favor to give me some specifications of the matters of fact to which you have referred.

I will, however, take this occasion to remark, that whatever statements you may have received in support of the insinuation apparently contained in your letter, that I have called in question, or even put any person in requisition to call in question, the oath or the word of a Governor of Georgia, during his continuance in office, is wholly destitute of truth. I have, indeed, believed, and have expressed to you my belief, that you have been greatly deceived by persons in whose honor you have placed reliance, but who were unworthy of your confidence.

But I am by no means disposed to yield my tacit assent to the high-toned rule of English law, which your remarks just now quoted call to mind, that "the King can do no wrong." Truth is a divine attribute, and the foundation of every virtue. "Truth is the basis of all excellence." This inestimable moral treasure, *truth*, is to be found in the cottage as well as in the *palace*, at the plough as well as at the official bureau of state.

Many of the unfortunate wanderers of the wilderness and its borders, are as firm votaries of truth as any men I have ever known. Some of them, who have been unfortunate in business, and whose regard to truth and honesty induce them to give up the last dollar justly due to their creditors, had they regarded money a little more, and *truth* a little less, might have *failed full handed*; and now, instead of being reduced to the condition of despised poverty, would wanton in the luxuries of plundered wealth. It is no longer possible, in America, to make freemen believe that "the King, (or he who governs,) can do no wrong."

The enlightened citizens of the Republic, having long since found it to be fruitless to look for *angels* in the form of *men* to govern them, know full well how to discriminate between the *high office* and the *man* who fills it.

Your Excellency will, I doubt not, always receive a degree of respect, proportioned, at least, to that which you are wont to bestow on other men in office; more than this could not be expected; less than this would not be just. That a great number of the citizens of Georgia are magnanimous, just, generous and chivalric, I well know; and that they are disposed to do justice to their Chief Magistrate, I am equally convinced; nor can I doubt that they will do equal justice to their *United States*, as well as their *State*, *officers*.

I rely upon the wisdom and justice and patriotism of at least nine-tenths of those with whom I have the pleasure of an acquaintance, many of whom are cultivators of the land; to which class, in this and every other State in the Republic, I look up with confident pleasure and pride, as they form the adamantine pillars of the *Union*; against which the angry vaporing paper squibs of the *little* and the *great demagogues* of all countries, may continue to be hurled for hundreds of centuries, without endangering the noble edifice. This beloved monument of American wisdom and valor and virtue, will stand unshaken, when the disturbers of its infantile repose will be remembered to be pitied or execrated.

The good people of Georgia, I am well aware, are anxious to obtain possession of the land upon their western border; but they would abhor the idea of fraudulent or lawless means being resorted to, to treat for, or, after treating, to obtain possession of it before the time authorized by treaty. And I am well convinced that the President of the United States is as sincerely desirous as any upright citizen of Georgia can be, that the Indian claims to the lands within her limits should be speedily extinguished, and that the Indians should remove therefrom as soon as they can justly be required to remove; but he owes them *protection* and *justice*, and both will be extended to them.

It is not to be denied that there is in Georgia, as well as every other State, a small class of men, who, like the "*Holy Alliance*," profess to employ themselves in the laudable work of enlightening and governing all other classes of the community, but whose labors consist of the vain and "daring efforts" to prove the light of truth is to be found only with the party to which they themselves respectively belong, and that all others go wrong. If you will take the trouble to read the newspaper essays with which the presses have been teeming for some years past, you will find that many of the essayists have had the hardihood to "refuse credence to the word of their Chief Magistrate," and yet we have no reason to despair of the Republic.

You say, "I do not like the complexion of things at all as disclosed by the Commissioners on the part of the State, and sincerely hope (you add) that you may never have cause to regret the part you have taken in them." Permit me then, Sir, to conclude with a sincere hope that the Commissioners, with whose report I am thus menaced, may prove by their conduct that they belong not to the aforementioned *one-sided enlightening* class; should their report be found to contain the *truth*, the *whole truth*, and *nothing but the truth*, your Excellency may dismiss your apprehensions, felt on my account, as I have nothing to apprehend. But if their report is not true, I can say only that the tongue and the pen of calumny can never move me from the path of duty, nor ever make me regret the course pursued by me in respect to the Indians, or the Commissioners, the State or the United States.

In tendering to your Excellency my acknowledgements for the prepossession in my favor, of which you speak, and which you say would have given you "pleasure to cherish in behalf of an officer who had rendered signal services to his country," permit me to observe that the approbation of my countrymen is more dear to me than any earthly treasure they could bestow, save that of an assured devotion to the Republic: if, indeed, it be in my power to win that approbation by a faithful discharge of my duty as a public officer, and as an honest man, I have long endeavored thus to win it. My best efforts are constantly exerted to ascertain the direct and proper course of duty prescribed by law and justice and honor, and to pursue that course without any regard to consequences. But I have seen, of late, with regret, that it is scarcely possible for an officer of the General Government to differ with you in opinion, without incurring your uncourteous animadversion or your acrimonious censure; neither of which shall ever induce me to forget what is due to myself or the venerated station you fill, and the relation in which you stand to the General Government, in whose service I have the honor to be placed.

Wishing you health and respect,

I have the honor to be

EDMUND P. GAINES,
Major-Gen. Com'g.

To his Excellency
George M. Troup,
Governor of Georgia.

The following from the Governor explains itself:

EXECUTIVE DEPARTMENT,
Milledgeville, 6*th Aug.*, 1825.

Sir: A letter, purporting to be yours, which appeared in the last Georgia Journal, and having every characteristic of an official one, could not fail to attract my attention.

Immediately, therefore, on my return to this place, inquiry was made, at the Department, for the original, and I learned, with surprise, that none such had been received. The proper means were then resorted to, to ascertain the authenticity of the published letter, and, having been satisfied that the same was in your proper handwriting, I have lost no time to direct you to forbear further intercourse with this Government. Having thought proper to make representations of your conduct to the President, I have ordered you to be furnished with a copy of every letter written on your subject, and which will reach you in due time. Any communication proceeding from the officer next in command in this military department, will be received and attended to.

G. M. TROUP.

E. P. Gaines,
Major-Gen. Commanding, Indian Springs.

The next day, Governor Troup addressed the following communication to the President of the United States:

EXECUTIVE DEPARTMENT,
Milledgeville, 7th Aug., 1825.

Sir: The letter of the Secretary of War, of the 18th May, introducing to this Government Major-General Gaines and Major Andrews, as Agents of the United States to inquire into the causes of the late disturbances, to adjust the differences subsisting between the Indians, and to inquire into the conduct of the Agent of Indian affairs, recommended them as officers distinguished for ability, prudence and discretion. They were received and treated accordingly. With the conduct of the one you have been already made acquainted: with that of the other it remains for me to place you in possession.

In the several conferences held with General Gaines, on his first arrival, I received repeated assurances from him of friendly dispositions; of upright intentions; of freedom from all kinds of bias or prejudice which could mislead his judgment, or influence his decisions, on any of the topics which, in the execution of his trust, might present themselves for discussion. Relying implicity on the sincerity of these declarations, I began with regarding Gen. Gaines as an honorable and disinterested arbiter between the United States, Georgia, and the Indians, and so continued to regard him until a short time before his insulting letter, of the 10th ult., was received at this Department. It was impossible for this Government not to repel that insult with indignation.

The Chief Magistrate, in his official message to the Legislature, had stated, explicitly, that McIntosh and his Chiefs had given their consent to the survey; and, in support of this statement, the letters of McIntosh were exhibited with his name subscribed in his own hand, of which General Gaines had full information: nevertheless, the certificate of an Indian Chief, who had deserted from the McIntosh party, and of a white man, of whom General Gaines himself does not pretend to know anything, is procured to discredit the statement of the Governor, and to exhibit him before the public as the dupe of the vilest and shallowest imposture; and, in his solicitude to accomplish this, he forgets that it is the consent given by McIntosh and his Chiefs to the survey, which, on the information of the Agent, you have taken for granted to be the sole cause of all the disturbances in the nation, and upon which you have recently issued the most offensive orders to this Government, connected with that survey, and in your last even denounced military vengeance against those who shall attempt to carry it into execution.

When Gen. Gaines is rebuked, in the mildest language which the unprovoked insult would admit of, he presents himself again before the public in a letter, indulging in most intemperate abuse of all the constituted authorities of a sovereign State, and the great body of its people, and which he causes to be published almost a week before it was received at this Department.

With regard to the first letter of General Gaines, to which I have called your attention, he does not seem to have been content with addressing a letter so exceptionable to the head of this Government: he assumes the authority to order its publication, on the allegation of some pretended and undefined malicious falsehoods in circulation, and which he makes the foundation of an appeal to the public—an appeal more censurable than that for which the gallant and meritorious Porter is now answering, before a Court Martial, assembled by your order; inasmuch as the latter only defends himself against the inculpatory charges made by his own Government, whilst the former, who was bound by equal respect to this Government, does not pretend that any charges, of any kind, had been preferred by it against him. It is in this letter, too, that General Gaines has fallen into the shocking extravagance of asserting, what nobody can believe, that the McIntosh party, which made the treaty, constituted but a fiftieth part of the nation; and it was in the same letter he made known, officially, to this Government, that he has happily concluded a pacification of the Indians, when at that moment he was as remote from the pacification as he ever had been, of which fact I have even within the passing hour received the most incontestable evidence.

With regard to the second letter, of the 28th ult., which, now that I am writing, has for the first time been put into my hands, and almost a week after its publication, I have to remark that the history of diplomacy will not furnish a parallel so marked with indiscretion, intemperance, disrespect, and the outrage of all decency. Gen. Gaines forgets as well what he owes to his own Government as to this. His duty to you required him to show respect to this Government in all his intercourse with it. If, in that intercourse, he had found himself wronged or aggrieved by the authorities here, it was not allowed him to take the redress into his own hands. Upon representation to you, you were competent to decide the nature and the extent of the injury he had received, and of the redress most suitable to it. He would not confide the exercise of this privilege to you, no doubt questioning your fitness or discretion for such matters, but chose to rely on his own dexterity and prowess.

He writes, among other things, of the "malignant villainy" which has been extensively practiced on the credulity of the good citizens of Georgia, and other States, in reference to the Indians and the treaty. A charge so vague cannot be easily understood, much less distinctly answered. Presupposing it to be directed against the authorities of this State, and to be in all respects true, who made Gen. Gaines the judge to pass this condemnatory sentence on the conduct of those authorities? It had been understood that you had reserved to yourself this power, and that General Gaines was here only as your Agent to collect the evidence upon which that power was to be exercised.

He proceeds to make another reference to the certificate of the Indian Chief and the white man—reiterates the expression of unlimited confidence in the veracity of Marshall—eulogizes him as among the most worthy of the "little treaty-making party," and comes again to the conclusion that the Chief Magistrate of Georgia, and others, are not to be credited against the certificate of such respectable personages.

Within this hour, I have received the testimony of the Chiefs of the friendly party, voluntarily given, "that the statement of Joe Marshall, to General Gaines, is false;" and I enclose you the certificate of my express,* a man of fairest character and undoubted veracity, to satisfy you that Marshall has added falsehood to treachery. In this part of his letter, he takes occasion to manifest his resentment towards the friends of McIntosh: he calls them "the little treaty-making party;" then, again, "the vassal Chiefs of McIntosh," and questions their right to give permission to make the survey. What a dispassionate and impartial umpire is this General Gaines! One would have supposed that, consulting the magnanimity of a soldier, if he had departed from the line of neutrality at all, he would be found at the head of the weaker—the innocent and injured party. But the General, consulting the better part of valor, and counting the odds against him as fifty to one, throws himself into the ranks of the stronger party, and thus commends himself again to you for that discretion which you had given to him in advance.

The General is correct in one of his positions, and, being in the right himself, he puts you in the wrong, and so conspicuously, that you stand on the insulated eminence, an almost solitary advocate for making and breaking treaties at pleasure.

General Gaines says, "the treaty, no matter how procured, had become a law of the land," &c., &c. He had said to the hostile Indians, at Broken Arrow, "that the treaty could not be annulled, and must be carried into effect," &c., &c. This is good sense. The day before yes-

* The certificate of the express, Jesse Prosser, dated 2d August, 1825, stated that on his way to the "Nation," and after he had got into the Indian country, (with a request from the Governor to McIntosh and the other Chiefs for their assent to the survey,) he fell in with Joe Marshall and William Edwards, who accompained him to McIntosh's house; that, on McIntosh's informing him that he had called a meeting of the Chiefs for 10th April, Marshall and Edwards being both present, Marshall (acting as Interpreter) informed witness that when the Chiefs were convened, and their wishes consulted, McIntosh would advise the Governor of it, and observed to witness, in presence of McIntosh, that he (Marshall) had no objection to the survey; that the survey would be an advantage to the Indians, as they could then dispose of a great deal of their provisions, and, after their growing crop was made, they could sell out their improvements and be ready, next spring, to set out for their new country; that Marshall informed witness that, although McIntosh requested it, yet it was not necessary for him (Marshall) to stay to the talk, as his consent was given; and that after Marshall, Edwards and witness left McIntosh's house, Marshall, several times during the journey, manifested his entire approbation of the survey, and observed that he had no doubt of the assent of the Chiefs being given when they should meet on 10th April, &c.—ED.

terday, I received your letter, in which you say, General Gaines having informed you that the treaty had been obtained by intrigue and treachery, it will be referred to Congress for reconsideration. General Gaines tells the Indians that no treaty has ever yet been annulled. You say this treaty shall be made an exception to all others, and upon the information received from General Gaines.

General Gaines proceeds to manifest his respect and complaisance for the Chief Magistrate of a sovereign State, by informing him that "he has been greatly deceived by persons in whom he placed reliance, but who were unworthy of his confidence," thus taking upon himself the responsibility to decide, for the Chief Magistrate, one of the most delicate of all questions connected with government and sovereignty, viz: the question, who are worthy of trust, and who, among the public servants, are or are not entitled to his confidence. In a little time, sir, with your countenance and encouragement, General Gaines would have dictated the appointments to office in this State, and, may be, the least hesitation or repugnance to comply with such dictation, would be subdued by a parade of United States troops.

After quoting a maxim, that "the king can do no wrong," and expatiating on the moral excellence of truth and her indiscriminate habitation at the palace and the cottage, the plough and the bureau of State—with the wanderers of the wilderness and the honest but unfortunate debtors, of all which I cannot, for the life of me, understand the application, much less the farrago which follows, about somebody regarding *money* a *little more* and *truth* a *little less*—condition of despised poverty and luxuries of plundered wealth, &c., &c., and which is equally unintelligible; General Gaines is scarcely more distinct and intelligible, when, in passing a meagre compliment to a portion of the citizens of Georgia, he professes to "rely on the wisdom, justice and patriotism of at least nine-tenths of those with whom he has the pleasure of an acquaintance," many of whom are cultivators of the land; and then, again, "that the cultivators are the adamantine pillars of the Union, against which the angry vaporing paper squibs of the *little* and the *great demagogues* of all countries may continue to be hurled for hundreds of centuries without endangering the noble edifice," &c., &c., all of which may be intended to convey some meaning and admit of ready explanation by General Gaines, but which, I assure you, sir, is altogether above my comprehension.

The General soon becomes a little more explicit, when he says there is in Georgia a small class of men, who, like the "holy alliance, profess to employ themselves in the laudable work of enlightening and governing all other classes of the community, but whose labors consist of vain and daring efforts to prove that the light of truth is to be found only with the party to which themselves respectively belong, and that all others go wrong." Party! Sir; an Agent representing the Government of the United States before the Government of Georgia, addressing to the Chief Magistrate of the State an official paper, in which, descanting on the state of parties, the writer places himself by the side of the one party, and fulminates a denunciation against the other!

Pray, Sir, suffer me to ask if Major-Gen. Gaines received special instructions at your hands so to deport himself—to pry into the state of parties to find out the relative strength of them—to place himself on the side of the strongest, giving it aid, countenance and co-operation—and from this strong-hold to issue insolent anathemas against the other, through the Governor of the State, thus directly intermeddling in our local politics and availing himself of our unhappy divisions to make the exasperations of party yet more bitter? Gen. Gaines will not permit us to mistake him—he proceeds to call the particular party to which he is opposed, the "one-sided enlightening class;" in another place he calls them "the small class."

The opportunities of General Gaines to inform himself of the state of parties in Georgia, have been no doubt much better than mine, which have indeed been very limited, but I have more generally heard from men better informed, that the relative strength of parties was somewhat different from the General's estimate of it. He seems to have adopted the same rule of enumeration, under the same optical delusion, as in measuring the strength of the Indian parties, and to have arrived at the very gratifying conclusion that the numerical strength was in the proportion of 50 to 1; undoubtedly a very incorrect conclusion.

This officer took umbrage at my request to permit the Commissioners, on the part of the State, to act in friendly concert with him, in making his investigation for the discovery of truth. Why he did so, I cannot conjecture. This, however, was passed by without notice, as was his subsequent refusal to admit them to a participation of the Councils in matters involving interests of Georgia. His indiscretion in declaring, before the Council at Broken

Arrow, that if the congregated world were to contradict the Chief Yoholo, he would not believe it—has been already noticed in the letter which I last had the honor to address to you. It is upon the authority of this Chief, Hambly, represented to be one of the most infamous of men, and of the Agent of Indian Affairs, that you have come to the conclusion to return the treaty to Congress, for revision, it having been procured by intrigue and treachery.

Gen. Gaines is reported to me to have said, in the presence of one of the Commissioners on the part of the State, that if 23 States out of the 24 were to pronounce the Agent guilty, he would not believe them.

Gen. Gaines has been guilty of the childish indiscretion of threatening to cut off the heads or ears of citizens of Georgia who happened to offend him, as if you had given him his sword for this special service.

But, indeed, Sir, it is high time to dismiss the subject of this officer.

In maintaining correspondence with the Government of the United States, I have not permitted any false considerations of dignity, or any false estimates of forms and ceremonies, which usually govern diplomatic intercourse between States, to interpose the least difficulty. So far from it, I have cheerfully descended to the level of every thing which it pleased you at any time to employ as your representative or organ—from the Clerks of your Bureaus, up to your Major-Generals by brevet, and have acted and treated with them as equals.

In the deportment of some of these, I have experienced arrogance, self-sufficiency, a haughty and contemptuous carriage, and a most insulting interference with our local politics; and these characteristics not exhibited to one but to all of the constituted authorities of the State. Now, Sir, suffer me, in conclusion, to ask if these things have been done in virtue of your own instructions express or implied, or by authority of any warrant from you whatsoever; and, if not so done, whether you will sanction or adopt them as your own, and thus hold yourself responsible to the Government of Georgia.

Be persuaded, Sir, that whenever hereafter you shall think proper, not deceiving yourself or us, to send gentlemen to represent you before this Government, of the character given to those by the letter of the Secretary of War of the 18th May, they will be received and respected as officers of the General Government would be by the most friendly States of the Union.

With great consideration,

G. M. TROUP.

We go back, now, in the order of time, and notice some other matters in this Indian controversy. Having, on 13th June, forwarded to the President the report and resolutions of the Legislature, with the evidence supporting them, all "having relation to the conduct of the Agent for Indian Affairs, as connected with the late disturbances in the Creek Nation," he received, soon after, a reply through Major Vandeventer, Chief Clerk of the War Department, dated 25th June, acknowledging the receipt of the letter and enclosures, and stating that the President would "give to them all the consideration which, coming from so high a source, they may merit." On the 15th June, the Chief Clerk had written to the Governor, acknowledging the receipt of his letter, of the 3d June, to the Secretary of War, and stating that the President had (in the absence of the Secretary,) directed him to say, in reply, "that if the Government of Georgia should undertake the project of surveying the lands ceded to the United States by the Creek Nation of Indians," &c., "before the expiration of the time specified by the 8th article of the treaty, for the removal of the Indians, it will be wholly upon its responsibility; and that the Government of the United States will not in any manner be responsible for any consequences which may result from that measure."

The Governor, on 25th June, replied, as follows, to the Chief Clerk:

I received, this morning, the note which, in the absence of the Secretary of War, the President of the United States directed you to address to me, and in which I am informed that the project of surveying the lands ceded to the United States by the Creek Nation of Indians, at the treaty of the Indian Springs, before the expiration of the time specified by the 8th article of the treaty for the removal of the Indians, will be wholly upon its (the Government of

Georgia's) responsibility, and that the Government (viz: the Government of the United States) will not in any manner be responsible for any consequences which may result from that measure." A very friendly admonition, truly. So that, whilst you referred your resistance of the survey to the evils already produced by the mere effort on the part of this Government to obtain permission to make the survey, and when the fact of that cause producing those effects is disproven, and it is made known to you that nobody here, either whites or Indians, ever conceived such a thing as possible before you had assumed it upon the representation of the Agent as undoubtedly true; and that your own Agent, to suit his own purposes, had fabricated it, to deceive and mislead you, nevertheless, you continue to issue order after order forbidding the survey, as if you had predetermined, from the beginning, that, under no circumstances, should we proceed to the survey without your express permission first had and obtained. Nay, more: You repeat this order to General Gaines, who is charged to promulgate it to the hostile Indians; so that, whether there be any thing obnoxious in the survey or not, they may seize it as a pretence, under the authority and with the support of the United States, to scalp and tomahawk our people as soon as we shall attempt that survey; and that, in fact, you adopt for the Indians, gratuitously, an imaginary wrong done to them, persuade them, even against their will, that it is a real one, and then leave them to indulge, in unbridled fury, the most tempestuous passions; and this, I presume, is the meaning, in part, of the responsibilities which we are to incur if we disregard the mandate of the Government of the United States.

You will, therefore, in the absence of the Secretary of War, make known to the President, that the Legislature, having, in concurrence with the expressed opinion of the Executive, come to the almost unanimous conclusion, that by the treaty, the jurisdiction, together with the soil, passed to Georgia, and in consequence thereof, authorized the Governor to cause the line to be run, and the survey to be made, it becomes me, in candor, to state to the President, that the survey will be made, and in due time, and of which Major-General Gaines has already had sufficient notice.

Whilst, in the execution of the decrees of our own constituted authorities, the Government of the United States will find nothing but frankness and magnanimity on our part, we may reasonably claim the observance, in like degree, of these noble qualities on theirs. When, therefore, certain responsibilities are spoken of, in the communication of the President, we can rightfully inquire, what responsibilities? Georgia, in the maintenance of her undoubted rights, fears no responsibilities; yet, it is well for Georgia to know them, so far as they are menaced by the United States. If it is intended that the Government of the United States will interpose its power to prevent the survey, the Government of Georgia cannot have too early or too distinct notice; for, how highly dishonorable would it be for the stronger party to avail itself of that power to surprise the weaker! If the Government only means that, omitting its constitutional duty, it will not pacify the Indians, and make safe the frontier, whilst the officers of Georgia are in peaceful fulfilment of their instructions, connected with the survey, it is important to the Government of Georgia to know it; that, depending on itself for safety, it shall not depend in vain. But, if the Government of the United States mean what is not even yet to be believed, that, assuming, like their Agent, upon another not dissimilar occasion, an attitude of neutrality feigned and insincere, it will, like that Agent, harrow up the Indians to the commission of hostile and bloody deeds, then, indeed, the Government of Georgia should also know it, that it may guard and fence itself against the perfidy and treachery of false friends. In either event, however, the President of the United States may rest contented that the Government of Georgia cares for no responsibilities in the exercise of its right and the execution of its trust, but those which belong to conscience and to God, which, thanks to Him, is equally our God as the God of the United States.

To this letter, Governor Troup received a reply from the Secretary of War, dated 21st July, in which that officer said:

Your letter, of the 25th of June, addressed to Major Vandeventer, has been received, the answer to which has been intentionally delayed till the result of Gen. Gaines' interview with the Indians, at Broken Arrow, should be received, as the President had anxiously hoped, in the acquiescence of the Indians to the treaty, to have found the necessity of replying to your inquiries entirely obviated.

But, as the communications from General Gaines, recently received here, have entirely destroyed that hope, a reply has become necessary.

The Indians, to the number of 1890, including a large majority of their Chiefs and Head-men of the tribe, have denounced the treaty as tainted alike with intrigue and treachery, and as the act of a very small portion of the tribe, against the express determination of a very large majority; a determination known to the Commissioners.

They urge that, to enforce a compliance with an instrument thus obtained, would illy become either the justice or the magnanimity of the United States, under which they claim to take shelter. These are allegations presenting a question beyond the cognizance of the Executive, and necessarily refers itself to Congress, whose attention will be called to it at an early day after the next annual meeting. Meanwhile, the President, acting on the treaty as though its validity had not been impeached, finds, by reference to the eighth article of the treaty, the faith of the United States solemnly pledged to protect the Creek Indians from any encroachment, till their removal in September, 1826. He therefore decided that the entering upon and surveying the lands before that period, would be an infraction of the treaty, whose interpretation and execution, should it remain uncanceled, are alike confided to him. I am, therefore, directed by the President to state distinctly to your Excellency, that, for the present, he will not permit such entry or survey to be made. The pain the President has felt, in coming to this decision, is diminished by the recollection that it interferes with no duty imposed on your Excellency by the laws of Georgia, as a discretion is given you, by the late law of the Legislature, in prescribing the time when the lands embraced by the treaty shall be surveyed. Under all the circumstances, the President permits himself to hope that you will acquiesce in his decision.

As General Gaines has been in communication with you on this subject, and as it is the wish of the President you should be in possession of every measure he may find himself constrained to take thereon, I am directed to enclose to your Excellency a copy of General Gaines' instructions of this date.

In his instructions to General Gaines, the Secretary of War said:

"It is still devoutly to be hoped that Governor Troup

will abstain from any act that may make it necessary to have recourse to the steps suggested: yet, should he persevere in sending persons to survey the lands embraced within the treaty, you are hereby authorized to employ the military, to prevent their entrance on the Indian Territory, or, if they should succeed in entering the country, to cause them to be arrested, and turn them over to the judicial authority, to be dealt with as the law directs."

To the foregoing letter of the Secretary of War, Gov. Troup replied on the 15th of August, and said:

I have received your letter of the 21st ult., giving the desired explanation of the former one of the 15th day of June last, in which you wrote of undefined responsibilities which this government must incur if it attempted the survey of the lands acquired from the Creeks, and which results in the employment of the bayonet on your part, and of the tomahawk and scalping-knife on the part of the Indians, if the survey be attempted. I thank you for this explanation; for, whether your intent were good or evil, it equally became you to make it. You make known, at the same time, the resolution of the President to refer the treaty to Congress, on the allegation that intrigue and treachery have been employed to procure it. This at once puts a stop to the survey, and you will inform the President that, until the will of the Legislature of Georgia is expresssed, no measures will be taken to execute the survey.

The Executive of Georgia has no authority, in the civil war with which the State is menaced, to strike the first blow, nor has it the inclination to provoke it—this is left for those who have both the inclination and authority, and who profess to love the Union best. The Legislature will, on their first meeting, decide what, in this respect, the rights and the interests of the State demand. In the mean time, the right to make the survey is asserted, and the reference of the treaty to Congress, for revision, protested against without any qualification. It is true, sir, that, according to my own opinion, if there be fraud and corruption in the procurement of the treaty, it ought to be set aside by the indignant expression of the nation's will—the taint of such corruption, according to that opinion, would suffice to render void an instrument of any kind purporting to pass a right of any kind.

But, of what avail is this opinion against your own established maxims and precedents? You would decry it as the visionary speculations of a wild enthusiast, because you would refer me to all your Indian treaties. You would present to me, in full relief, the decision of your Supreme Court, in the case of Fletcher and Peck, where, a feigned issue being made to settle the principle, the principle was settled that the Legislature of Georgia having, by bribery and corruption, sold the inheritance of the people for a mess of pottage, the grant passed a vested right which could by no possibility be divested, and therefore that the Congress had no alternative but to surrender the territory of Alabama and Mississippi, or compromise the claims. They chose the latter, and gave five millions of dollars to the claimants, of which we paid our full proportion.

Whilst, therefore, I present my own opinion on the one hand, you have, on the other, my public and official protestation in strict accordance and unison with your and all your constituted authorities' decisions, and which place the treaty upon such high ground, that, no matter by what execrable baseness it may have been elevated there, even the Congress of the United States cannot reach it.

It may be otherwise, but I do sincerely believe that no Indian treaty has ever been negotiated and concluded in better faith than the one which is the subject of this letter. If it be otherwise, having been concluded by your own officers, against your instructions, without any participation of the authorities of Georgia, I sincerely hope that those officers may, so far as you have power, be brought to trial and punishment. But yet, according to your own doctrines, this does not impair the validity of the treaty. The Legislature of Georgia will, therefore, on its first meeting, be advised to resist any effort which may be made to wrest from the State the territory acquired by that treaty, and no matter by what authority that effort be made.

The hostile Indians having resolved they will never surrender it but with their lives, and you having passively acquiesced in this resolution, because of the appeal made to your magnanimity and generosity, and it being obvious that our right, not asserted now, is lost to us forever; if the Legislature shall fail to vindicate that right, the responsibility will be theirs—not mine.

The Georgia Commissioners, Messrs. Jourdan, Williamson, Jones and Torrance, who had been appointed under the resolution of the Legislature, and acted under the in structions of the Governor, already noticed, made a report to the Governor on the 16th of July, appended to which were their correspondence with Gen. Gaines, Major Andrews and Col. Crowell, notes of their proceedings, and a mass of testimony, sufficient to make a volume. We can only make room for a few extracts from the report, which are of a general nature—a recapitulation of the report being embraced in the letter of the Governor to the President, dated 26th July, and which will be inserted in this chapter.

Speaking of one of their examinations, the Commissioners said: "We are unable to give you a proper idea of this examination. Suffice it to say, we became satisfied that any attempt on our part to obtain the truth from men living in the Indian nation, (whether white or red,) and under the influence and power of the Agent, into whose conduct we were then examining, must be fruitless." Again: "From the course pursued by the Agent, at that Council, and his permission to do so, (*for the omission to prohibit him was permission*,) his suspension was purely nominal—it was a mere mockery. We have no doubt but that his free admission into the Indian Councils, aided and assisted by his former sub-Agent, Mr. Walker, gave to him quite as much influence over the minds of the Indians as he ever exercised in the days of his utmost prosperity and authority." Again: "Upon the subject of a law which the hostile party allege that McIntosh violated, and which led to his death, you are referred to the report of Messrs. Jourdan and Williamson. We have no doubt, from the very many contradictory stories that we had heard in the Nation, touching the origin of the enactment of such a law, that no such law was ever known among the Creeks. We are confirmed in this opinion, by the reply of Gen. Gaines to the friendly Chiefs at the Indian Springs on the 20th ult. If we are correctly informed upon that point, he there stated that he had read their laws, and was gratified to find none so sanguinary as that alleged by their enemies to exist, under *color* of which it had been stated that the *murder* of McIntosh was perpetrated. The Chiefs in Council did not pretend that they had any such law reduced to record. A white man, who informed one of the Commissioners that he had resided in the Nation twenty or thirty years, stated that he knew of no such law. The very manner in which these unfortunate men were put to death, proves that the Indians did not execute them for having violated any law. We believe that when it became necessary to enforce such sanguinary edicts upon any of that tribe, the culprit is arrested and conducted to some town or public square in the Nation, and there undergoes a species of trial; sentence of death is then pronounced, the accused is thereupon publicly put to death by shooting.

"How unlike such a procedure was the foul murder of McIntosh and his friends: his house was surrounded at the dead hour of night, and set on fire by a band of lawless assassins, and there, encircled by the scorching flames produced by the conflagration of his own mansion, was he inhumanly and most unlawfully put to death. When witnesses are called on in the Nation, who, it is supposed, knew something of Indian laws and Indian policy, they account for these murders by saying, it was for violation of their law—which law, answers a Church Missionary, *was seen by nobody*. * * * * The gross inconsistencies in the statements of the Indians, and white men resident among them, to establish the existence of such a law, fix indelibly on the minds of the Commissioners that no such law is, or ever was.* The argument in support of such a law, proves too much: the Agent himself did not rely on it at the commencement of these Indian disturbances. * * * * * * * How far the whole of the testimony taken in support of the charges against the Indian Agent, sustains those charges, is not for us officially to determine; nor do we desire to express an opinion, of an official character, upon the subject. There is a subject not directly

* In his "Gazetteer of Georgia," page 265, third edition, Mr. Sherwood says: "But no such law ever existed. General Gaines and the Georgia Commissioners could find no traces of it. But if there had been such a law, all the others who signed the treaty ought to have shared a fate similar to that of McIntosh. If there had been such a law in existence, Colonel Crowell, the Agent, who witnessed the treaty, and who was the guardian of the Indians, must have known it, and he would not have suffered a brave warrior like McIntosh, a tried and steadfast friend to these United States, to sign his own death-warrant."—ED.

within the objects of our appointment, but it is inseparably connected with the treaty and its consequences, upon which we beg leave to offer a remark. It is upon the subject of the contemplated survey of the territory lately ceded. During the stay of the Commissioners at the Indian Springs, three of them were informed by several of the leading Chiefs of the friendly party, that they were willing and even desirous that the survey should be made during the ensuing fall, and assigned as a reason that the surveyors and their people being amongst them at that period, would afford them an opportunity of disposing of much of their products, that they could not transport with them to the westward; that they intended removing beyond the Mississippi before another crop was made, if the General Government would pay them the money, according to the terms of the treaty. Connected with this, Sir, we remark that it is somewhat strange that the Chiefs who reside *beyond* the limits of the territory ceded to the United States for the benefit of Georgia, are the only Chiefs, with a few exceptions, so far as we are informed, who are opposed to the survey."

The report concluded by stating that there was some other testimony to be taken, with which they would proceed as soon as practicable.

The reader is now referred to the following letter from Governor Troup to the President, giving a summary of the proceedings of the Commissioners, the obstacles they encountered, &c. It was dated July 26th, 1825:

In communicating the report of the Commissioners of the State, appointed under certain resolutions of the Legislature to take testimony in the case of the Agent for Indian affairs, and to investigate the causes of the late disturbances in the Creek Nation, it might be more satisfactory to you to receive it without comment. The report may indeed be said to carry with it its own commentary; nevertheless, a few remarks elucidatory of certain parts of it not easily understood by persons removed from the scene of action, may not be deemed objectionable.

I think, from the context of the report, but one impression will be made upon every fair and unbiased mind—that whatever may have been the motives which governed the conduct of the Agents on the part of the United States, in making the late investigations in the Nation, the results of those investigations have been such as to warrant a belief that, if the motives had been the suppression, and not the development, of truth, no other results could have followed.

[The rest of this paragraph, referring to the alleged refusal of certain persons to verify their statements by oath, &c., not deemed important for insertion here.]

The examination of Hambly, the interpreter, and confidential friend of the Agent, formerly reported to you by your own Commissioners as a base and unworthy fellow, was distinguished for its irregularity. The object of that examination was to lay a broad foundation for the rupture of the treaty, by showing it to be the offspring of bribery and corruption, and the most enormously wicked contrivances; and to traduce the characters and discredit the testimony of some of the most respectable men among us. How bad must that cause be which would employ such an instrument to accomplish such a purpose!

When Yoholo, a principal Chief in the Council, made a talk detailing circumstances connected with the late negotiations at the Indian Springs, Col. Williamson, one of the Commissioners, who was present, and who had also been a close observer of occurrences at the Springs, said to General Gaines that he knew, of his own knowledge, the statements of Yoholo to be false: the General answered, that he would not believe the congregated world, if it were to say so. Now you will have an opportunity of seeing that the statements of the Indian Chief are in direct contradiction to the statements of the Commissioners of the United States and their Secretary, of Col. Williamson himself, of all the friendly Chiefs, and of every respectable white man who was present at the Indian Springs.

The refusal of General Gaines to permit a separate examination of the Chiefs, in his presence, as the only mode of extracting the truth, and after having more than once promised it, is as unaccountable as it was unexpected.

It is understood that the Indians could produce no law authorizing the execution of McIntosh; yet, Gen. Gaines must have taken for granted the existence of such a law, for he passes by the murder as justifiable homicide. The whole body of evidence, as you will see, completely disproves the existence of the law.

The refusal of Gen. Gaines to admit the Commissioners of Georgia, as such, to a participation of the Indian Councils in all matters touching the interests of Georgia, was a wrong done to the State, and an indignity offered to its constituted authorities.

The interdict put upon our Commissioners, by General Gaines, to announce to the Indians, according to their instructions, the resolution of this Government to make the survey, and to represent to them the harmlessness and innocency of the act, whilst the General announced the resolution of his own Government to prevent it, was a further wrong done to the State, and a disrespect manifested of the authority which gave that instruction.

A gentleman of clear intellect, pure morals, honorable character, and great prudence, is selected by the Governor to hold a talk with the Indians—he performs that duty—makes his report, and that report is at once discredited on the naked word of the Indians. Gen. McIntosh writes three several letters to the Governor, subscribed by his own proper hand, giving his assent to the survey of the country; the friendly Chiefs, Marshall included, repeatedly assure the Governor, that they, one and all, consent to the survey; a certificate is obtained from this same Marshall and a white man, to prove that General McIntosh refused his assent; General Gaines immediately comes to the conclusion that this assent was never given.

The admission of free communication with the Indians, to every other description of persons, and the denial of it to the Georgia Commissioners, was a further wrong done to Georgia.

Indeed, sir, it would appear, from the reports of the Commissioners, that all or any description of testimony would be willingly received on the one side, and particularly that description of it which would exculpate the Agent, excuse the hostile Indians, prevent the survey of the lands, or effect the abrogation of the treaty; and that on the other side everything was to be discredited, or received, at best, with many grains of allowance, and every act or proceeding of the Commissioners of the United States, or of the constituted authorities of the State, resolved into corruption and depravity.

When General Gaines states, in one of his letters to the Governor, that the hostile party outnumber the friendly, in the proportion of something like fifty to one, it is not easy to understand him. If it be true, as the General seems to believe, that he has pacified and reconciled the two parties, there is no longer any McIntosh party—but if the General means there was any such disproportion between the strength of the two parties, whilst McIntosh lived, he is widely mistaken. If McIntosh had survived to this moment, the probability is his party would have been the strongest.

Suffer me to add a few particulars, which make the condition of the friendly party most pitiable. Independently of no atonement being offered for the blood of McIntosh, the money, according to the construction of the treaty, is taken from the pockets of the wives, children, brothers and friends of McIntosh, and paid over to the hostile Chiefs who murdered him, contrary to every principle of justice and stipulation of treaty, as if you intended it as the reward of gallant and meritorious acts commanded by yourselves; and this the friendly Chiefs cannot but feel most deeply. Nobody acquainted with the Indian character, can ever believe that General Gaines will ever make either a safe or permanent pacification until the offering of blood for blood has fulfilled the law and the usage of the country. An ephemeral peace may be patched up by force or menace—but ephemeral it will be, making, in the end, the catastrophe the more bloody.

I had written you of a certain personage of South Carolina having intermeddled in this matter, according to information communicated to me and submitted to you. There is a strong chain of corroborative circumstances, as you will see, to establish the facts there alleged, and running through the entire mass of evidence. The object undoubtedly was the annulment of the treaty.

Whatever knavery or folly may suggest, with the view to disannul the treaty, will, of course, be unheeded at Washington. But, indeed, Sir, I very much doubt, unless you have looked with a scrutinizing eye to the history of this matter, whether some of the self-interested oppugners of the treaty may not lead you into error. The idea that the entire Creek Nation is alone competent to make a treaty, is the most fallacious that could be entertained; it is so far from true in the general, that, unless by merest accident, it never happens to be true in any particular.

You have only to turn to the notes of Col. Hawkins, whose authority you cannot dispute, to be satisfied that, according to the laws and usages of the Nation, the most important public affairs, involving vital interests, are determined, not by a majority, but by a minority, and frequently a small minority of the Nation. In the whole course of his long residence among them, he never knew the most popular war concurred in by a majority; and all authorities and all custom will prove to you, that, with regard to the most important of their national acts, having relation either to peace or war, Coweta must take the lead. If a treaty be signed by the Chiefs of Coweta, it is considered good—if not signed by them, good for nothing. Georgia was settled in '32*: in '33 or '34 the first treaty with the Creeks was held; then I think in '36, and again in '39. The Cowetas are always foremost; their councils are invariably holden on the Coweta ground, and Gen. Oglethorpe paid them his first visit there. Hence, it is stated, in the evidence, that McIntosh had the power to sell the whole country, and hence the great efforts made to prevail on the old Coweta Chief, Etome Tustunnuggee, not to sell the country—efforts which succeeded at Broken Arrow; but this old and ill-fated chieftain came to me, afterwards, as you read in the documents, to say he had been deceived by bad white men, and was opposed to the sale at Broken Arrow, but then his eyes were opened, and he would follow the advice of his Father, the President, and sell the lands.

Having made this recapitulation and commentary, permit me to subjoin, that, for the gratification of a few mercenary and sordid characters in the Indian country, you threaten the most flagrant injustice to Georgia.

In the country to be surveyed, within the limits of Georgia, none, or very few, of the hostile party reside; and every one of the opposite party seeks the survey as a measure of convenience and interest. The survey will, in the first instance, extend no further West than the Chattahoochee, the act of the Legislature leaving it discretionary with the Governor, to run to that river before the boundary line between Georgia and Alabama shall have been ascertained.

Having corresponded with the Governor of Alabama upon this subject, and received his assurance that the Legislature of that State will immediately, on its first meeting in November, cordially co-operate with Georgia in running the line, and there being difficulty in ascertaining the precise point at which that line will commence, the running is

* Georgia was settled in 1733.—ED.

postponed to meet the wishes and expectations of the State of Alabama.

The evidence which remains to be taken by the Commissioners, will be forwarded as soon as received.

It will be remembered that, in his letter of 15th August, to the Secretary of War, the Governor authorized that officer to "inform the President that, until the will of the Legislature of Georgia is expressed, no measures will be taken to execute the survey." This put a stop, for the time, to one irritating cause of controversy. On the 31st of August, the Secretary wrote to the Governor, acknowledging, for the President, the receipt of certain letters from him, with their enclosures, &c., and stating that whilst the President deeply regretted the different views of the treaty which the Governor entertained, from those which the President had "found himself, upon the most deliberate consideration," &c., "compelled to take, he is anxiously desirous to avoid anything which, dictated by no absolute necessity, might have a tendency to widen differences, in his belief otherwise easily reconcilable," &c., &c. He stated, further, that the President "felt it, therefore, his duty to decline entering upon any discussion with you which can be forborne, and he perceives nothing in your letters which the interests of the people of Georgia, or of the rest of the Union, require to be discussed with you," &c., &c. After referring to the duties which the United States owed to the Indians, and expressing the President's hope that they had not been "violated in the conclusion of the treaty at the Indian Springs," he added: "He has heard, therefore, with the most lively satisfaction, the determination of your Excellency to proceed no further in the survey, till the Congress of the United States and the Legislature of Georgia shall have had an opportunity of acting on the subject, as, in their respective judgments, the rights, duties and obligations of all the parties concerned, may require." He referred to the death of McIntosh, the restoration of peace to the tribe, and stated that to "confirm this state of tranquillity, and to renew peaceable and reasonable efforts to reconcile the Indians to the measure of removing from the territory, appeared to the President to be his duty, in which he will not abandon the hope of being seconded by the Governor and authorities of Georgia." He concluded by saying: "The subject, in all its aspects, will be submitted to the consideration of Congress at the approaching session; and all the instructions of the officers of the United States, as well as their conduct under them, will be subject to the animadversions of that body upon them, for approbation or censure, as they may appear to have deserved."

We must now recur, once more, to Gen. Gaines. Having been forbidden to hold official intercourse with the Governor, he nevertheless proceeded to write insulting letters to him, through the newspapers. On the 23d of August, he addressed a letter to the Governor, through the columns of the Georgia Journal, dated "Head-quarters, Eastern Department, Indian Springs, 16th August, 1825," and signed "Edmund Pendleton Gaines, *Major-General Commanding*." We make room for a few extracts, at which the reader will be amused, if he is not instructed by them. He said: "I had seen with regret that for a U. S. officer to write to you, was, in fact, to write for the newspapers, and that to differ from you in opinion, was to be denounced as an offender. Since this was apparent to me, that is, since the receipt of yours of the 17th July, I have been well aware of the tax which our little differences of opinion would impose upon me—a tax which conscious innocence suffers under the groundless imputation of guilt.

"I was not, therefore, much surprised at the gross misrepresentations of your *dedimus protestatem* Commissioners, nor at the concluding paragraph of yours of the 6th, wherein you say, 'I have lost no time to direct you to forbear further intercourse with this Government.' These expressions, like others contained in some of your previous letters, (but of which I took no notice,) wherein you speak of my using the military against Georgia, &c., &c., appear to evince a very high degree of that prejudice and *inflated pride of office*, which might well be expected to prompt some little European despot 'to feel power and forget right.' Were you some little German Prince, for example, (the most self-important and overbearing of all the crowned tribe,) and I a Turk, it would in that case excite no surprise that the little German Prince should address the Turk as you have more than once addressed me, and, after freely indulging in words of learned length and thundering sound, conclude with the expressions above quoted, viz: '*I have lost no time to direct you to forbear further intercourse with this Government.*' But I am not a Turk, nor are you a prince! I am a plain native of Virginia, and an adopted citizen of Tennessee," &c., &c.

On the 30th of August, he published another letter, in the Georgia Patriot, dated the 29th, and headed and signed in the same military style. He said: "I have received your communication through Mr. Secretary Pierce, with two papers purporting to be copies of letters from your Excellency to the President of the United States, bearing date the 26th July and 6th August—wherein it appears you are pleased to write *at me* and *of me*, notwithstanding your avowed resolution not to write *to me*. To this wise expedient, to preserve the immense weight of dignity under which your Excellency labors, I can have no objection. I take this occasion, before noticing your assumed facts and arguments, to assure you that I have no authority whatever from the President of the United States or Department of War, to write or speak to you upon any other than public and official subjects—such as I have with perfect frankness and cordiality communicated to you, previous to the receipt of your letter of the 17th July." Again: "To your Excellency I have no apology to offer. I propose, however, that, in our future correspondence, after disposing of your futile charges against me, that you and I may confine ourselves *to our public and official duties*. When these are accomplished, I hereby promise, should you desire it, to correspond with you, *unofficially*, until 'we shall have exhausted the argument;' and then we will stand by our—goose quills, and talk of '*valor*'—about which you have written to the President."

The Governor wrote, as follows, to the President:

EXECUTIVE DEPARTMENT,
Milledgeville, 31*st Aug.*, 1825.

SIR: In the enclosed Gazette, you will find another insolent letter, dated the 16th inst., addressed by your Agent, Brevet Major-General Gaines, to the Chief Magistrate of this State. Having been betrayed by his passions into the most violent excesses, he is presented before you, at this moment, as your commissioned officer and authorized agent, with a corps of regulars at his heels, attempting to dragoon and overawe the constituted authorities of an independent State, and, on the eve of a great election, amid the distractions of party, taking side with the one political party against the other, and addressing electioneering papers almost weekly to the Chief Magistrate, through the public prints, couched in language of contumely and insult, and defiance, and for which, were I to send him to you in chains, I would transgress nothing of the public law. The same moderation and forbearance with which I have endeavored heretofore to deport myself, in my intercourse with you, and from which I trust there has in no instance been a departure, but on the highest necessity, have restrained me from resorting to harsh and offensive measures against him. You will see, however, if this officer has been thus acting by your authority or countenance, you have an awful atonement to make, both to your contemporaries and to posterity.

But if, contrary to either, he has assumed the responsibility, it is expected that your indignant reprobation of his conduct will be marked by the most exemplary punishment which the laws will enable you to inflict.

I demand, therefore, as Chief Magistrate of Georgia, his immediate recall, and his arrest, trial and punishment, under the rules and articles of war.

You will find, in the same paper, sundry affidavits proving the falsity of the certificate given by Marshall and Edwards to General Gaines, and which further prove that General Gaines must have obtained it to wield as an instrument, in the pending contest, on the side of one party against the other. As I write this, another Gazette has been put into my hands, containing another letter, of subsequent date and similar character, which is also enclosed for your information.

Very Respectfully,

G. M. TROUP.

The President of the United States,
Washington City.

To this letter the Governor received a reply from the Secretary of War, dated 19th September, saying:

"The President has decided that he cannot, consistently with his views of the subject, accede to your demand to have General Gaines arrested. He perceives no sufficient necessity to depart from the course he had determined to pursue before the receipt of your letter, and which I communicated to you fully in the last paragraph of mine of the 31st of August," &c., &c.

In this letter, the Secretary enclosed (to the Governor) a copy of his letter of same date, to Gen. Gaines, and said: "In so doing, I give you a new proof of the frankness by which the Executive has been guided in its intercourse with you," &c., &c.

In his letter to Gen. Gaines, the Secretary enclosed a copy of Gov. Troup's letter demanding the General's arrest, &c., and, after adding that the President had decided not to "accede to this demand," and expressing the President's regret that General Gaines had permitted himself to "indulge a tone whose effect will be to destroy that harmony which the President is so much disposed to cherish," &c., &c., and the President's determination to preserve the most scrupulous decorum in official intercourse with the State authorities, he said:

"In communicating to you the disapprobation of the President, as well for writing as publishing those letters, and his injunction that, in your official intercourse with Gov. Troup, in future, you abstain from anything that may be deemed offensive, I am directed to add, as an act of justice to you, that the President sees in the serious charges made against you by Gov. Troup, and the publicity given to them, and which the letters complained of were intended to repel, circumstances which go far, in his opinion, to palliate your conduct, and without which palliation the President would have found it his duty to have yielded to the demand of Gov. Troup."

The next letter from Governor Troup to the Secretary of War, will close our notice of this dispute with General Gaines. In that letter he is charged by the Governor with having aided in publicly traducing and vilifying him, "for the purpose of influencing the general election in this State, in behalf of his favorite candidate."* This was denied by Gen. Gaines, in a card published in the Georgia Patriot of 13th September, in which he said: "I have never, to my knowledge, endeavored to influence the vote or the political opinion of any man in the State of Georgia, in regard to the ensuing election." And yet there was the affidavit of one Michael Watson, who deposed, on the 10th of November, that in the month of August, "in a conversation that was held between and among several persons then at the Springs, General Edmund P. Gaines, of the United States Army, being present, the subject of conversation turned upon the late Indian treaty, and the proposed survey then about to be made by the order of his Excellency George M. Troup, Governor of the State of Georgia: he (Gen. Gaines) stated in public company, that if Governor Troup made the survey or attempted it, that he would be tried for treason and hung; that General Gaines also stated that Governor Troup and his friends were intriguing demagogues: that in the same conversation General Gaines manifested and expressed much warmth of hostile feeling towards Governor Troup and his friends," &c. The Hon. Christopher B. Strong, deposing, probably to the same occasion, said:

* At a dinner to Gen. Gaines, at Clinton, on 17th August, 1825, the following were among the partisan volunteer toasts:

His Excellency Governor Troup: A man of war! He "cares for no responsibilities;" as brave a knight as Don Quixote or his squire Sancho Panza.

Gen. John Clark: A former trouble to the *Indians*— a present trouble to some of their *kindred*.

Gen. John Clark: Too honest for intrigue, too independent to entreat for office, but always willing to serve his country; may he, on the first Monday in October, be elected Governor by the *people of Georgia*, and not, like the present incumbent, by *bribery* and *corruption*.—ED.

"On the 11th day of August, in the year 1825, at the Indian Springs, in the County of Monroe, of said State, he heard a conversation commence between Gen. Edmund P. Gaines, of the United States army, and Milton Cooper, of Putnam, in which General Gaines appeared to manifest much passion, and, after this deponent got near enough to hear what was said, he heard the said General say, 'he is a demagogue, his partisans are demagogues—unprincipled demagogues, *he* is guilty of treason,' 'and the Commissioners have stated wilfully, falsely,' or words to that effect. I was informed by several gentlemen then present, that the former epithets were used in relation and applied to Gov. Troup of Georgia. A severe controversy ensued betwixt the General and myself, which I deem it unnecessary here to detail. This deponent further saith, that, from what passed at that time, he has no doubt but that the first mentioned expressions of reproach were used by Gen. Gaines in direct relation to Governor Troup."

Joel Bailey also deposed that, in the month of July,

"Gen. Gaines said that he dared Governor Troup to attempt to survey the land lately ceded by the Indians; that he would have an armed force and arrest every Surveyor as fast as they crossed Flint river. That if the Governor of the little demagogue State of Georgia did not mind, that he (Gaines) would get hold of him, and that the people of Georgia were a set of demagogues."

Without professing to decide whether these affidavits proved Gen. Gaines to have been an active partisan of the opposition, we think it clear that the influence of his name and character was against the administration of Governor Troup; and, consequently, operated in favor of his enemies. We must do him the justice to say that, in his card in the Georgia Patriot, he said: "as I have been charged, however falsely, with an attempt to meddle with the political affairs of the State, with a view to the ensuing election, I have determined to suspend the publication of my promised exposition until after the election."

Governor Troup to the Secretary of War.

EXECUTIVE DEPARTMENT.
Milledgeville, 15*th Oct.*, 1825.

Sir: Notwithstanding the resolution of the President,

repeated in your letter of the 19th ult., to refer the complaints of this Government against the officers of yours, who have given it offence, to the consideration of Congress—a resolution considered here of most extraordinary character, inasmuch as it is the transfer of a subject over which the President, by the Constitution, has exclusive jurisdiction, to a power which has no jurisdiction of it at all—I cannot forbear calling his attention to a statement contained in your letter to Gen. Gaines, which, assumed to be true, although not true, is made the justification of the President in resisting the demand of the Governor of Georgia, and in extenuating the conduct of his officer. The paragraph in your letter embracing the statement, reads as follows: "I am directed to add, as an act of justice to you, that the President sees in the serious charges made against you by Governor Troup, and the publicity given to them, and which the letters complained of were intended to repel, circumstances which go far in his opinion to palliate your conduct." Now, sir, so far from this being true, the opposite is true. Nothing offensive or exceptionable was ever written to that officer, before he had sanctioned, by his approbation, an offensive letter written by your Special Agent on the 21st June, and addressed to the Agent for Indian Affairs, in which the authorities of Georgia are wantonly abused for injustice, oppression and tyranny practiced against that Agent; or before he had obtained a false certificate from two base and unworthy men, to traduce and vilify the character of the Chief Magistrate of Georgia, which he ordered to be published of his mere volition, on pretence that false rumors were in circulation, of what, or about whom, he does not say; and this, too, done, as was afterwards made manifest, for the purpose of influencing the general election in this State in behalf of his favorite candidate. That you may entertain no doubt of the correctness of this statement, and the incorrectness of the statement of the President, you have only to compare the dates of the various letters and of their publication. It will be seen that before Gen. Gaines could have received my letter of the 16th of July, of which he complained, he had already ordered the publication of his of the 10th of July, to which it was an answer.

You will be furnished, in time, with additional testimony, to show the very reprehensible conduct of the same officer, in his deportment towards the authorities of Georgia, not with any, the least, expectation that justice will be rendered by the President to those authorities, but in discharge of duties which they owe themselves.

I have the honor to be
Your obedient servant,
G. M. TROUP.

The Hon. James Barbour.
Secretary of War.

The Southern Recorder, of the 9th of August, contained a card "to the public," from Col. Crowell, to which was appended the following letter:

MILLEDGEVILLE, GEO., August 1st, 1825.

Sir: I acknowledge the receipt of your defence, accompanied by the testimony collected to rebut the charges preferred against you by his Excellency Governor Troup, as well as the testimony taken against you by a committee of the Legislature of Georgia, and that interspersed throughout the volume of documents furnished me by the Governor of Georgia.

After a diligent examination of all the testimony taken on both sides during the investigation, and coming before me, I feel it incumbent on me to say that I consider you, in reference to the charges made against you, not only an innocent, but a much injured, man. This result is the more honorable to you, as you have only had it in your power to avail yourself of *voluntary* testimony.

I shall make this report* to the Secretary of War, to whom you will look for the *decision* of the President, which will confirm or reverse this opinion. In the mean time you will consider your suspension withdrawn.

With respect, sir,
Your obedient servant,
T. P. ANDREWS,
Special Agent.

To Colonel John Crowell,
Indian Agent, &c., &c.

It is proper here to state the President *confirmed* this report.

In September, Major Andrews published, in the National

* The Report of Major Andrews to the Secretary of War, with the documents appended to it, occupies more than 150 pages of printed matter, in octavo form. It concludes with the expression of opinion in regard to Col. Crowell, the Indian Agent, that "he has fully succeeded in establishing his entire innocence of the charges preferred against him."—ED.

Journal and the National Intelligencer, a long "reply" to what he called the "Reports of the Georgia Commissioners," in which he was very severe in his strictures upon the official conduct of those gentlemen, and in which he did not hesitate to attack their characters as men, &c., &c.

In the mean time, the canvass for Governor was proceeding with much acrimony and bitterness. The papers teemed with articles of great warmth on both sides. "TROUP AND THE TREATY" was the rallying cry of the friends of the Governor, whilst it was contended by his enemies that his defeat was necessary to the repose of the country and the peaceful settlement of the Indian controversy. As early as the 4th of July, the celebration of the day was made the occasion of what were considered patriotic outbursts, but what were, in many instances, the offspring of party violence and heated controversy.*

Amongst other objections to Governor Troup, it was said his father had been a *Tory*; and then it was said General Clark's father was no better. Gov. Troup was charged with being an *alien*, born in Florida; General Clark was accused of being a Yazoo man, and with having shot at the effigy of Washington. It is hardly important to add, that none of these charges were made out to the satisfaction of the friends of the candidate against whom they were urged.

If party virulence had stopped with accusations, which, if true, would have affected the fitness for office or usefulness of either candidate, there would have been ground of excuse; but political rancor, in its opposition to Governor Troup, went beyond this. His domestic privacy was as-

* The following toasts drunk on the 4th of July, at an interior town, cannot be considered fair specimens. It is due to the Clark man to say that, in a card which he afterwards published, he declared that whilst his toast expressed "the sentiments of a large number," and *contained his real opinion*, yet he would not have given it, if another sentiment, *in favor* of Gov. Troup, had not been first offered at a dinner from which he had endeavored to keep out party politics. Here are the sentiments:

"*George M. Troup*—May he receive what he deserves, the infamy due to every man who attempts to excite civil war and destroy the Union."

"*George M. Troup*—May every hair on his head be a standing army, and every soldier be armed with a thundering cannon to drive his enemies to h—ll."—ED.

sailed; and it was basely and falsely insinuated by some, who had the cunning to do secretly what they had not the boldness to avow openly, that the ill health of the partner of his bosom was caused by conjugal ill treatment. That some dupes may have believed the slander, is probably true; but the high-minded and better informed even of his opponents refused to lend themselves to so cruel an expedient to defeat an honorable man.

Amidst the jarring elements of discord, and the turmoil of a fierce party war, Governor Troup remained as unmoved as it was possible for any man to be, under the circumstances. It is believed that not the slightest detail of business escaped his attention; and we have certainly seen that he kept the Indian question in full view. A silly rumor was started, that he was to be withdrawn, and Hon. William H. Crawford run in his stead. A short time before the election, his health became somewhat impaired, and it was at one time reported that he was dead.

The 3rd of October at length arrived. If public excitement had been great, public expectation and anxiety were now to be greater. The Georgia Journal, of the 11th of October, in noticing the election, said:

To a calm and indifferent spectator, Milledgeville, for the past week, would have furnished a wide field of amusement. The anxiety visible in all countenances, the avidity with which news from every quarter was sought after, the hailing of post riders, and the stopping of travelers as they entered the town, and the multitude crowding around them, all pressing forward to hear the result; and the alternate elevation and depression of spirits of one party or the other, according as the news agreed with, or differed from, what was expected—all together made up a spectacle which equaled anything seen in Athens on the invasion by Philip, or in Rome when Cæsar was marching upon it. But now all is comparatively quiet. The result is anticipated with much confidence to be in favor of Troup.

The same paper, of the 18th, announced the certain reelection of Gov. Troup. On the result being known in Savannah, the citizens fired a salute in honor of the victory; and another was fired by the Chatham Artillery, of which ancient corps Gov. Troup had been formerly a regular, and was then an honorary, member.

There were in Georgia, at that time, only sixty Counties. Governor Troup had resided in McIntosh, Chatham, Bryan, Montgomery and Laurens Counties. The vote in these Counties was, as follows:

McIntosh—	Troup,	117—	Clark,	83
Chatham,	"	595	"	132
Bryan,	"	125	"	1
Montgomery,	"	116	"	61
Laurens,	"	475	"	111

In Wilkes, the former residence of Gen. Clark, the vote was: Troup, 669; Clark, 644. In Baldwin, the residence of Gen. Clark, and where each had resided as Governor, the vote stood: Troup, 317—Clark, 482.

The official vote, in the whole State, as determined by the Legislature, was:

Troup,	20,545
Clark,	19,862
Majority for Troup,	683

The General Assembly met, at Milledgeville, on the 7th of November, when it was ascertained that *a majority, in each House, were political friends of the defeated candidate.* In the Senate, Allen B. Powell, of McIntosh, was elected President; and, in the House, Thomas W. Murray, of Lincoln, was elected Speaker.

The inauguration of the Governor took place on the 10th of November.

His inaugural address was, as follows:

Fellow-Citizens: I come, once more, and probably for the last time, to present myself before you and take the oath of office. Possessing no very great confidence in my own qualifications for the public service, I have not habitually or pertinaciously sought the public favor. It has been extended to me, freely, frequently, and by the people, in a spirit of abundant kindness, sometimes even in advance, always in a degree far transcending my merits and deserts. The late election by the people, approbatory of the former one by their representatives, inspires a belief that the acts of the administration have not been altogether censurable, and that the faults and errors which belong to them, being of the head, not of the heart, have, on that account, received a kind and indulgent judgment.

Resolved, as I am, at all times, to do what, under the constitution and laws, my judgment approves, it will be my consolation, in the midst of troubles and embarrassments, that what is intended well, will be well received; and that if, at the end of our labors, aught shall have resulted to the public of benefit or advantage, a due measure of praise and commendation will be awarded. Taking different views of the same subject, honest differences of opinion are to be regarded with mutual deference and respect. The utmost we can hope from our deliberations under free institutions, is, that, the love of country predominating over every other love, we will discard the partialities and prejudices which attach to men, and, forgetting the strifes and contentions of the day, will unite in support of every measure promotive of the public welfare.

To husband the resources of the State—to economize the public expenditure—to organize a system of Internal Improvement—to foster the institutions which direct the public Education—to give vigor and efficiency to the armed power to execute the laws and defend the State against her enemies—to vindicate, with firmness and dignity, all her rights; but, more especially, to assert, *practically*, those rights of sovereignty without which Georgia would be independent only in name; and to cultivate harmony between the different branches of the government, will be equally your duty, fellow-citizens, as mine; and, by cordial co-operation and patriotic efforts, I doubt not we will ultimately find our reward in the happiness and prosperity of the people.

The following is the message of the Governor, transmitted to the Legislature on the second day of the session.

EXECUTIVE DEPARTMENT,
Milledgeville, 8*th November*, 1825.

Fellow-Citizens of the Senate
and House of Representatives:

The political year just closed has not been without blessings, or without trials. Abundant thankfulness is due for the former, to the Giver of every good and perfect gift, not less for exemption from war, pestilence and famine, than for the enjoyment of more than ordinary health, propitious seasons, and an ample harvest. For the latter, as they belong to mortals, it is our holy duty, in the spirit of Christian resignation, to bow with reverential submission, and to implore the Omnipotent who orders all for the best, to convert them into blessings. The year has been rendered memorable, too, by the sojourn of the great and amiable LaFayette; the universal joy diffused by it—the display of all the charities and graces of life in the overflowings of grateful hearts, inseparable from his presence, and by the tears of millions, when, after giving to our country his last benediction, he re-embarked for his native land.

The recapitulation of the events of the last two years—the results of our intercourse and correspondence with the General Government, painful as it may be, is a duty too sacred to be omitted. In performing it, no apology is due for the prolix detail, so inconsistent with the analytical character of a State paper like this. The variety of topics, the multitude of facts, justify a departure from the ordinary usage. A tedious exposé may be more acceptable than a superficial survey, as the contemplation of the whole ground will enable you so to apply the resources of your wisdom and patriotism to the exigency, as, with the assistance of Divine Providence, to avert the mischiefs which threaten, make our own ways righteous in our own sight, and in the sight of all others, and bring back to a sense of justice those who, in their aberrations from it, have done us wrong.

I had, for the first time, come into office, when a subject of peculiar delicacy presented itself, and being intimately connected with the independence of the elective franchise, without which it would be vain for Georgia to claim for herself the attributes of a sovereign State, it was made known to the President, that, on the occasion of the election just then terminated, an officer in his employ, bearing a high and dignified commission, and being a citizen of another State, had abandoned his post to mingle in the strifes of that election; had espoused the cause of one of the parties, to the prejudice of the other, and, by the weight and influence of his office, united with the most enthusiastic ardor, had rendered himself so signally conspicuous, that the Chief Magistrate could not conscientiously forbear, among his first acts, to complain to the Executive Government of the Union of this outrage upon the most sacred of all the rights of sovereignty. An occasion offered, at the moment, to give weight to the presentation, and it was embraced. The head of the Missionary Establishment, in the Creek Nation, had been provoked by the ill usage and lawless conduct of the same officer, to prefer certain charges against him, which, if supported by truth, could not fail, it was believed, to bring upon him the severest animadversion of his own Government; and it was hoped that the remonstrance of the Governor of Georgia, thrown into the scale, would accomplish what seemed to him an important object, the removal from office of a man, who, by his prejudices and passions, would present the most formidable obstacles to the satisfaction of the just claims of Georgia against the General Government, at least so long as a certain person filled the first office of that State. They failed of their intent; and whatever sentence might have been passed on the memorial of the Missionary, the remonstrance of the Governor of Georgia was unheeded. The inference was inevitable, that, in virtue either of positive instruction, or of implied consent, the Agent of Indian Affairs, being a citizen of another State, and resident in the Nation, would, at any time, consult both duty and inclination in deserting his station to lend himself, with his insignia of office, to any party in the State, whose views it might be the interest of himself or of his Government to promote.

The State of Georgia had claims upon the General Government, of great magnitude; her territorial ones had been so long neglected, that time seemed to be running against them. The Indians were acquiring a permanency of foothold, under the direct encouragement of the United States, which would rivet them like their fixtures to the soil forever; and it was seen that a day or an hour was of precious import to her whom an act of limitations might bar, upon the arbitrary edict of a stronger power.

When, therefore, in a temper not discreditable, it is hoped, to the author, those claims were pressed upon the General Government, it was answered that everything had been done, which, in good faith, could be done, to satisfy the claims of Georgia, and that now nothing could be done, because the Indians had said nothing should be done. An answer so unkind, ungenerous and faithless, left no alternative but to abandon or strenuously assert them.

It was vain for the State of Georgia to prove to the United States, that, regardless of her claims, they had acquired immense tracts of country, from time to time, for other States and for themselves, and that, in the celebrated treaty of 1814, if the United States had been mindful of their engagements, they could as easily have acquired the whole country within our limits as a single acre.

By the treaty of 1814, the Creeks were treated as a conquered people, whom Georgia had assisted with her arms to conquer; their boundaries were marked by the sword; but charity, which begins at home, more potent than any stipulations of the articles of 1802, acquired for the United States a very large extent of rich country within the limits of Alabama, whilst twenty millions of acres within the limits of Georgia were reserved and guarantied to the Indians, and this guaranty subsequently produced against us to defeat our claim to the same territory. Georgia could not see, in all this, that scrupulous fidelity in the fulfilment of engagements asserted for the United States.

When, at last, the way seemed open to a further acquisition of territory, and Commissioners were appointed to negotiate with the Creeks, at Broken Arrow, Georgia found the Agents of the United States arrayed against her to defeat a treaty: so that it was difficult to understand whether the whole movement was a mockery, to sport with Georgia, or a perfidious betrayal by the Agents of the trust reposed in them. The treaty was defeated, and by their agency; the principal Agent appeared to rise in the esteem and confidence of his Government, and thus terminated this most disgusting scene.

The rehearsal of what happened immediately after, at the Indian Springs, would only revive recollections of the same odious practices of the same Agent, not less disgraceful because they were more covert and less successful. From this period are to be dated all the mischiefs, disorders and heart-burnings which followed, produced, chiefly, by the conduct of the same officer. But, in justice to him, it should be said, that, from this period, he is to be considered rather as an instrument than a principal; as his own Government, looking back upon the history of the past, had seemed to approve his actings and doings in the gross, and had given every token of undiminished confidence in him; so that, from that day thenceforth, whatever was said, done or written by him, seemed good in its sight. No evil report of him would be listened to; the word of no man taken against him; all testimony in his favor eagerly received, all against him promptly discredited: the expressed will of the constituted authorities of the State, which denounced him as an enemy to its interest, disregarded by his Government, and contemned by himself; in short, his single declaration in the face of truth, made by that Government the basis of the most offensive measures against this, even to the extreme one of threatening us with the sword, and actually drawing out a regular force for its execution.

The history of the treaty of 1825, and the character of the events which followed, will be best learned by the documents and evidence heretofore published, and those now laid before you. The epitome is, that the treaty was as untainted with fraud as most other Indian treaties—was made with an authority long since recognized by the United States as competent to make it—was acquiesced in at first by the great body of the Nation, and would have been cheerfully submitted to by the whole tribe, as the hostile Chiefs in Council indicated to Col. Lamar, if the Agent had not returned from his mission to Washington, and *altered it*. It was this ominous return from his defeat before the President and Senate, in which McIntosh foresaw the ruin which an infuriated man would bring upon him and his generation. "We are not in any danger until he comes home and commences hostility, and urges it himself upon us," says McIntosh. "If ratified, (meaning the treaty,) it may produce a horrid state of things among those unfortunate Indians," says the Agent. What the penetrating sagacity of the one foretold, soon came to pass. McIntosh was no more; and thus the evil genius of the other, which predicted the coming of the whirlwind, which rode in it, and directed the storm, saw, in one fell swoop, the triumph of his machinations and the fulfilment of his prophecy. McIntosh and his Chiefs had given their assent to the survey of the country, and this assent was seized by the Agent to divert the public odium from himself, and to fasten it on the Chief Magistrate of Georgia, who had sought and obtained that assent. The naked declaration of the Agent to this effect, unsupported by a tittle of proof, was sufficient to command the absolute credence of his Government, and, contrary to all opposing testimony of the most conclusive character, to warrant it in charging the calamities of the nation upon the same magistrate as the author of them all; to forbid the survey, and to embody a corps of regulars to prevent it, and to continue both its offensive orders and its offensive armament, even after another of its Agents, by false testimony, had proven, to its satisfaction, that no such assent was ever given, and had announced to it, moreover, what was not the fact, but what, on his authority, it implicitly believed to be the fact, that the pacification of the Indians had been concluded, and, of course, order and tranquillity permanently restored; nevertheless, the offensive mandate is unrevoked, and the parade of bayonets maintained.

The Indian right of occupancy is the only one acknowledged by the European powers, from the beginning; the only one acknowledged by all the public instruments through which Georgia derived her title; the only one conceded to the Indians by Georgia, in all her treaties with them, from the first settlement of the country, and the only one recognized by the United States themselves.

The Spaniards and the French, without respecting even this right, have forcibly appropriated to themselves entire countries, when and where it suited them. The English and Americans have so far respected it, as to make compensation for the relinquishment of claim or abandonment of use. It is true, that, with regard to this right of use, the United States, in their own territory, might have given to it any latitude which pleased them, because the soil and jurisdiction belonged to them; but, with regard to the territory of Georgia, where the soil and jurisdiction are indisputably hers, this right of use can only be construed to mean, what in all the treaties it did mean, the right of use for hunting. When, therefore, the United States, by changing the mode of life of the aboriginal upon the soil of Georgia, changed essentially this right, and caused her lands to be separately appropriated for the purpose of tillage, and gave every encouragement to fixed habits of agriculture, they violated the treaties in their letter and spirit, and did wrong to Georgia. It is not less strange than true, that, of all the various tribes of aborigines dispersed over the vast country within the limits of the United States, two of them, within the limits of Georgia, have been specially selected as most fit subjects for the operation of this great scheme of reclamation, and that the partial success of this scheme, (founded in wrong to Georgia, and continued in wrong,) should be held up to us now, as a mirror in which we are invited to see, at once, our own deformity and the moral beauty of its authors, and that this original and continued wrong should be set up in bar of our undoubted rights.

The State of Georgia contends that the jurisdiction over the country in question, is absolute in herself; she proves it by all the titles through which she derived her claim from the beginning, by the charters and proclamations of the mother country, by the repeated acknowledgments of the United States themselves, and by their solemnly expressed recognition in the first and second articles of the agreement and cession, of 1802. It was shown, that if Georgia had the jurisdiction, Georgia had never parted with it; and that, if she had it not, she can never have it in virtue of any authority of any power known to her. Yet, Georgia has been denied the right of survey of her own soil, within her own jurisdiction; a right as inseparable from that jurisdiction, and as innocent as a right of way; and this, notwithstanding the consent to that survey, as is verily believed, freely given by every Chief within the limits of the territory, who could, by any possibility, suffer harm or detriment from it; nay, more, it is confidently believed, that if the United States Government, or its Agents, had not extorted from one portion of the Indians, objections to the survey, there would not have been found a single individual who would have thought of entertaining any; and here it will not escape you, that, at the Council of Broken Arrow, where the Commissioners of Georgia were present, the military officer of the United States, under his instructions, made known to the Chiefs that his Government had resolved not to permit the survey; so that, if a spirit, at any time, from any cause, had animated the Indian to hostility against Georgia, the savage would have availed himself of the survey, as a pretext to fall upon our people, and with the more ferocity, because assured that he would be sustained by the arms of the United States.

The last pretext of the President, for resistance to the survey, is the obligation to execute the 8th article of the treaty, which guaranties protection to the friendly Indians. Under that guaranty, the United States passively suffer McIntosh and his friends to be murdered: in the hour of peril no arm is lifted to save or to protect; the danger past; the Chiefs massacred; their property destroyed or dispersed; the survivors in Georgia asking bread and protection of their lives, after abandoning to their enemies every thing valuable at home; the United States step forth with their armed power, to defend, under the 8th article of the treaty, these same Indians against all their enemies, and more particularly the Georgians, their only friends and protectors.

McIntosh having fallen in the cause of the United States, by the hand of treachery, the United States were bound, in honor, under the 8th article, to bring to punishment his murderers; to restore to his friends their rank, power and property, lost in the same cause, and to have coerced the execution of the treaty; all which could easily have been accomplished; but the Agents of the United States indulging more of sympathy for the hostile, than for the friendly Indians, prescribe to the latter the terms on which they shall make peace with their enemies; the blood of McIntosh, unwashed from their hands, the plundered property unrestored, the Agent unremoved; the hostile party are to be received into the bond of communion and fellowship, with a forgiveness of sins, as if these natives of the wilderness, at once the noble and fallen of their species, should, in the darkness of heathenism, do more than the philosophy of the heathen or the fortitude of the Christian ever did; the money stipulated to be paid to them exclusively, and by the Commissioners of the United States, ordered to be paid, in part, to their enemies, and by the hands of other Agents than those appointed by the treaty. These wrongs, done to the friends of McIntosh, are adverted to merely because they cannot be overlooked in the catalogue of wrongs done to Georgia, and to show that the friendly Indians may have suffered for indulging friendly sentiments towards Georgia, and Georgia, for indulging like sentiments towards the friendly Indians. The result of all which is, that, judging the motives and objects of human action by the results, the Agents of the United States, whether commissioned for that purpose, or not, must have been intent on vindicating the conduct of the Agent for Indian Affairs, and opening the way for the rupture of the treaty—for that conduct has been *vindicated* and approved by them, and all the materials, as it is understood, collected for that *rupture*, whilst the Indians remain unreconciled either to one another, or to the treaty, and a large portion of them more embittered and exasperated against the authors of it than ever.

The President having ultimately resolved to refer the treaty to Congress, for reconsideration, because of alleged intrigue and treachery practiced to obtain it, the resolution adopted by the Executive to prosecute the survey under the act of the Legislature, of the 9th day of June last, was changed, and the change immediately communicated to the President.

It would be uncandid, fellow-citizens, to disguise that, but for the proposed reference to Congress, the survey would have been commenced and prosecuted. So long as the controversy was confined to the Executive of the Union and the Executive of Georgia, there could be no hesitation as to the measures which it became the latter to pursue. Between States equally independent, it is not required of the weaker to yield to the stronger, because this would be settling controversies by the rule of force, not by the rule of right; and, between sovereigns, the weaker is equally qualified as the stronger to pass upon its rights. The immediate survey of the country, required certainly by the interest and convenience of Georgia, was not of that vital importance which would justify offensive measures to execute it. But the abandonment of a right, not considered doubtful by the only power competent to pronounce upon it, was another and very different matter. The concession of a right, without an equivalent, by a weaker to a stronger power, is never made without exposing the former to injurious imputation, and will always be followed by concession after concession to unjust demands, until nothing remains to be demanded on the one side, or conceded on the other. When, therefore, the President of the United States commanded the Governor of Georgia to forbear the survey, and when that command was followed by a distinct annunciation of the penalty which awaited the disobedience to it, the Executive of Georgia would not merely have surrendered a right already declared to be so by the supreme power of the State, but would have made a dishonorable surrender to a stronger power, with the sword suspended over his head. Whilst, therefore, the Governor would, in this respect, have treated the mandate of the President as unlawful, he did not hesitate, as soon as the contemplated reference of the treaty to Congress, for alleged intrigue and treachery, was officially known to him, to postpone the survey until the meeting of the Legislature; not because that reference was lawful, but that its legality or illegality was not so appropriately a question for his decision, as for that of the Legislature. So that, whilst the Government of Georgia denied the power of the Executive authority of the United States to pronounce upon her rights, it might not refuse to the assembled States of the Union the opportunity of investigating certain claims, or discussing certain questions in controversy, connected with the treaty, or with her own character and conduct in relation to it. So far as that character and conduct were in any manner involved in the negotiation or conclusion of the treaty, or in the events which preceded and followed, their purity, uprightness and justice might freely be canvassed before the whole world. Thus much was conceded for our own sake, until the meeting of the Legislature; the rights of the State were saved by protestation, and the Legislature is yet free to act upon the subject, as if no measure had been taken by the Executive in relation to that reference. The legality of the survey was asserted, the power to invalidate the treaty denied, and the absolute title of Georgia to the soil and jurisdiction vindicated.

The very limited knowledge of the history of the Creek tribes, possessed by the people of the United States, and the misconceptions and misrepresentations which could not fail to ensue, induced the Executive to direct the attention of J. V. Bevan, Esq., (already assiduously occupied under your appointment to collect the materials for a history of Georgia,) to the illustration of that part of the Creek story which had more immediate reference to the points involved in the discussion of the treaty. The result of his diligent research is submitted in the paper marked (A). You will find there the ground assumed by the Executive of Georgia in maïntenance of the treaty, viz: that the consent of Coweta was of itself sufficient, independently of all other considerations, to give force and efficacy to that instrument, is fully sustained, and by evidence derived from such authentic sources, as to leave nothing to cavil or to subterfuge.

In obedience to the will of the Legislature, expressed in their resolutions of the 11th day of June last, I proceeded to the appointment of Commissioners to carry the objects of them into effect. In selecting the members of this commission, I endeavored to have regard to the qualifications of uprightness, integrity and intelligence. It was believed that the selection would be approved by the moral and enlightened of our own community. Since, however, the censorship of the United States Agents has passed them in review, the Executive is informed by those Agents that he was mistaken and deceived; and, accordingly, you will see, in sundry documents accompanying this message, the characters of those Commissioners so portrayed that it would have been difficult to resist the belief that, by a strange fatality, they had been chosen from the least worthy and estimable of society, if the characters of the persons filling the highest offices of the State, both Legislative and Executive, had not previously been subjected to the same scrutiny and shared the same fate. The report will inform you of the treatment they received, and of the obstacles thrown in their way at every step, by which all investigation was rendered unavailing. The principal Agent having been instructed by the President to advise with the Governor of Georgia upon the measures necessary to the successful prosecution of his mission, when the Governor of Georgia appointed Commissioners to co-operate with him in the task of investigation, as well as to guard the interests of Georgia, the act of appointment is pronounced a usurpation—the commissioners treated as private persons—every obstruction opposed to the procurement of testimony—intercourse with the Indians denied them—the promises given of a separate examination of the Indians, violated—the word of an Indian Chief received as true against the testimony of the whole world—the Agent of Indian Affairs declared innocent, if condemned by 23 States of the 24—and Cherokee Chiefs, who had distinguished themselves, in the councils of their own Nation, for hostility to the interests of Georgia, permitted to sit in the councils, to aid with their advice, and to dictate the talks of the Creeks, whilst the confrontation with their enemies, sought by the friendly Chiefs, was refused.

In compliance with the requisitions of the same resolutions, I transmitted, without delay, a copy of the memorial addressed by the Legislature to the President, exposing the conduct of the Agent for Indian Affairs, and requesting his removal from office. The President, in this, as in every other case in which the authorities of Georgia have complained of the conduct of his Agents, has determined to refer the subject to the consideration of Congress; a decision as unexpected as unsatisfactory. It is the transfer of a matter by the President, who alone has the absolute control over it, to the Congress which has no such control. The President has authority to dismiss, at pleasure, the offending officer, or, if a military one, to order a court for his trial, whilst the Congress of the United States has no such power. The utmost the Congress can do, in an extreme case, is to impeach the officer, if impeachable; if not, repeal the law creating the office, and thus indirectly removing the incumbent, but without having any security that he would not immediately be appointed to another office, or restored to the same office if it should be re-established by law.

Having submitted, in detail, a narrative of the events to which our relations with the United States have given rise, and exposed the motives and principles which have governed the conduct of the Executive throughout, it is left to your wisdom to decide upon the measures necessary and proper to sustain the honor and defend the rights and independence of the State. It is confidently believed that the Constitution, the public law, nor the usages of nations, will justify an abrogation of the treaty; and it is recommended to you, therefore, in any and every event, to consider, as heretofore, the Indian claims to the territory as effectually extinguished by it, and that, whether the survey be suspended or not; to order the occupation of it on the day stipulated in that instrument, in the same manner as you would have done if its validity had not been questioned.

In the correspondence submitted to the Legislature, at their late extraordinary session, will be found the repeated and final resolution of the Cherokees never to abandon the territory they occupy within our limits. This resolution may be satisfactory to the Government of the United States; it cannot be so to you. Having taken theirs, it remains for you to take yours, and, in doing so, no time is to be lost. Your better judgment will suggest and approve the remedy. Whatever it may be, I recommend to you to adopt early and energetic measures for the removal of all white persons and others, not Indians, inhabiting that territory, with the exception only of such as are necessarily employed in the service of the United States, under the power granted to Congress to regulate commerce with the Indian tribes. By the second article of agreement and cession, you will find the following words inserted by our Commissioners out of abundant caution: The United States "cede to the State of Georgia whatever claim, right or title they may have to the jurisdiction or soil of those lands." Nothing remained to the Indians, therefore, but the right of temporary occupation for hunting. This right has been construed so liberally, that, in practice, a general usufructuary interest has been conceded to them. But this reservation of hunting grounds is confined to the Indians exclusively, and designed for their use and benefit only. The soil and jurisdiction being in Georgia, it was no more lawful for the United States to introduce other persons there, than it would have been for them to have introduced, within the settled limits of Georgia, a colony of free persons of color, of Indians, or of white people. The utmost allowable to the United States, in this respect, was the settlement, within the territory, of such of their own officers as were necessary to carry into effect their acknowledged power to regulate commerce with the Indians. The United States have, nevertheless, by permission, toleration, or encouragement, introduced there, from time to time, white persons, and others, who have made settlements, exercised ownership over the soil, and cultivated it in the same manner as if the United States, and not Georgia, possessed the right of soil and jurisdiction; and these very same persons, as it is confidently believed, have been chiefly instrumental in preventing the Indians from leaving the country; all such persons, therefore, are to be considered as trespassers and intruders upon the soil of Georgia, and treated accordingly. This is the theory and practice of the United States Government itself, with regard to its own lands. In every instance where the United States have claimed the soil and jurisdiction, whether the Indians be in occupation or not, the Government has exercised the power to treat all such persons as trespassers and intruders; and an act of Congress authorizes the President to expel them at the point of the bayonet. It is equally competent to the Government of this State, to adopt like measures for the removal of trespassers on her own soil; and, for this purpose, having made the necessary statutory provisions, it is recommended to you to extend the laws of Georgia over the country.

You have seen how our rights of sovereignty, those of the elective franchise, of territory and jurisdiction, have been infringed; you will see the same rights violated, in the independence, character and dignity of the constituted authorities occupied in the management of our affairs.

A special officer was commissioned by the President to inquire into the conduct of the Agent for Indian affairs, who, on presenting himself here, was received in the most friendly temper, and with assurance that every assistance would be rendered to promote the object of his mission; not doubting that the object, as he repeatedly professed, was justice to all the parties concerned—to the public, to his own Government, to Georgia, to the Indians, and to the officer implicated. Any deportment which might be construed into a disposition to bias or mislead him, was studiously avoided; all information required, promptly furnished; and not a suspicion admitted that he could have been actuated by other than honorable motives, until, in a conversation which a gentleman in the confidence of the Governor was instructed to hold with him, he betrayed very strong prepossessions in favor of the Agent; so much so, and at so early a period, that, with an intention to apprise his Government of the fact, a letter was addressed to him, marked (B), which, with his answer, marked (C), is submitted. In the latter, you will find repeated professions of impartiality and disinterestedness; but you will soon perceive, in his after conduct and writings, the hollowness and insincerity of them. They, and the report of the State Commissioners, show that the Special Agent came here, not to inquire into the conduct of the Agent of Indian affairs, but, as counsel or attorney, to advise with him, to lend him aid and countenance, to collect testimony for his vindication and acquittal, and, without giving ear to the testimony against him, to pronounce that acquittal as honorable for himself, and the prosecution as disgraceful to all the parties concerned in it; seeking, for this purpose, with great labor and assiduity, the evidence of the outcasts of society, wherever he could find it, and thus embodying for himself and his Government, a volume of impurest matter, by which to justify that acquittal. His patience would not permit him to wait the closing of the testimony on either side, as you will see in his letter of the 21st June, addressed to the Agent and published by him. It was this letter, proving incontestably that the question had been prejudged at Washington, and that a farce had been playing only to amuse the authorities of Georgia, which decided the Executive to address to him the note of the 28th June, instructing him to hold no further correspondence with this Government. The letter, of the 4th of July, was subsequently addressed to this Department, in which, after justifying his offensive one of the 21st June, he insults the authorities of Georgia, by referring the prosecution of the Agent to the most corrupt and reprehensible of motives; and, by the affected charity with which he excepted the Chief Magistrate from the charge, gave poignancy to his denunciation, and to his sentence a semblance of a legal character, as if pronounced by a competent magistrate from the judgment seat. It was not until after the return of this officer to Washington, that he caused to be published, under the eye of his Government, the declaration "that he was informed by the acting Agent for Indian Affairs, that the Commissioners of Georgia had carried with them into the Nation a large amount of money, say four to six thousand dollars," strongly insinuating, at the same time, that this money was carried there for the purposes of bribery and corruption. A charge against this branch of the Government, connected with the administration of the finances, so serious, proceeding from such a person, and made in a form so specific, deserves your attention, and the more, because the truth or falsehood of it can be easily established.

Another Special Agent had been deputed to this Government, in a civil and military capacity, to investigate the causes of the disturbances in the Indian country, to remove the causes of discontent, and to reconcile the contending parties. He likewise was received with the most friendly dispositions, and treated with all the respect due to his rank and character. He professed to be animated by the love of truth and justice, to be in the interest of no party, and, in the execution of his trust, to be governed by the dictates of duty only. Not doubting the sincerity of these professions, the aid and co-operation of the Executive of Georgia, in promoting the objects of his mission, were cheerfully tendered, and would undoubtedly have been afforded to any extent within the powers of the Department. The first manifestation given by this officer of dislike or aversion to the authorities of Georgia, which has come to the knowledge of the Executive, will be found in the representation of the Commissioners, and in the letter of the other Special Agent, in which, speaking of his obnoxious letter of the 21st of June, he says, " the letter is approbated by a man who for wisdom stands inferior to few, and in honor to none." If the inference was correct, that the person alluded to by the writer was the same Agent whose conduct is the subject of this review, it is certain that even at the time he could not have entertained for the authorities of Georgia those respectful sentiments which he professed, and which in duty he was bound to entertain ; for, in that obnoxious letter, those authorities were denounced for oppression, partiality and injustice of the most flagrant kind, practiced against the Indian Agent. On the 10th day of July, he wrote a letter to the Governor, enclosing a certificate of the Indian Chief, Marshall, and a white man named Edwards, to disprove the fact of McIntosh and his Council having given their assent to the survey. This officer could not have offered a greater insult to any independent Government. He had seen the public message, in which the assent of McIntosh and his Chiefs had been announced to the Legislature, and the incontestable evidence on which the annunciation was founded. Disregarding the authority of both, and professing to rely on the testimony of such persons as Marshall and Edwards, known to him to be infamous, he informs the Governor that no such assent was ever given. In aggravation of this insult, before any notice was taken of it, he causes the same letter, with the certificate, to be published on his own authority, alleging, as his excuse, that falsehoods and calumnies, by whom or about what, he did not inform us, were propagated; thus making his appeal to the public from the pretended rumor of the day, for the purpose of bringing the authorities of Georgia into disrepute with their own people, and separating the people from their Government. He was soon informed that he himself was the dupe of the certificate of Marshall, and that his own conduct was reprehensible in relying on it to reproach the Government of Georgia with misrepresentation and falsehood; and, of this his Government and the public were soon after furnished with abundant proof. When this officer is rebuked for an indignity which could, with no propriety, pass without censure, he loses all self-command, and, forgetting his own station and that of the person to whom he addresses himself, writes letter after letter to the Chief Magistrate, couched in the most offensive language, and which, from their manner as well as matter, and the immediate publicity given to them through the gazettes, must have been intended as electioneering papers, to subserve the cause of one of the contending parties in the State, to the prejudice of the other; an inference deriving abundant confirmation from the fact that the same officer was in the practice, in the common intercourse of society, of applying to the Chief Magistrate, and others in authority, the most contumelious and abusive epithets.

As no further intercourse could be held with him, without compromitting the dignity of the State, it was, in the first instance, forbidden; and when, afterwards, he had proceeded to the greatest extremity, his recall, arrest, trial and punishment were demanded of his Government. The Executive of the State would have been warranted by the public law and practice of nations, in a case so flagrant, to have ordered him to leave the territory of Georgia, and to have enforced that order. It was unwilling to resort to a measure of harshness or severity, however justifiable. The United States Government itself is not less tenacious of its own dignity than others. It has, at least on one occasion, interdicted intercourse with a foreign minister of first grade, representing a European power of first rank, for merely contradicting it abruptly; and the equally merited treatment of another minister, representing a first-rate power, for appeals to the people from their Government, is well known to you. More recently, the gallant Porter has been punished by his Government, for insulting the petty authorities of Foxardo, and for making an appeal from that Government, through the public prints, much less exceptionable than that made by this officer in the publication of his letter of the 10th July. Whether the constituted authorities of Georgia are of more or less importance than those of Foxardo, in the view of the General Government, will be seen in the answer of the President. The answer of the President to the demand of the Governor of Georgia, for his recall and arrest, is as little creditable to the functionary from which it comes, as satisfactory to the one to whom it is addressed.

The President is bound, by every constitutional obligation, to execute the laws. One of these laws declares, that "any officer or soldier who shall use contemptuous or disrespectful words against the Chief Magistrate or Legislature of any of the States, if a commissioned officer, shall be cashiered." The President acknowledges this officer to have used contemptuous and disrespectful words, for which his conduct is simply disapproved; and he is informed that if the Governor of this State had not previously used toward him offensive language, the demand would have been complied with. So that, according to this construction of the President, his military officers may conduct themselves as they please within the jurisdiction of the respective States, no matter how exceptionably; and the least reprehension or censure by the Chief Magistrate of a State, is their sufficient warrant to retort in abusive and insulting language, and to gratify their resentments, even at the expense of the independence of the elective franchise: a construction which makes the law a nullity, because it privileges the military officer to do that which, but for the law, he might legally have done; insult a Chief Magistrate of a State as he would insult a private citizen, for any real or imaginary grievance; a privilege which the law was intended to prohibit to him. But the fact assumed by the President as true, is not true. Nothing offensive was written to this officer before he had three several times offended the dignity of this Government, viz: by his approbation of the offensive terms of the letter of the other special agent, by his disrespectful treatment of the Commissioners, and by his procurement and publication of the false statement of Marshall and Edwards. This exposition of the law by the Executive of the United States, will satisfy you of the expediency of depending on your own measures for defence against the repetition of such outrages.

The Governor of Georgia denies the right of the President to excuse or justify his officer in the violation of the law of the United States, which he is bound to execute, because of any act or supposed act of the Governor, which is in violation of no law. The President, by such excuse or justification, takes the place of the Agent; and when, in one of his authorized communications, he says, "there is no part of his duty which the President more anxiously pursues than that of maintaining the most scrupulous decorum in his official intercourse with the State authorities, a line of conduct from which no circumstances, however aggravated, have or will tempt him to depart," he only means, that what he does not choose to do by himself he will do by his Agent.

The published addresses of the different agents are submitted with the rest, only to show the unity of feeling, sentiment and action, which has signalized the deportment of the United States officers of every grade, in their intercourse with the Government of Georgia. It can be submitted to no longer. The sovereignty, independence and dignity of the State must be maintained; and to support them you must depend on your own means. I advise you, therefore, to have recourse to those means: no matter whom you place in authority, all strangers must be compelled to respect, in their exterior demeanor at least, those authorities. The sacredness of the elective franchise can be protected by regarding every private person, not a citizen of Georgia, who interferes with that freedom, as an alien and stranger, violating a right of sovereignty, and exposing himself to punishment. If an officer of the United States, not being a citizen of Georgia, he renders himself the more obnoxious, from the double capacity in which he offends that sovereignty; and if an officer representing his Government, in a diplomatic character, before this Government, he can be made amenable under the sanctions of your own laws, and the laws and usages of nations, for offences committed against either; and to this end you have only to define the character of the offence, and to prescribe the punishment.

In the exposé of the state of our relations with the General Government, other grievances, minor and secondary in importance, are adverted to, not for the purpose of accumulating wrongs into a formidable mass, and making an appeal the louder and deeper to the justice of that Government, but to satisfy our fellow-citizens, that, if we have complained in vain, we have not complained without cause, and that our cup of bitterness is almost full.

[These two paragraphs—one relating to claims of the State against the United States, for militia services against Indian hostilities—and the other relating to claims of citizens of Georgia against the Creek Nation, under the treaty of 1821, are omitted.]

The Government of Georgia had reason to expect that the United States would not refuse their concurrence and co-operation in the running of the line between this State and the State of Alabama; 1st, because they were proprietors of the soil on one side of it; and, 2d, because Georgia was concerned that the presence and authority of the United States should be a security to the Indians that their rights should be respected—a security which would save to Georgia the expense of a military force in the prosecution of the work, as the Indians, in the absence of that security, might be excited by evil-disposed persons to interrupt its execution. The President, in the first instance, signified no objection to a co-operation, but the one founded on a mistake in fact, that Alabama had not given her assent. Subsequently, however, the co-operation was declined, it being, as was said, a matter in which Georgia and Alabama were alone concerned, and with which the United States had nothing to do. More recently, as you are informed, the State has been absolutely forbidden, at her peril, to enter her territory for the purpose of running a line or making a survey of any description; the sum of all which is, that the United States claim for themselves the power to enter upon their territory wherever the soil and jurisdiction are in them; to settle there whom they please, and to expel whom they please, even at the point of the bayonet; but deny the same power to Georgia, where the soil and jurisdiction are in her, and forbid her, under the pain of military chastisement, to run a line or make a survey there. The late correspondence with the Governor of Alabama, will show that we may soon expect the concurrence of that State in our resolution to run the line; and it is very desirable that no further obstacle should be suffered to prevent its execution.

A request made to the Executive of the United States, under authority of a resolution of the Legislature, to cooperate with this State in running the dividing line between it and the Territory of Florida, was also refused, on the allegation that Congress had made no provision for such cooperation.

[The portion of the message, here omitted, relates entirely to Internal Improvement, and has been copied into the eighth chapter of this work. The next three paragraphs are also omitted : the first relates to the Banks, the second recommends a "revision of our military system;" and the third, the establishment of a "Court of Errors or Appeals," as "a remedy for evils no longer tolerable."]

I transmit, as a matter of duty, two resolutions of the Legislatures of Connecticut and Illinois, received since the late extra session, recommending to the Congress, and to the States, the abolition of slavery.

Nothing has transpired to change my sentiments on a subject, to which, more than once, it has been made my duty to call your attention. It is my settled conviction, and the more confirmed than ever, that neither the other States, nor the Congress, have any right to bring that subject into question before them, in any form, and that every attempt to do so by either, should be regarded in the same manner as an attempt to destroy your sovereignty, of which it is an essential part; and that you will have no security for this property, against the efforts which will be made, from time to time, to impair its value, and eventually destroy it, but in the equally settled conviction on the part of the assailants, that you will defend it as you would defend your lives. Independently of any precautionary measures which you may deem proper for the permanent safety of this property, every proposition which may be addressed to you on the subject, either by the State or the United States authorities, being unconstitutional on the face of it, as it cannot be received otherwise than offensively, and consequently ought not to be received at all, should be returned to the authorities from which it emanated.

[These paragraphs, referring to various resolutions of the Legislature; to "Institutions for the instruction of youth;" to Franklin College, which was stated to be "in an onward course of prosperity;" to County Academies, and the Poor School Fund, omitted.]

In our lamented differences with the United States, the constituted authorities of Georgia have been ungenerously reviled—sentiments and feelings have been adopted for them, to which their hearts and understandings are strangers. The charge of hostility to the Union is indignantly repelled—Georgia is not behind the foremost of her sisters in devotion to the Union—she is laboring at this moment to cement and perpetuate that Union, by bringing it back to the principles of the Constitution. We mean a Union of definite signification—a Constitutional Union for all Constitutional objects—a Union for safety, for security of life, liberty and property—a Union to enforce the powers of the General Government, as well as to protect and defend the rights and powers of the States—a Union which means something, and which we love and cherish as a blessing. But the Union which is construed to mean any thing or every thing—a Union for absorption and consolidation, which would prescribe no limits to the powers of one Government, but the general welfare, and which would reduce the powers of all the rest to a shadow of sovereignty— which claims supremacy and exacts obedience—which construes the Constitution for itself, and issues its mandates to the States, backed by the purse and sword—which threatens to decide for us what is property and what is not property, and whether we shall hold any property of a certain kind, or not—which sends its officers and agents to insult and defy the public functionaries of the States, as if they were subaltern in rank and consequence to themselves—such a Union is not the Union adopted by the States, and it is believed is not such a one as the States will support. The Chief Magistrate especially disclaims any other motive as the governing one of his conduct, than the sincerest attachment to the Union, without tincture of prejudice against the persons who compose the councils of the United States; but, on the contrary, with the strongest predispositions to give every aid and support to those councils to promote the peace, interest and happiness of the country.

It is asserted, without fear of contradiction, that since Georgia was a party to the Revolution, the Confederacy, or the Union, she has fulfilled with sincerity and fidelity all her obligations and engagements; in peace and in war, under whatever administration, not merely answering with promptness to every requisition, but, according to her means, sustaining that Government with as much vigor and patriotism as any of her sisters—as little querulous as any of them—more complying than most of them, and never bringing into question the constitutionality of its ordinances or decrees, but when, from the honest impulses of her heart, and the strongest convictions of her judgment, she has believed them unconstitutional. If opposed to any particular administration, it has been an opposition of frankness and firmness; and if, with these characteristics, always honorable, she has at any time mixed a spice of indignation, it may well have been pardoned by the head and members of a family who cannot themselves claim exemption from the frailties of our nature, and who, when honor and principle were at stake, might have seen a color of virtue in a momentary departure from meekness, humility and patience. But Georgia can still contend, that, in respect to all questions of mere interest, to which her connection with the Union may have given rise, she has discovered as little of selfishness, as much of generosity, and of forgiveness, as could be expected from a sovereign and independent State, claiming rights of property of great value, demanded by the wants of her citizens, and indispensable to the complete organization of her social system. Georgia has not demanded justice of the Federal Government in her day of tribulation, of difficulty and of embarrassment, in war, or in the midst of divided councils, but at a moment when, with an ample treasury, at peace with all nations, and prosperous beyond example, she had her option to do us justice, or, refusing it, to present a military chest and armed men. If the United States choose to rely on these, and Georgia, taking counsel of her fears, shall make an inglorious surrender of her rights, what will remain of the fruit of her toil and blood and public virtue, but a consolidated Government, in which the sovereignty and independence of the States being merged, nothing is left her but the power of a municipal corporation to settle the strifes and contentions of individuals within the freedom of it?

By encroachment on the one side, and acquiescence on the other, every day brings us nearer to this result; and if we cannot find safety in the first principles of the Constitution, we can find it no where.

Your fellow-citizen,

G. M. TROUP.

One of the first duties of the new Legislature was the election of Judges, an Attorney and Solicitors-General. This is said to have been the first application of party rule to the choice of judicial affairs. Judge Wayne, of the Eastern District, was the only member of the Troup party who was re-elected—having had no opposition. Early in the session, the Governor communicated to the Legislature "copies of an official document" just received, "by which," he remarked, "you will see that the two Cherokee Chiefs,* who, on a late occasion, were admitted by the United States Agents to participate in the Councils at Broken Arrow, and dictate the talk there, have been denounced and punished by their own Government, for an unauthorized interference in the affairs of the Creeks."

On the 21st of November, he also sent to the Legislature "certain testimony recently taken by the Commissioners on the part of the State, additional to that furnished at the opening of the session," &c., &c.—a part of which, in the form of affidavits, we have already inserted; but we have not room for further extracts, or for the "exposition" of the United States Commissioners, Messrs. Campbell and Meriwether, "in relation to the late treaty concluded by them with the Creek Indians," which occupied two closely printed pages of the Georgia Journal. In the conclusion of the exposition, the Commissioners said:

"Let the treaty, then, be estimated according to the circumstances which attended its negotiation, or let it be tried by *itself*, and it seems to us that the most rigid observer would be at a loss to discover a competent reason for its revision. The circumstances were such as ordinarily attend such transactions, except the perfidious opposition which we encountered, and a treaty was never formed with Indians, *half* so beneficial to themselves as this. No error, then, being detected in the treaty itself, or in the manner of its obtainment, we are to look, for the cause of the mischief, to the manner in which both have been *misrepresented*. Let those who have originated the misrepresentations, and those also who have given them currency, be arraigned before their own consciences and their country, and we *know* that *their* trial will be more fearful than ours."

As an act of justice to these gentlemen, (now both dead,) and as intrinsic to the subject of the treaty, we should be glad to publish the preamble and resolutions *unanimously*

* John Ridge and David Vann, who were deposed from the National Council of the Cherokees, for "having thought proper to associate themselves as Secretaries to the Creek delegation," without authority of the General Council.—ED.

adopted by the Legislature, and approved by the Governor on 24th November. We make room for the resolutions:

Resolved, unanimously, therefore, by the Senate and House of Representatives of the State of Georgia, in General Assembly met, That they feel deeply and gratefully impressed with the important services of the honorable Duncan G. Campbell and James Meriwether, in obtaining the late cession of lands from the Creek Nation of Indians, and that their confidence remains unimpaired in the honor, uprightness and integrity of those gentlemen.

Resolved, further, That the General Assembly, representing the feelings and wishes of the good citizens of this State, do not hesitate in saying that they conceive that the treaty contains in itself intrinsic evidence of its own fairness, in the liberal and extended provisions which it contains for the removal, preservation and perpetuity of the Creek Nation: Such treaty, so beneficial to the United States, the State of Georgia, and the Indians themselves, having been negotiated under circumstances requiring the most devoted zeal, persevering industry and firmness, we pronounce upon the conduct of the Commissioners our most cordial approbation, and that a copy thereof be transmitted to each of said Commissioners, and also a copy to each of our Senators and Representatives in Congress.

The Committee on the state of the Republic, in the Senate, made a report on the subject of Indian relations, which was passed in both Houses, and approved by the Governor, concluding with resolutions expressive of their full reliance "in the late treaty," &c., "that the title of the territory obtained by said treaty, within the limits of Georgia, is considered as an absolute, vested interest, and that nothing short of the whole territory thus acquired, will be satisfactory; and that the right of entry, immediately upon the expiration of the time limited in the treaty, be insisted on, and accordingly carried into effect"; also approbatory of the conduct of the Governor; requesting the removal of Col. Crowell; and concluding with a protest against a reconsideration of the treaty, and expressing the opinion, in regard to that treaty, that "if there is to be a revision, it is due to the interests and rights of the State that she should be represented in the entire proceedings, as well preparatory as final."

During this session, the Legislature passed Acts for laying out and organizing the counties of Thomas, Lowndes, Baker, Lee, Taliaferro and Butts; and an Act "*to organize the territory lately acquired from the Creek Indians, lying between the Flint and Chattahoochee Rivers, and west of the Chattahoochee River.*" Four counties were thus laid out, and named, respectively, MUSCOGEE, TROUP, COWETA and CARROLL; the first, it is said, "in honor of McIntosh, and to perpetuate the memory of the Creek people."

The Legislature adjourned, without day, on 22d December, after enacting various other laws, which we cannot particularly notice.

CHAPTER XII.

New Treaty concluded, at Washington, with the Creek Indians.—Difficulties, Debates and Correspondence growing out of it.—More trouble with the Cherokees.—Position and firmness of Gov. Troup and the Georgia Delegation.—Gov. Troup pronounces a eulogium on Jefferson and Adams.—Dinner at Indian Springs.—Survey of lands ceded by old Treaty.—Threatened interruption of the Surveyors.—Boundary between Georgia and Alabama.—Meeting of the Legislature.—Governor's Message.—Legislative action.—Events of 1827.—Threatening posture of Indian question.—Settlement of it, &c., &c.

Whilst men of all parties in Georgia were uniting to give effect to the treaty of the Indian Springs, under which it was fondly expected Georgia was to come, within less than a year, into possession of the Creek Country, by the actual use and occupation of this valuable portion of territory within her acknowledged limits, controversy, of a most serious nature, and threatening discord and strife, unexpectedly arose. Congress had assembled on the first Monday of December, 1825; and the reports of General Gaines and Major Andrews, and the opposition of the hostile Indians, backed by the interference of others, had not failed to produce their effect on the mind of Mr. Adams. In his opening and first annual message, the President, after referring to the treaty of Indian Springs as having been "received at the seat of Government only a few days before the close of the last session of Congress and of the late administration," added:

"The advice and consent of the Senate was given to it, on the 3d of March, too late for it to receive the ratification of the then President of the United States; it was ratified on the 7th of March, under the unsuspecting impression that it had been negotiated in good faith, and in the confidence inspired by the recommendation of the Senate. The subsequent transactions in relation to this treaty, will form the subject of a separate message."

The "unsuspecting impression" of the President can be accounted for only on the idea, that, having just come into office, he was not aware of the existence of Col. Crowell's letter of 13th February, 1825, on file in the War Department; or that no faith was given to its statements; or that the statements, even if regarded as true, were not deemed sufficient to shake the President's "impression." Be these conjectures right or wrong, it is certain that on 24th January, 1826, the Secretary of War, by authority of the President, concluded a *new treaty* with certain persons styled the "Chiefs and Head-men of the Creek Nation of Indians," at Washington City, and that the President sent it in to the Senate on the 31st of the same month. The Chiefs, who signed, were thirteen in number, and the treaty was witnessed by (amongst others,) John Crowell, Agent for Indian Affairs. On communicating this treaty to the Senate, the President stated that the old treaty had been ratified by him under the firm belief "that it had been concluded with a large majority of the Chiefs of the Creek Nation, and with a reasonable prospect of immediate acquiescence by the remainder," &c., &c. He proceeded to state that this expectation had not merely been disappointed, but that troubles had ensued, resulting in the death of "the two principal Chiefs who had signed it," and that the "families and dependents" of these Chiefs, whilst in their "fugitive condition," &c., had "been found advancing pretensions to receive, exclusively to themselves, the whole of the sums stipulated," &c., "in payment *for all* the lands of the Creek Nation which were ceded by the terms of the treaty," &c., &c.

After referring to the anxious desire of the United States to carry into effect the treaty of Indian Springs, until that was found impracticable, &c., and the hope that the assent of the Indians would, at least, "have been given to a treaty, by which all their lands within the State of Georgia should have been ceded," and that this also had proved impracticable, the "excepted portion" being "of comparatively small amount and importance," he stated that he had assented to this exception, and placed it before the Senate, "only from a conviction, that, between it and a resort to the forcible expulsion of the Creeks from their habitations," &c., "there was no middle term." After stating that the "deputation" with which the new treaty had been concluded, consisted "of the principal Chiefs of the Nation, able not only to negotiate, but to carry into effect the stipulations to which they have agreed," and referring to another deputation, then also at Washington, which he characterized as "from the small party which undertook to contract for the whole Nation," &c., "but the members of which, according to the information collected by Gen. Gaines," did "not exceed four hundred," &c., he added:

"In referring to the impressions under which I ratified the treaty of the 12th of February last, I do not deem it necessary to decide upon the propriety of the manner in which it was negotiated. Deeply regretting the criminations and recriminations to which these events have given rise, I believe the public interest will best be consulted by discarding them altogether from the discussion of the subject. The great body of the Creek Nation inflexibly refuse to acknowledge or to execute that treaty. Upon this ground, it will be set aside, should the Senate advise and consent to the ratification of that now communicated, without looking back to the means by which the other was effected. And, in the adjustment of the terms of the present treaty, I have been peculiarly anxious to dispense a measure of great liberality to both parties of the Creek Nation, rather than to extort from them a bargain, of which the advantages on our part could only be purchased by hardship on theirs."

Accompanying this message, was a letter from the Secretary of War to the President, giving an account of the negotiation for the treaty, &c.

The principal differences* between the two treaties, were:

1st. By the new treaty, there was, with a small exception, no cession of any land *west* of the middle of the Chattahoochee—making, as was supposed, a difference to Georgia of about 1,000,000 acres of land, besides involving the ques-

* For the precise differences, the reader is referred to the treaties in the 7th vol. of United States Statutes at Large, the Governor's Annual Message of 1826, &c.—ED.

tion of jurisdiction, between Georgia and Alabama, of the western half of that river within the Creek limits.

2d. The new treaty fixed the time of removal of the Creeks at two years, instead of 1st September, 1826, as fixed by the old treaty: although possession was to be yielded on or before 1st January, 1827.

A supplementary article was added to the treaty, on 31st March, not important to be noticed here.*

As the matter of this treaty was an Executive, and therefore a secret, proceeding, until the ratification in April, nothing official was known when Governor Troup addressed the following letter to the President:

EXECUTIVE DEPARTMENT,
Milledgeville, 11*th February*, 1826.

SIR: As I will proceed, on the second day of September next, under the authority of the Legislature of Georgia, to occupy the country ceded by the treaty concluded at the Indian Springs, on the twelfth day of February, 1825; and as the running of the dividing line between this State and the State of Alabama must necessarily precede the survey which will immediately follow that occupation; as the Government of the United States, having been formally invited to co-operate, has, in declining it officially, made known to the Government of Georgia, that the running of the line is a matter in which Georgia and Alabama are alone concerned, and with which the United States have nothing to do; as Alabama did consent, and, it is believed, notified that consent to the United States, as she certainly did to Georgia; as Alabama is well disposed to co-operate with Georgia in the execution of the work; as it can have no assignable connection with the existence or non-existence of the treaty, it having been fixed unalterably by the Constitution and the Articles of Agreement, as the permanent boundary; and as the treaty recognizes and confirms it; as the Government of Georgia is resolved, after having encountered very many obstacles, equally unlooked for and unnecessary, to carry into effect its repeated decree; as the

* It was, evidently, in reference to the critical situation of Indian Affairs, that Gov. Troup, on 28th January, 1826, issued two military orders—one for enrolling and classifying the militia, and the other for their review and inspection. In this latter order, he said: "It is impossible that the General officers should be indifferent to the crisis in which the country finds itself; and, from his personal knowledge of them, the Commander-in-Chief would feel ashamed to address himself to their patriotism and military pride."—ED.

season will soon arrive most favorable to its execution with accuracy and precision; and, as General Gaines, in his letter of the 14th June last, had, in the name of his Government, expressly forbid the running of the line, as well as the survey of the lands, and had assembled troops* on the frontier, to enforce the prohibition; and, as the Secretary of War, by the order of the President, notified the Government, that no entry upon, or survey of, the country would be permitted; and, moreover, directed the Commanding General to employ a military force to prevent any such entry or survey; it is respectfully asked of the President, whether his resolution in these respects remains unchanged, and, if unchanged, whether the military force will be employed against us, with or without the auxiliary aid and co-operation of the savages, or whether these last will be restrained by the authority of the United States from interposing their arms at all; or whether they will be left to the indulgence of their natural feelings, under the artificial excitements of the day, to assume the character of neutrals, or of partisans and marauders, as those feelings and excitements may dictate? It is hoped and expected that the frankness of the President's answer will correspond with the importance of the occasion which prompts to this inquiry, so that nothing hereafter will be chargeable to the imperfection of our language, or the insincerity of either of the parties. And that the President may be in full possession of the considerations which influence this Government, and, more especially, that he may acquit the authorities here of precipitancy, prejudice, or undue diffidence in the wisdom and patriotism of the councils of the Union, I will take the liberty to submit the documentary and official evidence, which, it is trusted, will sustain and justify this Government in the eyes of the world, in the measures to which, for its own safety, it may be obliged to have recourse.

First—then, the running of the dividing line between Alabama and this State, has no assignable connection with the existence or non-existence of the treaty; the right to run the line having accrued to Georgia, by the articles of agreement and cession, of 1802; a right undisputed until now, and which ought to be indisputable now, because at that time made by the Constitution the permanent boundary of the State.

* Gen. Gaines is believed to have had one thousand regulars in the Indian country, at the time to which the Governor refers.—ED.

The Constitution, in the 23rd section of the 1st article, after defining the boundaries of the State, proceeds to authorize a sale to the United States, under the authority of the Legislature; but, that sale being effected, (as it was by the articles of agreement and cession, of 1802,) the remaining territory is declared to be the property of the whole body of the people, and inalienable but by themselves.

Secondly,—the repeatedly official assertion of the right of Georgia; the official concurrence of Alabama; and the official acquiescence of the Government of the United States.

Thirdly. The public acts and resolutions of Georgia, have kept separate and distinct the subject of running the line, and that of surveying the lands, any further than that the one must necessarily precede the other. But, with respect to the right to run the line at pleasure, never having entertained but one opinion concerning it, and disclaiming any authority on the part of the United States to bring it into controversy at all, whilst, in deference to the Councils of the Union, the Legislature consented to postpone the survey, they did not consent to postpone the running of the line, and of course left it where they found it, viz.: discretionary with the Executive to run it whenever he might deem proper. When the Legislature authorized the Executive to postpone the survey until the expiration of the time limited by the treaty, but to proceed in it immediately at the expiration of that time, they could not have intended to postpone the running of the line, because, as that must necessarily precede the survey, such postponement would defeat the survey.

Fourthly. The Legislature were therefore indifferent whether the treaty was declared null and void, or not, as regarded the running of the line; the running having been ordered long before the treaty was even in contemplation, had nothing to do with it, and therefore was to be carried into execution, whether such a treaty was ever brought into existence or not. If the treaty expedites the running now, it is only because the running must necessarily precede the survey, which will commence on the 2d day of September next, the day after the time limited by the treaty for the occupation of the Indians.

Fifthly. We are prohibited, by military force, from running the same description of boundary line which we are almost daily in the practice of running, without murmur or complaint from the General Government. I mean the exterior boundary line which separates our frontier counties from the Indians. Here the Indians are equally liable to trespass, encroachment, and interruption of all kinds, from the whites; to be cheated and defrauded of their effects, ill treated in their persons, and even their lands taken from them by the unskilfulness or dishonesty of surveyors. It has been shown, that, in the contemplated measure, the Government of the United States has been repeatedly invited to participate, not only to protect its own interests, but those of the Indians; the Indians themselves would have been invited. In running the line between the Cherokees and Georgia, under the treaty, both the United States and the Cherokees would be invited to be present. If the Indians, therefore, should, in either instance, suffer detriment by an act of the Government of Georgia, the Government of the United States would be there present to correct or redress it.

Sixthly. Other States have run lines, separating their territory from that of the Indians, without permission of the General Government; the States of Tennessee and North Carolina and Georgia have done so, and their legality has not been questioned by that Government. In many instances, too, these lines have passed through territory in the exclusive occupation of the Indians. (See the Reports of the Commissioners of the State, one dated 15th October, 1819, the other dated 13th July, 1818, running the lines between Tennessee and North Carolina and Georgia.)

Seventhly. The Executive of the United States has repeatedly, uniformly, and without reservation or condition, admitted the right of Georgia both to run the line and make the survey at the expiration of the time limited by the treaty; and, in the letter of the Secretary of War, so late as the 30th day of August last, viz: after the Government had been placed in possession of all the information which it now has, of the bribery and corruption and abuse of instructions, practiced to procure it, the Executive of the United States expressed itself highly gratified and delighted that the Executive of Georgia had consented to postpone the survey, even until the meeting of the Legislature of the State. It will be seen, on comparing the correspondence and official message of the Governor with the paragraph of the letter of the Secretary of War, (marked E) that the Secretary has committed a very great error. So far from the Governor consenting to await the decision of the Congress, he protested, in the most positive terms, against a reference of the treaty at all. The Governor never engaged to do more than to postpone the survey until the meeting of the Legislature of the State.

You have perceived, Sir, from every past indication of public sentiment, that nothing can shake the confidence of the Government and the people of Georgia in the validity of the treaty of the Indian Springs; and, as I flatter myself with the hope that the preceding illustration may afford some insight into the absolute right of the State of Georgia to run the dividing line between Georgia and Alabama, whensoever she pleases, I have taken the liberty to trouble you thus far.

It is my unpleasant duty to trespass upon your attention yet a little longer. Information, not wholly of official character, has been received, that, in the new treaty lately negotiated with the hostile Chiefs, a line has been designated as a true dividing line between the two tribes, by which something like 300,000 acres of land, as acquired by the treaty of the Indian Springs, are taken from us and given to the Cherokees. For this treaty, of course, we care nothing; because, in declaring the inviolability of the old, we have already proclaimed the invalidity of the new. But neither yourself nor myself can be altogether indifferent to the consequences of this ill-judged measure. A false line has been adopted, which favors the Cherokees; the true one, which favors the Georgians, blotted out. The true line will be the one followed by the Commissioners of Georgia, who are appointed to run it. The false line will be the one claimed by the Cherokees as the true one. I much fear you have not been made familiar with the territorial history of both tribes; it is short, but not, on that account, the more appropriate to the subject of this letter. But I cannot help saying to you, that, of all the measures which you have thought proper to adopt in relation to the matters in controversy between the two Governments, there is no one which has given me more pain or solicitude, because, no one partaking of more injustice, hardship, and oppression, than that now complained of. In giving a new boundary to the Cherokees, you have given them new feelings, hostile to the interests and people of Georgia; they will recognize no other line, in future, than that you have thought proper to prescribe; they will suffer none other to be run, but by coercion of the sword. Without any controversy between the Creeks and Cherokees, involving territorial boundary, or bringing this line into question, but such as might easily, according to their usages and customs, have been settled among themselves, you have become, gratuitously, a volunteer in the service of the Cherokees, to procure for them, by cession, from the hostile Chiefs, lands which belonged neither to them nor to the Cherokees, but which belonged more particularly to the friendly Creeks, and which now belong to us, by cession from both friendly and hostile Chiefs; thus giving to the Cherokees a little more space for the pursuits of agriculture and the civilized arts, by a permanent location assured to them, adverse to the claims and demands of Georgia, and preparing them for the promised admission into the Union as an independent State. Not only so; you will probably have caused, on all these accounts, an expenditure of blood and treasure to the State of Georgia, from which she would have been otherwise exempt. And suffer me, in no unkindly spirit, to inquire, if such be the consequences resulting from these, what will be those which must follow the ulterior and not distant assertion, by Georgia, of her right to all the territory of the Cherokees within the limits settled by the articles of agreement and cession.

One of two things has happened: either the people of Georgia, and the authorities who represent them, have, by the illusions of interest or prejudice, or both, been overwhelmed by sudden and impenetrable darkness, benumbing and stupifying their faculties; or the councils of those of whose measures they complain, have been directed by a strange infatuation.

The old treaty is proposed to be annulled, either because of corruption practiced to procure it; of an abuse of powers by the Commissioners; of an inadequate representation of the nation; or of the boundary on one side being an artificial, instead of a natural, boundary. If an irreversible sentence of denunciation and annulment is to be pronounced against the old treaty, because of these, what is to become of the new? The old treaty, negotiated by your own agents, in the woods, seven hundred miles from the seat of government, with nothing but their written instructions to direct them, in a simple, unostentatious manner, without any display of power, not even a guard or an escort, and with a comparatively limited command of money, with a fore-knowledge of their accountability to you, both for the fulfilment of their instructions and the appropriation of the money, and, finally, the formal ratification, agreeably to the forms enjoined by the Constitution.

The new treaty, negotiated at Washington, in the presence of the Government, with enough of pomp and circumstance to dazzle or over-awe; where a smile gives animation and buoyancy to despair; and where the lion-hearted savage himself can be made to quake and cower beneath a frown; where moneyed means lead into temptation, and the annals of Indian diplomacy furnish no moral nomenclature by which to estimate the terms, perfidious, treacherous, &c.; where instructions could be varied, from hour to hour, to every exigency; where, indeed, any party might be considered as the Nation, and any boundary a good one: it is under all these circumstances that, at Washington, we are to presume the existence of perfect freedom of will, uncontrolled and unconstrained, united to the romantic love of country, dictating every article and paragraph of the new treaty; whilst, in the woods of Georgia, the same freedom has been corrupted by gold, and the will misdirected to the ruin of Indian rights and interests.

We cannot look upon these things with the same eyes; but, when the effects and consequences come, however they may be regarded by others, I can assure you they will inflict a deep wound upon ourselves. The augmented expense, and the almost inevitable bloodshed, in running both the Alabama and Cherokee lines, to say nothing of the multiplied obstacles opposed to the Executive of Georgia, in the execution of his duties, by these unfortunate events, combine to make this a long, complaining, and, perhaps, importunate letter.

The same public duty which impels me to write, will incline you to a patient reading. We are never better employed than in hearing the griefs and lamentations of our friends, unless, in the kindliest of all offices, that of assuaging and comforting them.

With the highest consideration,

I am your obedient servant,

G. M. TROUP.

The President of the United States.

Accompanying this letter, as exhibits, were several documents; but their insertion here would be of no special importance.

The new treaty was ratified on the 22d April, 1826.*

* On advising and consenting to it, in the Senate, the following was the vote: YEAS—Messrs. Barton, Bell, Benton, Bouligny, Branch, Chambers, Chandler, Chase, Clayton, Dickerson, Eaton, Edwards, Findlay, Harper, Harrison, Hendricks, Johnson, of Ky., Kane, Lloyd, Marks, Mills, Noble, Randolph, Reed, Rowan, Seymour, Smith, Thomas, Tazewell, Willey—30.

NAYS—Messrs. BERRIEN, COBB, Hayne, King, Macon, White, Williams—7—ED.

As early as 24th December, 1825, the Secretary of War had addressed a letter to the Georgia Delegation,* in Congress, stating that, " with the strongest desire to relieve the controversy with the Creeks, so far as Georgia was particularly concerned," &c., the Executive had been " negotiating, for some time past, on the basis of a surrender of all their lands within the limits of Georgia," &c.—that " the prospect of success was, for a time, flattering," but " recent events" had " entirely dissipated it, as to the whole of their lands in Georgia ;" that they were, however, " willing to make a cession to the east of the Chattahoochee, insisting on the necessity of a natural boundary as a protection against those trespasses which they suffer when separated only from the white population by an artificial line,"&c.—that the Indians having " encumbered this proposition with some conditions which" were "exceptionable, " &c., the President had " refused to accept any proposition short of an entire cession within the limits of Georgia," &c.; that, " to a communication signifying this determination on the part of the Executive," the Indian Delegation had returned a " reply," which the Secretary of War submitted to the Georgia Delegation, stating that Georgia's " wishes on the question which the Executive finds itself obliged to decide, would have a great influence on its decision," &c., &c.

The substance of the " reply" of the Indians, may be condensed in the following paragraph :

" Our Nation respectfully demands the repeal of the treaty of the Indian Springs in February last. In doing this, sufficient reasons are assigned, and none stronger to be found on earth, than the fact that our Nation, in its legal capacity, was not a party to the treaty, and that they have refused to ratify a bargain calculated to annihilate the happiness of our people."

In replying to the Secretary, on 7th January, 1826, the Georgia Delegation stated that their answer had been delayed, by the absence from Washington of some of their

* Then consisting of Messrs. Berrien and Cobb, in the Senate, and Messrs. Cary, A. Cuthbert, Forsyth, Haynes, Meriwether, (one of the Commissioners who had negotiated the treaty at Indian Springs, of 12th Feb., 1825,) Tattnall and Thompson, in the House.—ED.

number, and "not that any difference of opinion among them would be anticipated," &c.—that they had learned with pleasure the anxiety of the President "to relieve the controversy with the Creeks from all difficulty," &c.—that whilst they had "no express instructions on the subject," and "did not feel authorized to determine what were the wishes of the State;" yet, in regard to the question "whether it is most advisable to refer the treaty, with the objections to its validity, to Congress, for their decision, or, accepting a new basis of the Chattahoochee as a boundary," &c., "to resume a negotiation, with a hope that certain exceptionable conditions coupled with it," &c., "may be satisfactorily modified," &c., they expressed the opinion that "neither branch of the alternative" proposed "would meet the wishes of the State of Georgia," &c. They said:

"The State, we believe, does not and cannot suppose that Congress will entertain a question concerning the original validity of a treaty ratified and promulgated by the proper departments, with all the solemnities required by the Constitution; to which no objections are now urged which were not distinctly presented to the President, prior to its submission to the Senate, and by him as distinctly brought to the view of that body, when asking their advice and consent," &c.

Adding a suggestion, that the "evidence" on which the treaty was assailed, had been "obtained by means totally adverse to and inconsistent with the just views of the President of the United States, because adverse to and inconsistent with the ascertainment of truth," they concluded:

"They know and they feel that the Indian Agent, profiting by the excitement of feeling into which the Special Agent of the Government had unhappily fallen, has unduly exerted the influence of his station, to obtain from persons, for the most part subject to his control, a statement of circumstances which have no foundation in fact, and, from those untutored savages who were committed to his protection, an expression of feelings which the great body of the Nation do not entertain. They know and they feel that to lift the veil from this transaction, to expose its real character to the President of the United States, it is only necessary that that influence should be withdrawn. They still hope that the earnest wishes of a faithful member of the American Confederacy, will not be urged, in vain, before the Chief Executive Magistrate; and, with this knowledge, this feeling and this hope, they cannot permit themselves to believe that the President will ultimately adopt either branch of the alternative which you propose. On the contrary, they rely, that, with a just respect to the rights of the State, and a paternal regard to the wishes and feelings of her people, he will, by the recall of this officer, remove the whole source of this unhappy controversy, give to Georgia peace throughout her borders, and tranquillity and happiness to the children of the forest."

With what effect these appeals were urged, has been seen. It is with deep regret we find our limits will not permit us to record here the efforts of Messrs. Berrien and Cobb, on the floor of the Senate, to prevent the ratification of the new treaty. Before he had learned of the action of the Georgia Delegation, as above detailed, Governor Troup wrote to them the following letter:

EXECUTIVE DEPARTMENT,
Milledgeville, *9th January*, 1826.

Gentlemen: I am supported on a sick bed, only to express my confident expectation that you will not entertain, for a moment, the proposition submitted by the United States, on the part of the hostile Indians, that proposition being inconsistent with the treaty of the Indian Springs, which is to be considered inviolable, and the more so, as the Legislature of this State has again explicitly recognized that inviolability, and directed the Executive, as heretofore, to carry the treaty into full effect, according to its stipulations. The treaty being the supreme law, and the Articles of agreement and cession having established the permanent boundary, in conformity with the 23d section of the first Article of the Constitution, no human authority exists to change or alter one tittle of it, save the whole people in convention assembled. I even regret that you should have considered it of any importance to make the concession that Georgia might have been satisfied by a further partial extinguishment of territory, as it had been my settled purpose, from the beginning, so far as depended on me, never to receive from the United States one square foot less than the entire country within the limits of Georgia. You now see that if Georgia had received less, she never would have received more; nevertheless, I know you to have been governed by the most pure and patriotic motives throughout.

With great consideration and respect,

G. M. TROUP.

Again, on 7th February, he wrote the Delegation, that, from a suggestion contained in a letter received by him from Washington, he was apprehensive that a sentence in the foregoing letter had been misconstrued; that, "in speaking of a concession made by the Delegation, nothing more was meant than the concession, which, in answer to the Secretary of War," the Delegation "thought it of sufficient importance to make, viz: that Georgia might have been satisfied, for the time, with an extinguishment of Indian claims to a less amount than that embraced within the limits prescribed by the Articles of Agreement and Cession; a most innocent concession, indeed," said he, "because you could not know that the Legislature would or would not accept such a treaty," &c. Referring to his "entire correspondence with the General Government," from his first letter to Mr. Calhoun, then Secretary of War, he said the Delegation would see that he had "considered the surrender of the whole as a *sine qua non*," &c. After speaking of "the hostile Indians dictating the permanent boundary of the State, to suit their convenience, and the Executive Government of the Union deigning graciously to receive that dictation," &c., he added:

"Not one word was written, or intended to be written, about your having made a concession of a right of any kind; a concession which the writer knew it would be as difficult to extract from you, as from your friend and humble servant."

Meanwhile, the Governor's health was suffering from the cares of office and too close confinement to business. The following extract from a private letter, is not without interest:

MILLEDGEVILLE, 20th Feb., 1826.

My Dear Sir: * * * * * * *

If I could spend a fortnight with you, my health and spirits would be restored. As it is, I am oppressed to death with business which it is impossible for me to turn my back on, and which is accumulating faster than I progress in physical ability to labor through it; so that, at bed-time, nature is not only wearied, but entirely exhausted. Hence, the snail-pace improvement of a condition of body, which, under more favorable circumstances, would have been comparatively vigorous and healthful, weeks ago. God knows what is to be the end of it; for I dread a relapse more than death: yet, the business must go on.

Very sincerely and affectionately,

Dr. Daniell. G. M. TROUP.

[1826.] On the 22d of April, Messrs. Berrien and Cobb wrote separate letters to the Governor, announcing the decision of the Senate on the new treaty, and their unsuccessful efforts so to modify its provisions, as to render them less objectionable to Georgia, and to do justice to the McIntosh Indians, &c., &c. The limits of this work do not permit the publication of these letters of the Georgia Senators. Mr. Cobb spoke of the able support of Judge White, of Tennessee; and Judge Berrien, of the "frank and cordial support from General Harrison, of Ohio, from Col. Hayne, of South Carolina, from Mr. Van Buren, of New York; and, though last, not least, from Judge White, of Tennessee."

To Messrs. Cobb and Berrien, Governor Troup wrote:

EXECUTIVE DEPARTMENT,
Milledgeville, 4*th May*, 1826.

Gentlemen: I have received the several communications which you did me the favor to write, explanatory of the proceedings of the Senate, connected with the amendment of the old, and adoption of the new, treaty. It gave me pleasure to learn that you had disapproved those proceedings, and voted against the instrument called the new treaty.

I recognize no power in the Senate of the United States, in conjunction with the President, to abrogate, for any political consideration whatever, any treaty constitutionally ratified; much less the power assumed by that body, to revoke an Article of the Convention of 1802, between the United States and Georgia, which establishes the boundary between Georgia and Alabama, and to prescribe a new boundary different from and inconsistent with it.

I recognize no power, in the President and Senate, to guaranty to the Indians, in perpetuity, those lands, which, by the Convention, they were pledged to surrender to Georgia at an early day, and which ought to have been surrendered long ago.

I cannot admit that the President and Senate can render null and void, an act of the Legislature of this State, founded on a treaty constitutionally ratified, by an arbitrary revocation of that treaty.

The cancelment of the old treaty had been resolved, right or wrong; for, this extraordinary and unheard of measure was taken on the naked allegation of the President, unsupported by a single document; whilst the ungenerous rebuke, by the President, of the friendly Chiefs, in his official message, shows the temper which dictated it.

Unless all the sources of information here, shall prove to be erroneous and deceptive, the State (if the validity of the new treaty be admitted,) has been defrauded of one million of acres of her very best lands.

Do me the favor to present my best thanks to General Harrison, Colonel Hayne, and Mr. Van Buren, and Judge White, for their able and liberal co-operation with you, in the cause of the weak against the strong; and, as I trust, of the just against the unjust.

With great respect and consideration,

G. M. TROUP.

To another letter from the Governor, Judge Berrien replied on 30th May, giving, more particularly, the grounds of opposition to the treaty, the injunction of secrecy having been previously removed from the proceedings of the Senate. Unable to insert the entire letter, we give the following synopsis.*

Speaking of the opposition of Mr. Cobb and himself, he said:

"Our course on this subject was plain and straightforward. We denied the power of Congress to annul the

* Mr. Cobb was absent, owing to domestic misfortunes, and could not join in this letter.—ED.

old treaty, without the consent of Georgia. We declared our readiness to investigate, and our ability to repel, any charge of fraud which could be brought against it; but we refused to consider the depositions taken by Gen. Gaines and Major Andrews, as evidence on this question, because they were *ex parte*, were taken in a collateral procedure, and while the Indian Agent, retaining his station substantially, though nominally suspended, was able to exercise an undue influence in the Nation."

After referring to some intermediate matters, the writer added:

"It was at this period that my colleague and Major Meriwether, after examining various maps, came to the conclusion which has been communicated to you by the former, and which was announced as our opinion to the Secretary of War; but he was, at the same time, told that the proposed cession, afterwards carried into effect in the supplemental Article, would not remove our objections to the treaty, nor would anything short of a surrender, in terms, of all the lands within the limits of Georgia. The course which we prescribed to ourselves, was this: First, to maintain the old treaty inviolate—Second, failing in this, to obtain a cession, in terms, of all the lands in Georgia, under the new treaty—Third, if this could not be done, to obtain as much land as we could, averring, at the same time, our determination to oppose the treaty as an infraction of the rights of Georgia."

Referring to various unsuccessful motions to amend, &c., the letter said:

"In all this we failed. The treaty was ratified, and we recorded our votes against it. The reason assigned for its ratification, and which appeared to influence the members generally, was, that there was no evidence that any of the Georgia lands were excluded; and that, if, when the line between Georgia and Alabama was run, it should appear that any had been left out, immediate measures would be taken to procure it. It was in vain that I replied that the wishes and immediate rights of a sovereign State ought not to be thus put to hazard—that the uncertainty under which we were acting, was the fault of the United States, as she had prevented or delayed the running of the line between Alabama and Georgia—that, unless we could have all our lands, we were entitled to ask that the old treaty should be maintained, or the charges against it proved, and that the Senate ought not to shrink from the investigation. My colleague reiterated these ideas, and made other suggestions; but they were unavailing. The Senate gladly avoided the unpleasant investigation which awaited them, if they rejected the new treaty; and ratified it, as I firmly believe, rather in the hope than the belief that all the lands within the limits of Georgia would be ceded by it.

"Defeated in these particulars, I still thought it an act of duty to the friends of McIntosh, and interesting to Georgia, to attempt something for their relief, and for the encouragement of their emigration. In this I have succeeded to an extent which you have no doubt seen, as the act has been published. Then came the bill appropriating money to carry the treaty into effect, and with it the discovery of the fraud which is developed in the report of the Committee of Conference, which I sent you. This completely turned the tables on our accusers, and such was the indignation of the Senate, that, if the new treaty had been then in our power, it would have been promptly rejected," &c.

The letter concluded:

"Such, Sir, is a brief narrative of this affair. We cannot say, with Francis, that we have lost everything but our honor; but we can say, with honest pride, that *it* is unimpaired."

The "fraud," to which Judge Berrien referred, as developed in the report of the committee, was shown up in that report made to the Senate on 17th May; from which the following is extracted:

"The paper, marked A, is a copy of the statement furnished to the Secretary, by the conferees; and, as appears by his last letter, corresponds with that spoken of by Mr. McKenney* in his report, as having been furnished to him by the Cherokees, Ridge and Vann, and by him shown to the Secretary. *From the facts stated in the documents submitted, it is manifest that it is the design of the delegation by whom the treaty was negotiated, to make a distribution of the greater part of the money to be paid by the United States, under the treaty, among themselves, three Cherokee Indians, who had no interest in the lands, and, consequently, were not entitled to any portion of the money,*

* Then at the head of the Bureau of Indian Affairs.—ED.

and a few selected individuals, in gross fraud of the rights of the Nation. The particulars of the contemplated distribution are stated in the paper marked A," &c.

We have italicized a portion of the above, that the reader may note some of the influences by which the new treaty was negotiated; and now submit "the paper marked A." The reader will bear in mind, that the "three Cherokee Indians" were John Ridge, Joseph Vann and Major Ridge, mentioned below.

A.

Statement referred to in the letter of James Barbour, Esq., Secretary of War, and communicated to him by the committee of conference, showing the terms of the agreement for the proposed distribution of the money to be received under the Creek treaty.

John Ridge, $15,000; Joseph Vann, $15,000; Opothle Yoholo, $10,000; John Stidham, $10,000; Menawee, $10,000; Charles Cornnells, $10,000; Mad Wolf, $6,000; Paddy Carr, $500; Tippee, a young man, $200; to the remaining members of the Delegation, each, (seven in number,) $5,000, $35,000; Little Prince, $10,000; Tookenehaw, of Tuckebatchie, $10,000; Tuskenuggee Mallow, $10,000; Major Ridge, of the Cherokees, $10.000; Tuckebatchie Tuskenuggee, $1,000; Tuskenehaw Cusseta, $2,-000; Hubi Hojo, $1,000; McGillivray, $4,000.

On the 9th of May, the bill to appropriate money to carry into effect the new treaty, being before the House, the Representatives from Georgia (through Mr. Forsyth,) presented a protest, signed by all of them, from which the following extracts are here made: * * * *

That, by a contract, made at the Indian Springs, between certain Chiefs of the Creek tribe, and the Commissioners of the United States, on the 12th of February, 1825, the claim of the Creek Indians to the land occupied by that tribe in Georgia, was extinguished, and provision made for their removal by the 1st day of September, 1826; that this contract was, on the 7th of March, 1825, duly and solemnly ratified and proclaimed by the President of the United States, acting by the advice and with the consent of the Senate; and that Congress, anticipating such contract, had appropriated the sum of 210,000 dollars towards the execution of it. This contract partially fulfilled, on the part of the United States, their obligation, under the compact with Georgia, of 1802, and removed every difficulty interposed by the occupation of the Creek Indians to the full exercise of all the vested rights of the State over a considerable portion of her soil and territory. That the undersigned are under the solemn conviction, that neither the President alone, nor the President and Senate conjointly, nor the Government of the United States, have any constitutional power, without the consent of Georgia, to interrupt or invalidate, on any pretense whatsoever, the right secured to that State, by this contract, made in obedience to an Act of Congress, and ratified with all due solemnity: That the new contract, for which an appropriation is now asked, differs from that of the Indian Springs, in this: that it does not provide for the removal of the Creek Indians, prior to 1827, and does not expressly provide for their removal from *all* the lands occupied by them in Georgia. The undersigned are, therefore, compelled, by a just sense of what is due to Georgia, to protest, as they do most solemnly protest, against it, as violating the rights of that member of the Union of which they are the Representatives, leaving it to the Constitutional organs of the State sovereignty to vindicate or to waive those rights, as their own sense of propriety, their duty to the people of the State, and their reverence for the Union of the States, under the Federal Constitution, may dictate.

A long and excited debate arose, in the House of Representatives, upon the bill to appropriate money to carry into effect the treaty, in which several of the Georgia Representatives, particularly Mr. Forsyth, Cols. Tattnall and Cuthbert, and General Thompson, took part. Mr. Forsyth denounced the whole affair of the new treaty as "a stupendous fraud," and, in several exceedingly able and eloquent speeches, vindicated the State of Georgia and her authorities, &c. Col. Tattnall, denying the power of the Federal Government to undo the old treaty, declared his readiness, if force should be resorted to, to shoulder his musket, to defend, at every hazard, the rights of Georgia, and to enforce that treaty.

Mr. Forsyth's speeches were the most elaborate of those

delivered by Representatives from Georgia, and were exceedingly pungent and able; but we cannot give even a synopsis. On the 8th of May, referring to the determination of Georgia to survey the lands, he said:

"This determination of the State peaceably to survey its own lands, was the pretext for one of the most high-handed measures ever witnessed in a free Government. The right was unquestionably with Georgia. Admitting it to have been doubtful; allow even that the President was correct; that his obligation was to interpose; see, sir, how that obligation was performed. No judge was called on, no magistrate sought to command the services of the Marshals, Sheriffs, or any other civil officer; but a direct appeal was made to force, in the most odious of its forms—military force—a portion of the standing army, of the hired soldiery, were the instruments ordered to be used against a State law—a military force previously carried to the scene of action, with the design of preserving peace among the Indians! I ask, by what authority the President employed this military force, in a time of profound peace, against one of the confederacy?"

On the 19th of May, the question being before the Senate, on the report of the committee of conference, considerable debate followed, in which Judge Berrien took part; and from his speech we extract the following:

"The murder of McIntosh—the defamation of the Chief Magistrate of Georgia—the menace of military force to coerce her to submission—were followed by the traduction of two of her cherished citizens, employed as the Agents of the General Government in negotiating the treaty—gentlemen, whose integrity will not shrink from a comparison with that of the proudest and loftiest of their accusers. Then the sympathies of the people of the Union were excited in behalf of 'the children of the forest,' who were represented as indignantly spurning the gold, which was offered to entice them from the graves of their fathers, and resolutely determined never to abandon them. The incidents of the plot being thus prepared, the affair hastens to its consummation. A new treaty is negotiated here—*a pure and spotless treaty*. The rights of Georgia and of Alabama are sacrificed; the United States obtain a part of the lands, and pay double the amount stipulated by the old treaty;

and those pure and noble and unsophisticated sons of the forest, having succeeded in imposing on the simplicity of this Government, next concert, under its eye, and with its knowledge, the means of defrauding their own constituents, the Chiefs and Warriors of the Creek Nation.

For their agency in exciting the Creeks to resist the former treaty, and in deluding this Government to annul it, *three Cherokees, Ridge, Vann, and the father of the former*, are to receive *forty thousand dollars* of the money stipulated to be paid by the United States to the Chiefs of the *Creek* Nation; and the Government, when informed of the projected fraud, deems itself powerless to avert it. Nay, when apprised by your amendment that you also had detected it, that Government does not hesitate to interpose, by one of its high functionaries, to resist your proceeding; by a singular fatuity, thus giving its countenance and support to the commission of the fraud. Sir, I speak of what has passed before your eyes, even in this hall.

One fifth of the whole purchase money is to be given to *three Cherokees.* TEN THOUSAND DOLLARS reward one of the heroes of Fort Mims—a boon which it so well becomes us to bestow. A few chosen favorites divide among themselves upwards of ONE HUNDRED AND FIFTY THOUSAND DOLLARS, leaving a pittance for distribution among the great body of the Chiefs and Warriors of the nation. But it is the price of blood—of the blood of McIntosh. Shall it not be freely distributed among those who shed it?"

Speaking of Gov. Troup, in connection with the "menace to employ the military force of the Union" to prevent the survey of the lands, Judge Berrien said:

"To this lawless mandate, her Chief Magistrate submitted. Unable to repress the feelings which had been excited by the contumely of the Government and its Agents, he nevertheless respected the peace of the Union, and the tyranny was unresisted. The Senate will permit me to say a passing word of this calumniated individual—the friend and companion of my earlier years—whose name has been associated, in the journals devoted to the Administration, with the epithets of madness and of treason. Sir, there is no man, however vindictive his feelings, however led astray by the reveries of a malevolent fancy, who, in the moment of retirement, communing with God and his own conscience, had the hardihood to avow to himself a belief of the calumnies which were uttered against the Chief Magistrate of

Georgia. Love for his country—indignation against her oppressors—these are the qualities of the patriot—these are the qualities which he has exhibited in this controversy."

Congress passed the bill; but it provided that the amount payable under the third article of the treaty, "*be paid to the Chiefs of the Creek Nation, to be divided amongst the Chiefs and Warriors of said Nation; and that the same be done under the direction of the Secretary of War*, IN A FULL COUNCIL OF THE NATION, *convened upon notice for that purpose.*"

Congress also passed another "Act to aid certain Indians of the Creek Indians in their removal to the west of the Mississippi." The Act provided for the payment and distribution of certain bounties, &c., amongst the warriors emigrating within a certain time, payment for improvements, &c.; and is the Act referred to by Judge Berrien, (in his letter of 30th May, to the Governor,) as an encouragement to the friends of McIntosh in their emigration, &c.

The following private letter may be properly inserted here:

MILLEDGEVILLE, 12th May, 1826.

My Dear Sir: It is true that something useful might have been accomplished for State rights, if my measures could have had their full effect. As it is, there may be some merit in having intended well and attempted so much. With the United States Government and the United States people against us, and a lean and shrinking majority at home, giving a feeble and reluctant support, it was not to be expected that measures of vigor, and adapted to the occasion, could succeed. I wished nothing more for their success, than a firm, unyielding majority; and, with such, I would have given no premium for the assurance of a triumph. It is most mortifying to me, that, whilst late events make it proper to have recourse to similar measures, we are likely to find similar results. To sustain the old treaty in its integrity, I would only ask the support of a firm, unyielding majority. Yet, what is to be done for principle or for State rights, if those, who are most concerned, retire from the defence, and leave me to sustain the burden of it? I cannot conceive a condition more pitiable than this; and I regard it with the more loathing, because you know how our enemies will rejoice. We have been defrauded of at least a million of acres of our very best land, besides being grossly insulted; and yet, you will hear it said 'tis not worth quarreling about.

Very affectionately, your friend,

G. M. TROUP.

Dr. W. C. Daniell,
Savannah.

The next subject claiming the attention of the Government of Georgia, was the running of the boundary line between that State and Alabama; a subject to which reference has already been made, and which derived additional importance from its connection with the Creek controversy. As early as 1822, the Legislature had recognized the fact that the line had never been run, and the Governor had been requested "to take as speedy measures as possible" on the subject. The same thing was substantially done at the session of 1823, and, again at the extra session of 1825; and in December, 1825, an appropriation was made to run this line as well as that between Georgia and Florida.

On 26th January, 1826, the Governor wrote to the Senators from Georgia, requesting them to learn from the Secretary of War, whether it was "the intention of the United States Government to prohibit the running of the dividing line between Alabama and this State." He added:

"General Gaines is explicit enough, but the Secretary of War is sometimes obscure on this subject. The object is to possess myself of an unequivocal declaration, which will admit of but one construction, and without delay."

In his reply to the application of the Georgia Senators, the Secretary of War wrote them on 20th February, stating that he had been instructed by the President to say, "that the uncertain posture of affairs in respect to the lands proposed to be surveyed, and through which the dividing line referred to, is to be run, renders it unnecessary, if not improper, that any definitive answer should be given to the questions contained in your letter, at this time:" but that "the earliest moment" which would relieve "the subject of these difficulties," would be seized to furnish the most satisfactory answer possible, &c.

On 9th March, Gov. Troup wrote to the President, and said:

I embrace, with great pleasure, the first instant, after having been myself corrected, to correct an error into which, from the indistinct information received here, of the provisions of the new treaty, I was inadvertently led, in the communication which I had the honor to address to you on the 11th day of February last.

Necessarily precluded from acting on official information, until the fate of the new treaty had been decided, it became my duty, for the purpose of averting apprehended evil, to act promptly upon the best which the nature of the case afforded; that, of course, is still the best I can resort to, and it warrants the belief that the 300,000 acres supposed to be given to the Cherokees, have not been given to them, but to the Creeks; and, consequently, that the dividing line between the two tribes, viz.: McIntosh's line of 1822, will, for any thing contained in the new treaty, remain unaltered. It is confidently hoped, therefore, that, with regard to the running of that line, we may experience no difficulty or obstruction from the Cherokees.

It is the alteration of the other, and most important one, viz: the line between the Big Bend and Nickajack, as guarantied by the Articles of Agreement and Cession, which remains a subject of specific and distinct remonstrance; and it is the inevitable permanency of that alteration, which, replete with evil and full of danger, produces here inquietude and alarm.

The new treaty having its foundation in the last resolution of the hostile Chiefs, officially declared, that they will never surrender the country, but with their lives; the inference is irresistible that our rights, depending, for the future, on that resolution, the new boundary is to be considered a permanent one; an inference the more warrantable, because the old treaty, being as much a matter of contract, passing vested rights, as the Articles of Agreement and Cession, if the new treaty can rescind the old, it can rescind the Articles of Agreement and Cession; and it is the boundary, as established by those articles, which now constitutes the chief value of them.

The articles of the treaty, either as negotiated or ratified, (if ratified at all,) not being before me, I can only write of what I understand them to be; with respect to other matters of fact, I may be equally deceived or mistaken; with respect to the inference drawn from them, I cannot be. To avert mischief by timely remonstrance, and not to misrepresent the views or proceedings of the Government of the United States, was the only object in addressing the letter to you of the 11th ultimo; and if, in this or that, there be anything else of error or misconception, none will be more ready to make acknowledgement and reparation, than,

Sir, very respectfully, your obedient servant,

G. M. TROUP.

On the 15th of February, Gov. Troup had written to the Georgia Delegation in Congress, stating that, in summoning the Board of Public Works to meet on the 3d Monday in March, he was "obliged, simultaneously, to make preparations for the running of the dividing lines between this State and Alabama, and between this State and the Cherokees." He added: "These preparations were in a state of forwardness, when I was unexpectedly informed that a new treaty had been negotiated, at Washington, with the hostile Chiefs, superseding the old one, and establishing new boundaries, not only with Alabama, but with the Cherokees." After expressing uncertainty as to the precise details of the projected treaty, &c., &c., he added: "You will see, from the tenor and spirit of the letter" (of 11th Feb.)" to the President, (a copy of which, with the annexed documents, is herewith forwarded for your information,) that no time was lost, on my part, if anything could be hoped from this last appeal to the Executive Government. You will, if you think proper, be pleased to make known to it, informally, what could not with so much propriety be submitted in that letter, as justificatory of the immediate exercise of an absolute right, that it will not be possible to commence the work of Internal Improvement, as authorized by the last Legislature, and apparently with the universal sanction of the people now warmly embarked in this interesting cause, and for which every necessary preparation can be made by the opening of the summer, unless our permanent Western and temporary Northern boundary are satisfactorily ascertained and marked."

On the 3d of February, Gov. Troup opened a correspondence with Gov. Murphy, of Alabama; and, in reply to the letter of the former, the latter wrote, enclosing to Gov. Troup a resolution of the Legislature of Alabama, authorizing the Governor of that State to appoint two fit persons, as Commissioners, to co-operate with the Georgia Commissioners, in ascertaining the boundary line between the two States, "according to the terms of the compact made between the United States and the State of Georgia, in the year 1802," &c. The Governor of Alabama having solicited the views of Gov. Troup, on the subject, a long, but interesting and very friendly, correspondence ensued, the result of which was the appointment of two Commissioners on the part of Alabama, (with a request, on her part, to the Secretary of War, to appoint U. S. Commissioners and an Engineer,) and the appointment of three Commissioners on the part of Georgia.

The Secretary of War, on 4th June, communicated (to Gov. Troup) his reply to the Governor of Alabama, in which he said no provision had been made by Congress, "for the appointment of a Commissioner," and no money had been appropriated "to meet the expenses of such an appointment"; and he added that the President "would fain hope that this subject may be equitably and satisfactorily adjusted by the two States, without the interposition of the Government of the United States," &c., &c. On the 17th June, Gov. Troup wrote to the Secretary of War: "It is not apprehended that any serious difficulty will occur between the two States; and the expression of this sentiment by the President, so favorable to the removal of one embarrassment, will prove, it is hoped, the precursor of the removal of all, in the unhappy differences which have occurred between the General Government and this, on other subjects connected with it."

[1826.] On this subject of the boundary line between Georgia and Alabama, it must suffice here to say, that the Alabama Commissioners, Arthur P. Bagby and Charles

Lewis, and the Georgia Commissioners, Richard A. Blount, Joel Crawford and Everard Hamilton, met at Fort Mitchell, on the 1st of July, ran an experimental or random line, and having failed to agree on the true line, the Georgia Commissioners proceeded alone to run the line, finishing their labors on the 19th of September; and that line, although not acquiesced in by Alabama during the administration of Gov. Troup, was virtually regarded as the true line then, and has ever since formed the dividing line between the two States. The reader will find this subject referred to in the annual message of 1826.

It is proper to add, in this connection, that, in June of this year, the Governor of Alabama renewed the correspondence, giving his own views of the construction of the articles of agreement and cession, so far as they related to boundary, "in return" as he said, for the views which Governor Troup had presented. He added: "I have great pleasure in doing so, as it affords another instance of the undisguised freedom of all our communications." The concluding part of Gov. Troup's reply to that letter, is, as follows:

"With respect to the new treaty and the rights violated by it, I am happy to find between us an entire accordance of sentiment. If history is philosophy, teaching by example, and the actions of men are to be referred to their true and appropriate causes, I do not know to what place in our story are to be assigned the strange proceedings connected with it, or what figure they will cut there. This much is certain, that, with regard to us, the old treaty is unimpaired; for it cannot be unknown even to those who sought its abrogation, that the rights vested by it are vested forever, and that the proclamation which announced its legal supremacy, remains an unchangeable record, to all future time, for the government of courts of justice, whose ministers through all ages, whether of refinement or of barbarism, must recognize it as passing interests to Georgia and Alabama, which, by the universal rule of natural justice and equity, no human power can divest. When the passions of the day shall subside, and a calm review is taken of the past, it is not to be doubted that the removal of the Indians will be considered as an indispensable act of justice and atonement both to Georgia and Alabama, and one of necessary precaution for the preservation and happiness of the Indians themselves."

The following private letter from Gov. Troup, to his friend Dr. W. C. Daniell, will be read with interest:

MILLEDGEVILLE, 8th June, 1826.

My Dear Sir: I have just returned from my plantation, and take the first occasion to write an answer to your last friendly and obliging letter.

The Government of the United States has long since been officially notified by the Governor of this State, that he would proceed to survey the lands, in conformity with the Act of the Legislature, passed in pursuance of the provisions of the old treaty, without regard to any thing which might be done on the part of the Government of the United States to impair or invalidate those provisions.

If any thing had subsequently transpired to satisfy me of the incorrectness or impolicy of this measure, be assured that, so far from its being persisted in for the sake of consistency, it would be most cheerfully and unhesitatingly abandoned. It has so happened, however, that every event which has followed that notification, has confirmed my belief in the propriety of it, and rendered the measure more indispensable than ever. It is impossible for me, believing, as I do, in the unconstitutionality of the new, and in the constitutionality of the old, treaty, to suspend the execution of a law express and mandatory in its character, whilst no justification could be rendered for such suspension, but my own honest conviction of the irrevocability of the old treaty and the utter worthlessness of the new. And this would be the very best reason which could be assigned in support of the resolution to execute the law: for I would never permit myself, even in extremity, to say that we had been deterred from doing what we had a right to do, what we had an interest to do, and what by the competent Constitutional power we were commanded to do, only because we were threatened with a good whipping if we attempted to do it. This, the people whose interest it is, have a right to say; but, should they say it, I assure you, my friend, I will not be with the people.

I think you will agree with me, now, that if my resolution to survey the lands, this time last year, had been backed by a strong and resolute majority, we might have been spared many humiliations and sacrifices. We had then good reason for changing the resolution—none now for changing this. The same reason which would postpone the survey, would postpone the running of the dividing line; for the one is equally forbidden as the other.

It is quite superfluous to say to you, that no man in my station respects public opinion more than myself. I believe it may sometimes be wrong—when it is so, it will be disregarded. If I am deserted, it will be no cause of complaint with me, because both the *honor* and the *interest* involved are theirs; my share is so small that it is not worth fretting about.

Affectionately, your friend,

G. M. TROUP.

Dr. Daniell.

The 4th of July, 1826, was rendered yet more memorable, by the decease, on that day, of THOMAS JEFFERSON and JOHN ADAMS.

By invitation of the citizens of Milledgeville, Governor Troup consented to pronounce a eulogium, "commemorative of the virtues, the talents and the public services" of these patriots. In consenting to deliver the eulogy on Jefferson, (the death of Mr. Adams not being then known at Milledgeville,) the Governor, in reply to the invitation of the committee, said:

"Nothing, but an early attachment to Mr. Jefferson, made stronger by every incident of his life to the hour of his death, could induce me to yield a willing obedience to your invitation of this morning. On any other occasion, the duties of my office, my utter incompetency to the task assigned me, and especially the obligation to be present at the approaching commencement of Franklin College, would have forbidden it."

The eulogy was delivered in the Baptist Church at Milledgeville, on 29th July, and did justice to both the illustrious dead; but we have not space even for extracts, and must refer to his equally eloquent notice of the deceased, in his annual message of that year. In furnishing a copy of the address, for publication, the Governor said:

"A copy of the address is reluctantly yielded to your request. Acceptable as it may have been to the enlightened auditory for whom only it was intended, and who only could make indulgent allowance for its imperfections, it is deemed unworthy of the press, and much more so of the occasion* which produced it."

On the 17th of July, Governor Troup, being on a visit to the Indian Springs, partook of a public dinner tendered him by the citizens of Forsyth and its vicinity, in consideration of the "eminent services" he had rendered and was still rendering the State. The fourth regular toast was:

"*Our distinguished guest*—Gratitude for his public services, honor for his integrity, and admiration for his talents."

In returning his thanks for the compliment, he said:

"It is not the less flattering because it is felt to be undeserved. 'T is true I have endeavored something for the public interest—'t is not the less true that I have, so far, endeavored to little or no purpose. You are not ignorant of the causes. If, however, for any thing, merit be due to any, it is most especially due to you, gentlemen, and to those like you, who have at all times, in the true spirit of patriotism, and in seasons of difficulty and trouble, been ready to lend a manly and liberal support in sustaining the rights and honor of the country."

He gave, in return, the following sentiment:

"*The prospect before us*—It is brightened by the union of honest men for the defence of State rights, and Georgia promises to be herself once more."

Some time in June, the Governor received information, from Mr. Fulton, Chief Engineer, and Hon. Wilson Lumpkin, a member of the Board of Public Works, then in the Cherokee country, of what seemed a determination by the Indians not to permit those gentlemen to proceed with their official examination, &c. In communicating to the Secretary of War, on 29th June, the letter of Mr. Fulton, Gov. Troup said:

The enclosed copy of a letter, this morning received, from our Chief Engineer, engaged in a reconnoissance under orders, and within the unsettled limits of Georgia, will inform you that he has been stopped by the Cherokees, and his further progress threatened to be arrested by force; and,

* Amongst the other distinguished citizens who pronounced eulogies on Jefferson and Adams, were Mr. Forsyth, at Augusta, Hon. T. U. P. Charlton, at Savannah, and Hon. Thomas Spalding, at Darien.—ED.

further, that these infatuated and misguided people threaten to resist, by force, the execution of the measure concerted by the Governments of Georgia and Alabama, for ascertaining the dividing line between the two States.

On the 6th of August, the Secretary of War, after noticing the receipt of the Governor's letter and enclosure, and stating that they had been laid before the President, said:

"I am directed to state to you, his opinion, that a survey or reconnoissance of the lands secured by treaties to the Cherokee Indians, to which treaties the United States are parties, and to the observance of which their faith is pledged, cannot be lawfully made without the consent of the Indians. To obtain that consent, the letter, a copy of which is herewith enclosed, has been written to the Agent of the United States with the Cherokee Indians. The President is persuaded that this consent may be obtained by amicable and pacific means. If, however, it cannot, he deems a resort to coercive measures as altogether unwarrantable. If, in the justness of this view, the constituted authorities of Georgia should coincide, it will be gratifying to the President. But, to guard against the consequences of different views on that part, he feels himself required to protest, in the name of the United States, against the use of forcible and hostile means to effect the purposes referred to in your letter."

Gov. Troup, in his reply, dated 26th August, said:

To my letter of the 29th June, announcing the resolution of the Cherokees to resist the officers of Georgia in the execution of their duties, I did not receive your answer until yesterday. Accept my thanks for your politeness in transmitting, by an enclosure, a copy of your communication to the United States Agent, and tender them, if you please, to the President, for the counsel he has thought proper to interpose on this occasion.

As, in my letter to which yours is an answer, no intimation had been given of an intention to resort to force to execute surveys or reconnoissances in the Indian country, I could not perceive on what authority such intention had been assumed, as the basis not only of a premonition that the employment of force by this Government, for such purposes, would be altogether *unwarrantable*, but of a formal protest, in behalf of the United States, against it. Whilst no doubt was entertained of the constitutional right of Georgia to protect from insult, and against any power, her officers employed within her territory, in execution of her own orders, whether that territory be in the occupation of Indians or not, it had not been resolved, as you seem to have imagined, to resort to force to execute the engineering reconnoissances or surveys in the Indian country; it was resolved to give effectual protection to our Commissioners engaged in running the dividing line between Georgia and Alabama; a measure which, if it had been provoked, the Executive Government of the United States should have been the last to complain of. It was not considered possible, that, after having given its cheerful acquiescence to the running of the line, it should have denied to Georgia and Alabama the only means by which, in a probable contingency, the measure could be executed; and that, whilst the two States, under the encouragement of the United States, were actually engaged in its execution, they should be enjoined by the United States to forbear the only means by which their officers could be protected from a threatened insult. It was resolved, therefore, to have recourse to force for the protection of the Commissioners. All the measures were taken to make this force available; and, it gives me pleasure to state, as highly honorable to the Chief of it, that for this purpose Georgia would have had the cheerful co-operation of the Government of Alabama.

If the President has considered it his duty to interpose his formal protest against the execution, by Georgia, of reconnoissances or surveys of any kind, in her own territory occupied by the Indians, much more is it conceived to be the duty of the Governor of Georgia to protest, most solemnly, against the doctrines on which that protest is founded.

Sir, it would be unavailing to open a discussion of this subject; the United States Government has long since concluded to discuss nothing with the States; it asserts supremacy, and in the spirit of supremacy it orders and executes. Within her chartered limits, Georgia is denied power to ask the Indians to sell to her, her own lands. She is denied the right of way or intercourse, by her own soil, with her sister States. Within her own territory she is divested of all the rights of sovereignty and jurisdiction, which appertain to it, as if she were the greatest stranger, and is treated, in relation to it, as if she had neither charter, title, claim, or pretence of claim. The Indians are the lords paramount, and, whilst we are not permitted to demand right at all, we are allowed the privilege of receiving favors from them, through you only. My word for it, Sir, these doctrines may be fashionable for the day, but they cannot last. Georgia must be sovereign upon her own soil, within her chartered limits; she has made no surrender of her territorial sovereignty and jurisdiction, by entering into the Union. The power to regulate commerce with the Indian tribes, is no diminution, much less renunciation, of either. It is not necessary to the regulation of commerce with the Creeks and Cherokees, that the Creeks and Cherokees should be kept within the limits of Georgia; it is sufficient for the exercise of your rights in this respect, that they are within your own limits; but, as in either case, they would be within the limits of the United States, you will readily perceive how vast the difference is between controlling things in a country which you justly claim, and in one to which you have no rightful claim; in a country where the sovereignty and jurisdiction would be acknowledgedly yours, and in one where, with regard to the sovereignty and jurisdiction, you are considered, and will be treated, as a foreign power. The United States Government, no more than any foreign Government, is permitted to insult officers of Georgia, within the territory of Georgia, occupied in the discharge of their lawful duty. Georgia has the right which she always had, in common with the colonies and colonizing countries, to prescribe limits, within her charter, to the territories of the aborigines. It is no derogation from this right, that Georgia has never exercised it but on terms of treaty; if she has forborne, from motives of humanity, she may deserve praise, but ought not to suffer loss. The exclusive right, claimed by the United States, to purchase lands from the Indians, is only the right to purchase those of which she claims the sovereignty and jurisdiction. She has no such exclusive right in relation to territory, the sovereignty and jurisdiction of which are claimed by Georgia.

If Georgia retains her colonial right under charter, to remove the Indians from her lands; *a fortiori*, she has a right to enter into peaceable purchase of the same lands. To have surrendered this right to the United States, would have been virtually to surrender her territory; yet, the United States have constantly exercised it, with our tolerance, over the territory of Georgia, as she has over her own. Georgia, with her rights of territorial sovereignty and jurisdiction, unimpaired by the Constitution, has, in practice, asserted none of these rights; she has forborne them for the sake of peace.

When, on a late occasion, she proposed an innocent act of survey, preparatory to the occupation of her territory, acquired under treaty—an act inconsistent neither with rights of the United States, nor with the occupancy of the Indians—she was threatened with a military force, as if she had been a stranger committing wilful trespass on the acknowledged property of the United States.

You will pardon this brief exposition; it is rendered necessary by your recurrence to principles and doctrines, the implied admission of which might involve the forfeiture or impair the rights of sovereignty and jurisdiction, which this State claims over her vacant territory, and of which she ought never to be divested, but with her voluntary and express consent.

It was a matter of sincere gratification, when, in a former correspondence, I perceived, or thought I perceived, symptoms of a kind and conciliatory spirit, which, met by one equally kind, would reconcile the parties in controversy, giving the past to oblivion, and opening a new way, upon lasting foundations, to concord and harmony; and now it is cause of the most painful regret to observe the slightest indications of a return to opposite principles, on the part of those with whom the authorities here have no wish or desire so strong as that of cultivating the most amicable and friendly intercourse.*

The Secretary of War wrote to Gov. Troup, on 16th September, and said:

By the treaty with the Creeks, negotiated at Washington, it was stipulated that they should retain possession of the lands ceded by that treaty, till the 1st January, 1827. Through their Agent, John Crowell, they have transmitted to this Department, a document of the following tenor:

[The document was an order issued 9th March, 1826, requiring the Surveyor-General to give notice to the Sectional Surveyors appointed under the Act of 9th June, 1825, to repair to Milledgeville, and qualify, on a given day, for the discharge of their duties required by that Act, &c., &c. The order contemplated the beginning of these surveys on

---

* On the 16th September, the Governor, in a private letter to Dr. Daniell, said:

"The only step as yet taken by the President against the survey, is the entry of a general and formal protest against a resort to force by Georgia to run lines or make surveys of any kind, in territory occupied by Indians, without intimating whether force will be resorted to by the United States to maintain that protest. Our Surveyors are, so far, uninterrupted, and by this time have, no doubt, carried their lines to the Chattahoochee."—ED.

1st Monday of September, 1826, and of the District surveyors as soon as they should be required. It is not important to insert the order entire.]

And direct him to say, in their behalf, that they are much disturbed at the idea of the Surveyors entering the country before they can secure their little crops, and remove their crops, and to express to the Executive their disapprobation of the measure. That while they are perfectly reconciled to the terms of the treaty, and will cheerfully comply with its provisions, on their part, they hope and believe that the Government of the United States will protect them in their rights, against the encroachments of Georgia; and they express their apprehensions that much mischief will ensue to them from the proposed premature survey, and the consequences of which it will be the cause. If the Indians had acquiesced in your measure, the President, so far from interfering, would have been pleased in the speedy fulfilment of the wishes of Georgia, in relation to the possession of these lands ; but, when they are dissatisfied, and have appealed to him to cause to be observed the Articles of that very treaty under which the lands were ceded, but possession retained to the 1st of January, 1827, he feels himself constrained, by the plighted faith of the Nation, to state to you, that he considers an entry on the ceded lands, for the purpose of surveying them, as a violation of the treaty. Ever disposed to promote the wishes of any member of the confederacy, to the uttermost of his power, the President has directed the Agent to use his best efforts to reconcile the Indians to the measures you propose, in which, if he succeed, you will be duly notified; but, if that be impracticable, it is expected that Georgia will desist from any further prosecution of the survey, till it is authorized by the treaty ; and when reference is had to the small portion of intervening time, the President can see no inducement, on the part of Georgia, to enter the territory of the Indians, against their will, and in violation of the supreme law of the land.

The following is the reply of the Governor :

EXECUTIVE DEPARTMENT, GEORGIA,
Milledgeville, *6th October*, 1826.

SIR: I did not receive your letter of the 15th ult., before the 30th, it having been delayed, as appeared by the postmark, at Charleston.

Be pleased to assure the President, that what has been

communicated to him, as a remonstrance of the Indians against the survey, is no remonstrance of theirs, but of some officious intermeddlers in their behalf, who, in misrepresenting the Indians, have only given a faithful representation of their own sordid interests and passions. Our surveyors, some of whom have already finished their work, and all of whom will have completed it in a very short time, have not only suffered no interruption, but have met with the most cordial and friendly reception, with the exception of a single instance, where two of the lower Chiefs, notoriously instigated by white men, had interposed threats, founded, as they alleged, on the authority of the Indian Agent: in truth, the subject of survey throughout, has been theoretically and practically treated by them as it deserved. The survey has not merely been regarded as an operation innocent in itself, and unproductive of harm, either to the persons or property of the Indians, but it has been considered as a source of accommodation and emolument, by opening a market for their surplus commodities, which are either perishable or not easily removable. The officers engaged in it having been appointed by the Legislature, are presumed to carry with them firmness of character, which not only forbids the supposition that they will commit trespass on the Indians, themselves, but warrants the belief that they will, to the utmost of their power, prevent others from doing so; and to this effect they are instructed. The surveyors operate as a check upon that description of persons, hundreds of whom, without authority of law, but according to custom, intrude upon the Indian occupancy, whom neither you nor I, with our utmost means, would be able to restrain, and whom nothing will restrain, but the laws, which, in a short time now, will be extended over the country.

The President concedes the right of occupancy and settlement to Georgia on the 1st day of January. If, according to the established rule, the concession of a right implies the concession of all the means, without which that right cannot be enjoyed, the survey on the 1st of September was an act of indisputable right, without which Georgia could not occupy the country on the 1st of January. The President cannot mean that the survey of the country is the occupation of the country, because that would be a perversion of language; and if he only means that the Indians are not to suffer the least disturbance in their persons or effects, before the 1st of January, I trust the President has found a sufficient guaranty for this, in the universal and joyous acquiescence of the Indians themselves; and here permit me to say to the President, in all frankness, that I believe himself, and yourself, and the Senate, have been grossly deceived and imposed on, in framing, at least, one of the stipulations of the instrument called the new treaty. Why, with regard to the time for the occupation of the country, was not the provision of the new treaty made to correspond with that of the old? This coincidence would at least have removed one difficulty; but it escaped his and your observation, that it was designed for the very purpose, in gratification of the worst of passions, by those who seek to embitter the controversy between the United States and Georgia, of postponing the settlement of the country one year; a postponement, which, to the President, might seem to be no very great evil, but which, I assure you, would be considered and felt as a very great one, not by ourselves only, but by the Indians and the United States.

The contrivers of this trick believed that you would prevent a survey before the 1st of January, and they well knew if you did that, consistently with our system, the country could not be occupied before the following year; and the reasons for this, which you may not fully comprehend, are universally understood and appreciated here. With a correct knowledge of the circumstances, the President, "consulting the views and interests of the people of Georgia," would never have suffered this despicable stratagem to have passed unexposed or unpunished.

The survey being disposed of, it only remains to invite the attention of the President to that part of the subject from which further embarrassment and misunderstanding may possibly arise: I mean the western boundary of Georgia, as prescribed contrary to her Constitution and the Articles of Agreement, by the instrument called the new treaty. My views on this subject have long since been submitted, in all possible candor, to the President. The President, however, consulting the views and interests of Georgia, as well as the interests of the United States, will not suffer, if he can avoid it, a conscientious difference of opinion to be a source of mischief and calamity to either. I may be mistaken or deceived, but the impression here has been uniform, from the beginning, that the Indians who negotiated that instrument, intended to cede to Georgia all the lands claimed by Georgia, and that the President, the Senate, and the Georgia Delegation, so understood it; rumor has lately said that the Indians still so understand it. Of, all this, however, you possess the more ample means of information; and it is only permitted to me to say, that if these things be true, it depends on the President to remove, by a single word, every obstacle to the adjustment of all the differences unhappily connected with this subject.

With great consideration and respect,

I have the honor to be

G. M. TROUP.

In the mean time, the surveys of the lands ceded by the old treaty, were proceeding; and, as is seen by the foregoing letter, some of the surveyors had already completed their work when that letter was written. There were many rumors and some threats of interruption; but these amounted to little, and the Governor took the proper precautions and measures to protect the surveyors.*

On the second day of October, the general election for Representatives in Congress and members of the Legislature, took place. It resulted in the choice of Edward F. Tattnall,† in the 1st; John Forsyth, in the 2d; Wiley Thompson, in the 3d; Wilson Lumpkin, in the 4th; Charles E. Haynes, in the 5th; Tomlinson Fort, in the 6th; and John Floyd, in the 7th, Congressional Districts; and in a decided majority of Troup men in each branch of the General Assembly.

The Legislature convened on the 6th day of November. In the Senate, Hon. Thomas Stocks, of Greene, was elected President; and, in the House, Irby Hudson, Esq., of Put-

* Nor was he inattentive to the interests of the Indians. Having received information that "certain disorderly and evil-disposed persons" had, "on divers pretenses, passed beyond the temporary limits of this State, into the vacant territory of the same, making settlements therein, or otherwise committing trespasses and depredations of various kinds, on the property of Indians, both Creeks and Cherokees;" he, on the 26th day of August, 1826, issued his proclamation, "warning and cautioning all such persons against the penalties which" awaited "their disobedience and violation of the laws of the United States and of this State, in the premises," and particularly ordering "all property unjustly or unlawfully taken, as aforesaid, and brought within the jurisdiction of this State, upon due proof thereof, to be restored," &c., &c.—ED.

† On the 23d July, 1827, Col. Tattnall resigned his seat in Congress, on account of ill health, and was succeeded by Hon. George R. Gilmer.

Mr. Forsyth having been elected Governor on the 1st Monday in October, 1827, resigned his place in Congress on the 13th of the same month, and was succeeded by Hon. Richard H. Wilde.

nam, was elected Speaker—both members of the dominant party. The result of these elections indicated a majority, on joint ballot, of twenty-five votes.

On the second day of the session, the Governor sent in the following message to the two Houses, which we are reluctantly compelled to abridge:

EXECUTIVE DEPARTMENT, GEORGIA,
Milledgeville, 7th November, 1826.

Fellow-Citizens: The political year just terminated has been distinguished by nothing so much as the decease of Thomas Jefferson and John Adams, who, after laying the foundation of American Independence, and filling the highest offices of State, through a long series of time, survived to the fiftieth anniversary of the Independence they had declared; and on that day, almost at the same hour, died, full of years and full of honor, deplored by the whole nation, whose grief was testified by a universal mourning, accompanied with every demonstration of love, respect and veneration. Among the many tokens of the tender mercies of Divine Providence toward our country, none have been more signal than those which accompanied this memorable dispensation; so much so, that our sorrows have found solace and comfort in the admiration and gratitude due to Almighty God, for the special interposition, which, by its circumstances, made their deaths not less glorious than their lives had been exemplary and illustrious.

It was known to the last Legislature, that, for certain reasons expressed by the President of the United States, he would call the attention of Congress, at their first meeting, to the validity of the treaty negotiated at the Indian Springs, in 1825; and, in his message to the Congress, at the opening of the session, after announcing that "the treaty had been ratified under the unsuspecting impression that it had been negotiated in good faith," he promised to lay before that body the subsequent transactions in relation to it. The President failed to do so. Toward the close of the session of Congress, he did submit to the Senate a new treaty, in abrogation of the old one, with a general declaration of the falsehood and deception practiced by the Commissioners, in their official communications with the Government, of the numerical inferiority of the party which signed it, and of their consequent inability to carry it into effect, but unaccompanied by a single document or voucher to support any fact or principle contained in that declaration. The Senate, as you know, ratified the treaty; and the one of the Indian Springs, of prior date, of prior ratification, and passing vested rights to Georgia, was declared null and void. The objections to this proceeding, considered altogether novel and unprecedented, were obvious. Georgia, for whose benefit alone the treaty was negotiated, was deprived, without her consent, of interests already vested. The party with whom the old treaty had been negotiated, was not recognized as a party at all in the conclusion of the new; and, in the execution of the new treaty, without their consent, and even against their consent, they have not merely been deprived of every right which they could claim, under the old or new, but have been, to all intents and purposes, denationalized, and forced either to submit unconditionally to the power of their enemies, or to abandon their country. It was with a knowledge of what was in prospect, from the first annunciation of the President to Congress, that the Legislature of Georgia, at the close of its session, again reviewed and again confirmed the validity of the treaty of the Indian Springs.

This confirmation was the more imposing, because the Legislature which first acknowledged the authority of that treaty, had returned to the people, its conduct had been passed in review, and of course a favorable verdict pronounced upon it. The act of the Legislature, founded on the provisions of the old treaty, having been, as it were, re-enacted by a succeeding Legislature, was to be regarded as mandatory and imperative, to be carried into effect by the Executive under his oath of office, according to its requisitions, unless forbidden by paramount considerations; there could be none paramount, but what would be found in the Constitution of the United States, and none such were found. The Constitution itself, in denouncing an act impairing the obligation of contracts, recognized the sacredness of the treaty of the Indian Springs. The Executive of Georgia, therefore, had no alternative but to carry that treaty into effect, in conformity with the repeatedly expressed will of the Legislature. His intentions were early communicated, in the most frank and ingenuous manner, to the Executive Government at Washington, and, from that time to the present moment, he has never ceased to remonstrate and protest, on every occasion requiring it, against any act injuriously affecting interests of Georgia derived under it. But there were other reasons for maintaining the inviolability of the treaty of the Indian Springs. By that treaty, Georgia had acquired all her territory within the Creek limits; by the new, she was to acquire less; and the difference between them was, by the stipulations of the new, guarantied to the Indians forever. The Governor could in no manner recognize the power of the President and Senate, by the abrogation of the old treaty, to violate the Constitution of Georgia. The Constitution of Georgia, as well as the articles of agreement, entered into in conformity with it, had settled her permanent boundaries irrevocably. The new treaty prescribed new boundaries for Georgia, and by its perpetual guaranty made them permanent. Lands, the rightful property of Georgia, were taken from her and ceded to the Indians forever, and the jurisdiction over the river Chattahoochee, which had been secured exclusively to her by the original Charter, by her Constitution, and by the articles of agreement and cession, was divided by the new treaty between Alabama and Georgia. As no power is given by the Constitution of the United States to the Government of the United States, to alter or revoke the Constitution of a State, it would have been not merely an unpardonable indifference to her rights and honor to have submitted in silence to these palpable infractions of them, but the Chief Magistrate would have believed himself guilty of a criminal desertion of the interests of the State, if his sanction or countenance had been given to such an instrument. If the difference between the provisions of the old and new treaties had been a nominal, not a real, difference, the United States and Georgia could have proceeded in good faith, and without collision of interest, to execute either, as the one or the other was believed to be the Constitutional law; but as those provisions were variant in several particulars involving essential rights, and as one of them especially, whether so designed or not, would have effectually postponed the settlement of the country for an entire year, it could not be expected that Georgia would surrender rights, interests, and principle too, because the President of the United States considered the new treaty the Constitutional law.

The Government of either State is to be considered as an independent moral agent, having a conscience of its own, the arbiter within itself of right and wrong, to be influenced or controlled only by Divine authority; and the conscience of this Government has already passed definitively on the validity of the treaty of the Indian Springs. And here permit me to remark, that, with regard to the rights of sovereignty and jurisdiction generally, which Georgia claims under her charter, to the territory within her limits in the occupancy of the Indians, there is such a radical difference of opinion between the authorities of Georgia and those of the United States, that the harmony and tranquillity of the two Governments, so much to be cherished by all good men, can never be maintained uninterruptedly until those Indians shall have been removed. In illustration of this, it is sufficient to inform you, that, on a recent occasion, the right of Georgia to make even a reconnoissance within that territory, with a view to eventual internal improvement, was denied, and that denial accompanied by a formal protest of the President of the United States against it; and, morever, that when, about the same time, there were indications of an hostile feeling on the part of the Indians, which threatened interruption to our Commissioners engaged in running, with the consent and approbation of the United States, the dividing line between Alabama and this State, and precautionary measures were taken for their safety, Georgia was given to understand that she had no right to extend her protection to her own officers, engaged on her own soil, in carrying into effect an act of her own Legislature, against such hostility. It is vain to look into the Constitution of the United States to find what rights of sovereignty and jurisdiction, acquired under the charter over the territory within her limits, Georgia has surrendered to the Federal Government. No such surrender has been made; and yet, Georgia, in her late intercourse with the United States, has been treated in this respect as if she had no rights of sovereignty or jurisdiction at all; and this, too, whilst the laws of the United States, as well as the Articles of Agreement and Cession, distinctly recognize and proclaim them, and of course to the very same extent as they are asserted by the treaty of Hopewell and others.

The forlorn and helpless condition to which the McIntosh or friendly party of the Creeks, have been reduced by the continued persecutions to which they have been exposed, is submitted to you as claiming your humane and benevolent consideration. This portion of the Creek tribe, having fought the battles of the United States, and vanquished the hostile part of it, who were at once their enemies and the enemies of the United States, it was hoped that they would have been regarded with some degree of favor by that Government and people, in whose defence they had expended their blood, and put to hazard everything dear to them. For a time this hope was not disappointed; General Jackson, by his treaty of 1814, had recognized their services and their claims; their chieftain was distinguished by the favor of the Government, and he and his followers were regarded not only as the faithful and devoted friends of the whites, but as the conquerors of the Red Sticks, then numbering two-thirds of the whole nation, whose rights of territory, by the laws of war, passed to the victors. It was the conviction of the justice of their cause, and of the rights acquired by it, which dictated the letter of the Secretary of War, of the 17th day of March, 1817, recognizing in full the power of McIntosh and his followers to sell the country. When, in obedience to the expressed wishes of the United States, McIntosh, with others, proceeded, at the treaty of the Indian Springs, to exercise this acknowledged power, the power was denied, and the murder of himself and chiefs, which followed, looked upon without emotion, whilst the murderers were cherished, caressed and honored by the Government of the United States; his followers, left without home, without protection, without bread, and finally denationalized and put under the ban; so that, at last, they were considered as no part of the nation, having no claim of territory, and, of course, no rightful participation in the consideration for which the territory sold; and, what is worse than all, the money which should have been given to them under the treaty, not only given to their enemies, but made the instrument of seducing from their allegiance the friends of McIntosh, who had no alternative but to take the bribe or share the calamities of the party. To complete their degradation as an unworthy and ignoble race, the President, in his official message to the Senate, has deigned to stigmatize them as "an impotent and helpless minority," "unable to execute their engagements;" "as fugitives instigated by a vindictive fury," "making extravagant and unwarrantable demands, whilst they were eating the bread and begging the protection of the United States:" and again, as "a party making unwarrantable pretensions and extravagant demands, and having no claims on the United States, other than of impartial and rigorous justice." Is it to be wondered, that, under such treatment, the friendly party should be reduced to a mere remnant, *an impotent and helpless minority;* or is it not a subject of wonder, that, instead of the 1000 which remain, there should be one left bearing the name or rallying under the standard of McIntosh? We cannot permit ourselves to believe that the Congress of the United States will not itself regard with tenderness and compassion a portion of the human family, reduced by reverses to piteous distress, deserted by the inconstancy of friendship, and abandoned to the sports of fortune.

Whether, in reference to that part of the territory of Georgia yet in the occupancy of the Cherokees, you will think proper, in conformity with the recommendation to that effect, contained in a late message, to extend the laws over it as a right resulting from your general sovereignty and jurisdiction, or whether you will abide the result of future negotiations by the United States to extinguish their claims, in virtue of the compact of 1802, will be for you, as the only competent authority, to decide. A state of things so unnatural and so fruitful of evil, as an independent Government of a semi-barbarous people coexisting within the same limits, cannot long continue; and wise counsels must direct, that relations, which cannot be maintained in peace, should be dissolved before any occasion can occur to break that peace. How ungenerously tantalizing to this unhappy tribe, would be a policy inviting them to a local habitation and repose, when the fates had already decreed their destiny to be fixed and irreversible upon another soil! To perpetuate the remnant of a noble race, we ask of the United States to give them a resting place within boundaries of their own, fruitful, ample and salubrious; such as they command, and such as in humanity they should bestow; where the arts of civilization and the lights of Christianity can reach them, unmixed with the corrupting and contagious vices of the whites, and where their perpetuity and independence can be assured. If the United States hesitate now, a few years will bring them to just reflections, but too late to save from irredeemable waste and decay the numerical strength and moral energies of a people, so far preserved by the encouragement and patronage of the United States, with the tolerance of Georgia.

[The portion which is here omitted, of this paragraph, refers to the running of the line between Georgia and Alabama, by the Georgia Commissioners, with the assistance of James Camak, as Mathematician, and E. L. Thomas, as Surveyor, also, the Chief Civil Engineer, &c., and to the Governor's "entire satisfaction;" and his regrets at the non-concurrence of the Alabama Commissioners, &c., &c.

If the first bend above Uchee and Coweta and Cussetah towns, from which a line to Nickajack did not strike the river, would not satisfy the requisitions of the articles of agreement and cession, it was not to be expected that any other bend above it, and farther removed from Uchee and the towns, would. It was the less to be expected that the Commissioners of Georgia would consent to pass that bend, for no other reason than that Alabama would take more, and Georgia less, of territory by it. And when the Commissioners, without the concurrence of those of Alabama, finally adopted the point of Miller's Bend, it was the point which was about midway between that assumed as the true one by the Governor of Alabama, and the one ultimately proposed by her Commissioners to ours. As the Commissioners of Alabama would not agree to run from the first bend, immediately above Uchee, and, as a line running from that bend intersecting the river, would have made the boundary not a straight one as contemplated by the articles, but a devious one, straight upon the land and meandering on the water, it is difficult to perceive how the Government of Alabama can withhold its assent from a boundary, which, contemplated in all its aspects, would seem, at least to us, to reconcile more differences, and present fewer objections, than any.

[The residue of this paragraph refers to the expense of running the line, &c., and is omitted.]

[This part of the message, referring to Internal Improvement, will be found copied into the eighth chapter of this work.]

It is proposed, in concert with the General Government, to commence running the dividing line between this State and Florida, on the first day of December next. The correspondence in relation to it, is submitted; and it will be seen that no difficulties can be expected to arise to embarrass the operation, or to prevent the most desirable conclusion of it.

You will receive, with other documents on this subject, a communication from the Governor of South Carolina, which looks to the improvement of the navigation of the Savannah river, by a concert of measures and combination of resources of that State and this, depending on the authority of their respective Legislatures, with my answer, which will disclose to you my own views and opinions in relation to the subject, and to which it may be only necessary to add that those views and opinions remain unchanged.

[This portion of the message, referring to the completion of Schley's Digest, its approval by the Executive, &c., and recommending a digest of Common and Statute law, similar to recommendation in message of 1824, and again advising improvement of the " defective organization of our own" Judiciary system, omitted.]

Our Academic Institutions continue to flourish, and Franklin College, at the head of them, sustains its merited reputation. To its other Professorships, a Chair of Moral Philosophy, Rhetoric and Belles Lettres, has been added; and the discipline and subordination maintained by the proper authorities, are not known to be surpassed by those which prevail in the best regulated Colleges of the country.

[These portions of the message, referring to the Poor School Fund, the Militia, the Banks, and especially the Bank of Darien, omitted.]

The organization of the territory lately acquired by the treaty of the Indian Springs, will be a subject of early attention. The public reservations will particularly require a provision, which will not merely place them beyond the probability of trespass or intrusion, but will make them available, with the least possible delay, for all the benefits and advantages expected to be derived from them.

[This portion, relating to militia claims, omitted.]

The militia claims, and the territorial claims of Georgia, remaining unsatisfied for twenty or thirty years, have given rise to the unhappy differences subsisting between the Federal Government and this. It is sincerely hoped that these differences approach to an amicable termination, and that enlightened counsels, united to better feelings, will restore the harmony which it is so much the interest of both parties to cultivate and cherish. Wrong has been done to Georgia; her views misrepresented, and her character traduced; but wrong will come to right, and what prejudice has misrepresented, history will correct. That history, from infancy to the present moment, falsifies the charges by which malignancy has sought to make her odious. In all her departments, her Representatives and Magistracy, in peace and in war, have failed in nothing of their duty to the United States. To the Constitutional law, a ready and cheerful obedience has been rendered at all times. In seasons of danger, her contributions have been given without stint, and her sword drawn upon the first appeal. If for these she claims no merit, she deserves no reproach. They are the righteous only whom we acknowledge as our peers; and to their judgment we submit our actions, without bespeaking for them anything but the award due to their intrinsic merits.

I cannot conclude this message, without congratulating you on the blessings communicated to society by that universal toleration of religion, (the guaranty of our political constitutions,) by which the intolerant himself, as well as the believing and unbelieving, are exempt from all responsibility, but to their Maker; whilst the numerous sectaries of the Christian Church, differing in creeds, but united in the faith given to the sermon on the mount, preach and worship securely, almost in the same temple, spreading the benign doctrines of that sermon far and wide, impressing their sacredness by precept and example, and laying the prosperity of society in the deep foundations of a pure morality.

It becomes nations and communities, like individuals, from time to time, to render homage and adoration to the Supreme Governor of the universe, the Author of every good; to acknowledge His power; to make confession of sins; to ask their forgiveness; to supplicate His mercy, and to deprecate His wrath. It especially becomes us, the most favored of the children of men, to display our gratitude and thankfulness for the continued dispensations of His paternal goodness, by which our Independence and liberties are preserved, our industry made fruitful, and its fruits protected—physical evils averted, and moral blessings multiplied; so that the prosperity and happiness we enjoy, not only transcend our deserts, but promise a destiny more elevated than any portion of the human family has attained. To set apart a day of thanksgiving and prayer, for these past manifestations of a superintending Providence, may be thought an act of moral and religious duty not inconsistent with the high political ones which you are required to perform, and may propitiate for us, in the time to come, a continuance of the same benignant smiles which our unworthiness may forfeit, but which His loving-kindness is ever ready to dispense to the humble supplications of the good and virtuous of all nations.

Your fellow-citizen, G. M. TROUP.

Although strongly supported at home, in all the prominent measures of his administration, the Governor was yet to encounter a strength of opposition to the chief of them all—his policy in regard to the Creek Territory—from the Government at Washington; an opposition, the extent of which was hardly foreshadowed by events then transpiring, and which threatened, for a time, to end in civil strife. Indeed, at the commencement of the session, and for some time afterwards, every thing seemed to betoken an early and amicable adjustment of the difference between Georgia and the General Government. In proof of this, we need only refer to what follows.

On the 27th of November, the Secretary of War wrote to Governor Troup, that "a long and distressing illness" had prevented his replying to the Governor's letter of 6th October; but, since his partial recovery, he had submitted it to the President, who instructed him to say that the Governor appeared " to labor under a most serious mistake, in supposing that the last treaty with the Creeks" had " affected, in any manner, the boundary of Georgia ;" that there was not "a tittle in the treaty that" had " the most distant allusion to that object ;" that, not " for one moment would a discussion have been admitted thereon, as it" lay " entirely out of the competency of the General Government." He added, further, that, in wishing, anxiously, to get a cession of all the Creek lands, every effort was made, but the Indians refused; that he thought the failure to run the line between Georgia and Alabama, was an impediment in the way, &c., &c.; and that, but for this, the President would have opened fresh negotiations, &c.; and that the President would embrace the first occasion, " to carry into effect, by fresh negotiation, if practicable, the entire cession," &c., &c.

On the 9th of December, the Governor communicated to the Legislature, the letter of Mr. Barbour, by which he said it appeared " to have been the intention of the parties to the instrument called the new treaty, that Georgia should acquire all the Creek lands within her limits," &c. He

60

denied having committed "the most serious mistake" imputed to him, &c., appealed, for his justification, to "the language of the new treaty;" said it was "not necessary for the President to anticipate difficulties between Georgia and Alabama," &c.; and that, until the boundary between the two States, as established by Georgia, should be changed by them, it must be considered the true one "by all the parties concerned."

To the Secretary's letter, received on 9th December, the Governor replied on the 11th; and, after acknowledging its receipt, and stating the pleasure it afforded him of hearing of Mr. Barbour's recovery from his "late illness," added:

Whilst I cannot admit the justice of the reproof, that I had committed a most serious mistake in believing the Western line of the new treaty to have been considered as the permanent boundary of Georgia, I have no hesitation in expressing my satisfaction that the President of the United States has thought proper to declare that it was the intention of the parties to that instrument to cede to Georgia all the lands claimed by her within the Creek limits. My practice has been, when I committed involuntary error, to make confession and ask pardon. You reprove me for a mistake which is not mine, but yours; and, instead of the double atonement which a fair course of moral reciprocity would exact, I ask nothing but a magnanimous acknowledgment of the wrong done me, and will be content with a denial of even that, if there shall be no occasion in future to ask it, either for myself, or for the State I represent. If the construction was a mistaken or erroneous one, it is made so only by your recent declaration of what your intentions actually were. The language of the new treaty fully justified my construction, and I was not permitted to seek your intentions through any other medium than the language; that language describes the Western line as a permanent one, because it expressly guaranties all the lands, lying West of it, to the Indians forever.

The permanent boundary line of Georgia, as established by her Constitution, having been run and marked by her Commissioners, and the Legislature having, within a few days, sanctioned and confirmed it, by an almost unanimous voice, it is now considered, and must be considered, by all parties, as the true and settled boundary, unalterable, but by the joint consent of Georgia and Alabama. This act of the Legislature of Georgia has been announced to the Government of Alabama, and her concurrence with it is not to be doubted, because it is in strict consonance with the most rational and disinterested construction which Georgia can give to the articles of agreement and cession, and is as favorable to Alabama as any other construction she could claim; unless, indeed, she would assume, what we are persuaded she would not, the exclusive right to dictate a boundary, regardless of the letter and spirit of the articles.

The joint committee on the state of the Republic, to whom was referred so much of the Governor's Message as related to the question of boundary between Georgia and Alabama, made a report, which passed both Houses, and was approved by the Governor on 8th December, expressing the hope that the citizens of Alabama would acquiesce "after the whole grounds of dispute" should be "maturely and deliberately considered;" and concluding with the following Resolution:

"That the line run and marked from Nickajack to Miller's Bend on the Chattahoochee, is the true line contemplated by the articles of cession of 1802, between the United States and Georgia; and that it be recognized as such by the State of Georgia.*"

On the 8th December, the Governor communicated the result to Gov. Murphy, of Alabama, in a very friendly letter, from which the following extracts are made:

"I cannot but flatter myself, both from the liberal views uniformly disclosed by your Excellency, and those not less liberal which must animate the Legislature of Alabama, that your concurrence may be asked with at least a reasonable prospect of success; and that two States so nearly allied by the ties of interest and of blood, may not be separated, even for a moment, on a question in which neither interest nor principle, of any great concernment, is involved. * * * * * * Suffer me to entreat your Excellency not to permit, so far as depends on you, a controversy to be opened, which is the more likely to prove interminable, not merely because it is a controversy of boundary, but because, accord-

* In the Senate, there was no division called for; in the House, there were only *ten* votes in the negative.—ED.

ing to my best judgment, Georgia will never be satisfied with any construction of the articles different from that now adopted; and ought not to be, because you can present to her none more rational or more disinterested."

On the 22d day of December, the Governor approved a report and resolution, (understood to have been drawn by the late Judge Clayton,) on the subject of the treaties with the Creek Indians, and the differences with the General Government. The whole document is one of great beauty and ability; but, for its details, we must refer to the State papers of that date. It asserted the soil and jurisdiction of Georgia to all the territory within her chartered and Constitutional limits; condemned the threat of military force against the State, the refusal of the President to arrest and punish General Gaines for "abusing and insulting the highest authorities of a State," the retention of Col. Crowell in office, the attempted abrogation of the treaty of the Indian Springs, the assertion of the President that the authorities of Georgia had no right to enter the Indian country without the consent of the Indians, &c., &c., &c.

The Governor, also on the same day, approved a report of the Senate committee on the state of the Republic, (and which had passed both Houses,) on the subject of his special message of 9th December, communicating the letter of the Secretary of War, of 27th November, and which report protested against the new treaty, &c., &c.

A joint resolution was also approved, requesting the President to hold a treaty for the cession of the Cherokee lands within the limits of Georgia; also one requesting the Georgia Delegation to procure some relief for the friendly Indians, and satisfaction to the citizens of Georgia for supplies, &c., afforded these Indians during the troubles in 1825, &c., &c.

A resolution was adopted by the Legislature, approving the Governor's measures for protecting the frontier settlements, and authorizing him to employ military force to repel savage invasion, &c., &c. An Act was also passed, extending, to 20th February, 1827, the time for District Surveyors to make their returns for the contemplated land lottery.

In response to the Governor's suggestion, the Legislature requested him to "set apart a day of general thanksgiving and prayer."*

Soon after the adjournment of the Legislature, the Governor wrote to the Secretary of War, giving information of his having called out a military force to protect the Southern frontier from threatened danger growing out of a sudden attack by Seminoles or Lower Creeks, &c., &c.

[1827.] The reply of the Secretary, dated 16th January, 1827, to that communication, and to the previous letter of the Governor, of 11th December, was a renewal of the Indian controversy. He stated that the President had approved the conduct of the Governor in calling out the military force, and that the expenses attending the means employed by the Governor, were "a proper debit against the United States." The concluding part is all that is important for insertion here:

"I trust you will, by reference to my letter, a small part of which only I have given you, perceive how greatly you have been mistaken, (if I have understood you correctly,) in supposing that the President had declared that all the Creek land, within the limits of Georgia, was intended to have been ceded by the new treaty."†

On the 26th January, 1827, the day of the receipt of the foregoing, Gov. Troup replied to the Secretary of War, in a long and able letter, which we would be glad to publish here, in full, but for which room cannot be made. After answering the preliminary portion of Mr. Barbour's letter, and stating "that the utmost precaution had been taken to

* In fixing the first Thursday in January, 1827, the Governor, in his Proclamation, recommended that the various religious denominations, "*with repentant hearts, make grateful acknowledgment for the blessings conferred by the Universal Parent, and, with holy piety and fervent devotion, beseech the forgiveness of sins, and the continuance of His gracious mercy and goodness to us as a People.*" Amongst other causes for thanksgiving, was an abundant treasury—reported, by the joint committee on finance, at $792,122.—ED.

† On 18th January, before the receipt of the foregoing, Governor Troup, in a private letter to Dr. Daniell, said: "Our red and white friends are determined to give me employment as long as I am in office."—ED.

make the expedition as little burdensome to the United States as possible," he proceeded to state his regret that he should, "on any occasion, however innocently, have misunderstood or misrepresented," the Secretary of War; that he had immediately informed the Legislature of what he had considered the "avowed intention of the President"; admitted that on the face of the new treaty "it did not appear to have intended to acquire all the lands," but that, when, "apart from the treaty, we sought the intention of the parties in matter foreign and extraneous to the treaty, there was some reason to believe it was the intention of the parties to acquire all the land," &c., &c. Amongst other things, he referred to the repeated disclaimer of the President "to interfere in settling the boundary" between Georgia and Alabama, the rejection by the President of the line as established by Georgia, his anticipation of a controversy between the two States, and his intimation "that if some other line more satisfactory to the United States, shall not be settled by Georgia and Alabama," measures would "not be taken to acquire the fragment," &c. The whole letter showed a sincere desire for the settlement of the controversy; and it gave an interesting exhibition of the unfortunate difficulties which, as the writer believed, without the fault of Georgia, had been thrown in the way of an adjustment. It concluded as follows:

"The United States will acknowledge no boundary for Georgia that is not acknowledged by Alabama. What is this but virtually to declare the right of Alabama to dictate the boundary—a dictation to which if Georgia will not submit, she incurs the penalty denounced by the United States, of fastening upon her and her people, forever, the boundary of the instrument called the new treaty, as the permanent boundary established by her constitution?"

The day following, (27th January,) he wrote to the President, giving him information of the "frequent interruptions" suffered by the Georgia surveyors "from the Indians of the Creek nation, accompanied by indignities and insults," &c., and stating that the surveyors were "still threatened with others of more violent and outrageous character." He further stated that there was reason to believe the "Agent of Indian Affairs" was "the prime mover and instigator of the same;" and, in support of that belief, enclosed certain papers; and he desired to be informed if that officer was acting by "authority" of the President, or with his "sanction and countenance." Not supposing that, in regard to the construction of treaties, &c., the President would "transfer the sovereign attributes to a subaltern agent," &c., he added:

"If these powers have been insolently assumed by such a subaltern, for such purposes, it is not for the Governor of Georgia to dictate to the President the measures which ought to follow, as well in vindication of the honor of the United States, as in reparation of the wrongs done to Georgia. The President is competent to judge them, and the Governor doubts not his willingness to judge them rightly."

The first "paper" referred to was a letter from Wiley Williams, a District Surveyor, dated in Carroll county, 22d January, 1827, in which, complaining to the Governor of the threatened interruption of the surveys, by Indians, he, amongst other things, said:

"Eight or ten lusty fellows rode up to my camp, last night, with a letter written by Crowell, and signed by several Chiefs, and ordered me to desist from surveying the land on the west side of the new treaty line," &c., &c.

James A. Rogers, another District Surveyor, wrote on the 23d:

"Enclosed, you will find a copy of an instrument of writing, which was handed to me by a parcel of Indians, on the 21st inst.; and, after I read the letter, they demanded of me my compass, which I had to surrender to them; but after a few minutes they agreed to give me back my compass," &c., &c.

He added: "They threatened me very severe if I should be caught over Bright's line again, a surveying. I have come on to McIntosh's old place, and have stopped my hands until I hear from you," &c., &c.

The Indian paper referred to, was directed "to the surveyors running the land west of the line of the late treaty," was dated 12th January, 1827, signed by Little Prince and six others, and said:

"We, the undersigned Chiefs and head-men of the Creek nation, having learnt, with great regret, that you are engaged in surveying the lands west of the line of the late treaty, and which was not ceded by that treaty, we have again to request and demand of you, in the most friendly terms, that you will desist from stretching a chain over any of our lands not ceded by the treaty," &c., &c.

In his opening message to Congress, the President had not alluded to the difficulties with Georgia; but, on the 5th February, 1827, he sent a special communication to both Houses, submitting "a letter from the Agent of the United States with the Creek Indians, who invoke the Government of the United States, in defence of the rights and territory secured," as the message said, "to that nation by the treaty concluded at Washington," &c., &c. After stating the nature of the complaint, &c., and the considerations which had induced him to abstain "from the application of any military force," &c., &c., and that it ought "not to be disguised that the Act of the Legislature of Georgia, under the construction given to it by the Governor of that State, and the surveys made, or attempted, by his authority, beyond the boundary secured by the treaty of Washington," were "in direct violation of the supreme law of the land, set forth in a treaty which" had "received all the sanctions provided by the constitution which we had sworn to support and maintain," the message added:

"Happily distributed as the sovereign powers of the people of this Union have been, between their General and State Governments, their history has already too often presented collisions between these divided authorities, with regard to the extent of their respective powers. No instance, however, has hitherto occurred, in which this collision has been urged into a conflict of actual force. No other case is known to have happened, in which the application of military force by the Government of the Union has been prescribed for the enforcement of a law, the violation of which has, within any single State, been prescribed by a legislative act of the State. In the present instance, it is my duty to say, that if the legislative and executive authorities of the State of Georgia should persevere in acts of encroachment upon the territories secured by a solemn treaty to the Indians, and the laws of the Union remain unaltered, a superadded obligation, even higher than that of human authority, will compel the Executive of the United States to enforce the laws, and fulfil the duties of the nation, by all the force committed for that purpose to his charge. That the arm of military force will be resorted to only in the event of the failure of all other expedients provided by the laws, a pledge has been given by the forbearance to employ it at this time. It is submitted to the wisdom of Congress to determine whether any further act of legislation may be necessary or expedient, to meet the emergency which these transactions may produce."

Accompanying this message, were sundry documents; the first in order being a letter from Col. John Crowell to the Secretary of War, dated at the Creek Agency, 15th January, 1827, stating that, a few days before, the Little Prince had complained to him that "the Georgia Surveyors were surveying lands West of the line of the late treaty;" that, at the request of that Chief, and in his name, he had written to the Surveyors, requiring them to desist, but that they "persisted in their surveys to the line run by the Georgia Commissioners as the line between Georgia and Alabama," &c., &c.; that, "at the request of a number of Chiefs, with the Little Prince at their head," he had again written to the Surveyors, "in the most friendly terms," "requiring of them to stop surveying the lands West of the line of the treaty of Washington," and that "a deputation of Chiefs" had "accompanied the bearer of the letter, with the avowed intention of stopping the Surveyors," &c.

The letter concluded:

"The Chiefs have requested me to apprise you that the authorities of Georgia had extended their surveys west of the line of the treaty of Washington, thereby violating the express stipulations of that instrument, which they held to be sacred; and to implore the Government to interpose its authority to protect them in their rights under that treaty. If Georgia is permitted to violate that treaty, with impunity, why may not Alabama? And they ask, where are they to look for protection, but to the Government of the United States?"

The next document, in order, was the reply of the Secretary of War to Col. Crowell, dated 29th January, 1827; in which, after acknowledging the receipt of Colonel Crowell's letter above noticed, with "the message of the Chiefs imploring the Government to interpose its authority," &c., the Secretary said:

"The President directs me to convey to the Little Prince, and the Head-men and Warriors of the Creek Nation, his assurances that he feels the binding obligation of the treaty of Washington no less forcibly than they; and that it is his intention to execute faithfully every clause and condition thereof. To this assurance he directs me to add, further, that he will take immediate steps to secure to them all the rights, as these are guarantied in said treaty. But the President expects it of the Creek Nation, that it will not frustrate his purposes by taking any steps of a hostile character, themselves; and he enjoins it on you so to counsel them in regard to this matter, as to induce them to rely upon the protection of the United States, and leave the subject in controversy wholly to the Government. They have very properly made known their grievances, as becomes good people; and further it will be expected of them they will not go, but wait for such measures as the wisdom of the Government may devise to secure to them their rights, as these are guarantied in the treaty of Washington."

The next document, in order, was a letter from the Secretary of War to Governor Troup, dated 29th January, 1827, as follows:

Sir: Complaints have been made to the President, by the Creeks, through the United States Agent, against the instrusions of the Surveyors of Georgia on their lands, guarantied to them by the treaty concluded with them at Washington, on the 24th January, 1826. With these complaints they have united an appeal to the President, calling for his interposition to protect them in their rights, by causing this treaty to be inviolably maintained.

The pretensions under which these surveys are attempted, are in direct violation of the treaty, and, if persevered in, must lead to a disturbance of the public tranquillity. The treaty of Washington, like all other treaties which have received the constitutional sanction, is among the supreme laws of the land. Charged, by the Constitution, with the execution of the laws, the President will feel himself compelled to employ, if necessary, all the means under his control, to maintain the faith of the nation, by carrying the treaty into effect.

I have the honor to be
Your obedient servant,
JAMES BARBOUR.

Besides the foregoing, were two letters from the Secretary of War—one to John H. Morel, U. S. Marshal, and the other to Richard W. Habersham, U. S. Attorney, for the District of Georgia; one dated 29th, and the other 30th January.

To the Marshal, (enclosing the letter to Mr. Habersham,) he said:

"I am instructed to charge you to lose no time, on the receipt of the process, which will be delivered you by the Attorney, in promptly executing it, and taking the steps directed by law in such cases," &c., &c.

In his letter to Mr. Habersham, the Secretary of War, after reciting that "official information" had been received by the President, "that certain persons, under the pretense of surveying," had "entered the lands of the Creek Indians, directly in violation of the late treaty," &c., "and directly in violation of the law of Congress, regulating intercourse with the Indian tribes," said:

"The chiefs and warriors of this tribe have appealed to the President for protection, by whom I am now instructed to direct you, without a moment's delay, to proceed to obtain the proper process with which to arrest them, which process you will cause to be delivered to the Marshal of the District, that they may be made amenable to law,"* &c., &c.

* It is hardly necessary to add that no arrests were made; but it is due to the memory of that patriotic Georgian, Richard W. Habersham, to state, that, after taking such preliminary steps as he deemed necessary to prevent embarrassment to the U. S. Government, he

The last paper, in order, was a letter from the Secretary of War to Lieut. J. R. Vinton, of the U. S. Army; in which, after stating the "official information" received by the President, in regard to the conduct of the surveyors, and other "information, though unofficial," that the Indians had "interposed and prevented" the completion of the surveys, and that the chiefs and warriors had "appealed to the President to protect them in their rights," he added:

"In this posture of affairs, it has been determined to dispatch a special agent, for the purpose of bearing dispatches to the Governor of Georgia, and to the District Attorney and Marshal of the United States for that State, and also to the Agent of the Creek Indians, to endeavor, if possible, to prevent a resort to violent measures, either by the authorities of Georgia or the Indians. Confiding alike in your zeal, capacity and discretion, I have determined to select you for this service.

"On the receipt of your instructions, you will proceed, with the least possible delay, to Milledgeville, and deliver the letter addressed to Governor Troup, with your own hands, as also to the Attorney and Marshal. Should Gov. Troup give you an answer, either verbal or written, you will communicate it by mail; as also the receipt from the District Attorney and Marshal, of the instructions with which you will be charged for them. Having accomplished this part of the duty assigned you, you will proceed to the Creek Agency, and deliver the letter addressed to Col. Crowell. Any information you may obtain in reference to the object of your mission, you will promptly communicate by mail; particularly, any acts of violence which may have occurred, or which may be threatened. Carefully abstain from any remarks which may disclose your object, and be still more careful not to indulge in any commentary on the affair, which may subject you to personal difficulty."

Lieut. Vinton delivered the Secretary's letter to Gov.

---

resigned his office, in a letter to the Hon. Henry Clay, Secretary of State, in which, after declining to appear for the prosecution, he added: "In a contest in which the interests and character of Georgia are so deeply involved, I should feel myself unworthy of the office I hold, and of the confidence which the President has hitherto reposed in me, if, contrary to my views of right, and the higher duties I owe to my native State, I could array myself against her."—ED.

Troup, on the 17th February. The following is the reply:

EXECUTIVE DEPARTMENT, GEORGIA,
Milledgeville, 17*th Feb.*, 1827.

Sir: I received, this afternoon, from Lieut. Vinton, your letter of the 29th ult., and read, within the same hour, both it and the copy of it as published in the National Intelligencer of the 7th inst. No room was left to mistake the meaning of this dispatch. Lieut. Vinton announced himself, in an introductory note, a copy of which is herewith transmitted, as the Aid of the Commanding General; and you are sufficiently explicit as to the means by which you propose to carry your resolution into effect. Thus the military character of the menace is established, and I am only at liberty to give it the defiance which it merits. You will distinctly understand, therefore, that I feel it to be my duty to resist, to the utmost, any military attack which the Government of the United States shall think proper to make on the territory, the people, or the sovereignty of Georgia; and all the measures necessary to the performance of this duty, according to our limited means, are in progress. From the first decisive act of hostility, you will be considered and treated as a public enemy; and, with the less repugnance, because you, to whom we might constitutionally have appealed for our own defence against invasion, are yourselves the invaders, and, what is more, the unblushing allies of the savages whose cause you have adopted.

You have referred me, for the rule of my conduct, to the treaty of Washington, "which, like all other treaties which have received the constitutional sanction, is among the supreme laws of the land," and which the President is therefore bound to carry into effect "by all the means under his control." In turn, I take the liberty to refer you to a treaty of prior date and prior ratification, concluded at the Indian Springs, a copy of the proclamation of which under the sign manual of the President, I have the honor to enclose. On a comparison of dates, the President may think proper to remind the Congress that the old grant claims preference to the new; and that, when vested rights have passed, the old treaty, like the old grant, has preference of the new.

You have deemed it necessary to the personal safety of Lieut. Vinton, to impose on him the injunction of profound secrecy, in the execution of your orders, whilst you cause to be published, at Washington, the very instructions which disclose those orders and enjoin that secrecy, and which in fact reached this place, by the public prints, even before Lieut. Vinton had had an opportunity to deliver your dispatch. You mistake the character of the people of Georgia. Officers of the United States, engaged in the performance of their lawful duties, have only to deport themselves as gentlemen, to find the same security and protection in Georgia, as under the ægis of the government at Washington.*

I have the honor to be your obedient servant,

G. M. TROUP.

Hon. James Barbour, Secretary of War.

The following orders were forthwith issued:

EXECUTIVE DEPARTMENT, GEORGIA,
Milledgeville, 17*th Feb.*, 1827.

Ordered, That the Attorney and Solicitors General of this State, in every instance of complaint made of the arrest of any Surveyor, engaged in the survey of the late acquired territory, by any civil process, under the authority of the Government of the United States, do take all necessary and legal measures to effect the liberation of the person so arrested, and to bring to justice, either by indictment or otherwise, the officers or parties concerned in such arrestation, as offenders against the laws and violators of the peace and personal security of the public officers and citizens of this State: That they give professional advice and assistance, in their defence against any prosecution or action which may be instituted against them as officers in the service of the State, and that they promptly make known to this Department their acts and doings in the premises. It is moreover enjoined on the civil magistrates of this State, having competent jurisdiction of the same, to be aiding and assisting in inquiring into the cause of every such arrest or detention, as aforesaid, that the person may be discharged forthwith, if illegally or unjustly detained, and in affording such redress to the aggrieved or injured party as by law he may be entitled to receive.†

By the Governor: E. H. PIERCE,
Secretary.

---

* In speaking of this reply, the Legislature of 1827 said it was "the more satisfactory, because, unlike some recreant threats, that are made for *effect* and *intimidation*, it was backed by a preparation so grave and determined, as to relieve it from all suspicion of being *idle* or *unmeaning*."—ED.

† Three days afterwards, the Governor addressed a "circular" to the Attorney and Solicitors General, in which he said: "In carrying into effect the order of the 17th inst., you are instructed to assume and support the inapplicability of the penal Statute of the United States, as quoted in the President's late message, to the case of an officer engaged in the service of a

HEAD-QUARTERS, Milledgeville, 17th Feb., 1827.

The Major-Generals commanding the 6th and 7th Divisions, will immediately issue orders to hold in readiness the several regiments and battalions within their respective commands, to repel any hostile invasion of the territory of this State. Depots of arms and ammunition, central to each Division, will be established in due time.

By the Commander-in-Chief:

JOHN W. A. SANFORD,
Aid-de-Camp.

It is unnecessary to detail the various measures which the Governor took, to put the State in an attitude of defence, according to the "limited means" at his command. The controversy had at length reached a crisis; the argument had been exhausted, and either party might be considered as saying to the other:

"My commission
Is not to reason of the deed, but do it."

Happily, however, better counsels were to prevail at Washington. It was soon perceived that the threat of military force could have no effect upon Georgia or her Governor; and, fortunately, a resort to arms was not tried.

The President's Message produced a sensation in Congress. In the Senate, it was referred to a special committee of *five*; and, in the House, to a committee of *seven*.*

---

sovereign State, under the authority of its laws—that Statute having relation only to private individuals trespassing upon lands in the possession of the Indians. The distinction, too, between trespasses committed on such lands, claimed by the United States, or by the State, will be obvious to you. You will not neglect, on any occasion requiring it, to assert, in its most ample latitude, the right of sovereignty and jurisdiction of the State over all the lands within her chartered limits, and, consequently, the absolute right of survey at all times, as necessarily appertaining to that sovereignty and jurisdiction."—ED.

* In moving its reference, with the accompanying documents, in the Senate, Mr. Berrien made a speech of some length; and, amongst other things, speaking of a resort to military force, said: "If such an exercise of power may find the color of justification, under existing laws, does it not become us, as the guardians of the rights of the States, by some clear and explicit act of legislation, to take from such an exercise of prerogative the shadow of pretense?"

In the House, Mr. Forsyth was the principal speaker from Georgia. Amongst other things, he said: "He rejoiced that, at length, the strange circumstances of this case had been presented to the House in such a form as to compel the rendering of a solemn decision between the Executive and the State of Georgia, and that it was called for at this time—not by them, for they had been demanding it for years past—but that now the call came from the Executive. He could not, however, as a Representative of Georgia, consent to sit and quietly hear the charges brought forward in this communication against the authorities of that State.

The report of the House committee, (which, with the documents appended to it, occupies more than eight hundred pages of printed matter,) was presented on 3d March, and was thoroughly against Georgia. It recommended the expediency of procuring "a cession of the Indian lands in the State of Georgia," and "that, until such a cession is procured, the law of the land, as set forth in the treaty of Washington, ought to be maintained, by all necessary constitutional and legal means."

On the report being read, Mr. Drayton, one of the committee, moved a substitute, recognizing, to the fullest extent, the rights of Georgia. "He expressed his readiness to discuss the questions, but preferred not to do so then."

The report of the Senate committee, presented on 1st March, although not so elaborate, took a conciliatory view of the questions, and deprecated, in such cases, "the resort to force," which, it said, "would be alike vain and nugatory." It concluded with recommending the following resolution:

"*Resolved*, That the President of the United States be respectfully requested to continue his exertions to obtain, from the Creek Indians, a relinquishment of any claim to lands within the limits of Georgia."

As Congress adjourned on the 3d of March, nothing further was done in the premises; and, indeed, the whole question was about to be settled speedily and peaceably.

On the 31st of January, two days after the date of his letter by Lieut. Vinton, the Secretary of War wrote, as follows, to Col. Crowell:

"Since my letter to you, of 29th inst., the Department has had information submitted to it, which appears to be entitled to respect, that, on a proper representation being made to the Chiefs, of the peculiar state of things as they now exist in regard to the remainder of their lands within the limits of Georgia, they will not object, for a suitable moneyed consideration, to sell. This information, and

---

They had done nothing which violated the Constitution of the country. *He would say this in the face of the Executive.*" The Senate Committee consisted of Messrs. Benton, Berrien, Van Buren, Smith, of S. C., and Harrison; the House Committee consisted of Messrs. Edward Everett, Powell, Cocke, Drayton, Whittelsey, Lawrence and Buckner.—ED.

which is from a source of great respectability, is, in substance, that the Indians would sell this remaining portion of their lands within the limits of that State, if they were assured of a prompt and suitable compensation. I therefore enjoin it on you, as a duty of great importance, to adopt such mode as may seem in your discretion to be best, to obtain their consent to relinquish their hold upon these pine barrens, which can be of no value to them; and thus secure that state of quiet, which it is so much the desire of the Executive to realize. On ascertaining the views of the Chiefs, you will communicate them to the Department; and also, at the same time, the amount of the consideration money which they will be willing to receive for those lands."

The publication of the foregoing letter presented to Gov. Troup the occasion for writing the following, which is amongst the noblest of his many noble productions. It was published, immediately, by the Georgia Delegation, through the columns of the National Intelligencer, and must have had a happy effect in tranquilizing the public mind on the subject of Georgia's Indian difficulties. How wide of the mark was the observation of the editor of Niles' Weekly Register, on republishing this letter, when he said: "We shall only say, for the present, that, if Gov. Troup *has been* right, this Union is held together only by a *rope of sand*, and is not worth an effort to preserve it!"

EXECUTIVE DEPARTMENT, GEORGIA,
Milledgeville, 21*st Feb.*, 1827.

Gentlemen: I was glad to learn, by the mail of to-day, that measures have been taken by the President, subsequently to the communication of the Secretary of War, of the 29th ult., to procure the lands left out by the instrument called the new treaty. I have uniformly urged this measure on the General Government, from the moment it professed a willingness, contingently, to adopt it, and in no part of the correspondence more strenuously than in my letter to the Secretary of War, of the 26th January, a copy of which was transmitted to you by the last mail. It was known to me, that a sincere desire to procure them, accompanied by corresponding efforts, could not fail of success, and I had felt both surprise and regret that any reluctance had been manifested to have recourse to the necessary measures without delay. The reasons assigned for the postponement, were, in no aspect of them, satisfactory; and so the President was informed in a candid and amicable spirit. You are at liberty to state to the councils before whom you represent the interests and rights of this State, what has been repeatedly represented to the President himself, that the Governor of Georgia has never, at any time, entertained the idea of resorting to military force to counteract measures of the Government of the United States, but on the occasion when it was deemed better in honor, in conscience, and in duty, to sacrifice every thing we hold dear, than unresistingly to submit. On the last occasion, when military coercion was threatened, the President was promptly and candidly informed of my resolution to meet that coercion in a military manner. So far as a determination was expressed to resort to the civil process, it was decided to resort to the like process to sustain, according to the Constitution and laws of the United States, and the Constitution and laws of the State, the public officers of Georgia engaged in the execution of their duties under the orders directly of its Legislative and Executive authorities —an obligation, on our part, enjoined by the very sanction which the President, in his late message, refers to, as being paramount to any human power, and, of course, equally imperative with us as with him. I cannot acknowledge a power in the United States, to bring before its judicial tribunals, for trial, and judgment, and punishment, the Governor, or Judges, or Representatives, or other officers, as such, acting under the authority of the Constitution and laws of the States. Whilst, therefore, no intention exists to resist the civil authority of the United States, I consider myself bound to afford to officers of Georgia, acting under my orders, all the protection I can, consistently with the Constitution and laws; and I can never admit that wrongs done by officers of the United States to officers of the State, shall not be inquired into and redressed by the State tribunals.

I consider all questions of mere sovereignty as matter for negotiation between the States and the United States, until the competent tribunal shall be assigned by the Constitution itself, for the adjustment of them.

I am not wanting in confidence in the Supreme Court of the United States, in all cases falling within their acknowledged jurisdiction. As men, I would not hesitate to refer our cause to their arbitration or umpirage. On an amicable issue made up between the United States and ourselves, we might have had no difficulty in referring it to them as judges, protesting, at the same time, against the jurisdiction, and saving our rights of sovereignty. If the United States will, with or without the consent of Georgia, make a question before the Supreme Court, it will be for the Government of Georgia ultimately to submit, or not, to the decision of that tribunal. But, acccording to my limited conception, the Supreme Court is not made, by the Constitution of the United States, the arbiter in controversies involving rights of sovereignty between the States and the United States. The Senate of the United States may have so considered it, because it has been proposed to make that honorable body itself the arbiter and umpire between them. The States cannot consent to refer to the Supreme Court, as of right and obligation, questions of sovereignty between them and the United States, because that Court, being of exclusive appointment by the Government of the United States, will make the United States the judge in their own cause. This reason is equally applicable to a State tribunal. Hence, the difficulties likely to arise even by a resort to the civil process; and thus you will perceive how infinitely preferable it is to carry into effect immediately the measure contemplated by the instructions to the Agent.

It is indeed to be lamented, that a person so well known here for his unfitness, should have been charged with such an office; but this very knowledge will make the failure, if the failure happen, not our fault, but the fault of his employers.

Of all the wrongs wantonly and cruelly inflicted, none have been borne with more patience than the charge of seeking a dissolution of the Union. My intentions have been to cement and perpetuate it, by preserving, inviolate, the rights of the parties to the compact, without which the compact would be of no value; and to this end I have unceasingly labored. Time may probably disclose that a very imperfect judgment had erred in the adoption of the best means; but the intentions will remain the same, and He who must finally judge, will certainly not mistake them.

Hoping that the President will not fail in the contemplated negotiation, and that the matters in difference may be speedily and amicably adjusted to the entire satisfaction of the parties in controversy, I have not hesitated to make you this frank disclosure and explanation, that you may use it, at your discretion, to promote the peace and harmony which ought ever to subsist between the States and the

United States, and in which I assure you none can feel deeper concern than

Yours, very respectfully,

G. M. TROUP.

The Honorable Senators and Representatives
from Georgia, in Congress of the
United States.

[1827.] On the first Monday in May, elections for county officers were held in the new counties laid off from the lands ceded by the treaty of the Indian Springs; and, the surveys having been completed, the Lottery was carried on with so much expedition, that the Georgia Journal, of 22d May, announced the organization and settlement of the new country. What had been a savage wilderness, was now becoming a garden; and although Gov. Troup's term of office expired before the recognition, by the discontented Creeks, of the title of Georgia to all their lands within her limits, yet this was accomplished by Articles of Agreement concluded with them at the Creek Agency on the 15th of November, 1827, and which were duly ratified on the 4th of March, 1828.

By these articles, it was expressed, that "they, the chiefs and headmen aforesaid, agree to cede, and they do hereby cede, to the United States, all the remaining lands now owned or claimed by the Creek Nation, not heretofore ceded, and which, on actual survey, may be found to lie within the chartered limits of the State of Georgia." [For these Articles, in full, see vol. 7 of United States Statutes at Large, pages 307, 308 and 309.]

The following letter will properly conclude this chapter:

MILLEDGEVILLE, Feb. 24th, 1827.

My Dear Sir: It was impossible for me, consistently with my views of right, to acquiesce in any of the measures proposed to be adopted by the General Government. It never was my intention to resist the civil process by a military force, unless they first resorted to a military force to enforce it. It always was my intention, when they resolved to proceed *civiliter*, to give our officers all the protection which our civil magistracy could afford them under the Constitution and laws. Our magistrates are bound to extend this protection, so far as it is not inconsistent with the Constitution of the U. S. The Constitution of the U. S. would not authorize an Act of Congress which would make the public officers of the State answerable to their judicial tribunals. The Act of Congress, referred to by the President, cannot, either in its letter or according to its intent, embrace such officers; and of this our own judicial tribunals are competent judges. What would be our situation, if the public officers were answerable exclusively to the judicial tribunals of the U. S., under any Acts of Congress which would make them criminals before such tribunals?—and what difference is there in this respect between the Governor, or Judges, and a surveyor? The President himself acknowledges, in his message, that the surveyors are not to be viewed as individuals, but as agents of a sovereign State, acting in obedience to authority which they believe to be binding on them. No State can have, rightfully, any claims to sovereignty, which makes its officers dependent for their protection, in the discharge of their duties, on the power of another State. I assure you, my dear friend, I have made as much of concession on this subject as I thought any of our friends could reasonably ask of me. Those at Washington have been extremely anxious about the measures which might be taken here; and I have endeavored, so far as propriety would permit, not to commit them by any of an odious or censurable character. I trust that the real friends of the country will nowhere so consider them. If they do, I will lament it, because it has been on their account that I have been particularly cautious to avoid it.

Remember me affectionately to the family, and particularly to my little friend. Tell him that I might have been to see him before this, but for John Quincy Adams.

Yours, very affectionately,

G. M. TROUP.

Dr. Daniell.

CHAPTER XIII.

Retirement of Governor Troup from the Executive Chair.—His last Annual Message.—Declines a Public Entertainment at Milledgeville, and a Public Dinner at Savannah.—Election to the United States Senate, in 1828.—Course in Congress.—Political opinions, &c.—His resignation and final retirement from public life.

WITH the exception of the events already noticed, the year 1827 was prolific of not much of interest in the history of Georgia. In March, Governor Troup received official notice of the adjustment of the claims of Georgia for payment of the troops that performed military services against the Indians in the years 1792, 1793 and 1794—a measure that had been urged for many years, before Congress, by himself and others of the Delegations from Georgia.

As soon as it was certainly known that Governor Troup would, under no circumstances, permit the use of his name in connection with the succeeding canvass for Governor, the public generally looked forward to Mr. Forsyth as his successor in that high office. Col. Duncan G. Campbell, whose name has been so frequently mentioned in connection with the Indian treaty of 1825, and one of the noblest men in the State, was brought forward by his friends, for the office, but he formally retired from the contest; and Capt. Matthew Talbot, who was then announced as a candidate, died before the election; so that Mr. Forsyth was chosen, with hardly a show of opposition.

On the 20th of October, a meeting of citizens of Milledgeville was held, with the view of tendering to the retiring Governor a public entertainment. To the letter of the committee, in which they spoke of the "personal regard" of the citizens of Milledgeville, the "high estimation" in which they held his "official conduct," and the "auspicious results, for the public good," to which he had brought his measures, "under every difficulty and embarrassment," he returned the following answer:

MILLEDGEVILLE, October 25th, 1827.

Gentlemen: I take the earliest opportunity to acknowledge the receipt, (last evening,) of your note of the 22nd inst., and to ask the favor of you—whilst you return my grateful thanks to my friends of Milledgeville for the undeserved testimony of their esteem and approbation, which it conveyed—to make known to them my resolution to decline the honor so generously intended. It is enough that they shall have been pleased to consider me worthy of such testimony; and my regrets at parting with them would only be increased in the degree in which they should, to the last hour, have increased their kindness to me.

Accept for yourselves, gentlemen, the expression of my sincere friendship and highest consideration.

G. M. TROUP.

Messrs. Camak, Lamar and
Boykin, Committee.

The Legislature convened on the 5th of November. Hon. Thomas Stocks was re-elected President of the Senate, and Irby Hudson, Esq., Speaker of the House. On the 6th, the Governor sent in, to each House, the following, being his last Annual Message, which is considerably abridged for want of space:

EXECUTIVE DEPARTMENT, GEORGIA,
Milledgeville, Nov. 6th, 1827.

Fellow-Citizens: In making known to you the events of the passing year, it is equally my duty to communicate those which give pain as those which afford pleasure, so that, without concealment or suppression, all may be embodied in the history of the times—our successors will take counsel from them, and the experience of the past will be equally profitable, whether it furnish examples of good to be imitated, or of evil to be avoided.

Before the close of the last session of the Legislature, hope was indulged that the controversy between the Government of this State and that of the United States, was happily terminating: and so indeed to all appearances it was. The surveys of the recently acquired territory, so long resisted, had proceeded with little or no interruption—

the last of them were about to be completed—the Indian irritation had exhausted itself in a few demonstrations of hostility; and when calmness and tranquillity had succeeded to excitement and clamor, and nothing remained to satisfy the Indian for his imaginary wrongs, but a trifling consideration in money, the Executive Government at Washington seized the occasion as a fit one to denounce the Executive of Georgia as the violator of the faith of treaties, and the lawless invader of Indian rights; to forbid the prosecution of the surveys, and to threaten the employment of military force to coerce obedience to its commands; a menace, which, without being unprecedented on the part of that Government, was yet so ill-timed and unexpected, that but one reception and but one treatment could be given to it. The documents, herewith transmitted, will disclose the manner of that reception and treatment; the message of the President to Congress, communicating this measure, left no doubt as to its motives and its objects. The councils and people of Georgia were to be subdued, at all events, into a recognition of the validity of the instrument called the new treaty; by civil process, if civil process would answer; by military force, if it would not; indeed, by all means civil or military, as enjoined by a superadded obligation, (to use the language of the President,) even higher than that of human authority. It could not be seen why, under a Government of laws, the civil remedy might not suffice, being, if not so prompt, at least ample and appropriate; or why, if resorted to at all, it should not be exclusively depended on. The alternative of a resort to the military, on failure of the civil remedy, or the resort to both, concurrently, for the redress of the same wrong, is not the theory, and has not been, hitherto, the practice of this Government; whenever it shall become so, there will be no longer any difference, in substance, between our own Constitution of Government and that of the most arbitrary and despotic. It was impossible to doubt, therefore, from the unconstitutional character of the menace, from its unreasonableness, and from the appalling consequences which must inevitably follow its execution, that the temper which dictated it was hostile to Georgia, and bent on her humiliation or destruction. The councils of Georgia could never recede, without the most degrading humiliation, from the positions taken in support of the treaty of the Indian Springs; it was the professed object of the menace to produce that recession; and it was obviously better for Georgia to run the hazard of being stricken from the roll of States, than by a passive submission to surrender, with important interests and essential rights, what was infinitely more important and more essential, character; but other rights and interests than those of Georgia were concerned. The doctrine assumed in justification of the menace, involved the rights of all the States; it asserts the broad power for the Executive of the General Government, in any controversy between a State and the United States, to decide the right and wrong of that controversy, promptly, absolutely and finally, without appeal, and to enforce such decision by the sword; a power most awful, tremendous, and unnatural, and not given by the Constitution even to the Congress. In such a contest, Georgia could make no sacrifice too dear, because she contended in a just and righteous cause, not for herself alone, but for all the States, whose honor, dignity and independence were alike at stake. Happily for the country, the enforcement of this measure has not been as yet attempted; whether on reconsideration it has been yielded to more deliberate suggestions and more prudent counsels, or decided as wholly indefensible, and therefore impracticable, or reserved for some other and future occasion, is not known to me, and can only be conjectured; it is reasonable, at least charitable to conclude, that, what in this respect ought to be done, has been done, and that wisdom and moderation can find no amends for the calamities of a civil war, in the transfer from Georgia to the Indians of a comparatively worthless fraction of territory, which, but for the principle involved, this Government would not deign to make a subject of angry contention with that of the United States.

[One of the paragraphs, here omitted, refers entirely to the extinguishment of the title to Cherokee lands, and is similar to views presented in the Annual Message of 1826; the other omitted paragraph refers to the memorial of the preceding Legislature to the President, on the same subject.]

Connected with other subjects of disagreement with the Government of the United States, is that of the dividing line between Florida and this State, directed to be run and marked by several resolutions of the Legislature. The concurrence of the General Government being necessary to the perfection of this measure, it was repeatedly invited and eventually obtained. A highly respectable gentleman, and late Governor of Virginia, Thomas M. Randolph, having been appointed the Commissioner on the part of the United States, and Thomas Spalding, the Commissioner on the part of Georgia, they proceeded in a spirit of harmony and concert to the execution of their trust; and I am happy to inform you, that, without bringing their labors to a termination most desirable, they closed them with no interruption of that spirit; on the contrary, with an improvement of it corresponding to the intelligence, patriotism and liberal sentiments which distinguish them.

[A portion of this paragraph is omitted; but it is believed that the concluding part embodies all that is necessary to the understanding of Gov. Troup's views on the subject of the line between Georgia and Florida.]

If the point established by Ellicott, had, by the Commissioners of the United States and Georgia, been found to coincide with the head or source of the St. Mary's, the Commissioner of Georgia would have been instructed to proceed. It was ascertained that they did not coincide, and his progress was accordingly arrested. You will observe that the first question presenting itself for settlement between the two Governments, is, whether the point arbitrarily agreed on by Ellicott and the Spanish Commissioner as the head of the St. Mary's, now ascertained not to be the head even of the stream pursued by Ellicott, shall be considered as the true head under the treaty of 1795. The other and only remaining question, will be, which is the true source or head of the St. Mary's. To enable you to act understandingly on these questions, as well as to afford some satisfaction to the Government of the United States, which must undoubtedly revise its proceeding, I had instructed a competent Agent, the same who acted as the Surveyor and Artist under the Commissioners, and who approved himself worthy of their highest confidence, to proceed to an examination of the several branches of the St. Mary's, for the purpose of ascertaining, by actual admeasurement, the true head or source of that river. The correspondence and documents on this subject, together with his report, are submitted. It will be seen that of the three branches forming the St. Mary's, viz.: the Northern, Western and Southern branches, the Southern is not only the longest by two or three miles, and having a direction corresponding most naturally with the general course and disemboguement of the river, but discharges eight times more water than either of the other branches, and one third more than both of them united, including various other tributary streams—that, of the three, the North branch, viz: that pursued by Ellicott, is the most inconsiderable, discharging, in proportion even to the Western branch, as two to three, and, in proportion to the Southern branch, as five to forty-three; and indeed that it is even more inconsiderable than another stream, (the Alligator,) south of it, and running between it and the Western branch. If these facts are confirmed to the satisfaction of the Government of the United States, the conclusion will be irresistible, even by itself, that we must follow, not the error or mistake of Ellicott, but the language of the treaty; not the point arbitrarily determined as the head of the St. Mary's, but the true head; and that the true head or source of the St. Mary's is to be found, not at the extremity of the Northern, but at the extremity of the Southern, branch; and that from this point the line must be run, according to the letter of the charter of Georgia, of the treaty of '83, of the treaty of '95, and of the Constitution of Georgia. This detail, so inconsistent with the generalizing character of a message, will find an apology in the extreme reluctance which I feel to open a new controversy with the Government of the United States—the great delicacy of the question, (being one of boundary,)—the extent of territory, (more than two thousand square miles,) which may be involved in it, and the obvious propriety, therefore, in stating the question for the first time, to state it fairly and fully.

It gives me great pleasure to inform you that recent acts of the General Government, and of its different departments, bespeak a return to good feelings, and give an earnest of future good understanding, which it has been the sincere desire, as it is the duty, of this Government, to cultivate. Our militia claims, so constantly and sedulously, but unavailingly, urged before that Government for twenty or thirty years, have been recognized, and, under circumstances, warranting the belief that some grains of prejudice had mingled with the former repeated considerations of them, and that nothing was wanting to a prompt acknowledgment of their justice at all times, but calm, dispassionate and impartial investigation. They are in a course of liquidation and settlement.

[The part of the message, here omitted, relates to expenses of military expedition for defence against Indians, and expenses of running and marking Georgia and Florida line.]

Among the various violations of the Constitution of the United States, the people of the Southern States have lately been made to feel and to complain of that prominent one which has taken from the States the general guardianship over the labor and industry of the people, which, it was supposed, exclusively belonged to them, and which, it is believed, they never have voluntarily relinquished. It is in the exercise of this guardianship that the Congress proceed, from session to session, to tax one portion of the community, not interested in a particular branch of industry, to sustain another portion interested in, and carrying on, that branch. Disregarding the liberal principles which would leave industry free to seek its own employment, and returning to the benighted policy long practiced by other nations, but now abandoned and abandoning by all enlightened ones, it claims an absolute dominion over it, to fetter, to restrain, to encourage, to prohibit, to cause it to take any or every direction—thus substituting, for the natural order of things, the artificial system of the darker ages. The power, which, in raising revenue or regulating commerce, incidentally protects manufactures, or encourages the fabrics which are indispensable to the national defence, is a very different power from that claimed by the Federal Government, to protect by any means, directly or indirectly, all or any of them, than which a more distinct substantive and important power could not be given by any constitution to any government. It is in vain that they ask for the grant of this mighty power to Congress. It is in vain we plead the cruelty of taking from the small profits of agriculture, to increase the large profits of manufactures. We are answered, from year to year, by an amended tariff, augmenting the tribute and multiplying the exactions. Nay, more: as if the Congress lacked vigor and animation for the work, a combination of States exclusively interested in perpetuating these abuses, resolve themseves into a body unknown to the constitution, and dictate to the Government at Washington the kind and amount of tax which the people of other States shall pay; so that we may soon have to ask ourselves, which is the Government of the United States, the assembly of States which passes the edict of taxation, or the authorities of more regular and constitutional appointment which receive it as law and order its registration. I recommend to you the adoption, without delay, of a firm remonstrance to the Congress against this system of usurpation, injustice and oppression. You will address yourselves, I know, to a formidable government, having the power, for certain purposes, over the purse and the sword, and now claiming and exercising the power to direct the national industry and national improvement, without limitation—in short, the absolute masters of the fortunes of twelve millions of people. But you can yet speak in the language of truth, if not in the spirit of freemen. Your complaints may be unheeded. If they should be, I recommend to you to address yourselves to the States having common interest with yourselves, and to suggest the expediency of concurring in a non-consumption agreement to be carried into effect by all the means which are constitutionally given to their respective Legislatures. It is painful to contemplate the consequences which must follow. That government, whose parental duty it is make us all friends and keep us so, is straining its faculties to fasten upon the country a system which cannot fail to set one part of it in hostile array against the other. In self-defence, we are first driven to a non-consumption, which, in the end, must prove a non-intercourse, and, as a necessary consequence of that, to the cultivation of more friendly relations with foreigners, who, supplying our indispensable wants, at least so long as the General Government suffers them to be supplied, will take the place of our own countrymen, in our feelings and affections, leaving nothing for them but bitterness and heart-burnings. We are not unwilling to give to our own countrymen the same profits we give to foreigners, provided they are fairly and constitutionally earned. It is the forced consumption of an article, unconstitutionally enhanced in price, which, like the forced consumption of the tea, we resist. All things being equal, we are not unwilling to consume the fabrics of our own country, and so far to encourage the fabricators; but we protest against the artificial encouragement given at our expense, when we are made to pay, not only the tax for that encouragement, but to lose the trade in our staple, which affords the only means of paying it. It is not to be expected that foreign nations will long continue to receive our raw material, if we refuse to receive their manufactures; and we are not used to that despotism which would constrain us, whether for or against our interest, to manufacture for ourselves against our inclination.

Conscientiously believing that the Government of the United States is not conducted according to the principles of the Constitution—that powers are claimed and exercised by it, in derogation of those principles, and that in practice it is virtually a consolidated government, and therefore essentially different from that formed and designed to be formed by the convention of '87, I would recommend to you, at the same time, to address a respectful and affectionate memorial to your sister States, requesting them to unite with you in all constitutional and legitimate measures to bring back the Government to the pure principles of Mr. Jefferson's administration, which are the true principles of the Constitution. It is a subject of sincere congratulation, that, notwithstanding your temptations have not been less than others', you remain uncorrupted by the assumed powers of the General Government over the Internal Improvement of the country. Other States which have surrendered this birthright, will find no compensation in the promised equivalent, as principle has never yet found its value in the weight or measure of the precious metals.

[A part of the message, here omitted, refers exclusively to Internal Improvement, and will be found copied into the Eighth Chapter of this work. The next thirteen paragraphs, referring to a Court of Errors, to the Penitentiary, reports on defects in the Penal Code, the Finances of the State, State Treasury, the University, Academies, the faults of the Militia system, encouragement of Agriculture, to Banks, and some matters of temporary interest, are here omitted.]

Retiring from office, after four years administration of the public affairs, it would have given me pleasure to congratulate you on the safety of the Republic, the flourishing condition of the country, and, above all, on the union and happiness of the people. That the Republic is yet safe, and that the country is still prosperous, we are indebted more to Divine Providence, than to our own merits. That the strifes and contentions of party have scarcely ceased to distract the public mind, to embitter social intercourse and impair the energies of society, we owe to the weakness and perverseness of human nature. The boisterous passions, the offspring of political dissensions, and in the conflicts of which reason is suspended, are not to be allayed on the instant, but by Him who can stay the tempest and bid the waves be still. No matter what the perils—no matter what the calamities which beset the country, experience has proven that in all countries these disastrous passions seek only a selfish gratification, regardless of the public interest. In our own, they have had their ferocious march, and their guilty triumphs. Formidable at the beginning, and fostered by events, they harrassed the progress of this administration under its greatest trials, and embarrassed its councils at every step. It is well that little could be claimed from abilities so moderate under circumstances so adverse. We may be content and thankful, that if nothing has been won, everything has not been lost—that the exasperations of the struggle are subsiding, and that, in the prospect before us, there is nothing so discourage or dismay. You have, therefore, fellow-citizens, every motive, as men, and every obligation, as Christians, to banish discord and to cultivate peace—to discard the passions which become children more than men—to separate yourselves from names, the best of which are comparatively worthless, and attach yourselves to principles, which are unchangeable, and which cannot fail you in your utmost need: in fine, to think and act as brethren of the same family, allied by a common interest and a common destiny, of which the universal Parent will be the guardian and protector. It is the best, as it is the last, advice I can give; and, returning to private life, I invoke the blessing of God upon our country, and bid you farewell.

G. M. TROUP.

The inauguration of Governor Forsyth took place on the 7th of November. The following is an extract from his inaugural address:

"The judgment formed of every administration, is the result of a comparison with that which immediately preceded it. Difficult, indeed, is the path before me, when the public mind is occupied, and will long continue to be so, by the recollection of the zeal, the fidelity and the success with which the Government has been administered by my respected and fortunate predecessor."

The Georgia Journal, of 12th November, said: "Few men have retired from office, under more flattering circumstances, than Gov. Troup. He has, certainly, during the four years of his service, had more difficulties to contend with than any of his predecessors ever had, not even excepting Gen. James Jackson."

After speaking of his trials and his triumphs, it added: "He left town, on Thursday last, for his private residence in Laurens County. It was proposed that a company of the young men of Milledgeville and the neighboring Counties, should escort him some distance from town; but this arrangement was abandoned, at his request. His friends, who were members of the Legislature, and strangers that were in town, of whom there were many, called in parties, at his lodgings, on Wednesday evening, and took their leave. And, on Thursday morning, a large number of the citizens of Milledgeville met at La Fayette Hall, and proceeded in a body to Mrs. Jenkins', for the same purpose. They were all received with kindness and cordiality; and they left him, expressing their regret at the separation which was about to take place."

Having visited Savannah, in February, 1828, the compliment of a public dinner was tendered him. In soliciting his acceptance, the committee, composed of personal and political friends, said:

"Your fellow-citizens feel assured that they have strong and peculiar claims upon your indulgence, as your public career commenced among them; and, during its continuance, has ever met with their warm and unqualified approbation."

From his letter, dated 6th February, declining the invitation, the following extract is made:

"On each occasion of revisiting your city, in which I had been reared from earliest infancy, I have felt myself at home; and it would have been most gratifying to me, if it had seemed most appropriate to you, to have been treated rather as a friend, which I am, than as a public man, which I am not. Born to many sorrows, I have sought consolation here, under every afflictive dispensation, and have found it in warm and generous bosoms, in which the most delicate sensibilities have been united to the most manly virtues. You must feel, therefore, how reluctant I have been in failing to receive your wishes as commands. The approbation of my public conduct is of the highest value to me, because it forces the conviction that that conduct has been right."*

The Georgian added: "It will be seen from his very feeling reply to the committee, that Col. Troup has declined the mark of respect tendered him by his fellow-citizens. It would have been, judging from the subscription list, the largest public dinner given here for many years."—ED.

One year after his retirement from the Executive office, Gov. Troup was, without solicitation on his part, elected to the Senate of the United States, for the full term to commence on the 4th of March, 1829. His election occurred on the 5th of November, 1828, and *without opposition.* Out of 183 votes cast, he received every vote but 15; and was, consequently, elected by a majority of 168—a thing believed to be unprecedented in the history of Georgia. In the sketch of Gov. Troup, in White's Statistics of Georgia, it is said:

"This appointment was accepted by him with unfeigned regret. Ill health and other circumstances had determined him to live in domestic seclusion. It is not generally known, that, when apprised of the Legislative intention to send him to Washington, he, to prevent it, hastened from his home in Laurens, to Milledgeville, where he arrived only a few hours after his election."

The term for which Gov. Troup had been elected to the Senate, was to begin on 4th March, 1829; but he was unable to attend the Executive session then held. On 22d January, 1829, he wrote to a friend:

"Letters received from Washington, express a wish that I would be present there on the 4th of March; and I may attempt it, at the risk of failure. * * * * I am very sick of politics and of public men, even more so than in body, which has had and still has sickness enough to complain of; but I will do anything I can to the contribution for the public interest, so long as there is a prospect of serving it."

In another letter, of 27th March, to the same friend, dated at Darien, after referring again to his health, &c., he said, in reference to the inaugural address of the new President:

"I like Gen. Jackson's prologue, much, and will like it still better, if time shall prove the plain-dealing and honest sincerity of the author," &c., &c.

Again, on the 8th of June, he wrote, from Laurens:

"I have postponed writing, that I might be able to give you a favorable account of my health. Hope is yet deferred; and I can only say, in this respect, that a

64

teasing cough harasses, without apparently wearing me away; and, because my strength does not decline, I flatter myself, or perhaps the disease flatters me, that my lungs are still whole. * * * * * The summer will decide my fate; and, if I cannot make myself useful at Washington, I will not go there."

On the 10th August, writing from Milledgeville, he said:

"My cough, without being worse, harasses me, and, although teasing, has not proved enfeebling."

The following, to the same friend, deserves a place here, as giving, not only an account of his health, but his views on Education.

LAURENS, 29th August, 1829.

My Dear Friend: My case is not a little perplexing and embarrassing to me. It may be affection of the lungs, or liver, or both, or neither. I am too little versed in your science, to trust myself with a conjecture. The cough and expectorations proceed: as to the former, I cannot say there is any thing fixed or settled about it; indeed, it gives me no trouble or uneasiness, compared with the hawking and spitting, or discharge of phlegm, (viscid,) which keeps my throat almost always sore. The cough gives me no trouble, at night, and sometimes is of rare occurrence in the day; the other proceeds quite independently of it. They are such symptoms which induce me to believe you may be right, when you suppose it a gastric affection, and not of the lungs. I am taking your remedy. * * * *

Schemes of Education have been multiplying for the last twenty years, in every part of the civilized world, without public opinion having rested on any one of them for a longer time than its novelty lasted. I have not much faith that our inventive faculties in this respect will enable us to make wiser men than the Greeks and Romans, although our Christian system may make better ones. Certainly, any contrivance which can make a school-room more captivating to a child, than a prison-house, must have its value; and, no doubt, the plan of the Infant Schools is the best which can be devised. It requires but little experience to determine its advantages, and the test is always unerring.

It has never been suggested that one nation had acquired a decided superiority over another, in intellectual endowment, all else being equal, by a *peculiar mode* of training the human mind. Undoubtedly, there are some modes of communicating knowledge, which have preference over others; but it is difficult to believe that at this time of day the modes are susceptible of much improvement. More cannot be communicated than is known; and I am much inclined to think that as much can be communicated, either by the ancient or modern *modes*, as the mind can receive. Well organized and disciplined Schools, with good instructors, have at all times been able to accomplish this. True, some are sanguine enough to think the mind can be made to master every department of human learning, when that learning shall have reached its highest perfection; but we remain without the *proof*. It is probable that no mind ever acquired more of *what is called* knowledge, than that of Aristotle, and it was probably far short of even the useful knowledge of his time. Pray excuse a treatise on Education. * * * * * * * * * * * * * *

Affectionately yours,

G. M. TROUP.

Dr. Daniell.

On the 25th November, he wrote, from Washington:

"I arrived safely, yesterday, and in as good condition as could have been expected. The route by Norfolk gave us some rest, and we lost no time—the Steamboat making up for the tardiness of the Stage. The members assembled early and in great number, as if something unusual were anticipated, and yet I hear nothing that can cause curiosity or anxiety. On Indian affairs and Internal Improvement, the President will do as we desire," &c., &c.

"Pennsylvania will, no doubt, fill the vacancy on the Supreme Bench. I am very anxious to get Mr. Cheves; but the prospect is far from flattering. The wishes of the State are to be consulted, and the State will probably not discover Pennsylvanianism enough in Mr. C. to recommend him. They speak of Binney, and Gibson, and Baldwin."*

He took his seat in the Senate, on 7th December, 1829, and, on the 9th, was appointed third on the Military Committee, and second on the Committee on Indian Affairs. The state of his health was such, during a great part of the time he continued in the Senate, as to unfit him for debate.

* Hon. Henry Baldwin was afterwards appointed to fill this vacancy, created by Judge Washington's death.—ED.

It was probably on leaving Georgia to take his place at the session of 1829—'30, that he expressed a doubt whether he would ever return from Washington. On 21st December, he wrote:

"I can give you no better account of my health, than to say it continues very much as when I left you, with the exception of increase of cough—being more troublesome by night as well as by day. * * * * * * We can accomplish nothing for Southern interests, here, unless perhaps the removal of the Indians; and this, if accomplished, will be done reluctantly and ungraciously; or, more properly, will be permitted only because it cannot but be vainly forbidden. I speak of the Congress; not of the Executive, who is sincerely with us."

On 8th January, 1830, he again wrote:

"I will leave this, for Athens, as soon as possible. If my health permit, will return to my duties immediately; otherwise, will resign, when I may hope to see you sooner than we once expected."

Again, on 4th March, he wrote, from Washington:

"Having resolved to resign, as I advised you, because of the uncertainty of my being able to return in time for any useful purpose, I wrote to our friend B.,* begging him to take my place. The idea was, if the constitutional difficulty could be removed, to prevail on the Governor to send the commission, forthwith; but he thought, and perhaps correctly, that a previous resignation would be necessary, which would have consumed too much time for our object. So many things occupy me, that I must hasten to beg my affectionate remembrance to the family," &c., &c.

And, on 20th March, he wrote:

"Those [members of Congress] who are most unprincipled, form an alliance to cheat the more scrupulous; and they are always a strong majority. The constitution stands in the way of nobody, and is never spoken of with any gravity, except in the way of a rhetorical flourish. A very common argument is held, that if the honest do not turn rogues, presently, the plunder will be all gone; and it is not difficult to see how the argument works. Our Indian affairs are likely to go well. * * * * * Pray re-

* Judge Berrien, probably, who was then Attorney-General of the U. S. Mr. Forsyth was at this time the colleague of Governor Troup; having been elected in Mr. Berrien's place, when the latter entered the Cabinet.—ED.

member me affectionately to Mrs. D. and the boys. Tell the latter that I always think of them, and do not despair of seeing them once more."

Whilst, however, Gov. Troup was unable to take part in debate, he was not inattentive to the duties of his station. Probably, a slight improvement in his health, and the unwillingness of his friends for his retirement, induced him to continue in the Senate. During all this time, and until his final retirement from public life, in 1833, it is confidently believed that the record of his votes, in the Senate, may safely be challenged to show any departure from the simplicity and honesty of his Republican faith, and those State Rights principles, which never forsook him in the most trying times. Although physically too weak to attempt a speech, his name was a tower of strength to his political friends. This will be shown by what follows.

The 13th day of April, 1830, the anniversary of the birth-day of Thomas Jefferson, was celebrated at Washington City, with great eclat. Hon. John Roane, of Virginia, presided, assisted by six Vice-Presidents. South Carolina having been toasted, Gen. Hayne responded to the sentiment, and, amongst other things, said:

"On a more recent occasion, GEORGIA, (in every sense, *our sister*,) under the guidance of one of the noblest of her distinguished sons, planted upon her borders the standard of STATE RIGHTS, and achieved a great and a glorious victory for the good cause. Neither denunciations nor threats could induce her enlightened and patriotic Chief Magistrate to recede from the proud stand he had taken in defence of the constitutional rights committed to his charge. Public opinion was rallied to his support, liberty triumphed, and the Constitution was saved."

He concluded with offering the following sentiment:

"*The State of Georgia*—By the firmness and energy of her *Troups*, she has achieved one great victory for *State rights*; the wisdom and eloquence of her sons will secure her another proud triumph in the councils of the Nation."

Hon. James M. Wayne, then a Representative from

Georgia, responded to this sentiment, in a speech, from which want of space forbids the making of extracts.

Speaking of the stand which Georgia had taken, even "when menaced with military coercion," &c., he said:

"Our appeal was heard by our brethren; the State triumphed; its principles prevailed; its rights are now fully acknowledged, and the cheering response given to the sentiments of the gentleman from South Carolina, assures us that Georgia, in her past relations with the General Government, stands vindicated and approved by the representative democracy of the Union."

Governor Troup gave the following toast, on the occasion:

"*The Government of the United States*—With more limited powers than the Republic of San Marino, it rules an Empire more extended than the Roman, with the absoluteness of Tiberius, with less wisdom than Augustus, and less justice than Trajan or the Antonines."

During the session of 1829—'30, Gov. Troup was generally at his post, and always voted as became the principles of his whole life. It was during this session that the celebrated debate, on Foot's Resolution, occurred, in which General Hayne and Mr. Webster so greatly distinguished themselves.

This session terminated on 31st May, 1830. We have abundant evidence that his health continued poor. During the recess, he was invited to a public meeting and dinner, by the friends of State Rights at Columbia, South Carolina.

In declining the invitation, he wrote, as follows:

LAURENS COUNTY, GEORGIA,
September 21st, 1830.

Gentlemen: Accept my thanks for your polite invitation to a public meeting and dinner at Columbia, directed to Milledgeville. Whether with you on that interesting occasion, or not, you have my best wishes for the results of the wise counsels and patriotic efforts which you cannot fail to carry to the discussion of the topics of the day: they are of first importance to the whole Union.

Whatever the people of South Carolina, in convention, shall resolve for their safety, interest and happiness, will be right, and none will have the right to question it. You can change your own government at pleasure; and, therefore, you can throw off the government of the Union, whenever the same safety, interest and happiness require it. If ambition and avarice shall make of the Federal Government a curse, and the States are to be held to it against their will, our condition differs in nothing from that of the Province of Turkey or Persia. The many-headed tyrant, in the habitual violation of the Constitution, vaunts his love of Union, as if ready to make a burnt-offering of his looms and spindles upon the altar of that Union—yet, not one jot of concession is made to the prayers and entreaties, which, if offered to the throne of Grace, would be received graciously and answered favorably. The cormorant who fastens and fattens on our substance, may not release his hold, so long as we are the willing subject of its remorseless passion. But I do not utterly despair—the American people will see that the Constitution and Union can only be preserved by a return to honesty and justice. It is impossible we can be wrong—ours is the cause of liberty—of freedom of industry—of the use of the faculties of mind and body for all purposes, merely innocent, without governmental interference; opposed to restraints and prohibitions and monopolies in every form. If, contrary to expectation, the existing system shall become the fixed and settled policy of the country, the Southern States must withdraw from the confederacy, cost what it may. No evil is more to be dreaded than a power in the General Government to regulate industry—a power which cannot with safety be confided to any government, but with the most guarded limitations. *Direct* taxes for the encouragement of manufactures, would not have been paid for a single year. The five cents a yard on our cotton bagging, levied for the professed purpose of enabling the Western States to supply the article on their own terms, when the proceeds were to make roads and canals for the same States, would have been opposed with a spirit not easily allayed. They have been borne, only, because being *indirect*, they are unseen; and because a portion of the evil may be avoided by the non-consumption of those articles which are not of first necessity. There cannot be a greater fallacy than that the Union is to be preserved by a power in the General Government to *coerce* the States. The existence of sovereignty excludes the idea of force. Ours is a Government of opinion, of consent, of voluntary association—the only guaranty for Union is justice. Justice secures good feeling, fidelity, affection; and nothing but justice can secure them. Of what value is that Union which is formed of unwilling and reluctant members, who, but for the sword suspended over their heads, would fly off from the common centre which burns only to destroy?

The Constitution, administered according to its letter and spirit, can dispense nothing but justice; and the character of the American people is a sufficient guaranty that no State would separate from the Union without justifiable cause. Regarding the Union as a family compact, the members of which can only be kept together by the practice of strict and impartial justice, it is better that the non-contents and the mal-contents should be suffered to depart in peace by common consent, than by common consent to constrain a reluctant obedience, which, if yielded to-day, may be forcibly withdrawn to-morrow. It is the shedding of blood which deters us from constitutional resistance to unconstitutional laws, and which ought to be postponed so long as the faintest hope remains of a returning sense of justice. You well know how the same infatuation is constantly pursuing an interest infinitely more sacred; the unhallowed touch of which we would be bound in honor to resist, and with a vengeance never to be appeased. But pardon so much on these distressing topics, and accept the tender of my regard and esteem.*

G. M. TROUP.

On 6th October, he wrote to his friend, Dr. Daniell, then a member of the Georgia Senate:

"I cannot ride on horseback, without suffering much inconvenience; the carriage is sufficiently irritating. Since my last, my condition is better.

"With regard to the Cherokees, I would say, enforce the laws strictly—set the Supreme Court at defiance, and occupy the *mineral* country. The last can either be worked by the State, or sold, or leased. Make it a high crime and misdemeanor, (treason, if you please,) for any person (no matter who,) within the jurisdictional limits of the State, (the chartered limits,) to issue or serve any judicial process, which shall, directly or indirectly, call in

* On the 16th of December, 1830, the following resolution was offered in the Georgia House of Representatives:

"That the people of Georgia disapprove of the political opinions of the Hon. George M. Troup, as expressed in his toast at the Jefferson celebration dinner, in Washington City, and in his letter replying to an invitation to the Columbia dinner."

The resolution was immediately laid on the table, for the remainder of the session, by yeas 93, nays 31.—ED.

question the sovereign jurisdictional or territorial rights of the State. This system, enforced as it ought to be, will soon move the Cherokees. They rely on their Northern friends; and, as soon as they see that to be a broken staff, they will surrender."

He wrote, again, on 2d November:

"The state of things at Milledgeville, from time to time, will be very acceptable. The majority against you, in the Senate, is stronger than I anticipated. The horizon is not very clear, either at home or abroad; and I fear poor human nature will work its own ruin at last. * * * * * * * * * * * * * Suffer much pain, at intervals, and do not know if I can accomplish the journey."

Governor Troup attended the session of 1830–31. Writing, from Washington, on 18th December, after referring to the action of the Legislature of Georgia in regard to the Cherokee lands, &c., he said:

"The poor University has met the fate* anticipated, and will never recover so long as party and bigotry have any thing to do with it. * * * * * * I do not look for any modification of the Tariff which would give us gratification. If any happen, it will be in furtherance of the system. We begin to rely somewhat upon a salutary change in public opinion, of which there are some signs."

On 4th January, 1831, in another letter, after referring to the resolutions of the Legislature of Georgia, requesting and enjoining the Governor and other officers of the State, to disregard the citation, &c., of the Chief Justice of the U. S. Supreme Court, in the case of the Indian Tassels, who had been convicted of murder before the Superior Court of Hall county, &c., &c., he said:

"The result has been hailed by our political friends here, as a signal triumph, although it may be but the onset. It is not believed they will venture to proceed in the contempt."

In another letter, written on 31st January, he said:

"The relations of public men here are worse than this time last year, and as bad as they can be. The President is almost the only man who has maintained his position as it was," &c., &c.

* It is proper to add, that, three days after the date of this letter, an Act was passed "to provide a permanent additional fund for the support of" the University, &c., &c.—ED.

Speaking of the protective system, he said, in a letter dated 11th May:

"The danger has become imminent, because it is evident, for the first time, that the entire capital and population of New England and other interested States, are embodying for the permanency of the system; and, if not resisted, we must be overthrown, horse, foot and dragoons."

This being the short session, not much of a general nature was done in Congress. Governor Troup voted on 2d February, in favor of granting leave to introduce a resolution "that the charter of the Bank of the United States ought not to be renewed." Congress adjourned on 3d March.

Meanwhile, the health of Governor Troup continued feeble. He was able, however, to attend the session of 1831–32. On 21st January, 1832, he wrote to Dr. Daniell:

"Public affairs are beginning to occupy more seriously the attention of everybody here, as it is seen in how much uncertainty they are involved. The present prospect is very gloomy, and we can only indulge the hope that events may transpire to favor the more desirable results. The Tariff party will attempt to reconcile the Southern people, by some trifling concession; which, if it should succeed, will rivet the system upon us. Our friends are, so far, very decided, and will not be content with anything short of justice and equality. For the Bank, there is no doubt a majority in both Houses, but not two-thirds; and the better opinion is that two-thirds will be required."

The following extract from a letter, to the same friend, dated 30th May, 1832, will show why Governor Troup took no part in debate:

"I would very gladly have availed myself of your friendly suggestion, and for the reason assigned, if it had been possible. Frequent occasions have occurred, making it very fit and proper, perhaps even useful, that my own opinions should have been expressed; but every essay of that kind would prove so distressing to myself and others, that it would be quite unwarrantable to attempt it. The least effort, in this way, is followed by a fit of coughing which is not easily allayed, and which, even in ordinary conversation, has more than once produced a spitting of blood. The effects, in relation to myself, would be of no consequence, if the object of the effort, on any profitable occasion, could be attained; but I know this to be physically impossible."

Of the tariff, he wrote, on 2d July:

"The bill from the House of Representatives, which is likely to pass the Senate, is essentially a bill for the further relief of the manufacturers, who will be exempted, in a great degree, from the only burthens to which they had been subjected under the old system."*

This was an exceedingly important session of Congress, the Bank and Tariff questions being the leading ones. It has been already stated, in a note to a previous chapter, that Governor Troup voted to sustain the President in his veto of the bill to re-charter the Bank of the United States, having previously voted against the bill itself. At this period, he was a cordial supporter of Gen. Jackson's administration; as may be seen by the following extracts from a private letter, written after the adjournment of Congress, and dated 29th August, 1832:

"Bad health carried me to the Virginia Springs, where, having acquired sufficient strength, we took the road by the higher country, direct for Athens, whence, (having first entered George of the Sophomore Class, and left his sisters with him, all in good health,) I proceeded homeward, where I arrived, ten days since, not much worse than I left the Springs.

"Have desired much to see you. Every thing, politically, is working badly for us, as you may perceive; and, amidst all the diversity of opinions, no rallying point, or principle of union, presents, by which the disorder may be corrected. * * * * * The cause of nullification is so generally connected with hostility to the President, that, even if it were more tenable, it would expose to jealousy any politician in Georgia who would seem to favor it. General Jackson deserves to be supported most liberally by every Georgian, and indeed by every Republican. No man would have hazarded more for correct principles."

* The bill was passed substantially as it came from the House, but, of course, against the vote of Governor Troup. It was entitled "An Act to alter and amend the several Acts laying duties on imports," and was approved by the President, on 14th July, 1832. This was one of the Acts embraced within the provisions of the South Carolina Ordinance of Nullification of 24th November, 1832.—ED.

[1832.] Congress re-assembled on 3d December. Gov. Troup was placed second on the Military Committee of the Senate, and was made Chairman of the Committee on Indian Affairs.

On the 10th December, the President issued his celebrated Proclamation, having reference to the nullification measures of South Carolina; the party divisions upon which, belong to the general history of the country.

The following letter from Gov. Troup finds its appropriate place here:

WASHINGTON, 13th Jan'y, 1833.

My Dear Friend: Within a few days, there has been a considerable abatement of excitement, and the Executive tone has moderated. It is now ascertained that force will not be resorted to, but to repel force*, and that regulars will not be employed against citizens.

The apprehension of civil war, which was for a time general, has disappeared before the promulgation of the State law, which is seen to allow the merchant to give and pay his bond. It now begins to be said, that, as a remedy, nullification has failed; and the manufacturers begin to think that reduction may yet be postponed. On this question, the Senate is more doubtful than the House.

In consequence of the repeated suggestions of yourself and others, as well as of a late censurable and ill-timed State paper, I have given my views and opinions generally. As Major Moore, of Oglethorpe, a very worthy patriot, was most pressing and mandatory, I have given them to him, and in a very familiar, homespun way. They will, of course, meet the reception and treatment which every thing, of like kind, emanating from myself, has in past time, and perhaps with very little favor from any quarter. * * * * *

Affectionately,

G. M. TROUP.

Dr. W. C. Daniell.

---

* On the 16th of January, Mr. Forsyth said, "he congratulated the Senate, that, notwithstanding the threatening appearance, there was no danger to the public peace. The Chief Magistrate pledges himself not to resort to any but defensive force; and the Senator from South Carolina tells us that South Carolina has no desire to use force, unless assailed. The hope might be indulged that all these pledges would be redeemed: if they were, force would not be used."—ED.

The "State paper," to which reference is made above, was the proclamation of the President. The letter to Major Moore, to which reference is also made above, will be found in the Appendix to this volume. On the 10th of February, Governor Troup wrote his celebrated letter to Major John H. Howard, which is also to be found in the Appendix.* Had he written nothing else, this letter would suffice to place him amongst the foremost men of the country. By the last of these letters, it will be seen that he was not an admirer of nullification as adopted by South Carolina, under the actual circumstances of the case, and for the reasons stated by himself. Believing, as he did, in the absolute and undivided sovereignty of each State, and that Carolina had a right to do as she did, he still thought she should have acted in concert with other States having identical interests. On 20th February, he wrote to Dr. Daniell:

"I am much gratified that the letter to Moore gave you pleasure. It does not appear to have been received as well elsewhere. I see it excepted to by 'BIBB,' in the last *Recorder*, who I take to be our excellent friend, * * * * * * . It is in this way that our cause is made hopeless. You must fall in with the whim-whams and crudities and conceits of every politician on one side, or you accomplish nothing for union. This sensitiveness is a prominent characteristic of nullification. It has its seat in the front of the cranium, and the subject of this infirmity reminds you of one in a fit of the gout, who is in dread of every thing that approaches his toes."

During the session of 1832–33, Gov. Troup was frequently absent, from severe indisposition. A more excited session never was held since the adoption of the Federal Constitution. The principles of the Government were sifted to their foundation, in the debates on the proclamation and the measures introduced to meet the crisis brought about by the nullifying ordinance of South Carolina, and General Jackson's

* These two letters are put in an appendix, reluctantly, and only because the limits assigned to this work do not permit their insertion in the large type selected for the body of this book. No admirer of Governor Troup's State Rights principles, will fail to read these letters attentively.—ED.

determination to put down what he deemed a political heresy. Some of the greatest men that ever figured in American history, as statesmen and debaters, were in that Congress. Calhoun, Clay and Webster were in the Senate, besides numbers of others who would have adorned any deliberative assembly.

The Revenue Collection Bill, more commonly known as the "Force Bill," came up for its engrossment and third reading, on 18th February. Although unable to take any part in debate, Governor Troup left his sick bed, and waited until nearly midnight, to record his vote against the measure. Out of forty Senators who voted, the only negatives were George M. Bibb, John C. Calhoun, William R. King, Willie P. Mangum, Stephen D. Miller, Gabriel Moore, GEORGE M. TROUP and John Tyler. On the passage of the bill, on 20th February, all the above named Senators were absent, except Mr. Tyler, whose voice was the only NAY. Gov. Troup was too sick to attend.* The following letter from him to one of the editors of the Georgia Messenger, appertains to this part of his history:

DARIEN, 1st December, 1833.

—— —— Of the misconstructions and misrepresentations connected with every thing I write, you are not insensible; so that, if I had been wilfully and deliberately mysterious in all things written or spoken, and conspicuously distinguished for ambiguity of purpose and indirection of conduct, all my life, I could not have expected any thing worse. Take, for example, the instance to which you emphatically call my attention—"the impression is attempted to be made that you (I) would have voted for the Force Bill of the last Congress, if you (I) had been in your (my) seat."

I went from my chamber to the Capitol, at an early hour of the afternoon, and, suffering much pain, kept my seat

* In the debate on this bill, on 19th February, Mr. Poindexter, in a long speech in opposition to it, quoting from Gov. Troup's annual message, of 1826, said: "Gov. Troup, than whom no man has maintained a more uniform and consistent political career; than whom a more pure and enlightened patriot has never adorned the councils of the country; and who, I rejoice to say, is now, as he was while Governor of Georgia, the sincere friend of State Rights and constitutional liberty, addressed a message to the Legislature of that State, an extract from which I submit, containing reflections well worthy the attention of honorable Senators in their deliberations on the pending question."—ED.

until midnight, when *I voted against the Force Bill. If on my death-bed, I would have been carried there to vote against it;* because it presented the strange political phenomenon of a mere government treating a sovereign State as if that State were a corporation or an unlawful assemblage of individuals. The vote was recorded, and *published in all* the newspapers of the day; and yet it is attempted to make the impression that I would have *voted for* the *Force* Bill if I had been in my seat. So the world goes.

Your friend, very truly,

G. M. TROUP.

The 22d Congress expired on the 3d of March, 1833. Governor Troup never returned to Washington as a public man. In November following, he resigned his seat, and bade a final adieu to public employment.

The following is a copy of his letter of resignation:

LAURENS COUNTY, November 8th, 1833.

To his Excellency, Gov. Lumpkin:

Sir: In execution of a deferred resolution, I resign my seat in the Senate of the United States. Reasons, merely personal, it would concern you very little to receive; and others, which are of higher import, belong to my constituents, who might not choose to be troubled with them. It may suffice, that, if the people of Georgia are as they were, another can serve them more usefully; and, if they are not, I would be the last whom they would select to serve them at all.

Your fellow-citizen,

G. M. TROUP.

CHAPTER XIV.

Governor Troup in retirement.—Nominated, by State Rights men, for the Presidency.—His political opinions, and views on various subjects.—State Sovereignty.—United States Bank and Independent Treasury.—Course in Presidential contest of 1840.—*Is opposed to admission of California, and Compromise measures of* 1850.—*Elected a Delegate to the Nashville Convention.—Nominated for the Presidency by Southern Rights Convention in Alabama.—Political and private correspondence.—Decline in health; last sickness and death.—Public testimonials to his worth.—Summary of his character.—Conclusion.*

ON retiring to his home in Laurens, Governor Troup lived in as complete seclusion from political affairs, as any man, of his commanding position and well known and decided principles, could. Without political aspirations, he was still unreserved in the expression of his opinions on all subjects of general interest, and willingly communicated them, in writing, to those who solicited his views.

A convention, composed of State Rights members of the Legislature, and delegates from various counties in the State, assembled at Milledgeville, on the 12th of December, 1833. At this meeting, Gov. Troup was nominated for the Presidency, in the following resolution:

"*Resolved*, That we recommend to the people of the United States, Col. GEORGE M. TROUP, as a suitable candidate for the next Presidency. His zealous advocacy of, and his firm attachment to, the principles of State Rights, designate him as the individual best calculated to promote the Republican doctrines we advocate."

It was evident that this recommendation was intended more as a compliment to Governor Troup, than as the expression of a belief that it could be successful. Nothing more was done about it. In reference, partly, to this demonstration, he wrote the following:

LAURENS, 1st January, 1834.

My Dear Friend: From the information given, and

desire expressed, in your and other letters, for the publication of the political letter,* I have given my consent; although I fear it may be construed as a political manœuvre in aid of the nomination—a measure, which, whatever may be my own views of its policy, having originated in the best feelings and with the best objects, I will say or do nothing to thwart. I hope, at the same time, that I will not be asked to do anything to promote it. The impossibility of success does not enter at all into my views of the subject; for, under circumstances much more favorable to it, my resolution would be the same. I consider it morally impossible to bring back the Government to its pristine principles; but that is no good reason that the virtuous men of the country should not make an effort. * * * * * * Remember me, as usual, to all, and believe me,

Very affectionately,

G. M. TROUP.

Dr. W. C. Daniell,
Savannah.

In July, 1834, Gov. Troup publicly identified himself, in feeling, with the State Rights party of Georgia. Being at Macon, on his way to the Indian Springs, he was invited to a public dinner. In declining the honor, he said, amongst other things: " the State Rights party of Georgia have my best wishes for their success." †

This announcement was the occasion of much comment by Georgia politicians, and will serve to explain the political part of the following:

LAURENS, 25th Sept., 1834.

My Dear Friend: * * * * * * G * * * * *, of * * * * * , wrote, in behalf of *. * * *. * *, to know if I approved of the prefatory editorial to my Macon letter. The letter being dictated in a very friendly spirit, I answered, thinking, it might possibly do some good. Not knowing him personally, but understanding his political position, I treated the matter with mildness and gentleness, but,

* For this letter, (to Major Howard,) see the Appendix to this volume.—ED.

† Such was the influence of his name and character, in Georgia, notwithstanding the decided tone of the letter from which the above quotation is made, that many of his old political associates, although not prepared to go the length of his extreme State Rights views, took the name of "Troup Union" men. Personally, he never lost their affections.—ED.

nevertheless, with decision. Among other things, (* * * * * having expressed his great abhorrence of nullification,) I requested him to say to my old friend, *. *. *., "that the denial of absolute sovereignty to the States, would be more mischievous and ruinous than 10,000 hydras to be raised from nullification." How it will take, I do not know—as apt to confirm the apostasy as to shake it. They force me to write political letters; and have written one to Hancock, cautioning, at the same time, * * * * * and * * * * *, if they hear of fragments from it, to challenge the production and publication. Have written another to Talbot, in answer to one from Breedlove and Graybill, whom I don't know, but who profess to be friends. If they are not, the letter will serve them no purpose. * * * * * * * * * *

Affectionately yours,

G. M. TROUP.

Dr. W. C. Daniell,
Savannah.

The following is the letter to Messrs. Breedlove and Graybill, to which reference is above made. It was extensively published, at the time, as a letter " to some State Rights gentlemen in Talbot county:"

Gentlemen: The States are sovereign, or they are not. We prove the affirmative, by the Declaration of Independence, and the Articles of Confederation—let the federal party prove the negative if they can. If a State is sovereign, it can do any thing—it can nullify any act of Congress, or secede; is subject only to the law of nature and nations, which it is bound to respect. This exercise of its sovereign power has nothing to do with the Constitution, much less with revolution—it is above the Constitution, because it has the law of nations for its constitution, and it can have no connection with revolution, because, of all acts of human power and authority, it is most commanding, peaceable, legitimate and sacred. Our opponents involve themselves in inextricable difficulty. The Federalists say that the powers of sovereignty have been divided between the State and Federal Governments—if so, the higher powers having been given to the latter, it possesses the greater sovreignty, and on that account must be the judge of its own powers, which makes it absolute. And yet the Federalists admit that sovereignty resides in the people, by which they mean the whole people of the United States; when or how they became one people, they cannot explain. The weaker among them are divided in opinion; some saying it resides in the United States, without being able to show a substantive, distinct and independent being called the United States, and capable of receiving sovereignty; and others that the Government is sovereign, because the people have vested their sovereign powers in the Government; as if a Government, a mere agent, were capable of receiving sovereign powers. Thus inconsistency follows inconsistency, and contradiction contradiction. If sovereign powers could vest in a Government, that Goverment could transfer them to any subject capable of receiving them, in virtue of that very sovereignty.

Carolina had a perfect right to do as she did; but, as we do not always wisely what we have right to do, I blamed Carolina for not acting in concert with those States having identical interests—if she had done so, a certain and complete triumph of the Constitution would have been the result.

You perceive, therefore, that the denial to a State of absolute sovereignty, is a surrender of the whole question; as, in any aspect of it, the Federal Government having the higher attributes of sovereignty, can, in no event, be checked, or restrained, or limited by a power possessing only the minor attributes.

Very respectfully, gentlemen,

G. M. TROUP.

The year 1837 is remembered for the severe commercial crisis through which the country passed. Having been invited by the State Rights party of Chatham county, to attend the celebration of the 4th of July, of that year, at Savannah, and being unable to attend, he wrote a letter, dated 30th June, from which the following extract is made:

"In all past time, and in every country, what is called a crisis, a panic, an excitement, or any temporary evil, natural or artificial, has been seized upon by the friends of arbitrary power, to strengthen the arm of Government already strong enough. The present state of things, full of distress, and moving the strongest passions, is also full of danger for posterity, who may weep in more sorrow and bitterness of heart, the doings of its ancestors, the fruits of a panic. Be pleased to accept, in the form of a toast, the expression of *a hope, an anxious hope, that the State Rights party of Georgia, if it cannot limit or restrain, will never, directly or indirectly, contribute to increase, the power of the Federal Government.*"

To a friend, who desired to know his views on the currency question, Gov. Troup wrote a long letter,* on 16th May, 1840, which the reader will find in the Appendix to this volume. "The use and abuse of his name in connection with" the Presidency, had reference to the circumstance of his name having been used in one or more of the news-papers in Georgia, for that office, before their conductors came out in support of Gen. Harrison against Mr. Van Buren.

On 25th July, 1840, he wrote to his friend, Dr. Daniell, and said:

"Have been much plagued by political letters, and hoped, by abusing every body, I might rid myself of them; but it is not so, and all I can now do is to beg they will not publish."

In the same letter, he expressed a preference for Mr. Van Buren over the other party, and added: "but it is only between arsenic and hellebore; and why need we make choice, when we can refuse both?"

The following letter, to the same friend, (then at Gainesville,) shows that the writer of it was not indifferent to the pleasures of social intercourse, and that he could indulge in the sallies of pleasantry:

LAURENS, 15th June, 1841.

My Dear Friend: Many thanks for your kind invitation. My brother, the Doctor, proposes to accompany me, in July—George probably making a third; and it is even possible my brother Robert will make us count four in all. We will not fail to see you, and to remain with you as long

* The sub-Treasury scheme, to which this letter refers, was enacted into a law passed 4th July, 1840, which was repealed 13th August, 1841. The present system of collecting, keeping, transferring and disbursing the public revenue, was adopted by Act of Congress, passed 6th August, 1846. See 5th and 9th vols. United States Statutes at Large.—ED.

as we can. * * * * * * * *
I am so much afraid, in these Harrisonian days, of judges, sheriffs, bailiffs, and their precepts, that, apart from all other motive or consideration, any one of them would as easily conduct me to the river Styx as a gaol; and you know gaol or Styx is the alternative—at least, it is so with us. I hope better things, in your quarter, than molten lead for a man who is not yet entitled to a place on that side of the gulf; and shall content myself with the fare of Lazarus, which, as I remember, was a little worse than I have been accustomed to under the roof of a gentleman who shall be nameless.

Many kind remembrances to all yours.

G. M. TROUP.

To the same friend, he said, on 15th September, 1842:

"I had heard something of * * * * *, aforetime, which prepared me for his present decided attitude. By the by, is it not saying something for a good cause, that such men cannot follow the lead of their would-be leaders, and on questions, too, not only leading, but, to their party, essentially vital? Why cannot our friend * * * * *, one of the best of men, renounce his Bankism, and suffer the real friends of the Southern country to vote for him? The enlightened men, who are opposed to a Bank, believe it to be unconstitutional, and most disastrous to Southern interests; and they cannot conscientiously vote for even such a patriot as *."

Again, on 7th November, 1842, speaking of the Presidential question, and of some things that he regarded as errors in the Democratic party, he said:

"You are a very bad party, but your adversary is the d—l; and as Milton, an excellent Republican, did most excellently and transcendentally overcome and defeat him, so I have no doubt you will, and by the same means—the intrinsic merit and virtue of your cause, according to profession, at least; and profession is something."

On the 3d of April, 1844, he wrote to the same friend:

"Do me the favor to say to Ben, that, when he resolves to take up Blackstone, I recommend to him the edition of Tucker. Although it is not a commentary on Blackstone, it is a most excellent comparison of English and American constitutions and laws, illustrated with much clearness and ability, with sufficient candor and impartiality, and affording, at the same time, the best exposition of the Federal

Constitution and government of any work extant. I fear the Federal lawyers will proscribe and banish it their libraries."*

On the 3d of June, 1844, in reply to a question from two gentlemen of Putnam county, whether it would be "politic and expedient, or rather just, on the part of the Government of the United States, considering its existing relations to Mexico, and its geographical position to that of Texas, to incorporate immediately the latter Government into the Union, without the formal acknowledgment on the part of Mexico," Governor Troup wrote a letter, in which he said he had "not the least doubt" in regard to "that measure, not merely as one of expediency and sound policy, but as vital, in every sense of the word; without which," he added, "the southern and western country are in imminent peril." We make a few more extracts:

"If Texas, following the example of Mexico, were to pass an act of emancipation, well knowing that the same population would simultaneously cross the line to poison and corrupt and incite their own color to cut the throats of the women and children on this side, no doubt could be entertained by the strictest casuists, of the right of the Southern States (the Federal Government refusing its aid,) to protect themselves by all the means in their power, as a case of imminent peril, and one not admitting of delay. * * * * * * * * * * * When the United States acknowledged the independence of Texas, Mexico knew that such acknowledgment would qualify Texas to make a treaty of cession, or any other treaty; and she did not then choose to make it a cause of war with the United States."

He stated, as the substance of his views, that it was "better, every thing considered, to take the treaty of cession as a good and valid treaty, than to run the hazard of occupying Texas by force, (whether a territory of Mexico or

---

* In the same letter, he said: "Ever and anon, I hear of old friends falling in with the Federal current--even *. *. *. * * * * * * * * * * Pray tell me how you find Mr. *——*, in health and spirits, and if our excellent friend *——* is yet proof against black cockade and blue-lights. Amongst all the going, gone, he would be the last one on whom a shade of suspicion would rest; but the world is changeable; and, without the tardy process of precession, the equator and the poles may come into juxtaposition before we can turn round."—ED.

Texas,) as a measure of self-preservation against the threatened aggressions of England, Mexico, or Texas, or all of them," &c.

From private letters written by him, about this time, it would be interesting to make extracts, did the limits of this work permit. They all breathe the spirit of contentment, and evince a keen relish for the pleasures of social life. Without active participation in politics, he yet took an interest in what was going on.

On the 14th of June, 1845, he wrote:

"The Federal party seems to be losing ground, fast, in every quarter, and in a fair way to be reducible to cipher. May such be its fate, if the omnipotency of the other should not make it forgetful of its duties and principles."

Of his health, he said, on 20th May, 1846:

"To tell you the truth, my health is bad, very bad—an increasing aggravation of my old asthmatic affection—one of the consequences of old age."

The treaty of Guadalupe Hidalgo, concluded in 1848, between the United States and Mexico, secured to the former that vast extent of country then known as New Mexico and part of California. The controversy growing out of the attempt to form Governments for these Territories, and the connection of the question of slavery with the agitation which grew out of those attempts, are of too recent occurrence and too closely allied to the general history of the times, to require particular notice here. It was in reference to these absorbing questions, that Gov. Troup, in 1849, wrote two letters to a friend, in Mobile, and which, for a reason already assigned, we are forced to place in the Appendix. Although the writer was then in his seventieth year, and abstracted from public employment of every sort, these letters show a vigor of intellect, and a spirit of patriotic devotion to the rights of the South, entitling them to the careful consideration of the reader. Of the same character, are the two letters to his friend Dr. Slappey; the latest of these two having been written when Gov. Troup was nearly seventy-five years old.

Of Governor Troup's allusion to "fanaticism in the person of the good and gallant La Fayette," a passing notice is proper. From the second letter to his Mobile friend, it will be seen that "the illustration of fanaticism in the character of Gen. La Fayette, was not designed to detract any thing from the merits of that really excellent man." Gov. Troup was too candid to give countenance to what he deemed political error, when it came in his way. It was well understood, at the time, that, during La Fayette's visit to Georgia, he uttered some imprudent remarks on the subject of slavery, in presence of Gov. Troup, which made the interview unpleasant.*

In February, 1850, the General Assembly adopted resolutions approving the recommendation for a convention to be held at Nashville, in June, of that year, by the people of the slave-holding States, "as eminently conducive to harmonious and efficient action among them, in defence of the institution of slavery," &c., &c., and for the appointment, by the Legislature, of four delegates from the State at large; and two from each of the Congressional Districts, to be elected by the people on the first Tuesday in April. The people of Chatham county having determined to appoint a committee "from each of the political parties," &c., to recommend one candidate and one alternate, each, for the first Congressional District, the Democratic Committee unanimously recommended Governor Troup as the Democratic candidate.† It is almost superfluous to add

* From an article which appeared in a Columbus news-paper, in 1850, the following is extracted: "When Gen. La Fayette departed, Governor Troup, having waved his hand in parting salutation, turned to his Staff, and said, 'gentlemen, I heartily welcomed General La Fayette to the soil of Georgia, but I am more than rejoiced to see him depart.'"

It is due, we think, to Gov. Troup and Gen. La Fayette, to suppose that when the former speaks of the latter having been "prime mover in the destiny of St. Domingo," &c., he meant no more than that the tragedy on that Island was the natural result of anti-slavery or emancipation sentiments. His reference to Mr. Jefferson's Notes on Virginia, shows Governor Troup's perfect independence in thought and speech.—ED.

† The committee said: "This has necessarily been done without consultation with him. The committee, however, have full confidence that he who commenced his brilliant career of public duties in this Congressional District, and in this county, will now, after a long life of

that he was elected. On the 3d of April, two days after the election, he addressed a note to Hon. R. M. Charlton, in which, after stating that he had received the announcement, only the day before, "in consequence of very bad weather and high waters," he added:

"I trust, notwithstanding, that the First Congressional District may have elected a gentleman who will serve them at Nashville, with more certainty and more ability than myself. Be pleased to say to the Committee, and, through them, to my fellow-citizens of Chatham county, without distinction of party, that there is scarcely any thing they would ask me to do, which, if I thought I could do it well, I would not consent to do for them. In inviting me to represent them in the assembly contingently to be held at Nashville, they have, on their part, but performed an act of pure and exalted patriotism; on mine, by accepting the invitation, I would only have performed the duty of a good citizen."

The Convention met on the first Monday in June, and adjourned over to a day in November. Governor Troup did not attend either session.* Public opinion was much divided in Georgia, as to the propriety or probable usefulness of the Convention.

In 1852, Governor Troup was nominated for the Presidency of the United States, by a convention of the Southern Rights party of Alabama, with Gen. Quitman for the Vice-Presidency. To the Committee who informed him of the nomination, he replied, as follows:

disinterested and devoted patriotism, yield, with a lively satisfaction, to the call of those whose fathers matured and cherished his early aspirations, and gave to the State an eminent patriot and statesman, and who has proved himself faithful to his first friends, by being true to our common country. The committee deem it of the first importance, at such a juncture as the present, to call into the public service, men of the purest virtue, the most exalted patriotism, and the highest grade of talent. All these unite eminently in Governor Troup."—ED.

* On 10th October, he wrote to a friend: "Finding things getting every day worse and worse, and particularly after the miscalled Pacification by Congress, I resolved, even if able, not to attend the second Convention at Nashville, if one should be holden; and accordingly, a few days since, informed the Governor that I would not; so that, if he deems it best, he may nominate a successor, whether there be really any vacancy or not. It would have given me much pleasure, if I could have represented the few counties, especially Chatham, which voted for me."

The "Pacification" to which this letter referred, embraced the so called "compromise" measures of Congress, including the Act proposing Northern and Western boundaries for Texas, to establish a Territorial Government for New Mexico, &c., the Act for "admission of California into the Union," and the Act "to establish a Territorial Government for Utah;" all approved on the 9th September, 1850. See U. S. Statutes at Large, vol. 9, pages 446 to 458.—ED.

VALDOSTA, LAURENS COUNTY, GA.,
September 27, 1852.

Gentlemen: I am now seventy-two years old, and, for the last twenty or thirty years, if the Presidency had been offered spontaneously by the people of the United States, I would not have accepted it, because of my physical disqualification to execute the duties of the office. At no period within that time, could I, as an honest man, have done so. Not many years ago, the State Rights party of Georgia were pleased to make that nomination; and my acquiescence was placed on the footing that the acceptance would fulfil the object of the demand, viz: that, otherwise, that party which had very strong claims on me as a native and citizen of Georgia, and could not conscientiously vote for any other candidate, who had a fair prospect of success, were at liberty to vote for me, while other persons had none.

It was the partiality of friendship which suggested a similar movement of distinguished citizens of South Carolina, on another occasion, and which I discountenanced for similar reasons.

Your decided nomination, on the present occasion, leaves me no alternative but to submit myself cheerfully to the will of the State Rights convention of Alabama, recently assembled at Montgomery, in that State; but for the sole purpose of organizing that party. It, as well as the State Rights party of any portion of the United States, may rightfully demand that which it has only asked, because, in my day and generation I had labored to contribute a mite, according to my humble abilities, to sustain its principles. They are the only principles worth any thing to the Southern country; and as long as a party of two or three can be gathered together for such a purpose, the contribution of my name is the least I could think of making—at least, for the purpose of merely organizing that party; but, for that purpose only.

The increasing pressure of disease forewarns me that I have but a short breathing spell; and I hasten to my conclusion.

I would vote for Pierce and King. Mr. King is a most excellent man, and I have not expected ever to be able to vote for a Northern man so pure and disinterested as Mr. Pierce; and you may never have such another opportunity. Embrace it—and use my name, as long as you please, for organizing the State Rights party, and maintaining and consecrating its principles.

It is honorable to have such an associate in the nomination, as Gen. Quitman. He deserves and would adorn any office.

G. M. TROUP.*

To Messrs. Thomas Williams,
J. A. Elmore, G. B. DuVal,
Montgomery, Ala.

Letters from him to his friends, written between this time and the period of his death, show much mental vigor, if not bodily health. They relate to various subjects; and extracts from them would be interesting—especially those relating to agriculture—if space permitted. Composed in the privacy of retirement and the confidence of friendship, they evince a tenderness of regard for those whom he loved, and an affection which age had not lessened. His recreations seem to have consisted in attention to his farming interests, and occasional fishing excursions. In early life, he was particularly fond of the chase; the relish for which he indulged to a comparatively late period. The time, however, was approaching, when he was to leave the scenes of earth, and the associations which had contributed to make his decline of life tranquil and placid.

Being on a visit to his Mitchell place, in Montgomery county, in April, 1856, Governor Troup was taken with hemorrhage of the lungs, which there terminated his life, on 26th April, 1856, after an illness of five days. His remains were interred at Rose Mount, in the same county, beside those of his brother, Robert L. Troup. A granite monument, with a suitable inscription, marks the spot—the whole being enclosed by a fence of native sand-stone.

Considering the length of time he had been out of public service, the testimonials, throughout the State, on the occasion of his death, were highly honorable to his memory, and showed the estimation in which his virtues and public services were held by the people of Georgia. A detail of these testimonials would lead to undue prolixity.

* In the publication of this letter, at the time, an error occured, not important to be noticed here. The Troup and Quitman ticket got a few thousand votes in Alabama.—ED.

At Savannah, a meeting of citizens, irrespective of party, and presided over by the Mayor, was held on the 5th of May; at which, feeling and suitable resolutions were adopted. One of these resolutions contained a request that the Honorable John C. Nicoll "deliver a eulogy on the life and character of the deceased." Another resolution was, to the effect, that "the Chatham Artillery, of which Gov. Troup was an honorary member, be requested to fire minute-guns corresponding with the number of years of the deceased," &c., &c.*

To Hon. Joseph Henry Lumpkin, we are indebted for an elegant tribute to the memory of Governor Troup, contained in a letter dated 15th September, 1857. The following extracts are made:

* * * * * * * * "A more modest man never lived, than George M. Troup. He arrogated to himself no credit for any thing he had ever done. And in this, as in most other respects, how widely he differed from the politicians of the present day! Still, I remember, distinctly, that he was better satisfied with his speeches and efforts in Congress, in bringing on the last war with Great Britain, after her dastardly and disgraceful attack upon the Chesapeake, than any other portion of his past political life.

"Your letter has brought vividly to my feelings, the fact not only that the great head, but that nearly all the members, of his military family, are dead: Brailsford, and Jackson, and Bailey, and Randolph; men without fear and without reproach, are not alive to testify to the more than Roman purity and patriotism of our glorious old chief. I rejoice to have the opportunity of contributing my humble mite to the merits of one whom I loved as a man and venerated as a magistrate beyond all others. Georgia will never look upon his like again.

"None dared approach him with any other than public considerations as motives for his conduct." †

* It is greatly to be regretted that Judge Nicoll's engagements did not permit him to pronounce a eulogy. On 12th May, minute-guns were fired by the Chatham Artillery. The following is an extract from the minutes of the corps: "Marching to Forsyth Place, seventy six minute-guns were fired, agreeably to the resolution of the corps, passed at the meeting on the 5th inst." For a transcript of the entire proceedings of the corps, we are indebted to Lieut. C. C. Jones; but we have not space for their insertion. The City Court of Savannah adjourned over, for one day, as a token of respect for the memory of Gov. Troup.—ED.

† We regret that room cannot be made for more of this letter. Judge Lumpkin was one of Governor Troup's Staff, and a warm personal and political friend. Of the Governor's

In person, Gov. Troup was of the ordinary height, with light complexion, blue eyes and sandy hair. His carriage was erect, and his step slow and measured. He would have passed for a military man, anywhere; and those who knew him best, accorded to him military talents of a high order. The gravity of his mien, and the guttural and almost solemn tones of his voice, led strangers to suppose that his dignity partook of austerity; but this was not so. Reserved, even in boyhood, he was still open and affable with his associates; adding, early in life, a tinge perhaps of melancholy, to that native dignity which never forsook him. Perfect candor and the strictest truthfulness were eminent characteristics. Where principle was involved, he was a stranger to the spirit of compromise.*

His domestic life was embittered by the early and sudden death of his first wife; and, afterwards, by the prostration of health, and death of the second, at a time, when, amid the cares of office and the active engagements of life, the weary heart looks for comfort and repose at home; and his declining years were saddened by the death of his older daughter, and the wreck of health of his only son. Nevertheless, he retained a degree of cheerfulness to the last; enjoying the social intercourse of friends at his secluded homestead; numbers of whom were attracted there, as well by the cordiality of his welcome and the simplicity of his manners, as by the amount of information he imparted, and the stores of political wisdom which he was ever ready to unlock. Of the qualities of his mind and his heart, his writings are the best delineators. To a vigorous intellect, he added the faculty of a sound judgment, and the quality of almost intuitive perception of the characters of men and the tendency of measures. Whilst his firmness was as conspicuous as that of any man, his perfect purity of intention, and his disinterested zeal for the public good,

message, at the extra session in 1825, he says: "Portions of it have long become as familiar as household words; and the day is not distant when its concluding paragraph will become the watch-word of the patient, long-suffering and down-trodden South."—ED.

* On the 19th of April, 1856, just one week before his death, in the postscript to a letter, written to the overseer at his Turkey Creek place, he said, in reference to a threatened dispute with a neighbor, about a piece of land: "If I have not right on my side, I will surrender, but not compromise."—ED.

were a standing rebuke to the timidity of the wavering politician, and the selfishness of the demagogue. Well instructed in the principles of law, he was deeply read in history, and was a thorough master of the English language. The productions of his pen are amongst the most eloquent on record, and his style was as free from redundancy, as his language was remarkable for directness of expression and force of utterance. Whilst Governor Troup was not usually ranked with the great intellects of the day, there are those who believe that some of his writings will compare, favorably, with any of the political essays to which the theory of our federative system of government has given rise. As specimens of profound thought, and forcible and clear argumentation, they deserve to rank with the best treatises of any age. In what were considered his extreme views of the absolute sovereignty of the American States, Governor Troup was certainly in a minority; yet, those who condemn these views as impracticable, have nowhere shown the fallacy of his reasoning, or proved that there is less danger from practically maintaining the opposite opinions. Every day's observation tends to confirm the truth of Governor Troup's apprehension of danger from the usurpations of the central government.

Consequent upon his ardent temperament, Gov. Troup's oratory, in the earlier portion of his life, was impassioned and vehement; but not open to the jeering criticism of his enemies, that he frothed at the mouth. In later life, his utterance, whether in public or private, was slow, distinct and emphatic. A gentleman*, who heard his address before the Board of Public Works, in 1826, pronounced him a fine public speaker.

Of mere outward appearance, few men were more careless. In the matter of dress, he had little taste; and on this subject several amusing anecdotes are told. There is no doubt, that, during the canvass for Governor, before the Legislature of 1823, some of his supporters requested one of his most devoted friends to give him a hint, that the election would be lost, if he did not appear in better trim.

* J. Hamilton Couper, Esq., who was a member of the Board.—ED.

The duty was delicately performed, and the wish of his friends was at once gratified. Something similar had occurred, in 1816, when he passed through Savannah to take his seat in the U. S. Senate. This did not proceed from parsimony, or a disposition to appear eccentric. His clothes were usually of good quality, but often of the oddest colors or the worst fit. His peculiar and perhaps only fancy was for a blue coat with metal buttons, a buff vest, and a fur cap. Whilst his habits were retiring, and most of his private life was spent at his plantation; yet it was usual for him to pass a portion of the warm season, at the Indian Springs, or some other watering-place in Georgia. He exercised, even at these places, much on horseback. His principal diversions, at home, consisted in riding over his crops, in fishing and hunting; but more of his time was spent in reading. Possessed of an ample fortune, he lived in abundance, if not elegance, delighting in the society and conversation of friends. His memory of historical events is said to have been remarkable; and his published and official correspondence shows the readiness and facility of the action of his mental powers. No one can contemplate his executive career, without awarding to him administrative talents of first grade. Add, to all this, an iron will, and a resolution that quailed before no difficulty and no foe; we have, if not the very model of a statesman, one at least who could not only inspire confidence in the doubting, but lead his countrymen through any crisis.

There is no doubt that he would have made any honorable sacrifice to avoid the shedding of blood, especially in civil strife; and yet it is true, that, rather than yield the principles involved in the Indian controversy, he would have marshaled the whole military power of the State, and have led her troops to victory or annihilation. The wonder is, that the authorities at Washington, who were not ignorant of his character, or of the people of Georgia, could have supposed that the threat of military coercion would cause him or them to falter in their purpose.*

* There is, probably, truth in the statement which has been made, that, in a conversation between Gov. Troup and a leading Carolina statesman who did not precisely understand the difference in the position of Georgia on the Indian, and that of South Carolina on the

On the subject of "intensest interest" to the Southern people, Gov. Troup spoke in no equivocal tones; and his writings show his decided opposition to the folly of forever arguing a question which is entirely beyond the right of Federal interference. Treating it as such, he was always ready, on this as on every other question of undoubted right, that the enemies of the Constitution exercise the "option to do us justice, or, refusing it, to present a military chest and armed men."

Of his religious views, not much is known, beyond what is disclosed in his messages and correspondence. These show a deep reverence for the Supreme Being, and a realizing sense of the pure and holy truths of the Christian religion. He made no public profession of faith; but it is evident that he was far removed from the taint of infidelity or scepticism.* He is said to have been an attendant on the services of the sanctuary, when opportunity offered; and his preference is believed to have been for the Episcopal forms of worship.

By resolution of the General Assembly, adopted in 1857, a life-size portrait of Governor Troup has been painted, and hangs on one side of the President's chair in the Senate-Chamber of Georgia—the portrait of General John Clark being on the other. That of Governor Troup is said to be an excellent likeness. The engraved likeness in this volume, is also said to be a life-like delineation of him, who was pronounced by a devoted and discriminating friend, "a Roman in feature, and a Roman in soul."

A county in Georgia, the county site of another, a ward and square in Savannah, and perhaps other places, commemorate the name of TROUP; but his enduring monument is the love of the people of Georgia for the memory of one who was first in their affections.

Tariff, question, the former cut the matter short, by the remark: *Yes; but whilst you were arguing the question, we would have had our troops in the field!*"

* An intimate friend of Governor Troup assures us that he considered him a pious man. On one occasion, as related to us by another friend, a conversation occurred, in Governor Troup's presence, on the subject of prayer for rain. One of the party, expressing a doubt on the point, appealed to Governor Troup for his opinion. The reply was: "Pray for *rain*, Sir? pray for EVERY THING!"—ED.

APPENDIX.

[The following is the letter to Major John H. Howard, noticed in the thirteenth chapter of this work. The "namesake," to whom reference is made, was the late Honorable George Troup Howard, who died in September, 1856. The letter was published in the early part of 1834.]

WASHINGTON, February 10th, 1833.

My Dear Sir: Knowing that you wish to possess my views of the present state of affairs, and of the measures connected with them, I sit down to their exposition, with the conviction, that, whether they happen to be in accordance with your own, or not, they will receive a kind and hospitable treatment, more than proportioned to their deserts; and, if valueless, be dismissed with the generosity and urbanity so congenial to your nature: otherwise, it may be a little legacy to your son, my name-sake, who, if he inherit the patriotism of the father, and virtues of the mother, may find them useful to him, in sustaining, in many an hour of trial, as we have done, the rights of the States, against a very strong Government created by the States, now threatening, by a most unnatural action, to cripple, to humble, and finally to destroy, its creator, which, in the natural and healthful action of the system, would be also its preserver.

I am not certain that you are aware of my early and uniform disrelish of the doctrine of Nullification, as maintained by the ruling party in a sister State. My objections to that doctrine were unconnected with party of any kind, and were founded on the difficulty of reconciling the peacefulness and constitutionality which it asserted, with that powerful remedial process, by which the wheels of the Federal Government would be stopped, as well as that resort to construction, (the old Federal sin,) by which alone the doctrine could be maintained, which has involved us in all our troubles, and which is equally good at any time to establish a veto against the General Government, a power to protect manufactures, or a power to do any thing a majority in Congress pleases. It was easy to perceive, that such a remedy might, by possibility, be peaceful; that depending on the other party; but not certainly peaceful. It was more difficult to see how it could be constitutional, because, as no power was given by the Constitution to the States to resist the laws of the United States, none such could be derived by implication or construction:* the derivation of remedies or powers, by construction, being, according to the republican doctrines, inadmissible. Indeed, no Constitution would authorize resistance to the laws, without defining explicitly, how, in what manner, and by whom, such resistance could be lawfully made. It is assumed, therefore, that the laws must be executed; and at all events, according to the *stipulations* of the federal compact. But who, in the last resort, are the judges of these stipulations? None are created by the compact, other than the Courts of the United States. The jurisdiction of the Courts of the United States must be confined to judicial cases, to the exclusion of political questions between sovereigns: and, so far,

* What are called the reserved rights or powers in the Constitution, are very erroneously deemed the sovereign power. They, on the contrary, are only those rights and powers which are usually exercised by governments, or enjoyed by the people, and which have not been given to the Federal Government. If they were construed to mean sovereign power, then, indeed, it would follow, that a State had conceded a portion of its sovereignty to the Government of the United States, and retained only a portion for itself, which would be making that Government sovereign, when it is only servant. Sovereignty protects both delegated and reserved powers, but is neither the one nor the other.

the Courts of the United States have paramount jurisdiction. The "controversies between two or more States," mean only such judicial questions as are presented by "cases in law or equity," to which their jurisdiction is limited by the Constitution. Political controversies, or questions between Governments, could not have been intended, they not admitting the interpretation of cases in law or equity; much less could political controversies between the States and Federal Government have been intended, they not being recognized by the Constitution as parties in any cases.

If, therefore, in controversies between those parties, no independent tribunal has been established for their adjustment, we can have no alternative but the resort to one or both of the parties—if to one, which one?—if to both, why? If the parties were equal in all respects, reason would prescribe equal participation in the adjustment, which would be an adjustment by negotiation. If they were not equal, but the one was in power and authority superior to the other, the same reason might claim for the superior party a participation in the adjustment, proportioned to that superiority. Between the government of a State and the Government of the United States, this equality, as they both represent sovereigns, must be admitted. No superiority can be claimed for the Government of the United States because of its representation of more sovereigns than one; as all their powers, in mass, amount only to the powers of one sovereign. Regarding the Government of the United States, therefore, apart from the Constitution, in the light of any other independent government, the equality between it and a State Government establishes the right of equal participation in the adjustment of any political controversy which may arise between them. But, as between the Government of the United States and the sovereignty of a State, there can be no such equality, the same sovereignty having created both governments, and standing in relation to each other of creator and creature—hence the right of a sovereign State to decide for itself, without appeal; still it is among the most sacred of its duties, to fulfil, strictly, all its engagements, especially its constitutional engagements, they being of the highest and most solemn import, not engagements to the Government of the United States, but to the other sovereign States. There is no sovereignty in what is called the United States. The United States is nothing but a government or a confederacy, the style of which is, "the United States;" and Government, according to our doctrine, is not sovereign, but is agent or servant of the sovereign. The sovereign must be found in the States, that is, in the people of the States. It is in virtue of this sovereignty that the State Government is formed; and it is in virtue of the same sovereignty that the United States Government is formed. This sovereignty, wherever it exists, is omnipotent; it is the same in one independent community as another, and is insusceptible of division, of increase or diminution; it can only be destroyed, by destroying the community in which it exists. Constitutions and governments are emanations from it, as light from the sun, which parts with it constantly, without itself being impaired, or wasted, or weakened. Hence it is, that it makes and unmakes at pleasure, and knows no superior but Divinity, and no law but the universal law ordained by that Divinity, which is the law of right and justice. According to our theory and practice, the mode of action of this sovereign, is to form Constitutions, which prescribe the rules for the conduct of the agent or servant called the Government. If the sovereign is dissatisfied either with the rule or with the conduct of the agent, it can abolish or change it, at pleasure. If it can abolish or change the rule, it can destroy the agent, because the rule is of higher power and authority.

Admitting, therefore, that a State may, at any time, destroy its own State Constitution, can a State, of its own pleasure, destroy the Constitution of the United States? The same power which created the one, has created the other—and may it not, for causes which shall seem good to itself, change or destroy the one, as well as the other? The answer is, no: Because other States, equally sovereign as itself, are equal parties to it. But, although a State may not for this reason alter or destroy the Constitution, it may throw it off; it may release itself; it may, by its own volition, for justifiable causes, cease to be a party to it. Are there no such good and justifiable causes? Yes—there are such as will justify the breach of a compact between sovereigns, by one of the parties to that compact; many of which causes are to be found in that public law, which is the Divine law, which is the law of right and justice, and which being the paramount law, is as controlling over compacts and constitutions, as the sovereign itself. Let it not be said that the Government of the United States, formed by the compact is paramount, because it is a compound of all the sovereignties of all the States. Sovereignty, it is repeated; admits of no degrees. It is the same in a small State as in a great one; the same in the State of Delaware or Rhode Island, as in the greatest community. It is said that the States have parted with many of their sovereign powers, as the power to make war—the power to make treaties, the power to regulate foreign commerce, &c., &c., &c. But this is a mistake; they have not parted with them: they have merely authorized the common agent to exercise them, under prescribed rules and limitations; the powers themselves residing in the States, and inseparable from them as independent communities. It is true, the Constitution speaks of powers granted and powers reserved; but this only means powers of the States to be exercised by the Government of the United States, and powers of the States to be exercised by the States. And, with regard to the powers prohibited to the General Government and to the States, it is only a declaration by each to the other States, that it will not exercise, itself, nor permit the exercise by the common agent, of such powers—the sovereignty still retaining the unity and indivisibility which are essential to it, and which are indestructible. The fundamental error has been to consider the United States as self-existent, and independent, and sovereign, as a party to a compact between sovereigns, and as capable of imparting as well as receiving sovereign powers under stipulated engagements; but this error is dissipated simply by asking, what is the United States? Territorially speaking, there is no such separate and identical thing as the United States. "United States," in the preamble to the Constitution, means the thirteen sovereign and independent States, *united* for certain defined and limited purposes therein expressed. The same words were used in the articles of confederation, one of which asserted expressly the absolute sovereignty of each State—in this sense it was universally understood by the States immediately after the ratification of the Constitution—for when it was attempted to bring one of these sovereigns before the Courts of the United States, it was indignantly resented by all of them as an insult, and the Constitution was so amended, (and, I think, by unanimous consent,) as to prevent the possibility of its recurrence. "We, the people," means the people of the several States, who alone were competent to ordain and establish constitutions of government, whether for the management of foreign or domestic concerns. If New Hampshire and Georgia had not ratified the Constitution, they might have confederated and adopted the same Constitution, in precisely the same words. We, the people of the United States. What States? The several States of New Hampshire and Georgia, "united" for certain defined purposes, do "ordain and establish" this Constitution, &c.—"united" having reference to States, and not to the people-and the words "ordain and establish," having reference to people and not to the States. Nay, further, Georgia or New Hampshire might, each of them, have formed two governments and two constitutions, the one for the conduct of its foreign relations, the other for the conduct of its domestic, on the same principles, and with the same powers as their present State and Federal Governments; yet no one would believe, that, in the first case, the people of Georgia and the people of New Hampshire were one people, or that, in the last, either State had parted with its sovereignty to one or both governments; it would still possess the same right to alter, new model or destroy both. The nature and extent of the powers delegated, could not impair the sovereignty of the States. If the convention had delegated all powers, Executive, Legislative and Judicial, to Gen. Washington and his successors forever, the sovereignty of the States would have remained entire. When the monarchists of the Convention, who labored the destruction of State sovereignty, had thrown every thing into disorder, and Dr. Franklin had advised the Convention to go to praying, and the members were returning home in despair of anything being accomplished but mischief, Gunning Bedford, a noble patriot of the now misrepresented or apostate State of Delaware, turned the fortune of the day, by warning them, if they dared to touch the sovereignty of his State, that State would call in the aid of foreign powers to protect her sovereignty; and so the Constitution passed, explicitly recognizing that sovereignty, by the organization of the Senate; and not in the least impairing it by the representation of the people of each State in the House of Representatives. Politically speaking, there is no such being as the United States; distinct from the States, no such community or people. There is such a thing as the Government of the United States, an artificial creature, an incorporeal hereditament—but a government is not a nation, or a people, or a community, any more than it is a sovereign.

The Constitution, to be sure, speaks of "we the people;" but it only means the people of the States who formed that Constitution, and who were the only rightful framers of Constitutions. As one people or community, they have never performed a single act either to originate the Government or to carry it on, nor will they nor can they, perform any to end it—no such people or community could have been formed, but by breaking up all the communities called the States, and consolidating them into one mass, which never could be done but by force or consent. We speak of boundaries between the United States and foreign States—but they are only such, because they are the boundaries between the States and such foreign powers. The Government of the U. S., if the boundaries were theirs, could alter them at pleasure, which it cannot do—it cannot acquire territory within a State, for the erection of needful buildings, without the consent of that State; and then may have no jurisdiction within the same, if withheld by that authority. The Government of the United States, is, in fact, a corporate body, with a common seal and common flag, representing the States according to a defined and limited charter, which cannot be violated but at the risk of forfeiture, of which the sovereign creating it must judge. But is it competent to one State to judge of the violation of the charter? Yes—but it judges for itself alone—every other State, in virtue of the same sovereignty, has the same right. Why should it not? The answer is, it would be too liable to abuse; the Union would be in constant danger of agitation and dismemberment, by capricious and irregular movements of the States. Here is another fundamental error:—Instead of ascribing wisdom, prudence, moderation and discretion, to a sovereign State, it is taken for granted that such State wil not understand her true interest, will not pursue it, will act from the whim or caprice or passion of the moment. But this is not the history of States; on the contrary, experience has proven, that all well regulated communities are most generally governed by a wise, judicious, and temperate regard to their own true interests. Now, what is the strongest ligament which binds this Union together? It is interest. Remove this motive of interest, and how long would the Union last?—just as long as it would take the States, ceasing to have interest in the Union, to withdraw from it. It is the beauty of the system, while it is the surest foundation for its perpetuity, that each State is left to pursue its own interest, in its own way, only asking the Government of the United States, which it has itself constituted, to protect it from foreign powers stronger than itself, and to let it alone in all matters which it has not specially confided to its care. How different is this from the idea of keeping the States together by force—to keep together by force, those who were brought together by consent; to keep Union by force, to keep amity by force, to keep brotherly love by force, to keep peace by force! It is absurd, and fortunately it is as impossible as it is absurd. If a single State, standing upon her sovereignty, resists the invasion of her rights, this is not to be endured, because it endangers the Union. If some half dozen States unite and secede, this, though it so far dissolves the Union, must be submitted to, because it cannot be resisted. So that the rightfulness of force depends, not on the rightfulness of the cause, but on the relative strength and weakness of the parties. But let us see what are the nature and extent of the risk and danger to the Union, of admitting the right of a State to repose itself upon its sovereignty, to resist an aggression by the Government of the United States. The danger and risk must be measured by the probable frequency of its recurrence: how often has it occurred since the date of the Union, and how often is it likely to occur? Surely, it is not intended to deny to a State the right which is given to the worm, the right to defend itself, and to preserve itself; this, indeed, consists with the denial of all sovereignty, but I trust that in our downward course to the grave, we have not reached a point so near its brink. A State has engaged, with other States, that it will do certain things, and omit certain other things; and that their common agent shall be authorized to do, in their name and in virtue of their authority, certain other things. Here, then, is a contract, involving rights and obligations on the face of it; it purports to be perpetual and irrevocable; but is it so in fact? Can it be so between independent communities, who are bound, by the laws of God and nature, to protect and defend themselves, to take care of their own happiness and interests—are these communities to be bound, from generation to generation, without the possibility of finding absolution? Is it permitted to us of the present degenerate day, to disinherit posterity, by sending down to it a worn, debased and abraded shilling, which they cannot refuse, but at the peril of their lives? No—every generation must take care of itself, and by all the moral, political and physical force it can; always bound by the great law of eternal justice, which it is not permitted to individuals or communities to violate—but contracts and engagements can be violated by communities, under the sanction of that supreme law. This happens when the sovereign judges that the safety, happiness and interest of the community, require such violation. Nothing is or can be required of it afterwards, but to repair whatever injury or damage it may have done to the parties interested, of which, of course, they are the judges in equal degree, in virtue of the same equal rights and prerogatives. The declaration by the contract, that the Union shall be perpetual, only means that it shall be so under the higher and supreme law, which permits the parties to consult their safety, happiness and interest. But with regard to the rights of the other parties: What can they do? As sovereigns they can demand satisfaction: they can go to war; they can annihilate the party resisting—they may satisfy vengeance, but they may not compel that party to send Senators and Representatives to Congress, or electors of President to an electoral College. If the party make all the atonement and reparation in its power, this is all that can be lawfully demanded—and where the public law is satisfied, the party wronged can make its appeal, under that same law, to all the sovereigns of the civilized world, who would then be the arbiters between the party doing wrong, and the party suffering wrong. I have said they may go to war, but certainly not by any power of the Constitution.

The Constitution authorizes the Federal Government to declare war—but not against a State. The articles of the Confederation expressly recognized the absolute sovereignty and independence of the States; and the Congress, like the present Congress, had the power to declare war. It was not believed to be a power to declare war against a State. The Confederation was dissolved to make way for the new Government, not that the new Government should have the power to coerce a State, but because, as no Government could possess that power, it should possess the power which the Confederation had not, to coerce individuals. This power it amply possesses, for all authorized purposes, and more than this it cannot claim. In the exercise of this power, it can proceed to any extremity which the Constitution authorizes. But if, in proceeding to that extremity, it encounters the sovereign power of a State, it must stop, because it is a mere Government without sovereignty, acting against a sovereign power. It is true, that, if the action and counter action proceed from the two Governments merely, and not from the sovereign power, the Federal Government has the advantage resulting from the stipulations of the compact, which its own courts, in all cases mere judicial, may enforce; but if the State, acting by convention of the whole people, shall throw itself upon its sovereignty, the other party may not proceed without an act of war. It is not admitted that the Congress has power to declare war against a State. Other States may combine to declare it, but they do so as sovereigns, to enforce stipulations of the contract, if they please, or for any other purposes they please. If they declare war and subjugate a State, they may divide it and make it parts of two adjacent States with the consent of those States; but these are the rights of war and of conquest. They have no right to deal with individuals captured or vanquished, otherwise than as prisoners of war. But it is said that the powers conferred by the Constitution shall be the supreme law, any thing in the laws or Constitution of a State to the contrary, notwithstanding—thus making the authority of the Constitution of the United States superior to that of the States—and this is all true; but who ordained that superiority? Why, the sovereign which ordained both Constitutions. Might not the same sovereign have given that superiority to the State, over the United States Constitution? Certainly. They are both alike the creatures of that sovereign, who could mould and fashion them at its will, without limitation or restraint, other than by the laws of God and nature. The Government of the United States passes a law; it is in conformity with the Constitution; it is arrested in its execution by the sovereign power of a State, which decides that the law is inconsistent with its safety: has a State the right to take care of itself? It decides a law to be null and void May not the power, of which the Constitution is but an emanation, so decide it? Why not as rightfully as the Supreme Court, which is but the creature of a creature, and which stands, in relation to the sovereign, but as a servant or agent? Here, then, is an exercise of sovereign power, in a case where the legislation of the United States Government is admitted to be constitutional. If, for its safety or preservation, the sovereign can so act in such a case, *a fortiori*, it can so act when the law is in fact unconstitutional, or of doubtful constitutionality. You would cheerfully trust the decision to the Supreme Court, the members of which are appointed by the agent created by the instrument, which instrument is itself ordained by this sovereign power; and you would not trust it to the same sovereign power. After all, it is seen that every thing turns on the existence of the sovereignty and independence of the States. If they are not sovereign and independent, where is sovereignty to be found? In the United States Government? That doctrine has long since been exploded.

Sovereignty was claimed for the Governments of Europe, founded on fraud and usurpation or conquest; but our modern doctrine recognizes no sovereignty but the sovereignty of the *people;* even the modern public law regards the people, or community, or State, as the only sovereign. Sovereignty cannot be parceled out and divided among different communities, any more than that primary and paramount allegiance which is due to it. The sovereign prescribes obedience, decrees to whom it shall be owing, and measures the extent of it in the Constitution. The power to punish treason, is given to the Government of the United States; and treason is defined to be "the levying of war against the United States, or adhering to their* enemies,"—not the levying of war against the Government, but against the United States, the States of the Union; not against the Government of the States, but against the people of the States; in short, against the sovereign. Let it be remembered that the Articles of Confederation expressly declared that "each State retained its sovereignty and independence," without any qualification; and yet, almost all the powers now granted, were then granted, and many of them in the very same terms; the words, "United States," being used in both instruments in the same manner, and conveying the same meaning. Now, it is evident that if the States were sovereign and independent then, they must be so now, unless an express and formal surrender by the sovereign power be shown, it being universally conceded that sovereignty cannot be lost by implication or construction. It is equally evident that if any of the sovereign States had failed to become parties to the present Constitution, such States would have remained to this day as sovereign and independent as any States or potentates of the world.

On these principles and with these limitations, the Government of the United States is still the strongest in the world, for all the objects of the Constitution—certainly, for external relations it is so; and it is so because it is sustained by the sovereignty of the States. It only becomes weak, and sometimes degraded and contemptible, when, forgetting its obligation as a servant, it usurps the prerogative of the master, and plays the tyrant, without pretensions to the authority or dignity of the sovereign. If allegiance had been due to the United States in virtue of its sovereignty, there would have been no necessity for defining treason against the United States. Perhaps the apprehension was entertained, that, as no allegiance was due to the United States, inconsistent with that which is due to the States, the United States Government would not have had authority to punish treason, unless the power was expressly given; and that, if the Government assumed it without definition, it would be exercised as arbitrarily and capriciously as by the governments of Europe. If allegiance is due to the sovereign, and not to the government, how can the citizens obey the government and disobey the sovereign? If it be due to the government, and not to the sovereign, the people of all the States know no other allegiance than that which is due to the Government of the United States; and of course that Government is a consolidated one, based on the existence of one people or community, and not on the existence of so many sovereign and independent States. The obedience owing to the Government of the United States by citizens of the States, is that which is required by the act of the sovereign in the Constitution of the United States, and of course cannot be inconsistent with that which is due to the States. Otherwise, it would be a government of the most odious character, by which a corrupt, vicious, interested majority, might dispose of the lives, liberties and fortunes of the smaller number, without check or control—than which it is impossible to conceive a tyranny more hateful, or a despotism more absolute. The actual state of things proves it. For years, many of the States of this Union have been most earnestly remonstrating against certain proceedings of Congress, avowing at the same time their unalterable resolution not to submit to them—regardless of consequences, this Government has moved on with a fixedness of purpose, which almost extinguished all hope of reform or amelioration, until one of the complaining States has resolved to submit no longer. In this extremity we find ourselves; and, instead of calmly and deliberately reviewing the whole ground, for the purpose of deciding whether we are in all things on the side of right, justice and the Constitution, before the sword is drawn, we begin by denying to that State, and of course to all other States, any rights whatsoever that are in their estimate of the least value; and

---

* Nothing is more strikingly illustrative than the use of the word "*their*," which cannot be relative to a singular noun; but must be relative to the word "*States*," against which alone an act of treason could be committed. It would not be English, to say, in the Constitution of France, treason shall consist in levying war against France, and adhering to *their* enemies—the word, *its* or *her*, would have been employed as relative to a single nation.

above all, their right of sovereignty, without which they consider themselves, as all the world must consider them, nothing more than petty corporations, the members of which are bound to the Government of the United States, by a paramount, indissoluble allegiance, in virtue of which, they are (members, officers and all,) amenable to it, on charges of high treason, and punishable accordingly. I think, according to the doctrines of the day, the most important right conceded to them is the right to petition and remonstrate. Having thus degraded the States, they resolve to draw the sword: for one, I cannot go with them. I cannot go with them, until I satisfy myself, that in all things they are strictly right: as long as there is a shadow or suspicion of wrong, I will not go with them to shed blood. If they were right beyond doubt, I would defer it to the last moment, and then I would execute the laws only against those who unlawfully resist them; against those who resist by commission and authority from a State, I would not. You shed blood without executing the laws, because you force the State out of the Union, and place her out of the reach of the laws. Let those who please to indulge in the revery of keeping this Union by force, go on in their mad career. Deity can do any thing: It can arrest the motion of the planets, and turn the sun into blood; it can extinguish the fixed stars, and make darkness cover the face of the heavens; but it is infinitely more easy for Deity to accomplish this, than for the Government of the United States to keep in its orbit, against its will, one of the States of this Union.

Let the State, therefore, be ever so vicious or wicked in its designs, I would forbear the resort to bloody measures, leaving her peaceably to depart the Union, as a nuisance to be gotten rid of, or as a prodigal, the repentant return of which to the fold, might one day be hoped for. But how different is the actual state of things! Four millions of people complain of the injustice and unconstitutionality of the laws, and we are ready to shed blood in their defence. These laws are founded on asserted power to regulate the industry of the country. Now, if such a power is sustained for the General Government, nothing can render that Government more worthless and insupportable in the contemplation of all the American people, opposed to restraints, monopolies and privileges; and it may expect, of course, that entire portion of them to be embodied against it. They would as soon think of making a Turkish bashaw the regulator of their industry, as the Congress of the United States; and for the simple reason, that, for flagrant abuses one could be made responsible; whereas, the Congress, by its multitude, is as irresponsible as the most multitudinous assembly, where the innocent cannot be separated from the guilty; and the public vengeance, if it fall at all, must fall alike upon the just and the unjust. Why is it, therefore, that, on a disputed question of doubtful right, or justice, or constitutionality, Congress will run the hazard of a civil war, when, by an easy operation, not costing them four days, they can adjust the controversy? The Union is to be lost by a squeamish delicacy, or a reckless obstinacy. The Lilliputian will not yield to the Brobdignag, and the Brobdignag will not make a concession of justice to the Lilliputian. The twenty-three States say to the twenty-fourth, if we do not take your blood as an atonement and propitiation for the rashness and intemperance of your conduct, we will be set down in history as cowards. Shame! Shame! Is it not enough for the stability of the Union, that the laws will, in ordinary cases, be peacefully executed by the courts of justice, and that, in extraordinary cases, they will be enforced, by all means, against unlawful obstructions and assemblages? To attempt their execution, by military power, against a State, is almost the only mode by which a State can be driven from the Union. A single State will not withdraw, until rendered desperate by the madness or tyranny of the General Government. A single State cannot maintain her independence; and, therefore, could not hope long to maintain her liberty. Her rights and obligations, as an isolated sovereign, would devolve on her very great expense, and expose her to difficulties and troubles from which the greatest wisdom could not exempt her.

The Union is much more exposed to danger, by a combination of States, who could maintain independence and liberty, at a cheaper rate, and with better security against vexatious and humiliating annoyances from abroad; and, when such combinations happen, what will their *denial* of the right to secede avail? Would they take sides with thirteen weak States against eleven strong ones, and make war to preserve the Union? This would, indeed, present our puissant Government in a light of no enviable majesty and supremacy, and is only an instance, among very many of analogous character, to show how much this Union must depend, for its duration, upon moderation and mutual concession. The power is asserted, to protect United States officers, in all cases which may arise under the laws of the United States, by asserting for the United States Courts, exclusive criminal jurisdiction, even where the parties are citizens of the same State. Now, no such power can be derived in criminal cases, but by construction; and thus it is, in a crisis like the present, the criminal jurisdiction of a State, always contemplated as a paramount interest, is attempted to be wrested from it, and transferred to the party whose long and continued infractions of the Constitution, in other respects, have produced this crisis; so that, by construing the words, "all cases in law and equity," to mean criminal as well as civil cases, the power may be claimed to authorize the commission, by the citizen of a State, of an act of treason against that State, and who would be sure to find his justification and acquittal before the tribunals of the United States, because he had acted in obedience to a law which they were bound to adjudge to be the supreme law, &c., &c., &c. Now what is the amount of all this? It is:

1st. That the exercise of certain powers, which would otherwise have been exercised by the States, has been granted to the Government of the United States.

2nd. That it has all the means admissible to any Government to carry those powers into effect.

3rd. Those powers have been derived from the sovereignty of the States, and were derivable from no other source; that such sovereignty is, notwithstanding, unimpaired and undiminished—the Government acting as a common agent or servant, merely, to carry them into effect.

4th. That, being so derived, the Government of the United States being charged with their execution, is of inferior authority to the Constitution which confers them; which is itself inferior and subordinate to the sovereign which created it.

5th. That, the Constitution of the United States being a compact, contract or agreement, between sovereigns, equal in all respects, the parties to it are bound in good faith, each to the others, and according to the terms and letter of the instrument, to abide by it, and to fulfil its obligations, without any qualifications, save

6th. That which results from a still higher authority, the law of God and nature, by which law the sovereign power is bound to watch over, and take care of, to defend and preserve the State or community from which it is inseparable.

7th. That when, by the action of the common agent or Government, the safety, happiness and interests of a State are endangered, it is the right, and becomes the duty, of the sovereign power, to interfere for its security—that such interference being justifiable under the public law when the action shall have been constitutional, is the more justifiable when the action shall have been unconstitutional, null, and void.

8th. That the States cannot, even by their sovereignty, bind themselves forever by engagements, stipulations or contracts, of any kind, but with the qualifications and reservations implied under the higher sanctions of the public law, which admits many causes of justification for the non-observance, non-fulfillment or violation, of the most solemn compacts. That it is enough that every generation should be permitted to bind itself; but that the idea of the power or competency of one generation to bind all successive generations, is unnatural and preposterous.

9th. That it is more reasonable and just to confide the ultimate decision on the rights and obligations of the compact, to the State sovereign, than to the Supreme Court or any other tribunal, the first being indeed supreme, and the last only the creature of a creature, whose decision must, finally, from the nature of things, be subjected to the revision of the creator of all.

10th. That the Government of the United States is authorized to make war only on foreign powers, and not upon the States; that if not so, the Government of the United States, the common agent of all, might be found on the side of twelve States, making war against the other twelve; thus illustrating its paternal care over union, justice, domestic tranquillity, general welfare and liberty, as enumerated in the preamble to the Constitution, and all in the name of the people of the United States.

11th. That the allegiance of the citizen, primary and paramount, is due to the State or sovereign. That obedience is due to the Government, as it represents the sovereign, and, as it is ordained by the sovereign; and, of course no obedience can be claimed by the Government inconsistent with the allegiance due the sovereign.

12th. That, admitting the above propositions to be true, the Government of the United States is still the strongest government in the world, for all the purposes for which it was constituted—that being a Government founded on consent, and supported by opinion, it must, to be sustained by that consent and opinion, be just and righteous; that it can never fail to be just and righteous, so long as its action conforms to the strict letter of the Constitution—that the slightest departure from that letter, is an abuse, whether it amounts to usurpation, or the exercise of doubtful powers, and may and will give rise to complaint, to discontent, and with a people so enlightened and free as ours, eventually to resistance.

13th. That a State, for the violation of the articles of compact, is responsible under the public law to the other States, and may, as between sovereigns, be compelled to make reparation for any injury or damage which may ensue to them in consequence of such violation; and that this is one of the great securities against hasty and precipitate action on the part of the States.

14th. That the words, "we the people," in the Constitution, are to be construed as meaning the people of the several States, who alone, in virtue of their sovereignty, were capable of forming Governments; and that all the powers conferred by all of them on the Federal Government, as well as all the powers retained to be exercised by themselves, are only such powers as each State would have possessed and exercised, if there had been no Constitution or Union; and, therefore, that the Federal Government has no more authority than it would have had, if the same powers had been conferred by a single State.

Your affectionate friend,

G. M. Troup.

[At the annual session of 1832, the General Assembly of Georgia adopted a preamble, looking to an amendment of the Federal Constitution, in the matter of "the principle involved in a Tariff for the direct protection of domestic industry," and "a system of Federal taxation," which should be "equal in its operation," &c.; and it passed a resolution, making "application to the Congress of the United States, for the call of a convention of the people, to amend the Constitution aforesaid, in the particulars herein enumerated, and in such others as the people of the other States may deem needful of amendment." It was in reference to this action of the Legislature, that the following letter to Major John Moore, of Oglethorpe county, was written. It was published in the Southern Recorder, of 30th January, 1833.]

Washington, Dec. 26th, 1832.

Dear Sir: What could have induced our people to think of holding a general convention of the States? Have they resolved to enter the lion's den, from which no returning footsteps can ever be seen? Is not the Constitution good enough for them?—or is it so bad that they would commit it to the hands of their enemies to fashion it as they will? The power to make amendments was given to answer no such exigency as the present; it was given to make that instrument more perfect, when, by the workings of the Government, experience having detected defects to be cured and evils to be remedied, the application of it could be made by general concurrence, and without hazard to the public peace. Hence it was that so soon as it was seen that a State might, by construction, be sued by an individual, an amendment was proposed and carried to correct the evil. So, too, when it became apparent that the designation of the electoral vote for President and Vice-President, was necessary to preserve the harmony of the States, the States concurred in an amendment accordingly; and so, too, when a young prince was born of an American alliance with the Bonaparte family, the States concurred in an amendment excluding from office any citizen who should accept a title of nobility or honor, from any Emperor, King, Prince or foreign power. These several amendments were made in the true spirit of the Constitution. At this moment, public sentiment is favoring two proposed amendments, which I think would be an improvement of that instrument: one, to limit the President to a single term; the other, to prohibit the appointment of members of Congress to office, during the period for which they shall have been elected.

Now, by a sudden and very strange after-thought, as it seems to me, this provision of the Constitution is to be made applicable, in times of excitement, to great and extraordinary exigencies: so that, whenever five or six States shall become dissatisfied with the Constitution, they may command the rest to assemble in convention, to alter, new-model or amend it. As I do not read any thing like this in that instrument, and as our old Republican doctrine rejects every power but that derived from its strict letter, opposed to all construction, I cannot unite with our fellow-citizens in the call of a General Convention. If the power is granted, it must be an efficient, not a nugatory, power. The minority States must command the majority States to assemble, and it must be the duty of the majority States to obey; they cannot, by silence, or evasion, or direct negation, escape. If they refuse, if they evade, if they are silent, it must be shown how, according to the letter of the Constitution, that silence or evasion or negation is to be taken. Is a sovereign State compellable, at the point of the bayonet, to answer aye or no? And how is silence to be construed? It is easy to see how a majority, claiming a given power, may ask the minority to concur in making that power more explicitly a part of the Constitution; but it is difficult to understand how a minority, protesting against the exercise of the power, can constrain the majority, either to make it a part of the Constitution, or to abandon it, unless it can be shown that the Constitution has so expressly provided, &c.

The Congress of the United States, supported by public sentiment, has, for a long time, by abuses and usurpations, so disfigured and disgraced the Constitution, that if all hope of its restoration were abandoned, it would be mattter for grave consideration whether that instrument was not utterly destroyed, and had, in every legal and moral contemplation of the subject, ceased to be binding on the parties to it. It is inconceivable how, in the eye of justice, a compact between two or more parties could be so construed as that the one party should be bound, and the other free. The immutable law is that all are bound or all are free. Nevertheless, a majority of Congress, whether considered as a mere agent to carry the powers expressly delegated into effect, or not, have assumed the right to interpret the Constitution at pleasure; and have so interpreted it, that whatever is resolvable into common defence and general welfare, has been claimed as a fair and legitimate power to be exercised by the General Government, until, at last, instead of a limited government for defined purposes, we have had one either actually engrossing or claiming to engross all the powers belonging to any government, and even some which ought not to belong to any. Now, it is under such circumstances, my good Sir, that you propose to go into a convention of the States, either *general* or *special*—if into a *General Convention*, then you must be prepared to receive, at the hands of the majority, a consolidated government, one and indivisible, a denial to the States (if permitted to exist at all,) of even the shadow of sovereignty, and, of course, a formal reclamation of all those rights and privileges, which, in the exchange of equivalents, you had expressly reserved as attaching essentially to your peculiar position and condition:—if into a *special* Convention, then you must be prepared for a prompt rejection of your amendatory propositions, (if these look to a further security for your rights and interests,) and eventually for the re-assertion and incorporation into the Constitution, of the very powers so long and strenuously denied by you, and long claimed and exercised by them. The indications of public sentiment at this moment are unerring, that an overwhelming majority favors a consolidated government; and it may behoove you, in all wisdom, to prepare, not for an improvement of your condition, but for a Cæsar and the purple. If, therefore, it be true, that you are to come out of a convention, shorn and despoiled, it may be well to think of some other and better course, by which the perils of the day are to be turned aside. Can you think of any better than the old Republican landmarks, by which, so far, although we have not escaped from storms, we have from shipwreck? You want no better Constitution, if the government be administered according to its letter—no body asks more than justice; and justice it secures, so far as written instruments can secure it. For all external relations, the government is stronger than the strongest in the world—its strength depends not less on the integrity of the States, than on that common consent and enlightened opinion, on which all our institutions are founded, and by which they must be held together: and what, after all, is the foundation of these, but justice, justice, justice?—all that the right of representation can give, it secures. Within the pale and letter of the Constitution, the man of Massachusetts is, to to be sure, as much our representative in Congress as the man of Georgia—beyond that pale and letter, however, he is as much a stranger as the representative of Scotland or Ireland in the British Parliament; and this is all, in this respect, that we could ask. Are there no means, then, by which Congress can be held to the letter of the Constitution? I answer, no constitutional means but the *ballot box*, unless the power of amendment, in the sense I have interpreted it, be so considered. The right of petition, of remonstrance, of discussion, are only auxiliaries by which the one or the other may be supported. But if these fail; if that power which decrees its own supremacy, perseveres to enforce it; must every thing yield to force? Force may vanquish everything—reason, right, truth, justice; and it is because force may do so, that we have erected barriers to defend reason, right, truth and justice. These barriers are the sovereign States of this Union, which, whatever the old federalists and monarchy men may say of them, were absolute sovereigns on the Declaration of Independence, are sovereigns now, and will remain so, until, by the voluntary surrender of their sovereignty, they please to make themselves slaves—but I trust, of all who shall make that surrender, Georgia will be the last.

But, you will ask, how is this doctrine to work? I see no more difficulty than is inseparable from the management of all human affairs. You have the passions and interests of men to encounter at every step; and these must be so met, as to make them work rather for good than for evil.

For ordinary grievances, we have said there is no constitutional remedy but the ballot-box —for extraordinary and extreme ones, there is no remedy but the sovereign power of the States; and in extreme cases, you repose yourself upon the sovereign power, for the very reason that the constitutional remedy fails. This sovereign power, at last, is in communities little more than the right of self-defence and self preservation—of the exercise of which, it is the sole judge, because, in this respect, it is independent as well as sovereign. It acknowledges no law but the law of nature and nations, which, in the settlement of controversies between States, acknowledges no *means* but *negotiation* and *force*. Shall we stop here to inquire which will serve us best, in the long run, the doctrine which acknowledges the sovereignty of the States; which recognizes, in extreme cases, the right of this sovereignty to defend itself, to negotiate, to make treaties; which, in a spirit of amity that consigns the past to oblivion, will re-unite dissevered States, who, being generous enemies, are, once more, and on that account, cordial, and, perhaps, inseparable friends; or *that* which admits the absolute *supremacy* of the Federal Government, its right to whip a State into the Union, and to hold it there forever, by brute force? I know it is said this power in the States is inconsistent with the power confided to the Federal Government; that for light and trivial causes, States may and will have recourse to it, by which the Union will be constantly agitated, and, finally, dissolved. Let us see if this apprehension is well founded. A State has the undoubted right, (undoubted even yet,) to change its own Government at pleasure, consulting only its interests and happiness, regulating all its internal concerns, with its right of soil and jurisdiction so absolute that the Federal Government cannot claim to erect an arsenal or fort or dock-yard within its limits, without its express consent. Here, then, is a community, by the power of self-government, made free and happy at home, wanting, for the consummation of that happiness, scarcely anything but protection against powers stronger than itself. Will these be put to hazard for light and trivial causes? Reason says no—the public law says no. The public law forbids the presumption that communities will act imprudently—it presumes them to be governed by a sound discretion—not that they are always so governed, but that their acts alone shall speak for them. Experience justifies the public law. Fifty years of Union, without convulsion, is no trifling evidence of intelligence, of prudence, of subordination, of contentment. How many guarantees, besides, are to be found against hasty and inconsiderate action, by which great blessings are to be lost. An insulated State may, for a moment, rescue liberty; but liberty is not to be maintained without independence, and independence cannot long be maintained by an insulated State. A solitary State resting on its own limited resources, with great wants for internal and external objects, surrounded by other States, (united for common defence,) must be exposed to evils and annoyances, from which the wisest councils cannot exempt her. Possessing sovereign rights, herself, she must so exercise those rights as not to interfere with the sovereign rights of others. The right of *way* and of *free passage*, the *regulation of trade and commerce*, so apt to conflict with those of others, framed in a different spirit—these, and many of kindred character would be sources of endless embarrassment and vexation. I would rather say, upon the whole, that the States would not secede for light and trivial causes—that grave and weighty considerations alone could influence them—that only some grievous oppression or frightful tyranny, driving them to despair, could divide them from the Union. Are there not some reasons for this belief? We hear the cry of Union, Union, from all quarters, as if there were nothing left in this world worth preserving, but Union—so that the friends of liberty and union may well doubt whether the people love liberty less or union most. See what has been submitted to for many years, with a degreee of patience and forbearance, which might be construed into something not to be named: Unnecessary taxes, to make a splendid, of what was designed to be a simple and economical, Government—the taxes levied on the many to promote the interests of the few—the revenues distributed for objects of Internal Improvement, where the taxes were not levied—every scheme and device for the extravagant expenditure of public moneys—dormant claims on the Government revived, and pension systems established on principles so loose, as to offer the strongest temptations to fraud and perjury. As if it were not enough for the Federal Government to regulate commerce, which it is authorized to do, it assumes the care and regulation of manufactures; and then the transition is easy to the care and regulation of agriculture—so is the transition, sometimes, from the grave to the ridiculous. Who, of the Convention who framed the Constitution, would have believed it possible, that even in our time committees of agriculture would have been organized in both Houses of Congress, to instruct our people how to sow and to reap, to weave and to spin, to milk and to churn? It is because they employ themselves with all these follies, abuses and usurpations, that the Congress which should, in ordinary and peaceful times, dispatch its constitutional business in three short months, is occupied through five, six and seven; and a portion, and a large portion too, of this time, devoted to the manœuvres of factions, who seem to have been congregated here for the single purpose of making Presidents, to make the leaders of those factions Presidents in turn. Are not these things, good Sir, enough to disturb the harmony of the States? If a single State, fretted and tortured by such abominations, shall, by an unwise and hasty movement, resolve to shake them off, is she to be bound, neck and heels, and consigned to the Cave of Trophonius or the Cyclops? The almost universal answer is, yes, yes! down with the rebels, down with the traitor State. But whose turn comes next? If the Federal Government is not stopped in its career of encroachment, by some counteractive agent, what, reasoning from what has been done to what may be done, will it not do? It gives countenance to colonization and other voluntary associations, which keep in ferment large sections of country, which, by a single false movement, would be excited to the most desperate resistance. It may, for any thing we know, pass acts of attainder and proscription, by which, masses of society may be cut off. It has, on occasions, stopped the liberty of speech and of the press. It may ordain a State religion, or decree a universal emancipation. Its supreme judicial tribunal, which, it contends, is, in the last resort, to pass on the constitutionality of all laws, may send its warrants into the States, commanding its marshals to hang up, by the lamp posts, A., B. and C. These, you will say, are extreme cases. So they are. It may pronounce null and void, charters by which States claim their rights of *soil, jurisdiction* and *sovereignty*. It may erect one sovereignty within another. It may decide that one portion of the community, within the chartered limits of a State, is sovereign and independent, and entitled to the right of self-government. It may control the criminal jurisdiction and arrest the criminal laws of a State by writs of error and appeal. *Are these, too, extreme cases?* If they are, extreme cases require extreme remedies; and if these are to be sought in the power of the States, it is because the States are sovereign, and may protect and defend themselves. But does this consist with that unity, one and indivisible, claimed for the United States as a nation? Certainly not. But then it becomes those who make that claim, at the same time to make it good. For ourselves, we protest against it, as most wild, extravagant and fallacious. The States formed the Government of the United States—the States ratified it. From that day to this, it exists and breathes but by permission of the States. Though three-fourths of the States are necessary to amend or alter it, a majority, or less than a majority may dissolve it. If the States refuse Electors of President, it is prostrate. If they refuse their Senators, it stops. If they withhold their Representatives, it is the same thing. There is, indeed, no one act required of the people of the United States, as one people, either to begin it, to conduct it, or to end it—it would be just as rational to make the Congress of Vienna a nation, deriving its authority from the people of all Europe. The old confederation must have been a confederation of States; for I have never yet heard of a confederation of the people. The confederation was abandoned for the new government, because it had no power to coerce the States. But was the new government adopted to coerce the States? Certainly not. It was adopted to coerce individuals, for the very reason that States could not be coerced. The statesmen of that day perceived that every thing was gained by making a government strong enough to operate effectually on *individuals*—that the idea of coercing States was an absurdity, and that the new government would answer all the ends of its creation, without the least danger of collision, so long as it confined itself to its constitutional limits.

It is the departure from those limits; it is the exercise of powers not delegated; it is the exercise of doubtful powers, equally prohibited by the Constitution, which has at any time brought the General Government into collision with the States.

In scribbling thus much, I think I may have answered, out of order, no doubt, all your inquiries. The result, according to my poor opinion, is, that there is no power given by the Constitution to resist the laws of the United States.

The only Constitutional remedy for unconstitutional laws, is the ballot-box.

Amendments of the Constitution, petition, remonstrance, conventions, correspondence and consultations of the States—these (if you please to call them remedies,) are not unconstitutional.

Under a government founded on consent and opinion, evils are to be borne as long as possible.

The States, in virtue of their sovereignty, when evils are no longer supportable, must judge the evil and the remedy.

The sovereign knows but two modes of settling controversies, negotiation and war.

Negotiation admits of arbitration; and controversies may be referred to other States; but this is by *consent*, and not by the Constitution. It is, of course, not permissible to one of the parties to refer it to its own Courts and Juries.

When States cease to have an interest in the Union, or suffer extreme oppression, it is better that they withdraw peaceably, than that blood should be shed in contests, which seldom decide any thing, and which are apt to separate the parties forever.

As States may do very imprudently and unwisely, what they have a right to do, it becomes them to act very deliberately and cautiously; because it is lawful for other States to unite against them to compel a fulfilment of their obligations under the public law.

You ask what Georgia ought to do? My worthless opinions had been given on former occasions, and you know what use has been made of them. Those opinions were unchanged, and are, as I think, unchangeable—they amounted to this: if the abuses and usurpations, of which we complain, are continued, and become the settled policy of the Government, the States having identical interests, ought to withdraw—but it was indispensable to a movement like this, that there should be union; that this union should be the result of a deep and settled conviction, that such policy was inconsistent with the paramount peace, interest, prosperity and happiness of the State; and not a temporary union produced by an artificial excitement. A united people, even of one State, might rescue *liberty* for a time; but, without the means of maintaining *independence*, *liberty* could not be preserved.

It was necessary, therefore, that other States having common interests, should be prepared to think and act with us; and it was altogether proper, that, for this purpose, a system of correspondence and consultation should be organized, as the best means of producing union. My own belief was, that the Tariff would not yield, and could not be made to yield, but to some interest stronger than the interest in manufactures; and I knew but one that was so, and that was the interest in Union. It could not be doubted that the Northern States were as much concerned in preserving the Union as ourselves; and it was altogether fair, that, in the last resort, we should present to them the plain alternative, either *"to return to the bargain and stick to the bargain, or give up the Union."* If, unhappily, it should turn out that they take more interest in manufactures than in Union, it is my deliberate opinion the Union is not worth preserving. In all this we have considered not so much what might be done, and rightfully done, by the sovereign States of this Union, as what may be wisely done. Do what we may, and let what of evil come, we will have the consolation, that, from the beginning to the end, we have been passive subjects, and the adverse party active agents. The abuses and usurpations practiced, and the burdens imposed, have been of a positive character—we have done nothing but beg relief from them.

You have insisted on my opinions, and I have given them. No one could ask them with more propriety than yourself. You have been, all your life, a uniform, consistent Republican, and as much devoted to the prosperity of the State, and States too, as any man in it. The stake which you and all of your name and family have in it, is pledge sufficient for your loyalty and discretion; and the passion for liberty that was born with you, is absolute security that you cannot be a slave.

Your friend,

G. M. Troup.

[The following letter is the one to which reference is made in the fourteenth chapter of this work, as relating to the Currency question.]

LAURENS COUNTY, GEORGIA, May 16th, 1840.

My Dear Sir: It is a long time since I have taken any part in President-making. When Mr. Crawford was smitten by the hand of Providence, I advised my friends at Washington to take up Mr. Macon. He was a plain farmer, of Revolutionary merit, of sound common sense with great knowledge of men and things, and of sufficient political experience to administer the Government of the United States. He could say no, when it was fitting, and was no dealer in ifs. It struck me it would do well for an experiment at least, and that if it succeeded, the people of the United States might contract a taste for such men, rather than for your well-trained and thorough-bred politicians. One thing would have been certain—you would have had no violations of the Constitution, or other abuses, to complain of, and the Government would have been known and felt only in its salutary, constitutional action. But these were so many objections to him.

If I failed in my second trial of President-making, surely you would not have me, at this time of day, to join in the cry of Loafers, Loco Focos, Shinplasters, Log Cabin, Hard Cider, and the like—let those who have a fancy for such things, settle the matter among them—they who have the least to do with it, always excepting a fraction of the office-hunters, will be the better off.

As to the *use* and *abuse* of my name in connection with the same office, all I have to say is, that if those who used it were genuine State Rights men, they had a right to use it, and were the only men who had—if they used it for the office, they were wrong—if they used it because they could not consistently vote for either of the persons who were the only candidates for it, then they were right, and then they were thrice welcome to use and abuse it. I must confess the use did give me some annoyance; but that was personal, and not worth a complaint; the abuse in a general sense, I had been used to, and, therefore, could bear with it; but, in the sense which excited your friendly indignation, it was indeed the most signal and heart-felt gratification.

The relation in which you have stood, and the warm feelings constantly manifested toward me, give you a claim to my poor political opinions, when you please to ask them; and you have them briefly, but frankly.

What is called the sub-Treasury, (if it means the dealing by the Government in gold and silver, exclusively,) I consider not only constitutional, but an extremely wise and very expedient measure. It ought never to have been a dealer in any thing else—at least, such has been always my opinion. I thought the Constitution required it; and it seemed to me to be most unreasonable, that a government which was compelled to pay all its *debts* in gold and silver, should, at the same time, be compelled to receive any or every kind of paper, which might be, called money, in payment of debts due to itself. You would, no doubt, at this moment, feel it somewhat comfortable and refreshing to look upon a great dealer in gold and silver, a dealer without premium and without discount, and therefore without profit; dealing to the amount of many millions per annum, and to the amount of many thousands per diem, constantly receiving and as constantly paying out. The gratification of the senses, in such sad times, would be something; and the chance of a dime finding its way to your pocket, would be something more; but if this dealer so dealt, that we soon began to see we could command as many dimes as would do for market money, we would feel we had derived a precious benefit by his dealing, and that indeed a benefit had fallen upon the country. If the dealer happened so to deal, as to supply, constantly and uniformly, a small-change circulation, or pocket money, sufficient for the every day wants and business of life, then, indeed, a new era would have opened, which the past had never seen; which would be in glaring contrast with the present, and which the future would hail with thanksgiving and praise; and the more joyously, as what was, will be no more, and what is, will be and must be forever, at least as long as the dealer lasts and deals in gold and silver exclusively. Now, if this can be accomplished by a great dealer, it is more likely to be accomplished by the Federal Government than by any other agency we know anything about. 1st, its dealings will be large enough. 2dly, it will be to the same amount, or nearly so, from year to year, in times of peace increasing gradually, perhaps in proportion to an increasing population, and a consequently increasing expenditure. 3dly, paying and receiving equal amounts in equal times, or nearly so, the small change circulation could never be suddenly contracted or enlarged. I will not pretend to say what the amount of small change in circulation should be in a such a country; it is sufficient, if it give you only the change for a shin of beef to the butcher, and a loaf of bread to the baker, per diem. But it must necessarily give a great deal more—perhaps all we want. Stating the average revenue and expenditure at twenty millions, some four or five millions of specie will suffice to carry on the annual operation; the balance in the country, whether it be forty, fifty, sixty or seventy millions, will be left to sustain the paper, which, whether it amounts to one hundred and twenty or two hundred and ten millions, will be quite ample for all the demands of trade and commerce—perhaps quite enough to satisfy the cravings of the most extravagant of the paper-money lovers. This paper will be so much the sounder than it would otherwise be, because, instead of comparing paper with paper, as you are now forced to do, you would compare it with an ever present standard of gold and silver. An additional and certain effect of a merely metallic currency for governmental purposes, would be the check it would furnish to the extravagances and aberrations of Government, an effect not to be lightly estimated.

You perceive I am sanguine in my predictions of the salutary consequences of this much condemned measure, of which you have a simple statement of my opinion or belief, without the *argument*. I supposed you asked no more. An argument on a financial subject is not worth much; what would appear a good system on paper, might turn out to be a bad one in practice, and an indifferent or objectionable one on paper, a very good one in practice; but an argument against a system, founded on the dishonesty of mankind, is a very false one; men must carry into effect systems; men must collect and men must disburse the public revenue; and it matters nothing whether that revenue be of gold and silver or of paper. If, indeed, the paper be good for nothing, that is sufficient security against embezzlement; if equally good, it is more easy of embezzlement than gold and silver. Will it matter much if the men who collect and disburse, happen to be Whigs or Democrats? I have pretty much the same confidence in both; the one set have been already there to steal and plunder; the other have yet to come.

From this project to deal in gold and silver, I have never been able to conjecture how, by any possibility, loss or detriment can accrue to any body. Is it true the mass of the community is so corrupt, that it is willing to deal in nothing but bad paper; or do the politicians persuade them they will have a bank, the extinguisher of all other banks, whose paper will be equal to gold and silver? Instead of loss or detriment, I have seen no inconvenience to result to any body, except, indeed, in the first instance, to the merchant: to him it will be a novel operation, for a time, but for a short time; if it costs him more trouble and expense to be always ready to meet the custom-house demand, he knows how to charge that expense to his customer; and, my word upon it, the consumer of his merchandise will be the last to complain, if he sees nothing in an insignificant charge, but a redemption from evil suffering, and a restoration to the comforts and enjoyments of life, to which, in every country, the pocket and traveling money in gold and silver coinage so eminently contribute. The very fraction of a per cent., charged by the merchant, for his trouble and expense of keeping gold and silver to answer occasional demands, will be more than repaid by the direct tendency of the operation to keep that gold and silver at home, which might otherwise go abroad: it will be by so much the more valuable at home, and therefore cannot leave the country.

But enough; every body tires of this dry and hitherto unproductive subject. The President should long since have compelled his party to carry out the measure.

Very sincerely and truly,

G. M. Troup.

[The two next letters are those addressed to the gentleman at Mobile, and to which reference is made in the fourteenth chapter of this work.]

Valdosta, Laurens County, Georgia, 15th Sept. 1849.

My Dear Sir: I have just received and read, with great pleasure, your excellent letter of the 2nd inst. Its complimentary part evinced so much of disinterestedness and sincerity, that I rose from its perusal, thinking better of myself, and almost believing that indeed I had done some little service to the State. A few hours before the receipt of it, the Montgomery letters came to hand, announcing the Barbecue; and the committee of invitation were so kind as to make the same request which yourself, from the best motives in the world, have made. You may conceive the reluctance and unfeigned regret with which I was obliged to decline a compliance with theirs, and now to decline a compliance with yours. The general suggestion in my letter, was the disinclination, amounting almost to abhorrence, to appearing in the newspapers so often, and especially upon the same subject, as if I had resolved to force my poor opinions on a tired and unwilling public. I had given my views, in and out of Congress, formerly and recently, and so frankly, and I trust so intelligibly, that I began to indulge hope that for the future I might safely, even with my best friends, excuse myself from a repetition of what had, on former occasions, been received, frequently with ridicule, and always with abuse. It is of no consequence, to me, who knows those views; and therefore you are at liberty to use them as you please, provided you keep me out of the newspapers.

I will give you an illustration of fanaticism in the person of the good and gallant La Fayette. It was one of his virtues to be consistent, even in his faults—his heart was the milk of human kindness. He had passed by Mount Vernon, and shed tears—burning tears on the tomb of Washington. You received him, before that, with open arms, and exhausted your generous hospitalities upon him. In the same hour, he would have seen the throats of your women cut, and your streams run blood, smiling at the havoc he had made. He had been prime mover in the destiny of St. Domingo, and, to the last hour of his life, he sighed for a new St. Domingo. The irreligious and immoral French, now unable to govern themselves, are, by the legacy he bequeathed them, destroying their last colonies as they destroyed St. Domingo, and would draw the sword, at any moment, in union with the Federal Government, to destroy our Southern country.

It is worse than useless to conceal anything from ourselves—it is far better to lay bare the naked truths, and in good time. Are we to surrender because the civilized world, and, it may be, more than one-half of our own countrymen, are against us? This is the only question worth considering—and, I begin, by answering No! by no means. If you are divided, you can do nothing—perfect unanimity is not to be hoped for, but an approach to it might be realized; what then? I say a perfect preparedness for the last resort, by the establishment, in every State, without delay, of Military Schools, Founderies, Armories, Arsenals, Manufactories of powder, &c. Have you not seen that our adversaries are constantly growing stronger, and ourselves comparatively weaker, in all the elements of power—population—wealth—education—military resources of all kinds; and these sustained by a Government strong in its military and naval power—ready for combat at any time, and at any place, and already the terror of the world? Have you not remarked, also, that in the very proportion our weakness was disclosed, in the same proportion our adversary advanced, until he assaults us to our teeth, and at our firesides? I say, then, ceasing all bluster and bravado, prepare to meet them on that last field, in which, if you be well prepared, they will receive harder blows than they can give; and they know it. General La Fayette would not have been deterred by the fear of death, from carrying into practice his anti-slavery notions; but most men will; and it is only the dread of death, that in the United States will stay the hand or stop the machinations of the fanatic. That dread you must present to him, in a visible, palpable form. They know you have courage; but where is the flying artillery, the most formidable arm in modern warfare—where the munitions, the arms, the discipline—and where the science to serve them in the field? If united and ready for the last recourse, the Union might yet be saved by the very knowledge of our adversary, that, to a bloody field—more bloody than that of Ghengis or Tamerlane—might be added the loss of Union, and the loss of the very object they seek to accomplish. Victory is not always to the strong; and Alexander conquered the world with little more than thirty thousand men. To be sure, if the abolitionists seek disunion, they may have disunion, by peaceful means—nothing would be more easy, and as peaceful as easy, because we want no better Constitution for our Government, than that which governs the abolitionists and ourselves; but if the Union is to be dissolved by force—that is to say, if the abolitionists resolve to force emancipation, or to force dishonor on the Southern States by any act of Congress, then it is my decided opinion, that, with the military preparation here indicated, conjoined to a good volunteer, instead of a militia, system, the States should march upon Washington, and dissolve the Government; and just as soon as such overt act of treason shall have been committed by Congress.

We have always been in the right—are still in the right, and I advise you to keep so. They are the active agents of mischief and persecution: we the passive subjects. There are good men on the other side of Mason and Dixon's line, and they might incline to the side of an innocent and injured people. Even their neutrality might be useful to us—so with the army and navy; the justice of our cause might divide them. I assure you, my dear sir, few men would be more averse from this latter alternative, than myself; but I have never thought of any cure for our evil, short of it; and if you cannot unitedly make up your minds for it or something better, the talk about it only makes the matter worse. In this familiar and informal scribbling manner, I write to you, because I believe you would like it best.

As long as we maintain braggadocia style, the Northern people will laugh at us; and I do no t care to be laughed at, and despoiled of what we know to be our own, at the same time. If the abolitionists do not wish disunion, they would keep us in the Union by the argument of Gen. Jackson. Once in the Union, always in the Union, is the Federal argument; but perhaps not as strong as Gen. Jackson's. I would like to be always well prepared to resist these arguments, whether offered in the form of paper or iron bullets. When the adversary becomes strong enough to alter the Constitution and abolish slavery, what are you to do? You must submit, or withdraw, or resist; but withdrawal or resistance would be vain, without adequate preparedness.

Without fatiguing you, I dismiss the heart-rending subject, with my best wishes for your health and happiness.

G. M. Troup.

Valdosta, Laurens County, October 1st, 1849.

My Dear Sir: I have deemed it best to submit a few general observations, in addition to those which I took occasion to offer in answer to your late very able, kind and friendly letter, and in elucidation of them. They embraced a few reasons or motives for declining, most respectfully, a very reasonable and most patriotic request, which, without a good reason, ought not to have been declined; and I was willing to submit to your courtesy and generosity the sufficiency of the reasons. I superadded a word on the subject of remedy for our present grievances, to which you were pleased to invite my attention; and now I take leave to trouble you with a second but very short letter, explanatory, a little more fully, of my poor opinions in connection with that remedy.

The illustration of fanaticism in the character of Gen. La Fayette, was not designed to detract any thing from the merits of that really excellent man. It was his fault—his blot—his sin, in our sight. In the sight of our adversary, it was his crowning jewel. At no period of our history has the South not suffered from the false opinions, or open treachery, of Southern men. It cost Mr. Jefferson a life of useful service to his country to compensate the injury done to his own South by his Notes on Virginia; and your President, General Taylor, has just escaped from his responsibilities by a trick. In despite of every thing, men will have their thoughts; and our Constitution, as it ought, gives freedom to the expression of them. May it always be so. But when the overt act follows the expression, the overt act being evil, and of the temptation of the devil, then it is, that a matter of such concernment becomes a deeply agitating question to all concerned; and the more, if such act be the act of a Government. It is then, that, in such a controversy as ours, the overt act is likely to prove an act of treason, and that the action on the one side should be met by correspondent action on the other, and so I have advised you to meet it.

Now, the probable action of Congress will be to prevent you, by force of arms, from inhabiting territory of the United States with your negro property, where she has forbidden you to carry it. I say you have a right to go there with your negro property, and the act of forbidding it is an act of treason* against the South; producing an actual state of war, by an open declara-

* I do not use the word in its legal acceptation. If we owe duties and obligations to the Federal Government, this latter owes duties and obligations to the States; and an act, tantamount to an act of war against them, is moral treason.

tion on the part of the Federal Government, and making us the defendants in that war.* It is not worth our time to consider how Congress derive their power over the subject of slavery. They do not claim it as a power exercisable within the States—the most inveterate abolitionists renounce it—but they claim it in the Territories, as if they had any more power over a subject of property there, than they had over the trial by jury—freedom of speech—of religion—of the press—of bearing arms, or any right secured equally to all the citizens of the United States, wherever they might be within the limits of their own country.

They in vain seek for power in the Constitution—they affect to derive it from the Ordinance of '87. The Ordinance of '87 gave no pretence to Congress to assert any other right, than the right to prohibit slavery in the North-western Territory. By the terms of the Ordinance they were bound to interdict it there, but no where else. It was a *contract* between the United States, Virginia, and the inhabitants of that Territory, present and future, not to be violated by either party. It was made under the Articles of Confederation, and it is vain and useless now to inquire whether rightfully and constitutionally made, or not. The present Constitution ratified and confirmed it, by ratifying and confirming all contracts or agreements binding on the Confederation.

This Ordinance, so far from authorizing Congress to make a new move on the subject of slavery, beyond the limits of that territory, impliedly forbids it. It says, in substance, "slavery being universally established among the States, we, the parties to the contract, have prohibited slavery there, and there only, leaving it established and confirmed elsewhere, until the separate States of the Union shall otherwise decree." If Congress were now to pass an act for the establishment of slavery in the North-west Territory, the people would most rightfully protest against it as a breach of faith—as violative of the present Constitution, and as violative of the Ordinance under the Confederation; proof conclusive, I think, that, unless by contract between all the parties, Congress could not, even under the Confederation, pass an Ordinance, or any other act, interdicting slavery in the Territories. When, therefore, Congress subsequently undertook, of its own authority, by virtue of the Ordinance, to limit slavery elsewhere, it was guilty of a mere usurpation.

In the Missouri case, Congress had not even the pretense of contract to excuse the usurpation. If France had contracted with the United States, and with the consent of the inhabitants of Louisiana, that slavery or involuntary servitude should be abolished forever within the limits of Louisiana, such portion of the treaty would have been merely void—Congress having no power, by the present Constitution, to touch the subject of slavery in any manner whatsoever, either by treaty or by legislation. But there was no such contract made; and Congress had no more right to prohibit slavery in any portion of Louisiana, than to abolish it where it already existed. Its silly contract with England, to unite in abolishing the slave trade, is not in virtue of any power which Congress has over slavery, but in virtue of the power which it has over foreign trade and commerce. But it is one thing for Congress to assert the power to prohibit slavery in Missouri, and another and very different thing for the people of the slave States to concede that power. The character of compromise does not alter the case. You cannot compromise a power or principle of the Constitution. If you could, it would soon be a very different thing, both from what it is and from what it was intended to be. It was, in truth, a voluntary surrender, on your part, without the shadow of a *quid pro quo*—not even a blackberry. Indeed, it seemed as if you had been whipped into it by the rope's end, or cat o'nine-tails. Still, at last, it was a voluntary surrender. You bound yourselves by it; and, as in the case of the Ordinance, it is vain now to be raising constitutional questions. Nevertheless, it is true, that you surrendered no more than what you actually agreed at the time to surrender, the prohibition of slavery north of latitude 36° 30′, and within what was formerly the limits of Louisiana. Beyond that, (shameful and scandalous as the surrender was,) you surrendered nothing, nothing of territory, to be sure, but you surrendered the argument. The great argument was: "If we make a voluntary concession of what you have no right to claim, it will only afford you a pretext, in future, to ask more—to insist on the ell, because we had given the inch. You will not even promise not to ask for more, and

* It will not be less a declaration of war against us, if we are simply treated as squatters, to be turned out at the point of the bayonet. If by voluntary associations, 50 or 100,000 men had gone into California, Congress would have had no remedy but by recourse to the army and navy.

We foresee, distinctly, that with regard to the future acquisition of territory, either by purchase or by conquest, this line of 36-30 will be regarded as equally surrendered—for, being a line, marking a boundary of climate, into which we have not, and never will have, any inducement to carry our slave property, the argument, if it be good for any thing, is as good for future as for present territory." By the by, although this may have been the view taken of it at the time, it has since turned out that, for all mining purposes, slave labor would be as applicable to countries north of 36-30, as south of it. African slavery had its origin in the necessity of substituting black for Indian servitude, for mining. So that, really, when it was supposed we had only surrendered a right, we had in fact surrendered a substantial interest likewise.

Now, the question is, will you, having once, for the sake of preserving the Union, made a voluntary concession of rights and interests, be willing to make a like concession to preserve the same Union now? I would not have done so then, nor would I do so, now; but I am only one of the million. How far are we willing to go, and how much more are we willing to give up to preserve the Union? It is known to you, that there are some who are prepared to give up everything. I trust there never will be found a majority for this. What then shall we do? I say, let us begin and put our trust in a condition of full preparedness to meet the worst contingency, in defence of all our rights and interests. As we have most unwisely surrendered our birth-right for less than a mess of pottage—as we have surrendered, in the same manner, valuable interests—as, at the same time, we surrendered almost the only argument that ought to have proved available for their preservation, may we, myself not included, not again make more sacrifices by consenting to extend the same line indefinitely, on the single condition, that all countries South of it shall be opened to us forever, with a distinct understanding that not a man or a dollar would be supplied to any future wars, but with the full assurance, on their part, that we were to share equally in their benefits as in their burthens? So much might be yielded to avert the greatest of all evils—a civil war. But, still, I am persuaded that these sacrifices would not, by our adversary, be considered enough, if not supported by an attitude and posture so palpably formidable as not to be mistaken. To bring about these ends, I fear a convention—more paper resolutions—I would prefer a general informal understanding, each State engaging earnestly and heartily in the work of preparation, as if the result of a common sense of duty and safety. The States that are willing to co-operate, would soon be known and distinguished from those who are unwilling; and so you would be able to estimate your strength, and then, if it were deemed sufficient, a convention might follow, not for paper resolutions, but for the purpose of counseling as to the best modes of carrying into effect your already fixed and settled purpose.

December 1, 1849.—Two or three days after forwarding my first letter, I had written thus much, when I decided not to send it, but to await the action of the Convention of California. If the prescribed boundaries are finally adopted, giving the entire Pacific coast to the new State, and all the country north and south of 36-30 to the southern line of Oregon, besides, and Congress should adopt the same, then I advise that you take the remedy as suggested in my first letter, or the expedient of an armed emigration of slave-holders into the territory south of 36-30, with a resolution to hold it forever as a slave country, or until eventually its population, as a State, shall determine otherwise.

And now, as California itself has prepared the way for the problem to be solved by Congress, I have no hesitation in relieving you from the injunction heretofore imposed; and you are thus at liberty to make what use you please of my crude letters, with the single restriction, that you must first believe that some public usefulness may follow.

Very sincerely and respectfully,

G. M. Troup.

[The two remaining letters have been noticed in the fourteenth chapter of this work.]

Valdosta, Laurens Co., Ga., 29th October, 1850.

Dear Sir: It would have afforded me great pleasure to have been able to comply with your very reasonable and patriotic request; but it is rendered impossible for the following reasons, which I trust will prove satisfactory to you and my other friends:

1st. I am decidedly averse to appearing in the public prints.

2d. I have repeatedly, of late, declined compliance with similar applications.

3d. With very great reluctance, I had consented to the publication of a letter addressed to a gentleman of Mobile, on the same subject, which I saw afterwards in the newspapers, and which contained my deliberate and unchangeable sentiments, both in regard to the grievance and the remedy—as to which, of course, I would add or subtract nothing.

It is true that since the date of that letter, acts have been passed by Congress, which have been called a compromise of the agitated questions; but still my opinions remain the same, and it would be idle repetition and waste of words to offer you the same substance dressed in different language.

Congress has merely consummated a scheme conceived and begun by the Executive in fraud, falsehood and trickery, and has effectually excluded you from every square foot of territory acquired from Mexico, and 40,000 square miles taken from Texas, besides, as if they had enacted the Wilmot Proviso, word for word; and they have done this without violating the letter of the Constitution—nor would they have forborne the Wilmot Proviso, word for word, had they not believed that the law of God and the law of Mexico had effectually done the same thing without it.

Now, if Congress had enacted the Wilmot Proviso, and had abolished slavery in the District, and the slave trade between the States, and had even made the first move to abolish slavery in the States, I could have advised nothing more nor less than I advised in that Mobile letter. I would have rejoiced if I had had the power to call you to arms, but even in that case you would have had none. I therefore advised the arming of the Southern States, without delay—a good musket and bayonet in the hand of every man capable of using it, and good parks of artillery, well officered and well trained volunteers, &c., &c., in all of which you are deficient. I know of but one State, on this side of the Potomac, that is not so—it is South Carolina. If S. C. shall unhappily resolve to secede alone, she will be able to fight a good fight—if cloven down, she will fall with honor. If any one believes there can be dissolution without the most bloody contests, he deceives himself; and he who is best armed is likely to be most successful. For dissolution, two things are necessary. 1st—The will—2d.—The means. Carolina is the only State having the will, and the only one having any degree of preparedness to carry that will into effect. In every other State there is neither the one nor the other. Some of the States are, almost to a man, satisfied with what Congress has done—all the rest are divided. Their Representatives and Senators have divided; with respect to Georgia, none can tell on which side a majority is, either for submission or resistance. I would consider it extremely unwise and imprudent to dissolve, unless a majority of the States of coterminous boundaries could be formed into a Confederacy sufficiently strong to resist all foreign aggression. It would be exceedingly desirable that all the States having identical interests, should join in the same confederacy; but I would not wait for this if the enemy continued to force the separation.

All remedies, short of force or conventional agreement, I reject—every other remedy, whether of non-intercourse, or restrictive duties, or discriminative taxes on trade or commerce, is unconstitutional, and, until we are driven to the last alternative, I wish every unconstitutional movement to proceed from the North. I wish our people to be constantly on the side of morality, good faith and the Constitution, until that alternative is offered. Violations of the Constitution admit of no degrees,* and I would abstain from following the example of the North. Let her go on in the career of violation, until she has heaped so many coals of fire on her head, and then present to her the bayonet, with a good conscience, and with an energy that will make her, if not a friend, a better and a more honest neighbor.

Nothing is more easy, if you will permit yourselves, than to be drawn into an experiment of remedies that are extra-constitutional. They exclude you from Territories which are as much yours as theirs—may you not exclude Northern men from Territories which are exclusively yours? Northern men exclude your property from California and the Territories—may not you exclude their property from the boundaries of Georgia? On a principle of retaliation, you would be justifiable; but you would not be justified by the Constitution.

A voluntary non-intercourse would be good, and might be remedial, but this would require a

* The effects and consequences of different violations, may be very different; but, whilst in the Union, every wilful violation is criminal.

unanimity for which there is no hope—less than unanimity would defeat it. Discriminating taxes violate the Constitution, because Congress have exclusive power to regulate commerce between the States; and the regulation of commerce does not mean destruction, but encouragement. And now, sir, I have only to repeat, for the hundredth time, and for all that time unheeded, there is no remedy for our present grievance, but armed States, bidding defiance and presenting such array that the one party must withdraw from its unjust pretensions, or the other assert its rights of equality and independence. Whether continued aggression, resistance to or repeal of the Fugitive Act, or something worse, will rally the people of the South and bring them to think and feel and act like brothers, remains for the future to disclose. In the mean time, we have thrown ourselves upon a Convention, and it will become good citizens to abide its action.

Having thus presented my general views in as few words as I could employ to make myself at all intelligible, I trust you will see in those few an additional reason why they should not be published. They proclaim our weakness, by proclaiming our divisions, and thus encouraging the North to proceed in her course of aggression, which is what the enemies of Union desire and the friends of Union deplore. No State can act with safety in the direction of dissolution, without a majority strong enough to expel the non-contents and drive them into the arms of the enemy.

Very respectfully, dear Sir,

G. M. TROUP.

Dr. John G. Slappey,
Newton, Georgia.

VALDOSTA, July 4th, 1855.

Dear Sir: You are quite welcome to do as you please with any thing of mine you may have in possession, provided you think good may come of it.

I have neither taste, inclination, nor spirits, for controversial politics; but am, notwithstanding, far from being indifferent to the welfare of our country. If a word from me could subserve its interest, in any sense, it would not be wanting. We see with different eyes, or I would be amazed at the opposition to the present administration, especially in the Southern country.* The present is, in truth, the least exceptionable of all the administrations we have ever had, Gen. Washington's, Mr. Jefferson's and Mr. Polk's not excepted. People seem to be opposed to it because there is really nothing to find fault with. The Southern people are bound by honor, gratitude and patriotism, to sustain it with all their might.

† *Catholic Church and foreign emigration* are mere pretenses—the administration has nothing to do with either. The first has existed at all times, without complaint; the second has not only existed, but has been almost uniformly encouraged by people and government; and now a party is formed to destroy the administration because it will not destroy the Roman Catholics and put down the foreigners. This is not to be believed. The true grounds of opposition are:

1st. The very small number of offices at the disposal of the President, when compared with the very great number of those who seek them. 2nd. The faithful and unfaltering integrity with which the public treasure is guarded against the thieves who prowl, by night and by day, to break in and steal; and 3rd. The inflexible courage with which the President, in defending the Constitution, defends the dearest rights and most sacred interest of the South. The most formidable power against the administration, is the party occupying the latter ground; and what a spectacle is here presented for the Southern country! Mr. Pierce and Mr. Hale,

* Elected by a vast majority of his countrymen, in a manner most honorable to himself, he is threatened with overthrow by a majority almost as formidable, for, (as I think,) not even plausible reasons. [The reader will readily understand the allusion here to be to President PIERCE.—ED.]

† This Church is more innocent now, in the eyes of all Protestant sects, than it has been before for two hundred years; and there is not beneath the sun a finer people than the people of Maryland, who are made to fall under the common proscription.

both from New Hampshire—the one an honest man; the other a bigot, fanatic and abolitionist! What a contrast! What effulgence! What blackness! And yet, there are Southern men, acting with the latter, to humble and prostrate the former, and with scarcely any better pretext than that the former had appointed to two conspicuous offices, two prominent men, one failing in his duty, and the other doing his with honor and advantage to the country. Mistaken and deluded men! Our very safety depending on union among ourselves, they would sow discord and division. Our highest interests depending on the veto, they would take the veto from Mr. Pierce to bestow it on Mr. Hale, or Mr. Anybody. Such men seek to restore the administration of the past, when peculation and plunder and swindling were the order of the day in every administrative department, and when the only security of the public against rapine and spoliation, was the exhaustion and beggary of the treasury.

Very respectfully, dear Sir,

G. M. TROUP.

Dr. John G. Slappey,
Newton, Georgia.

P. S. The President has had nothing to do with the disgraceful bidding for the Presidency, going on for some time in the Senate of the U. S., where the public lands and the public offices have been offered to any or every body who had a vote to give, and any or every body might be qualified to vote.

www.ingramcontent.com/pod-product-compliance
Lightning Source LLC
LaVergne TN
LVHW021233110826
845150LV00002B/322

9781425562601